Lecture Notes in Computer Science 4228

Commenced Publication in 1973
Founding and Former Series Editors:
Gerhard Goos, Juris Hartmanis, and Jan van Leeuwen

Editorial Board

David E. Lightfoot   Clemens A. Szyperski (Eds.)

Modular Programming Languages

7th Joint Modular Languages Conference, JMLC 2006
Oxford, UK, September 13-15, 2006
Proceedings

 Springer

Volume Editors

David E. Lightfoot
Oxford Brookes University
School of Technology
Department of Computing
Oxford, OX33 1HX, UK
E-mail: dlightfoot@brookes.ac.uk

Clemens A. Szyperski
One Microsoft Way
Redmond WA 98052, USA
E-mail: cszypers@microsoft.com

Library of Congress Control Number: 2006932028

CR Subject Classification (1998): D.3, D.2, D.1, D.4, F.3

LNCS Sublibrary: SL 1 – Theoretical Computer Science and General Issues

ISSN	0302-9743
ISBN-10	3-540-40927-0 Springer Berlin Heidelberg New York
ISBN-13	978-3-540-40927-4 Springer Berlin Heidelberg New York

Springer is a part of Springer Science+Business Media

springer.com

© Springer-Verlag Berlin Heidelberg 2006
Printed in Germany

Typesetting: Camera-ready by author, data conversion by Scientific Publishing Services, Chennai, India
Printed on acid-free paper   SPIN: 11860990   06/3142   5 4 3 2 1 0

Preface

On behalf of the Steering Committee we are pleased to present the proceedings of the 2006 Joint Modular Languages Conference (JMLC), organized by Oxford Brookes University, Oxford, UK and held at Jesus College, Oxford. The mission of JMLC is to explore the concepts of well-structured programming languages and software and those of teaching good design and programming style. JMLC 2006 was the seventh in a series of successful conferences with themes including the construction of large and distributed software systems, and software engineering aspects in new and dynamic application areas.

We were fortunate to have a dedicated Program Committee comprising 41 internationally recognized researchers and industrial practitioners. We received 36 submissions and each paper was reviewed by at least three Program Committee members (four for papers with an author on the Program Committee). The entire reviewing process was supported by the OpenConf system. In total, 23 submissions were accepted along with two invited papers and are included in this proceedings volume.

For the successful local organization of JMLC we thank Muneera Masterson, Ali McNiffe and Fiona Parker and other staff and student helpers of Oxford Brookes University as well as Rosemary Frame and Jo Knighton and other staff of Jesus College, Oxford. The proceedings you now hold were published by Springer and we are grateful for their support. Finally, we must thank the many authors who contributed the high-quality papers contained within these proceedings.

September 2006

David Lightfoot
Clemens Szyperski

Organization

JMLC 2006 was the seventh conference in a successful series, with past events held in:

1987 in Bled, Slovenia;
1990 in Loughborough, UK;
1994 in Ulm, Germany;
1997 in Linz, Austria;
2000 in Zürich, Switzerland;
2003 in Klagenfurt, Austria.

Steering Committee

László Böszörményi, University of Klagenfurt, Austria
Michael Franz, UC Irvine, USA
Jürg Gutknecht, ETH Zürich, Switzerland
David Lightfoot, Oxford Brookes University, UK (Program Co-chair and Local Organizer)
Hanspeter Mössenböck, University of Linz, Austria
Clemens Szyperski, Microsoft, USA (Program Co-chair)
Niklaus Wirth, ETH Zürich emeritus, Switzerland

Program Committee

Jonathan Aldrich, CMU, USA
Pierre America, Philips Research, Netherlands
Uwe Assmann, TU Dresden, Germany
Nick Benton, Microsoft Research Cambridge, UK
László Böszörményi, University of Klagenfurt, Austria
Gilad Bracha, Sun Java Software, USA
Michael E. Caspersen, Aarhus University, Denmark
Craig Chambers, University of Washington, USA
Michael Franz, UC Irvine, USA
K. John Gough, Queensland UT, Australia
Dominik Gruntz, Fachhochschule Aargau, Switzerland
Jürg Gutknecht, ETH Zürich, Switzerland
Thomas Henzinger, EPF Lausanne, Switzerland
Nigel Horspool, University of Victoria, Canada
Zoltán Horváth, Budapest University (ELTE), Hungary
Mehdi Jazayeri, TU Vienna, Austria
Helmut Ketz, Fachhochschule Reutlingen, Germany

Table of Contents

Separating Concerns with Domain Specific Languages

Steve Cook

Microsoft UK Ltd, Cambridge
steve.cook@microsoft.com

Abstract. I'll talk about the separation of concerns in the development of large distributed enterprise systems, how to manage it using domain specific languages, and how to build these languages. This brief note outlines some of the topics I'll cover.

1 Separation of Concerns

Most developments in programming language design are intended to improve the ability of the programmer to separate the expression of different concerns. This has progressively led to the development of language features such as procedures, abstract data types, objects, polymorphic type systems, aspects, and so on.

We're now moving into an era when the normal case of software development is distributed and heterogeneous, with the internet playing a pivotal role. It's simply not practical today to use a single programming language to create all aspects of a large and complex computing system. Different technologies are used to implement user-interfaces, business subsystems, middleware, databases, workflow systems, sensors, etc. Enterprise programming stacks include as first-class participants a variety of inter-related programming and scripting languages, databases, metadata and configuration files. Most programming projects involve interoperating with what is already there, which requires interfacing to existing technology stacks.

In such a world, concerns such as the structure and organization of business data and processes inherently span multiple technologies. A given business concept will show up in the user interface, in the formats used to communicate between components, in the interfaces offered from one component to another, in the schemas for databases where business data is stored, and in the programming logic for manipulating all of the above. Even the simplest change, such as changing the name of the business concept, impacts all of these pieces. Such concerns cannot possibly be effectively separated by improving programming language design. How then can we approach this problem?

2 Development Using Domain Specific Languages

A promising approach has been described variously as "Language-Oriented Programming" [1], "Language Workbenches" [2], "Generative Programming" [3] and "Model Driven Engineering" [4]. All of these phrases essentially describe the same

D. Lightfoot and C. Szyperski (Eds.): JMLC 2006, LNCS 4228, pp. 1–3, 2006.

pattern: given a class of problems, design a special-purpose language – a Domain Specific Language or DSL - to solve it.

A simple (and old) example of this pattern is the language of regular expressions. For example, using the .Net class System.Text.RegularExpression.Regex, the regular expression "(?<user>[^@]+)@(?<host>.+)" applied to a string of characters will find email addresses in it, and for each address found, appropriately extract the user and host variables. Programming such a procedure directly in a general-purpose language is a significantly larger and more error-prone task.

In developing complex enterprise systems, it is increasingly the case that graphical languages can be used to express certain concerns most effectively. Business workflows, business data, and system, application and data centre configuration are obvious candidates for graphical representation. Also textual languages, while effective for inputting large programs, may not be the most effective medium for displaying, analyzing and interpreting these programs.

Putting these ingredients together provides the motivation for an emerging class of graphical language-processing tools, which includes the DSL Tools from Microsoft [5], the Generic Modeling Environment (GME) from Vanderbilt University [6], and commercial examples from MetaCase, Xactium and others. These tools enable the language author to design and implement the abstract and concrete syntax for a DSL, together with the ancillaries needed to integrate the language into a development process.

Of course it is not sufficient simply to design what a DSL looks like; it is also necessary to give its expressions meaning, which in practical terms means to generate executable artifacts from it: these will most likely be programs in more general-purpose languages, together with configuration files, scripts and metadata, that can be deployed together to implement the intention of the developer.

As soon as generation is introduced into the development process, there is the possibility of developers changing the generated artifacts. Uncontrolled, this will break the process: the source form of the DSL will become out of date and useless. Alleviating this issue is one of the main challenges of making DSLs successful. Not all artifacts can be generated from DSLs, so it is essential to be able to interface generated artifacts with hand-coded ones: various language techniques such as partial classes [7] can enable this.

3 Software Factories

A DSL can provide a means to simplify the development of one area of concern. But the development of large distributed applications involves the integration of multiple areas of concern, with multiple stakeholders manipulating the system via multiple different viewpoints.

Managing the complexity of such a development involves delivering appropriate languages, tools and guidance to individual participants in the process at the right place and time. Enabling this is the province of Software Factories [8], an approach to software development that focuses on the explicit identification of viewpoints in the development process, the definition of DSLs, tools and guidance to support these viewpoints, and the delivery of these capabilities to individuals during the enactment of the process.

References

1. Dimitriev, S. Language-Oriented Programming: The Next Programming Paradigm, http://www.onboard.jetbrains.com/is1/articles/04/10/lop/
2. Fowler, M. Language Workbenches: The Killer App for Domain Specific Languages? http://martinfowler.com/articles/languageWorkbench.html
3. Czarnecki, K. and Eisenecker, U.W. Generative Programming – Methods, Tools and Applications. Addison-Wesley (2000).
4. Bézivin J., Jouault F, and Valduriez P. On the Need for Megamodels. Proceedings of the OOPSLA/GPCE: Best Practices for Model-Driven Software Development workshop, 19th Annual ACM Conference on Object-Oriented Programming, Systems, Languages, and Applications (2004).
5. DSL Tools Workshop. http://msdn.microsoft.com/vstudio/DSLTools/
6. Akos Ledeczi, Miklos Maroti, Arpad Bakay, Gabor Karsai, Garrett, J., Thomason, C., Nordstrom, G., Sprinkle, J. and Volgyesi, P. The Generic Modeling Environment. Proceedings of WISP'2001, May, 2001. http://www.isis.vanderbilt.edu/Projects/gme/GME2000Overview.pdf
7. C# programming guide, http://msdn2.microsoft.com/en-us/library/wa80x488.aspx
8. Greenfield, J., Short, K., Cook, S., Kent, S. Software Factories: Assembling Applications with Patterns, Models, Frameworks and Tools. Wiley (2004).

Event-Based Programming Without Inversion of Control

Philipp Haller and Martin Odersky

École Polytechnique Fédérale de Lausanne (EPFL)
1015 Lausanne, Switzerland

1   Introduction

Concurrent programming is indispensable. On the one hand, distributed and mobile environments naturally involve concurrency. On the other hand, there is a general trend towards multi-core processors that are capable of running multiple threads in parallel.

With *actors* there exists a computation model which is especially suited for concurrent and distributed computations [16,1]. Actors are basically concurrent processes which communicate through *asynchronous message passing*. When combined with *pattern matching* for messages, actor-based process models have been proven to be very effective, as the success of Erlang documents [3,25].

Erlang [4] is a dynamically typed functional programming language designed for programming real-time control systems. Examples of such systems are telephone exchanges, network simulators and distributed resource controllers. In these systems, large numbers of concurrent processes can be active simultaneously. Moreover, it is generally difficult to predict the number of processes and their memory requirements as they vary with time.

For the implementation of these processes, operating system threads and threads of virtual machines, such as the Java Virtual Machine [22], are usually too heavyweight. The main reasons are: (1) Over-provisioning of stacks leads to quick exhaustion of virtual address space and (2) locking mechanisms often lack suitable contention managers [12]. Therefore, Erlang implements concurrent processes by its own runtime system and not by the underlying operating system [5].

Actor abstractions as lightweight as Erlang's processes have been unavailable on popular virtual machines so far. At the same time, standard virtual machines are becoming an increasingly important platform for exactly the same domain of applications in which Erlang–because of its process model–has been so successful: Real-time control systems [23,27].

Another domain where virtual machines are expected to become ubiquitous are applications running on mobile devices, such as cellular phones or personal digital assistants [20]. Usually, these devices are exposed to severe resource constraints. On such devices, only a few hundred kilobytes of memory is available to a virtual machine and applications.

This has important consequences: (1) A virtual machine for mobile devices usually offers only a restricted subset of the services of a common virtual machine

D. Lightfoot and C. Szyperski (Eds.): JMLC 2006, LNCS 4228, pp. 4–22, 2006.

for desktop or server computers. For example, the KVM[1] has no support for reflection (introspection) and serialization. (2) Programming abstractions used by applications have to be very lightweight to be useful. Again, thread-based concurrency abstractions are too heavyweight. Furthermore, programming models have to cope with the restricted set of services a mobile virtual machine provides.

A common alternative to programming with threads are event-driven programming models. Programming in explicitly event-driven models is very difficult [21].

Most programming models support event-driven programming only through *inversion of control*. Instead of calling blocking operations (e.g. for obtaining user input), a program merely registers its interest to be resumed on certain *events* (e.g. an event signaling a pressed button, or changed contents of a text field). In the process, *event handlers* are installed in the execution environment which are called when certain events occur. The program never calls these event handlers itself. Instead, the execution environment dispatches events to the installed handlers. Thus, control over the execution of program logic is "inverted".

Virtually all approaches based on inversion of control suffer from the following two problems: First, the interactive logic of a program is fragmented across multiple event handlers (or classes, as in the state design pattern [13]). Second, control flow among handlers is expressed implicitly through manipulation of shared state [10].

To obtain very lightweight abstractions without inversion of control, we make actors *thread-less*. We introduce *event-based actors* as an implementation technique for lightweight actor abstractions on *non-cooperative* virtual machines such as the JVM. Non-cooperative means that the virtual machine provides no means to explicitly manage the execution state of a program.

The central idea is as follows: An actor that waits in a receive statement is not represented by a blocked thread but by a closure that captures the rest of the actor's computation. The closure is executed once a message is sent to the actor that matches one of the message patterns specified in the receive. The execution of the closure is "piggy-backed" on the thread of the sender. If the receiving closure terminates, control is returned to the sender as if a procedure returns. If the receiving closure blocks in a second receive, control is returned to the sender by throwing a special exception that unwinds the receiver's call stack.

A necessary condition for the scheme to work is that receivers never return normally to their enclosing actor. In other words, no code in an actor can depend on the termination or the result of a receive block. We can express this non-returning property at compile time through Scala's type system. This is not a severe restriction in practice, as programs can always be organized in a way so that the "rest of the computation" of an actor is executed from within a receive. To the best of our knowledge, event-based actors are the first to (1) allow reactive behavior to be expressed without *inversion of control*, and (2) support arbitrary blocking operations in reactions, at the same time. Our actor library outperforms other state-of-the-art actor languages with respect to message passing

---

[1] See http://java.sun.com/products/cldc/.

speed and memory consumption by several orders of magnitude. Our implementation is able to make use of multi-processors and multi-core processors because reactions can be executed simultaneously on multiple processors. By extending our event-based actors with a portable runtime system, we show how the essence of distributed Erlang [31] can be implemented in Scala. Our library supports virtually all primitives and built-in-functions which are introduced in the Erlang book [4]. The portability of our runtime system is established by two working prototypes based on TCP and the JXTA[2] peer-to-peer framework, respectively.

All this has been achieved without extending or changing the programming language. The event-based actor library is thus a good demonstrator of Scala's abstraction capabilities. Beginning with the upcoming release 2.1.7, it is part of the Scala standard distribution[3].

Other Related Work. Actalk [8] implements actors as a library for Smalltalk-80 by extending a minimal kernel of pure Smalltalk objects. Their implementation is not event-based and Smalltalk-80 does not support parallel execution of concurrent actors on multi-processors (or multi-core processors).

Actra [29] extends the Smalltalk/V virtual machine with an object-based real-time kernel which provides lightweight processes. In contrast, we implement lightweight actors on unmodified virtual machines.

Chrysanthakopoulos and Singh [11] discuss the design and implementation of a channel-based asynchronous messaging library. Channels can be viewed as special state-less actors which have to be instantiated to indicate the types of messages they can receive. Instead of using heavyweight operating system threads they develop their own scheduler to support continuation passing style (CPS) code. Using CLU-style iterators blocking-style code is CPS-transformed by the C# compiler.

SALSA (Simple Actor Language, System and Architecture) [30] extends Java with concurrency constructs that directly support the notion of actors. A pre-processor translates SALSA programs into Java source code which in turn is linked to a custom-built actor library. As SALSA implements actors on the JVM, it is somewhat closer related to our work than Smalltalk-based actors or channels. Moreover, performance results have been published which enables us to compare our system with SALSA, using ports of existing benchmarks.

Timber is an object-oriented and functional programming language designed for real-time embedded systems [6]. It offers message passing primitives for both synchronous and asynchronous communication between concurrent *reactive objects*. In contrast to event-based actors, reactive objects cannot call operations that might block indefinitely. Instead, they install call-back methods in the computing environment which executes these operations on behalf of them.

Frugal objects [14] (FROBs) are distributed reactive objects that communicate through typed events. FROBs are basically actors with an event-based computation model, just as our event-based actors. The goals of FROBs and

---

[2] See http://www.jxta.org/.
[3] Available from http://scala.epfl.ch/.

```
class Counter extends Actor {
  override def run(): unit = loop(0)

  def loop(value: int): unit = {
    Console.println("Value: " + value)
    receive {
      case Incr()   => loop(value + 1)
      case Value(a) => a ! value; loop(value)
      case Lock(a)  => a ! value
                       receive { case UnLock(v) => loop(v) }
      case _        => loop(value)
    }
  }
}
```

Fig. 1. A simple counter actor

event-based actors are orthogonal, though. The former provide a *computing model* suited for resource-constrained devices, whereas our approach offers a *programming model* (i.e. a convenient syntax) for event-based actors, such as FROBs. Currently, FROBs can only be programmed using a fairly low-level Java API. In the future, we plan to cooperate with the authors to integrate our two orthogonal approaches.

The rest of this paper is structured as follows. Section 2 shows how conventional, thread-based actors are represented as a Scala library. Section 3 shows how to modify the actor model so that it becomes event-based. Section 4 outlines Scala's package for distributed actors. Section 5 evaluates the performance of our actor libraries. Section 6 concludes.

2   Decomposing Actors

This section describes a Scala library that implements abstractions similar to processes in Erlang. Actors are self-contained, logically active entities that communicate through asynchronous message passing. Figure 1 shows the definition of a counter actor. The actor repeatedly executes a `receive` operation, which waits for three kinds of messages:

- The `Incr` message causes the counter's value to be incremented.
- The `Value` message causes the counter's current value to be communicated to the given actor a.
- The `Lock` message is thrown in to make things more interesting. When receiving a `Lock`, the counter will communicate its current value to the given actor a. It then blocks until it receives an `UnLock` message. The latter message also specifies the value with which the counter continues from there. Thus, other processes cannot observe state changes of a locked counter until it is unlocked again.

Messages that do not match the patterns `Incr()`, `Value(a)`, or `Lock(a)` are
ignored. A typical communication with a counter actor could proceed as follows.

```
val counter = new Counter
counter.start()
counter ! Incr()
counter ! Value(this)
receive { case cvalue => Console.println(cvalue) }
```

This creates a new `Counter` actor, starts it, increments it by sending it the
`Incr()` message, and then sends it the `Value` query with the currently executing
actor `this` as argument. It then waits for a response of the counter actor in a
`receive`. Once some response is received, its value is printed (this value should
be one, unless there are other actors interacting with the counter).

Messages in this model are arbitrary objects. In contrast to channel-based
programming [11] where a channel usually has to be (generically) instantiated
with the types of messages it can handle, an actor can receive messages of any
type.

In our example, actors communicate using instances of the following four
message classes.

```
case class Incr()
case class Value(a: Actor)
case class Lock(a: Actor)
case class UnLock(value: int)
```

All classes have a **case** modifier which enables constructor patterns for the class
(see below). Neither class has a body. The `Incr` class has a constructor that
takes no arguments, the `Value` and `Lock` classes have a constructor that takes
an `Actor` as a parameter, and the `UnLock` class has a constructor that takes an
integer argument.

A message send `a!m` sends the message `m` to the actor `a`. The communication
is asynchronous: if `a` is not ready to receive `m`, then `m` is queued in a mailbox of
`a` and the send operation terminates immediately.

Messages are processed by the `receive` construct, which has the following
form:

```
receive {
  case p₁ => e₁
  ...
  case pₙ => eₙ
}
```

Here, messages in an actor's mailbox are matched against the patterns $p_1, \ldots, p_n$.
Patterns consist of constructors and variables. A constructor pattern names a
case class; it matches all instances of this class. A variable pattern matches every
value and binds the value to the variable. For example, the pattern `Value(a)`

matches all instances v of the `Value` class and binds the variable `a` to the constructor argument of v.

A `receive` will select the first message in an actor's mailbox that matches any of its patterns. If a pattern p_i matches, its corresponding action e_i is executed. If no message in the mailbox matches a pattern, the actor will suspend, waiting for further messages to arrive.

Looking at the example above, it might seem that Scala is a language specialized for actor concurrency. In fact, this is not true. Scala only assumes the basic thread model of the underlying host. All higher-level operations shown in the example are defined as classes and methods of the Scala library. In the rest of this section, we look "under the covers" to find out how each construct is defined and implemented.

An actor is simply a subclass of the host environment's `Thread` class that defines methods ! and `receive` for sending and receiving messages.

```
abstract class Actor extends Thread {
  private var mailbox: List[Any]
  def !(msg: Any) = ...
  def receive[a](f: PartialFunction[Any, a]): a = ...
  ...
}
```

The ! method is used to send a message to an actor. The send syntax `a!m` is simply an abbreviation of the method call `a.!(m)`, just like `x+y` in Scala is an abbreviation for `x.+(y)`. The method does two things. First, it enqueues the message argument in the actor's mailbox, which is represented as a private field of type `List[Any]`. Second, if the receiving actor is currently suspended in a `receive` that could handle the sent message, the execution of the actor is resumed.

The `receive { ... }` construct is more interesting. Here, the pattern matching expression inside the braces is treated in Scala as a first-class object that is passed as an argument to the `receive` method. The argument's type is an instance of `PartialFunction`, which is a subclass of `Function1`, the class of unary functions. The two classes are defined as follows.

```
abstract class Function1[-a,+b] {
  def apply(x: a): b
}
abstract class PartialFunction[-a,+b] extends Function1[a,b] {
  def isDefinedAt(x: a): boolean
}
```

So we see that functions are objects which have an `apply` method. Partial functions are objects which have in addition a method `isDefinedAt` which can be used to find out whether a function is defined at a given value. Both classes are parameterized; the first type parameter a indicates the function's argument type and the second type parameter b indicates its result type[4].

A pattern matching expression { case p_1 => e_1; ...; case p_n => e_n } is then a partial function whose methods are defined as follows.

- The isDefinedAt method returns **true** if one of the patterns p_i matches the argument, **false** otherwise.
- The apply method returns the value e_i for the first pattern p_i that matches its argument. If none of the patterns match, a MatchError exception is thrown.

The two methods are used in the implementation of receive as follows. First, messages m in the mailbox are scanned in the order they appear. If receive's argument f is defined for some of the messages, that message is removed from the mailbox and f is applied to it. On the other hand, if f.isDefinedAt(m) is **false** for every message in the mailbox, the thread associated with the actor is suspended.

This sums up the essential implementation of thread-based actors. There is also some other functionality in Scala's actor libraries which we have not covered. For instance, there is a method receiveWithin which can be used to specify a time span in which a message should be received allowing an actor to timeout while waiting for a message. Upon timeout the action associated with a special TIMEOUT() pattern is fired. Timeouts can be used to suspend an actor, completely flush the mailbox, or to implement priority messages [4].

Thread-based actors are useful as a higher-level abstraction of threads, which replace error-prone shared memory accesses and locks by asynchronous message passing. However, like threads they incur a performance penalty on standard platforms such as the JVM, which prevents scalability. In the next section we show how the actor model can be changed so that actors become disassociated from threads.

3   Recomposing Actors

Logically, an actor is not bound to a thread of execution. Nevertheless, virtually all implementations of actor models associate a separate thread or even an operating system process with each actor [8,29,9,30].

In Scala, thread abstractions of the standard library are mapped onto the thread model and implementation of the corresponding target platform, which at the moment consists of the JVM and Microsoft's CLR [15].

To overcome the resulting problems with scalability, we propose an event-based implementation where (1) actors are thread-less, and (2) computations

---

[4] Parameters can carry + or - variance annotations which specify the relationship between instantiation and subtyping. The -a, +b annotations indicate that functions are contravariant in their argument and covariant in their result. In other words Function1[X1, Y1] is a subtype of Function1[X2, Y2] if X2 is a subtype of X1 and Y1 is a subtype of Y2.

between two events are allowed to run to completion. An event in our library corresponds to the arrival of a new message in an actor's mailbox.

3.1   Execution Example

First, we want to give an intuitive explanation of how our event-based implementation works. For this, we revisit our counter example from section 2.

Let c be a new instance of a lockable counter (with an empty mailbox). After starting c it immediately blocks, waiting for a matching message. Consider the case where another actor p sends the message Lock(p) to c (c ! Lock(p)). Because the arrival of this Lock message enables c to continue, send transfers control to c. c resumes the **receive** statement that caused it to block. Instead of executing the receiving actor on its own thread, we reuse the sender's thread.

According to the semantics of **receive**, the new message is selected and removed from the mailbox because it matches the first case of the outer **receive**. Then, the corresponding action is executed with the pattern variables bound to the constituents of the matched message:

```
{ case Incr()   =>  loop(value + 1)
  case Value(a) =>  a ! value; loop(value)
  case Lock(a)  =>  a ! value
                    receive { case UnLock(v) => loop(v) }
  case _        =>  loop(value)
}.apply(Lock(p))
```

Intuitively, this reduces to

```
p ! value
receive { case UnLock(v) => loop(v) }
```

After executing the message send p ! value, the call to **receive** blocks as there are no other messages in c's mailbox. Remember that we are still inside p's original message send (i.e. the send did not return, yet). Thus, blocking the current thread (e.g., by issuing a call to **wait()**) would also block p.

This is illegal because in our programming model the send operation (!) has a non-blocking semantics. Instead, we need to suspend c in such a way that allows p to continue. For this, inside the (logically) blocking **receive**, first, we remember the rest of c's computation. In this case, it suffices to save the closure of

```
receive { case UnLock(v) => loop(v) }
```

Second, to let p's call of the send operation return, we need to unwind the runtime stack up to the point where control was transferred to c. We do this by throwing a special exception. The ! method catches this exception and returns normally, keeping its non-blocking semantics.

In general, though, it is not sufficient to save a closure to capture the rest of the computation of an actor. For example, consider an actor executing the following statements:

```
val x = receive { case y => f(y) }
g(x)
```

Here, `receive` produces a value which is then passed to a function. Assume `receive` blocks. Remember that we would need to save the rest of the computation *inside* the blocking `receive`.

To save information about statements following `receive`, we would need to save the call-stack, or capture a (first-class) continuation. Virtual machines such as the JVM provide no means for explicit stack management, mainly because of security reasons. Thus, languages implementing first-class continuations have to simulate the run-time stack on the heap which poses serious performance problems [7]. Moreover, programming tools such as debuggers and profilers rely on run-time information on the native VM stack which they are unable to find if the stack that programs are using is allocated on the heap. Consequently, existing tools cannot be used with programs compiled using a heap-allocated stack.

Thus, most ports of languages with continuation support (e.g. Scheme [18], Ruby [24]) onto non-cooperative virtual machines abandon first-class continuations altogether (e.g. JScheme [2], JRuby[5]). Scala does not support first-class continuations either, primarily because of compatibility and interoperability issues with existing Java code.

To conclude, managing information about statements following a call to `receive` would require changes either to the compiler or the VM. Following our rationale for a library-based approach, we want to avoid those changes.

Instead, we require that `receive` *never returns normally*. Thus, managing information about succeeding statements is unnecessary. Moreover, we can enforce this "no-return" property at compile time through Scala's type system which states that statements following calls to functions (or methods) with return type `Nothing` will never get executed ("dead code") [26]. Note that returning by throwing an exception is still possible. In fact, as already mentioned above, our implementation of `receive` relies on it.

Using a non-returning `receive`, the above example could be coded like this:

```
receive { case y => x = f(y); g(x) }
```

Basically, the rest of the actor's computation has to be called at the end of each case inside the argument function of `receive` ("continuation passing" style).

3.2   Single-Threaded Actors

As we want to avoid inversion of control `receive` will (conceptually) be executed at the expense of the sender. If all actors are running on a single thread, sending a message to an actor A will resume the execution of `receive` which caused A to suspend. The code below shows a simplified implementation of the send operation for actors that run on a single thread:

---

[5] See http://jruby.sourceforge.net/.

```
def !(msg: Any): unit = {
  mailbox += msg
  if (continuation != null && continuation.isDefinedAt(msg))
    try { receive(continuation) }
    catch {
      case Done => // do nothing
    }
}
```

The sent message is appended to the mailbox of the actor which is the target of the send operation. Let A denote the target actor. If the continuation attribute is set to a non-null value then A is suspended waiting for an appropriate message (otherwise, A did not execute a call to receive, yet). As continuation refers to (the closure of) the partial function with which the last blocking receive was called, we can test if the newly appended message allows A to continue.

Note that if, instead, we would save receive(f) as continuation for a blocking receive(f) we would not be able to test this but rather had to blindly call the continuation. If the newly appended message would not match any of the defined patterns, receive would go through all messages in the mailbox again trying to find the first matching message. Of course, the attempt would be in vain as only the newly appended message could have enabled A to continue.

If A is able to process the newly arrived message we let A continue until it blocks on a nested receive(g) or finishes its computation. In the former case, we first save the closure of g as A's continuation. Then, the send operation that originated A's execution has to return because of its non-blocking semantics. For this, the blocking receive throws a special exception of type Done (see below) which is caught in the send method (!). Technically, this trick unwinds the call-stack up to the point where the message send transferred control to A. Thus, to complete the explanation of how the implementation of the send operation works, we need to dive into the implementation of receive.

The receive method selects messages from an actor's mailbox and is responsible for saving the continuation as well as abandoning the evaluation context:

```
def receive(f: PartialFunction[Any, unit]): Nothing = {
  mailbox.dequeueFirst(f.isDefinedAt) match {
    case Some(msg) => continuation = null
                      f(msg)
    case None      => continuation = f
  }
  throw new Done
}
```

Naturally, we dequeue the first message in our mailbox which matches one of the cases defined by the partial function which is provided as an argument to receive. Note that f.isDefinedAt has type Any => boolean. As the type of the resulting object is Option[Any] which has two cases defined, we can select between these cases using pattern matching. When there was a message dequeued we first reset the saved continuation. This is necessary to prevent a former continuation to be called multiple times when there is a send to the current actor inside the call f(msg).

If we didn't find a matching message in the mailbox, we remember the continuation which is the closure of f. In both cases we need to abandon the evaluation context by throwing a special exception of type Done, so the sender which originated the call to receive can continue normally (see above).

3.3   Multi-threaded Actors

To leverage the increasingly important class of multi-core processors (and also multi-processors) we want to execute concurrent activities on multiple threads. We rely on modern VM implementations to execute concurrent VM threads on multiple processor cores in parallel.

A scheduler decides how many threads to spend for a given workload of concurrent actors, and, naturally, implements a specific scheduling strategy. Because of its asychronous nature, a message send introduces a concurrent activity, namely the resumption of a previously suspended actor. We encapsulate this activity in a *task item* which gets submitted to the scheduler (in a sense this is a *rescheduling send* [28]):

```
def send(msg: Any): unit = synchronized {
  if (continuation != null
      && continuation.isDefinedAt(msg)
      && !scheduled) {
    scheduled = true
    Scheduler.putTask(new ReceiverTask(this, msg))
  } else mailbox += msg
}
```

If a call to send finds the current continuation of the receiving actor A to be undefined, A is not waiting for a message. Usually, this is the case when a task for A has been scheduled that has not been executed, yet. Basically, send appends the argument message to the mailbox unless the receiving actor is waiting for a message and is able to process the argument message. In this case, we schedule the continuation of the receiving actor for execution by submitting a new task item to the scheduler.

The scheduler maintains a pool of worker threads which execute task items. A ReceiverTask is basically a Java java.lang.Runnable that receives a specified message and has an exception handler that handles requests for abandoning the evaluation context:

```
class ReceiverTask(actor: Actor, msg: Any) extends Runnable {
  def run(): unit =
    try { actor receiveMsg msg }
    catch {
      case Done => // do nothing
    }
}
```

`receiveMsg` is a special form of `receive` which processes a given message according to the actor's continuation.

Actors are not prevented from calling operations which can block indefinitely. In the following we describe a scheduler which guarantees progress even in the presence of blocking operations.

3.4   Blocking Operations

The event-based character of our implementation stems from the fact that (1) actors are thread-less, and (2) computations between the reception of two messages are allowed to run to completion. The second property is common for event-driven systems [17] and reflects our assumption of a rather interactive character for most actors. Consequently, computations between arrival of messages are expected to be rather short compared to the communication overhead.

Nevertheless, we also want to support long-running, CPU-bound actors. Such actors should not prevent other actors from making progress. Likewise, it would be unfortunate if a single blocking actor could cause the whole application to stop responding, thereby hindering other actors to make progress.

We face the same problems as user-level thread libraries: Processes yield control to the scheduler only at certain program points. In between they cannot be prevented from calling blocking operations or executing infinite loops. For example, an actor might call a native method which issues a blocking system call.

In our case, the scheduler is executed only when sending a message leads to the resumption of another actor. Because send is not allowed to block, the receiver (which is resumed) needs to be executed on a different thread. This way, the sender is not blocked even if the receiver executes a blocking operation.

As the scheduler might not have an idle worker thread available (because all of them are blocked), it needs to create new worker threads as needed. However, if there is at least one worker thread runnable (i.e. busy executing an actor), we do not create a new thread. This is to prevent the creation of too many threads even in the absence of blocking operations.

Actors are still thread-less, though: Each time an actor is suspended because of a blocking (which means unsuccessful) receive, instead of blocking the thread, it is *detached* from its thread. The thread now becomes idle, because it has finished executing a receiver task item. It will ask the scheduler for more work. Thereby, threads are reused for the execution of multiple actors.

Using this method, an actor-based application with low concurrency can be executed by as few as two threads, regardless of the number of simultaneously active actors.

Implementation. Unfortunately, it is impossible for user-level code to find out if a thread running on the JVM is blocked. We therefore implemented a simple heuristic that tries to approximate if a worker thread which executes an actor is blocked, or not.

```
def execute(item: ReceiverTask): unit = synchronized {
  if (idle.length > 0) {
    val worker = idle.dequeue
    executing.update(item.actor, worker)
    worker.execute(item)
  } else {
    val iter = workers.elements
    var foundBusy = false
    while (iter.hasNext && !foundBusy) {
      val worker = iter.next
      ticks.get(worker) match {
        case None => foundBusy = true
        case Some(ts) => {
          val currTime = System.currentTimeMillis
          if (currTime - ts < TICKFREQ)
            foundBusy = true
        }
      }
    }
    if (!foundBusy) {
      val worker = new WorkerThread(this)
      workers += worker
      executing.update(item.actor, worker)
      worker.execute(item)
      worker.start()
    } else tasks += item
  }
}
```

Fig. 2. Scheduling work items

The basic idea is that actors provide the scheduler with life-beats during their execution. That is, the send (!) and `receive` methods call a `tick` method of the scheduler. The scheduler then looks up the worker thread which is currently executing the corresponding actor, and updates its time stamp. When a new receiver task item is submitted to the scheduler, it first checks if all worker threads are blocked. Worker threads with "recent" time stamps are assumed not to be blocked. Only if all worker threads are assumed to be blocked (because of old time stamps), a new worker thread is created. Otherwise, the task item is simply put into a queue waiting to be consumed by an idle worker thread. Figure 2 shows the main part of the scheduler implementation.

Note that using the described approximation, it is impossible to distinguish blocked threads from threads that perform long-running computations. This means basically that compute-bound actors execute on their own thread.

For some applications it might be worth using a scheduler which optimizes the number of spare worker threads depending on runtime profiles. User-defined schedulers are easy to implement and use with our library.

In summary, additional threads are created only when needed to support (unexpected) blocking operations. The only blocking operation that is handled without thread support is `receive`. Thus, a large number of non-cooperative actors (those using blocking operations other than what our library provides), may lead to a significant increase in memory consumption as the scheduler creates more and more threads.

On the other hand, our approach adds significant flexibility, as the library does not need to be changed when the user decides to use a blocking operation which has no special library support. This also means that actors and standard VM threads can be combined seamlessly. We discovered an important use case when porting our runtime system to use JXTA as transport layer: Providing an actor-based interface to a thread-based library.

4   Distributed Actors

With the help of a portable runtime system actors can be executed in a distributed fashion. More specifically, message sends are location transparent and actors can be spawned on remote nodes. As we also target resource-constrained devices, runtime services need to be runnable on virtual machines which offer only a subset of the functionality of standard desktop virtual machines. For example, the KVM[6] does not support reflection. Thus, our serialization mechanism is not based on a general reflective scheme. Instead, we provide a combinator library which allows efficient picklers for custom datatypes to be constructed easily. The pickler combinators are based on Kennedy's library for Haskell [19]. The generated byte arrays are compact because of (1) structure sharing, and (2) base128 encoded integers.

Our runtime system is portable in the sense that network protocol dependent parts are isolated in a separate layer which provides network services (connection management, message transmission, etc.). Two working prototype implementations of the service layer based on TCP and JXTA, respectively, establish portability in practice. TCP and JXTA are protocols different enough that we expect no difficulties porting our runtime system to other network protocols in the future.

We are currently working on the addition of the SOAP[7] XML-over-HTTP protocol as transport layer. One of the goals is to provide an actor-based interface to web services such as the publicly exposed APIs of Google and Amazon. Moreover, we want to build web services in terms of actors.

5   Performance Evaluation

In this section we examine performance properties of our event-based implementation of actors. In the process, we compare benchmark execution times with SALSA [30], a state-of-the-art Java-based actor language, as well as with

---

[6] See http://java.sun.com/products/cldc/.

[7] See http://www.w3.org/2000/xp/Group/.

a thread-based version of our library. As a reference we also show the performance of a straight-forward implementation using threads and synchronized data structures. In addition to execution time we are also interested in scalability with respect to the number of simultaneously active actors each system can handle.

Experimental Set-Up. We measure the throughput of blocking operations in a queue-based application. The application is structured as a ring of n producers/consumers (in the following called *processes*) with a shared queue between each of them. Initially, k of these queues contain tokens and the others are empty. Each process loops removing an item from the queue on its right and placing it in the queue on its left.

The following tests were run on a 1.60GHz Intel Pentium M processor with 512 MB memory, running Sun's Java HotSpot Client VM 1.5.0 under Linux 2.6.12. We set the JVM's maximum heap size to 256 MB to provide for sufficient physical memory to avoid any disk activity. In each case we took the median of 5 runs.

The execution times of three equivalent actor-based implementations written using (1) our event-based actor library, (2) a thread-based version of a similar library, and (3) SALSA, respectively, are compared.

Benchmark Results. Figure 3 shows start-up times of the ring for up to 2000 processes (note that both scales are logarithmic). For event-based actors and the naïve thread-based implementation, start-up time is basically constant. Event-based actors are about 60% slower than pure threads. However, we have reasons

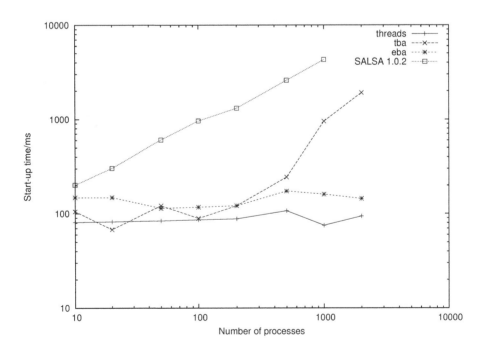

Fig. 3. Start-up time

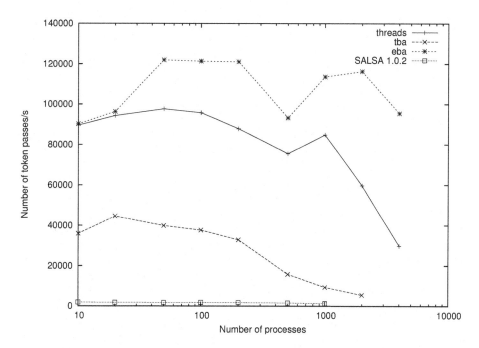

Fig. 4. Throughput (number of token passes per second) for a fixed number of 10 tokens

to suggest that this is due to the different benchmark implementations. In all actor-based implementations, start-up time is measured by starting all actors and letting them wait to receive a special "continue" message. In contrast, the thread-based implementation only *creates* all required threads without starting them. Our measurements suggest that the used JVM optimizes thread creation, potentially creating required runtime structures lazily on start-up. For thread-based actors, start-up time increases exponentially when the number of processes approaches a thousand. With 4000 processes the JVM crashes because of exhaustion of maximum heap size.

Using SALSA, the VM was unable to create 2000 processes. As each actor has a thread-based state object associated with it, the VM is unable to handle stack space requirements at this point. In contrast, using event-based actors the ring can be operated with up to 310000 processes that are created in about 10 seconds.

Looking at the generated Java code shows that SALSA spends a lot of time setting up actors for remote communication (creating locality descriptors, name table management, etc.), whereas in our case, an actor must announce explicitly that it wants to participate in remote communications (by calling `alive()`). Creation of locality descriptors and name table management can be delayed up to this point. Also, when an actor is created in SALSA, it sends itself a special "construct" message which takes additional time.

Figure 4 shows the number of token passes per second depending on the ring size. We chose a logarithmic scale for the number of processes to better depict effects which are confined to a high and strongly increasing number of processes. For up to 1000 processes, increase in throughput for event-based actors compared to pure threads averages 22%. As blocking operations clearly dominate, overhead of threads is likely to stem from context switches and contention for locks. Interestingly, overhead vanishes for a small number of processes (10 and 20 processes, respectively). This behavior suggests that contention is not an issue in this case, as uncontended lock management is optimized in Sun's HotSpot VM 1.5. Contention for locks becomes significant at about 2000 processes. Finally, when the number of processes reaches 4000, the threads' time is consumed managing the shared buffers rather than exchanging tokens through them. At this point throughput of event-based actors is about 3 times higher.

For SALSA, throughput is about two orders of magnitude lower compared to event-based actors. The average for 10 to 1000 processes amounts to only 1700 token passes per second. Looking at the generated Java source code revealed that every message send involves a reflective method call. We found reflective method calls to be about 30 times slower than JIT-compiled method calls on our testing machine.

For thread-based actors, throughput is almost constant for up to 200 processes (on average about 38000 token passes per second). At 500 processes it is already less than half of that (15772 token passes per second). Similar to pure threads, throughput breaks in for 2000 processes (only 5426 token passes per second). Again, contended locks and context switching overhead are likely to cause this behavior. The VM is unable to create 4000 processes, because it runs out of memory.

Performance Summary. Event-based actors support a number of simultaneously active actors which is two orders of magnitude higher compared to SALSA. Measured throughput is over 50 times higher compared to SALSA. A naïve thread-based implementation of our benchmark performs surprisingly well. However, for high numbers of threads (about 2000), lock contention causes performance to break in. Also, the maximum number of threads is limited due to their memory consumption.

6   Conclusion

Scala is different from other concurrent languages in that it contains no language support for concurrency beyond the standard thread model offered by the host environment. Instead of specialized language constructs we rely on Scala's general abstraction capabilities to define higher-level concurrency models. In such a way, we were able to define all essential operations of Erlang's actor-based process model in the Scala library.

However, since Scala is implemented on the Java VM, we inherited some of the deficiencies of the host environment when it comes to concurrency, namely low maximum number of threads and high context-switch overhead. In this paper we have shown how to turn this weakness into a strength. By defining a new event-based model for actors, we could increase dramatically their efficiency and scalability. At the same time, we kept to a large extent the programming model of thread-based actors, which would not have been possible if we had switched to a traditional event-based architecture, because the latter causes an inversion of control.

The techniques presented in this paper are a good showcase of the increased flexibility offered by library-based designs. It allowed us to quickly address problems with the previous thread-based actor model by developing a parallel class hierarchy for event-based actors. Today, the two approaches exist side by side. Thread-based actors are still useful since they allow returning from a receive operation. Event-based actors are more restrictive in the programming style they allow, but they are also more efficient.

In future work we plan to extend the event-based actor implementation to other communication infrastructures. We are also in train of discovering new ways to compose these actors.

References

1. Gul A. Agha. *ACTORS: A Model of Concurrent Computation in Distributed Systems*. Series in Artificial Intelligence. The MIT Press, Cambridge, Massachusetts, 1986.
2. Ken Anderson, Tim Hickey, and Peter Norvig. Jscheme.
3. J. Armstrong. Erlang — a survey of the language and its industrial applications. In *INAP'96 — The 9th Exhibitions and Symposium on Industrial Applications of Prolog*, pages 16–18, Hino, Tokyo, Japan, October 1996.
4. Joe Armstrong, Robert Virding, Claes Wikström, and Mike Williams. *Concurrent Programming in Erlang, Second Edition*. Prentice-Hall, 1996.
5. Joe L. Armstrong. The development of erlang. In *ICFP*, pages 196–203, 1997.
6. A. Black, M. Carlsson, M. Jones, R. Kieburtz, and J. Nordlander. Timber: A programming language for real-time embedded systems, 2002.
7. Yannis Bres, Bernard P. Serpette, and Manuel Serrano. Bigloo.NET: compiling scheme to.NET CLR. *Journal of Object Technology*, 3(9):71–94, 2004.
8. Jean-Pierre Briot. Actalk: A testbed for classifying and designing actor languages in the smalltalk-80 environment. In *ECOOP*, pages 109–129, 1989.
9. Legand L. Burge III and K. M. George. JMAS: A Java-based mobile actor system for distributed parallel computation. In *Proceedings of the Fifth USENIX Conference on Object-Oriented Technologies and Systems*, pages 115–129. The USENIX Association, 1999.
10. Brian Chin and Todd Millstein. Responders: Language support for interactive applications. In *ECOOP*, Nantes, France, July 2006.
11. Georgio Chrysanthakopoulos and Satnam Singh. An asynchronous messaging library for c#. In *Proceedings of Workshop on Synchronization and Concurrency in Object-Oriented Languages (SCOOL), OOPSLA*, 2005.
12. Adam Dunkels, Björn Grönvall, and Thiemo Voigt. Contiki - A lightweight and flexible operating system for tiny networked sensors. In *LCN*, pages 455–462, 2004.
13. E. Gamma, R. Helm, R. Johnson, and J. Vlissides. *Design Patterns*. Addison-Wesley, 1995.

14. Benoit Garbinato, Rachid Guerraoui, Jarle Hulaas, Maxime Monod, and Jesper H. Spring. Frugal Mobile Objects. Technical report, EPFL, 2005.
15. John Gough. *Compiling for the .NET Common Language Runtime*. .NET series. Prentice Hall, 2002.
16. Carl Hewitt, Peter Bishop, and Richard Steiger. A universal modular ACTOR formalism for artificial intelligence. In *IJCAI*, pages 235–245, 1973.
17. Jason Hill, Robert Szewczyk, Alec Woo, Seth Hollar, David E. Culler, and Kristofer S. J. Pister. System architecture directions for networked sensors. In *ASPLOS*, pages 93–104, 2000.
18. Richard Kelsey, William Clinger, and Jonathan Rees. Revised[5] report on the algorithmic language Scheme. *Higher-Order and Symbolic Computation*, 11(1):7–105, 1998. Also appears in ACM SIGPLAN Notices 33(9), September 1998.
19. Andrew Kennedy. Pickler combinators. *J. Funct. Program.*, 14(6):727–739, 2004.
20. George Lawton. Moving Java into mobile phones. *Computer*, 35(6):17–20, June 2002.
21. P. Levis and D. Culler. Mate: A tiny virtual machine for sensor networks. In *International Conference on Architectural Support for Programming Languages and Operating Systems, San Jose, CA, USA*, Oct. 2002.
22. T. Lindholm and F. Yellin. *The Java Virtual Machine Specification*. Addison-Wesley, 1996.
23. Jeremy Manson, Jason Baker, Antonio Cunei, Suresh Jagannathan, Marek Prochazka, Bin Xin, and Jan Vitek. Preemptible atomic regions for real-time java. In *RTSS*, pages 62–71. IEEE Computer Society, 2005.
24. Yukihiro Matsumoto. *The Ruby Programming Language*. Addison Wesley Professional, 2002.
25. J. H. Nyström, Philip W. Trinder, and David J. King. Evaluating distributed functional languages for telecommunications software. In Bjarne Däcker and Thomas Arts, editors, *Proceedings of the 2003 ACM SIGPLAN Workshop on Erlang, Uppsala, Sweden, August 29, 2003*, pages 1–7. ACM, 2003.
26. Martin Odersky and al. An overview of the scala programming language. Technical Report IC/2004/64, EPFL Lausanne, Switzerland, 2004.
27. F. Pizlo, J. M. Fox, David Holmes, and Jan Vitek. Real-time java scoped memory: Design patterns and semantics. In *ISORC*, pages 101–110. IEEE Computer Society, 2004.
28. Erik Stenman and Konstantinos Sagonas. On reducing interprocess communication overhead in concurrent programs. In *Proceedings of the 2002 ACM SIGPLAN Workshop on Erlang, Pittsburgh, PA, USA, October 7, 2002*, pages 58–63. ACM, 2002.
29. D. A. Thomas, W. R. Lalonde, J. Duimovich, M. Wilson, J. McAffer, and B. Berry. Actra A multitasking/multiprocessing smalltalk. *Proceedings of the ACM SIGPLAN Workshop on Object-Based Concurrent Programming, ACM SIGPLAN Notices*, 24(4):87–90, April 1989.
30. Carlos Varela and Gul Agha. Programming dynamically reconfigurable open systems with salsa. *SIGPLAN Not.*, 36(12):20–34, 2001.
31. Claes Wikström. Distributed programming in erlang. In Hoon Hong, editor, *Proceedings of the First International Symposium on Parallel Symbolic Computation, PASCO'94 (Hagenberg/Linz, Austria, September 26-28, 1994)*, volume 5 of *Lecture Note Series in Computing*, pages 412–421. World Scientific, Singapore-New Jersey-London-Hong Kong, 1994.

Programming Language Concepts for Multimedia Application Development

Oliver Lampl, Elmar Stellnberger, and László Böszörményi

oliver.lampl@hollomey.com, estellnb@yahoo.de,
laszlo.boeszoermenyi@itec.uni-klu.ac.at

Abstract. Multimedia application development requires features and concepts currently not supported by common systems programming languages. This paper introduces two new minimal language extensions increasing expressive power, safety and optimization possibilities in multimedia programming. New loop statements are presented to shorten multidimensional array access and optimize its execution. Furthermore, a new data type concept is presented to allow quality of service (QoS) definition on data type declaration level. Both have been implemented in Modula-3 and C#.

1 Introduction

Substantial parts of programs processing multimedia data follow some very common patterns:

1. In the compression/decompression/transformation part of such programs, large multidimensional numerical arrays are partitioned into small independent blocks and processed by algorithms, like the Discrete Cosine Transformation (DCT).
2. In the video streaming and play-back part, long sequences of data (e.g. video frames) are processed and/or transmitted periodically, under so-called "soft real-time" constraints.

The manually created code for these recurring patterns is typically cumbersome, error-prone and inefficient. These observations suggest that we could give good support for multimedia programming on the level of a programming language. A vast number of multimedia query languages resp. language extensions exist [15], nevertheless, to our knowledge, no language support for multimedia systems-programming exists. We argue in our paper that such a support is advantageous and easily possible.

The first pattern obviously calls for a simple, automatic parallelization. To handle the second pattern, we need a notion of time, and a way to express Quality of Service (QoS) constraints. Instead of defining a brand new language, we investigated the possibilities of extending some existing programming languages with the minimal necessary features, considering the following basic principles: Add an extension to a language only if the following conditions are fulfilled:

1. The new feature enhances the expressive power of the language considerably.
2. The safety of programs using the new feature is enhanced.
3. The new feature enables some automatic optimizations.

D. Lightfoot and C. Szyperski (Eds.): JMLC 2006, LNCS 4228, pp. 23–36, 2006.

Everything else should rather be put into a library than applied as a language extension. Under these premises we suggest the following extensions for general purpose programming languages:

1. A *foreach* and a *forall* statement enabling compact and safe expression, and automatic parallelization of typical video transformation code, operating on independent blocks of data.
2. A time dimension, which can be added to any existing scalar or array type as an n+first dimension.
3. A very simple first-order logic based language extension, enabling to express QoS constraints.

The actual language extensions were designed both in Pascal- and C-style and were implemented in two well-known representatives of these language families: Modula-3 [13] resp. C# [11]. The parallel development helped us a lot to separate the essence of a new construct from the syntactic sugar and it was - by the way - the source of a lot of fun.

2   Related Work

2.1   Parallelism

Generally, two different approaches exist to introduce parallelism. In the synchronous approach one instruction is used to work on multiple data elements. The asynchronous approach on the other hand allows the execution of different instruction streams simultaneously.

In [3] Philipsen and Tichy implement a machine independent *forall* loop both in a synchronous and asynchronous version targeting multiple architectures with shared and distributed memory. Furthermore they showed in [4] that with the use of an adequate working environment debugging of parallel programs written with *forall* loops is feasible and does not pose a big problem.

In [2] Knudsen introduces a queue to distribute the workload of an asynchronous *forall* loop on multiple execution units of a shared memory system as provided by multi processor and multi core computers. Implementing dynamic workload generation via distributing nested procedures by a queue causes very little overhead in the range of a few percents. This approach reaches a high utilization even in the last loop iterations without the need of static analysis.

We have adopted his approach both in our Modula-3 and C# implementation. In the latter, however, we pass objects instead of using nested procedures because nested procedures are not supported in C#. Supplying an asynchronous *forall* seems to be sufficient in most cases of multimedia programming. Asynchronous *foralls* are also open to vectorization thus allowing a further possibility for speedups.

In [14] Zima presents how dependence analysis can be used by compilers to automatize vectorization and parallelization. Source to source transformation using *forall* loops as a target construct is suggested. Explicit synchronization barriers are used rather than implicitly inserted barriers at the end of each parallel loop. The described techniques can also be used to verify the mutual independence of different loop iterations, a condition which is demanded but not yet checked by Knudsens approach, nor by ours. Loop carried dependencies would require explicit assumptions about loop behavior.

2.2 Quality of Service

Quality of service (QoS) is another important aspect of multimedia applications. A lot of different notations and specifications can be found to express QoS-related mechanisms like resource reservation, admission control, and adaptation. Jin and Nahrstedt provide a classification over existing QoS specification languages [9]. These specification languages try to cover most aspects of QoS and are defined on application-, user-, or resource-level to allow a user-friendly notation.

To apply QoS constraints directly at the programming language level not all aspects of QoS have to be met. When applying QoS on displaying of a video the most important QoS constraints are frame rate, delay, and jitter. These timing limitations can be expressed using temporal logic. In [1] Blair and Stefani introduce the first order logic based language QL to define and formally analyze QoS constraints. QL is based on an event model basically identified by three components: event types (1) , events (2) and histories (3).

1. Event types represent a particular state transition in a system (e.g. the arrival of a frame of video).
2. An event is an occurrence of an event type (e.g. the arrival of a particular frame of video).
3. The history represents a discrete sequence of events of the same event type.

To reflect a special occurrence of an event in the history the function $\tau(\varepsilon, n)$ is used, where n represents the nth occurrence and ε the event type. By applying this model, we can express a wide range of quality of service constraints. E.g. the throughput of video can be expressed (ε_r stays for frame reception):

$$\forall n, \tau(\varepsilon_r, n+k) - \tau(\varepsilon_r, n) \leq \delta$$

To be precise, this formula specifies that for all video frames, the difference in time between the arrival of the frame n + k and the frame n is less than a given value δ. The next example shows the definition of bounded execution time (ε_e stays for the emission, ε_r for the arrival of a frame):

$$\forall n, \left| \tau(\varepsilon_{e,n}) - \tau(\varepsilon_r, n) \right| \leq \delta$$

In this case, the maximum allowed delay between two different event types is specified for all of their occurrences.

In [1] Esterel is used for QoS monitoring. It is an imperative language specifically developed in order to assert the QoS compliance of networked applications. An

Esterel program consists of a set of parallel processes which execute synchronously and communicate with each other. Apart from its fancy signaling concept Esterel is quite minimalistic. Programmers may prefer a better integrated approach that is easy in practical deployment and that allows them to make use of their existing knowledge. However, we chose a different approach, see *QoS Monitoring*.

Our work concerning QoS is based on the event model of QL. It can describe most of the QoS constraints required in multimedia applications. Nevertheless it is limited and some constraints cannot be expressed like general reliability requirements such as Mean Time Between Failure or Mean Time To Repair.

3 Parallelism and Loops

3.1 Extended Loop Statement

Pixel manipulations can be implemented using multidimensional arrays. A lot of encoder or decoder implementations make use of such data structures. In programming languages like Modula or C/C++, such arrays are iterated using simple *for* statements. In Java and C# new loop statements have been developed in order to iterate over collections or arrays.

In C# the *foreach* statement [11] is used to iterate over expressions that can be evaluated to a type that implements the *IEnumerable* interface, or a type that declares a *GetEnumerator* method which then returns an object of type *IEnumerator* [8].

```
foreach ( type identifier in expression )

      embedded-statement
```

These enumerators iterate over the stored elements. For each element the embedded statement is executed.

In multimedia applications we often want to refer to the index of the elements accessed. Therefore we extended the *foreach* statement to define the expression for retrieving the elements of the array. This enables the programmer to define index variables which can be accessed during the loop. To avoid unpredictable side effects index access is read only.

```
foreach ( type identifier = expression in expression )

      embedded-statement
```

The following example represents a simple implementation of the discrete cosine transformation (DCT) as used for JPEG implementations [10] implemented in C#.

```
double value = 0;

for (int u = 0; u < 8; u++) {
  for (int v = 0; v < 8; v++) {

    for (int i = 0; i < 8; i++) {
      for (int j = 0; j < 8; j++) {
```

```
      value += (source[i,j] - 128)
            * Math.Cos(((2*i + 1) * u * Math.PI) / 16)
            * Math.Cos(((2*j + 1) * v * Math.PI) / 16);
  }
  }
  coefficients[u,v] = value / 4;
 }
 }
```

Instead of using four conventional nested *for* statements the code fragment can be reimplemented by applying two extended *foreach* loops without considering the size of the array being iterated over.

```
foreach (double c = coefficients[u,v]
            in source) {
  foreach (int p = source[i,j] in source) {
   value += (p - 128)
            * Math.Cos(((2*i + 1) * u * Math.PI) / 16)
            * Math.Cos(((2*j + 1) * v * Math.PI) / 16);
  }
  coefficients[u,v] = value / 4;
 }
```

The extended *foreach* has been implemented in Modula-3 too.

```
FOREACH c = coefficients[u,v] IN coefficients VIA u,v DO
 FOREACH p = source[i,j] IN source VIA i,j DO
    value := value + ( FLOAT(p-128,LONGREAL)
            * cos(FLOAT((2*i+1)*u,LONGREAL)*Pi/16.0D0)
            * cos(FLOAT((2*j+1)*v,LONGREAL)*Pi/16.0D0));
 END
 coefficients[u,v] := value / 4.0D0;
END
```

The extended *foreach* loop expresses more clearly how elements are assigned within the loop. Furthermore, no array ranges have to be considered. The compiler internally generates the correct code for iteration and therefore provides more safety. No infinite loops can be created and the statement enables the programmer to express index based calculations with arrays. Like the original *foreach* in C#, the current element of the loop can be directly accessed.

3.2 Parallel Loop Execution

To optimize performance, parallelism can be added to the loop to distribute its execution into several threads. This executional optimization can be reached due to the fact that a *foreach* statement as defined in [11] does not necessarily guarantee a special order of execution. The semantic only defines that each element of the given collection or array is accessed. This fact can be used to implement a *foreach* loop in which each of the iterations can be executed simultaneously. The syntax is very similar to the shown *foreach* or the extended *foreach* statement, but the semantics differ.

```
forall ( type identifier in expression )
        embedded-statement
forall ( type identifier = expression in expression )
        embedded-statement
```

The block executed each time the loop iterates is embedded into a *job class*. The instance of this class represents a job which is executed for each loop iteration. Instead of executing the jobs in sequential order, they are put into a queue to feed workers which can operate in parallel. These workers are controlled by a management framework which observes the execution of all workers. Furthermore, it ensures that sequential execution follows after all parallel work is done. The compiler itself generates code to fork the workers, distribute the work to each worker and synchronize all workers when all work has been completed. After all parallel work is done, the program continues normally.

3.3 Parallel Processing Framework and Results

The default worker pool implementation is integrated into the system class library of Mono [7]. To give programmers the ability to implement their own worker pools the default behavior of jobs and the worker pool is defined by the interfaces *IJob* and *IworkerPool* (see figure 1). The worker pool can be exchanged during runtime by replacing the default worker pool implementation with the *WorkerPoolFactory*.

Each time a *forall* statements loop body is executed, an *IJob* object is created and added to the worker pool. At the end of the loop the *waitTillFinished* method is called to ensure that work has been done before continuing. The implementation uses the default multithreading libraries. The same behavior can be achieved using asynchronous method invocation. This feature of the Common Language Runtime [12] can be used to inherently introduce concurrency into a program. The *forall* statement has also been implemented in Modula-3 using nested procedures [5, 6, 16] instead of passing objects.

But parallelism is not without issues. The programmer has to consider the overhead for thread creation, control and the cost of object initialization. Normal loops can be terminated using *return* or *break* statements. This cannot be easily achieved when using parallelized execution. So the use of these statements has been forbidden, because of the misleading semantics. If *break* or *return* is used, the programmer wants the execution of the loop to stop, but the parallel execution disables immediate loop termination. Another problem is exception handling within the loop. This is achieved by catching exceptions within the worker threads, and throw them at the end of the execution to allow the programmer to use the default exception handling mechanisms of the language.

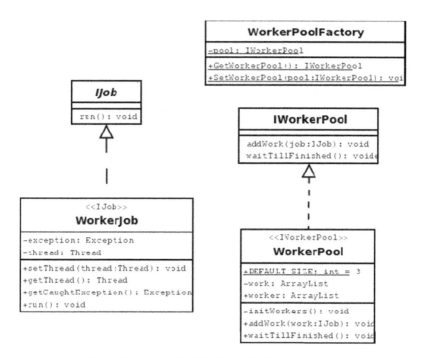

Fig. 1. Classes involved in the parallel loop statement

The performance enhancement is demonstrated using the simple block based DCT (see prior example). The *forall* statement is applied to parallelize the processing of blocks where the number of threads and the number of blocks are varied. The measurement was done on a quad processor machine showing linear scalability and little overhead (see figure 2 and 3).

The execution time of the *forall* statement using one single thread is only a few percents higher than the execution time of an implementation using *for* statements. This overhead is caused by object initialization and thread control. When increasing the number of threads, the execution time decreases significantly, but when the number of threads reaches the number of processors, the management overhead grows considerably. Similar results are presented in [2] which proofs the efficiency of our implementation.

At this point the presented concept will be evaluated according to the criteria defined at the beginning of this paper:

1. The expressive power of the extended *foreach* statement has been demonstrated by rewriting a DCT. The new statement tries to express the array loops with more simplicity in syntax but of course higher complexity in semantics.
2. The safety of the programs is enhanced due to the fact that the loop termination condition is hidden in the compiler generated code and guarantees that the loop comes to an end after it has accessed all elements of the data structure.
3. The *forall* loop can be used to optimize the execution time of the program (demonstrated by examples and graphs), where the loop body is separated into work packages and put into an efficient parallel processing framework.

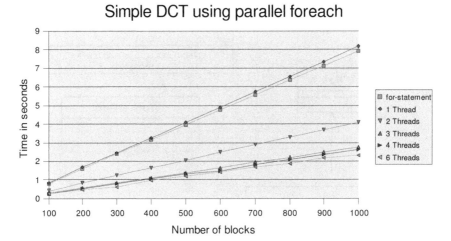

Fig. 2. The amount of time needed to process a given number of blocks using a set of threads

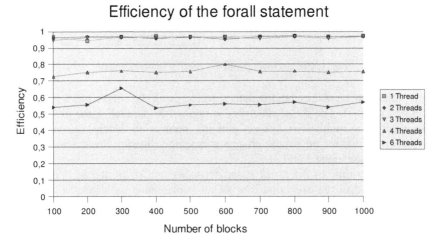

Fig. 3. The efficiency of the distribution to multiple workers

4   Monitoring QoS Constraints

4.1   Quality Aware Data Types

Instead of implementing QoS monitoring with Esterel as shown in [1], we introduce the concept of quality aware data types. The declaration of said types allows the programmer to specify the quality of service contract for a simple data type. A special assignment operation is used to examine declared constraints and cause exceptions in case of constraint violations.

The intent of quality aware data types is not to enforce a specified constraint. To achieve this, real time systems have to be used. In case of multimedia applications users might agree to quality of service changes if the cost is reduced, so we just have to check possible violations and inform about their occurrence.

Quality aware data types are declared by an additional dimension of time. This n+first dimension is declared using the token [~].

```
type [~] identifier
```

The dimension of time can be parameterized to specify quality of service constraints. The initialization of the type can be expressed in a static way for primitive data types with a constant constraint or using the *new* command to allow dynamic creation. The dynamic way provides exchangeability of the quality of service object to implement adaptive quality of service features.

```
type[~(IQoSObject)Identifier]

type[~] identifier = new type
                    [~(IqoSObject)identifier]
```

The quality of service parameter definition is encapsulated within an *IQoSObject*. This interface is used to implement QL like quality of service constraints, which are controlled automatically by compiler generated code. The programmer may use available implementations of QoS constraints and can also add own code.

4.2 Implementation Issues

Quality aware data types are implemented using event histories. Such events can be evaluated by an *IQoSObject* which then decides whether the given constraint can be held or not. The event happens at the assignment statement and is recorded in the history. In order to distinguish between an assignment and a QoS monitored assignment we define the timed assignment operation "~=".

Each time a quality aware data type is assigned using the timed assignment operation, its currently embedded constraints are checked. If the check fails a *QoSException* is thrown, which is used to react upon constraint violation. This allows easy implementation of adaptive quality of service constraints, e.g. the frame rate can be changed or the size of frames can be reduced. The definition of an additional assignment statement is advantageous because it allows the programmer to decide if the quality aware data type is monitored for the current assignment or not. This can be compared to video processing. If we playback a video, we monitor QoS constraints to achieve correct frame rate, jitter and delay. In case of management operations on videos, e.g. format conversion or video analysis for meta data retrieval, we do not necessarily need to monitor QoS.

The first example demonstrates a quality aware numerical type which is assigned within a *for* statement to values of a given array. The quality aware variable *value* is defined with the constraint *QoSDelay*. This object is initialized with the variable to be monitored and a numerical value expressing the delay in milliseconds to slow down execution. Each time *value* is assigned using the timed assignment statement the execution is delayed to print one value per second to the console. The numerical value is streamed.

```
int[~new QoSDelay("value", 1000)] value;
int[] data = {1,2,3,4,5,6,7,8,9};
for (int i = 0; i < data.Length; i++) {
        value ~= data[i];
        Console.WriteLine(value);
}
```

The control structure for video transcoding applications is implemented using quality aware data types. The variable *output* is declared as a quality aware data type and initialized with th QoS constraint *QoSThroughPut*. The QoS constraint is used to monitor the throughput of frames. It is initialized to monitor that every 1000 milliseconds 25 frames are processed. The short code for transcoding ensures that the quality of service constraint for display is held if not, an exception is thrown to terminate the execution of the loop. If the programmer implements the quality of service check manually, the code would be much more complicated. The quality aware variable *output* limits its execution time while being assigned using the timed assignment statement.

```
public void transcode(FrameIterator frames) {
  IQoSObject constraint =
            new QoSThroughput("output", 1000, 25);
  Frame[~] output = new Frame[~constraint];
  try {
   foreach(Frame f in frames) {
    output ~= transcodeFrame(f); // transcoding function
    display(output); // display output
   }
  } catch (QoSException e) {
   Console.WriteLine("QoS Constraint Violation!");
  }
}
```

4.3 QoS Management Framework

The history of the events are recorded with the implementation of the *IQoSHistoryManager* (see figure 4). This class registers events, assigns quality of service constraints to these events, and stores their histories within a time frame. The default implementation available in the system class library is used by the compiler by default. To enable the programmer to provide its own implementation, the default history manager can be exchanged using the *QoSHistoryManagerFactory*.

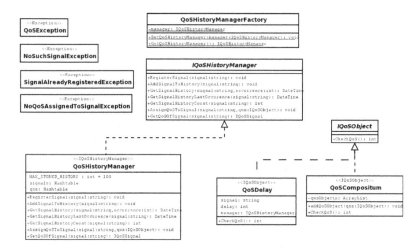

Fig. 4. Classes involved in quality of service management used in the default implementation

As the history manager can observe many events, we can define quality of service constraints applying these events. The bounded execution time of video frame processing can be used to demonstrate the implementation of a quality of service object.

```
private string input, output;

private long execTime;

public int CheckQoS() { // bounded execution time
  int delta =
    (int)((TimeSpan)(this.manager
.GetSignalHistoryCurrent(this.output) -
                  this.manager
      .GetSignalHistoryLastOccurrence(this.input)))
            .TotalMilliseconds;
  // check if delay can be held,
  // if not throw exception
  if (delta > this.execTime) {

    throw new QoSException(
              "Bounded execution time of "
              + delta + "ms exceeds limit of "
              + this.execTime + "ms!");

  }
  return 0; // go on normally
}
```

The quality of service constraints are specified by implementing the interface definition *IQoSObject*. The method *CheckQoS* must implemented which monitors the

QoS constraint. It throws an exception if the constraint cannot be held or slows down execution by returning a numerical value. This values is interpreted as time in milliseconds to wait after the timed assignment. If zero is returned, the code following the timed assignment statement is executed without delay.

The history manager is used to calculate time ranges between events and compare these ranges to specified values. Predefined constraint implementations are provided by a system class library and can be used by the programmer.

```
private string signal;

private int count, delay;

public int CheckQoS() { // throughput

  int delta =
       (int)((TimeSpan)(this.manager
            .GetSignalHistoryCurrent(this.signal)-
                   this.manager
            .GetSignalHistory(this.signal,
                   this.manager
            .GetSignalHistoryCount() - this.count)))
            .TotalMilliseconds;

  // check if delay can be held
  // if not throw exception,
  // otherwise delay execution to

  // reach expected delay value

  if (delta > this.delay) {

    throw new QoSException(
                "Throughput of " + this.count
                + " exceeds limit of "
                + this.execTime + "ms!");

  }

  return delta - this.delay; // slow down execution

}
```

4.4 Results

To justify the concept of quality aware data types it is evaluated against the criteria defined at the beginning of this paper:

1. The expressive power is enhanced because quality of service constraints can be expressed on the data type declaration level. This allows the developer to use embedded QoS without worrying about the implementation. Although the system libraries should include lots of default constraints that can just be used, the developer is enabled to express a new constraint by just implementing a simple interface which emphasizes the extensibility in case of constraint implementation.

Furthermore, one can use polymorphism or other object oriented language concepts to implement, extend, or vary given quality of service constraints. Moreover, we consider the possibility to access a history not only as an aid for the implementation but as something that imposes a basic structure upon QoS monitoring thus improving readability. With the use of a history manager it becomes possible to write programs that are quite close to a specification.

2. The automatic and implicit generation of events triggered at every assignment to the QoS monitored structure increases the safety of the program. Instead of the error-prone task of registering every event manually, this is done by compiler generated code.

3. Optimization of the code can be seen by comparing length and simplicity. Currently no further optimization possibilities can be presented. More investigations are needed to show how the concept of quality aware data types can help to generate more efficient code.

However, our concept is non interruptive in comparison to Esterel. Esterel allows to terminate the execution of a code block prematurely if the result is outdated before its calculation finishes. We claim that this is only a minor restriction. The time gain of immediate cancellation will be small in many cases, whereas subsequently inserting test operations for the case that no sufficient operating system support should be given could slow down the overall performance drastically.

5 Conclusion and Future Work

The aim of this paper is to introduce two new minimal language extensions to improve multimedia application development. New loop statements are presented which can be applied when accessing large multidimensional arrays often used in parts of encoder or decoder software. The extended *foreach* statement is used to allow index access during the loop, and the *forall* loop inherently introduces parallelization to the loop execution. Furthermore the concept of quality aware data types is shown to define QoS monitoring on a data type declaration level which helps us to implement QoS based streaming. These extensions are justified by three basic principles: expressive power, safety and optimization possibilities. This is emphasized by examples of the current implementations in Modula-3 and C#.

Both Modula-3 and C# and their actually used language environments show a lot of pleasant features, and none of the two languages can be declared as a definite winner. Despite of the well-known stylistic differences, the existence of nested procedures in Modula-3 eased the implementation of some features considerably.

In the search towards a multimedia language we want to identify challenges in current programming languages and their embedded concepts. The concepts described in this document still raise a lot questions. Our aim is to define quality of service constraints not directly with code, but with syntax extensions to allow a compact and declarative definition. Furthermore, we want to analyze the possibility of compile time optimizations on code generation based on the compile time knowledge of such constraints.

References

[1] Gordon S. Blair, Jean-Bernard Stefani: Open distributed processing and multimeda. - Addison Wesley Longman Ltd., 1998 ISBN 0-201-17794-3

[2] Svend Erik Knusen: Statement-Sets .- Third International ACPC Conference with Special Emphasis on Parallel Databses and Parallel I/O Klagenfurt, Austria: September 1996

[3] Michael Philippsen, Walter F. Tichy: Modula-2* and its Compilation .- Universität Karlsruhe, 1991 First International appeared in: First International Conference of the Austrian Center for Parallel Computation, Salzburg, Austria, 1991, Springer Verlag, Lecture Notes In Computer Science 591, 1992

[4] Stefan U. Hänßgen, Ernst A. Heinz, Paul Lukowicz, Michael Philippsen, Walter F. Tichy: The Modula-2* Environment for Parallel Programming, 1993

[5] Michael Philippsen, Markus U. Mock: Data and Process Alignment in Modula-2*, Department of Informatics, University of Karlsruhe, 1993

[6] Laszlo Böszörményi, Carsten Weich: Programming in Modula-3 - An Introduction in Programming with Style. - Springer Verlag, Heidelberg 1996

[7] Mono: Open Source .NET Development Framework - http://www.mono-project.com

[8] Microsoft Developer Network: C# Programmer's Reference, http://msdn.microsoft.com

[9] Jingwen Jin, Klara Nahrstedt: QoS Specification Languages for Distributed Multimedia Applications: A Survey and Taxonomy – IEEE Multimedia Magazine, July 2004, pp. 74-87

[10] Ralf Steinmetz, Klara Nahrstedt: Multimedia Systems – Springer Verlag, 2004, ISBN 3-540-40867-3

[11] Standard ECMA-334 - C# Language Specification, 3rd Edition June 2005

[12] Don Box, Chris Sells: Essentials .NET Volume 1 – The Common Language Runtime. - Addison Wsley 2004, ISBN 0-201-73411-7

[13] Greg Nelson: Systems Programming with Modula-3. - Prentice Hall, 1991 ISBN 0-13-590464-1

[14] Zima,H.P., Chapman,B.M.: Supercompilers for Parallel and Vector Computers ACM Press Frontier Series/Addison-Wesley (1990); Japanese Translation, Ohmsha (1995)

[15] J. Z. Li, M. T. Ozsu, and D. Szafron. MOQL: A multimedia object query language. Technical Report TR-97-01, Department of Computing Science, University of Alberta, January 1997

[16] Elmar Stellnberger: Enhancing the Usability of Nested Procedure Values in a Multi Threaded Environment. Manuscript

Implicit and Dynamic Parameters in C++

Christian Heinlein

Dept. of Computer Science, University of Ulm, Germany
`christian.heinlein@uni-ulm.de`

Abstract. Implicit and dynamic parameters are proposed as a general means to reduce the length of argument lists of function calls without resorting to dangerous global variables. In C++, these new kinds of parameters constitute a generalization of parameters with default arguments, whose values can be omitted in function calls. In contrast to the latter, however, the values of implicit and dynamic parameters are not obtained from a function's definition context, but rather from its different calling contexts. This is in turn similar to so-called dependent names in function templates, but offers a higher degree of flexibility and comprehensibility.

1 Introduction

There are basically two ways to pass information from one procedure or function of a program to another: parameters and global variables. Even though the former are usually preferred for good reasons and use of the latter for this purpose is generally discouraged, there are circumstances where parameters turn out to be inconvenient and cumbersome and therefore the use of global variables becomes tempting. In particular, if functions require large numbers of parameters, most of which are simply passed down to other functions, providing this information via global variables could significantly reduce the size of many parameter and argument lists. Furthermore, if major parts of this information usually remain unchanged during a program execution, the use of global variables is even more appealing. Finally, if it becomes necessary to retroactively extend the parameter list of some deeply nested function, each call of this function must be augmented with additional arguments, which usually requires the parameter lists of all functions containing these calls to get extended, too, etc.

On the other hand, using global variables to pass information between functions is dangerous, especially in multi-threaded programs, where one thread might inadvertently change the value of variables needed by other threads. But even in single-threaded applications, it might happen that global variables required by a particular function are modified by a subordinate function called from it. Finally, if exceptions cause unexpected and premature terminations of functions, temporary modifications to global variables performed by these functions might not be undone as expected.

To dissolve this longstanding tension between using parameters and global variables, *implicit parameters* [7] and *dynamic variables* [3] have been proposed

D. Lightfoot and C. Szyperski (Eds.): JMLC 2006, LNCS 4228, pp. 37–56, 2006.

earlier as different means to provide the benefits of global variables, i.e., short and comprehensible parameter and/or argument lists, without suffering from their drawbacks. While the former are specifically tailored to functional programming languages and provide static type checking, the latter also address imperative languages, but lack static type safety. Building on these approaches, the main contribution of this paper is their combination into a single coherent framework for imperative languages, i.e., *implicit and dynamic parameters*, that provides a large degree of flexibility combined with static type safety. More specifically, language extensions for C++ are proposed which generalize its notion of parameters with *default arguments* and also provide a superior replacement for *dependent names* in templates. Nevertheless, the basic concept of implicit and dynamic parameters is actually language-independent and might be incorporated into many other languages, too.

After reviewing in Sec. 2 the basics of functions, overloading, and default arguments in C++, the concept of implicit and dynamic parameters is introduced and developed in Sec. 3. Its basic implementation ideas as a precompiler-based language extension for C++ are described in Sec. 4, before concluding the paper with a discussion of related work in Sec. 5.

2   Functions, Overloading, and Default Arguments in C++

Even though C++ provides a large number of different function kinds, including global functions, virtual, non-virtual, and static member functions, constructors, and function call operators [10], their basic principle is always the same: a function consists of a name, a parameter list, a (possibly `void`) result type, and a body. Therefore, examples will be limited to global functions and constructors in the sequel.

All kinds of functions can be statically *overloaded* by defining multiple functions of the same name (in the same scope) with different parameter lists, e.g.:

```
int max (int x, int y) { return x > y ? x : y; }
double max (double x, double y) { return x > y ? x : y; }
```

When resolving a call to such a function, the *static types* of all arguments are used to determine the *best viable function* at compile time. If no viable function is found at all or several viable functions remain where none is better than the others, the call is ill-formed. For example, `max(1, 2)` and `max(1.0, 2.0)` will call the first resp. second version of `max` defined above, while `max("a", "b")` and `max(1, 2.0)` cannot be resolved due to missing resp. ambiguous definitions.[1]

The trailing parameters in a function definition might have *default arguments*, i.e., associated expressions whose values will be used to initialize these parameters if corresponding arguments are missing in a call, e.g.:

---

[1] Note that in C++ an `int` value is implicitly convertible to `double` *and vice versa*, and both conversions are *equally ranked*.

```
// Print floating point number d on standard output stream
// with minimum field width w and precision p.
void print (double d, int w = 10, int p = 5) { ...... }
```

This function can be called with one, two, or three arguments, where `print(d)` and `print(d, w)` are equivalent to `print(d, 10, 5)` and `print(d, w, 5)`, respectively. Therefore, the single definition of `print` above is similar in effect to the following three definitions:

```
// Print d with field width w and precision p.
void print (double d, int w, int p) { ...... }

// Print d with field width w and precision 5.
void print (double d, int w) { print(d, w, 5); }

// Print d with field width 10 and precision 5.
void print (double d) { print(d, 10, 5); }
```

In the first case, however, a *single* function is defined which might be *called* with different numbers of arguments, while in the second case, there are actually three different overloaded functions.

A default argument is not restricted to a simple value such as 10, but might be any expression, which is evaluated *each time* it is used in a call. Names appearing in such an expression are interpreted and bound in the context of its *definition*, not in the context of a call, e. g.:

```
int width = 10;
void print (double d, int w = max(width, 20), int p = 5);
```

If `print` is called with a single argument `d`, its second argument `w` is initialized with the value of the expression `max(width, 20)`, where `width` corresponds to the global variable defined before, even if the calling function contains a local variable of the same name that basically hides the global one. Therefore, *literally* adding a default argument expression to a function call might lead to a quite different result than omitting the argument.

Default arguments might be specified later on, after a function has been declared or defined for the first time, and it is even possible to specify different default arguments for the same function in different local scopes, e. g.:

```
// Initial definition without default arguments.
void print (double d, int w, int p) { ...... }

// Later declaration with one default argument.
void print (double d, int w, int p = 5);

// Client function.
void client (double d) {
  // Local declaration with two default arguments.
```

```
    void print (double d, int w = 10, int p = 4);

    // Call equivalent to: print(d, 10, 4).
    print(d);
}
```

When an overloaded function is called, only the *explicitly specified arguments* are considered to determine the best viable function. However, functions possessing more parameters than arguments given will be included in the set of *candidate functions* if the missing arguments could be provided by default arguments. If the selected function actually has more parameters than arguments given, the corresponding default arguments will be supplied afterwards, e. g.:

```
    void f (int x, int y);
    void f (double x, int y = 0);
```

Here, a call such as f(0) would select the second function since the explicitly specified argument 0 of type int is compatible with its first parameter of type double and the second parameter can be satisfied from its default argument, while the first function cannot be called with only one argument. On the other hand, f(0, 0) would select the first function since the arguments (0, 0) exactly match its parameters, while the second function would require a conversion of the first argument from int to double. Again, literally adding a default argument expression to a function call might lead to a different result than omitting the argument. Furthermore, if a *member function* has default arguments, these expressions might refer to private or protected members of the class, which are inaccessible to clients calling the function; in that case, literally adding a default argument expression could even lead to a compile time error.

3   Implicit and Dynamic Parameters

This section introduces *implicit and dynamic parameters* as language extensions to C++. Their basic idea is similar to parameters with default arguments, as corresponding arguments can be omitted in function calls, too. However, the way to obtain values for missing arguments is quite different.

Implicit and dynamic parameters as well as parameters with default arguments will be collectively called *optional parameters* in the sequel, and the original C++ rules for parameters with default arguments are generalized to all kinds of optional parameters, i. e.:

- If a particular parameter of a function is declared optional, all subsequent parameters must be optional, too.
- Parameters might be declared optional later on, and the same function might have different optional parameters in different scopes.
- During overload resolution, only the arguments which are explicitly specified in a call are used to select the best viable function. Afterwards, if the selected function has more parameters than arguments given, values for optional parameters will be added as required.

3.1   Implicit Parameters

Function parameters are declared *implicit* by prefixing their declaration with the C++ keyword using[2], e. g.:

```
void print (double d, using int width, using int prec);
```

If an argument corresponding to an implicit parameter is missing in a call, an entity with the *same name* as the parameter from the *calling context* is substituted. If no such entity is found there, or if its type is incompatible with the parameter's type, the call is rejected by the compiler. For instance, the call print(d) is equivalent to print(d, width, prec) where the names width and prec are looked up and bound in the calling context. This implies that the names of implicit parameters are mandatory in declarations and significant for callers, in contrast to ordinary parameters whose names are irrelevant for clients and might even be omitted in function declarations.

According to the general rules about optional parameters stated above, it is possible to declare a parameter implicit later on, possibly in a different scope, and it is also possible to change its name on that occasion, including the possibility to introduce a name for a formerly anonymous parameter, e. g.:

```
void print (double d, int w, int);
......
void print (double d, using int width, using int prec);
```

Usually, the "entity" that is used to satisfy an implicit parameter of a called function is some kind of variable, including local variables and parameters of the calling function, member variables of an enclosing class, and global variables. In particular, the calling function might itself possess an implicit parameter of the same name (and a compatible type). If the implicit parameter has a function pointer or reference type, however, the entity might also be a function of an appropriate type, e. g.:

```
// Sort vector v using function less to compare its elements.
void sort (vector<string>& v,
   using bool less (const string&, const string&)) { ...... }

// Namespace N1 containing a definition of less
// and a client function calling sort with the latter.
namespace N1 {
   bool less (const string& s1, const string& s2) { ...... }
   void client (vector<string>& v) {
     sort(v); // calls: sort(v, N1::less)
   }
```

---

[2] At first sight, a different keyword such as implicit might be more appropriate. However, to avoid incompatibilities with C++ code using this as an identifier, the existing keyword using has been "re-used."

```
}

// Namespace N2 containing a different definition of less
// and a client function calling sort with the latter.
namespace N2 {
  bool less (const string& s1, const string& s2) { ...... }
  void client (vector<string>& v) {
    sort(v); // calls: sort(v, N2::less)
  }
}
```

3.2 Constructors with Implicit Parameters

If a constructor has implicit parameters, their values are also supplied from the calling context if necessary, no matter whether the constructor is called directly in so-called *functional notation* or indirectly in variable initializations (or *member initializers* of other constructors), e. g.:

```
// Hash table for strings.
class HashTable {
  ......
public:
  // Create hash table with given size and hash function.
  HashTable (using int size, using int hash (const string&));
};

// Preferred hash table size and hash function.
int size = 193;
int hash (const string& s) { ...... }

// Direct constructor call.
HashTable t1 = HashTable(101); // calls: HashTable(101, hash)

// Indirect constructor call.
HashTable t2;                  // calls: HashTable(size, hash)
```

In this example, the direct constructor call `HashTable(101)` used in the declaration of `t1` is equivalent to `HashTable(101, hash)`, using the definition of `hash` given before, while the declaration of `t2` contains an indirect call to the *default constructor* `HashTable()` (because the variable is not explicitly initialized), which is equivalent to `HashTable(size, hash)`.

In other contexts, however, where constructor calls are completely invisible, these calls must not depend on implicit parameters in order to avoid too much implicitness and consequent incomprehensibility. This includes implicit *copy* and *conversion constructor* calls as well as implicit default constructor calls in *ctor-initializers* [10]. For example, even though the `HashTable` constructor defined above may be called with a single argument of type `int` if the second parameter

hash can be satisfied from the calling context (as shown in the declaration of **t1**), this constructor cannot be used as a conversion constructor to implicitly convert an **int** value to a **HashTable** object.

3.3   Dynamic Parameters and Environment Variables

EEven though implicit parameters need not be specified explicitly in function calls, the compiler checks that corresponding entities are found in the calling context and rejects calls otherwise. While this avoids run time errors or undefined behaviour due to missing parameter values, it leads to a rather tight coupling between callers and callees. In particular, it is not generally possible to transparently add another parameter to an existing function, even if it is declared implicit, because an entity of the same name must be present in every calling context.

To relax this strict rule and to support more loose couplings between callers and callees, *dynamic parameters* are introduced. Syntactically, dynamic parameters look like implicit parameters with default arguments, i. e., their declaration is preceded by the keyword **using** and followed by an equals sign and an accompanying expression, e. g.:

```
void print (double d,
  using int width = 10, using int prec = 5);
```

As with implicit parameters, the value for a dynamic parameter is retrieved from the calling context if the corresponding argument is missing in a call. In contrast to implicit parameters, however, the value need not be provided by the *direct* caller, but might also come from an *indirect* caller, i. e., from the complete *dynamic scope* of the call.

However, since the compiler normally does not know the set of all callers of a function (and recursively their callers etc.), it can no longer check statically whether a value required for a dynamic parameter is actually provided. Therefore, dynamic parameters always possess a default argument which will be used in cases where no value can be found in the dynamic scope of the call. As with normal default arguments, the corresponding expression is evaluated each time it is used, i. e., whenever a call is made that neither provides an explicit argument nor an implicit value for the parameter, and names appearing in the expression are interpreted and bound in the context of its definition.

As another significant difference to implicit parameters, entities intended to provide values for dynamic parameters must be explicitly marked as such to avoid accidental matches with local variables defined in indirect callers, which might not even know about a particular dynamic parameter. The underlying model employed for that purpose is quite similar to the concept of *environment variables* found in operating systems: At any point in time during the execution of a program (or a single thread within a multi-threaded program) there is a *dynamic scope* or *environment* containing variables which have been declared by so-called *export declarations* described below.

To give an example, if `print(d)` is called (with the declaration of `print` given above), this call is always accepted by the compiler and will actually call `print(d, width, prec)` if variables `width` and `prec` are found in the current environment, or `print(d, 10, 5)` if no such variables are found (or a combination of these if only one of the variables is found).

Because the compiler cannot and does not check whether the value for a dynamic parameter will be actually present at run time, it is indeed possible to transparently add additional parameters to existing functions without needing to check or change their direct callers.[3] Of course, to be actually useful, values for such parameters should be exported to the environment by some indirect caller.

3.4 Export Declarations

An *export declaration* is a definition of a global or local variable prefixed by the keyword `export`[4], e.g., `export int width = 10;`
The *environment variable* declared that way is initialized just like a regular variable by evaluating the optional initializer expression and/or executing an appropriate constructor. Furthermore, the variable is destroyed in the same way as a regular variable by executing its destructor when it gets out of scope, i.e., when the statement block containing the export declaration terminates (either normally or abruptly by executing a jump statement or throwing an exception) or (for a globally declared environment variable) when the entire program terminates.

In contrast to a regular variable, however, the variable is not inserted into any *static* scope at *compile time* (i.e., it will not be found by normal static name lookup), but rather added to the current *dynamic* scope (i.e., the environment) when the declaration is executed at *run time*. It is automatically removed from there immediately before it is destroyed, i.e., at the end of the enclosing statement block (if it is declared locally) or at the end of the program (if it is declared globally). If a variable of the same name and type as a newly exported variable is already present in the environment, the former is hidden by the latter until the latter is removed again, i.e., the environment is organized in a stack-like manner, and a dynamic parameter always receives the value of the top-most matching variable, if any. For example:

```
void print (double d,
   using int width = 10, using int prec = 5);

void client1 (double d) { print(d); }

void client2 (double d) {
```

---

[3] It will depend on the implementation strategy whether or not it is necessary to recompile the callers.

[4] Again, an existing C++ keyword is re-used, which is used for a similar purpose in Unix shells.

```
  client1(d);      // client1 calls print(d, 10, 5)
  { export int width = 20;
    client1(d);    // client1 calls print(d, 20, 5)
    { export int width = 30, prec = 10;
      client1(d);  // client1 calls print(d, 30, 10)
    }
    client1(d);    // client1 calls print(d, 20, 5)
  }
  client1(d);      // client1 calls print(d, 10, 5)
}
```

3.5   Environment Variables with Constant and Reference Types

The type of an environment variable might be any suitable C++ type including const-qualified and/or reference types. Accordingly, dynamic parameters might possess such types, and an environment variable is said to *match* a dynamic parameter if the following conditions hold:

- the names of the variable and the parameter are equal;
- the *core types*, i.e., the types without any top-level const or & qualifier, of the variable and the parameter are identical;
- if the common core type is T and the parameter's type is T&, the variable's type is T or T&, but not const T or const T&.

The last rule is in accordance with normal C++ rules, which do not allow to bind a constant object to a non-constant reference via which it could be modified inadmissibly. On the other hand, the rule about identical core types is much stricter than normal C++ type compatibility rules, as it completely excludes any implicit type conversions such as standard conversions between numeric types or conversions from derived classes to base classes. The main reason for not allowing such conversions is to avoid confusion and unpleasant surprises due to unexpected or unintended conversions, which already happen occasionally with normal parameters. Combined with the loose coupling between dynamic parameters and environment variables, the danger of an accidental match would become even greater. Furthermore, when exporting a variable to the environment, one should have a clear conception about the dynamic parameters this variable is intended to match, and thus it should be easily possible to choose the appropriate type exactly, without relying on any implicit conversions. (And if really necessary, one might export several variables of the same name with different types.) Finally, an efficient implementation of more flexible matching rules would be extremely difficult, since it would actually require to perform extensive analyses at run time which are normally carried out at compile time. (For the same reason, the C++ rules for finding a matching handler for a thrown exception do not allow the full range of implicit type conversions either. However, to support the typical idiom of catching exceptions of multiple classes with a single handler for a common base class, conversions from derived to base classes are considered in this context.)

Declaring an environment variable of some core type T with or without const or & qualifiers has important consequences for its usage and actually sets up different "access rights" for it:[5]

- If its type is simply T, it will match dynamic parameters with all kinds of qualification. In particular, it will be possible to change the variable's value indirectly via dynamic reference parameters of type T&, even though direct manipulations of the variable are impossible since it is not part of any static scope!
- To forbid such indirect modifications of an environment variable, a const-qualified type, i.e., const T or const T&, can be chosen, because a variable of such a type does not match a parameter of type T&. In the former case (const T), the variable becomes completely immutable.
- When using a reference type, i.e., T& or const T&, the environment variable can be initialized with a regular variable of type T in both cases and then actually constitutes an *alias* for the latter. Therefore, modifications to the regular variable are immediately reflected in the environment variable, i.e., the latter can be directly manipulated through the former, no matter whether its type is T& or const T&. However, the distinction between these types decides whether indirect manipulations via dynamic parameters are possible or not: A variable of type T& matches a parameter of the same type which allows such manipulations, while a variable of type const T& does not match such a parameter and therefore cannot be modified indirectly.

3.6 Correspondence to Checked and Unchecked Exceptions

The conceptual distinction between implicit and dynamic parameters exhibits interesting parallels with *checked* and *unchecked exceptions* in Java [2].

If the signature of a Java method declares a checked exception, the compiler checks that each caller of this method either catches the exception or declares it in its own signature. Likewise, if a function declares an implicit parameter, the compiler checks that each caller of this function either passes an explicit argument for it or provides an entity to satisfy it, including an implicit parameter of its own. Therefore, both scenarios are statically safe: a checked exception is guaranteed to be caught somewhere, while an implicit parameter is guaranteed to receive a value.

On the other hand, since unchecked exceptions need not be declared, the compiler cannot and does not check that they will be caught somewhere. Likewise, the compiler cannot and does not check that a dynamic parameter always receives a value from the current environment. However, the default value provided

---

[5] For experienced C++ programmers, the following considerations are quite obvious, since they are completely in line with standard C++ rules about constant and reference types. For less experienced or novice C++ programmers, however, they might require some time of accommodation.

for such cases guarantees well-defined behaviour anyway, while an uncaught exception leads to program termination.

In the same way as both checked and unchecked exceptions have useful applications in practice (even though some programmers tend to avoid the former to circumvent the strict checks performed by the compiler), both implicit and dynamic parameters turn out to be useful for different kinds of applications: If it is essential that a value for a particular parameter is provided (e. g., the comparison function for a sort routine) – and there is no reasonable general default value –, an implicit parameter should be used. If, on the other hand, a value is dispensable and/or a reasonable default value can be specified (e. g., the field width for a print function), a dynamic parameter is usually more appropriate as it allows greater flexibility.

3.7   Replacing Dependent Names in C++ Templates

If a normal C++ function such as max calls another function such as less, the latter must have been declared earlier, e. g.:

```
bool less (int x, int y) { return x < y; }
int max (int x, int y) { return less(x, y) ? y : x; }
```

For functions called from function *templates*, however, this simple declare-before-use rule is replaced with rather complicated rules about *dependent names*, the *point of instantiation* of a template, etc. [10]. For example, the following generic definition of max is accepted by the compiler without any preceding definition of less, since the latter is a *dependent name* because its arguments x and y depend on the template parameter T:

```
template <typename T>
T max (T x, T y) { return less(x, y) ? y : x; }
```

If, however, max is actually called with arguments x and y of a particular type T0, a definition of less accepting these arguments must be found, either in the *definition context* of max or in the current *instantiation context*, i. e., in the calling context of the function. In this regard, dependent names are similar to implicit parameters, which are also interpreted in the calling context of a function. Therefore, the fact that max requires a matching definition of less, which is *hidden* in its *body* above, can be specified *explicitly* in its *signature* by means of an implicit parameter:

```
template <typename T>
T max (T x, T y, using bool less (T, T)) {
  return less(x, y) ? y : x;
}
```

Similar to the original definition of max shown before, this function is also accepted by the compiler without any preceding definition of less, and a matching definition is required only when max is called. This time, however, no special rules about dependent names are required, since the usage of less in the func-tion's body obviously refers to the parameter declared in its signature, whose context-dependent binding is achieved by the much simpler rules for implicit parameters. Furthermore, using an implicit parameter is actually more flexible than a dependent name, since it might naturally be bound to different functions less in different calling contexts (cf. Sec. 3.1), whereas a dependent name is required to refer to the *same* function in *all* instantiation contexts, even across multiple translation units.[6] Finally, it is even possible to pass a function with a different name as an explicit argument.

In summary, implicit parameters constitute a superior replacement for de-pendent names in function templates, since they reveal hidden dependencies by moving their names from a function's body to its signature and provide more flexible means for their context-dependent binding. On the other hand, calling a function such as less that is passed as an argument to another function such as max might be less efficient than a direct, inlined call to less in max. However, if the code of both max and less is visible, a call such as max(x, y, less) might be completely inlined by an optimizing compiler, too, yielding, e. g., x < y ? y : x if less is defined as shown above.

4   Prototypical Implementation

Implicit and dynamic parameters have been implemented prototypically in a pre-compiler for C++ that is based on the EDG C++ Front End (cf. www.edg.com). In contrast to a real implementation in a compiler, a precompiler-based ap-proach has the advantage that it is independent of any particular compiler and requires much less implementation time and effort. Both of these aspects im-prove the possibility to experiment with the new language constructs early and quickly and thus gain important practical experience, which might help to im-prove the concepts before hard-wiring them in real implementations. Of course, a precompiler-based approach does usually not achieve the same performance as a direct implementation in a compiler, but for typical experimental applications this does not really constitute a problem.

4.1   Dynamic Parameters and Environment Variables

Conceptually, the environment or dynamic scope of a program (or a single thread within a multi-threaded program) can be represented by a *stack* whose entries each contain a pointer or reference to a variable plus information about the vari-able's name and type, where the name could be stored as a string of characters, while the type could be represented by its typeid [10]. To find the topmost variable that matches a given dynamic parameter, the stack must be searched in top-down order for the first entry whose name and type are equal to the parameter's name and type.

---

[6] And to make things worse, a compiler is not forced to diagnose violations of this rule!

Although possible in principle, this representation of the environment suffers from both unnecessary storage consumption for the name and type of each variable and unnecessary run time overhead to find the topmost matching variable. To reduce these costs, the environment can be represented by a *set* of stacks, where each stack contains only references to variables of the *same* name and type. In this case, the topmost variable matching a given dynamic parameter is directly referenced by the topmost entry of the appropriate stack, which can be found rather quickly, e. g., with binary search or hashing, if names and types are still represented as strings and `typeids`, respectively.

Even though much better than the initial solution, this approach still suffers from avoidable run time overhead to find the appropriate stack matching a dynamic parameter. To completely eliminate these costs, the name of a variable can be encoded *statically* as a (dummy) type, which can be used as one of two *template arguments* for a template class `Dyn`, where the actual type of the variable is used as the second argument:

```
// Entry of stack identified by Name and Type.
template <typename Name, typename Type>
struct Dyn {
  Type& var; // Reference to variable.
  Dyn* prev; // Pointer to previous stack entry.

  // Pointer to topmost stack entry (initially null).
  static Dyn* top;

  // Constructor pushing variable v on the stack.
  Dyn (Type& v) : var(v), prev(top) { top = this; }

  // Destructor popping topmost stack entry.
  ~Dyn () { top = prev; }
};

// Dummy template class to encode variable names as types.
template <char head, typename Tail = void>
struct Name {};
```

Using the template class `Name`, a variable name such as `x` or `xyz` is uniquely identified (even across different namespaces and translation units) by the dummy type `Name<'x'>` and `Name<'x', Name<'y', Name<'z'> > >`, respectively. Therefore, the stack containing all references to variables of type `int` and name `x` (more precisely, the pointer to its topmost element) is *statically* identified by `Dyn<Name<'x'>, int>::top`. Consequently, the topmost variable matching a dynamic parameter of type `int` and name `x` can be immediately accessed as `Dyn<Name<'x'>, int>::top ->var`, without any overhead for comparing strings or `typeids` at run time.

Since variable export operations are performed explicitly by means of export declarations, while the corresponding remove operations shall happen

automatically when the enclosing statement block (or the entire program) terminates (cf. Sec. 3.4), it is advantageous to embed these operations in the constructor resp. destructor of class Dyn, as already shown above. Then, an export
declaration such as

```
export int x = expr;
```

can be transformed to a corresponding declaration of a regular variable with
some unique internal name such as x__1234 (internal, since the original name x
shall not appear in any static scope, and unique, since multiple environment
variables of the same name might be defined), followed by a declaration and
initialization of an additional dummy variable _x__1234 of the corresponding
Dyn class:

```
int x__1234 = expr;
Dyn<Name<'x'>, int> _x__1234(x__1234);
```

When the control flow of the program reaches these declarations, x__1234 is
initialized with expr and afterwards the constructor of _x__1234 is called, receiving a reference to x__1234 as an argument and pushing it onto its stack. The
corresponding destructor performing the matching pop operation is automatically executed when the enclosing statement block (or the entire program) is
terminated.

By implementing the stacks as linked lists whose elements are global or local variables of type Dyn<...> declared at the corresponding export points, no
dynamic storage management is necessary for maintaining the stacks. Instead,
they are "threaded" through the normal run time stack and possibly the global
data segment of the program.

Based on this representation of the environment, a dynamic parameter declaration as in the following example:

```
void print (double d, int w, using int prec = 5);
```

is transformed to an ordinary parameter declaration with a default argument:

```
void print (double d, int w, int prec =
  Dyn<Name<'p', Name<'r', ...> >, int>::top ?
  Dyn<Name<'p', Name<'r', ...> >, int>::top->var : 5);
```

If the function print is called with three arguments, the default argument is
simply ignored. If it is called with only two arguments, the default argument
is evaluated as follows: If the pointer top of the stack identified by the name
prec and the type int is not null, i.e., if this stack is not empty, the variable
referenced by its topmost entry is used; otherwise, the original default argument
of the dynamic parameter (which is simply 5 in the example) is evaluated. In
particular, the original default argument is evaluated only if necessary, i.e., if
no suitable value is found in the environment.

To simplify the presentation, the above description has ignored two details: First, if the type of an environment variable is `const T` or `const T&`, it must not match a dynamic parameter with a non-`const` reference type `T&`. To accomplish this, all `Dyn` classes actually have a second static data member `nctop` as well as a second link field `ncprev` that points to the topmost resp. previous stack entry referencing a non-`const` variable. Furthermore, two different constructors for pushing a `const` resp. non-`const` variable are provided which do not resp. do modify the `nctop` pointer. To find the topmost variable matching a non-`const` reference type `T&`, the `nctop` pointer is used instead of `top`, while for all other kinds of types (i.e., `T`, `const T`, and `const T&`) `top` is used as described above.

Second, if multi-threaded programs shall be supported, the static data members `top` and `nctop` must not directly point to stack entries, but rather refer to some kind of thread-local objects which contain such pointers, in order to maintain a separate environment for each thread.

4.2 Implicit Parameters

While the implementation of dynamic parameters is rather simple and straightforward – and the conceptual decoupling between export declarations and function calls using exported entities leads to an analogous decoupling in the implementation –, the precompiler-based implementation of implicit parameters turns out to be more difficult.

A rather obvious idea is to simply add missing arguments to function calls, e. g., to transform a call such as `print(d, w)` to `print(d, w, prec)` if `print`'s third parameter `prec` is implicit. If the identifier `prec` is not known in the calling context or has an incompatible type, this approach would naturally lead to a corresponding compiler error message in that case.

However, there are two important problems with this approach, which have already been pointed out in Sec. 2: First, the process of overload resolution might lead to different results if an argument for any kind of optional parameter is either explicitly specified or omitted. Second, if an implicit parameter is preceded by a parameter with a default argument (including a dynamic parameter), and the corresponding argument is also omitted in a call, it would have to be explicitly added, too. However, this is generally difficult for a precompiler operating on source code for two reasons: First, the meaning of names occurring in the default argument expression might be different when it is evaluated in the calling context instead of its definition context; second, some of these names might be inaccessible in the calling context if they refer to private or protected data members of a class (if the function to be called is a member function of this class).

The problem regarding overload resolution can be solved as follows: Similar to a dynamic parameter, an implicit parameter is also transformed to a parameter with a (dummy) default argument. This allows overload resolution to be performed before adding any missing arguments, i. e., by considering only the explicitly specified arguments. Afterwards, any implicit type conversions which are necessary to convert the arguments to the exact parameter types of the selected function are made explicit. (In the example given at the end of Sec. 2, the call f(0), which will be resolved to the second definition of f and thus requires an implicit conversion of its argument 0 from int to double, would be transformed to f((double)0).) Finally, missing arguments corresponding to implicit parameters are added to the call, again using explicit conversions to the corresponding parameter types. (If the second parameter y of f would be implicit, the resulting call would be f((double)0, (int)y).) By inserting explicit type conversions for all arguments of the augmented call, the process of overload resolution will in fact resolve it to the same function as the original call without any additional arguments.[7]

The problem regarding preceding parameters with default arguments can be solved in principle by encapsulating default argument expressions into parameterless auxiliary functions with unique compiler-generated internal names. Calling such a function will always execute the encapsulated expression in the context of its definition, without any interference of the calling context. Furthermore, if a default argument belongs to a member function of a class, the corresponding auxiliary function can be defined as a member function of the same class in order to have access to private and protected members of the class. By using these auxiliary functions, it is in fact possible to explicitly add all missing arguments to a function call, no matter whether they belong to parameters with default arguments, to dynamic parameters, or to implicit parameters.

However, since the actual generation of these auxiliary functions is amazingly complicated in practice (in particular for function templates, where the auxiliary functions must be templates, too, and for member functions defined outside their class, where the auxiliary functions must be predeclared in the class), it has not actually been implemented yet. As a consequence, the current prototypical, precompiler-based implementation does not allow parameters with default arguments (including dynamic parameters) to appear in a parameter list *before* a dynamic parameter. For practical applications, this does not constitute a severe restriction, since it is always possible to place implicit parameters before any other kind of optional parameter. Of course, in a real compiler, the problems discussed above do not exist at all, since it is always possible to appropriately add missing arguments to a function call in assembly or machine code.

Based on the preceding considerations, a function declaration such as

```
void print (double d, using int width, int p = 5);
```

will be transformed to

```
void print (double d, int width = *(int*)0, int p = 5);
```

where *(int*)0 is a dummy expression of type int, actually dereferencing a null pointer of type int*. A call to print such as print(d) will be transformed to print((double)d, (int)width), i.e., by explicitly adding an argument for the second parameter width, its default argument expression will never get executed

---

[7] Except in very strange situations where multiple functions with the same parameter types defined in different namespaces are visible simultaneously.

at run time. Furthermore, by not adding an explicit argument for the third parameter p, its default argument will be used correctly as expected.[8]

To summarize, the transformation of a function call generally proceeds as follows: First, the normal process of overload resolution is performed to select the best viable function according to the explicitly specified arguments. (For that purpose, a complete semantic analysis of the source program is necessary, which is indeed performed by the EDG C++ Front End.) Then, it is checked whether the selected function has implicit parameters whose values are not provided by the explicit arguments. If this is the case, the names and types of these parameters are used to add corresponding arguments to the call. If one of these names is not known in the calling context, or its type is incompatible with the type of the parameter, this automatically causes the Front End to issue a corresponding error message.[9] Furthermore, implicit type conversions of the explicitly specified arguments are made explicit to guarantee (in most circumstances) that the process of overload resolution will select the same function as for the original call.

In contrast to dynamic parameters, where an exact match of core types is required (cf. Sec. 3.5), implicit parameters naturally allow implicit type conversions: If the type of the entity denoted by the respective name x in the calling context is different from the type T of the implicit parameter, a corresponding conversion is performed automatically (if possible) when the augmented argument expression (T)x is evaluated.

4.3 Constructor Calls with Implicit Parameters

Constructor calls depending on implicit parameters can be transformed in exactly the same manner as calls to ordinary functions, i.e., by adding corresponding arguments, no matter whether they appear directly in so-called functional notation [10] or indirectly in variable and member initializers. For example, the declarations of t1 and t2 shown in Sec. 3.2 will be transformed as follows:

```
HashTable t1
   = HashTable((int)101, (int (*) (const string&))hash);
HashTable t2((int)size, (int (*) (const string&))hash);
```

In the same way, so-called mem-initializers of constructors can be transformed.

4.4 Invisible Constructor Calls

If a constructor call is completely invisible, it must not rely on implicit parameters in order to avoid too much implicitness and consequent incomprehensibility

---

[8] Basically, this could cause overload resolution to fail for the transformed call, if another definition print (double, int) accepting the same arguments is visible. Since such a function is not directly callable due to ambiguity, such cases are not expected to be practically relevant. In the worst case, the programmer must specify all arguments explicitly in order to select the desired function.

[9] In particular, no attempt is made in such a case to find a worse matching function that does not require these implicit parameters.

(cf. Sec. 3.2). Therefore, an appropriate error message is produced by the pre-compiler if such a constructor call is encountered.

5   Related Work and Discussion

The most obvious related work to implicit parameters as proposed in this paper are implicit parameters as proposed by Lewis et al. [7]. Even though the motivation for introducing such a concept as well as the basic idea is very similar in both cases, there are several differences in detail, however: Most obviously, Lewis et al. present their work in the realm of functional programming languages, while this paper specifically addresses imperative languages. Apart from that, Lewis et al. draw a clear syntactic distinction between implicit and regular parameters of a function: The former are not specified in the function's parameter list, but simply used in its body, where they are distinguished from other identifiers by prefixing their name with a question mark. Nevertheless, the *type* of a function, which is usually inferred from its body by the interpreter or compiler, but might also be specified explicitly in an additional *signature*, contains the information about implicit parameters. By that means, a function calling another function with implicit parameters implicitly inherits the latter's implicit parameters in its own type. Furthermore, since implicit parameters do not belong to the regular parameter list of a function, special syntax is required to explicitly pass their values in a call.

In contrast, implicit and regular parameters are treated uniformly in our approach, i. e., both are explicitly declared in a function's parameter list and both are used homogeneously in a function's body. In fact, since the implicitness of a parameter might be declared later on, there is no distinction whatsoever between implicit and regular parameters in a function's body. As a consequence of this uniformity, explicit values for implicit parameters are passed in the same way as values for regular parameters, i. e., via the normal argument list of a call.

The fact that implicit parameters are part of a function's type in both approaches enables static type checking and guarantees that functions cannot be called without directly or indirectly supplying values for all implicit parameters. The other side of the coin, i. e., the drawbacks of this tight coupling between calling and called functions, is also pointed out by Lewis et al.: If another implicit parameter is added to a function later on, its own signature as well as the signatures of all direct and indirect callers have to be modified if they have been specified explicitly. To avoid this bother, they suggest as a compromise to use ellipses to obtain signatures with only partially specified *context information*. However, since the type of a function that is inferred by the compiler still contains complete information about all implicit parameters, this approach does not really relax the tight coupling mentioned above.

For exactly this reason, *dynamic parameters* and *environment variables* are proposed in this paper as a dual concept to implicit parameters, that allows a more loose coupling between callers and callees. This part of our proposal is similar to *dynamic variables* as proposed by Hanson and Proebsting [3], again with some important differences, however: First of all, dynamic variables have no relationship with function parameters; they are created and "exported" to the environment with a `set` statement corresponding to our export declarations, and accessed anywhere in a program with a matching `use` statement. Therefore, similar to the implicit parameters of Lewis et al., the uses of dynamic variables are "hidden" in function bodies, i. e., a function's dependency on the value of a dynamic variable is not documented in its signature. In contrast, dynamic parameters in our approach integrate the effect of a `use` statement with a parameter declaration and therefore explicitly reveal the uses of environment variables in a function.

Furthermore, in the C++ implementation of dynamic variables, their types are restricted to pointers to "polymorphic" classes [10], i. e., pointers which might be used in `dynamic_cast` operations, while dynamic parameters and environment variables might possess any C++ type. In particular, the different combinations of `const` and reference types described in Sec. 3.5 allow a very fine-grained control of "access rights" to an environment variable, ranging from completely immutable variables to those that can be modified (directly or indirectly) both in their export context and in any using context. On the other hand, dynamic variables support a more flexible matching between `set` and `use` statements by allowing a pointer to a derived class object to match a pointer to a base class, while the types of dynamic parameters and environment variables are required to match exactly except for differing `const` and reference qualifiers. In addition to the conceptual reasons for this restriction outlined in Sec. 3.5, this enables a maximally efficient implementation that does not require any kind of searching for matching variables at run time. In contrast, any implementation of dynamic variables, whether straightforward or more sophisticated, requires a linear search through the environment stack (which might be threaded through the normal run time stack) to find the first variable with a matching name and type. Even if variable names would be encoded as dummy types and used as template arguments as described in Sec. 4.1 (which is even better than any kind of hashing proposed in [3]), a search for a matching type cannot be avoided if a pointer to a derived class object shall match a pointer to a base class.

Similar to Sec. 3.6, Hanson and Proebsting also point out that dynamic variables are a data construct based on dynamic scoping, while exception handling is actually a dynamically scoped control construct. We add the observation, that the distinction between checked and unchecked exceptions has conceptual parallels to our distinction between implicit and dynamic parameters.

Other control constructs based on dynamic scoping include *control flow join points* in aspect-oriented languages [6, 8], Costanza's *dynamically scoped functions* [1], and the author's *local virtual functions* [4, 5]. As shown in [4], the latter can actually be used to simulate both exception handling and dynamically scoped variables (called semi-global variables there), even though the latter is somewhat cumbersome in practice.

The general concept of *dynamically scoped variables* can be traced back to early implementations of Lisp, where it was actually a bug instead of an intended feature. Nevertheless, since it is still considered a useful concept in addition to the usual static scoping, the basic idea has survived in Common Lisp's *special variables* [9]. Similarly, scripting languages such as PostScript, Tcl, Perl, etc. also provide similar concepts. Finally, as already mentioned in Sec. 3.3, environment variables found in operating systems are another embodiment of basically the same idea.

Of course, any kind of implicitness in a program bears the danger of obscuring important details and thus making programs harder to understand and debug. On the other hand, however, explicitly passing around large numbers of parameters also bears the danger of obscuring a few important ones with many unimportant ones. Therefore, just like any other language construct, implicit and dynamic parameters should be used with care and perceptiveness to make programs easier to read and understand in the end.

References

1. P. Costanza: "Dynamically Scoped Functions as the Essence of AOP." *ACM SIG-PLAN Notices* 38 (8) August 2003, 29–36.
2. J. Gosling, B. Joy, G. Steele, G. Bracha: *The Java Language Specification* (Third Edition). Addison-Wesley, Reading, MA, 2005.
3. D. R. Hanson, T. A. Proebsting: "Dynamic Variables." In: *Proc. 2001 ACM SIGPLAN Conf. on Programming Language Design and Implementation (PLDI)* (Snowbird, UT, June 2001). ACM, 2001, 264–273.
4. C. Heinlein: "Local Virtual Functions." In: R. Hirschfeld, R. Kowalczyk, A. Polze, M. Weske (eds.): *NODe 2005, GSEM 2005* (Erfurt, Germany, September 2005). Lecture Notes in Informatics P-69, Gesellschaft für Informatik e. V., Bonn, 2005, 129–144.
5. C. Heinlein: "Global and Local Virtual Functions in C++." *Journal of Object Technology* 4 (10) December 2005, 71–93, http://www.jot.fm/issues/issue_2005_12/article4.
6. G. Kiczales, E. Hilsdale, J. Hugunin, M. Kersten, J. Palm, W. G. Griswold: "An Overview of AspectJ." In: J. Lindskov Knudsen (ed.): *ECOOP 2001 – Object-Oriented Programming* (15th European Conference; Budapest, Hungary, June 2001; Proceedings). Lecture Notes in Computer Science 2072, Springer-Verlag, Berlin, 2001, 327–353.
7. J. R. Lewis, M. B. Shields, E. Meijer, J. Launchbury: "Implicit Parameters: Dynamic Scoping with Static Types." In: *Proc. 27th ACM Symp. on Principles of Programming Languages* (Boston, MA, January 2000). ACM, 2000, 108–118.
8. O. Spinczyk, A. Gal, W. Schröder-Preikschat: "AspectC++: An Aspect-Oriented Extension to the C++ Programming Language." In: J. Noble, J. Potter (eds.): *Proc. 40th Int. Conf. on Technology of Object-Oriented Languages and Systems (TOOLS Pacific)* (Sydney, Australia, February 2002), 53–60.
9. G. L. Steele Jr.: *Common Lisp: The Language* (Second Edition). Digital Press, Bedford, MA, 1990.
10. B. Stroustrup: *The C++ Programming Language* (Special Edition). Addison-Wesley, Reading, MA, 2000.

Reconciling Virtual Classes with Genericity

Erik Ernst

Department of Computer Science, University of Aarhus, Denmark
eernst@daimi.au.dk

Abstract. Type abstraction in object-oriented languages mainly embodies two techniques with different strenghts and weaknesses. The first technique is extension, yielding abstraction mechanisms with good support for gradual specification; the prime example is inheritance. The second technique is functional abstraction, yielding more precise knowledge about the outcome; the prime example is type parameterized classes. This paper argues that they should be clearly separated to work optimally. We have applied this design philosophy to a language based on an extension mechanism, namely virtual classes. As a result, a kind of type parameters have been introduced, but they are simple and only used where they excel. Conversely, final definitions of virtual classes have been removed from the language, thus making virtual classes more flexible. The resulting language presents a clearer and more flexible trade-off between extensibility and predictability, empowering programmers to choose the right balance.

1 Introduction

Sometimes the world is full of possibilities to explore, and sometimes it is like a dangerous mountain precipice where every step must be secured. Ideally, one should be able to explore freely when that is safe, and watch every step when that need arises, but the two modes should not be mixed at all times. Common type abstraction mechanisms actually force developers to mix the two. This paper describes a language design process in which virtual classes are optimized for unrestricted extensibility and complemented by a simple kind of type parameters providing stricter predictability, thus improving the separation of the two modes.

Extensibility lies at the heart of inheritance. Traditional inheritance is hardly powerful enough to express statically typed contemporary software, but enhanced with virtual classes it is a viable platform. Virtual classes [13] were invented along with the language BETA [14] in the seventies and, briefly, they apply late binding to inner classes such that the meaning of a class name can depend on the object from which it is obtained. Functional abstraction over types has been known since the sixties in the shape of parametric polymorphism [22]. In System F [10], Girard explicitly applied functions to types, but even in languages such as Standard ML [17] where these applications are implicit, the properties of the type system are highly influenced by it. Recently such mechanisms have become main-stream in statically typed object-orientation, due to the inclusion of type parameterized classes in Java 1.5 [11] and $C^{\#}$ 2.0 [16]. However, these two mechanisms have a different fundamental structure.

An extension mechanism takes a value from a given domain A, extends it with a value from a different domain B, and produces a new value from A, i.e., $A \rightarrow B \rightarrow A$.

D. Lightfoot and C. Szyperski (Eds.): JMLC 2006, LNCS 4228, pp. 57–72, 2006.
© Springer-Verlag Berlin Heidelberg 2006

The prototypical example is that inheritance produces a new class (e.g., `ColorPoint`) by extending a given class (`Point`) with an incremental entity (a class body `{ String color; ... }` or, with a slight generalization, a mixin [1,9]). A is here the domain of classes and B the domain of incremental entities. The crucial point is that the outcome belongs to the same domain as the entity being extended, such that the process can be repeated.

Functions used for type abstraction apply a value from a domain A to a value from a different domain B, producing a value in B, i.e., $A \rightarrow B \rightarrow B$. The prototypical example is that a parameterized type may be applied to a type, yielding a type. There is often a shortcut such that parameterized *classes* are applied to type arguments to produce a *class*, but an implicit coercion from classes to types preserves the functionality $A \rightarrow B \rightarrow B$. Note that this is in fact required in order to allow nested type applications such as `List<List<String>>`. The crucial point is that the outcome belongs to a different domain than the entity being applied, which makes it a one-step process.

Extension mechanisms are *inclusive* because they allow for repeated extensions and it is generally only known that *at least* some specific extensions are present; in return for this freedom it is both hard and inappropriate to try to establish guarantees about extensions which are not present. Conversely, type parameterization is *exclusive* because it allows for just one explicit step from the parameterized type to the resulting type; in return for this strict discipline, information about the type arguments can safely be used to reason about the outcome.

This is the ideal situation. In reality, the mechanisms have been polluted by attempts to give each of them the qualities which come naturally for the other, and it is a main point of this paper that they should be allowed to coexist in a clean form rather than overstretching each of them to do it all. The contributions of this work are as follows:

- Identifying the fundamental structural difference between type abstraction based on extension and on function application, and concluding that the former should aim for flexibility and the latter should focus on predictability.
- Revising the semantics and type system of the full-fledged programming language gbeta to follow these guidelines; introducing a new mechanism in this process, namely virtual constraints.
- Implementing the revised language design, and rewriting several hundred programs to use the revised language.

The next section presents the two mechanisms, and the following section outlines some well-known problems. Section 4 describes how simple parameterized types are added as a complement to virtual classes, and Sect. 5 describes how this allows for simpler virtual classes. The following section shows that the expressive power of the language is preserved. Finally, the implementation status is described in Sect. 7, related work is described in Sect. 8, and Sect. 9 concludes.

2   Existing Type Abstraction Mechanisms

We use Java 1.5 genericity to illustrate type parameterization. It supports type parameters for classes, constrained by bounds including recursive ones known as F-bounds [4], and co-/contra-variance in type applications by means of wildcards [11,25].

```
class Box<X> {
  X x;
  X getX() { return x; }
  void setX(X x) { this.x=x; }
}

class BoxBox<X extends BoxBox<X>> extends Box<X> {
  void selfwrap() { setX((X)this); }
}

class ColoredBoxBox<X extends ColoredBoxBox<X>>
                    extends BoxBox<X> {
  String color;
}

class BoxBoxF extends BoxBox<BoxBoxF> { }

<X extends BoxBox<X>> X unwrap(X cb) {
  return cb.getX();
}
```

Fig. 1. Boxes, expressed using Java parameterized classes

Figure 1 shows a parameterized class Box with a type parameter X. BoxBox is a subclass of Box, which is able to contain a BoxBox. It propagates the type parameter to its superclass and also constrains it with an F-bound. Hence, all type applications BoxBox<T> are checked to ensure that the actual type argument T is a subtype of BoxBox<T>, which is useful because classes instantiated from this parameterized class have a certain recursive structure, namely that the type X is "similar" to BoxBox. ColoredBoxBox shows how this technique can be extended to handle inheritance.

The method unwrap illustrates that the F-bound succeeds in expressing that getX returns an object of similar type as its argument, e.g., that the return value from unwrap applied to a ColoredBoxBox has a color. However, the method selfwrap in BoxBox, which makes the receiver wrap itself, must use a dynamic cast '(X)this' because the F-bound does not ensure that this is of type X.[1]

The class BoxBoxF is a subclass of BoxBox with type argument is BoxBoxF. This idiom is known as "taking the fixed point" of the parameterized class because it appears as the type argument to itself. This is a standard technique (presented in [2]) for using F-bounds to establish mutual recursion which can be preserved under inheritance.

---

[1] In current Java implementations, this cast is 'unchecked' because the representation of types does not support a run-time check, but this is a problem with the type erasure implementation strategy, not with parameterized classes as such. E.g., $C^\#$ does not use type erasure.

This paper uses virtual classes in gbeta [5,6,7,8] as the target of the language re-design process. At this point virtual classes are briefly introduced, with examples in the language before the redesign.[2] Later examples show the redesigned language.

Figure 2 mimics Fig. 1 using virtual classes for type abstraction. As mentioned, virtual classes were introduced in BETA, but they have been generalized in the language gbeta, and adapted to a Java-like context and in some ways clarified in the language Caesar [15]. A virtual class is a feature, similar to an inner class because it is a class and it is nested in an instance of the enclosing class; it is similar to a (virtual) method because it is accessed using late binding. A virtual class is introduced by the keyword **virtual**. Subclasses of the enclosing class may redefine an inherited virtual class, and it must then be marked with the keyword **extended**. The effect is that the value of that virtual class becomes a subclass of its inherited value, computed by adding the contributions in the **extended** definition. This often amounts to the application of a mixin to the inherited value of the virtual class; in general it is a class combination operation defined by linearization. Redefinition of a virtual class replaces it with a sub-class of its inherited value, so we use the word 'extension' rather than 'redefinition'. If the extension definition is marked with **final** then further extension of that virtual class in subclasses of the enclosing class is prohibited. This paper is intended to be self-contained, but because of the limited space we must refer to additional litera-ture [5,6,7,8] for more details about virtual classes.

Virtual classes provide type abstraction because a virtual class name (such as X inside Box in Fig. 2) denotes some subclass of its statically known value (here Object), but the actual value is determined at run-time. To establish the recursive structure we make BoxBox a virtual class and refer to itself in the extension of X. As a result, BoxBox is now a subclass of Box whose X is BoxBox itself. Note that this is the case for inherited usages of X as well as newly added ones. The selfwrap method corresponds to the one in Fig. 1, but it does not need a dynamic cast because the receiver is known to have type BoxBox or a subtype. (BoxBox is not a 'MyType' [3], but it is known to be a supertype thereof). Next, BoxBox is equal to X, because the extension of X is final. Finally, X is the argument type of setX, so setX(**this**) is type safe.

The enclosing class CB is needed in order to make BoxBox a virtual class such that the relation between BoxBox and its virtual X is preserved for extended versions of BoxBox, e.g., the one in ColoredCB. The recursive structure need not be redeclared when the color is added, as opposed to the situation with parameterized classes. In-stances of CB and subclasses can be used to specify the type of BoxBox, with whatever extensions the given subclass of CB has added. This phenomenon is known as *family polymorphism* [6,21,18]. For instance, the method unwrap accepts an argument aCB of type CB, and an argument cb of type aCB.BoxBox, and the return value is of the same type. In particular, it is again possible to access the color of the return value from unwrap applied to a BoxBox from an **object** known to be a ColoredCB.

Note that the type of the second argument cb depends on the *object* aCB. Such a type would not be well-defined if it were possible to change aCB during the life-time of cb, and the return type of the method also depends on aCB remaining unchanged

---

[2] For main-stream readability, the syntax of gbeta examples has been changed to follow the Java style.

```
class Box {
  virtual class X extends Object;
  X x;
  X getX() { return x; }
  void setX(X x) { this.x=x; }
}

class CB {
  virtual class BoxBox extends Box {
    final extended class X extends BoxBox;
    void selfwrap() { setX(this); }
  }
}

class ColoredCB extends CB {
  extended class BoxBox { String color; }
}

aCB.BoxBox unwrap(final CB aCB, aCB.BoxBox cb) {
  return cb.getX();
}
```

Fig. 2. Boxes, expressed using gbeta virtual classes (transformed to a Java-style syntax)

throughout the method invocation. Because of this aCB is **final**, which means that it cannot be changed after initialization. An object used in the type of a variable or method argument is a *family object*, and the immutability restriction applies to all family objects. If a mutable variable were used as a family object then types declared from it would be useless, because no object can be shown to have such a type.

3 Problems with Existing Mechanisms

The given examples exhibit some problems characteristic of the two mechanisms. First, the method selfwrap in Fig. 1 has a dynamic cast because the F-bound does not ensure any particular relation between X and the type of the receiver. Next, the type bound of the method unwrap in Fig. 1 must re-declare the recursive structure of BoxBox. It is a case of bad encapsulation that this supposedly internal recursive structure of BoxBox must be restated whenever it is used or passed on to another piece of code.

In comparison, the method selfwrap in Fig. 2 is safe and does not need the dynamic cast. The method unwrap receives the extra argument aCB which—like a "dynamic package"—provides the other types used in the method signature. This extra argument often causes objections, but the notion of a dynamic package is quite simple after getting used to it, and it remains equally simple no matter how complex the contained structure is. In contrast, restating the recursive structure grows in complexity with the square of the number of members of the class family. Moreover, virtual classes are more flexible because one can use family-polymorphic references to BoxBox objects:

```
... final CB myCB = ...
myCB.BoxBox cb1,cb2;
... cb1 = new myCB.BoxBox(); cb2.setX(cb1); ...
```
Ex. 1

In Ex. 1 a family object myCB is in scope—it could be a final argument to a method, or a final instance variable of an enclosing object. By ordinary reference polymorphism it could be an instance of CB, ColoredCB, or any other subclass of CB. Using the type myCB.BoxBox it is possible to declare variables of that specific BoxBox type and operate safely on them because it is known to always be the same version of BoxBox, namely the one in myCB. Hence, myCB works like a package because it provides access to a set of classes. There is no corresponding "package polymorphism" with parameterized classes, because the class families consist of individual classes with no common identity. It is, however, possible to create a polymorphic reference using Java wildcards which is capable of referring to BoxBox<T> objects with varying type argument T, as in the following example:

```
BoxBox<?> cb1,cb2; /* type arg variation is allowed */
...cb2.setX(cb1); /* not type correct! */
...cb1 = new BoxBox<?>(); /* cannot use ? here! */
```
Ex. 2

But there is no way wildcards in the type of these variables can express that the type argument of cb1 and cb2 is the same at run-time. Consequently, expressions like cb2.setX(cb1) in Ex. 2 are not type safe. It is also impossible to create new instances of BoxBox in "the right family" because the '?' denotes an arbitrary type rather than the type argument given to BoxBox in the type of cb2 or any such thing.

In summary, type parameterized classes with F-bounds can go a long way to describe recursive type structures, but some problems remain, especially because the recursive structure is imposed from the outside rather than built-in.

Turning to the world of virtual classes, there are also some well-known problems. Collection classes using virtual classes for type abstraction have distinct type for each subclass created just in order to specify its element type. The Box class could be seen as a very simple collection class, and we could create some boxes to hold numbers:

```
class NumBox extends Box {
   final extended class X extends Number;
}
NumBox nb = new NumBox();
... nb.setX(new Integer(3)); ...

class NumBox2 extends Box {
   final extended class X extends Number;
}
NumBox2 nb2 = new NumBox2();
... nb2.setX(new Double(.5)); ...
```
Ex. 3

It is important that X is **final** in Ex. 3, to ensure that it is safe to insert elements into the "collection", i.e., to call setX(). Large projects would have many locations where a collection of a given type is created. Each time a class like NumBox is created the result is a distinct class, unrelated to all the other classes which are also boxes holding numbers. Consequently, we cannot write generic code that polymorphically accesses a NumBox or a NumBox2, preserving the information that the elements are Numbers.

This is a nontrivial problem because it is hard to reconcile virtual classes with structural type equivalence. In [23] it was in fact proposed to support a kind of structural equivalence for virtual classes, and Fig. 8 in that paper shows a family of mutually recursive classes with this kind of structural equivalence. However, no details are given, and several years of experience with the static analysis of gbeta suggests that the entire environment of enclosing scopes all the way out to the global namespace must be included in the structure which represents a type for this to work. In that case, two distinct declarations would hardly ever be structurally equivalent unless they are declared in the same scope. Obviously, this eliminates most of the benefits of structural equivalence.

Another hard problem with virtual classes is that their inherently extensional nature makes it hard to reconcile them with lower bounds. In particular, it is difficult to use virtual classes to describe contravariance, i.e., that supertypes of a type argument create subtypes in type applications. Essentially, contravariance is useful in order to achieve polymorphism over a type parameter X of a data structure that accepts method arguments of type X (an "X sink" data structure). E.g., if List is a parameterized type in Java and objects of type T should be inserted into such a list, but the actual type argument of the list should be allowed to vary within the bounds of type safety, the proper type would be List<? **super** T> which uses **super** to specify contravariance and is allowed to refer to instances of List<S> for all types S such that T is a subtype of S. A detailed example of non-trivial and useful contravariance which can easily be expressed using wildcards has been given in a solution to the so-called expression problem [24]. The feature described in the next section is able to express this solution directly.

4   Adding Lightweight Type Parameters

This paper solves the problems described in the previous section by adding a simple version of type parameterization to virtual classes. As a consequence of this, virtual classes are simplified and made more flexible, as described in the next section.

The new type abstraction mechanism is based on *constraints* on virtual classes. It is only applicable to types, i.e., the declared type of an instance variable, a local variable, or a method argument, and in particular they cannot be applied to class definitions. They are not higher-order, there is no support for aliasing, and they do not allow F-bounds. The rationale for these design choices is that virtual constraints should be able to express certain typing properties known from parameterized classes with wildcards as in Java, but they should not be used for the specification of recursive type structures, because virtual classes are better at that anyway. Syntactically, virtual constraints are similar to type applications in Java:

```
class List {
  virtual class X extends Object;
  ...
}


List<X extends Number> ro_nums;  // covariance
List<X super Number> wo_nums;    // contravariance
List<X equals Number> rw_nums;   // invariance
```

Ex. 4

To check these types for correctness, it is required that List is statically known to contain a virtual class named X and the right hand side of each constraint is again a correct type. The main difference to Java type applications is that the constrained virtual is mentioned by name, e.g. X in the example, whereas wildcards are denoted by question marks and identified with specific type arguments by their position in the argument list. This is a natural consequence of the fact that virtual constraints are not passing arguments, they specify relations that must be verified to hold for the actual virtual classes in question. This also makes it possible to give multiple constraints on the same virtual class, and it enables constraining a subset of the virtual classes. When there is exactly one virtual class, an equality constraint on that virtual class is the default; e.g., the last line in Ex. 4 could have used List<Number>. The names of the declared variables have been chosen to support a useful intuition about variance, namely that a covariant data structure is read-only, a contravariant data structure is write-only, and only an invariant data structure allows both writing and reading.

These variables can be assigned to each other according to the rules for use-site variance [12] which can also be used to explain the treatment of wildcard types in the Java programming language (when disregarding wildcard capture [25]). These rules allow assignment among variables of the same type and from an invariant type to both variant types (e.g., from rw_nums to wo_nums and from rw_nums to ro_nums), and prohibits all other combinations.

We can also verify that constraints are satisfied based on direct knowledge about virtual classes, especially because creation of a new object is as monomorphic as the class denotation (e.g., 'new C()' is known to be an instance of C whereas the value of a variable of type C is only known have type C or a subtype). In particular, the following assignments are type correct (assuming that Integer is a subtype of Number which is again a subtype of Object):

```
ro_nums = new List() {
  extended class X extends Integer
};


wo_nums = new List() {
  extended class X extends Object
};


rw_nums = new List() {
  extended class X extends Number
};
```

Ex. 5

We need not make the virtual class **final**, because the new object is known to be an instance of the denoted anonymous class, so X cannot be further extended.

Virtual constraints solve the problem of accidentally incompatible collection types, because the constrained types are structurally equivalent even though the classes are distinct. Virtual constraints can also express contravariance as with **super** bounded wildcard types. Finally, constraints can of course be nested as in the following example:

```
List<List<Number>> numss;
List<X extends List<X super Number>> ro_wo_numss;
```
Ex. 6

This declares numss to be a list of list of Number, and ro_wo_numss to be a read-only list of write-only lists of numbers. With the latter it is possible to iterate over the outer list and insert numbers into each of the inner lists. In fact, an inner list might be a LinkedList<Object> because the outer list might actually be a list of LinkedList<X **super** Number>, which can hold a LinkedList<Object>.

The constrained virtual classes are looked up in the base class of the nearest enclosing type—e.g., X is looked up in List in the examples—and the right hand side of the constraints are looked up in the same scope as the entire type. This rule is simple and ensures that recursion (F-bounds) cannot occur inside a virtual constraint, thus avoiding the abovementioned problems with F-bounds as well as others such as the lack of principal types.

The decision to add virtual constraints to a language with virtual classes can now be evaluated and motivated. First, note that type parameterization of classes does not interact well with inheritance because the two mechanisms are fundamentally different: inheritance is based on extension and class parameterization is based on type functions. Hence, it did not seem attractive to add type parameters to classes, which would also produce a very complex and redundant language design. However, a coercion from class to type takes place—implicitly, but at well-known locations—for the declared type of each instance variable, local variable, and method parameter, and this process fits very well with type functions because it is inherently a single step process. Moreover, the addition of virtual constraints does *not* add much complexity to gbeta; the static analysis already computed the information needed to determine whether virtual constraints are satisfied in connection with types without virtual constraints, and the variance rules used to determine subtyping among types with virtual constraints are very simple. It adds complexity to the grammar, but the new constructs should be quite easy to understand for most programmers, and they are (even in the actual gbeta syntax) modeled to be syntactically similar to type application in main-stream languages.

As a result, a useful amount of structural type equivalence is now available, in a familiar syntax, with variance that corresponds to Java wildcards, and the new features are tightly integrated with virtual classes because it is virtual classes which are constrained, and because the right hand sides of constraints can also refer to virtual classes.

5   Simplifying Virtual Classes

It is tempting to consider language design as a matter of designing new language features. However, it has always been a core design criterion for BETA that there should be few language features; each of them should be powerful; they should work well to-gether; and they should be orthogonal, i.e., their application areas should not overlap. The language gbeta was created in the same spirit. Hence, we consider it useful to *re-move* features during a language design process, and this is exactly what is described in this section: final extensions of virtuals are removed from the language. The reason why this is so important is that it removes constraints from an extension mechanism, hence enabling unrestricted usage of extensions—with final extensions, dynamic class combination will inevitably be unsafe.

As mentioned in Sect. 2, a **final** virtual class extension implies that no more ex-tensions to this virtual class can be made in subclasses of the enclosing class. This implies that more information can be established about the value of this virtual class: Normally, a virtual class is only known by upper bound when the class of the enclosing object is not known exactly; for instance, in the class body of Box in Fig. 2 it is known that X denotes some subclass of Object, but it cannot be assumed that any given type is a subtype of X because it is only bounded from above. (The type of null may be considered a 'bottom' type, but that is the only exception). Consequently, a variable or method argument of type X cannot be assigned any value unless this value is already of type X. For a collection, e.g., this means that we can reorganize contained objects, but we cannot insert objects obtained from elsewhere. Final definitions of virtual classes thus play an important role of making it safe to assign externally provided objects to variables or method arguments whose type is a virtual class. For instance, a list is not so useful if we cannot put anything into it (except null).

However, adding virtual constraints as described in Sect. 4 solves this problem in almost all cases: Collections and other objects for which it is important to have a lower bound on a virtual class should be accessed via variables whose type has a lower bound on the virtual, e.g., List<X **super** Number> or List<X **equals** Number>. Us-ing an **equals** bound is the typical choice for important references to such an object, because it preserves the possibility to both deliver and receive objects whose type is the virtual class (e.g., giving method arguments, and receiving method return values).

The remaining—hard—case is exemplified by BoxBox in Fig. 2. In this case it is not possible to use a type with virtual constraints to establish the required typing properties because the constraints are concerned with an object rather than virtual classes of an object, and that object is the current object, **this**.

The final extension of X ensures that it is exactly equal to BoxBox. This is be-cause the contributions to X are known to be Object and BoxBox, and the combina-tion of these two contributions is statically known to be BoxBox, even though this is a virtual class and its actual value is not known statically (just like $\emptyset \cup A = A$ for any set A). Since the current object **this** in any class body on the right hand side of a virtual class definition is an instance of that virtual class or a subclass thereof, we conclude that **this** has type BoxBox and hence also type X.

If we remove **final** from the extension of X in BoxBox, it is no longer known that **this** has type X, which means that the method call setX(**this**) would be rejected by the compiler because it would not be type safe. It is easy to create an example show-ing that it would be unsound to consider it type safe, so this is an essential difference rather than a matter of improving the type analysis. A dynamic cast would have to be used, and the situation would then be just as bad as it is with parameterized classes.

However, there is a quite general approach which makes it possible to achieve the effect of a final declaration of a virtual class, and this is the topic of the next section. Based on this opening, virtual classes were simplified as follows: It is no longer possible to use **final** in a virtual class extension; a language mechanism known as 'disownment' [5, p.197] which was used to avoid multiple conflicting final extensions of virtual classes is no longer needed and is removed from the language. Finally, the implementation of the type checker has been simplified.

6   Emulating Final Declarations

Final extensions of virtual classes can be emulated based on a surprisingly simple mechanism, namely that of binding a final instance variable to an object, i.e., binding a name to a simple, opaque run-time value which is an address in the heap.

Binding a name to a simple value is inherently a one-step process, so extension is wasteful because there will not be "multiple extensions". The language gbeta has had a one-step binding mechanism for several years [5, p.193], known as 'virtual objects'. This mechanism is in fact what is used to express **final** method arguments such as aCB in Fig. 2 in the original gbeta syntax, but the semantics is simply that of binding a name immutably to a value. Syntactically, virtual objects are different from method arguments, because they are class features. The class and method concepts are in fact unified to one concept in BETA and in gbeta, namely *patterns*. So virtual objects are really features of objects created as instances of patterns, and it is a matter of taste whether one wants to consider a given pattern as a class or as a method, and correspondingly its instances as objects or as method activation records. For simplicity, virtual objects will be shown as class features, and the relation to methods is not made explicit.

A virtual object is introduced in a declaration marked with **virtual**, and for each virtual object introduction there must be at most one virtual object final declaration. If there is no final declaration of a virtual object, the declared class of the object given in the introduction is used to create a new instance (it turns out to be convenient to get fresh objects by default). If there is a final declaration then it specifies an object, which must be of the type given in the declaration or a subtype thereof, e.g.:

```
myCB.BoxBox myBoxBox;

class StickyBox {
  virtual object bx isa Box;
  bx.X x;
}

class MyStickyBox extends StickyBox {
  final object bx is myBoxBox;
}
```
Ex. 7

Instances of StickyBox contain a virtual object of type Box or a subtype thereof, as well as an ordinary mutable instance variable x. The subclass MyStickyBox contains a corresponding **final** declaration of the virtual object, which binds the name bx in instances of that class to the object myBoxBox (assuming myCB is declared as in Ex. 1). It is essential for the typing that a virtual object is immutable, because this makes it possible to use it as a family object. For example, x is declared to have the type bx.X, which means that it is known to be safe to execute statements like x=**new** bx.X(), bx.setX(x), and x=bx.getX().

Moreover, x has type myBoxBox.X in MyStickyBox, which establishes that it is also safe to execute x.setX(x) ... except that this only holds when the extension of X in BoxBox is **final**, and we are in the middle of reconstructing that property after having removed **final** extensions from the language.

```
//  Original Code
class C {
  virtual class X extends Number;
  X x;
  ...
}
class D extends C {
  final extended class X extends Integer;
  ...
}

//  Transformed Code
class Xholder { virtual class X extends Number; }
class C {
  virtual object Xh isa Xholder;
  Xh.X x;
  ...
}
class D extends C {
  final object Xh is new Xholder() {
    extended class X extends Integer;
    ...
  }
}
```

Fig. 3. Emulation of a final extension

The emulation uses the transformation shown in Fig. 3. Assume that a class C is given that introduces a virtual class X and uses it (in the example: as the type of an instance variable x). The subclass D of C contains a **final** extension of X. There are no ordinary (non-**final**) extensions of X. The transformation expresses an equivalent situation without using **final** extensions of virtual classes. Transformed declarations use a virtual object, and the virtual class will then be looked up in that virtual object, as shown in the transformed code.

The only difference is that the virtual class is now wrapped inside a virtual object. For the virtual object, the transition from unbound to bound is registered by the type analysis and will occur exactly once (by a final declaration or by default). Hence, any given **final** declaration of a virtual object is the only such declaration for that attribute, and hence whatever is known about that particular object will hold for the attribute. In particular, it is known for all instances of D or subclasses thereof that their Xh virtual object is an instance of the given anonymous class (and not a subtype thereof!), and this means that Xh.X is exactly Integer. In other words, Xh.X was introduced as being some (unknown) subtype of Number in C and then fixed to be exactly Integer in D and its subclasses, just like X in the original code. Note that the default binding of the virtual object corresponds to using the declared bound as a default for a type parameter in type parameterized classes.

In essence, we use a virtual object to achieve strict two-phase abstraction, then use it as a family object to provide the virtual class. The technique can be used to emulate all cases where a virtual class is used for introduction and **final** extension, which corresponds closely to the two-phase abstraction of a type parameter—first declaration of the formal, later passing actual arguments. Note that one virtual object may provide several virtual classes, possibly a mutually recursive family.

Trying this out in practice, several hundred small gbeta programs (about 20.000 lines of code in total) were redesigned to use the revised language, and this technique was sufficient to remove all usages of **final** virtual extension.

Static checking of virtual objects in the gbeta compiler is currently based on considering every program location where two classes are combined (including the degenerate case where a single mixin is added to a class). This includes every virtual extension declaration and every explicit class combination operation (explicit class combination is a kind of multiple inheritance that gbeta supports). If the two classes being combined are statically known then the combination can be performed statically and the result checked directly. If one of the classes is statically known and does not contain any **final** virtual object declarations then the combination cannot create conflicts, and the operation is accepted. In the remaining cases a warning is issued, and the merging operation is checked dynamically. Note that every gbeta program in this paper (expressed in the original gbeta syntax) compiles without warnings.

7   Implementation Status

Apart from the fact that the original gbeta syntax has been transformed to a style similar to the Java programming language and all directives concerned with the module system have been left out, the example programs in this paper are actual, running gbeta code. The design and implementation of virtual constraints took place in 2003, but some adjustments were made more recently, particularly in the handling of nested constraints. About 20.000 lines of gbeta code in about 650 programs (most of them small, but up to 2500 lines of code) have been updated along the way to use the revised language, thereby helping to evaluate the new language design. The implementation is available at http://www.daimi.au.dk/~eernst/gbeta/.

8   Related Work

Several related research efforts have been mentioned already, so at this point we just add a few extra remarks.

In [2] the relation between type parameterized classes and virtual classes is described as if the significant difference in the treatment of families of mutually recursive classes is in the verbosity of parameterized classes (and type safety, but that discussion has changed since then). This paper demonstrates that there are also some deeper differences between the abilities of these two approaches to express complex typing structures.

We mentioned that virtual constraints are similar to wildcards [11,25], but deferred discussion of wildcard capture. Wildcard capture is a mechanism that enables invocation of a polymorphic method on an argument whose type includes a wildcard as a type argument, effectively giving a name to the type argument which is otherwise only known as '?'. In fact, this capability is just a special case of the general ability of accessing "type arguments" (virtual classes) in a language with virtual classes—in such a language the type argument is never nameless and access is as simple as `obj.X`.

The language SCALA [19,20] features abstract type members which share many properties with virtual classes. However, abstract type members must *always* have a final declaration; introductory and overriding declarations are subtype and/or supertype constraints, and only when the type member is finally bound to a concrete class (which must satisfy all the constraints) it can be used for such things as creating new objects. Hence, this mechanism is clearly divided into two phases. Moreover, it is possible in Scala to specify types by means of a combination of names and structural *refinements*, which may override declarations of abstract type members in the named type. This mechanism is similar in nature to the virtual constraints of gbeta, but based on a strict two-phase model rather than the extension based model of gbeta virtual classes.

9   Conclusion

This paper argues that virtual classes and type parameterized classes are fundamentally different kinds of type abstraction mechanisms, and that they should be kept separate in order for each of them to work optimally. Starting from the language gbeta which is based on virtual classes, this philosophy is applied in a language redesign process. A simple use-site type parameter mechanism is added, based on constraints on virtual classes, and virtual classes themselves are simplified by removing final definitions of virtual classes from the language. As a result, the support for variance and structural type equivalence is improved due to the virtual class constraints, and the powerful extension support provided by inheritance and virtual class extensions is made more flexible because the potential for final definition conflicts has disappeared.

References

1. Gilad Bracha and William Cook.   Mixin-based inheritance.   In *Proceedings OOP-SLA/ECOOP'90, ACM SIGPLAN Notices*, volume 25, 10, pages 303–311, October 1990.
2. K. Bruce, M. Odersky, and P. Wadler. A statically safe alternative to virtual types. *Lecture Notes in Computer Science*, 1445:523–549, 1998.

3. K. B. Bruce, R. Van Gent, and A. Schuett. PolyTOIL: A type-safe polymorphic object-oriented language. *Proceedings ECOOP'95*, LNCS 952:27–51, 1995.

4. Peter Canning, William Cook, Walter Hill, John Mitchell, and Walter Olthoff. F-bounded polymorphism for object-oriented programming. In *Fourth International Conference on Functional Programming and Computer Architecture*. ACM, September 1989. Also technical report STL-89-5, from Software Technology Laboratory, Hewlett-Packard Laboratories.

5. Erik Ernst. *gbeta – A Language with Virtual Attributes, Block Structure, and Propagating, Dynamic Inheritance*. PhD thesis, DEVISE, Department of Computer Science, University of Aarhus, Aarhus, Denmark, June 1999.

6. Erik Ernst. Family polymorphism. In Jørgen Lindskov Knudsen, editor, *Proceedings ECOOP'01*, LNCS 2072, pages 303–326, Heidelberg, Germany, 2001. Springer-Verlag.

7. Erik Ernst. Higher-order hierarchies. In Luca Cardelli, editor, *Proceedings ECOOP'03*, LNCS 2743, pages 303–329, Heidelberg, Germany, July 2003. Springer-Verlag.

8. Erik Ernst, Klaus Ostermann, and William R. Cook. A virtual class calculus. In *Proceedings POPL'06*, pages 270–282, Charleston, SC, USA, 2006. ACM.

9. Matthew Flatt, Shriram Krishnamurthi, and Matthias Felleisen. Classes and mixins. In *Conference Record of POPL '98: The 25th ACM SIGPLAN-SIGACT Symposium on Principles of Programming Languages*, pages 171–183, San Diego, California, 19–21 January 1998.

10. Jean-Yves Girard. *Interprétation fonctionelle et élimination des coupures de l'arithmétique d'ordre supérieur*. PhD thesis, Université Paris VII, 1972. A summary appeared in the Proceedings of the Second Scandinavian Logic Symposium (J.E. Fenstad, editor), North-Holland, 1971 (pp. 63–92).

11. James Gosling, Bill Joy, Guy Steele, and Gilad Bracha. *The Java Language Specification – Third Edition*. The Java Series. Addison-Wesley, third. edition, 2004.

12. Atsushi Igarashi and Mirko Viroli. On variance-based subtyping for parameteric types. In Boris Magnusson, editor, *Procedings ECOOP'02*, LNCS 2374, pages 441–469. Springer-Verlag, June 2002.

13. Ole Lehrmann Madsen and Birger Møller-Pedersen. Virtual classes: A powerful mechanism in object-oriented programming. In *Proceedings OOPSLA'89, ACM SIGPLAN Notices*, volume 24, 10, pages 397–406, October 1989.

14. Ole Lehrmann Madsen, Birger Møller-Pedersen, and Kristen Nygaard. *Object-Oriented Programming in the BETA Programming Language*. Addison-Wesley, Reading, MA, USA, 1993.

15. M. Mezini and K. Ostermann. Conquering aspects with Caesar. In *Proceedings AOSD'03*, pages 90–99, Boston, USA, 2003.

16. Microsoft Corporation, Seattle, USA. *C# – Version 2.0 Specification*, May 2004.

17. R. Milner, M. Tofte, R. W. Harper, and D. MacQueen. *The Definition of Standard ML*. MIT Press, 1997.

18. Nathaniel Nystrom, Stephen Chong, and Andrew C. Myers. Scalable extensibility via nested inheritance. In *Proceedings OOPSLA'04*, pages 99–115. ACM Press, 2004.

19. Martin Odersky and al. An overview of the scala programming language. Technical Report IC/2004/64, EPFL Lausanne, Switzerland, 2004.

20. Martin Odersky and Matthias Zenger. Scalable component abstractions. In *Proceedings OOPSLA'05*, pages 41–57, New York, NY, USA, October 2005. ACM Press.

21. Klaus Ostermann. Dynamically composable collaborations with delegation layers. *Lecture Notes in Computer Science*, 2374:89–110, 2002.

22. Christopher Strachey. Fundamental concepts in programming languages. Lecture Notes, International Summer School in Programming Languages, Copenhagen, Denmark, 1967.

23. Kresten Krab Thorup and Mads Torgersen. Unifying genericity - combining the benefits of virtual types and parameterized classes. In *Proceedings ECOOP'99*, pages 186–204, 1999.

24. Mads Torgersen. The expression problem revisited – four new solutions using generics. In Martin Odersky, editor, *Proceedings ECOOP'04*, LNCS 3086, pages 123–143, Oslo, Norway, 2004. Springer-Verlag. To appear.
25. Mads Torgersen, Erik Ernst, Christian Plesner Hansen, Peter von der Ahé, Gilad Bracha, and Neal Gafter. Adding wildcards to the java programming language. *Journal of Object Technology*, 3(11), 2004. `http://www.jot.fm/issues/issue_2004_12/article5`.

Oberon Script: A Lightweight Compiler and Runtime System for the Web

Ralph Sommerer

Microsoft Research, 7 J J Thomson Avenue,
Cambridge, United Kingdom
som@microsoft.com

Abstract. Oberon Script is an experimental scripting language and runtime system for building interactive Web Client applications. It is based on the Oberon programming language and consists of a compiler that translates Oberon Script at load-time into JavaScript code, and a small runtime system that detects and compiles script sections written in Oberon Script.

1 Introduction

Oberon is the name of a modular, extensible operating system for single user workstations [19], and also of an object-oriented programming language specifically developed to implement the former [17]. Although originally designed as the native operating system for custom built workstations, Oberon was subsequently ported to various different computing platforms including personal computers [2][4] and Unix workstations [1][14][15].

With the recent emergence and proliferation of sophisticated Web client applications, the *Web browser* has become a computing platform on its own. It offers the Web application programmer scripting facilities based on the JavaScript language [3] to programmatically interact with a Web server, and to manipulate the Web page in-place and without reloading. It thus allows the construction of rich Web application user interfaces that are not limited to the page-based hypertext model anymore and approach those of desktop applications.

As the Web browser morphs into a runtime system and operating platform for Web client applications, the question arises whether it can provide a suitable target platform for another installment of Oberon, especially in light of all previous porting efforts that have shown Oberon's demands of the host platform to be very limited. While attempting to answer this question we can explore in particular the suitability of JavaScript as a "portable object code" to compile Oberon to, and the feasibility of performing the compilation online, i.e. on the browser itself. Oberon promises to strike the right balance between being simple enough to make this experiment feasible and powerful enough to make it meaningful.

In this paper we present *Oberon Script*, an experimental effort to develop a simple and lightweight application programming framework for building complex Web client applications in Oberon. The system consists of a load-time Oberon-to-JavaScript compiler and a small runtime system to process and run script sections written in Oberon Script.

D. Lightfoot and C. Szyperski (Eds.): JMLC 2006, LNCS 4228, pp. 73–83, 2006.
© Springer-Verlag Berlin Heidelberg 2006

2 Web Client Programming

The page based hypertext model of the Web is unsuitable for rich Web applications user interfaces because the unit of interaction – the execution of a link and the corresponding loading of a new page even for simple interactions – is too coarse to provide a smooth and pleasant user experience. Simple interactions such as attaching a file to an email message in a Web based email client require as many as 3 page loads. Recently, however, Script-based Web applications have started to emerge, that employ a so-called Ajax-style of application design. Ajax stands for *Asynchronous JavaScript and XML* [10]. In applications built using these techniques the page is modified on-the-fly by programs written in browser-run scripting languages, thus avoiding the reloading of the page even for complex user activities or display updates. This application style was popularized by Google through their e-mail [7] and mapping [8] services, although neither was pioneering in relying on Ajax techniques.

2.1 Ajax

The Ajax-style of Web application programming is usually recognized by the use of the following techniques: HTML DOM [16] manipulation via client-side scripting languages, mainly JavaScript [3], and the use of XML as the data exchange format between server and client. The core foundation of Ajax, however, is a built-in browser component called *XMLHttpRequest* [10] that allows JavaScript code to interact with a Web server "behind the scenes" and without having to reload the page. The use of XML is not essential, and other data formats are commonly employed, including plain text or a linearization of JavaScript objects (JSON) [12].

2.2 JavaScript

JavaScript is an object-based scripting language for the Web. Originally developed under the name of *LiveScript* it was later re-branded as JavaScript because of its superficial syntactical similarities with the programming language Java [9], but also in order to benefit from the publicity around the then new language. JavaScript is now standardized as ECMAScript [3], and all modern Web browsers support the language using different brand names, such as JScript or JavaScript.

JavaScript does not support classes. Instead, it supports a prototype-based inheritance model with shared properties (fields and methods). Objects are created using a *constructor function* that initializes the object's instance variables. Fields and methods that were defined via the constructor function's *prototype* property are subsequently available as instance fields and methods.

JavaScript objects are implemented as hash tables, and instance fields are stored as entries in those tables. The following ways of accessing instance fields are therefore interchangeable: obj.field (field access), obj[field] (hash table access).

The JavaScript runtime system also features a small collection of predefined objects such as strings, arrays, regular expression objects, and so on, some of which also have a correspondence in the language (e.g. string constants in the language are instances of the *String* object).

3 Oberon Script

3.1 Language

Oberon Script is a subset of the Oberon programming language as defined in [17]. "Subset" is to be understood not so much with respect to *language* as to *semantics*. Indeed, the Oberon Script compiler compiles the *full language* as specified in the language report referenced above, i.e. the language Oberon and some of the additions introduced by *Oberon-2* [13]. However, for reasons of simplicity and compactness, and also to be compatible with the underlying runtime system that is based on JavaScript, some of the rules are relaxed. Thus, some of what would be syntactical errors in Oberon is permissible in Oberon Script.

The decision to support the full language was based chiefly on the following principles: First, we consider an effort to port a language to a new computing environment to be incomplete as long as the full language is not supported. Changing the language to simplify its porting is tantamount to adjusting a question to fit an answer. Problems encountered during such an endeavor should be regarded as challenges, and not opportunities to shortcut. Dropping or adjusting features later for purposes of optimization or simplicity are acceptable but only once the system has proved working. Second, we believe the Oberon language to be sufficiently concise such that stripping it down any further will likely harm its expressiveness. The language report specifying the syntax and semantics of Oberon is one of the shortest around (28 pages). The JavaScript language specification, in comparison, covers 188 pages [3]. Third, by basing our experiment on the full language Oberon instead of a cut-down toy language we can assess more accurately the limits of a language's complexity that can be reasonably compiled and processed in the browser on-the-fly.

3.2 Compiler

The Oberon Script compiler is a simple one-pass recursive-descent parser [18] that performs very basic syntax analyses and emits JavaScript constructs as a side-effect. Manual translation of Oberon constructs into JavaScript revealed that many features and constructs of the former have a structure that is very similar to those in the latter. For example, designators, expressions, statements, and control structures look basically the same in both languages, apart from trivial differences such as the symbols used to express them. This similarity suggests employing regular expressions to translate Oberon's syntax into that of JavaScript. However, after some initial experiments we decided against it. Apart from very simple expressions, most syntactical elements require the translator to have a certain minimal understanding of their structure in order to translate them into correct JavaScript. For instance, a simple designator, such as a local variable, can be discovered using regular expressions, but a moderately complex one, e.g. one involving arrays, type tests, or even a combination of these, requires at least *some* (recursive) parsing to establish its extent. But if *some* parsing is required in any case for any moderately complex program, it stands to reason that we can as well parse the *whole* program.

While the syntactical differences of Oberon with the resulting JavaScript code are too big to allow using regular expressions to translate one into the other, they are small enough to greatly simplify the compiler. For example, in many places it is only necessary to identify syntactical *patterns* instead of their details. The same parsing routine can therefore be employed in different places in our compiler where the different semantics of such constructs would require different routines in a regular compiler. Consider for example the following syntactical constructs:

```
FieldList = [IdentList ":" type].
VariableDeclaration = IdentList ":" type.
FPSection = [VAR] ident {"," ident} ":" FormalType.

IdentList = identdef {"," identdef}.
identdef = ident ["*"].
```

Although it is obvious that field lists (of record type declarations), variable declarations, or formal parameter sections (FPSection) are different syntactical constructs and require different processing in a regular compiler (such as different allocation methods), for our purposes they are simply lists of identifiers followed by a type. Their different processing requirements can easily be accommodated for by passing an appropriate handler method, but the compiler doesn't need to parse them differently. A single parser method thus suffices for all three.

For reasons of simplicity and compactness of the compiler – and interoperability with regular JavaScript – only very minimal semantics analyses are performed, and only where it is necessary to establish a certain condition in order to proceed with the parsing. Designators, for example, are fully developed, including the type of the current selector, in order to determine certain features of the designated object, e.g. to distinguish procedure calls from type tests, or to handle reference parameters correctly. Expressions, as a counter example, are not developed at all, and are simply output to the JavaScript generator. Therefore, a standard procedure call such as the following (where s is a string variable):

```
INC(s, "hello world")
```

which is illegal in Oberon, is not only permissible in Oberon Script, its translation in JavaScript actually makes perfect sense:

```
s+="hello world"  //concatenation
```

3.2.1 Modules

Oberon modules can be described in object-oriented terms as singleton objects [6], with static fields and methods representing the global variables and procedures. This is also the approach used in Oberon Script to implement modules.

An Oberon Script module is translated into a JavaScript object constructor function bearing the name of the module. In the body of that function, all exported items, including (record) types, constants, variables, and procedures are assigned as static members of the function object. They can thus be accessed from the "outside" (other Oberon Script modules or regular JavaScript) using the familiar "dotted" qualified identifier notation consisting of the module name and that of the object in the form *Module.Object*.

Example of an Oberon Script module and its representation as JavaScript object.

```
(*Oberon Script module*)
MODULE Mod;

CONST
  N*=1024;

TYPE
  Point*=RECORD x,y:INTEGER END;

VAR
  pt*, pt0:Point;

PROCEDURE Move*(dx,dy:INTEGER);
BEGIN INC(pt.x,dx); INC(pt.y,dy)
END Move;

PROCEDURE SetOrg*(x,y:INTEGER);
BEGIN pt0.x := x; pt0.y := y
END SetOrg;

BEGIN pt0.x := 0; pt0.y := 0; pt := pt0
END Mod.
```

```
//JavaScript translation
function Mod
{
  Mod.N=1024;
  Mod.Point=function(){this.x=0;this.y=0}
  Mod.pt=new Mod.Point();
  var pt0=new Mod.Point();
  Mod.Move=function(dx,dy){pt.x+=dx;pt.y+=dy}
  Mod.SetOrg=function(x,y){pt0.x=x;pt0.y=y}
  pt0.x=0;
  pt0.y=0;
  _cpy(pt,pt0); //value copy
}
Mod(); //execute body
```

Non-exported objects (variables, types and procedures) are translated as local functions and/or variables in the body of the constructor function that represents the module. Note that this use of local objects (variables, functions) as "private global" objects is perfectly legal in JavaScript, and possible due to its *execution contexts* in which a local function can reference objects of an outer scope and keep them alive even if their containing scope dies. The global variable *pt0* the example above is referenced in the exported (hence static) procedure *SetOrg* and thus kept alive even if the body of the function *Mod* terminates. If *SetOrg* were not exported both it and the global variable *pt0* would disappear (i.e. be garbage collected) when *Mod* terminates. However, this is perfectly valid, since objects that are not referenced need not be kept alive, irrespective of whether they are dynamic data structures, or functions and global variables.

3.2.2 Record Types

JavaScript distinguishes only a few type *classes* (e.g. numbers, objects, and strings), but doesn't support *types*. Objects in JavaScript are considered compatible if they support the same fields.

An Oberon record type is represented in JavaScript by a constructor function that initializes the record's fields and thus renders it "compatible" with one of equal or extended type. The identity of the type (as opposed to its compatibility) is only required for type tests. It is represented by a (static) array of constructor functions that encodes the record's extension hierarchy. The constructor function also gets as part of its *prototype* properties (remember that those are shared by all instances of the object) a base-type initializer function and a type check function that implements the IS operator. Those features are assigned to the constructor function by a runtime *extension initializer* function called *_ext*.

```
TYPE
  R0=RECORD x,y: INTEGER END;
  R1=RECORD(R0) b:BOOLEAN END;

VAR
  r:RECORD(R0)k:INTEGER END;
  r1:R1;

function R0(){this.x=0;this.y=0}
_ext(R0);

function R1(){this._b();this.b=false}
_ext(R1,R0);

var r=new function(){this._b=R0;this._b();this.k=0}();
var r1=new R1();
```

The example above illustrates a named record type declaration, a named type extension and an anonymous record declaration. The field *_b* holds the base-type initializer. In the example above the value of *_b* in *R1* is *R0*, and will initialize the inherited fields *x* and *y* of *R1*. In multi-level extensions, the corresponding base-type initializer call will cascade through all levels until all fields are initialized.

The anonymous record type (3rd example above) does not get an extension list because it cannot appear on the right-hand side of a type test (left-hand side appearances can be checked by the compiler). Therefore, the extension initializer *_ext* is not called for the record type, and the base-type initializer *_b* needs to be assigned in-place before it can be called.

As a consequence of records being JavaScript objects special care is required to handle record assignments correctly. Assignments to record variables and value parameters require copying the record contents (recursively if necessary). A generic runtime function is provided for that purpose. It copies all fields of the source record for which there is a correspondence in the target record, by enumerating all target field names and then using them to copy the corresponding source values to the respective target fields. This is not the most efficient way of handling record assignments, but record value assignments are relatively rare in Oberon. For reference parameters (see below) passing the pointer of the record object is sufficient.

3.2.3 Reference Parameters

In Oberon, reference parameters (*var parameters* in Oberon lingo) allow addresses of variables to be passed to functions instead of their values. This usually serves one of two purposes: either to return structured and/or multiple values from functions (return values are scalar in Oberon), or to pass complex sizeable structures to functions even if there's no intention to modify (any of) their values, in order to save the computing effort of copying the structures onto the argument stack. In JavaScript arguments are always passed to functions by value.

In contrast to their conceptual simplicity, implementing reference parameters in an environment that does not support them natively often requires a disproportionate effort to handle them correctly under any circumstances [11]. The reason is the rare but non-negligible possibility of *aliasing*, i.e. the possibility that the variable (memory location) referenced using a reference parameter might be changed using a different designator. For instance, a field of a record might be passed as a reference parameter to a function that later overwrites the complete record (and hence also the field). Although such aliasing effects are rare, they need to be provided for because they are almost impossible to detect by the compiler.

JavaScript offers a relatively simple way to simulate passing a variable instead of its value to a function, but care has to be taken that the passed value behaves correctly under possible aliasing effects. The basic idea is to pass an *execution context* as the actual reference parameter to the function rather than the *value*. The execution context is that of an anonymous function defined in-line, that contains a reference to the variable, such that all modifications prompted through the execution context affect the original variable. Assuming the following declarations in Oberon Script and a call to procedure *P*:

```
PROCEDURE P(VAR x:INTEGER);

VAR k:  INTEGER;
...
P(k);   //procedure call
```

The translation to JavaScript looks as follows:

```
function P(x) {...}
...
var k=0;
P(function(v){return(v?k=v:k)});
```

Note that the body of the function passed to *P* in above example operates on the *k* of the outer, i.e. calling scope. If the passed function is called without an argument, it returns the value of k, and if it's called *with* an argument it sets the value of k. For all scalar values (including pointers) above solution is resistant to aliasing effects.

The situation is a bit more involved for complex designators denoting instance fields, values accessed via pointers, and arrays. In these cases the "access path" to the variable must be evaluated like in a regular compiler to determine the "final" variable that is passed to the function by reference. To use the technique introduced above the variable must be referenced in the execution context. To avoid passing a copy instead of the variable itself, the last selector must be evaluated in the execution context. In case of arrays, this means that the last array dimension must be evaluated in the execution context using a cached index expression. The following code segment illustrates passing arguments by reference using multi-selector designators. The three situations shown are the following: (1) a pointer dereferencing chain, (2) a field of a multidimensional array of records, and (3) an element of a multidimensional array. They are based on the type declarations below. The examples list alternately the call in Oberon and then the translation in JavaScript.

```
TYPE
  PR=POINTER TO R;
  R=RECORD k:INTEGER; ptr:PR END;
VAR
  ptr:PR;
  a:ARRAY N,N,N OF R;
  b:ARRAY N,N,N OF INTEGER;

P(ptr.ptr.ptr.k);       // Oberon (1)

var _0= ptr.ptr.ptr;   //JavaScript (1)
P(function(v){return(v?:_0.k=v:_0.k}));

P(a[i,j,k].k);          // Oberon (2)

var _0= a[i][j][k];     //JavaScript (2)
P(function(v){return(v?:_0.k=v: _0.k}));

P(b[i,j,k]);            // Oberon (3)

var _0= b[i][j];_1=k; //JavaScript (3)
P(function(v){return(v?:_0[_1]=v: _0[_1]}));
```

From the discussion above it is obvious that the complexity of handling reference parameters can hardly be justified in light of the simplicity of the original concept. Reference parameters are therefore likely candidates for being discarded if an effort to simplify Oberon Script is ever considered. Structured return values could provide an alternative to reference parameters that are far simpler to realize in JavaScript.

3.2.4 Code Quality

The compiler is effectively a syntax translator that transforms code written in Oberon into equivalent JavaScript code. It specifically does *not* emit JavaScript that resembles artificial "assembly code". Therefore, the resulting code carries no significant runtime overhead compared to equivalent manually written JavaScript (disregarding the different "styles" of programming in the different languages). Furthermore, the most salient transformations required when compiling Oberon to JavaScript are those that deal with *declarations*, especially those that have no counterparts in JavaScript (modules, records). These incur only an insignificant execution overhead. With regard to *statements* there is more or less a one to one correspondence of Oberon's features to those of JavaScript. Their respective execution times are therefore equivalent. The most significant additional execution costs can be expected for features not present natively in JavaScript that therefore need to be simulated with extra code. These include type tests, reference parameters, and local record variables which must be allocated each time a procedure is entered.

3.3 Runtime System

The runtime system consists of the above Oberon-to-JavaScript compiler and a small set of utility functions that includes JavaScript and DOM bindings, and a facility that detects script sections written in Oberon Script and subjects them to the compilation process.

Oberon Script is activated on a Web page by specifying in the header section of the page a link to the Oberon runtime scripts using a <script> element, and a call to *Oberon.Init()* in the *onload* event handler of the Web page body. As part of the initialization process, the runtime system identifies all code sections that contain Oberon Script. These need to be specified using the type attribute on the <script> element. Oberon Script is specified by the experimental MIME [5] type of "text/x-oberonscript". The runtime system then extracts the code from these sections and compiles them one after the other using the compiler, resulting in a collection of JavaScript sections. The compiler then replaces the original <script> elements containing Oberon Script code with new ones containing the compiled JavaScript code. Control is then passed to the compiled code. The following code illustrates the core of the Oberon Script detector and compiler.

```
function findLang(scp,typ)
{
  var code=[];
  for(var i=0;i<scp.length;++i){
    if(scp[i].type.toLowerCase()==typ){
      code.push(scp[i].text)
    }
  }
  return code
}

function addScript(par,code)
{
  var scp=document.createElement("script");
  scp.text=code;
  par.appendChild(scp)//this will also execute the code
}

function compileAll(typ,compile)
{
  var scp=document.getElementsByTagName("script");
  if(scp.length>0){
    var par=scp[0].parentNode;
    var code=findLang(scp,typ);
    for(var i=0;i<code.length){
      var res=compile(code[i]);
      if(res)addScript(par,res)//else error
    }
  }
}

compileAll("text/x-oberonscript",Oberon.Compile);
```

Although the compiler is usually not needed after it has finished compiling all Oberon Script sections, it stays around, in case further Oberon Script is created programmatically, and then compiled and executed on-the-fly.

4 Summary and Conclusions

In this paper we have presented an experimental runtime system called *Oberon Script* for using Oberon as a scripting language in the Web environment. It consists of an Oberon Script detector and a simple compiler that translates Oberon into JavaScript as a portable runtime code. We have shown that it is possible to process and compile the *full language* albeit with some effort to handle the few features in Oberon that are difficult to port without native support such as its reference parameters.

For a scripting language it is acceptable to sacrifice some of the parent language's features to simplify its implementation. Supporting the full language, however, makes it possible in theory to port the whole Oberon *system* to the browser, thus turning the latter into a virtual machine. How difficult it is to accomplish this task – and whether it is sensible to attempt it in the first place – needs to remain the subject of further study.

The current version of the Oberon Script compiler which is not optimized for efficiency or code size consists of 1081 lines of JavaScript code (24452 bytes). On a personal computer equipped with a 1.2 GHz CPU and 512 Mbytes of RAM it compiles an Oberon module of 268 lines (7933 bytes) in 783 ms (average of 10 runs).

References

1. Brandis, M., Crelier, R., Franz, M., Templ, J.: The Oberon System Family. Tech. Report ETH 174, (1992)
2. Disteli, A. R.: Oberon for PC on an MS DOS Base. Tech. Report ETH 203, (1993)
3. ECMA International, ECMAScript Language Specification, Standard ECMA-262, 3rd ed. (1999)
4. Franz, M.: Emulating an Operating System on Top of Another. Software - Practice and Experience, Vol. 23:6, 677-692, (1993)
5. Freed, N., Borenstein, N.: Multipurpose Internet Mail Extensions (MIME) Part Two: Media Types, RFC 2046 (1996)
6. Gamma, E., Helm, R., Johnson, R., Vlissides, J.: Design Patterns: Elements of Reusable Object-Oriented Software, Addison-Wesley (1994)
7. Google Mail, http://gmail.google.com
8. Google Maps, http://maps.google.com
9. Gosling, J., Joy, B., Steele, G., Bracha, G.: The Java Language Specification, 3rd edition. Addison-Wesley (2005)
10. Garrett, J. J.: Ajax: A New Approach to Web Applications, http://www.adaptivepath.com/ublications/essays/archives/000385.php
11. Gough, K. J., Courney, D.: Evaluating the Java Virtual Machine as a Target for Languages Other Than Java. Proc. Joint Modular Languages Conf. (JMLC 2000), Zurich, Switzerland. Lecture Notes in Computer Science Vol. 1897, 278-290, Springer (2000)
12. JavaScript Object Notation (JSON), http://www.json.org

13. Mössenböck, H., Wirth N.: The Programming Language Oberon-2. Structured Programming, Vol. 12:4, 179-196. (1991)
14. Supcik, J.: HP-Oberon (TM). The Oberon Implementation for HP 9000 Series 700. Tech. Report ETH 212, (1994)
15. Templ, J.: Design and Implementation of SPARC-Oberon. Structured Programming, Vol. 12, 197-205. (1991)
16. W3C: Document Object Model (DOM). http://www.w3.org/DOM/
17. Wirth, N.: The Programming Language Oberon. Software - Practice and Experience, Vol. 18, 671-690. Springer-Verlag, Berlin Heidelberg New York (1989)
18. Wirth, N.: Compiler Construction. Addison-Wesley (1996)
19. Wirth, N., Gutknecht, J.: The Oberon System. Software - Practice and Experience, Vol. 19, 857-893. Springer-Verlag, Berlin Heidelberg New York (1989)

Efficient Layer Activation
for Switching Context-Dependent Behavior

Pascal Costanza[1], Robert Hirschfeld[2], and Wolfgang De Meuter[1]

[1] Vrije Universiteit Brussel, Programming Technology Lab, B-1050 Brussels, Belgium
{pascal.costanza, wdmeuter}@vub.ac.be
[2] Hasso-Plattner-Institut, Universität Potsdam, D-14482 Potsdam, Germany
hirschfeld@hpi.uni-potsdam.de

Abstract. Today's programming platforms do not provide sufficient constructs that allow a program's behavior to depend on the context in which it is executing. This paper presents the design and implementation of programming language extensions that explicitly support our vision of Context-oriented Programming. In this model, programs can be partitioned into layers that can be dynamically activated and deactivated depending on their execution context. Layers are sets of partial program definitions that can be composed in any order. Context-oriented Programming encourages rich, dynamic modifications of program behavior at runtime, requiring an efficient implementation. We present a dynamic representation of layers that yields competitive performance characteristics for both layer activation/deactivation and overall program execution. We illustrate the performance of our implementation by providing an alternative solution for one of the prominent examples of aspect-oriented programming.

1 Introduction

In Context-oriented Programming, programs consist of partial class and method definitions that can be freely selected and combined at runtime to enable programs to change their behavior according to their context of use. In [18], we have introduced this idea and presented the programming language ContextL which is among the first language extensions that explicitly realize this vision.[1] As a motivating example in that paper, an alternative implementation of the model-view-controller framework is illustrated that avoids any secondary non-domain classes and thus increases understandability and flexibility at the same time.

Context-oriented Programming encourages continually changing behavior of programs according to the context of use, and employs repeated changes to class and method definitions at runtime. Therefore, efficient implementation strategies are needed for Context-oriented Programming to become practical.

The contribution of this paper is a novel design and implementation that addresses these needs, yielding the desired efficiency characteristics.

---

[1] For example, we are also working on similar extensions to Smalltalk and Tweak called *ContextS* and *ContextT* respectively.

D. Lightfoot and C. Szyperski (Eds.): JMLC 2006, LNCS 4228, pp. 84–103, 2006.

2   Context-Oriented Programming

2.1   Motivation

In the following, we present examples that motivate the need to be able to write code with a meaning that is not fully self contained, but partially depends on the context in which it is deployed and executed.

- *Mobile applications* running on mobile devices might need to dynamically adjust their behavior according to the geographical context in which they are used [12].
- *Mobile code* typically depends on the context of the runtime environment in which it is executed, such as applets or software agents [21].
- *Exploration environments* create safe contexts in which to execute applications and can considerably help users to learn how to use them, as has been shown by research in the field of Human-Computer Interaction [46].

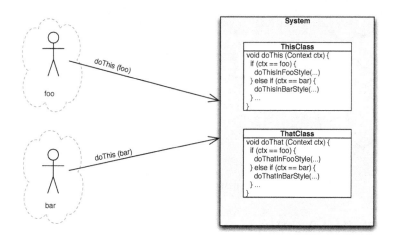

Fig. 1. Context-dependent behavior through `if` statements

With contemporary mainstream programming languages, the only way to introduce context-dependent behavior into a program is either by inserting `if` statements everywhere that check for the context in which a program is running (Fig. 1), violating one of the fundamental principles of object-oriented programming, namely to avoid `if` statements for achieving polymorphic behavior, or else by factoring out the context-dependent behavior into separate objects that can be substituted according to the context in which a program is used. Both approaches lead to unnecessarily complicated code that is hard to comprehend and even harder to maintain. Furthermore, they can only be applied for context dependencies that are anticipated in the software development process. There are cases in which it is clearly not possible to foresee all context-dependent issues and without explicit support, it is difficult to write maintainable and robust code that handles them well. With Context-oriented Programming on the other hand, we can factor out partial class definitions into separate layers. As illustrated in Fig. 2, we can then, depending on the context of use, select different layers for further program execution. The principal notion of such layers as partial program definitions has been suggested before ([3,40], cf. the section on related work in this paper). In our approach, we extend this idea with the notion of dynamically scoped layer activation (see Sect. 2.4), resulting in a viable approach for expressing context-dependent behavior.

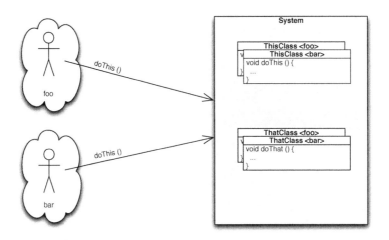

Fig. 2. Context-oriented Programming with layers

2.2 ContextJ/ContextL

ContextL is one of our first programming language extensions that explicitly support a context-oriented programming style [18]. While it is an extension to the Common Lisp Object System (CLOS, [4]), the features we describe are conceptually independent of that particular object model. In order to ease the accessibility of this paper, code examples are given in a Java-style syntax instead of the original Lisp syntax. This is possible because in this paper, we only deal with a subset of CLOS that is compatible with a similar subset of Java. Consequentially, we call this hypothetical Java-style language extension ContextJ, which we refer to in this paper when we discuss Java-specific issues. Since we are concerned with illustrating ContextL features using a Java-style syntax, we do not consider advanced Java language constructs that are not available or necessary in CLOS, like inner classes or generic types, but restrict ourselves to essentially the feature set of JDK 1.0. Adapting Java-specific features, like its static type system, to match the new constructs can be a topic for future work.

2.3   The Figure Editor Example

The figure editor [42] is a popular example widely used to motivate aspect-oriented programming. It is a variation of a similar example used to illustrate the notion of *jumping aspects* [8]. In this example, there is a class hierarchy for graphical objects of which instances are to be presented on a display. Some of these graphical objects are implemented by other, simpler graphical objects. So for example, a line is described by two end points. In order to move such objects to a different location, the contained simpler objects must be moved individually. Whenever the description of a graphical object is changed, its presentation on the screen should be updated accordingly.

The basic class hierarchy can be implemented in a plain object-oriented language as shown in Fig. 3: A figure element is described by an interface which is implemented by concrete classes, such as `Point` and `Line`.[2] Note that the required update of the display is not part of the code yet, but will be added in the following.

2.4   Layers

Layers are the essential extension provided by ContextL on which all subsequent features of ContextL are based. Layers can be defined by the `layer` construct:

```
layer DisplayLayer { /*...*/ }
```

Layers have a name and comprise partial class definitions, as shown in Sect. 2.5. There exists a predefined root layer. All class definitions that are not explicitly placed in a particular layer are by default associated with the root layer.

Layers can be activated and deactivated in the dynamic scope of a program:

```
with (DisplayLayer) { /* ... contained code ... */ }
without (DisplayLayer) { /* ... contained code ... */ }
```

Dynamically scoped layer activation/deactivation has the effect that the layer is active/inactive during execution of the *contained code*, including all the code that the *contained code* executes directly or indirectly. When the control flow returns from the dynamically scoped layer activation/deactivation, a layer's activation state is reverted to the previous state. This time interval between activation/deactivation of a layer and subsequent reversal to the previous activation state is also called the *dynamic extent* of the `with`/`without` block.

Layer activation can be nested, meaning that a layer can be activated/deactivated more than once in an individual flow of control. Furthermore, dynamically scoped layer activation/deactivation only affects the activity state of layers applied in the context of the current thread. The activity state of layers in other threads will remain unaffected.

---

[2] Since ContextJ would not need to change any of the existing Java language constructs, we can define and use interfaces, classes, fields, and methods as before.

```
interface FigureElement {
  void move (int dx, int dy);
}

class Point implements FigureElement {
  int x, y;

  Point(int newX, int newY) { this.x=newX; this.y=newY; }

  void setX(int newX) { this.x=newX; }
  void setY(int newY) { this.y=newY; }
  int getX() { return this.x; }
  int getY() { return this.y; }

  void move(int dx, int dy) { /*...*/ }
}

class Line implements FigureElement {
  Point p1, p2;

  Line(Point newP1, Point newP2) { this.p1=newP1; this.p2=newP2; }

  void setP1(Point newP1) { this.p1=newP1; }
  void setP2(Point newP2) { this.p2=newP2; }
  Point getP1() { return this.p1; }
  Point getP2() { return this.p2; }

  void move(int dx, int dy) { /*...*/ }
}
```

Fig. 3. A basic implementation of the figure editor example

2.5   Layered Classes

A class definition, or parts of it, can be associated with a specific layer:

```
layer DisplayLayer {
  class Display { /*...*/ }
  // ...
}
```

Here, such an association does not have a useful effect yet: The class can still be instantiated from any other layer. However, placing a class definition in a specific layer gets interesting when we use layers to add to the definition of a class that is already defined in another layer. In Fig. 4, we add the display update mechanism: The layer DisplayLayer contains a class Display that implements the code for updating the graphical representation of an object on a screen (not shown here). It also contains additional definitions for our classes Point and Line as well as the interface FigureElement, introducing after methods for the state changing

```
layer DisplayLayer {
  class Display {
    // ...
    static void update(FigureElement elm) { /*...*/ }
  }

  interface FigureElement {
    after void move (int dx, int dy) {
      Display.update(this);
    }
  }

  class Point {                      class Line {
    after void setX (int newX) {       after void setP1 (Point newP1) {
      Display.update(this);              Display.update(this);
    }                                  }

    after void setY (int newY) {       after void setP2 (Point newP2) {
      Display.update(this);              Display.update(this);
    }                                  }
  }                                  }
                                   }
```

Fig. 4. The `DisplayLayer` for the figure editor example

methods `setX`, `setY`, `setP1`, `setP2` and `move`. All these `after` methods contain calls to the `update` method of the `Display` class.

It is important to observe that the original classes `Point` and `Line`, and the interface `FigureElement` are not replaced. They still have their original definitions. The fact that the new extensions are placed in the `DisplayLayer` ensures that the respective `after` methods are executed when and only when the `DisplayLayer` is active. So an update of the display is just visible when the figure elements are changed in the dynamic extent of a `with (DisplayLayer)` `{...}` activation.

ContextJ would have to add `before`, `after` and `around` method qualifiers along the lines of `before`, `after` and `around` methods in CLOS.[3] They are methods of their own and are combined with other methods of the same signature. This is different from the advice-construct in AspectJ. AspectJ-style advice code adds behavior to pointcuts, that is collections of join-points, which are not necessarily methods, and not necessarily of the same signature. In our example, the `after` methods are all executed after the respective primary methods associated with the "root" layer in Fig. 3, but only if the `DisplayLayer` is active.

Due to the fact that layer activation/deactivation is confined to the current thread, display updates occur only in threads in which `DisplayLayer` is active, but not in other threads unless `DisplayLayer` is utilized within them as well.

---

[3] Indeed, the corresponding `before`, `after` and `around` methods in ContextL are just taken over from CLOS of which ContextL is an extension.

2.6 Nested Layer Activation/Deactivation

ContextL does not automatically activate layer definitions. Layers must be explicitly activated via the `with` construct to take effect. Indeed, layer activation is provided as a base-level language construct, so layers *can* be activated anywhere in a ContextL program, including layers that are loaded while a program is already running and also in classes that are loaded after a program is already running. One especially interesting case is the nesting of activation and deactivation of the same layer within the same control flow because this allows solving the phenomenon of *jumping aspects* without using AOP-style pointcuts, as shown below.

The figure editor example has been introduced in [8,42] to illustrate the jumping aspects phenomenon: Whenever we change the state of a simple graphical object, we can immediately update its presentation on the screen. However, when we change the state of a complex object that consists of other, simpler objects, the change has to be propagated to those simpler objects, but screen updates should be deferred and combined until all objects are changed that the complex object comprises. This has led to the introduction of `cflow`-style constructs in AspectJ and subsequent AOP approaches [31].

ContextL's `with` and `without` are base-level language constructs that allow us to achieve the effect of deferring the update on the screen by providing `around` methods instead of the above `after` definitions. Figure 5 contains a revised version of the `DisplayLayer` where `after` methods are replaced by `around` methods that deactivate the `DisplayLayer` before they proceed[4] to the respective primary method. This has the effect that the method definitions of the `DisplayLayer` are not executed during the extent of these calls to `proceed`, so no display update will take place here. Only after leaving the `without` block, the `update` method is called eventually, and only once.

Now, a crucial question is whether continually activating and deactivating layers is a reasonable approach with regard to efficiency considerations. Sect. 4 discusses this question after the presentation of our implementation approach.

3 Implementation

This section presents an implementation of the language constructs introduced in the previous section. ContextL is an extension to CLOS. In our description we focus on the implementation strategy that is reusable in other languages, without going too much into the CLOS-specific details. The general idea is this:[5]

- Layers are implemented internally as classes.
- Combinations of currently active layers are represented as classes that inherit from the primary layer classes using multiple inheritance.

---

[4] Similar to `proceed` in AspectJ and `call-next-method` in CLOS.

[5] Some of these building blocks do not exist in languages like Java and C#, especially multiple dispatch and multiple inheritance. However, Section 3.4 refers to existing approaches that can be used for implementing them in those languages.

```
layer DisplayLayer {
  class Display {
    // ...
    static void update(FigureElement elm) { /*...*/ }
  }

  interface FigureElement {
    around void move (int dx, int dy) {
      without (DisplayLayer) { proceed(); }
      Display.update(this);
    }
  }

  class Point {                        class Line {
    around void setX (int newX) {        around void setP1 (Point newP1) {
      without (DisplayLayer)               without (DisplayLayer)
        { proceed(); }                       { proceed(); }
      Display.update(this);                Display.update(this);
    }                                    }

    around void setY (int newY) {        around void setP2 (Point newP2) {
      without (DisplayLayer)               without (DisplayLayer)
        { proceed(); }                       { proceed(); }
      Display.update(this);                Display.update(this);
    }                                    }
  }                                    }
}
```

Fig. 5. The DisplayLayer with around methods to defer the update of the display

- A dynamically scoped variable contains a prototype instance of such a layer combination class.
- Multiple dispatch is used to dispatch on both the currently active combination of layers and the receiver of a message.
- Efficiency is gained by providing fast caches for layer combinations and reusing efficient implementations for multiple inheritance and multiple dispatch.

3.1 Layers as Classes

Primary layers. Layers which are explicitly introduced by a programmer are called *primary layers.* For example, the following declaration defines a primary layer.

```
layer DisplayLayer { /*...*/ }
```

In the ContextL implementation, such primary layers are internally supplemented by dynamically generated layers which programmers cannot directly refer to (see below).

Layers are implemented as classes. Each layer declaration is represented internally by a corresponding class. So for example, the above `DisplayLayer` is internally represented by the following class.

```
class DisplayLayer { /*...*/ }
```

Active layers are combinations of such primary layers. Active layers are represented by dynamically generated *combination classes* which are ordinary classes that inherit from the classes that represent primary layers. Multiple inheritance is used to connect the various static and dynamic layer representations to create a chain of active layers. In Fig. 6, a combination of `Layer1`, `Layer2`, `Layer3`, and the `RootLayer` is realized as a combination class named `Layer1+2+3*` that inherits both from `Layer1` and a combination class named `Layer2+3*` that represents `Layer2`, `Layer3`, and the `RootLayer`. The latter combination class is in turn formed by inheriting from both `Layer2` and a combination class named `Layer3*` that represents `Layer3` and the `RootLayer`, and so forth.

Multiple inheritance typically results in the possible occurence of conflicting inherited members and thus in the need to determine a linearization of all superclasses [2]. However, in our case the linearization of layers is trivial: Each dynamically generated combination class has exactly two superclasses, one static layer representation (such as `DisplayLayer`, `Layer1`, `Layer2`, etc.) and one previous dynamic layer representation (such as `Layer1+2+3*`, etc.). For each combination class, the static layer representation takes precedence over the previous dynamic layer representation. Therefore after each layer activation, the most recent combination class comes first, followed by the most recently activated layer, followed by the previous combination class, and so on, which naturally leads to the required ordering of layers. For example in the combination illustrated in Fig. 6, the linearization of the class hierarchy starting from `Layer1+2+3*` is `Layer1+2+3*`, `Layer1`, `Layer2+3*`, `Layer2`, `Layer3*`, `Layer3`, `RootLayer` in that order.

Different layer combinations can coexist in the same program. Figure 7 illustrates how both a combination of layers `Layer1` and `Layer3` and a combination of layers `Layer1` and `Layer2` can exist at the same time. Indeed, any combination can be built without interfering with other combinations. Note that this allows the implementation to reflect the order in which layers are activated and deactivated: Whenever a layer is activated, it is ensured that it will be placed in front of all other already active layers. When it is already active itself, it will nevertheless be placed in front of all other already active layers from which it is implicitly removed beforehand as part of the activation process.

For example, assume layers `Layer1` and `Layer3` are already active in that order. An activation of layer `Layer2` will lead to a chain of layers `Layer2`, `Layer1` and `Layer3` in that order. Given that latter order, an activation of the (already active) layer `Layer1` will internally lead to first a deactivation and a subsequent reactivation of layer `Layer1`, and thus to a chain of layers `Layer1`, `Layer2` and `Layer3` in that order.

The various possible combinations do not have to be determined at compile time, but can be created on demand at runtime if the given language allows for creating classes at runtime (as is possible in CLOS, Smalltalk, Java, and so on)

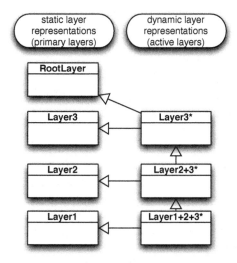

Fig. 6. Static and dynamic layers

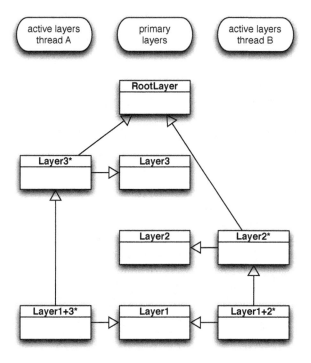

Fig. 7. Different layer combinations in different threads

so that only the actually required combinations are ever created. Layer combinations only need to be created once, because when they have been created they can be cached and reused. Layers are always activated/deactivated relative to the currently active layer combination. Therefore, such caches can be associated with the dynamically generated classes that represent layer combinations and only need to include the new combinations relative to those combinations. This enables the use of very small and fast caches.

3.2 Dynamic Scoping

The `with` and `without` constructs activate/deactivate layers with dynamic extent, that is, they effectively implement dynamic scoping for layers, including the fact that activations/deactivations are confined to the current thread and so do not interfere with activations/deactivations in other threads.

Such a dynamically scoped activation scheme can be easily implemented if the underlying language offers dynamically scoped variables which can already be rebound without affecting other threads [15]. We can then instantiate the class that represents the currently active combination of layers and store it in a dynamically scoped variable. By default, that variable contains an instance of the root layer representation, and can later be rebound to contain instances of the corresponding layer combinations. Such instances are called *prototypical* because they do not contain any state or behavior of their own, but are just used to select the correct behavior for layered classes and methods (see below).

Common Lisp provides dynamically scoped variables directly [41] and Java allows their simulation by storing a stack data structure in a thread-local variable [11]. Thread locality ensures non-interference with other threads, and the stack allows shadowing a previous layer combination with a new one by pushing the new layer combination at the beginning of the execution of a `with`/`without` block, and by popping it at the end.

3.3 Method Invocation

Having modelled layers as classes and layer combinations as dynamically generated classes, we turn to the question of which methods to execute in response to a message. It becomes obvious that this depends on both the class that represents the currently active layer combination and the class of the message receiver. In other words, we need *multiple dispatch*. Common Lisp already has multimethods, and it is possible to add multimethods to Java – see for example MultiJava [13]. To illustrate this further, Figure 8 shows how the method `move` from our figure editor example can be understood to be internally mapped to a multimethod definition using a combination of MultiJava and ContextJ syntax. The `Layer@SomeLayer` notation used in Fig. 8 is taken from MultiJava and specifies that the corresponding parameter is of the (static) type `Layer` but further specialized to be applicable only when the respective parameter is an instance of

```
// in the root layer
class Point implements FigureElement {
  // ...
  void move (Layer@RootLayer layer, int dx, int dy)
  { /*...*/ }
}

layer DisplayLayer {
  // ...
  class Point {
    // ...
    around void move (Layer@DisplayLayer layer, int dx, int dy)
    { /*...*/ }
  }
}
```

Fig. 8. Internal mapping of layered methods to multimethods

SomeLayer at runtime. How multimethods in MultiJava are translated into Java bytecode on a per-compilation-unit basis is described in [13].[6]

3.4   Putting It All Together

We have implemented ContextL as an extension to CLOS in a relatively straight-forward way. This is because CLOS provides all the necessary ingredients described above, namely dynamic class generation, multiple inheritance, dynamically scoped variables, and multiple dispatch. As indicated, a similar implementation could in principle be achieved in a Java-based implementation as well: Classes can indeed be generated at runtime [20], a variant of dynamically scoped variables is already present in the form of thread-local variables [11], and it has already been described how to add multiple dispatch [13]. Currently, it is not obvious to us how to incorporate the required multiple inheritance mechanism into Java. However, subsets of multiple inheritance and their implementation have already been described, for example, for C# based on traits [37] and for Java based on interfaces with default implementations [35]. It is likely that such subsets are sufficient to support our model, but this needs to be explored further to be answered appropriately.

Note that the implementation we describe is only one possible implementation of layers and dynamically scoped layer activations. For example, we have a prototypical implementation of a minimal version of ContextL that is solely based on dynamically scoped instance variables, a construct of ContextL not described here ("special slots", see [18]). However, the implementation described

---

[6] Note that MultiJava implements symmetric dispatch while CLOS implements asymmetric dispatch by default. This issue would need to be addressed in an implementation of ContextJ. In the current ContextL implementation, the layer argument in a layered function/method has least priority with regard to argument precedence order.

in this paper yields competitive performance characteristics because multiple active layers are always represented by exactly one generated class. In comparison, straightforward implementation techniques for cflow-style constructs in aspect-oriented language implementations introduce if-tests for each pointcut that contains a cflow expression which is reported to lead to substantial runtime overheads [19]. In our approach, computational overhead occurs exclusively on the first activation/deactivation of a previously unused combination of layers and on the first message send in a previously unused combination of methods [30]. After that, both lookups of layer combinations and method dispatches take advantage of highly efficient caches.

4   Benchmarks

We have used the figure editor example described in Sect. 2.3 as the basis for a benchmark that measures the effect of layer activation and deactivation. In order to measure only the method dispatch and layer activation/deactivation overhead, no actual updates on the screen are implemented, but instead a global counter is incremented on each call of the Display.update() method to check the correct number of issued updates at the end of a test run.

We have implemented the benchmark in ContextL and have run the benchmark on six different Common Lisp implementations. We have run two versions of the benchmark, one without and one with layer activations/deactivations. In other words, we have compared the program in Fig. 3 that does not issue any display updates with the program in Fig. 5 that continually switches the DisplayLayer on and off: on to enable display updates and off to disable display updates for calls to proceed in the around methods of the DisplayLayer. The main loop of the latter version looks as follows:

```
for (int i=0; i<1000; i++) {
   for (Line line: lines) {
      with (DisplayLayer) {
         line.move(5, -5);
      }
   }
   for (Line line: lines) {
      with (DisplayLayer) {
         line.move(-5, 5);
      }
   }
}
```

The main loop of the version without layer activations/deactivations just omits the with blocks around the line.move() calls. It is important to note that the version without layer activations/deactivations is essentially just a plain CLOS program.

The results of the various runs on different Common Lisp implementations is presented in Fig. 9. Each run creates a collection of 100 lines, with each line being

Implementation	Platform	Without Layers	With Layers	Overhead
Allegro CL 7.0	Mac OS X	2.292 secs	2.540 secs	10.82% slower
CMUCL 19b	Mac OS X	0.7812 secs	0.7361 secs	7.8% *faster*
LispWorks 4.4	Mac OS X	3.0928 secs	3.1768 secs	2.72% slower
MCL 5.1	Mac OS X	2.3506 secs	2.6412 secs	12.36% slower
OpenMCL 0.14.3	Mac OS X	2.2448 secs	2.5066 secs	11.66% slower
SBCL 0.9.4	Mac OS X	0.8363 secs	0.7795 secs	7.29% *faster*
CMUCL 19a	Linux x86	0.76 secs	0.836 secs	10% slower
SBCL 0.9.4	Linux x86	0.5684 secs	0.638 secs	12.24% slower

Fig. 9. The results of running the figure editor example in various Common Lisp implementations

moved 1000 times. Time required for creating the collection of lines and filling it is not taken into account. The entries in Table 9 are average measurements of five runs. The respective platforms are an Apple PowerBook 1.67 GHz PowerPC G4 running Mac OS X 10.4.2 and a Dell PowerEdge 1600SC dual Xeon 2.8 Ghz running Linux 2.6.12. The overheads in runtime range from very moderate 2.72% in LispWorks for Macintosh to still reasonable 12.36% in Macintosh Common Lisp (MCL), especially when taking into account that we have an additional update of a global counter for each call of `line.move()`. Two implementations show the anomaly that the runs that repeatedly switch layers on and off are actually *faster* than the runs without layers: On CMUCL 19b, the runs without layers are on average 7.8% slower, and on SBCL 0.9.4 they are 7.29% slower. These two environments are based on the same Common Lisp compiler, so this provides an explanation for them showing similar efficiency characteristics. The performance anomaly as such may seem surprising, but in fact such anomalies occur frequently in performance benchmarks [25]. Obviously, factors beyond layer activation/deactivation and method dispatch play a more important role for the overall performance of our test program. Since applications typically spend less than 10% of the overall time in call overhead [28], our numbers suggest an overall estimated cost of 0.3% to 1.3% for inclusion and repeated switching of layers. This is a noteworthy result, despite the fact that, of course, more benchmarks are necessary to measure the effects of, for example, combinations of multiple layers.

This excellent performance is evidently the result of a combination of finding an appropriate runtime representation of layers and reusing existing optimizations for implementing object-oriented language constructs as described in the previous section. It stems from folding all active layers into a single class that represents current combination of active layers, and specializing the involved methods on an implicit argument in addition to the receiver of a message. Ultimately, our implementation relies on efficient multiple dispatch as provided by modern CLOS implementations. See [30] for a discussion of implementation techniques for multiple dispatch in CLOS, and [10] for a general overview.

5   Related Work

5.1   Dynamic Aspect Weaving

The only aspect-oriented technologies we are aware of approaching our notion of dynamically scoped activation of partial program definitions are AspectS [26,27], LasagneJ [43], CaesarJ [34] and the Steamloom virtual machine [6]. They all add constructs for thread-local activation of partial program definitions at the base-program level. However, CaesarJ is limited in that it does not provide a corresponding thread-local deactivation construct, and LasagneJ is even further limited in that it restricts the use of thread-local activation to the `main` method of a Java program [36]. Their lack of thread-local deactivation constructs makes `cflow`-style constructs necessary in those approaches to implement the figure editor example. Our approach allows its modular implementation without using AOP-style pointcuts. Global (non-thread-local) activation/deactivation constructs, like in CaesarJ and ObjectTeams [45] are not sufficient in this regard. Steamloom provides undeployment of thread-local aspects, but cannot thread-locally undeploy a globally active aspect.

With regard to efficiency considerations, it is important to note that the straightforward technique to implement activation/deactivation by using thread-local flags that are subsequently checked for each message impose a substantial runtime overhead, as is reported in [19]. We are aware of two approaches that specifically address efficiency improvements for `cflow`-style constructs and thread-local aspect activation/deactivation respectively.

In [1], optimizations are described that reduce the number of flags to be checked at runtime, with considerable efficiency improvements for `cflow`-style pointcuts. However, the basic implementation as described above remains the same. The main disadvantage of their approach is its reliance on a time-consuming static global program analysis.[7]

In contrast, we gain high runtime performance without limiting applicability of layers to those that have already been available at compile time. In our approach, no dedicated global analysis is required.

The Steamloom virtual machine [6] is another attempt to reduce the overhead of `cflow`-style poincuts. It implements a `deploy` statement that can be used to activate aspects in its dynamic extent by modifying the Jikes virtual machine for Java. It avoids the use of flags for checking applicability of aspects by recompiling the program at each context switch. That paper reports a considerable efficiency improvement for the remaining part of the program execution in the dynamic extent of a `deploy` block when compared to traditional implementation strategies for similar `cflow`-style constructs. However, the `deploy` statement as such is extremely expensive since it recompiles all parts of the program that are affected by such aspect deployment. The benchmark results provided in that paper suggest a performance decrease by a factor of 30, compared to their

---

[7] For example, a simple AspectJ program that takes less than 5 secs to be compiled with the plain AspectJ compiler can easily take more than 5 mins with their compiler.

original example program without any aspects. [8] The Steamloom manual discusses these "remarkable performance penalties" [5] in conjunction with the display updating aspect in their version of the figure editor example which is triggered by frequently entered and exited control flows.

The latest implementation of Steamloom explicitly addresses the above issues and is described in [7]. That paper reports considerable performance gains of `cflow`-style constructs, and would therefore be a viable candidate for an implementation of ContextJ. As future work, we plan to explore this option and compare the implementation approaches of ContextL and Steamloom.

5.2 Delegation Layers

Delegation layers, as in the prototype-based languages Slate [39] and Us [40] and also combined into a class-based programming language in [38], are very similar to our approach. As in ContextL, delegation layers define layers that group behavior for sets of objects in [39,40] and for sets of classes in [38]. However, the hierarchy of layers is globally fixed in [38]. One can select a layer from which to start a specific message send, but all the other layers below are then predetermined by the original configuration of layers. In [39] and [40], the selection and ordering of layers is not fixed but layers can be arbitrarily recombined in the control flow of a program. However, layer selection and combination has to be done manually, there are no dedicated `with/without` constructs like in ContextL. Providing these constructs as high-level abstractions allows for less straightforward, but more efficient implementation strategies.

5.3 Other Related Work

Related work for special functions, precursors for combinations of methods from different layers, is discussed in [15,16]. Related work for special slots is discussed in [16,17]. Related work for delegation is discussed in [18].

The term Context-oriented Programming has already been used in two other contexts. Gassanenko [22,23] describes an approach to add object-oriented programming concepts to Forth without turning it into an actual object-oriented programming language. Instead, a notion of context is added that essentially comes down to some form of first-class environments [24]. This allows code to behave differently when executed in different environments. The description in Gassanenko's papers focuses on Forth-specific details and it is very hard to tell how much overlap, if any, exists with our approach. For example, it is not clear whether Gassanenko's contexts must be fully defined or can be partial and combinable. The examples provided in [23] only cover fully specified, but no partial contexts. Furthermore, Gassanenko's contexts seem to cover functions only, neither state nor class definitions, the latter due to the explicit goal not to turn Forth into a fully object-oriented programming language. Therefore, it seems

---

[8] See column "no aspect" compared to column "`cflow`/dynamic" in the Steamloom row of Table 2 in that paper.

that those contexts are most likely similar to dynamically scoped functions [15], one of our own precursors to ContextL.

Keays and Rakotonirainy [29] use the term context-oriented programming for an approach that separates code skeletons from context-filling code stubs that complete the code skeleton to actually perform some behavior. The claimed advantage is that the code stubs can vary depending on the context, for example the device some code runs on. A proof-of-concept implementation using Python and XML is described. Their approach appears to be a reverse macro expansion framework in which code skeletons and code stubs need to be combined at runtime. Furthermore, there is no mention whether different combinations of skeletons and stubs can coexist at the same time.

In contrast, ContextL is essentially an extension to an object-oriented approach that does not rely on runtime source code transformation. ContextL's root layer, whose behavior can be altered in other layers, can already be fully operational, and different combinations of different layers can be simultaneously active in multiple threads.

6   Conclusions

Several examples suggest the need for programming language constructs that allow explicit association of the meaning of code not only with its position in a static hierarchy, but also with the context in which it is running. This is what we call Context-oriented Programming. The essential ideas are exemplified by ContextL's layers which are presented using a Java-style syntax. ContextL allows for partial class definitions that belong to individual layers. Layers can be activated and deactivated with dynamic extent.

We present an implementation of ContextL that relies on CLOS's multiple dispatch, and an analysis on how ContextL constructs can be implemented in more mainstream programming languages such as Java. The experiments with ContextL show that the concepts presented in the paper can be implemented efficiently. A ContextL program with repeated activations and deactivations of layers is about as efficient as one without.

We show that context-dependent layers can be used to implement the popular figure editor example in an elegant and very efficient way, without using aspect-oriented features. Most notably, no `cflow`-style construct is necessary to implement the full example because ContextL includes constructs not only for thread-local activation, but also for thread-local deactivation of layers.

Acknowledgements

We thank Thomas F. Burdick, Brecht Desmet, Johan Fabry, Michael Haupt, Bjoern Lindberg, Oscar Nierstrasz, Andreas Raab, Christophe Rhodes, Dave Thomas, Peter J. Wasilko, and JonL White for fruitful discussions and valuable contributions.

References

1. Pavel Avgustinov, Julian Tibble, Aske Simon Christensen, Laurie Hendren, Sascha Kuzins, Jennifer Lhotak, Ondrej Lhotak, Oege de Moor, Damien Sereni, Ganesh Sittampalam. Optimizing AspectJ. Proceedings of the 2005 ACM SIGPLAN conference on Programming Language Design and Implementation.
2. Kim Barrett, Bob Cassels, Paul Haahr, David A. Moon, Keith Playford, P. Tucker Withington. A Monotonic Superclass Linearization for Dylan. OOPSLA '96, Proceedings.
3. Daniel Bobrow and Ira Goldstein. Representing Design Alternatives. Proceedings of the Conference on Artificial Intelligence and the Simulation of Behavior. Amsterdam, July 1980.
4. Daniel Bobrow, Linda DeMichiel, Richard Gabriel, Sonya Keene, Gregor Kiczales, David Moon. Common Lisp Object System Specification. Lisp and Symbolic Computation 1, 3-4 (January 1989), 245-394.
5. Christoph Bockisch, Tom Dinkelaker, Michael Haupt, Michael Krebs. The Steamloom Manual, December 2004. Available: http://www.st.informatik.tu-darmstadt.de/static/pages/projects/AORTA/Steamloom.jsp
6. Christoph Bockisch, Michael Haupt, Mira Mezini, Klaus Ostermann. Virtual Machine Support for Dynamic Join Points. AOSD 2004, Proceedings, ACM Press.
7. Christoph Bockisch, Sebastian Kanthak, Michael Haupt, Matthew Arnold, Mira Mezini. Efficient Control Flow Quantification. OOPSLA 2006, Proceedings, ACM Press.
8. Johan Brichau, Wolfgang De Meuter, Kris De Volder. Jumping Aspects. ECOOP 2000 International Workshop on Aspects and Dimensions of Concerns, 2000.
9. Martin Büchi and Wolfgang Weck. Generic Wrappers. ECOOP 2000, Proceedings, Springer LNCS.
10. Craig Chambers and Weimin Chen. Efficient Multiple and Predicate Dispatching. OOPSLA '99, Proceedings.
11. Patrick Chan. *The Java Developers Almanac 1.4, Volume 1: Examples and Quick Reference.* Addison-Wesley Professional, 2002.
12. Guanlin Chen and David Kotz. A Survey of Context-Aware Mobile Computing Research. Technical Report TR2000-381, Dept. of Computer Science, Dartmouth College, Hanover, USA, November 2000.
13. Curtis Clifton, Todd Millstein, Gary T. Leavens, and Craig Chambers. MultiJava: Design Rationale, Compiler Implementation, and Applications. ACM Transactions on Programming Languages and Systems (TOPLAS), 28, 3 (May 2006), 517-575.
14. Pascal Costanza, Günter Kniesel, Armin Cremers. Lava – Spracherweiterungen für Delegation in Java. JIT '99 – Java-Informations-Tage 1999. Springer, Informatik Aktuell, 1999.
15. Pascal Costanza. Dynamically Scoped Functions as the Essence of AOP. ECOOP 2003 Workshop on Object-oriented Language Engineering for the Post-Java Era, Darmstadt, Germany, July 22, 2003. ACM Sigplan Notices 38, 8 (August 2003).
16. Pascal Costanza. A Short Overview of AspectL. European Interactive Workshop on Aspects in Software (EIWAS'04), Berlin, Germany, September 23-24.
17. Pascal Costanza. How to Make Lisp More Special. International Lisp Conference 2005, Stanford. Proceedings.
18. Pascal Costanza and Robert Hirschfeld. Language Constructs for Context-oriented Programming. ACM Dynamic Languages Symposium, San Diego, USA, 2005. Proceedings.

19. Bruno Dufour, Christopher Goard, Laurie Hendren, Oege de Moor, Ganesh Sittampalam, Clark Verbrugge. Measuring the dynamic behavior of AspectJ programs. In: *OOPSLA 2004*, Proceedings, ACM Press.
20. Ira R. Forman and Nate Forman. *Java Reflection in Action*. Manning Publications Co., 2004.
21. Alfonso Fugetta, Gian Pietro Picco, Giovanni Vigna. Understanding Code Mobility. IEEE Transactions on Software Engineering, Vol. 24, No. 5, May 1998.
22. Michael Gassanenko. Context-oriented Programming: Evolution of Vocabularies. Proceedings of the euroFORTH'93 Conference. Marianske Lazne, Czech Republic.
23. Michael Gassenenko. Context-oriented Programming. euroFORTH'98, Schloss Dagstuhl, Germany.
24. David Gelernter, Suresh Jagannathan, Thomas London. Environments as First Class Objects. POPL '87, Proceedings.
25. Matthias Hauswirth, Peter F. Sweeney, Amer Diwan, Michael Hind. Vertical Profiling: Understanding the Behavior of Object-Oriented Applications. OOPSLA 2004, Proceedings.
26. Robert Hirschfeld. AspectS – Aspect-Oriented Programming with Squeak. In M. Aksit, M. Mezini, R. Unland (eds.), *Objects, Compononts, Architectures, Services, and Applications for a Networked World*, pp. 226-232, LNCS 2591, Springer, 2003.
27. Robert Hirschfeld and Pascal Costanza. Extending Advice Activation in AspectS. European Interactive Workshop on Aspects in Software (EIWAS 2005), Brussels, Belgium, 2005.
28. Urs Hölzle, personal communication, 1999.
29. Roger Keays and Andry Rakotonirainy. Context-oriented Programming. International Workshop on Data Engineering for Wireless and Mobile Access, San Diego, USA, 2003. ACM Press.
30. Gregor Kiczales and Luis Rodriguez. Efficient method dispatch in PCL. Proceedings of the 1990 ACM conference on LISP and Functionl Programming.
31. Gregor Kiczales, Erik Hilsdale, Jim Hugunin, Mik Kersten, Jeffrey Palm and William G. Griswold. An Overview of AspectJ. ECOOP 2001, proceedings.
32. Günter Kniesel. Type-Safe Delegation for Run-Time Component Adaptation. ECOOP '99, Proceedings, Springer LNCS 1628.
33. Henry Lieberman. Using Prototypical Objects to Implement Shared Behavior in Object-oriented Systems. OOPSLA '86, Proceedings.
34. Mira Mezini and Klaus Ostermann. Conquering Aspects with Caesar. In: *2nd International Conference on Aspect-Oriented Software Development* (AOSD 2003). Boston, USA, March 17-21, 2003, 90-100. ACM Press.
35. Markus Mohnen. Interfaces with Default Implementations in Java (extended abstract). Conference on the Principles and Practice of Programming in Java, Dublin, Ireland, June 2002. Proceedings.
36. Adriaan Moors, Jan Smans, Eddy Truyen, Frank Piessens, Wouter Joosen. Safe language support for feature composition through feature-based dispatch. Position paper at 2nd Workshop on Managing Variabilities Consistently in Design and Code (MVCDC2005), OOPSLA 2005, San Diego, California, USA, October 20, 2005.
37. Oscar Nierstrasz, Stéphane Ducasse, Stefan Reichhart, Nathanael Schärli. *Adding Traits to (Statically Typed) Languages*. Technical report no. IAM-05-006, Institut für Informatik, Universität Bern, Switzerland, December 2005.
38. Klaus Ostermann. Dynamically Composable Collaborations with Delegation Layers. ECOOP 2002, Proceedings, Springer LNCS.
39. Lee Salzman and Jonathan Aldrich. Prototypes with Multiple Dispatch: An Expressive and Dynamic Object Model. ECOOP 2005, Proceedings, LNCS.

40. Randall Smith and David Ungar. A Simple and Unifying Approach to Subjective Objects. Theory and Practice of Object Systems, 2, 3 1996.
41. Guy L. Steele. *Common Lisp the Language, 2nd Edition.* Digital Press, 1990.
42. Perri Tarr, Maja D'Hondt, Lodewijk Bergmans, Cristina Videira Lopes. Worshop an Aspects and Dimensions of Concerns: Requirements on, and Challenge Problems For, Advanced Separation of Concerns. In: *Object-oriented Technology: ECOOP 2000 Workshops, Panels, and Posters*, Sophia Antipolis and Cannes, France, June 2000. Proceedings. Springer LNCS 1964.
43. E. Truyen, B. Vanhaute, W. Joosen, P. Verbaeten, B.N. Jorgensen. Dynamic and Selective Combination of Extensions in Component-Based Applications. In: *Proceeedings of the 23rd International Conference on Software Engineering*, Toronto, Ontario, Canada, May 12-19, (2001) 233-242.
44. David Ungar and Randall Smith. Self: The Power of Simplicity. OOPSLA '87, Proceedings.
45. Matthias Veit and Stephan Herrman. Model-View-Controller and ObjectTeams: A Perfect Match of Paradigms. In: *2nd International Conference on Aspect-Oriented Software Development* (AOSD 2003). Boston, USA, March 17-21, 2003, 90-100. ACM Press.
46. Volker Wulf and Björn Golombek. Exploration Environments: Concept and Empirical Evaluation. In: *Proceedings of GROUP 2001*, ACM 2001 International Conference on Supporting Group Work. Boulder, Colorado, USA, September 30 - October 3, 2001. ACM 2001.

Object-Oriented Language Processing

Pietu Pohjalainen

Department of Computer Science,
University of Helsinki
pietu.pohjalainen@cs.helsinki.fi

Abstract. Compiler architecture often follows an imperative layout. Different actions in the compiler are modeled as functions that operate over defined data structures. In this work, we present existing methodologies for writing object-oriented language-processing tools. As a contribution, we explore possibilities of writing a compiler based on recursive descent parsing in an object-oriented way. As a proof of the concept, we present a parser generator that employs the presented constructs both in its internal structure and in generated output.

1 Introduction

Object-oriented design has been available to programmers and designers for decades. Compiler reference architectures, however, usually follow an imperative paradigm, as the architecture presented in most text books, such as Aho, Sethi and Ullman [1], discuss in terms of data structures and a stream of modules (scanning, parsing, semantic analysis, etc.) that operate on the data.

We feel that modeling a language processor in an object-oriented way gives benefits in implementation easiness, understandability, and maintenance operations. In our understanding, the object-oriented design for compilers is most beneficial for small, special-purpose languages that are embedded inside a larger object-oriented application, as there already exist many fine and powerful tools for full-scale compiler construction.

2 Background

When given a task of designing and implementing a domain-specific language processor for some application, the individual in question has multiple choices of how to proceed. Choosing an object-oriented implementation is natural if the surrounding application is already written in a language that supports object orientation. Within the language subsystem, choosing the right path depends on trade-offs in many dimensions, such as performance requirements, amount of maintenance work expected, and general knowledge on language processors available within the organization.

Even a small language implementation requires some amount of theory knowledge in areas of context-free languages and compiler writing. Because different developers have different specialization areas, it is not expected that there would be too many compiler specialists available in the development project. For this reason, it would be

D. Lightfoot and C. Szyperski (Eds.): JMLC 2006, LNCS 4228, pp. 104–115, 2006.
© Springer-Verlag Berlin Heidelberg 2006

beneficial if the interface to the domain-specific language for the regular application developer ('user of the language') would be as simple as possible. On the other hand, for the case of modification of the target language and/or compiler, we would wish to provide structures that allow modification with minimal knowledge related to compiler construction.

As an illustrative example, we will carry on with a simple language of single-digit numbers with two operators, as expressed as a context-free grammar in Figure 1.

```
Expression   -> Digit | ParenthExpr
Digit        -> '0' | '1' | '2' | .. | '8' | '9'
ParenthExpr -> '(' Expression Operator Expression ')'
Operator     -> '+' | '*'
```

Fig. 1. A context-free grammar for a limited desktop calculator

For processing this kind of language inside another application, there would be few basic operations in the exposed interface: transmitting input from the application to language processor and evaluation of the input. Other additional tasks could be e.g. code generation for faster execution or automatic documentation in the spirit of literate programming. The language processor provides a programmatic interface to the application developer.

The ideal case for the application developer is that the programming interface of a language processor is no different than any other object handling on the application side. Language constructs could be instantiated using regular object construction methods and the programmatic interface would expose methods for efficient usage. So, for the example grammar above, the client code accessing this language would be similar to the one shown in Figure 2.

```
Expression expr   = new Expression("1+2");
int          result = expr.eval();

System.out.println(result);                      // prints 3
```

Fig. 2. Example application code using the desktop calculator

Depending on the chosen implementation language and parsing method, the internal structure of the language processor gets different forms. This simple example also introduces a problem with evaluation of expression trees. The return type of *expr* is defined to be an int. Integrating a type system over the host language type system will be briefly discussed in section 4. It still remains a problem, which we have not been able to find a clean solution to.

2.1 Object-Oriented Context–Free Grammars

In the example grammar, we see that an Expression is either a Digit or a ParenthExpr. The other type of grammar rule, for ParenthExpr, is a concatenation rule, which states that such production consists of all the symbols on the right-hand side. This grammar is in an example of object-oriented context-free grammar [2], OO-CFG for short, which allows the implementing class hierarchy to mirror the original grammar. In OO-CFGs, the grammar productions are either *or*-rules or *and*-rules, having the meanings of selection between one of possible forms and catenation of terminals and nonterminals, correspondingly[1].

In object terminology an *or*-rule can be called an IS-A -relationship, which can be implemented using inheritance. Correspondingly, an *and*-rule is implemented using object composition, as it is a HAS-A -relationship.

2.2 Top–Down Parsing

Recursive-descent parsing is a well-known technique for parsing, as discussed in every compiler textbook, e.g. [1, 3, 5, 6]. A grammar in LL(1) form can be straight-forwardly converted into a set of mutually recursive functions that handle parsing. For every nonterminal A, there exists a routine for parsing the nonterminal in question. When the production's right-hand side definition contains another nonterminal B, the corresponding routine is called.

In the object-oriented world, Grune et al. [3] present a methodology for construct-ing an object-oriented compilation and interpretation system. In this system, the grammar rules are systematically converted into classes in the implementation lan-guage. Each class contains methods for processing the language structure in question, e.g. how to evaluate the parsed expression. A snippet of class hierarchy for the exam-ple grammar is shown in Figure 3.

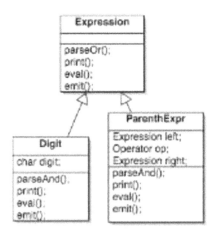

Fig. 3. Class hierarchy for the example grammar

There exists a small problem when expressing object constructors in this system. The authors would like to start parsing using the regular object construction system, by writing new Expression(input); This, however is problematic because the

---

[1] See exact definition in the appendix.

language operator *new* is responsible for allocating enough space for the created object. However, on entry to the constructor for the Expression class, it is not known whether the object to be instantiated should be a Digit or a ParenthExpr.

To express this problem another way, we can say that the semantics of the operator *new* in most object languages statically binds the name of the instantiated object's class. In this situation, the class of the parsed structure is not known until parsing has proceeded far enough to determine which class to instantiate.

To work around this problem, the authors use static factory methods [4] that are parameterized according to the grammar specification to handle instantiation of objects during parsing. This way, the recursion strategy is reduced to two standard templates, one for *and*-productions, and another for *or*-productions. For example, pseudo-code for parsing the production Expression is shown in Figure 4.

// in class Expression	// in class Digit
public static Expression parseOr() {	public boolean parseAnd() {
// try to parse a digit	if(Lexer.tokenClass == DIGIT) {
Digit d = new Digit();	digit = Lexer.tokenValue;
if(d.parseAnd()) return d;	Lexer.nextToken();
	return true;
// try a parenthesized expression	}
ParenthExpr pe = new ParenthExpr();	return false;
if(pe.parseAnd()) return pe;	}
return null;	// Conceptually similar parseAnd()
}	// in class ParenthExpr

Fig. 4. Code following parsing template

While this solution works, the authors are not satisfied by it because they do not think it as a natural way of constructing objects.

2.3 Bottom-Up Parsing

When using a bottom-up parsing method, this problem disappears. As the bottom-up parser does a reduction once all components of a grammar structure are available and recognized, there is no confusion about which class should be instantiated.

Maybe for this reason, existing language implementation systems that employ object-oriented context-free grammars, such as TOOLS [5] use bottom-up parsing. Another systematic approach of using bottom-up parsing for constructing an interpreter/compilation system is shown in [6]. Their approach is to employ YACC [7] to automatically generate the parser and C++ [8] to program semantic actions to the system. To the application programmer, their approach looks very similar to this work, as only a simple interface with few operations is exposed to the client code.

3 Parsing in Object Constructors

In this section, we show how it is possible to write recursive descent parsing of an object-oriented context-free grammar into object constructors. While using bottom-up parsers solves the problem, implementation of a bottom-up parser is generally considered harder to understand than a top-down parser [1, pp. 216, 6 pp. 117]. In the code generated by most parser generators, the structure of the parser is encoded into parsing tables that are driven through a generic driver algorithm. While the representation of the parser is compact, it is rather hard for the human reader to comprehend at first sight. For this reason, we feel that studying top-down parsing is viable.

Using object constructors as the recursive descent parsing routines is not a new idea. An early suggestion of this for C++ appears in [9]. However, this discussion stops at the idea of making object constructors to replace regular methods as the parsing routines. Because he considers only the case of simple production rules, the approach is only of little use.

We approach the problem by concentrating on the contract between the client of an object and the object itself. The client of the object does not care how the serving object implements the requested service (the main idea of encapsulation and information hiding). Depending on features offered by the implementation language, the service interface of an object can be directly or indirectly changed during the lifetime of an object.

In the example setting, an object that promises to be of type `Expression` can delegate its actual operations to another object that knows which kind of expression was encountered during parsing.

3.1 Class-Based Languages

In class-based languages, such as C++ and Java [10], using this kind of delegation is known as applying the Bridge design pattern [4]. The implementation for delegation requires additional work in the object constructing code, because the target of the message '*new*' is statically bound, and is required to return an object of its own class. An example of class hierarchy for a bridge-based solution is presented in Figure 5.

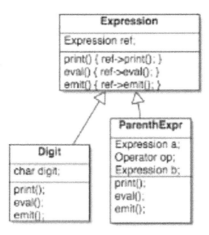

Fig. 5. Class hierarchy for bridge-based parsing

In bridge-based parsing, the base class that implements an *or*-rule in the grammar contains a reference to another object of the same class. By convention, an instance of the correct subclass is assigned to this attribute. In each method that belongs to the public interface of the language processor, there is a delegating method call. This makes this particular instance of the base class behave like an instance of the subclass it is delegating to.

```
class Expression {                        void print(PrintStream out) {
    private Expression ref = null;            ref.print(out);
    public Expression(){// for subclasses }  }

    public Expression(Lexer lex) {        void eval() {
        try {                                 ref.eval();
            ref = new ParenthExpr(lex);       }
            return;
        } catch(ProductionException pe) {  void generateClass(PrintStream out) {
            ref = new Digit(lex);             ref.generateClass(out);
            return;
        }                                     }
    }
}                                         } // of class Expression
```

Fig. 6. Class Expression in bridged parsing

An example of the `Expression` class in Java when using bridged parsing is shown in Figure 6. In this implementation, failure to recognize a grammar structure is signaled by raising an exception, `ProductionException`. A simple optimizing and clarifying change would be to change the parsing constructor to use LL(1)-lookahead tokens to predict the subclass which should be instantiated; this has been left out in order to retain semantic compatibility with the listing presented in Figure 5.

3.1.1 Prototype–Based Languages

Some object languages allow this kind of bridging to be done on the language level. Languages such as JavaScript and Ruby [11, 12] allow redefinition of methods of an object during runtime. In a prototype-based solution, each of the methods defined in the interface are redefined once the concrete type of the grammar construct gets known. The idea is the same as in the bridging solution – to have an object change its behavior – but redefinition of the object's methods and attributes makes the solution much cleaner.

Figure 7 shows a sketch of an implementation of the operator production in the example grammar. The idea is that the object that represents a calculation operation in the grammar can be either an addition or a multiplication operation. This information becomes known during parsing. Once this happens, the same object is redefined to contain routines that are associated with the corresponding mathematical operation.

When comparing prototypical and bridged implementations of parsing in object constructors, it is interesting to see how the differences in structures created by each

// object 'operator'
abstract eval();
expression lhs, rhs;
operator() {
   if (token == '+') { eval ⇐ plus.eval; }
   else if (token == '*') {
     eval ⇐ times.eval;
   }
}
	// methods plus.eval and times.eval
	plus.eval() {
	   return lhs.eval() + rhs.eval();
	}
	
	times.eval() {
	   return lhs.eval() * rhs.eval();
	}

Fig. 7. Prototypical implementation of the Operator production

of the methods resemble the differences between a parse tree and an abstract syntax tree (AST). A parse tree is a structure that shows which derivations were chosen during parsing, while the abstract syntax tree drops the 'unnecessary' intermediate nodes. In prototypical implementation the rules of this dropping are written into method redefinition parts of the parsing code. Once the behavior of an object gets fixed with meaningful operation, the object in question is a node in the abstract syntax tree. For this reason, there is only one level of indirection regardless of the complexity of the grammar.

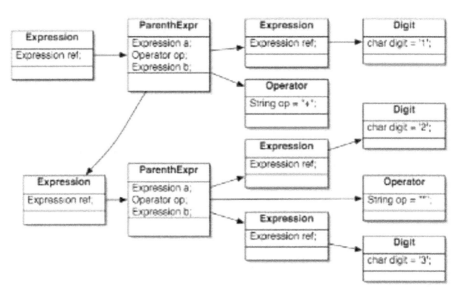

Fig. 8. A bridging parse structure for expression (1 + (2*3))

In a bridged solution, illustrated in Figure 8, there exists an object for each derivation step. When interpreting this kind of a structure, each call gets delegated through a series of nodes. In this solution, it is possible to leave out grammar symbols that are only used to guide parsing (e.g. left and right parenthesis in ParenthExpr). When these symbols are included, the resulting structure of the object tree is very similar to a parse tree.

4 A Case Study

In order to assess the feasibility of the presented language processor architecture, a real world case study has been made. It is an OO-CFG parser generator that reads an input specification (an OO-CFG) and outputs the class hierarchy with parsing constructors.

4.1 A Recursive Descent–Parser Generator

As a testing tool for the concepts presented in this paper, we have implemented a small parser generator for object-oriented context-free grammars. Given an OO-CFG, the tool constructs a stub program in Java that encodes the corresponding class hierarchy and parsing routines. The input language for the tool is written as an OO-CFG, as illustrated in Figure 9.

```
RULENAME "->" (OR_PROD "|")* OR_PROD
RULENAME "->" (AND_PROD)*
```

Fig. 9. OO-CFG for the parser generator input language

Classes that implement this grammar offer only two operations to the client: `print()` and `generateClass()`. The first operation is used to (re)print the input grammar, mostly for testing purposes. The second operation writes out the specified class hierarchy along with constructors for parsing the specified language.

Grammar specifications for this tool tend to be very compact. For example, the limited desktop calculator grammar shown in Figure 1 can be given to the tool just as it is, in four lines. For comparison, a similar specification for the JavaCC tool [13] takes from 50 to 100 lines of specification. On the other hand, a parser generated by JavaCC allows semantic actions to be associated with parsed constructs directly. This approach is powerful for languages that have exactly one semantic interpretation in the client side.

For situations where multiple interpretations, such as both evaluation and code generation are needed, additional constructs are required. In our approach, this is achieved by defining a sound interface method for each of the operations. Unfortunately, finding a clean solution to generating interface methods for anything more complicated than a desktop calculator with one data type is a non-trivial task. An alert reader has noticed that while in Figure 2 we specified that writing

```
int result = expression.eval();
```

is the way to evaluate the parsed structure, in every other Figure we have avoided specifying the interface of that method. This is because we have not been able to find a good way to specify evaluation interfaces for generated objects. In the example above, the return type of integer would imply that every expression evaluated would have a return type of integer – which clearly is not the case.

Other compilation/interpretation systems such as [6] and HotScheme [14] take the approach of defining one base class (e.g. SchemeObject) for all values that can be passed within interpreting methods. This solution is unfavorable for multiple reasons. It is quite heavyweight in terms of object creation and destruction rate. If the domain-specific language requires only integer arithmetic, forcing the evaluation system to capsulate every value into an object seems an unclean solution. Also any type checking that could be done on the host-language's type system cannot be utilized efficiently, as the type information is obscured into a class hierarchy of its own.

Another problem in the traditional view of object-oriented interfaces gets exposed along with the usage of a parser generator. Once the object-oriented grammar has been successfully translated to a class hierarchy, the semantic methods for e.g. evaluation should be inserted into stubs provided by the generator. This works as long as there is no need to change the grammar of the input language, because re-running the generator will overwrite any changes made to the classes generated on the previous run. The generator tool could employ sophisticated analysis to target code generation only to constructors of the classes in the generated hierarchy.

Our solution is simpler. We have defined an interface for objects that follow the Visitor pattern [4]. When generating the class hierarchy we also generate a visitor base class `Walkabout` that mirrors the structure of the grammar, as characterized by [15]. This organization gives surprisingly good robustness against different kinds of changes both in semantic actions and in grammar rules. Because the structure of the traversed structures is known, there is no need to rely on runtime reflection techniques in the Walkabout base class. This greatly improves performance during execution.

Adapting the Visitor pattern and a Walkabout class to OO-CFGs happens by defining a new method, `Accept(Visitor v)` to the object interface of the language processor. For each production in grammar, a callback to the visitor is added. For the grammar in Figure 1, the accept method for production `ParenthExpr` is shown in Figure 10.

```
// accepting a visitor for ParenthExpr
public void accept(Visitor guest) {
   expr.accept(guest);
   oper.accept(guest);
   expr2.accept(guest);

   guest.visitParenthExpr(this);
}
```

Fig. 10. Accept method of class ParenthExpr

The Walkabout base class defines virtual callback methods with no-operations for every production in the grammar. Overriding suitable methods by the subclassed visitor does the adaptation of the Walkabout class for certain interpretation of the grammar.

For example, a visitor that generates Java virtual machine bytecode for a given Expression structure is shown in Figure 11.

class JVM extends Walkabout {	public void visitOperator(Operator oper)
void visitDigit(Digit d) {	{
emit("iconst"+ d.value);	if("+".equals(oper.value))
}	{
	emit(" iadd");
Void visitParenthExpr(ParenthExpr pe)	} else if("*".equals(oper.value)) {
{	emit(" imul");
pe.expr.accept(this);	}
pe.expr2.accept(this);	}
pe.oper.accept(this);	
}	} // class JVM

Fig. 11. Java bytecode generating visitor

Whenever a parenthesized expression is visited, the visiting order is changed to follow reverse polish order. Otherwise, bytecodes for corresponding operations are emitted: imul for multiplication and iadd for addition.

This separation of structure-defining Walkabout base class and semantics-defining Visitor-class is surprisingly robust to changes. In case of modifications that add productions to the grammar, the base class is re-generated, but no changes are required in the subclass. When a definition of production changes and there is a reference to that particular production in the visitor, the host language compiler (Java in this case) gives an error message stating which part of the system has experienced the incompatible modification. The same applies to removal of productions that are used within the semantics providing visitors.

5 Conclusions

Originally it was believed that recursive descent parsing could not be performed in any object-oriented language using object constructors [3, pp. 708]. We have shown a possible way of constructing language processors that can provide a suitable programming interface that sufficiently hides implementation details from an application developer. Although the technique is not applicable to speed-sensitive production compilers, it might be possible to use the presented structures for writing domain-specific processing systems and/or for educational use.

A small-scale recursive descent parser generator was constructed and its most important aspects were discussed. As the generated parser is in human-readable form instead of driver code that executes parsing tables, we believe that the constructed parser is easier to understand for an application developer without former knowledge of language technologies.

The discussion of the work finds some surprising connections between concepts previously thought unrelated. When a recursive descent parser is written by using object constructors and bridges, the resulting object reference web can be a straight representation of a parse tree. This compares to a prototypical implementation, which constructs an abstract syntax tree during parsing.

References

1. A.V. Aho, R. Sethi, and J.D. Ullman. Compilers: Principles, Techniques, and Tools. Addison – Wesley, 1986
2. K. Koskimies, Object-orientation in attribute grammars. In *Attribute Grammars, Applications and Systems* (H. Alblas & B. Melichar, ed.) pp. 297-329. Springer-Verlag, 1991
3. D. Grune, H.E. Bal, C.J.H. Jacobs, K.G. Langendoen: Modern Compiler Design. Wiley publishing, 2000
4. E. Gamma, R. Helm, R. Johnson, J. Vlissides, Design Patterns: Elements of Reusable Object-Oriented Software. Addison – Wesley, 1995
5. K. Koskimies, J.Paakki, Automatic language implementation, Ellis Horwood, 1990
6. J. Holmes, Object-Oriented Compiler Construction. Prentice Hall, 1995
7. S.C. Johnson, YACC, yet another compiler compiler. Rep. CS-TR-32, Bell Laboratories, 1975
8. B. Stroustrup, The C++ Programming Language (3rd edition). Addison—Wesley, 1997
9. P.W. Hall, Parsing with C++ Constructors, ACM SIGPLAN Notices, vol. 28, no. 4, pp. 67-68, April 1993
10. K.Arnold, J.Gosling, D.Holmes, The Java(TM) Programming Language (3rd Edition). Addison—Wesley Professional, 2000
11. Standard ECMA-262. ECMAScript Language Specification. (3rd edition), 1999. http://www.ecma.ch/stand/ecma-262.htm
12. D. Thomas and C. Fowler and A. Hunt, Programming Ruby: The Pragmatic Programmers' Guide (2nd edition). Pragmatic Bookshelf, 2004
13. V. Kodaganallur, Incorporating Language Processing into Java Applications: A JavaCC Tutorial. IEEE Software, vol. 21, no 4, pp 70-77, July 2004
14. G. Callahan and B. Clark, Design Parameters in a Java Interpreter. Java Developer's Journal, January 1999. http://jdj.sys-con.com/read/36098.htm
15. J. Palsberg, C.B. Jay, The Essence of the Visitor Pattern. COMPSAC '98: Proceedings of the 22nd International Computer Software and Applications Conference, Washington, 1998

Appendices

Context-Free Grammars

A Context-free grammar is a 4-tuple, G = (V, T, P, S) where
- V is a finite set of terminals
- T is a finite set of nonterminals
- P is a finite set of production rules
- S is an element of Vn, the distinguished starting non-terminal.
- elements of P are of the form Vn -> (T $\cup$ V)*

Object-Oriented Context–Free Grammars

An object-oriented context-free grammar is a context-free grammar with the following definitions and restrictions (as defined in [5, pp 64]):

- G is cycle-free if for each nonterminal NT the derivation $NT \Rightarrow +NT$ is impossible (a class cannot be its own base class).
- G is reduced if each symbol X is used in some derivation $S \Rightarrow +\alpha X\beta \Rightarrow * \omega, \ \omega \in T$.
- A production $NT \rightarrow \alpha$ is a chain production if $\alpha \in N$.

A CFG is an OO-CFG if it is reduced and cycle-free and for each nonterminal A either

1) there is only one A-production and this production is not a chain production
2) all the A-productions are chain productions
3) all the A-productions have only terminal symbols on their right-hand sides
additionally, each nonterminal appears on the right-hand side of a chain production at most once.

A Framework for Modular Linking in OO Languages

Sean McDirmid[1], Wilson C. Hsieh[2], and Matthew Flatt[2]

[1] École Polytechnique Fédérale de Lausanne (EPFL), 1015 Lausanne, Switzerland
sean.mcdirmid@epfl.ch
[2] University of Utah, 84112 Salt Lake City, UT, USA
{wilson, mflatt}@cs.utah.edu

Abstract. The successful assembly of large programs out of software components depends on **modular reasoning**. When the linking of component code is modular, components can be compiled and type checked separately, deployed in binary form, and are easier to reuse. Unfortunately, linking is not modular in many mainstream OO languages such as Java. In this paper we propose an intuitive and formal framework for enhancing a language with modular linking, which is applied to the specific problem of making linking in Java modular. In our proposed framework, the degree to which components can be reasoned about modularly is adversely affected by language features that limit abstraction. We show that most of Java's core language features, such as inheritance, permit a high degree of modular linking even in the presence of cyclic dependencies.

1 Introduction

Reasoning is *modular* if it can be divided into separate reasoning of a system's parts, all of which can be combined into a reasoning of the entire system. General modular reasoning is indispensable in developing large programs out of third-party software components [24], because developers do not need to understand the implementations of the components they reuse. *Modular linking* is a specific kind of modular reasoning where component code can be compiled, linked, and statically type checked separately. Modular linking avoids many "DLL hell" problems related to the link-time binary compatibility [9,18] of components. Although modular linking is a common feature of functional languages because of the elegance and simplicity of functions, modular linking in object-oriented (OO) languages is problematic because of complex language features related to classes and objects.

The degree to which components can be separated by modular reasoning depends on what can be hidden, or "abstracted," between components. Abstraction in Java is complicated by **inheritance**: reasoning about a class defined in a component separate from its inherited superclasses is similar to reasoning about a *mixin* [4,14]. Mixins have well-known type-checking challenges related to **ambiguous methods**, where a subclass may "introduce" a method that conflicts with a method unknowingly provided by a superclass, and **cyclic inheritance**, where mixins are applied recursively. As a result, statically-typed OO languages that support modular linking have done so by restricting inheritance [3], disallowing cyclic dependencies between components [12,17], or by severely limiting abstraction [3,12].

D. Lightfoot and C. Szyperski (Eds.): JMLC 2006, LNCS 4228, pp. 116–135, 2006.

In this paper, we propose a framework that intuitively and formally describes how linking can be made modular independent of a specific language. We apply this framework to the problem of making compilation, linking, and type checking, modular in the Java language, which models our design and implementation of Jiazzi [19]. Jiazzi enhances Java with support for externally linked and separately compiled components based on program units [13].

Issues related to modular linking in OO languages have been previously explored in the areas of managing virtual method namespaces [22,25], merging module systems and OO languages [3,12,17], and reasoning about mixins [4,14]. The work presented in this paper is the first to show how modular linking can be added to a language using a general framework, which directly considers the effects of a language's features, such as OO inheritance. We show that inter-module inheritance restricts abstraction in a way that does not significantly decrease the degree of modular reasoning.

Section 2 motivates modular linking in the Java language. Section 3 describes an intuitive and formal framework for adding modular linking to a language that does not already support it. Section 4 shows how this framework is used to add modular linking to the Java language, and describes how we have dealt with inheritance and cyclic dependencies. Section 5 briefly discusses how our modular linking framework can be used to evaluate language features other than inheritance, such as abstract methods and symmetric multi-methods. Section 6 discusses related work and Section 7 summarizes our conclusions.

2   Motivation

Programs can be assembled out of separately developed and deployed containers of code, which we refer to as *components*. Such components in Java can be physically realized as Java archive (JAR) files that contain compiled classes. The linking of components is important in the development of a program. During linking, type checking is performed to ensure that safety properties are not violated that could result in segmentation faults or circumvent security of the program. When compared to other mainstream languages, Java's support for program linking is advanced: linking always guarantees program type safety, can occur dynamically, and supports laziness. Unfortunately, the linking of components in Java is not modular: the entire code of all components linked into a program is always type checked together. Because the linking of components in Java is not modular, interactions between components can result in errors that can only be debugged by inspecting the source code for all components involved.

In Java, the source code of each component is compiled in an environment where the implementations of all used classes are available, even if those classes are implemented in other components. These classes that originate from other components can differ between compile-time and link-time. For example, the component *icon* illustrated in Figure 1 uses the class Cowboy, which is provided by the component *cowboy_cmpl* when component *icon* is compiled but later is provided by the component *cowboy_lnk* when component *icon* is linked.

The fact that the class Cowboy is different between the compile-time and link-time of the component *icon* is significant because the class Icon, provided by the component

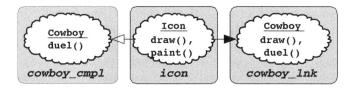

Fig. 1. The components *icon*, *cowboy_cmpl*, and *cowboy_lnk*; throughout this paper, components are illustrated as gray-filled rounded rectangles; classes are clouds whose names are underlined over their methods; clear arrows point from a class to its direct superclass as its containing component is compiled; solid arrows point from a class to its direct superclass as its containing component is linked

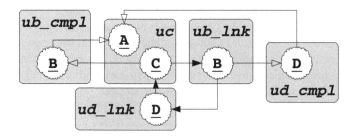

Fig. 2. The components *uc*, *ub_cmpl*, *ub_lnk*, *ud_cmpl*, and *ud_lnk*

icon, is a subclass of Cowboy. The class Icon implements a *draw* method, as in "drawing an icon." When the component *icon* is compiled against the component *cowboy_cmpl*, the class Cowboy does not have a *draw* method, but when the component *icon* is linked against the component *cowboy_lnk*, a *draw* method, as in "drawing guns in a cowboy duel," exists in the class Cowboy. Assuming both *draw* methods are public and have the same signature, the *draw* method in the class Icon should not override the *draw* method in the class Cowboy: the *draw* method was not visible when the component *icon* was compiled so overriding was not the programmer's intention. However, unintended overriding occurs in Java because unmodular linking disregards compile-time intentions.

Changes in the inheritance hierarchies that occur between compilation and linking can also "break" programs in Java. In Figure 2, the component *uc* is compiled against the component *ub_cmpl*, but it is linked against component *ub_lnk*, and the component *ub_lnk* is compiled against the component *ud_cmpl*, but linked against the component *ud_lnk*. When component *uc* is compiled against the component *ub_cmpl*, class B appears as a direct subclass of the class A, so it is safe for the class C, implemented in component *uc*, to subclass the class B. However when the component *uc* is linked against *ub_lnk*, the class B is an indirect subclass of the class C, so an inheritance cycle is created. Although linking in Java rejects this program, "blame" to one component cannot be assigned for this error. Instead to understand why this error occurs, and thus be able to fix it, the changes that occur from the component *ub_cmpl* to *ub_lnk* and from the component *ud_cmpl* to *ud_lnk* must be understood together.

The problems in linking the components illustrated in Figures 1 and 2 are created by inheritance between classes across component boundaries. In Figure 1, the class Icon inherits from the class Cowboy; in Figure 2, the class C inherits from the class B. The superclasses, the classes Cowboy and B, are implemented in components that change between compile-time and link-time. Such changes can lead to the typing problems of *mixins* [4,14], which are classes with explicitly parameterized superclasses. Compared to mixins, the superclasses of classes Icon and C are implicitly parameterized through linking.

In Java, differences between a component's compile-time and link-time environment are governed by special *binary compatibility* [9,18] guidelines, which specify what changes to components can occur after compile-time that will still allow linking to succeed. Additive changes between link-time and compile-time, such as adding new methods or new superclasses to a class, are generally considered safe according to binary compatibility. In Figure 1 a method is added to the class Cowboy, while in Figure 2, the class D is added as superclasses of the class B.

Even though the changes in Figures 1 and 2 are additive, linking in these examples still breaks. In Figure 1, linking is technically type safe; the components are linked in Java without errors even though programmer intent is not be adhered to. In Figure 2, the components have *cyclic dependencies*: they each use each other's classes and their dependency graph contains a cycle. Binary compatibility primarily accommodates changes to libraries, such as AWT, which cannot have cyclic dependencies with programs. Adding a new superclass to a class is always safe if the containing component does not have any cyclic dependencies with other components in the system, which is not the case in Figure 2.

Perhaps inheritance of classes should be restricted across component boundaries or perhaps cyclic dependencies between components should be disallowed. However, inheritance is an essential mechanism in using the OO paradigm to develop entire programs, not just individual components. The use of cyclic dependencies is the most natural way to codify two-way interactions that commonly occur between classes in different components. Restricting either inheritance or cyclic dependencies disallows the language-supported use of OO design throughout a program. Mixin-style inheritance of classes across component boundaries and cyclic dependencies between components also enables *open classes* [6], which are classes that can be extended with new fields and methods without breaking their existing subtypes.

Modular linking of components can be used to implement open classes with what we call an *open class pattern* [19]. The components illustrated in Figure 3 demonstrate the mechanics of the open class pattern. The class BButton is a subclass of the class BWidget in the component **base**, but rather than directly subclass the class BWidget, the class BButton is a direct subclass of the class FWidget from the component **fixed**. This creates a cyclic dependency between the components **base** and **fixed**, because the class FWidget is also an indirect subclass of the class BWidget. The class in the inheritance hierarchy between classes FWidget and BWidget depends on whether the components **base** and **fixed** are linked with the component **color_1** or the components **color_2** and **font**. With the former linking, one new method setColor is visible in the class FWidget, while in the latter linking two new methods setColor

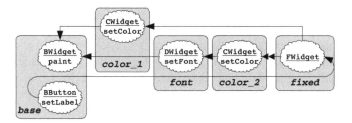

Fig. 3. The components **base**, **color_1**, **color_2**, **font**, and **fixed**; double-head arrows point from classes to direct superclasses in an alternative way to link these components together

and *setFont* are visible in the class FWidget. Regardless of which linking occurs, the class BButton inherits any new methods added because it subclasses the class FWidget rather than the class BWidget.

In Java, the components illustrated in Figure 3 can be linked together into a valid program. However, the linking is fragile because type checking is not performed in a modular way. Jiazzi, our enhancement to Java that supports modular linking of components, supports the open class pattern with additional renaming mechanisms, not discussed in this paper, so that components can be "mixed-and-matched" to form classes with a desired feature set [19].

3   Modular Linking

When modular reasoning is applied to the linking of component code, type checking is "solved" in two phases: first when the component code is initially compiled, and later when the component code is linked with the code of other components to create a program. Type checking performed during compilation is not duplicated during linking. The benefit of modular linking is that the phases of compilation and linking are truly separate: they occur at separate times and can be performed by different parties.

To better understand modular linking, we propose a formal framework that describes how modular linking can be implemented in an arbitrary language. An intuition of how our framework works is illustrated in Figure 4. Linking that is not modular, which we refer to as *whole linking*, is shown in the top part of Figure 4: the code of components are compiled directly against the code of other components. In our framework, the key to making linking modular is to provide an **abstraction** between the compilation of a component and its linking with other components in a system. Rather than compile a component against other components in a system, a component is compiled against its abstraction, as shown in the bottom part of Figure 4. The abstractions of components are then used during linking to ensure they are compatible. Because components are not compiled directly against each other, as in whole linking, modular linking can reuse the results of compilation to avoid inspecting component code when ensuring static type safety of the system during linking.

A formal description of our framework is expressed over systems written in some language L, where linking of a system ensures the system conforms to the static type

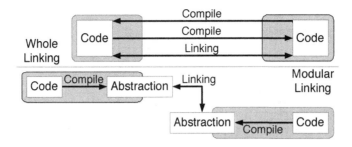

Fig. 4. A comparison between whole linking (top) and modular linking in our framework (bottom); single directed arrows labeled "compile" point from code being compiled to what the code is being compiled against

safety properties of L. Before modular linking is formally described, a corresponding whole linking can be formally described with the definition of the rule **WHOLE-OK**:

$$\frac{\vdash_L \textbf{ENV-OK } \overrightarrow{\| \textbf{c} \|} \qquad \overrightarrow{\| \textbf{c} \|} \vdash_L \overrightarrow{\textbf{IMPL-OK } \textbf{c}}}{\vdash_L \textbf{WHOLE-OK } \textbf{p} = \overrightarrow{\textbf{c}}}$$

Notation: Lower-case letters designate instances of constructs, and the same letters (differing only with subscripts) are used to designate instances of the same construct. Rules are in small caps; e.g., **RULE-OK**. Directed overbars are vectors that designate unordered sets; e.g., $\overrightarrow{\textbf{c}}$ is a set of construct instances designated by c. A rule within a vector applies to all elements of any sets under the same vector, but any elements adjacent to the rule not within the same vector are duplicated as the rule is applied to these elements; e.g., if $\overrightarrow{\textbf{c}} = \textbf{c}_0, \textbf{c}_1, \textbf{c}_2$ then enforcement of $\overrightarrow{\textbf{s}} \textbf{ RULE-OK } \overrightarrow{\textbf{c}}$ expands to enforce $\overrightarrow{\textbf{s}} \textbf{ RULE-OK } \textbf{c}_0$, $\overrightarrow{\textbf{s}} \textbf{ RULE-OK } \textbf{c}_1$, and $\overrightarrow{\textbf{s}} \textbf{ RULE-OK } \textbf{c}_2$.

For the rule **WHOLE-OK**, a system p consists of syntactically separated, but not modular, parts designated by c and written in the language L. We refer to these parts as *L-parts*, which have *shapes* that can be used to reason about interactions between L-parts. An L-part shape can be extracted from an L-part using the double bar operator ($\| \textbf{c} \|$). L-part shapes are combined to form a *typing environment*, which is used to reason about the type correctness of a group of L-parts. A typing environment can be used to ensure the type correctness of L-part implementations, which is enforced by the rule **IMPL-OK**, if it is closed and well-formed, which is enforced by the rule **ENV-OK**. The rules **ENV-OK** and **IMPL-OK** depend on the language L. In Section 4, each L-part models a Java class and definitions for the rules **ENV-OK** and **IMPL-OK** model type checking for the Java language.

In the definition of rule **WHOLE-OK**, only a single "whole" typing environment formed from the shapes of all the system's L-parts ($\overrightarrow{\| \textbf{c} \|}$) is used to type check the system. Linking according to the rule **WHOLE-OK** is not modular because type checking occurs over a single whole typing environment. For linking to be modular in our framework, the system's L-parts are placed inside special kinds of components referred

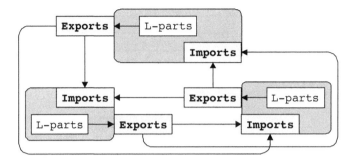

Fig. 5. An illustration of how abstraction enables modular linking in a system of three units; abstraction relationships are solid directed lines from what is being abstracted to the abstraction

to as *unit* constructs, designated by u. Modular linking is then defined in our framework as follows:

$$\frac{\vdash_L \overline{\textbf{COMPILE-OK } \vec{u}} \qquad \vdash_L \textbf{LINK-OK } \overline{\| u \|}}{\vdash_L \textbf{MODULAR-OK } p = \vec{u}}$$

For the rule **MODULAR-OK**, a system p consists of a set of units $\vec{u}$, where each unit has a *signature*, designated by $\| u \|$, which describes the unit's interactions with other units in the system without revealing the unit's implementation. The units of a system each undergo separate *compile-time typing* that is performed by the rule **COMPILE-OK**. Compile-time typing can examine the private implementation of a unit, but does not look at how the unit is used in a system. All units of a system also collectively undergo *link-time typing* that is performed by the rule **LINK-OK**. Link-time typing only examines the signatures of the system's units ($\overline{\| u \|}$).

To bridge type checking between the compile-time and link-time typing phases, the signature of each unit abstracts its interactions with other units in the system. The abstraction process is illustrated in Figure 5. A unit signature is divided into two sections: *exports* that abstract the unit's L-parts to other units in the system for use in link-time typing; and *imports* that abstract the exports of other units in the system to the unit for use in its compile-time typing. As a result, the use of a foreign L-part in a unit is abstracted twice: first, when it is exported from its originating unit; and second, when it is imported into the unit.

An L-part c can be described in a signature by an L-part shape designated by s. The format of a unit is $u = U \, \vec{s_i} \, \vec{s_e} \, \vec{c}$, where U uniquely identifies the unit u in a system, $\vec{s_i}$ describes u's imports, $\vec{s_e}$ describes u's exports, and $\vec{c}$ are the L-parts that make up u's private implementation. The signature of a unit only consists of its identifier, imports, and exports, and does not include its private implementation, so $\| U \, \vec{s_i} \, \vec{s_e} \, \vec{c} \| = U \, \vec{s_i} \, \vec{s_e}$. The definitions of the rules **COMPILE-OK** and **LINK-OK** are as follows:

$$\frac{\vdash_L \text{ENV-OK } \overrightarrow{\mathbf{s}_i} \cup \overrightarrow{\|\mathbf{c}\|} \quad \vdash_L \text{ENV-OK } \overrightarrow{\mathbf{s}_i} \cup \overrightarrow{\mathbf{s}_e} \quad \overrightarrow{\mathbf{s}_i} \cup \overrightarrow{\|\mathbf{c}\|} \vdash_L \overrightarrow{\text{IMPL-OK } c}}{\vdash_L \overrightarrow{\mathbf{s}_i} \cup \overrightarrow{\mathbf{s}_e} \text{ ABSTRACTS-OK } \overrightarrow{\mathbf{s}_i} \cup \overrightarrow{\|\mathbf{c}\|}}$$
$$\vdash_L \text{COMPILE-OK } \mathbf{u} = \mathsf{U} \overrightarrow{\mathbf{s}_i} \overrightarrow{\mathbf{s}_e} \overrightarrow{\mathbf{c}}$$

$$\frac{\vdash \text{UNIQUE } \overrightarrow{\mathsf{U}} \quad \vdash_L \text{ENV-OK } \overrightarrow{\mathbf{s}_e} \quad \vdash_L \overrightarrow{\mathbf{s}_i} \cup \overrightarrow{\mathbf{s}_e} \text{ ABSTRACTS-OK } \overrightarrow{\mathbf{s}_e}}{\vdash_L \text{LINK-OK } \overrightarrow{\|\mathbf{u}\|} = \mathsf{U} \overrightarrow{\mathbf{s}_i} \overrightarrow{\mathbf{s}_e}}$$

More notation: Multiple sets can be combined into a larger set with the union ($\cup$) operator. A set of structures is designated by adjacent elements under the same overbar, where an element of the structure can be pulled out to form its own set; e.g., $\mathsf{U} \overrightarrow{\mathbf{s}_i}$ can be used to form $\overrightarrow{\mathsf{U}}$ and $\overrightarrow{\mathbf{s}_i}$. The construct $\overrightarrow{\mathbf{s}}$ is not a set of $\mathbf{s}$ sets; it is a single set that is formed by unioning the $\mathbf{s}$ sets together.

The definition of the rule **COMPILE-OK** combines a unit's imports ($\overrightarrow{\mathbf{s}_i}$) with the shapes of the L-parts in its internal implementation ($\overrightarrow{\|\mathbf{c}\|}$) to form a *compile-time typing environment*, which is used to reason about the unit's internal implementation using the rules **ENV-OK** and **IMPL-OK**. These rules are the same as those used in the definition of whole linking (**WHOLE-OK**), whose definitions only depend the language L, and do not depend on whether linking is modular or not. The rule **LINK-OK** combines the exports of all units ($\overrightarrow{\mathbf{s}_e}$) in the system to create an *link-time typing environment*, which is used to type check interactions between units in the system.

The key to modular linking in our framework is an *abstraction relationship* that is symmetrically enforced between compile-time and link-time typing environments. We say that a unit's imports and exports ($\overrightarrow{\mathbf{s}_i} \cup \overrightarrow{\mathbf{s}_e}$) "abstracts" a typing environment correctly if the two following criteria hold: the imports and exports collectively specify a subset of the abstracted typing environment; and the imports and exports do not hide anything about the abstracted typing environment that could confuse or create ambiguity in modular linking. "Correctly abstracts" is enforced by the rule **ABSTRACTS-OK**, whose definition depends on how type checking can be made modular in language L.

The rule **ABSTRACTS-OK** represents only part of the extra work that must occur to make linking modular; the rest of the extra work is performed by *link reduction*, which transforms a system of units into a linked system of just L-parts. Link reduction rewrites the L-parts of units so that no ambiguities in typing occur over the resulting linked system. Names locally used in a unit must be renamed so that they do not conflict with the names used in other units of the system. In our framework, link reduction allows a modular system to be subjected to program evaluation, and allows us to express a necessary relationship between whole and modular linking as Lemma 1:

Lemma 1 (MODULAR-IMPLIES-WHOLE)

$$\vdash_L \text{MODULAR-OK } \mathbf{p_u} = \overrightarrow{\mathbf{u}} \quad \overrightarrow{\|\mathbf{u}\|} \vdash_L \overrightarrow{\mathbf{u} \to \overrightarrow{\mathbf{c}}} \quad \Rightarrow \quad \vdash_L \text{WHOLE-OK } \mathbf{p_c} = \overrightarrow{\overrightarrow{\mathbf{c}}}$$

Link reduction occurs with the arrow ($\to$) operator, and only depends on the signatures of a system's units ($\overrightarrow{\|\mathbf{u}\|}$) when linking each unit. Lemma 1 states that if modular linking ensures that a modular system of units ($\mathbf{p_u}$) is statically type safe, then whole linking ensures that the corresponding linked system (p_c) is statically type safe. It is possible that the linked system is statically type safe when modular linking has determined that the modular system of units is not; modular linking is more conservative than whole linking.

When Lemma 1 can be proven, modular linking is sound when the corresponding whole linking is sound. A proof of Lemma 1 depends on link reduction and the rule **ABSTRACTS-OK**, where more than one set of definitions may be able to facilitate a proof of Lemma 1. **ABSTRACTS-OK** can be defined in a trivial way that always ensures a proof of Lemma 1:

$$\frac{\overrightarrow{s_i} \cup \overrightarrow{s_e} == \overrightarrow{s_r}}{\vdash_L \overrightarrow{s_i} \cup \overrightarrow{s_e} \ \text{NO-ABSTRACTS-OK} \ \overrightarrow{s_r}} \qquad \overline{U_a \ \overrightarrow{s_{ia}} \ \overrightarrow{s_{ea}} \vdash_L U \ \overrightarrow{s_i} \ \overrightarrow{s_e} \ \overrightarrow{c} \ \rightarrow \ \overrightarrow{c}}$$

The definition of the rule **-ABSTRACTS-OK** forces a unit's imports and exports to always be equivalent to the unit's compile-time and the system's link-time typing environment, which means no abstraction occurs at all! The entire shape of every L-part in the system would be exposed in the imports and exports of each unit, and any trivial change of any unit in the system would invalidate linking of the entire system. Modular linking is only useful if a sufficient amount of abstraction can be supported. How much abstraction can be supported depends on the features of the core language L.

4   MiniJiazzi

The modular linking framework in Section 3 can be applied to the task of modular linking of programs written in a small Java-like core language, which models the addition of modular linking into Java. Language L is bound to language J, where J is our small Java-like language called core MiniJiazzi. We refer to the resulting language enhanced with modular linking as MiniJiazzi because it models Jiazzi [19]; Jiazzi enhances the full Java language with modular linking. Our experience with Jiazzi is the primary basis for our modular linking framework.

4.1   Core language

Core MiniJiazzi is similar to other small Java-like languages; e.g., ClassicJava [14] or Featherweight Java [16]. The syntax and type-checking rules of core MiniJiazzi are shown in Figure 6. So that we can focus our discussion on how modular type checking must deal with inheritance and virtual methods, core MiniJiazzi does not support fields, constructors, or casting. Besides class implementations (c) and class shapes (s) (the L-parts and L-part shapes in our modular linking framework), the syntax of core MiniJiazzi also defines method implementations (m), method shapes (n), types (t), and expressions in methods (e). Expressions can instantiate classes, access arguments and this, and call virtual methods on objects. The extends operator (◁) is used to specify a class's apparent direct super type, which is either another class or the root type Object.

To aid in our reasoning, we have added two features to the MiniJiazzi core language that do not have equivalent support in the Java language but are easily derived from conventional Java class definitions. First, a class shape describes only the "fresh" methods

$$s = \quad C[U] \triangleleft t_{super} \ \overrightarrow{n_{fresh}} \qquad n = \quad t_{return} \ M[U](\overrightarrow{t_{arg} \ x})$$

$$c = \quad s_{sig} \ \overrightarrow{m_{impl}} \qquad\qquad m = \quad n_{sig} \ \{ \ e_{return} \ \}$$

$$t = \quad \text{Object} \mid C[U]$$

$$e = \quad \text{new } C[U] \mid x \mid \text{this} \mid e.M[U_a](\overrightarrow{e_x})$$

$$\frac{\vdash \textbf{UNIQUE } \overrightarrow{C[U]} \quad \vdash \textbf{UNIQUE } \overrightarrow{M[U_a]} \quad \overrightarrow{s} \vdash_m \overrightarrow{M[U_a]} \notin t_s}{\overrightarrow{s} \vdash_t t_s \cup \overrightarrow{t_{ret}} \cup \overrightarrow{t_x} \quad \overrightarrow{s} \vdash_t \overrightarrow{C[U]} < \text{Object}}{\vdash_J \textbf{ENV-OK } s = C[U] \triangleleft t_s \ n = t_{ret} \ M[U_a](\overrightarrow{t_x \ x})}$$

$$\frac{\overrightarrow{s} \vdash_m \overrightarrow{t_r \ M[U_a](\overrightarrow{t_x \ x})} \in C[U] \quad \overrightarrow{n_{fresh}} \subseteq \overrightarrow{t_r \ M[U_a](\overrightarrow{t_x \ x})}}{\overrightarrow{\Gamma(x) = t_x} \quad \overrightarrow{\Gamma(this)} = C[U] \quad \overrightarrow{s}, \Gamma \vdash_e \overrightarrow{e_r \in t} \quad \overrightarrow{s} \vdash_t t \le t_r}{\overrightarrow{s} \vdash_J \textbf{IMPL-OK } C[U] \triangleleft t_s \ \overrightarrow{n_{fresh}} \ m = t_r \ M[U_a](\overrightarrow{t_x \ x}) \ \{ \ e_r \ \}}$$

$$\frac{\overrightarrow{s} \vdash_t C[U] < \text{Object}}{\overrightarrow{s}, \Gamma \vdash_e \text{new } C[U] \in C[U]} \qquad \frac{\overrightarrow{s}, \Gamma \vdash_e x \in \Gamma(x)}{\overrightarrow{s}, \Gamma \vdash_e \text{this} \in \Gamma(this)}$$

$$\frac{\overrightarrow{s}, \Gamma \vdash_e e \in C_b[U_b] \quad \overrightarrow{s} \vdash_m t_r \ M[U_a](\overrightarrow{t_x \ x}) \in C_b[U_b]}{\overrightarrow{s}, \Gamma \vdash_e \overrightarrow{e_x \in t_y} \quad \overrightarrow{s} \vdash_t \overrightarrow{t_y \le t_x}}{\overrightarrow{s}, \Gamma \vdash_e e.M[U_a](\overrightarrow{e_x}) \in t_r}$$

Fig. 6. The syntax and type-checking rules of core MiniJiazzi; evaluation reduction is not shown

of a class, which must not exist in the class's superclass. Next, to accommodate link reduction, class and method names are enhanced with *linking offsets*. Linking offsets are significant parts of class and method names; e.g., $C[U_a]$ and $C[U_b]$ identify different classes when $U_a \ne U_b$. Linking offsets are used during link reduction to distinguish names that may clash after linking.

The type-checking rules of core MiniJiazzi consists of definitions for the rules **ENV-OK** and **IMPL-OK**. The rule **ENV-OK** ensures the following (in the top part of the judgment that defines **ENV-OK**; from left to right, top to bottom):

1. The names of all classes, taking into account their linking offsets, are unique in the typing environment;
2. The shapes of fresh methods are unique in each class;
3. No fresh methods of a class exist in the class's superclasses, which ensures that a method can always be unambiguously referred to in a class by its name;
4. All types referred to in a class shape are defined in the typing environment;
5. Each class is a subtype of Object, which ensures there are no inheritance cycles in the typing environment.

For simplicity, the definition of rule **ENV-OK** does not allow for method overloading; overloading can always be handled through renaming. Typing relationships ($\vdash_t$) and method relationship ($\vdash_m$) are used in the definition of **ENV-OK** but are not defined in Figure 6. They have their traditional meanings: subtyping ($\leq$) is reflexive and transitive ($\leq$ adds associative); the $\in$ operator queries whether or not a method is visible in a class. Both typing relationships and method relationships depend only on a typing environment.

The definition for rule **IMPL-OK** ensures the following (again top to bottom, left to right): all methods implemented by a class are declared by the class or one of its superclasses; all fresh methods of the class are implemented; and all implemented methods are well-typed; $\Gamma(\ldots) = \ldots$ defines an expression typing environment.

Expression-level typing ($\vdash_e$) is a judgment over recursive expression structures that determines the static compile-time types of expressions. It takes the form $\vec{s}, C[U], \Gamma \vdash_e e \in t$. The typing of expressions is standard; e.g., typing of method calls at the bottom of Figure 6 only ensures that the method exists in the statically determined type of the calling expression, and that the argument expressions are typed as subtypes of the argument types.

The evaluation reduction rules and the proof that shows that whole type checking in core MiniJiazzi is sound are similar to those in other ClassicJava [14] and Featherweight Java [16]. In this paper, we concentrate on a proof of Lemma 1 from Section 3. To do this, we apply our modular linking framework to core MiniJiazzi by defining the rule **ABSTRACTS-OK** and link reduction.

4.2   Modular Linking

MiniJiazzi is a small model of Jiazzi, which enhances Java with *program units* [13]. We focus on how Jiazzi units make linking in Java modular and not the novel features of Jiazzi units, such as externally-specified linking and hierarchical structuring.

Modular linking is implemented in MiniJiazzi as follows. MiniJiazzi specifies an abstraction relationship that allows for the modular detection inheritance cycles and name clashes, but also allows for enough hiding to permit expressive linking organizations, such as those that use the open class pattern. In MiniJiazzi, potential name clashes (method and class name ambiguity) that could occur with modular type checking are prevented through link reduction.

The structure of units is described in Section 3 as $U \ \vec{s_i} \ \vec{s_e} \ \vec{c}$. The class shapes described by a unit and the classes in a unit's private implementation initially have empty linking offsets ([∘]). Linking offsets will not be specified until link reduction of the modular system occurs. The fact that linking offsets are empty does not have any effect on the rules **ENV-OK** or **IMPL-OK**.

At minimum, abstraction in MiniJiazzi must ensure that the signature of a unit is a "subset" of the compile-time and link-time typing environments of its unit. This criteria is described by the definition for weak abstraction:

$$\frac{\overrightarrow{s_i \cup s_e} = \overrightarrow{C[\circ] \lhd t_s \ \vec{n}} \qquad \overrightarrow{C[\circ]} \subseteq \overrightarrow{|s_r|} \qquad \vec{s_r} \vdash_m \overrightarrow{\vec{n} \in C[\circ]} \qquad \vec{s_r} \vdash_t \overrightarrow{C[\circ] < t_s}}{\vdash_J \overrightarrow{s_i} \cup \vec{s_e} \ \textbf{WEAK-ABSTRACTS-OK} \ \vec{s_r}}$$

The unit's typing environment abstraction is designated by $\vec{s_i} \cup \vec{s_e}$, which is the imports and exports of a unit. The abstracted typing environment is designated by $\vec{s_r}$, which is either the compile-time typing environment of the unit or a link-time typing environment of a system. The single bar operator takes a class shape and returns its class identifier; e.g., $\lfloor \vec{s_r} \rfloor$ is a set of class identifiers for classes described in the abstracted typing environment $\vec{s_r}$.

The definition of the rule **WEAK-ABSTRACTS-OK** ensures the following (top to bottom, left to right):

1. Every class described by the abstraction is described by a same-named class in the abstracted typing environment;
2. The methods of each class described by the abstraction exists in a class with the same identifier or its superclass of the abstracted typing environment;
3. The superclass of each class described by the abstraction is a superclass of a class with the same identifier in the abstracted typing environment.

The definition of the rule **WEAK-ABSTRACTS-OK** does not enable modular type checking to detect irresolvable method ambiguity or inheritance cycles, and so cannot be used in a proof of Lemma 1. The problem is that the abstracted typing environment contains the superclass relationships specified by the abstraction ($\vec{s_r} \vdash_t \overrightarrow{\mathtt{C}[\circ] < \mathtt{t_s}}$), but the abstraction is free to hide any superclass relationships expressed by the abstracted typing environment. Take as an example the components illustrated in Figure 2 from Section 2, where an inheritance cycle occurs because the fact that class B is a subclass of class C at link-time can be hidden from component **uc** during its compile-time. A stronger definition of abstraction, which does not allow for the hiding of subclassing relationships, is as follows:

$$\frac{\vec{s_i} \cup \vec{s_e} = \overrightarrow{\mathtt{C}[\circ] \lhd \mathtt{t_s} \ \vec{n}} \qquad \overrightarrow{\mathtt{C}[\circ]} \subseteq \lfloor \vec{s_r} \rfloor \qquad \vec{s_r} \vdash_m \overrightarrow{\vec{n} \in \mathtt{C}[\circ]} \qquad \overrightarrow{\mathtt{C}[\circ] \lhd \mathtt{t_s} \ ...} \subseteq \vec{s_r}}{\vdash_J \vec{s_i} \cup \vec{s_e} \ \textbf{STRONG-ABSTRACTS-OK} \ \vec{s_r}}$$

The definition of the rule **STRONG-ABSTRACTS-OK** differs from **WEAK-ABSTRACTS-OK** only in that it prevents the hiding of superclass relationships in the abstracted typing environment by the abstraction with $\overrightarrow{\mathtt{C}[\circ] \lhd \mathtt{t_s} \ ...} \subseteq \vec{s_r}$. While this stronger abstraction does enable modular type checking—it rejects the linking in Figure 2 and can be used in a proof of Lemma 1—it does not permit enough information hiding through abstraction; e.g., it prevents useful applications of the open class pattern.

In Figure 3 from Section 2, the class DWidget may or may not be one of the superclasses of class FWidget, depending on whether or not the components *color_2* and *font* are linked with the components *base* and *fixed* in a system. With the rule **STRONG-ABSTRACTS-OK**, the fact that the class DWidget is a superclass of class FWidget, and indirectly a superclass of class BButton, would have to be apparent during the compile-time of the components *base* and *fixed*. Unfortunately, this also eliminates the possibility of linking components *base* and *fixed* with the component *color_1* instead, where the class DWidget is not provided.

We have discovered an effective compromise between the weakest and strongest abstraction relationships: superclass relationships are hidden by the abstraction of a

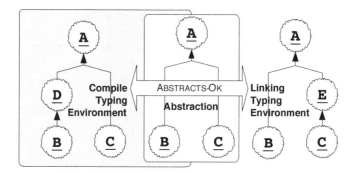

Fig. 7. An example of how the inheritance graph of an abstraction can hide inheritance relationships of classes in compile-time and link-time typing environments not visible in the abstractions

unit if and only if the classes involved are hidden by the abstraction. With help from an auxiliary rule **Super-Ok**, this best definition of the rule **Abstracts-Ok** is as follows:

$$\frac{C[\circ] \lhd t_s \ \ldots \in \vec{s_r}}{\vec{s_i} \cup \vec{s_e}, \vec{s_r} \vdash_J C[\circ] \ \textbf{Super-Ok } t_s} \qquad \frac{C[\circ] \lhd C_a[\circ] \ \ldots \in \vec{s_r} \qquad C_a[\circ] \notin \overrightarrow{|s_i|} \cup \overrightarrow{|s_e|}}{\vec{s_i} \cup \vec{s_e}, \vec{s_r} \vdash_J C_a[\circ] \ \textbf{Super-Ok } t_s}}{\vec{s_i} \cup \vec{s_e}, \vec{s_r} \vdash_J C[\circ] \ \textbf{Super-Ok } t_s}$$

$$\frac{\vec{s_i} \cup \vec{s_e} = \overrightarrow{C[\circ] \lhd t_s \ \vec{n}} \qquad \overrightarrow{C[\circ]} \subseteq \overrightarrow{|s_r|}}{\vec{s_r} \vdash_m \vec{n} \in \overrightarrow{C[\circ]} \qquad \vec{s_i} \cup \vec{s_e}, \vec{s_r} \vdash_J \overrightarrow{C[\circ] \ \textbf{Super-Ok } t_s}}{\vdash_J \ \vec{s_i} \cup \vec{s_e} \ \textbf{Abstracts-Ok } \vec{s_r}}$$

This definition of rule **Abstracts-Ok** permits the hiding of classes between units even if the classes occur in the middle of the inheritance hierarchy of two classes that are visible in the unit; e.g., class DWidget can be hidden from the components *base* and *fixed* in Figure 3. However, it also prevents the hiding of subtyping relationships between visible classes; e.g., a subtyping relationship between the Cowboy and Icon classes cannot be hidden if these classes are visible in the same scope.

The rule **Super-Ok** ensures that a unit's abstraction ($\vec{s_i} \cup \vec{s_e}$) expresses every direct and indirect inheritance relationship in the abstracted typing environment ($\vec{s_r}$) for classes visible in the abstraction. This relationship is illustrated in Figure 7, where the inheritance graph of the abstraction (center) expresses the proper inheritance relationships of classes A, B, and C, but ignores classes D and E, which are not visible in the abstraction. The relationship just discussed in English is expressed as Lemma 2, whose proof follows directly from the definition of rule **Super-Ok**:

Lemma 2 (Super-Abstraction)

$$\vec{s_i} \cup \vec{s_e} = \overrightarrow{C[\circ] \lhd t_s \ \ldots} \quad \overrightarrow{C[\circ]} \subseteq \overrightarrow{|s_r|} \quad \vec{s_i} \cup \vec{s_e}, \vec{s_r} \vdash_J \overrightarrow{C[\circ] \ \textbf{Super-Ok } t_s} \quad \Rightarrow$$

$$\forall C_a[\circ] \in \overrightarrow{|s_i|} \cup \overrightarrow{|s_e|}, \forall C_b[\circ] \in \overrightarrow{|s_i|} \cup \overrightarrow{|s_e|} \ . \ \vec{s_i} \cup \vec{s_e} \vdash_t C_a[\circ] < C_b[\circ] \leftrightarrow \vec{s_r} \vdash_t C_a[\circ] < C_b[\circ]$$

Our chosen definition of the rule **Abstracts-Ok** can be used in a proof of Lemma 1 in Section 3 and allows for a sufficient amount of abstraction to make modular type checking useful.

When units are combined together into a linked program, linking must ensure that name clashes between unit implementations do not cause ambiguities during evaluation of the program. Name clashes in OO languages result from classes from different units with the same name, or distinct methods with the same names that are defined in compatible classes that originate from different units. While modular type checking can detect name clashes between units if the names involved are exposed in unit signatures, MiniJiazzi's abstraction relationship permits hiding between units. Classes and methods hidden within a unit's implementation should not clash with classes and methods from other units. MiniJiazzi's definition of link reduction ensures that references to hidden classes and methods are disambiguated during linking.

MiniJiazzi achieves disambiguation with *linking offsets*. Every class and method reference within a unit implementation is qualified with a linking offset that is used disambiguate these references. Method implementations also have linking offsets to ensure that they implement or override the appropriate method from a superclass. Linking offsets are always treated as parts of class and method names. Unlike names, however, linking offsets are not provided by the programmer; they are assigned during link reduction, in much the same way as branch offsets are rewritten when a dynamically-linked library (DLL) is loaded into memory. Before link reduction occurs, all linking offsets of a unit's implementation are empty. Link reduction then binds linking offsets according to the unit that the class or method originates from.

The core judgments of link reduction specify class and method linking offsets. Other judgments are merely used to traverse the structure of a unit and are not shown in this paper. The following pair of judgments determines how linking offsets are bound for class references:

$$\frac{\mathsf{C}[\circ] \notin \overrightarrow{|\mathsf{s}_{ia}|}}{\mathsf{U}\,\overrightarrow{\mathsf{s}_i}\,\overrightarrow{\mathsf{s}_e}, \mathsf{U}_a\,\overrightarrow{\mathsf{s}_{ia}}\,\overrightarrow{\mathsf{s}_{ea}}\,\overrightarrow{\mathsf{c}_a} \vdash_J \mathsf{C}[\circ] \;\to\; \mathsf{C}[\mathsf{U}_a]} \qquad \frac{\mathsf{C}[\circ] \in \overrightarrow{|\mathsf{s}_{ia}|} \quad \mathsf{C}[\circ] \in \overrightarrow{\mathsf{s}_{eb}} \quad \mathsf{U}_b\,\overrightarrow{\mathsf{s}_{eb}} \in \mathsf{U}\,\overrightarrow{\mathsf{s}_e}}{\mathsf{U}\,\overrightarrow{\mathsf{s}_i}\,\overrightarrow{\mathsf{s}_e}, \mathsf{U}_a\,\overrightarrow{\mathsf{s}_{ia}}\,\overrightarrow{\mathsf{s}_{ea}}\,\overrightarrow{\mathsf{c}_a} \vdash_J \mathsf{C}[\circ] \;\to\; \mathsf{C}[\mathsf{U}_b]}$$

These judgments are used to specify linking offsets of any class referred to in a unit. References to classes that are not imported into the unit must be to classes that originate in the unit, so such references are assigned the linking offset of the referring unit, which is identified in the judgments as U_a. References to imported classes are resolved to the unit that exports those classes in a system. Linking offsets for method reference are bound using a similar but more complicated pair of judgments:

$$\frac{\overrightarrow{\mathsf{s}_{ia}} \cup \overrightarrow{\|\mathsf{c}_a\|} \vdash_m \mathsf{M}[\circ] \in_{fresh} \mathsf{C}_b[\circ] \quad \overrightarrow{\mathsf{s}_{ia}} \cup \overrightarrow{\|\mathsf{c}_a\|} \vdash_t \mathsf{C}[\circ] \le \mathsf{C}_b[\circ] \quad \mathsf{C}_b[\circ] \notin \overrightarrow{|\mathsf{s}_{ia}|}}{\mathsf{U}\,\overrightarrow{\mathsf{s}_i}\,\overrightarrow{\mathsf{s}_e}, \mathsf{U}_a\,\overrightarrow{\mathsf{s}_{ia}}\,\overrightarrow{\mathsf{s}_{ea}}\,\overrightarrow{\mathsf{c}_a} \vdash_J \mathsf{C}[\circ]{:}\mathsf{M}[\circ] \;\to\; \mathsf{M}[\mathsf{U}_a]}$$

$$\frac{\begin{array}{c}\overrightarrow{\mathsf{s}_{ia}} \cup \overrightarrow{\|\mathsf{c}_a\|} \vdash_m \mathsf{M}[\circ] \in_{fresh} \mathsf{C}_a[\circ] \quad \overrightarrow{\mathsf{s}_{ia}} \cup \overrightarrow{\|\mathsf{c}_a\|} \vdash_t \mathsf{C}[\circ] \le \mathsf{C}_a[\circ] \quad \mathsf{C}_a[\circ] \in \overrightarrow{|\mathsf{s}_{ia}|} \\ \mathsf{U}_b\,\overrightarrow{\mathsf{s}_{eb}} \in \mathsf{U}\,\overrightarrow{\mathsf{s}_e} \quad \overrightarrow{\mathsf{s}_e} \vdash_m \mathsf{M}[\circ] \in_{fresh} \mathsf{C}_b[\circ] \quad \mathsf{C}_b[\circ] \in \overrightarrow{|\mathsf{s}_{eb}|} \quad \overrightarrow{\mathsf{s}_e} \vdash_t \mathsf{C}_a[\circ] \le \mathsf{C}_b[\circ]\end{array}}{\mathsf{U}\,\overrightarrow{\mathsf{s}_i}\,\overrightarrow{\mathsf{s}_e}, \mathsf{U}_a\,\overrightarrow{\mathsf{s}_{ia}}\,\overrightarrow{\mathsf{s}_{ea}}\,\overrightarrow{\mathsf{c}_a} \vdash_J \mathsf{C}[\circ]{:}\mathsf{M}[\circ] \;\to\; \mathsf{M}[\mathsf{U}_b]}$$

Each method reference ($\mathsf{C}[\circ]{:}\mathsf{M}[\circ]$) is associated with a class ($\mathsf{C}[\circ]$) that must implement the method being referred to. To determine the method's linking offset, the class that introduces the method must be first found in the compile-time typing environment of

```
unit cowboy {
 import
 export class Cowboy[o] ◁ Object
 { Object draw[o](), Object dual[o]() }
} {
 class Cowboy[cowboy] ◁ Object
 { Object draw[cowboy]()  { /* a gun duel */ },
   Object dual[cowboy]()  { this.draw[cowboy]() }  }
}
unit icon {
 import class Cowboy[o] ◁ Object {  }
 export class Icon[o] ◁ Cowboy { Object paint[o]()  }
} {
 class Icon[icon] ◁ Cowboy[cowboy]
 { Object paint[icon]()  { this.draw[icon]() },
   Object draw[icon]()  { .../* draw icon */ } }
}
unit main {
 import class Icon[o] ◁ Object
 { Object paint[o](), Object draw[o]() }
 export class Main[o] ◁ Object { Object main[o]()  }
} {
 class Main[main] ◁ Object
 { Object main[main]()  { this.draw[cowboy]() } }

}
```

Fig. 8. The units *cowboy*, *icon*, and *main* that are linked together into a system; linking offsets that result from link reduction are shown

the unit. In the top judgment, the introducing class is not an import of the unit, so the method must originate from the referring unit (U_a). In the bottom judgment, the introducing class is an import, so the class that introduces the method must be found with respect to the link-time typing environment. The unit that the introducing class is exported from is used as the method's linking offset.

The MiniJiazzi units shown in Figure 8, based on the illustration of Figure 1 from Section 2, demonstrate how link reduction resolves method ambiguity. The unit *icon* specifies what it expects from other units through its imports. Since the unit *icon* does not import the method *draw* from the *cowboy* unit, link reduction binds the linking offset of the call to method *draw* in class Icon to the unit *icon*. Since the unit *cowboy* exports the method *draw*, whereas the unit *icon* does not, link reduction binds the linking offset of the call to *draw* within the class Main to the unit *cowboy*.

In Java, method scope is established by packages and access flags. If the above example was written in normal Java using packages and access flags (the method *draw* in a package *cowboy* would be public, and the method *draw* in a package *icon* would be package-only), ambiguity between the *draw* methods could not be avoided and the Java source compiler would even reject such a construction. In this MiniJiazzi program a source compiler error does not occur: the scopes of the *draw* methods are separated by abstraction and the unintended ambiguity is avoided through link reduction.

Rather than use linking offsets, other approaches [22,23,25] disambiguate between methods using dictionaries that are based on unit-like scopes. With dictionaries, a link reduction phase is not necessary; rather dictionaries are queried during evaluation. The advantage of using link reduction is the ability to easily express Lemma 1, which would be much more complicated if the evaluation of a modular system were different from the evaluation of a non-modular system.

Link reduction only binds linking offsets and does not need to otherwise change the structure of class expressions within a unit. The abstraction relationship ensures that referenced classes and methods exist within the program typing environment and that method implementations override methods correctly. The only nontrivial aspect of proving Lemma 1 is showing that the typing environment formed by the shapes of the resulting link-reduced classes is well-formed. We express this as Lemma 3:

Lemma 3 (LINK-REDUCED-ENV-OK)

$$p = \overrightarrow{\mathsf{u} = \mathsf{U}\ \vec{s_i}\ \vec{s_e}\ \vec{c_x}} \quad \vdash_J \textbf{ENV-OK}\ \overrightarrow{\vec{s_i} \cup \| \mathsf{c}_x \|}, \quad \overrightarrow{\vec{s_i} \cup \vec{s_e}}, \quad \vec{s_e}$$

$$\vdash_J \overrightarrow{\vec{s_i} \cup \vec{s_e}}\ \textbf{ABSTRACTS-OK}\ \overrightarrow{\vec{s_i} \cup \| \mathsf{c}_x \|} \quad \vdash_J \overrightarrow{\vec{s_i} \cup \vec{s_e}}\ \textbf{ABSTRACTS-OK}\ \vec{s_e}$$

$$\vdash \textbf{UNIQUE}\ \vec{\mathsf{U}} \quad \overrightarrow{\| \mathsf{u} \| \vdash_J \mathsf{u}} \ \rightarrow \vec{\mathsf{c}_y} \ \Rightarrow \ \vdash_J \textbf{ENV-OK}\ \overrightarrow{\| \mathsf{c}_y \|}$$

The proof of Lemma 3 primarily depends on using Lemma 2 to show that the signature of each unit abstracts the inheritance graph of the link-reduced classes. That is, the linking typing environment of the modular system forms an inheritance graph that abstracts the inheritance graph formed by the non-modular system ($\overrightarrow{\| \mathsf{c}_y \|}$), which is expressed as Lemma 4 that has the same antecedents as Lemma 3:

Lemma 4 (MODULAR-WHOLE-SUBTYPING)

$$\ldots \ \Rightarrow \ \forall \mathsf{U}_a\ \vec{s_{ia}}\ \vec{s_{ea}}\ \vec{c_a}, \mathsf{U}_b\ \vec{s_{ib}}\ \vec{s_{eb}}\ \vec{c_b} \in \overrightarrow{\mathsf{U}\ \vec{s_i}\ \vec{s_e}\ \vec{c_x}}, \forall \mathsf{C}_a \in |\vec{s_{ea}}|, \forall \mathsf{C}_b \in |\vec{s_{eb}}|.$$

$$\vec{s_e} \vdash_t \mathsf{C}_a[\circ] < \mathsf{C}_b[\circ] \leftrightarrow \overrightarrow{\| \mathsf{c}_y \|} \vdash_t \mathsf{C}_a[\mathsf{U}_a] < \mathsf{C}_b[\mathsf{U}_b]$$

The last consequent of Lemma 4 states that all subtyping relationships in the linking environment between pre-linked classes ($\mathsf{C}_a[\circ]$ and $\mathsf{C}_b[\circ]$) must be preserved in the post-linked classes ($\mathsf{C}_a[\mathsf{U}_b]$ and $\mathsf{C}_a[\mathsf{U}_b]$). Lemma 4 represents the core of our proof of Lemma 1 for MiniJiazzi.

Proof sketch: Our proof of Lemma 4 proceeds by using induction and showing that contradictions necessarily occur if this consequent does not hold. Our inductive base case is based on the fact that segments in the inheritance hierarchy remain unchanged between pre-linking and post-linking as long as they do not contain imported or exported classes. As a result, the following two implications always hold:

$$\vec{s_e} \vdash_t \mathsf{C}_a[\circ] \lhd \mathsf{C}_b[\circ] \rightarrow \overrightarrow{\| \mathsf{c}_y \|} \vdash_t \mathsf{C}_a[\mathsf{U}_a] < \mathsf{C}_b[\mathsf{U}_b]$$

$$\overrightarrow{\| \mathsf{c}_y \|} \vdash_t \mathsf{C}_a[\mathsf{U}_a] \not< \mathsf{C}_b[\mathsf{U}_b] \rightarrow \vec{s_e} \vdash_t \mathsf{C}_a[\circ] \not\lhd \mathsf{C}_b[\circ]$$

These base cases will be reached reached as long as the the post-linked inheritance graph is acyclic, which is given by ENV-OK already being enforced on the linking environment.

4.3   Comparisons with Jiazzi

MiniJiazzi formally describes Jiazzi linking system that was introduced in [19]. Jiazzi contains many features that make linking more convenient. Jiazzi supports *package signatures* that describe the shapes for a package of classes and can be reused between units. Package signatures are used to generate import class stubs that enable unit compilation to occur with a standard Java complier. When implementing a unit from scratch, package signatures can also be used to generate skeletons for exported classes. Alternatively, package signatures can be inferred automatically from existing Java classes by assuming public and protected classes and methods should appear in the signatures. Linking occurs after compilation with Java bytecode rewriting of method and class names to implement linking offsets. Unit imports and exports are supported with extension that simplifies usage of the open class pattern that was described in Section 2. Using this mechanism, a unit can extended a package of classes without creating new subtypes. For this purpose, the abstraction we have shown to be safe and possible with MiniJiazzi is very essential as it makes the open class pattern possible.

5   Beyond Inheritance

When considering modular linking, inheritance in Java permits a sufficient amount of abstraction; e.g., the open class pattern as illustrated in Figure 3 from Section 2 can be expressed. Abstract methods in Java, however, cannot be abstracted, despite their name: abstract methods can never be hidden in visible classes and Java interfaces, because modular type checking must ensure concrete subclasses implement all abstract methods. This becomes a significant expressiveness problem when abstract methods are used aggressively in "framework classes," or when components evolve to provide new functionality that require adding new abstract methods to classes.

Binary compatibility in Java allows new abstract methods to be added to library classes. It also allows concrete classes to have abstract methods that are not implemented [18]; e.g., the AWT class `Graphics` is often enhanced with new abstract methods as the AWT library evolves. This is only safe when there are assurances that unimplemented abstract methods are never invoked; e.g., a program compiled against the old AWT library will not cause the new abstract methods added to the class `Graphics` to ever be called. Such assurances cannot be automatically verified with static type checking, so Java uses run-time type checking to detect and reject attempts to invoke unimplemented abstract methods.

Our proposed modular linking framework can be used to reason about modular linking in other languages, OO or otherwise. It can also be used as a metric for new experimental language features. Consider symmetric multi-methods, which support dispatch over arbitrary arguments. Compilation and linking of symmetric multi-methods require the detection of cases where a multi-method is overridden ambiguously [21], that is, where two or more specializations of the multi-method are equally applicable to a combination of argument bindings. When this is enforced in the most direct way, multi-methods cannot support much abstraction under our modular linking framework because any class used in the specialization of a visible multi-method can never be hidden within a component. However, like inheritance, there is probably a middle ground similar to the rule SUPER-OK, where class hiding can be permitted if ambiguous multi-method overriding is type checked more conservatively.

6 Related Work

Separate compilation and modular linking are explored extensively by Cardelli [5] with linksets. In comparison, the work presented in this paper tackles modular linking from a different direction: rather than build modular linking into a newly designed language, we show how modular linking can be added to an existing language after it has been designed. Cardelli also does not address mutually-dependent modules or language features such as inheritance. On the other hand, Cardelli's correctness criteria are more rigorous including issues such as non-termination. In another direction, MTAL (modular typed-assembly language) [15] explores the low-level implications of binaries and modular linking. In contrast, our framework does not deal with low-level details such as Java bytecode, and instead focuses on high-level language abstractions. Effective modular systems must deal with both issues. Our modular linking framework is based on program units, which initially were conceived for Scheme and ML [10], and have been considered in OO extensions of Scheme [10]. With Jiazzi, we have shown how program units can be added to statically-typed OO languages.

Drossopoulou et al. extensively explore and formalize binary compatibility [9] and linking [8] in Java. Jiazzi eschews Java's binary compatibility in favor of modular linking, which we believe is more appropriate for component software. Both modular linking in Jiazzi and binary compatibility in Java address the technical "fragile base class problem." Ancona et al. [1] use a notion of a compilation schema to explore separate source code compilation and runtime linking in Java. The task of separate compilation in Jiazzi, as modeled by MiniJiazzi, is simplified because compile-time and link-time typing environments are explicitly separated by our modular linking framework.

The language JavaMod [3] explores adding a module system to the Java language, while the ML-like language Moby [11,12] explores modular linking for a class-based core language. Unlike Jiazzi, neither JavaMod nor Moby support mixin-style inheritance with abstraction. In JavaMod, methods hidden in a superclass are not visible in a subclass, while in Moby, methods provided by a superclass can only be invoked by explicitly specifying the superclass. Like most ML-like languages, Moby does not support modules with cyclic dependencies. MiniJiazzi is the first formalization of a statically-typed module system that supports cyclic dependencies, full mixin-style inheritance, and abstraction for an OO language. The language SmartJavaMod [2] enhances JavaMod with a form of signature inferencing and class overriding. It is an open question whether signature inferencing is feasible in a MiniJiazzi-like system because of abstraction.

The languages Dubious [21] and EML [20] explores modular type checking of symmetric multi-methods, while MultiJava [6,7] explores how symmetric multi-methods can be added to Java in a modular way. The hiding of abstract methods is also restricted in these languages to preserve modular type checking. Imports are not expressed in the module interfaces of these languages, which leads to a different definition of abstraction than we model in our modular linking framework. Even without multi-methods in the Java language, Jiazzi can implement the open class idiom that multi-methods enable, as illustrated in Figure 3 from Section 2.

Enforcing the privacy of methods in OO languages has been explored extensively in the literature. Riecke and Stone [22] formally explore method privacy in structurally typed OO languages by using method dictionaries, while this work is extended by Stone [23] and Vouillon [25] in the context of class and mixin-based languages. Mini-Jiazzi differs by using linking offsets rather than dictionaries to enforce method scopes and disambiguate between method namespaces.

7   Conclusion and Future Work

We have shown how modular linking can be added to statically-typed OO languages such as Java while allowing several expressive features: cyclic dependencies between components, inheritance across component boundaries, and non-trivial abstraction between components. Our modular linking framework provides the intuitive and formal foundation for our work, and we have used this framework to formally reason about how modular linking can be added to Java with MiniJiazzi. MiniJiazzi models Jiazzi, which is an enhancement of Java whose implementation is available for download:
http://www.cs.utah.edu/plt/jiazzi
Although we have shown that inheritance is a modular language feature because it permits an adequate amount of abstraction, abstract methods are problematic, while multi-methods are still an open question. Future work should explore how our modular linking framework and language features such as abstract methods and multi-methods can be made to support more abstraction.

Modular reasoning is what makes developing software out of components possible. This reasoning goes beyond linking, compilation, and type checking to also include execution, testing, debugging, semantic correctness, and so on. Future work should explore how these other kinds of reasoning can be made modular through a more general modular reasoning framework.

References

1. D. Ancona, G. Lagorio, and E. Zucca. A formal framework for Java separate compilation. In *In Proc. of ECOOP*, pages 609–636, June 2002.
2. D. Ancona, G. Lagorio, and E. Zucca. Smart modules for Java-like languages. Submitted for publication, Dec. 2005.
3. D. Ancona and E. Zucca. True modules for Java classes. In *Proc. of ECOOP*, pages 354–380, June 2001.
4. G. Bracha and W. Cook. Mixin-based inheritance. In *Proc. of OOPSLA*, pages 303–311, Oct. 1990.
5. L. Cardelli. Program fragments, linking and modularization. In *Proc. of POPL*, pages 266–277, Jan. 1997.

6. C. Clifton, G. Leavens, C. Chambers, and T. Millstein. MultiJava: Modular open classes and symmetric multiple dispatch for Java. In *Proc. of OOPSLA*, pages 130–146, Oct. 2000.

7. C. Clifton, T. Millstein, G. T. Leavens, and C. Chambers. MultiJava: Design rationale, compiler implementation, and applications. Technical Report 04-01b, Iowa State University, Dept. of Computer Science, Dec. 2004. Accepted for publication, pending revision.

8. S. Drossopoulou, S. Eisenbach, and D. Wragg. A fragment calculus: Towards a model of separate compilation, linking and binary compatibility. In *Proc. of Logic in Computer Science*, July 1999.

9. S. Drossopoulou, D. Wragg, and S. Eisenbach. What is Java binary compatibility? In *Proc. of OOPLSA*, pages 341–361, Oct. 1998.

10. R. Findler and M. Flatt. Modular object-oriented programming with units and mixins. In *Proc. of ICFP*, pages 98–104, Sept. 1998.

11. K. Fisher and J. Reppy. The design of a class mechanism for Moby. In *Proc. of PLDI*, pages 37–49, May 1999.

12. K. Fisher and J. Reppy. Extending Moby with inheritance-based subtyping. In *Proc. of ECOOP*, pages 83–107, June 2000.

13. M. Flatt and M. Felleisen. Units: Cool modules for HOT languages. In *Proc. of PLDI*, pages 236–248, May 1998.

14. M. Flatt, S. Krishnamurthi, and M. Felleisen. Classes and mixins. In *Proc. of POPL*, pages 171–183, Jan. 1999.

15. N. Glew and G. Morrisett. Type-safe linking and modular assembly language. In *Proc. of POPL*, Jan. 1999.

16. A. Igarashi, B. Pierce, and P. Wadler. Featherweight Java: A minimal core calculus for Java and GJ. In *Proc. of OOPSLA*, pages 132–146, Oct. 1999.

17. X. Leroy, D. Doligez, J. Garrigue, D. R'emy, and J. Vouillon. The Objective CAML system, documentation and user's manual, 2000. http://caml.inria.fr/ocaml/htmlman/.

18. S. Liang and G. Bracha. Dynamic class loading in the Java Virtual Machine. In *Proc. of OOPSLA*, Oct. 1998.

19. S. McDirmid, M. Flatt, and W. C. Hsieh. Jiazzi: New-age components for old-fashioned Java. In *Proc. of OOPSLA*, pages 211–222, Oct. 2001.

20. T. Millstein, C. Bleckner, and C. Chambers. Modular typechecking for hierarchically extensible datatypes and functions. In *Proc. of ICFP*, Oct. 2002.

21. T. Millstein and C. Chambers. Modular statically typed multimethods. In *Proc. of ECOOP*, pages 279–303, July 1999.

22. J. G. Riecke and C. A. Stone. Privacy via subsumption. *Theory and Practice of Object Systems*, 1999.

23. C. Stone. Extensible objects without labels. In *Proc. of FOOL*, Jan. 2002.

24. C. Szyperski. *Component Software: Beyond Object-Oriented Programming*. ACM Press and Addison-Wesley, 1998.

25. J. Vouillon. Combining subsumption and binary methods: An object calculus with views. In *Proc. of POPL*, pages 290–303, Jan. 2001.

Flexible Type-Safe Linking of Components for Java-Like Languages*

Davide Ancona, Giovanni Lagorio, and Elena Zucca

DISI, Univ. of Genova, v. Dodecaneso 35, 16146 Genova, Italy
{davide, lagorio, zucca}@disi.unige.it

Abstract. We define a framework of components based on Java-like languages, where components are binary mixin modules. Basic components can be obtained from a collection of classes by compiling such classes in isolation; for allowing that, requirements in the form of type constraints are associated with each class. Requirements are specified by the user who, however, is assisted by the compiler which can generate missing constraints essential to guarantee type safety.

Basic components can be composed together by using a set of expressive typed operators; thanks to soundness results, such a composition is always type safe.

The framework is designed as a separate layer which can be instantiated on top of any Java-like language; a prototype implementation is available for a small Java subset.

Besides safety, the approach achieves great flexibility in reusing components for two reasons: (1) type constraints generated for a single component exactly capture *all possible* contexts where it can be safely used; (2) composition of components is not limited to conventional linking, but is achieved by means of a set of powerful operators typical of mixin modules.

1 Introduction

It has been argued that the notion of software component is so general that cannot be defined in a precise and comprehensive way [12]. For instance, [20] provides three different definitions, that adopt different levels of abstraction. However, most researchers would agree that the following features are essential prerequisites for component technology: *modularity*, *type safety*, and *independence* from a particular programming language.

Modules and components share several common characteristics. The important software engineering principle of maximizing cohesion and minimizing dependencies of code applies as well to modules and to components. Furthermore, both modules and components are meant as units of composition which can be developed independently.

---

* This work has been partially supported by APPSEM II - Thematic network IST-2001-38957, and MIUR EOS - Extensible Object Systems.

D. Lightfoot and C. Szyperski (Eds.): JMLC 2006, LNCS 4228, pp. 136–154, 2006.

Type safety is an important property which guarantees a correct integration between components; separate development of components requires explicit interfaces not only for the provided services, but also for the requirements which ensure safe assembly of components. In order to maximize reuse, required interfaces should capture as many as possible contexts where a component can be safely used.

While modules are often tied to a specific programming language, components are usually meant as binary units, and therefore should not depend on a particular language; of course, basic components still need to be constructed by using some language. For instance, .NET assemblies do not strongly rely on any particular language, but can be created, for instance, from both C# and Haskell code. However, assembling components is a process which should involve only binary units and, therefore, is expected to be language independent. The benefits of this independence are a better integration and interoperability of components, especially when the binary form is some kind of intermediate language.

Among the several varieties of modules which can be found in programming languages or have been proposed in literature, *mixin modules* are one of the closest approximations of the notion of software component.

Module systems based on the notion of mixin module offer a framework largely independent from the core language with well-established and clean foundations [7,6,14]. Differently to parametric modules, like, for instance, ML functors, which offer only one composition operator roughly corresponding to function application, mixin modules are equipped with a richer set of operators that support *mutual recursion* across module boundaries and declaration of *virtual* entities which can be redefined via an *overriding* operator. For this reason, mixin modules seem a good starting point for defining a language independent framework for flexible composition and reuse of components in a type safe way. The main difference between a mixin module and a component is that the former is modeled as a collection of classes in source form, while the latter is modeled as a collection of classes in binary form. Of course, in practice there are other differences which we deliberately do not model in this paper: for instance, in general a component is a collection of more heterogeneous entities including not only code, but also resources like, for instance, multimedia data.[1]

Nowadays component technology is mainly based on mainstream object-oriented languages; nevertheless, object-oriented languages alone fail to provide important features for developing and assembling components. Compositional compilation is not supported by mainstream object-oriented languages, even though this property is important for allowing separate development of components: users should be able to obtain a basic component from a collection of classes by simply compiling such classes in total isolation. Furthermore, linking is the only available mechanism for manipulating and assembling binary components.

In this paper, we investigate how to build a framework for component-oriented programming based on Java-like languages. The framework is meant as a

---

[1] We refer to [20], Section 4.1.4, for more details.

logically separate layer constructed on top of the Java-like language used for creating basic components.

In the framework, components are modeled as mixin modules in binary form, by following and further developing the approach presented in [5]. Furthermore, separate development of components is possible by adopting the type technology we have developed for Java-like languages in a previous work [2]. Thanks to this technology it is possible to specify the minimal requirements needed by a component for being safely used by a set of *polymorphic type constraints*. Compilation in total isolation of classes into components is supported by the notion of *polymorphic bytecode*, a bytecode annotated with type variables which can be instantiated according to the context where a component is deployed.

The framework allows separate compilation of classes into basic components starting from the declarations of such classes in a Java-like language and from the specification of the requirements needed by the classes. Then, components in polymorphic bytecode can be assembled together in a type safe way by means of five composition operators: *bind*, *merge*, *renaming*, *unbind*, and *restrict*.

Other interesting features of the framework are the following:

- Since specifying the requirements needed by a class can be a tedious activity, the framework assists the programmer by generating those constraints which have not been explicitly specified by the user, but are nevertheless necessary for guaranteeing a type safe composition. The interface obtained in this hybrid way is then permanently associated with the polymorphic bytecode of the class in the components.
- Classes in a component are all implicitly considered *virtual*, that is, their definition can be later replaced when composing the component with others.
- In addition to composition operators typical of mixin modules [7,6], the framework provides two novel operators[2] *bind* and *unbind*, designed for better supporting unanticipated software evolution.

The paper is organized as follows. Section 2 is a gentle introduction to the framework; some examples are used for explaining its main features and its ability to support software reuse and unanticipated software evolution. In Section 3 we formally define syntax and reduction semantics of the framework, by listing the ingredients the underlying Java-like language should provide. Section 4 is devoted to the implementation of the framework: a prototype is available[3] for testing all the examples shown in Section 2. Finally, Section 5 outlines related work, summarizes paper contribution and draws directions for future developments.

A preliminary presentation of the ideas developed in this paper can be found in [3]. The full formal definition of the framework can be found in [4], notably including the definition of the type system modeling compilation of component expressions into binary components and soundness results. Moreover, [4] provides

---

[2] Which, however, can be encoded in lower-level operators of module calculi such as CMS [6].

[3] http://www.disi.unige.it/person/LagorioG/SmartJavaComp/

the formal description of an instantiation of the framework on top of Featherweight Java [15], and more examples.

2   A Gentle Introduction to Components

This section is a brief introduction to our component-oriented system: its main features are presented through some simple, but still meaningful, examples showing its expressive power. A more involved example showing how to deal with the classical *expression problem* (or *extensibility problem*) [21] can be found in [4].

Even though our operators handle components in binary form (more precisely, in polymorphic bytecode), in the examples we write components in source format for readability. In particular, we choose Java as source language, but all code could be easily rewritten in, say, C#.

2.1   Basic Components

Let us start our introduction with an example[4] of declaration of basic component:

```
component LinkedList = {
  deferred class N;
  class List {
    requires { N(N); }
    N first;
    void addFirst() {
      first=new N(first);
    }
  }
  class Node {
    requires { & N; }
    N next;
    Node(N n) { next=n; }
    N getNext() { return next; }
  }
}
```

A basic component is a collection of declarations of classes which are either *deferred*, that is, whose definition has to be imported later, like N, or *defined* inside the component, like List and Node. Class definitions are those in the Java-like language under consideration, enriched by a requires part which specifies *type constraints* on deferred classes, which of course also depend on the language. In the example, constraint N(N) means that class N is required to have a constructor applicable to an argument of type N, whereas constraint &N means that class N must exist. Other forms of constraints are subtyping constraints and constraints requiring a class to have a field of a certain type or a method applicable to

---

[4] For simplicity, we will avoid access modifiers.

certain argument types; moreover, constraints are *polymorphic* in the sense that types can be type variables, as will be illustrated below.

As it will be shown, deferred classes can be bound to a definition by means of the *bind* and *merge* operators. Within this example, the intuition is that N *could be* Node; indeed, if we replaced all occurrences of N with Node, then we would obtain the classic example of single-linked lists with a header node. However, having used a deferred class instead of the already defined class Node allows us to bind N to something more specific than Node later, for instance a class DoubleNode (which, presumably, extends Node).

This particular use of a deferred class allows one to simulate the idea of type *mytype* [10], or ThisClass of LOOJ [9], where inside a class, say Node, we can use *mytype* instead of Node with the effect that in any subclass of Node, say DoubleNode, this type will be interpreted by DoubleNode rather than Node.

However, our approach allows a step further: N can be bound to *any class* that satisfies the type constraints declared in class List and Node. For instance, class Node simply requires an existing declaration for N, since N is used in Node only as a type, while the correctness of List relies on a stricter constraint[5] asking N to provide a constructor which takes an argument of type N (hence, with a single parameter whose type is a supertype of N).

Note that constraints are declared at the level of each class definition, rather than at the level of the component declaration. As we will see, this is due to the fact that classes declared in components are all *virtual:* for instance, a new component could be derived from LinkedList by overriding the declaration of Node. In this case, the constraints associated to Node, and only those, are analogously replaced.

Component LinkedList supports an important feature for promoting component-oriented programming: each class is explicitly equipped not only with the interface of the provided services, (what is usually, and improperly, called the provided interface), but also with the interface of the required features. (what is usually, and improperly, called the required interface). Indeed, provided and required interfaces for classes List and Node can be easily extracted from their code:

```
class List {
  requires { N(N); }
  provides { N first;
             void addFirst();
  }
}
class Node {
  requires { & N; }
  provides { N next;
             Node(N n) ;
             N getNext() ;
  }
}
```

---

[5] Indeed, the constraint N(N) implies & N.

Providing the required interface should allow compilation of a component in *total isolation* (no other sources or binary files are needed) and composition with other components (already in binary form) in a *type safe* manner. To this end, the required interface should specify, on the one hand, all the requirements on deferred classes which are needed to compile the component; on the other hand, it should not specify requirements which are not strictly necessary, in order to allow safe composition with as many other components as possible. For Java-like languages, this can be achieved by using the approach we propose based on type constraints, whereas cannot be achieved by using other forms of required interfaces. For instance, compilation in isolation of the component above cannot be achieved by using the approach based on only subtyping constraints adopted for Java generics [8]; there is no way to guarantee that class N has a constructor which is type compatible with the call in method `addFirst` by simply requiring class N to extend some already defined class or interface.

Conversely, an approach where the required interface has to specify for each deferred class its expected signature (that is, constructor, field and method signatures), as done, e.g., in our previous work [5], is too restrictive, since it rejects components which do not match this type but can still be linked in a safe way with the given component. We will illustrate better this point in the following when introducing the merge operator.

Since specifying required interfaces by listing all the needed type constraints may be a tedious and error prone activity, the specification of required interfaces is assisted by the compiler: the most general constraints which are required by a component, but are not explicitly specified by the programmer, are automatically generated and added to the required interface. In this way the compiled code will contain the complete required interface, including both the user constraints and the missing ones inferred by the compiler. Of course, the user can always specify constraints which are not strictly necessary to guarantee type safety, but that are needed for contractual reasons.

For instance, in class `List` the user could specify the requirement `N <= Node` which requires N to be a subclass of `Node`, even though this condition is not necessary for the type safety of the code of the class. However, the required interface generated with the code will contain both the user-defined constraint `N <= Node` and the inferred constraint `N(N)`.

As shown in the following, the generated required interface will be used together with the provided interface, to check type safety of component composition.

2.2 Open and Closed Components

A component with deferred classes, as `LinkedList`, is called *open*; analogously, a component with no deferred classes is called *closed*. Classes declared inside an open component, as `List` and `Node`, cannot be accessed through qualified names (see 2.5).

```
LinkedList.List l=new LinkedList.List(); // type error
```

The qualified name `LinkedList.List` is used for denoting class `List` at component `LinkedList`.[6] An unqualified class name is called a *simple class name*. A *soft link* to a class is any of its unqualified occurrences except those which introduce the declaration of either the class itself, or any of its constructors. Analogously, qualified occurrences are called *hard links* (see more in Section2.5).

There are two different composition operators for deriving closed components from open ones: *bind* and *merge*.

Bind. A closed component can be obtained by binding the deferred classes of some open component to definitions in the same component. For instance, a new component `ClosedLinkedList` could be obtained from `LinkedList` by binding N to `Node`, since class `Node` satisfies all required constraints on N:

```
component ClosedLinkedList=bind(LinkedList,N->Node);
```

The component we obtain in this way is equivalent to (that obtained compiling) the following, where we have copied the definition of `LinkedList` and replaced each occurrence of N by `Node`.

```
component ClosedLinkedList = {
  class List {
    requires { Node(Node); }
    Node first;
    void addFirst() {
      first=new Node(first);
    }
  }
  class Node {
    requires { & Node; }
    Node next;
    Node(Node n) { next=n; }
    Node getNext() { return next; }
  }
}
```

Now classes `List` and `Node` can be used:

```
ClosedLinkedList.List l=new ClosedLinkedList.List();
```

When closing a component, all type constraints in the class types must be verified, otherwise a type error is issued.

For instance, the expression `bind(LinkedList,{N->List})` is not type correct, since `List` does not satisfy the constraint `List(List)`.

---

[6] For simplicity, we use here the dot notation for qualified class names since it is likely the most natural choice for Java programmers. However, while this poses no ambiguity problems for the simple Java subset we have implemented so far, this would be the case in an extension to full Java.

Note that the constraints in `ClosedLinkedList` cannot be removed by the compiler even though they are clearly satisfied. Indeed, a closed component is not permanently "sealed", but can be reopened using operators *restrict* and *unbind*, which will be discussed in Section 2.4.

Merge. Assume we want to extend the code in `LinkedList` in order to support doubly linked lists. This extension can be isolated in a separate component:

```
component Double = {
  deferred class N, List, Node;
  class DoubleList extends List {
    requires { N(N,N);
               'a List.first;
               N<='a;
               'a N.next;
               'a 'a.prev; }
    N last;
    void addLast() {
      N n = new N(last, null);
      if (first==null) first = n;
      if (last!=null) last.next = n;
      last = n;
    }
    void addFirst() {
      N n=new N(null, first);
      if (first!=null)
        first.prev = n;
      first = n;
      if (last==null) last=n;
    }
  }
  class DoubleNode extends Node {
    requires { Node(N); }
    N prev;
    DoubleNode(N n) { super(n); }
    DoubleNode(N p,N n) {
      super(n); prev=p; }
    N getPrev() { return prev; }
  }
}
```

Before explaining how the merge operator behaves, let us focus on the user requirements in `DoubleList`: the type variable `'a` is used for expressing the general[7] requirement that class `List` must provide the field `first` with a type

---

[7] For sake of simplicity we have omitted to specify the most general requirements as they would be inferred by the compiler.

'a such that 'a is a supertype of N (N<='a), and provides a field prev having the same type 'a ('a 'a.prev). Note that, as anticipated above, we could not achieve the same effect by using a required interface which specifies for each deferred class its expected signature. Indeed, in this case we should have fixed for instance the type of field f in List, e.g., requiring this type to be N, whereas in fact any supertype of N would work as well.

A new component DoubleLinkedList can be defined by merging LinkedList with Double:

```
component DoubleLinkedList=merge(LinkedList,Double);
```

In DoubleLinkedList the two deferred classes List and Node of component Double are bound to the corresponding classes declared in LinkedList, whereas class N remains deferred (indeed binding of deferred classes is by name matching). Note that, while it is possible to merge components with deferred classes having the same name, name conflicts for defined classes are not allowed.

Finally, it is possible to bind N to DoubleNode in DoubleLinkedList:

```
component ClosedDoubleLinkedList = bind(DoubleLinkedList,N->DoubleNode);
```

2.3   Renaming Facilities

Since binding of deferred classes is by name matching, a renaming operator might be useful in some circumstances.

For instance, if in Double the two deferred classes List and Node were named L and Nd, respectively, then a renaming would be necessary before merging LinkedList with Double.

```
component DoubleLinkedList =
               merge(LinkedList,rename(Double,{L->List,Nd->Node}));
```

The rename operator allows renaming of a single class name at time, therefore the expression rename(Double,{L->List,Nd->Node}) is just a convenient shortcut for the more verbose one:

```
rename(rename(Double,L->List),Nd->Node)
```

Renaming of more classes is accomplished sequentially from left to right. Both deferred and defined classes can be renamed. Since the operator allows only bijective renamings, the newly introduced name must be unused in order to avoid conflicts.

2.4   Unbind and Restrict

Let us consider again component ClosedLinkedList as defined in Section 2.2. As already noted, the constraints on class Node cannot be removed by the compiler without compromising type safety. This is due to the fact that it is possible to derive an open component from a closed one by making some class deferred. This can be accomplished by using either the *unbind* or the *restrict* operator.

Unbind. The unbind operator can be considered the inverse of bind; for instance, as `ClosedLinkedList` could be derived from `LinkedList` with the bind operator, the opposite could be obtained by deriving `LinkedList` from `ClosedLinkedList` with the unbind operator.

```
component LinkedList=unbind(ClosedLinkedList,Node->N)
```

The class to be unbound (`Node` in the example) must be defined in the component while the new name (`N` in the example) must be unused. The effect consists in adding the deferred class `N` and replacing all soft links to `Node` with `N`.

This example shows also that in general requirements cannot be safely removed by the compiler; indeed, requirements on `Node` specified in `ClosedLinkedList` cannot be simplified, since after applying the unbind operator, soft links to the defined class `Node` could be redirected to some deferred class (`N` in the example). The unbind operator offers an effective way to deal with unanticipated code modification due to poor component design; although unanticipated code modification should be better addressed when designing and developing components, unbind gives a chance to recover from this problem when components are assembled and are not available in source form.

Restrict. The restrict operator provides another mean for opening closed components. It is mainly used jointly with the merge operator to override class definitions. For instance, a new component could be obtained from `ClosedLinkedList` by overriding the definition of `Node` with that contained in component `AnotherNode`:

```
component AnotherNode = {
  class Node {
    Node next;
    int elem;
    Node(Node n) { next=n; }
    Node(Node n,int e) { next=n; elem=e; }
    Node getNext() { return next; }
    int getElem() { return elem; }
  }
}
component ClosedIntLinkedList =
            merge(AnotherNode,restrict(ClosedLinkedList, Node));
```

First, the restrict operator makes class `Node` in `ClosedLinkedList` deferred by removing its definition. Then the new definition of `Node` in `AnotherNode` is added by the merge operator.

Note the difference between the unbind and the restrict operator: for class `C` defined in component `Comp`, `unbind(Comp, C->U)` does not remove the definition of `C`, but redirects soft links to `C` to an unused class `U`; `restrict(Comp,C)`, instead, makes class `C` deferred by removing its definition, but does not redirect soft links to C. Hence `rename(restrict(Comp,C),C->U)` is still different from `unbind(Comp, C->U)` since in the latter the definition of C is kept.

As for renaming, convenient shortcuts are provided for unbinding and restricting multiple classes.

2.5   Qualified Class Names

As already explained, references to classes defined in other components are allowed by using qualified class names:

```
component AnotherList = {
  class List {
    requires { AComponent.Node(AComponent.Node); }
    AComponent.Node first;
    void addFirst() { first=new AComponent.Node(first); }
  }
}
```

Component `AnotherList` directly depends on component `AComponent` which is expected to define a class `Node` satisfying the constraint specified in class `List`. While soft links can always be redirected by the composition operators, hard links cannot and establish direct dependencies between components. However, these dependencies are always made explicit by the required interface. The same consideration applies to hard links to classes declared in the same component.

```
component YetAnotherList = {
  class List {
    requires { YetAnotherList.Node(YetAnotherList.Node); }
    YetAnotherList.Node first;
    void addFirst(){first=new YetAnotherList.Node(first);}
  }
  class Node{
    requires { & YetAnotherList.Node; }
    YetAnotherList.Node next;
    Node(YetAnotherList.Node n){next=n;}
    YetAnotherList.Node getNext(){return next;}
  }
}
```

In component `YetAnotherList` all hard links to `Node` are permanently bound to the definition of `Node` in the same component and can no longer be unbound.

While it is not possible to transform a hard link into a soft link, the opposite can be achieved via the bind operator. For instance, `YetAnotherList` could be equivalently obtained from `ClosedLinkedList`:

```
component YetAnotherList =
             bind(ClosedLinkedList,Node->YetAnotherList.Node);
```

3   A Framework of Components

The full formal definition of the framework of components we have introduced through examples in the previous section is given in [4]. In this paper, for lack of space, we only report syntax and reduction rules, to give the reader a precise, yet rather intuitive, definition of the behaviour of the operators. However, in the real scenario (see Section 4) a component expression is not reduced at the source level, but rather generates a binary component in a context where binary components for component names used inside the expression are already available. This is modeled by the type system given in [4].

The framework is parametric, in the sense that syntax and reduction rules can be instantiated on top of a programming language providing some syntactic categories and judgments. We use a Java-oriented terminology, since our aim is to instantiate the framework on Java-like languages (in particular, in [4] we present an instantiation on Featherweight Java [15]). However, the framework could in principle be applied more in general, thinking of "class" as "language entity".

In order to define syntax and reduction semantics of our component language, we first list the syntactic categories the used programming languages must provide.

- Simple class names (c). A qualified class name has the shape M.c, where c is a simple class name, and M is a component name. The meta-variable n ranges over both the sets of simple and qualified class names.
- (Source) class definitions (cd^s). We assume that each source class definition introduces a simple class name c that can be extracted by a function *out*. Sequences of source class definitions $cd_1^s \ldots cd_n^s$ will also be denoted by S.

The syntax used for creating and composing components is given in Fig.1. We assume that order in sequences is immaterial and use a bar notation for sequences following the same conventions as in [15]   (for instance, $\overline{c}$ stands for $c_1 \ldots c_n$).

An application program corresponds to an executable application obtained by assembling together and deploying some components as specified in the environment MDS, and by providing a main expression e^s from which execution must start in the context of components MDS.

A component environment is a sequence of component declarations (possibly mutually dependent), each one associated with a distinct name.

A basic component BM is a sequence of class names (the deferred classes), followed by a sequence of class definitions. We assume that all class names (deferred or defined) introduced in BM are distinct.

Moreover, we assume that class definitions can only contain soft links to classes which are explicitly declared in BM, either in $\overline{c}$ or in S. If $S = cd_1^s \ldots cd_n^s$, then $out(S) = out(cd_1^s) \cup \ldots \cup out(cd_n^s)$ denotes the set of all classes defined in S, whereas $in(S)$, whose definition depends on the used language, is expected to denote the set of all soft links in S. Recall that a soft link to a class is any of its

$$
\begin{aligned}
\texttt{P} &::= (\texttt{MDS}, \texttt{e}^s) & \text{application program} \\
\texttt{MDS} &::= \overline{\texttt{MD}} & \text{(source) component environment} \\
\texttt{MD} &::= \texttt{M} = \texttt{ME} & \text{component declaration} \\
\texttt{ME} &::= \texttt{M} \mid \texttt{BM} \mid \texttt{merge}(\texttt{ME}_1, \texttt{ME}_2) \mid \texttt{restrict}(\texttt{ME}, \texttt{c}) \mid & \text{component expression} \\
& \quad \texttt{rename}(\texttt{ME}, \texttt{c} \mapsto \texttt{c}') \mid \\
& \quad \texttt{bind}(\texttt{ME}, \texttt{d} \mapsto \texttt{n}) \mid \texttt{unbind}(\texttt{ME}, \texttt{c} \mapsto \texttt{d}) \\
\texttt{BM} &::= \{\overline{\texttt{c}}; \texttt{S}\} & \text{basic component}
\end{aligned}
$$

where: component/class names declared in MDS/BM are distinct;
$in(\mathsf{S}) \subseteq \overline{c} \cup out(\mathsf{S})$ in BM

Fig. 1. Syntax

unqualified occurrences except those which introduce the declaration of either
the class itself, or any of its constructors.

For instance, in `component M={class C{ C(){...} M.C m(C arg){...}}}`
only the last occurrence of C is a soft link to C, whereas M.C is a hard link, that
is, a link permanently anchored to the declaration of C inside M.

Defined class names are not associated permanently with a class definition in
the component, but their definition can be changed later when composing the
component with others. In other words, classes are all considered *virtual*.

Composition operators include `merge`, `restrict`, `rename`, `bind`, and `unbind`.
The reduction relations over programs, component environments, declarations
and expressions are defined by the rules in Figure 2. For simplicity, we use the
same symbol for the reduction relations over the four different sets of terms,
since such sets are mutually disjoint.

Values for component expressions are basic components BM, whereas a component declaration M = ME is expected to reduce to a declaration of a basic
component M = BM. Analogously, component environments are expected to reduce to environments of basic components $\overline{\texttt{M} = \texttt{BM}}$.

Rule (*prog*) corresponds to the intuition that the component environment of
the program needs first to be reduced to a collection of declarations of basic
components; then, the reduced component environment is closed by completing
simple class names with their corresponding qualified version, and, finally, in
the context of the class definitions extracted from the elaborated component
environment, the reduction of $\texttt{e}^s$ can start (*prog2*) according to the reduction
relation $\rightarrow_{core}$ at the level of the programming language.

The auxiliary functions *classes* and *close* are trivially defined by

$$
\begin{aligned}
classes(\overline{\texttt{M} = \{\overline{\texttt{c}}; \texttt{S}\}}) &= \overline{\texttt{S}} \\
close(\overline{\texttt{M} = \{\overline{\texttt{c}}; \texttt{S}\}}) &= \overline{\texttt{M} = \{\overline{\texttt{c}}; close_{\texttt{M}}(\texttt{S})\}}
\end{aligned}
$$

The definition of $close_{\texttt{M}}$, though trivial (simple class names are qualified by
M), depends on the used language; the instantiation for FJ can be found in [4].

$$(prog)\frac{\text{MDS} \rightarrow \text{MDS}'}{(\text{MDS}, e^s) \rightarrow (\text{MDS}', e^s)}$$

$$(prog2)\frac{(S, e^s) \rightarrow_{core} (S, e^{s'})}{(\overline{M = BM}, e^s) \rightarrow (\overline{M = BM}, e^{s'})} \quad S \equiv classes(close(\overline{M = BM}))$$

$$(mdecs)\frac{\text{MD} \rightarrow \text{MD}'}{\overline{M = BM} \text{ MD MDS} \rightarrow \overline{M = BM} \text{ MD}' \text{ MDS}}$$

$$(mdecs2)\frac{}{\overline{M = BM} \text{ MD MDS} \rightarrow \overline{M = BM} \text{ MD}' \text{ MDS}} \quad \begin{array}{l} \text{MD}' \equiv \text{MD}[\overline{BM/M}] \\ \text{MD}' \not\equiv \text{MD} \end{array}$$

$$(mdec)\frac{\text{ME} \rightarrow \text{ME}'}{M = \text{ME} \rightarrow M = \text{ME}'}$$

$$(merge)\frac{}{\text{merge}(\{\overline{c}_1; S_1\}, \{\overline{c}_2; S_2\}) \rightarrow \{\overline{c}; S_1 S_2\}} \quad \begin{array}{l} \overline{c} = \overline{c}_1 \overline{c}_2 \setminus out(S_1 S_2) \\ out(S_1) \cap out(S_2) = \emptyset \end{array}$$

$$(restrict)\frac{}{\text{restrict}(\{\overline{c}; S \, cd^s\}, c) \rightarrow \{\overline{c} \, c; S\}} \quad out(cd^s) = c$$

$$(rename)\frac{}{\text{rename}(\{\overline{c}; S\}, c \mapsto c') \rightarrow \{\overline{c}; S\}[c'/c]} \quad \begin{array}{l} c \in \overline{c} \cup out(S) \\ c' \notin \overline{c} \cup out(S) \end{array}$$

$$(bind)\frac{}{\text{bind}(\{\overline{c} \, d; S\}, d \mapsto n) \rightarrow \{\overline{c}; S[n/d]\}} \quad n \text{ qualified or } n \in out(S)$$

$$(unbind)\frac{}{\text{unbind}(\{\overline{c}; S\}, c \mapsto d) \rightarrow \{\overline{c} \, d; S[d/in \, c]\}} \quad \begin{array}{l} c \in out(S) \\ d \notin \overline{c} \cup out(S) \end{array}$$

Fig. 2. Reduction rules

In a component environment, component declarations are sequentially processed from left to right. The leftmost declaration MD which is not fully reduced yet is selected, and, either a reduction step can be applied to MD (*mdecs*), or some name M_i of previously declared components can be substituted with the corresponding basic expression (*mdecs2*). Note that even though the two rules are not mutually exclusive, the reduction relation turns out to be confluent. The side condition MD' $\not\equiv$ MD avoids loops, whereas MD[$\overline{BM/M}$] denotes parallel substitution of M_i with BM_i, for $i \in 1..n$, in MD. The inductive definition of such substitution is standard, except for the following case: $\{\overline{c}; S\}[\overline{BM/M}] = \{\overline{c}; S\}$. Substitution is not propagated inside components, since hard links are allowed to establish mutual dependencies between components.

Rule (*mdec*) is straightforward.

We denote by $S[c'/in\ c]$ the class definitions obtained from S by replacing every soft link to c by c'. Recall that references to c are all occurrences of c except those which either occur in qualified names, or introduce the declaration of either c, or one of its constructors.

Finally, $\overline{c}[c'/c]$ denotes the replacement of c with c' in $\overline{c}$, if present, and $S[c'/c]$ denotes the replacement of simple class name c (but not of qualified names of shape $M.c$) with c'. That is, $S[c'/c]$ differs from $S[c'/in\ c]$ since it also replaces declaring occurrences. Again, the precise definitions of $\_[\_/in\ \_]$ and $\_[\_/\_]$ depend on the core language.

The reduction relation for component expressions is defined as the compatible closure of the corresponding rules, since, for brevity, we have omitted the usual congruence rules. Even though it is not deterministic, the reduction relation is clearly confluent by orthogonality.

Merging two basic components (*merge*) corresponds to just putting together their class definitions ($S_1\ S_2$), provided that there are no conflicts ($out(S_1) \cap out(S_2) = \emptyset$), whereas the deferred classes are those of the two components which do not match with a defined class ($\overline{c}_1\overline{c}_2 \setminus out(S_1 S_2)$); note that deferred classes are shared.

The restrict operator (*restrict*) removes the definition of a class c in a basic component, and makes c a deferred class.

The rename operator (*rename*) performs a bijective renaming of a class c into c' in a basic component BM: c must be either a deferred or a defined class in BM, whereas c' must be new, that is, neither deferred nor defined in BM. Recall that qualified names are not affected by the substitution.

The bind operator (*bind*) replaces all soft links to a deferred class[8] with the name of a defined class of the same component or with a qualified class name. Conversely, the unbind operator (*unbind*) replaces all soft links to a defined class with a new deferred class.

As final remark, note that all the composition operators can be expressed as a combination of operators in (mixin) module calculi, such as CMS [6]. Indeed, **merge** (called *link* in [6]) and **restrict** are exactly the corresponding operators of the CMS version with virtual components, whereas **rename**, **bind** and **unbind** can all be obtained as special instances of the CMS *reduct* operator which allows independent renaming of input and output names (in **rename** names which are both input and output are renamed in the same way, and only bijective renamings are considered; in **bind** an input name is renamed to an output name; finally, in **unbind** an input name is renamed to a fresh name). Hence, the semantics of our component language could be equivalently given by translation into CMS. However, we preferred here a direct semantics since it is more intuitive for most readers. Note also that **unbind** operator, which seems at a first sight to change the inner structure of a component, actually can safely be expressed by module operators which consider a component as a black box, relying on the CMS distinction between (external) names and (internal) variables which

---

[8] Note that all soft links to a deferred class are just all unqualified occurrences of c, hence $S[n/d]$ and $S[n/in\ d]$ coincide here.

we have omitted here for simplicity: that is, only the input name is changed, whereas the variable used in internal code is kept. This model exactly reflects what happens at the implementation level.

4   Implementation

In this section we discuss how we have implemented a prototype compiler for the framework we have presented; it can be downloaded (along with its sources and some examples) at: `http://www.disi.unige.it/person/LagorioG/SmartJavaComp/` This compiler supports a small Java subset, which extends the language used in the instantiation of the framework described in [4]; in addition to some syntactic shortcuts it supports primitive types, assignments, implicit use of `this`, the literal `null`, `void` methods, constructor overload and basic statements. All examples shown in the paper can be tested.

Our prototype consists of two programs: the *compiler* and the *deployer*. The former generates `.bc` component binary files from `.sjc` component source files, and the latter assembles component binary files into standard `.jar` files. These resulting JAR files are directly executable on any JVM (Java Virtual Machine). A `.sjc` file contains a single component declaration MD as in Fig.1, where the language used for writing class definitions is the small Java subset described above. A `.bc` file (a binary component) is (roughly) a collection of Java classes in polymorphic bytecode format, each one equipped with its constraints. A basic component is compiled by compiling in isolation any class definition, by implementing the type system for separate compilation defined in [2], extended to the considered language.

Component declarations where unbound component names appear only in qualified names can be compiled in total isolation. On the other hand, component declarations which depend on other components can be compiled only if these components are already available in binary form. In this case, our compiler acts also as a linker, that is, it generates a new `.bc` file by also using those binary files.

When components are compiled, type constraints are checked for consistency; unfortunately, some errors could be undetected as long as components remain open. Luckily, verification of constraints is complete in case of closed components [2].

Because binary components contain polymorphic bytecode, they cannot be directly loaded, much less executed, by a standard JVM. In order to obtain a standard Java "executable" (that is, a JAR archive containing a proper *manifest*) from a set of `.bc` binary files, we must *deploy* them.

The deployer can assemble components into a single executable, after having checked that these components complete each other without clashing; that is, when the collection of Java class signatures extracted from these components is well-formed[9] and all type constraints of components can be simplified in this environment of class signatures.

---

[9] The class hierarchy is acyclic and there is no bad overriding/overloading.

5   Conclusion

We have presented a parametric framework of components for Java-like languages where a component is a collection of (binary) classes, each one equipped with type constraints on used classes. These type constraints guarantee *safe* linking of components; moreover, linking is *flexible*, in the sense that type constraints are abstract enough to never reject safe compositions, and components can be combined by a set of powerful (mixin) module operators.

A concrete instantiation of the framework can be provided by giving a suitable intermediate language: Java bytecode or .NET intermediate language does not allow fully adaptive components since, roughly speaking, they do not abstract away from all the possible contexts where open components can be safely used. However, as shown in [2], it is possible to define more abstract binary languages which are adequate to this aim. Our work until now, both in [2] and in the prototype accompanying this paper, has focused on extending Java bytecode, by adding type variables and type constraints. However, instantiations based on .NET intermediate language are feasible and interesting as well; moreover, they would be even more appealing, being .NET an intermediate language which does not rely on a particular source language, so the corresponding component framework would allow interoperability among components written in any language which targets .NET. We plan to investigate this possibility further.

Basic components are constructed, as mentioned above, in a particular language. Again, the framework can be instantiated on any source language which allows compilation in isolation of classes in the given binary language.

The semantics of the component language is defined in terms of reduction into basic components, that is, collection of class declarations.

To show the effectiveness of the approach, we have provided in [4] a complete formal description of an instantiation of the framework on Featherweight Java [15], which uses the type system for compositional compilation in [2]. Moreover, we have developed a prototype implementation on a small Java subset, which implements a large extension of this type system.

In literature there exist several proposals to better support component programming in object-oriented languages.

MzScheme [13] and Jiazzi [17] components are mixins which can be statically linked, in a way similar to our approach. MzScheme is built on top of Scheme and is not statically typed; Jiazzi is inspired by MzScheme, but is defined on top of Java, and is statically typed.

Other related papers propose language level abstractions for component-oriented programming allowing components to be first-class entities. ComponentJ [18], ArchJava [1], and ACOEL [19] are Java-like component-oriented languages, where components can be dynamically composed by explicitly connecting their *ports*. Ports basically play the role of required and provided interfaces in our framework.

ComponentJ promotes black-box object-oriented component programming style, by avoiding inheritance in favor of object composition.

ArchJava is an extension of Java with component classes; its type system allows for static checking of structural conformance between architecture and implementation.

ACOEL is an extensional language for supporting black-box components which uses mixins and virtual types to build adaptable applications.

Finally, Zenger [22] follows a more scalable approach, by proposing a component model where components are composed by type-safe high-level composition operators.

Differently to our approach, all the works above are less focused on the problem of programming language independence and interoperability of binary components. There are several short term enhancements on the design of the component language which could be considered: for instance, adding the possibility of hiding classes in components by making them private, or allowing non virtual classes (classes statically bound).

Long term future work includes at least two important directions. First, our binary components are linkable units, but not loadable units, that is, they cannot be replaced or serviced after application execution has started. Hence, we plan to study the possibility of considering a different semantics for the composition operators based on dynamic rather static linking, following the approach taken in [11,16] where models for virtual machines able to execute polymorphic bytecode have been defined.

Another limitation of the approach is that mutual consistency of components only means that type correctness is guaranteed, but of course does not imply that components satisfy some expected behaviour. To go more towards preservation of also semantic properties, one should develop an assertion-based version of both required and provided interfaces.

References

1. J. Aldrich, C. Chambers, and D. Notkin. Architectural reasoning in ArchJava. In B. Magnusson, editor, *ECOOP'02 - Object-Oriented Programming*, number 2374 in Lecture Notes in Computer Science, pages 334–367. Springer, 2002.
2. D. Ancona, F. Damiani, S. Drossopoulou, and E. Zucca. Polymorphic bytecode: Compositional compilation for Java-like languages. In *ACM Symp. on Principles of Programming Languages 2005*. ACM Press, January 2005.
3. D. Ancona, G. Lagorio, and E. Zucca. Smart modules for Java-like languages. In *7th Intl. Workshop on Formal Techniques for Java-like Programs 2005*, July 2005.
4. D. Ancona, G. Lagorio, and E. Zucca. A flexible and type-safe framework of components for Java-like languages. Technical report, Dipartimento di Informatica e Scienze dell'Informazione, Università di Genova, 2006. Submitted for journal publication.
5. D. Ancona and E. Zucca. True modules for Java-like languages. In J.L. Knudsen, editor, *ECOOP'01 - European Conference on Object-Oriented Programming*, number 2072 in Lecture Notes in Computer Science, pages 354–380. Springer, 2001.
6. D. Ancona and E. Zucca. A calculus of module systems. *Journ. of Functional Programming*, 12(2):91–132, 2002.

7. G. Bracha. *The Programming Language JIGSAW: Mixins, Modularity and Multiple Inheritance*. PhD thesis, Department of Comp. Sci., Univ. of Utah, 1992.
8. G. Bracha, M. Odersky, D. Stoutmire, and P. Wadler. Making the future safe for the past: Adding genericity to the Java programming language. In *ACM Symp. on Object-Oriented Programming: Systems, Languages and Applications 1998*, pages 183–200. ACM Press, October 1998.
9. K. B. Bruce and J. N. Foster. LOOJ: Weaving LOOM into Java. In *ECOOP'04 - Object-Oriented Programming*, number 3086 in Lecture Notes in Computer Science, pages 389–413, 2004.
10. K.B. Bruce, M. Odersky, and P. Wadler. A statically safe alternative to virtual types. In *ECOOP'98 - European Conference on Object-Oriented Programming*, number 1445 in Lecture Notes in Computer Science, pages 523–549, 1998.
11. Alex Buckley and Sophia Drossopoulou. Flexible Dynamic Linking. In *6th Intl. Workshop on Formal Techniques for Java Programs 2004*, June 2004.
12. Krzysztof Czarnecki and Ulrich Eisenecker. *Generative Programming: Methods, Tools, and Applications*. Addison-Wesley, 2000.
13. R.B. Findler and M. Flatt. Modular object-oriented programming with units and mixins. In *Intl. Conf. on Functional Programming 1998*, September 1998.
14. T. Hirschowitz and X. Leroy. Mixin modules in a call-by-value setting. In D. Le Métayer, editor, *ESOP 2002 - European Symposium on Programming 2002*, number 2305 in Lecture Notes in Computer Science, pages 6–20. Springer, 2002.
15. A. Igarashi, B. C. Pierce, and P. Wadler. Featherweight Java: a minimal core calculus for Java and GJ. *ACM Transactions on Programming Languages and Systems*, 23(3):396–450, 2001.
16. G. Lagorio. Dynamic linking of polymorphic bytecode. In *8th Intl. Workshop on Formal Techniques for Java-like Programs 2005*, July 2006.
17. S. McDirmid, M.Flatt, and W. Hsieh. Jiazzi: New age components for old fashioned Java. In *ACM SIGPLAN Conference on Object-Oriented Programming, Systems, Languages and Applications (OOPSLA 2001)*. ACM Press, October 2001.
18. J. Costa Seco and L. Caires. A basic model of typed components. In E. Bertino, editor, *ECOOP'00 - European Conference on Object-Oriented Programming*, number 1850 in Lecture Notes in Computer Science, pages 108–128. Springer, 2000.
19. V. C. Sreedhar. Mixin'up components. In *Proceedings of the 22rd International Conference on Software Engineering, ICSE 2002*, pages 198–207. ACM, 2002.
20. Clemens Szyperski. *Component Software: Beyond Object-Oriented Programming, 2nd Edition*. Addison Wesley, 2002.
21. M. Torgersen. The expression problem revisited. In M. Odersky, editor, *ECOOP'04 - Object-Oriented Programming*, number 3086 in Lecture Notes in Computer Science, pages 123–143. Springer, 2004.
22. M. Zenger. Type-safe prototype-based component evolution. In *ECOOP'02 - Object-Oriented Programming*, number 2374 in Lecture Notes in Computer Science, pages 470–497, Berlin, 2002. Springer.

Towards a Formal Semantics for AspectJ Weaving[*]

Nadia Belblidia and Mourad Debbabi

Computer Security Laboratory (CSL)
Concordia Institute for Information Systems Engineering
Concordia University
Montreal, H3G 1M8, Quebec, Canada
na_bel@ece.concordia.ca, debbabi@ciise.concordia.ca

Abstract. This paper ascribes a formal semantics to advice weaving in AspectJ. Since the version 1.1, AspectJ language is developed using bytecode weaving, which combines aspects and classes to produce ".class" files that run in a Java Virtual Machine (JVM). In AspectJ, advice weaving is done statically by inserting the advice functionality in some regions of the code. These regions are join points that are declared using pointcuts. In this paper, we focus only on static pointcuts, i.e., pointcuts that correspond directly to locations in the bytecode. AspectJ dynamic pointcuts such as `target`, `this`, and `cflow` are not in the focus of this paper.

1 Motivations and Background

Aspect Oriented Programming (AOP) [1] is a new computational paradigm that complements the Object Oriented Programming (OOP) paradigm by supporting modular implementation of a range of crosscutting concerns such as security and synchronization.

The acceptance of this new approach is growing rapidly due to the popularity of AspectJ [2], an aspect oriented extension to the Java programming language. The fundamental concepts of AspectJ approach are: Join points, pointcuts, and advices. A join point is an identifiable point in the execution of a program. A pointcut is a constructor that designates a set of join points. Advices are pieces of code attached to pointcuts and executed when the join points satisfying their pointcuts are reached. This is made possible thanks to the process of "advice weaving" that combines the base functionality of the application with advices. The process of advice weaving is implemented differently in the AOP languages. In AspectJ, it is done statically by inserting the advice functionality in certain regions of the program that correspond to the join points that are matched by the advice pointcut. These regions are called join points shadows and represent the textual part of the program executed during the considered join points. Since

---

[*] This research is the result of a fruitful collaboration between Concordia University, the Canadian Department of National Defense and Bell Canada under an NSERC DND Research Partnership Program.

D. Lightfoot and C. Szyperski (Eds.): JMLC 2006, LNCS 4228, pp. 155–171, 2006.

AspectJ-1.1, the advice weaving is based on bytecode transformation rather than on source code transformation. In this case, the AspectJ compiler is composed of two components. The first component (front-end compiler) is implemented as an extension to the Java compiler and compiles applications and aspects into pure Java bytecode that is enriched with additional annotations to handle non-pure Java information as advices and pointcuts. The second component (back-end compiler) weaves compiled aspects with compiled applications producing woven class files.

AOP is a very appealing approach, however most of the research contributions target practical implementation efforts rather than theoretical underpinnings. Furthermore, in spite of the fact that AspectJ is the defacto standard for AOP in Java, only one paper [3] described its advice weaving implementation.

In this paper, we present a formal description for AspectJ advice weaving. We are interested only in static pointcuts. A static pointcut operates and uses only compile-time information. Such pointcuts can be directly mapped to code and the advice weaving is represented by a direct call to the advice functionality. Contrarily to static pointcuts, dynamic pointcuts cannot be mapped to places in code but include some conditional logic (called residuals) in order to check some dynamic properties. This is the case of the dynamic pointcuts: `cflow`, `cflowbelow`, `if`, `this`, `target`, and `args` and the implementation of the residuals can be less or more complex depending on the pointcut in question. We plan to extend the proposed semantics in the near future by taking into account the dynamic pointcuts as well.

The rest of the paper is organized as follows. Section 2 discusses the state of the art on AspectJ semantics. Section 3 presents the syntax of a subset of JVML (Java Virtual Machine Language) and Section 4 is devoted to the description of the static pointcuts, the join points shadows, and the advices that we consider. Section 5 describes the ingredients that are used in the semantic description. The weaving semantics is given in Section 6 and finally some concluding remarks are reported in Section 7.

2   Related Work

The most relevant research contribution on this topic is the one advanced by Hilsdale and Hugunin in [3] where a complete description of the advice weaving implementation in AspectJ is reported. It was the first discussion of the implementation concerns in AspectJ. However, this description is not formal and the purpose of our paper is the formalization of this work.

Other relevant frameworks present a formalization of the AOP paradigm. Wand, Kiczales and Dutchyn [4] present a denotational semantics for point-cuts and advices for an AOP language defined in the Aspect Sand Box (ASB) project [5]. Jagadeesan, Jeffrey and Riely [6] present an operational semantics for an un-typed base language with multithreads, classes and objects. They enrich the syntax of the base language to handle aspects. Walker, Zdancewic and Ligatti [7] present an operational semantics for a simply-typed lambda calculus extended with two central new abstractions: Explicitly labelled program points and advices. The labels serve to trigger advice and to mark continuations that the advice may return to. The system is not intended to model constructs directly like AspectJ, but it is a calculus into which source-level AOP constructs can be translated. It could be considered more general than the existing AOP languages. Douence, Motelet and Sudholt present an operational semantics of an AOP system [8]. They describe a domain specific language for the definition of crosscuts. The system is based on a monitor that observes the behavior of the programs. The monitored program calls the monitor when an event is emitted and the monitor will then check if there is any crosscut at this point. This approach is called EAOP for Event Aspect Oriented Programming.

In contrast to all this research, our aim is to develop a formal semantics that describes the aspectJ back-end compiler task. The semantics that we propose shows how the back-end compiler uses the front-end compiler information in order to produce pure JVML code that can be executed by a JVM.

3   JVML Syntax

This section describes a concrete syntax for our JVM set of instructions. It contains simple instructions such as local variable access and stack manipulation as well as other more tricky instructions like thread creation, mutual exclusion and exceptions.

Table 1. JVML Bytecode Grammar

$JVMLInstruction ::=$	aload i		iload i		astore i
|	istore i	|	pop	|	push n
|	dup	|	iadd	|	new i
|	ifeq adr	|	ifne adr	|	goto adr
|	return	|	ireturn	|	areturn
|	athrow i	|	monitorenter	|	monitorexit
|	invokevirtual i	|	invokespecial i	|	invokestatic i
|	invokeinterface i,n	|	getstatic i	|	putstatic i
|	getfield i	|	putfield i		

4   Pointcuts, Joinpoint Shadows and Advices

This section presents the join points, the join points shadows and the pointcuts considered in this paper. A join point is a point in the control flow graph of a running application whereas a pointcut determines a set of join points. A join point shadow represents the textual part of the program executed during the execution of the corresponding join point. AspectJ provides a number of base pointcuts that can be logically combined, using boolean operations, to construct more complex ones. An AspectJ pointcut is either a static pointcut or a dynamic pointcut. A static pointcut describes join points that can be determined by a

static analysis whereas a dynamic pointcut describes join points that cannot
be determined statically. The following AspectJ pointcut is a static one and
describes all the join points that are in the class A and call the void method
"logging" of class B.

    pointcut callLoggingFromAtoB(): `call`(void B.logging()) `&& within`(A);

whereas the next pointcut depends on the type of the executing object. A call
of a void method "logging" in a superclass of A might be a valid join point if
the object is an instance of A.

    pointcut callLoggingFromA(): `call`(void *.logging()) `&& this`(A);

In this paper, we address only AspectJ static pointcuts because they do not
require adding conditional logic (called residuals) in order to check the dynamic
properties. More precisely, we consider eight base pointcuts: "Method call",
"method execution", "advice execution", "within method code", "field get",
"field set", "static class initialization" and "within class"[1]. These base pointcuts can be combined with boolean operators as described in the formal syntax
in Table 2. The set of corresponding join points and join point shadows where
advice weaving may intervene is given in Table 3. As we can notice, there are two
cases of join point shadows: The case where the shadow is exactly one instruction and the case where the shadow is an entire method. Notice also that the
pointcuts "within method code" and "within class" do not by themselves define
new shadows. They use the shadows defined by the other six static pointcuts.

In this paper, we consider an advice as either a `Before` advice or an `After` advice. The shadows that correspond to a method execution (including the "clinit"
method) or advice execution are entire methods and we need to delimit the beginning and the end of such shadows. For this purpose, we will assume that
the front-end compiler has inserted a special code `impdep1`[2] to mark the start
of a method or advice execution. The end of method or advice execution are
determined by the "return" instructions. For this reason, we introduce the notions of "before shadow" and "after shadow". We consider that an instruction
in the code of the pre-compiled application can be a before shadow, an after
shadow or none of them. In case of a `Before` advice, all the before shadows are
checked for an eventual matching with the advice pointcut. In case of an `After`
advice, all the after shadows are checked for matching with the advice pointcut.
Each instruction among: `invokevirtual`, `invokestatic`, `invokeinterface`,
`invokespecial`, `getfield`,
`getstatic`, `putfield`, or `putstatic` is both a before shadow and an after
shadow because it can be a candidate for a weaving either for a `Before` advice or an `After` advice and should be considered in both cases. The mnemonics `impdep1` are before shadows and all return methods `return` or `ireturn` or
`areturn` are after shadows.

---

[1] In order to ease the semantics reading, we do not use any regular expression patterns
for pointcuts, such as m(..) or *.

[2] AspectJ compiler inserts `idemp1` mnemonics before and after all the join points
shadows. In our case, we insert this code just before the execution shadow.

Table 2. Pointcut Syntax

Pcut	::= *BasePcut*	|	*BooleanPcut*
BasePcut	::= `mcall`(*MethodPattern*)	|	`mexecution`(*MethodPattern*)
	`aexecution`()	|	`withincode`(*MethodPattern*)
	`get`(*FieldPattern*)	|	`set`(*FieldPattern*)
	`staticInit`(*ComponentType*)	|	`within`(*ComponentType*)
BooleanPcut	::= *Pcut* **or** *Pcut*	|	**not** *Pcut*
	Pcut **and** *Pcut*		

MethodPattern	::= ⟨ methodModifiers: (*MethodModifier*)`-set`,
	methodSignature: *MethodSignature*,
	componentType: *ComponentType* ⟩
FieldPattern	::= ⟨ fieldModifiers:(*FieldModifier*)`-set`,
	fieldSignature:*FieldSignature*,
	componentType: *ComponentType* ⟩
MethodSignature	::= ⟨ name:`Identifier`,
	argumentsType:(*Type*)`-list`,
	resultType:*Type* ⟩
FieldSignature	::= ⟨ name:`Identifier`,
	type:*Type* ⟩
MethodModifier	::= `public` | `private` | `static` | `synchronized`
FieldModifier	::= `public` | `private` | `static`
ComponentType	::= *ReferenceType* | *AspectType*
ResultType	::= *Type*
	| `void`
Type	::= *PrimitiveType*
	| *ReferenceType*
ReferenceType	::= *ClassType*
	| *InterfaceType*
ClassType	::= `Identifier`
InterfaceType	::= `Identifier`
AspectType	::= `Identifier`

Table 3. Join Points Shadows

DYNAMIC JOIN POINT	JOIN POINT SHADOW
Method call	`invokevirtual` *i*
	`invokespecial` *i* (for private methods)
	`invokestatic` *i*
	`invokeinterface` *i,n*
Field get	`getfield` *i*
	`getstatic` *i*
Field set	`putfield` *i*
	`putstatic` *i*
Method execution	Entire method's code
Advice execution	Entire advice's code
Static initialization	Entire `clinit` method code

5   Semantics Ingredients

In this section, we define the ingredients that are used in the semantic description. Accordingly, we introduce and define the notions of environment and configurations. We will use the following notation along this paper.

Notation

- Given two sets A and B, $A \xrightarrow{m} B$ denotes the set of all mappings (maps for short) from A to B (partial functions from A to B). A map $m \in A \xrightarrow{m} B$ could be defined by extension as $[a_0 \mapsto b_0 \ldots a_{n-1} \mapsto b_{n-1}]$ to denote the association of the elements b_i's to a_i's, where $a_i \in A$ et $b_i \in B$.
- Given a map m from X to Y, the domain of m, X, is written $\mathrm{Dom}(m)$.
- Given a partial map f, we write $f[x \mapsto v]$ to denote the updating operation of f that yields a map that is equivalent to f except that x is from now on associated with v.
- Given a record space $D = \langle f_1 : D_1, f_2 : D_2, \ldots, f_n : D_n \rangle$ and an element e of type D, the access to the field f_i of e is written $e.f_i$ and the update of the fields $f_{i1}, \ldots, f_{ik}$ in e by the values $v_{i1}, \ldots, v_{ik} \in D_{i1}, \ldots, D_{ik}$ is written $e[f_{i1} \leftarrow v_{i1}, \ldots, f_{ik} \leftarrow v_{ik}]$.
- Given a type τ, we write (τ)-list to denote the type of lists having elements of type τ.
- Given a type τ, we write (τ)-set to denote the type of sets having elements of type τ.
- The type Identifier classifies identifiers whereas *NoneType* classifies the unique value None.

5.1   Environment

We define hereafter the environment as prepared by the front-end stage of the compiler. We assume that the reader is familiar with the class file format as described in the official specification of JVML [9]. The environment as described in Table 4 models the different program declarations and is represented as a record containing a Java environment and advices.

The Java environment is quite similar to the dynamic environment under which the execution will be done after the weaving. The only difference is the existence of the idemp1 code in the method codes. The front-end compiler injects at the beginning of all methods (or advices) an idemp1 code to mark the beginning of the method (or advice) execution. After the weaving, the idemp1 codes are removed from the method and advice codes.

The Java environment is a map that associates a set of classes to a set of component types. We consider that an aspect can be viewed as a class and its advices are represented by the methods of the class. A class is a record containing a constant pool, a super-class, a set of interfaces, a list of fields, a map that associates values to static fields, a list of methods, three flags that indicate whether the class is initialized or not, is an interface or not, is an aspect or not and a monitor. A constant pool is a map that associates a set of integers with a set of constant pool entries. A constant pool entry can be a class type, a pair of a method signature and a supposed class, or a pair of a field signature and a supposed class. Whenever a constant pool entry is a class type, this means it has been created when the compiler encountered a Java instruction of the form A a = new B(). The compiler then generates the corresponding new and invokespecial instructions and a class constant pool entry initialized to B. In the two other cases of constant pool entries, the supposed class represents the class in which the method or the field is supposed to be found. The value None for the super class indicates that the class does not have a super class. The monitor associated with a class is a record of three components: *threadOwner*, *depth* and a *waitList*. If the class is not locked the monitor is set to the value $\langle \text{None}, 0, [\ ] \rangle$. Otherwise the monitor contains the thread identifier that locked the class, the number of times this class has been locked by the same thread and a list of all the threads blocked waiting for this class. A method consists of a method signature, a class name in which the method has been defined, a set of modifiers, an initial code idemp1 followed by a bytecode sequence, and a list of method variables. A method signature is a record that contains the method name, the types of arguments and the result type. The list of the method variables contains the default values of all local variables defined inside the method. The method parameters are not considered in the method variables. A field is represented by a record that contains a field signature, a class type to which the field belongs to, and a set of modifiers. An advice is represented by a record containing its kind, its pointcut, its signature, and the aspect where the advice has been defined.

5.2 Configurations

The operational semantics is based on the evolution of configurations that are defined hereafter. Weaving a class with some aspects is the result of weaving all its methods with the considered aspects. For this reason, we restrict ourselves to describe only the weaving inside one method and a configuration will then have the following form:

$$\langle \mathcal{E}, m, pc, ads, nextpc \rangle$$

where:

- $\mathcal{E}$ represents the environment.
- m is the current method.
- pc represents the program counter that contains the address of the instruction to be advised in the method m.
- ads represents the advices to consider.
- $nextpc$ represents the program counter for the next instruction to consider.

Table 4. Environment Before Weaving

Environment	::=	⟨ javaEnvironment: *JavaEnvironment*,
		advices: (*AdviceInfo*)-`list` ⟩
JavaEnvironment	::=	*ComponentType* $\xrightarrow{m}$ *Class*
Class	::=	⟨ constantPool: *ConstantPool*,
		superClass: *ClassType* | *NoneType*,
		interfaces: (*ClassType*)-`set`,
		fields: (*Field*)-`list`,
		staticMap: *Field* $\xrightarrow{m}$ *Value*,
		methods: (*Method*)-`list`,
		initialized: *Int*,
		interface: *Int*,
		aspect: *Int*,
		monitorClass: *Monitor* ⟩
ConstantPool	::=	*Int* $\xrightarrow{m}$ *ConstantPoolEntry*
ConstantPoolEntry	::=	*ClassType* | *MethodPoolEntry* | *FieldPoolEntry*
MethodPoolEntry	|	⟨ methodSignature: *MethodSignature*,
		supposedClass: *ClassType* ⟩
FieldPoolEntry	|	⟨ fieldSignature: *FieldSignature*,
		supposedClass: *ClassType* ⟩
Monitor	::=	⟨ threadOwner: *ThreadOwner*,
		depth: *Nat*,
		waitList: *WaitingList* ⟩
ThreadOwner	::=	*ThreadId* | *NoneType*
WaitingList	::=	(*ThreadId*)-`list`
ThreadId	::=	*Nat*
Field	::=	⟨ fieldSignature: *FieldSignature*,
		fromClass: *ComponentType*,
		fieldModifiers: (*FieldModifier*)-`set` ⟩
Method	::=	⟨ methodSignature: *MethodSignature*,
		fromClass: *ComponentType*,
		methodModifiers: (*MethodModifier*)-`set`,
		code: *Code*,
		methodVariables: *MethodVariables* ⟩
AdviceInfo	::=	⟨ kind: {`Before`, `After`},
		pointcut: *Pcut*,
		fromClass: *AspectType*,
		adviceSignature: *MethodSignature* ⟩
Code	::=	*ProgramCounter* $\xrightarrow{m}$ *Instruction*
Instruction	::=	*JVMLInstruction* | `impdep1`
ProgramCounter	::=	*Nat*
MethodVariables	::=	(*Value*)-`list`

6   Weaving Semantics

This section is devoted to the description of the semantics, which contains five rules. All the utility functions used inside the rules are described in the appendix of this paper.

The first rule of the semantics describes the case where the instruction in the method m at the program counter pc is not a shadow or the advice list is empty (all the advices have been treated for this instruction). In such cases, the current instruction is skipped and the list of advices is reset to its initial value (all the advices of the environment).

$$\frac{(\neg\mathsf{isBeforeShadow}(m, pc) \wedge \neg\mathsf{isAfterShadow}(m, pc)) \vee ads = [\,]}{\langle \mathcal{E}, m, pc, ads, nextpc \rangle \longrightarrow \langle \mathcal{E}, m, nextpc, \mathcal{E}.\mathsf{advices}, nextpc + 1 \rangle}$$

The second rule fires in the case where the head of the advice list is a `Before` advice but is not applicable to the current instruction. This advice is then removed and we reconsider the possibility of weaving the same instruction with the remaining list of advices.

$$\frac{\begin{array}{c}\mathsf{head}(ads).\mathsf{kind} = \mathtt{Before} \\ \neg\mathsf{isBeforeAdviceApplicable}\ (\mathcal{E}, m, pc, \mathsf{head}(ads))\end{array}}{\langle \mathcal{E}, m, pc, ads, nextpc \rangle \longrightarrow \langle \mathcal{E}, m, pc, \mathsf{tail}(ads), nextpc \rangle}$$

The third rule of the semantics represents the case where the head of the advice list is a `Before` advice and is applicable to the current instruction. In this case, the method and the environment are changed because of the `Before` advice merging. The program counter of the current instruction will change also because of the `Before` advice injection.

$$\frac{\begin{array}{c}\mathsf{head}(ads).kind = \mathtt{Before} \\ \mathsf{isBeforeAdviceApplicable}(\mathcal{E}, m, pc, \mathsf{head}(ads)) \\ (\mathcal{E}', m', pc') = \mathsf{insertBeforeAdvice}(\mathcal{E}, m, pc, \mathsf{head}(ads))\end{array}}{\langle \mathcal{E}, m, pc, ads, nextpc \rangle \longrightarrow \langle \mathcal{E}', m', pc', \mathsf{tail}(ads), pc' + 1 \rangle}$$

The fourth rule depicts the case where the head of the advice list is an `After` advice but is not applicable to the current instruction. The head of the advice list is then removed and we reconsider the possibility of weaving with the remaining list of advices.

$$\frac{\begin{array}{c}\mathsf{head}(ads).\mathsf{kind} = \mathtt{After} \\ \neg\mathsf{isAfterAdviceApplicable}\ (\mathcal{E}, m, pc, \mathsf{head}(ads))\end{array}}{\langle \mathcal{E}, m, pc, ads, nextpc \rangle \longrightarrow \langle \mathcal{E}, m, pc, \mathsf{tail}(ads), nextpc \rangle}$$

The fifth and last rule of the semantics represents the case where the head of the advice list is an `After` advice and is applicable to the current instruction. In this case, the method and the environment are changed because of the `After` advice merging. The program counters of the current instruction and next instruction will change also because of the **After** advice injection.

$$\frac{\begin{array}{c}\mathrm{head}(ads).kind = \texttt{After}\\ \mathrm{isAfterAdviceApplicable}(\mathcal{E}, m, pc, \mathrm{head}(ads))\\ (\mathcal{E}', m', pc', nextpc') = \mathrm{insertAfterAdvice}(\mathcal{E}, m, pc, \mathrm{head}(ads), nextpc)\end{array}}{\begin{array}{c}\langle \mathcal{E}, m, pc, ads, nextpc\rangle \longrightarrow\\ \langle \mathcal{E}', m', pc', tail(ads), nextpc'\rangle\end{array}}$$

We assume that the operational semantics stops when there are no more instructions in the method to be treated.

7 Conclusion and Future Work

In this paper, we reported a formalization of the static weaving in AspectJ. More precisely, the semantics allows to describe the weaving in presence of static pointcuts. To handle the case where join points shadows are complete methods as for method-execution, advice execution, and static initialization, we introduce two kinds of shadows "before shadow" and "after shadow". This allows us to delimit the start of the shadow and its end. We believe that our work is a first step in developing a formal semantics for AspectJ weaving. As future work, we intend to extend this semantics in order to take into account dynamic pointcuts as cflow.

References

1. Gregor Kiczales, John Lamping, Anurag Menhdhekar, Chris Maeda, Cristina Lopes, Jean-Marc Loingtier, and John Irwin. Aspect-oriented programming. In Mehmet Akşit and Satoshi Matsuoka, editors, *Proceedings European Conference on Object-Oriented Programming*, volume 1241, pages 220–242. Springer-Verlag, Berlin, Heidelberg, and New York, 1997.
2. Gregor Kiczales, Erik Hilsdale, Jim Hugunin, Mik Kersten, Jeffrey Palm, and William Griswold. An Overview of AspectJ. Budapest, 2001. Springer Verlag.
3. Erik Hilsdale and Jim Hugunin. Advice weaving in AspectJ. In *3rd International Conference on Aspect-oriented Software Development (AOSD)*, pages 26–35, 2004.
4. M. Wand, G. Kiczales, and C. Dutchyn. A Semantics for Advice and Dynamic Join Points in Aspect-Oriented Programming. *ACM Trans. Program. Lang. Syst.*, 26(5):890–910, 2004.
5. C. Dutchyn, G. Kiczales, and H. Masuhara. Aspect Sand Box Project. http://www.cs.ubc.ca/labs/spl/projects/asb.html, 2002.
6. R. Jagadeesan, A. Jeffrey, and J. Riely. A Calculus of Untyped Aspect-Oriented Programs. In *ECOOP*, pages 54–73, 2003.
7. D. Walker, S. Zdancewic, and J. Ligatti. A Theory of Aspects, 2003.
8. R. Douence, O. Motelet, and M. Südholt. A Formal Definition of Crosscuts. *Lecture Notes in Computer Science*, 2192:170–184, 2001.
9. T. Lindholm and F. Yellin. *The Java Virtual Machine Specification, Second Edition*. Addison Wesley, 1999.

APPENDIX: Utility Functions

1. The function changeMethods changes a given method contained in a given list by another given method:

   changeMethods   : $(Method)$-list$\times Method \times Method \rightarrow (Method)$-list
   changeMethods(l,m,m') = head(l)::changeMethods(tail$(l),m,m'$)
                             if head(l).signature $\neq m$.signature
   changeMethods(l,m,m') = m'::tail(l)
                             if head(l).signature $= m$.signature

2. The function head returns the first element in a given list:

   head   : (τ)-list $\rightarrow \tau$
   head$(v$::$l)$ = v, $\forall$ $(v, l) \in \tau \times (\tau)$-list

3. The function insertAfterAdvice takes an environment, a method, a program counter, an advice and the program counter of the next instruction as arguments and returns a new environment, a new method (where the advice has been injected), and the program counters of the two next instructions to treat. It injects the advice in the method by injecting two JVML instructions: The call to the static "aspectOf" method of the advice aspect, and the advice call itself. This corresponds to the injection of two bytecodes: invokestatic i and invokevirtual j where i and j are added as new entries to the constant pool of the method class. It is necessary to call the static "aspectOf" method of the aspect to obtain an instance for use as the receiver of the advice call. The "aspectOf" method is automatically generated when compiling the aspect into a class:

   insertAfterAdvice : $Environment \times Method \times ProgramCounter \times AdviceInfo \times$
        $ProgramCounter \rightarrow Environment \times method \times ProgramCounter \times ProgramCounter$
   insertAfterAdvice$(\mathcal{E},m,pc,ad,nextpc) = (\mathcal{E}',m',pc',nextpc')$ if

   $\left(\begin{array}{l} \neg\text{isReturn}(m, pc) \\ \wedge \ \mathcal{JE} = \mathcal{E}.javaEnvironment \\ \wedge \ c = \mathcal{JE}(m.fromClass) \\ \wedge \ cpool = c.constantPool \ //Getting \ the \ Constant \ pool \ of \ the \ class \ of \ m. \\ \wedge \ ms = \text{signatureAspectOf}(ad) \\ \wedge \ cpool1 = cpool[i \mapsto \text{newPoolEntry}(ms, ad.fromClass)], \ i \notin Dom(cpool) \\ \wedge \ cpool2 = cpool1[j \mapsto \text{newPoolEntry}(ad.adviceSignature, ad.fromClass)] \\ \qquad j \notin Dom(cpool1) \\ \wedge \ code1 = m.code[k + 2 \mapsto m.code(k)], \ \forall \ k \in Dom(m.code) \ / \ k >= pc + 1 \\ \wedge \ code2 = code1[pc + 1 \mapsto \text{invokestatic} \ i] \ //Adding \ invokestatic \ i \ to \ m. \\ \wedge \ code3 = code2[pc + 2 \mapsto \text{invokevirtual} \ j] \ //Adding \ invokevirtual \ j \ to \ m. \\ \wedge \ m' = m[code \leftarrow code3] \ //Setting \ the \ code \ of \ m \ with \ the \ updates. \\ \wedge \ c1 = c[constantPool \leftarrow cpool2, \\ \qquad methods \leftarrow \text{ChangeMethods}(c1.methods, m, m')] \\ \wedge \ \mathcal{JE}1 = \mathcal{JE}[m.fromClass \mapsto c1] \ //Updating \ the \ class \ where \ m \ is \ defined. \\ \wedge \ pc' = pc \ //Considering \ the \ same \ instruction \ for \ next \ advice \ weaving. \\ \wedge \ netxtpc' = nextpc + 2 \ //Shifting \ next \ instruction. \\ \wedge \ \mathcal{E}' = \mathcal{E}[javaEnvironment \leftarrow \mathcal{JE}1] \end{array}\right.$

insertAfterAdvice : insertAfterAdvice($\mathcal{E}$,m,pc,ad,$nextpc$) =($\mathcal{E}$',m',pc',$nextpc$') if

$$\begin{cases} \text{isReturn}(m, pc) \\ \wedge\ (\mathcal{E}', m', pc') = \text{insertBeforeAdvice}(\mathcal{E}, m, pc, ad) \\ \wedge\ nextpc' = nextpc + 2 \end{cases}$$

4. The function insertBeforeAdvice takes an environment, a method, a program counter, and an advice as arguments and returns a new environment, a new method, and a new program counter after injecting the advice in the method. It works as the insertAfterAdvice except that the injection is done before the shadow:

insertBeforeAdvice : $Environment \times Method \times ProgramCounter \times AdviceInfo \rightarrow$
$$Environment \times method \times ProgramCounter$$

insertBeforeAdvice($\mathcal{E}$,m,pc,ad) =($\mathcal{E}$',m',pc') if

$$\begin{cases} \mathcal{JE} = \mathcal{E}.javaEnvironment \\ \wedge\ c = \mathcal{JE}(m.fromClass) \\ \wedge\ cpool = c.constantPool \\ \wedge\ ms = \text{signatureAspectOf}(ad) \\ \wedge\ cpool1 = cpool[i \mapsto \text{newPoolEntry}(ms, ad.fromClass)]\ i \notin Dom(cpool) \\ \wedge\ cpool2 = cpool1[j \mapsto \text{newPoolEntry}(ad.adviceSignature, ad.fromClass)] \\ \qquad\qquad j \notin Dom(cpool1) \\ \wedge\ code1 = m.code[k+2 \mapsto m.code(k)]\ \forall\ k \in Dom(m.code)/k >= pc \\ \wedge\ code2 = code1[pc \mapsto \texttt{invokestatic}\ i] \\ \wedge\ code3 = code2[pc+1 \mapsto \texttt{invokevirtual}\ j] \\ \wedge\ m' = m[code \leftarrow code3] \\ \wedge\ c1 = c[constantPool \leftarrow cpool2, \\ \qquad\qquad methods \leftarrow \text{ChangeMethods}(c1.methods, m, m')] \\ \wedge\ \mathcal{JE}1 = \mathcal{JE}[m.fromClass \mapsto c1] \\ \wedge\ pc' = pc + 2 \\ \wedge\ \mathcal{E}' = \mathcal{E}[javaEnvironment \leftarrow \mathcal{JE}1] \end{cases}$$

5. The function isAfterAdviseApplicable returns true if the given **After** advice is applicable in the method m at the program counter pc:

isAfterAdviseApplicable : $Environment \times Method \times ProgramCounter \times AdviceInfo$
$$\rightarrow Boolean$$
isAfterAdviseApplicable($\mathcal{E}$,m,pc,ad) =true if
$$\begin{cases} \text{isAfterShadow}(m, pc) \\ \wedge\ \text{matchAfterPcut}(\mathcal{E}, ad.pointcut, m, pc) \end{cases}$$
isAdviseApplicable(m,pc,ad) =false otherwise

6. The function isAfterShadow returns true if the instruction at the position pc in the method m can be a join point shadow for an **After** advice:

isAfterShadow : $Method \times ProgramCounter \rightarrow Boolean$
isAfterShadow(m,pc) =true if
$$\begin{cases} \text{isBeforeOrAfterShadow}(m, pc) \\ \vee\ m.Code(pc) = \texttt{return} \\ \vee\ m.Code(pc) = \texttt{ireturn} \\ \vee\ m.Code(pc) = \texttt{areturn} \end{cases}$$
isAfterShadow(m,pc) =false otherwise

7. The function isBeforeAdviseApplicable returns true if the given **Before** advice is applicable in the method m at the program counter pc. We distinguish between the case of execution shadow and the other shadows:

isBeforeAdviseApplicable : $Environment \times Method \times ProgramCounter \times AdviceInfo$
$\rightarrow Boolean$
isBeforeAdviseApplicable$(\mathcal{E},m,pc,ad)$ =true if
$\begin{cases} (m.Code(pc) = \texttt{impdep1} \wedge \texttt{matchBeforeExecut}(ad.pointcut, m)) \\ \vee \, \texttt{matchBeforeOtherExecut}(\mathcal{E},ad.pointcut,m,pc) \end{cases}$
isBeforeAdviseApplicable$(\mathcal{E},m,pc,ad)$ =false otherwise

8. The function isBeforeOrAfterShadow returns true if the instruction at the position pc in the method m can be a join point shadow for either a **Before** advice or an **After** advice:

isBeforeOrAfterShadow : $Method \times ProgramCounter \rightarrow Boolean$
isBeforeOrAfterShadow(m,pc) =true if
$\begin{cases} m.Code(pc) = \texttt{invokevirtual } i \\ \vee \, m.Code(pc) = \texttt{invokespecial } i \\ \vee \, m.Code(pc) = \texttt{invokestatic } i \\ \vee \, m.Code(pc) = \texttt{invokeinterface } i, n \\ \vee \, m.Code(pc) = \texttt{getstatic } i \\ \vee \, m.Code(pc) = \texttt{putstatic } i \\ \vee \, m.Code(pc) = \texttt{getfield } i \\ \vee \, m.Code(pc) = \texttt{putstatic } i \end{cases}$
isBeforeOrAfterShadow(m,pc) =false otherwise

9. The function isBeforeShadow returns true if the instruction at the position pc in the method m can be a join point shadow for a **Before** advice:

isBeforeShadow : $Method \times ProgramCounter \rightarrow Boolean$
isBeforeShadow(m,pc) =true if
$\begin{cases} \texttt{isBeforeOrAfterShadow}(m, pc) \\ \vee \, m.Code(pc) = \texttt{impdep1} \end{cases}$
isBeforeShadow(m,pc) =false otherwise

10. The function isFpatternMatched returns true if a given field matches a given field pattern:

isFpatternMatched : $FieldPattern \times Field \rightarrow Boolean$
isFpatternMatched(fp,f) = true if
$\begin{cases} fp.fieldSignature = f.fieldSignature \\ \wedge \, fp.componentType = f.fromClass \\ \wedge \, fp.fieldModifiers = f.fieldModifiers \end{cases}$
isFpatternMatched(mp,m) = false otherwise.

11. The function isMpatternMatched returns true if a given method matches a given method pattern:

isMpatternMatched :$MethodPattern \times Method \rightarrow Boolean$
isMpatternMatched$(mp,m) =$ true if
$\begin{cases} mp.methodSignature = m.methodSignature \\ \wedge\ mp.componentType = m.fromClass \\ \wedge\ mp.methodModifiers = m.methodModifiers \end{cases}$
isMpatternMatched$(mp,m) =$ false otherwise.

12. The function isReturn returns true if the instruction in the method m at the position pc is one of the "return" JVML instructions:

    isReturn :$Method \times ProgramCounter \rightarrow Boolean$
    isReturn$(m,pc) =$ true   if
    $\begin{cases} m.code(pc) = \texttt{return} \\ \vee\ m.code(pc) = \texttt{areturn} \vee \\ \vee\ m.code(pc) = \texttt{ireturn} \end{cases}$
    isReturn$(m,pc) =$ false otherwise.

13. The function matchAfterAexecut returns true if the given method is an advice and the instruction at the given program counter is a "return" instruction:

    matchAfterAexecut :$Method \times ProgramCounter \rightarrow Boolean$
    matchAfterAexecut$(m,pc) =$ true if
    $\begin{cases} (m.fromClass).aspect = 1 \\ \wedge\ \text{isReturn}(m, pc) \end{cases}$
    matchAfterAexecut$(m,pc) =$ false otherwise.

14. The function matchAfterMexecut returns true if the given method pattern argument matches with the given method and the instruction at the given program counter is one of the "return" JVML instructions:

    matchAfterMexecut : $MethodPattern \times Method \times ProgramCounter \rightarrow Boolean$
    matchAfterMexecut$(mp,m,pc) =$ true if
    $\begin{cases} \text{isMpatternMatched}(mp, m) \\ \wedge\ \text{isReturn}(m, pc) \end{cases}$
    matchAfterMexecut$(mp,m,pc) =$ false otherwise.

15. The function matchAfterPcut returns true if the given **After** advice is applicable in the method m at the program counter pc:

    matchAfterPcut : $Environment \times Pointcut \times Method \times ProgramCounter \rightarrow Boolean$
    matchAfterPcut$(\mathcal{E},pcut1$ **and** $pcut2,m,pc) =$
           matchAfterPcut$(\mathcal{E},pcut1,m,pc) \wedge$ matchAfterPcut$(\mathcal{E},pcut2,m,pc)$
    matchAfterPcut$(\mathcal{E},pcut1$ **or** $pcut2,m,pc) =$
           matchAfterPcut$(\mathcal{E},pcut1,m,pc) \vee$ matchAfterPcut$(\mathcal{E},pcut2,m,pc)$
    matchAfterPcut$(\mathcal{E},$**not** $pcut,m,pc) = \neg$ matchAfterPcut$(\mathcal{E},pcut,m,pc)$
    matchAfterPcut$(\mathcal{E},pcut,m,pc) =$ matchPcut$(\mathcal{E},pcut,m,pc)$
           if $(pcut \in BasicPcut) \wedge (pcut <>\texttt{mexecution}(mp)) \wedge$
           $(pcut <>\texttt{staticInit}(ct)) \wedge (pcut <>\texttt{aexecution}())$

matchAfterPcut($\mathcal{E}$,mexecution(mp),m,pc) = matchAfterMexecut(mp,m,pc)
matchAfterPcut($\mathcal{E}$,staticInit(ct),m,pc) = matchAfterStaticInit(ct,m,pc)
matchAfterPcut($\mathcal{E}$,aexecution(),m,pc) = matchAfterAexecut(m,pc)

16. The function matchAfterStaticInit is called when the advice is an **After** advice and its pointcut is **staticInit**(ct). The function returns true if the given method is the "**clinit**" method of the class ct and the instruction in the method m at the position pc is one of the "return" JVML instructions:

matchAfterStaticInit : $Component Type \times Method \times Program Counter \rightarrow Boolean$
matchAfterStaticInit(ct,m,pc) = true if
$\begin{cases} m.fromClass = ct \\ \wedge\ (m.methodSignature).name = \text{"clinit"} \\ \wedge\ \mathsf{isReturn}(m, pc) \end{cases}$
matchAfterStaticInit(ct,m,pc) = false otherwise.

17. The function matchBeforeExecut returns true if the given pointcut $pcut$ of a **Before** advice matches as a method or advice execution of the given method :

matchBeforeExecut : $Pointcut \times Method \rightarrow Boolean$
matchBeforeExecut($pcut1$ **and** $pcut2$,m) =
        matchBeforeExecut($pcut1$,m)$\wedge$ matchBeforeExecut($pcut2$,m)
matchBeforeExecut($pcut1$ **or** $pcut2$,m) =
    matchBeforeExecut($pcut1$,m)$\vee$ matchBeforeExecut($pcut2$,m)
matchBeforeExecut(**not** $pcut$,m) = $\neg$ matchBeforeExecut($pcut$,m)
matchBeforeExecut(mcall(mp),m) = false
matchBeforeExecut(get(fp),m) = false
matchBeforeExecut(set(fp),m) = false
matchBeforeExecut(withincode(mp),m) = isMpatternMatched(mp,m)
matchBeforeExecut(within(ct),m) = ($m.fromClass{=}ct$)
matchBeforeExecut(mexecution(mp),m) = isMpatternMatched(mp,m)
matchBeforeExecut(staticInit(ct),m) =
    (($m.fromClass{=}ct$)$\wedge$ (($m.methodSignature).name{=}\text{"clinit"}$))
matchBeforeExecut(aexecution(),m) = (($m.fromClass$).aspect=1)

18. The function matchBeforeOtherExecut returns true if the given pointcut pc of a **Before** advice matches with the instruction at the position pc in the method m not as method or advice execution:

matchBeforeOtherExecut : $Environment \times Pointcut \times Method \times Program Counter \rightarrow$
                $Boolean$
matchBeforeOtherExecut($\mathcal{E}$,$pcut1$ **and** $pcut2$,m) =
matchBeforeOtherExecut($\mathcal{E}$,$pcut1$,m,pc) $\wedge$ matchBeforeOtherExecut($\mathcal{E}$,$pcut2$,m,pc)

matchBeforeOtherExecut($\mathcal{E}$,$pcut1$ **or** $pcut2$,m) =
matchBeforeOtherExecut($\mathcal{E}$,$pcut1$,m,pc)$\vee$ matchBeforeOtherExecut($\mathcal{E}$,$pcut2$,m,pc)

matchBeforeOtherExecut($\mathcal{E}$,not $pcut$,m,pc) =
¬ matchBeforeOtherExecut($\mathcal{E}$,$pcut$,m,pc)

matchBeforeOtherExecut($\mathcal{E}$,$pcut$,m,pc) = matchPcut($\mathcal{E}$,$pcut$,m,pc)
if ($pcut \in BasicPcut$) $\wedge$ ($pcut$ <>mexecution(mp)) $\wedge$
($pcut$ <>staticInit(ct)) $\wedge$ ($pcut$ <>aexecution())

matchBeforeOtherExecut($\mathcal{E}$,mexecution(mp),m,pc) = false
matchBeforeOtherExecut($\mathcal{E}$,staticInit(ct),m,pc) = false
matchBeforeOtherExecut($\mathcal{E}$,aexecution(),m,pc) = false

19. The function matchPcut is called from the functions matchBeforeOtherExecut, matchAfterPcut. The pointcut argument is one of the the following base pointcuts: mcall(mp), get(fp), set(fp), withincode(mp) and within(ct). The function returns true if the given pointcut matches with the instruction at the position pc in the method m:

matchPcut : $Environment \times Pointcut \times Method \times ProgramCounter \rightarrow Boolean$
matchPcut($\mathcal{E}$,$pcut$,m,pc) = true if

$$\left\{ \begin{array}{l} pcut = \text{mcall}(mp);\ mp \in MethodPattern \\ \wedge\ (m.code(pc) = \text{invokevirtual } i\ \vee \\ \quad m.code(pc) = \text{invokestatic } i\ \vee \\ \quad m.code(pc) = \text{invokeinterface } i\ n\ \vee \\ \quad (m.code(pc) = \text{invokespecial } i) \\ \wedge\ \mathcal{JE} = (\mathcal{E}.javaEnvironment) \\ \wedge\ mPoolEntry = \mathcal{JE}(m.fromClass).constantPool(i) \\ \wedge\ msign = mPoolEntry.methodSignature \\ \wedge\ calledm = \text{retrieveM}(msign, \\ \qquad \mathcal{JE}(mPoolEntry.supposedClass).methods) \\ \wedge\ ((m.code(pc) = \text{invokespecial } i) \Rightarrow (\text{isPrivate}(calledm) \\ \qquad \wedge\ calledm.methodSignature.name <> \text{``init''})) \\ \wedge\ \text{isMpatternMatched}(mp, calledm) \end{array} \right.$$

matchPcut($\mathcal{E}$,$pcut$,m,pc) = true if

$$\left\{ \begin{array}{l} pcut = \text{get}(fp);\ fp \in FieldPattern \\ \wedge\ m.code(pc) = \text{getfield } i \vee m.code(pc) = \text{getstatic } i \\ \wedge\ \mathcal{JE} = (\mathcal{E}.javaEnvironment) \\ \wedge\ fPoolEntry = \mathcal{JE}(m.fromClass).constantPool(i) \\ \wedge\ fsign = fPoolEntry.fieldSignature \\ \wedge\ getF = \text{retrieveF}(fsign, \\ \qquad\qquad \mathcal{JE}(fPoolEntry.SupposedClass).fields) \\ \wedge\ \text{isFpatternMatched}(fp, getF) \end{array} \right.$$

matchPcut($\mathcal{E}$,$pcut$,m,pc) = true if

$$\left\{ \begin{array}{l} pcut = \text{set}(fp);\ fp \in FieldPattern \\ \wedge\ m.code(pc) = \text{putfield } i \vee m.code(pc) = \text{putstatic } i \\ \wedge\ \mathcal{JE} = (\mathcal{E}.javaEnvironment) \\ \wedge\ fPoolEntry = \mathcal{JE}(m.fromClass).constantPool(i) \\ \wedge\ fsign = fPoolEntry.fieldSignature \\ \wedge\ setF = \text{retrieveF}(fsign, \\ \qquad\qquad \mathcal{JE}(fPoolEntry.supposedClass).fields) \\ \wedge\ \text{isFpatternMatched}(fp, setF) \end{array} \right.$$

matchPcut($\mathcal{E}$,*pcut*,*m*,*pc*) = true if
$\left\{ \begin{array}{l} pcut = \texttt{winthincode}(mp); \; mp \in MethodPattern \\ \wedge \; \text{isBeforeOrAfterShadow}(m, pc) \\ \wedge \; \text{isMpatternMatched}(mp, m) \end{array} \right.$
matchPcut($\mathcal{E}$,*pcut*,*m*,*pc*) = true if
$\left\{ \begin{array}{l} pcut = \texttt{winthin}(ct); \; ct \in ComponentType \\ \wedge \; \text{isBeforeOrAfterShadow}(m, pc) \\ \wedge \; m.fromClass = ct \end{array} \right.$
matchPcut($\mathcal{E}$,*pcut*,*m*,*pc*) = false otherwise.

20. The function newPoolEntry returns a constant pool entry for a method given the signature of the method and its class:

newPoolEntry : $MethodSignature \times Class \rightarrow ConstantPoolEntry$
newPoolEntry(ms,c) = c if
$\left\{ \begin{array}{l} c.methodSignature = ms \\ \wedge \; c.supposedClass = c \end{array} \right.$

21. The function retrieveF searches for a field contained in a list of fields given its signature:

retrieveF   : $FieldSignature \times Fields \rightarrow Field$
retrieveF(fs,l) = head(l) if head(l).*fieldSignature* = fs
retrieveF(fs,l) = retrieveF(fs,tail(l)) if head(l).*fieldSignature* $\neq$ fs

22. The function retrieveM searches for a method contained in a list of methods given its signature:

retrieveM   : $MethodSignature \times Methods \rightarrow Method$
retrieveM(ms,l) = head(l) if head(l).*methodSignature* = ms
retrieveM(ms,l) = retrieveM(ms,tail(l)) if head(l).*methodSignature* $\neq$ ms

23. The function signatureAspectOf returns the signature of the method "aspectOf" of the advice aspect:

signatureAspectOf : $AdviceInfo \rightarrow MethodSignature$
signatureAspectOf(ad) = ms if
$\left\{ \begin{array}{l} ms.name = \text{``aspectOf''}, \\ \wedge \; ms.argumentsType = [\,], \\ \wedge \; ms.resultType = ad.fromClass \end{array} \right.$

24. The function tail returns the tail of a given list:

tail   : $(\tau)\text{-list} \rightarrow (\tau)\text{-list}$
tail([ ]) = [ ]
tail(v::l) = l, $\forall \; (v, l) \in \tau \times (\tau)\text{-list}$

Symbolic Analysis of Imperative Programming Languages

Bernd Burgstaller[1], Bernhard Scholz[1], and Johann Blieberger[2]

[1] The University of Sydney[*]
[2] Technical University of Vienna

Abstract. We present a generic symbolic analysis framework for imperative programming languages. Our framework is capable of computing all valid variable bindings of a program at given program points. This information is invaluable for domain-specific static program analyses such as memory leak detection, program parallelisation, and the detection of superfluous bound checks, variable aliases and task deadlocks.

We employ path expression algebra to model the control flow information of programs. A homomorphism maps path expressions into the symbolic domain. At the center of the symbolic domain is a compact algebraic structure called supercontext. A supercontext contains the complete control and data flow analysis information valid at a given program point.

Our approach to compute supercontexts is based purely on algebra and is fully automated. This novel representation of program semantics closes the gap between program analysis and computer algebra systems, which makes supercontexts an ideal intermediate representation for all domain-specific static program analyses.

Our approach is more general than existing methods because it can derive solutions for arbitrary (even intra-loop) nodes of reducible and irreducible control flow graphs. We prove the correctness of our symbolic analysis method. Our experimental results show that the problem sizes arising from real-world applications such as the SPEC95 benchmark suite are tractable for our symbolic analysis framework.

1   Introduction

Static program analysis is concerned with the design of algorithms that determine the dynamic behaviour of programs without executing them. Symbolic analysis is an advanced static program analysis technique. It has been successfully applied to memory leak detection [32], compilation of parallel programs [17,22,37,10], detection of superfluous bound checks, variable aliases and task deadlocks [31,13,6,7], and to worst-case execution time analysis [4,8]. The results gained using symbolic analysis provide invaluable information for optimising compilers, code generators, program verification, testing and debugging.

---

[*] This work has been partially supported by the ARC Discovery Project Grant "Compilation Techniques for Embedded Systems" under Contract DP 0560190 and the ARC Discovery Project Grant "Distributed Data Processing for Wireless Sensor Networks" under Contract DP 0664782.

D. Lightfoot and C. Szyperski (Eds.): JMLC 2006, LNCS 4228, pp. 172–194, 2006.

		val_u	val_v
1	integer::u,v;		
2	read (u,v);	u	v
3	u := u + v;	u+v	v
4	v := u - v;	u+v	u
5	u := u - v;	v	u

Fig. 1. Simple Statement Sequence

Symbolic analysis [17,29,23] uses symbolic expressions to describe computations as algebraic formulæ over a program's problem space. Symbolic analysis consists of two steps:

(1) the computation of symbolic expressions that describe all valid variable bindings of a program at a given program point, and
(2) the formulation of a specific static analysis problem in terms of the computed variable bindings.

As an example, consider the statement sequence depicted in Fig. 1. After the declaration of two scalar variables, the read statement in line 2 assigns both variables a new value. The subsequent assignment statements change the values of both variables. Symbolic analysis applies symbolic values for program variables. Assuming that the read statement in line 2 yields the symbolic value u for variable u, and v for variable v, then a simple sequence of forward substitutions and simplifications computes the symbolic values depicted in the table at the right of Fig. 1. Each row in the table denotes the symbolic values val_u and val_v of variables u and v after execution of the corresponding statement. These symbolic values describe the variable bindings that are valid at the corresponding program points. Comparing the variable bindings depicted with line 2 and line 5, it is clear that the values of the variables u and v are swapped in the example in Fig. 1. Due to the symbolic nature of the analysis this is true irrespective of the concrete input values for u and v. Based on the computed variable bindings an optimising compiler can derive that the expression u−v in line 4 of the example program will always yield u, which makes an overflow check of this expression redundant. (Note that variables u and v are of the same type!)

The above example reflects the clear-cut division of symbolic analysis into (1) the computation of valid variable bindings, and (2) the formulation of the specific analysis problem under consideration (e.g., range check elimination) in terms of those variable bindings.

In this paper we propose a generic symbolic analysis framework that automates step (1) above. The need for such a generic symbolic analysis framework stems from the observations

- that step (1) is a prerequisite common to all static analysis problems to be solved by symbolic analysis, and
- that existing approaches to this problem are of limited applicability (i.e., they cannot compute a solution for program points within loops, they are not applicable to irreducible control flow graphs, and they are often tailored to a specific application).

Our generic symbolic analysis framework extends the applicability of existing symbolic analysis applications to a larger class of programs. It allows the application of symbolic analysis to other static analysis problems.

Our symbolic analysis framework accurately models the semantics of imperative programming languages. We introduce a new representation of symbolic analysis information called *supercontext*, which is a comprehensive and compact algebraic structure describing the complete control and data flow analysis information valid at a given program point.

We encode the side-effect of a single statement's computation as a function from supercontexts to supercontexts. We then extend this functional description from single statements to program paths and sets of program paths. By doing so, we gain a functional description of the input program in the symbolic domain.

With our approach the control flow information of the input program is modelled by means of path expressions first introduced in [34]. A path expression is a regular expression whose language is the set of paths emanating from the start node of a control flow graph to a given node. We provide a natural homomorphism that maps the regular expressions representing path sets into the symbolic domain. We define these mappings by reinterpreting the $\cdot$, $+$, and $*$ operations used to construct regular expressions. The technical part of our work shows that these mappings are indeed homomorphisms and that the symbolic functional representation is correct.

With our approach we represent the infinitely many program paths arising due to a loop by means of a closure context, which is an extension of a program context (cf. [17]) that incorporates symbolic recurrence systems. In this way a supercontext consists of a finite number of closure contexts. Symbolic analysis at this stage reduces to the application of the functional representation of the input program to a closure context representing the initial execution environment.

The *contribution* of our paper is as follows: Our approach is the first to prove the semantic correctness of symbolic analysis with respect to the underlying standard semantics. Second, we show the correctness of the meet over all paths solution and the modelling of loops as symbolic recurrence systems. Third, our approach does not restrict symbolic analysis to reducible flowgraphs, and it can derive solutions for arbitrary graph nodes (even within nested loops). Fourth, our approach is purely algebra-based and fully automated. It closes the gap between static program analysis and computer algebra systems, which makes supercontexts an ideal intermediate representation for all domain-specific static program analyses. Fifth, the feasibility of our approach was proven by conducting experiments with the SPEC95 benchmark suite. A high portion (i.e. 94%) of the functions in SPEC95 has less than 10^5 closure contexts to analyse, with the majority of those 94% involving even fewer than 4000 closure contexts.

The paper is organised as follows: In Sect. 2 we outline notations and background material. In Sect. 3 we define syntax and semantics of a flow language that we use to develop our symbolic analysis methodology. In Sect. 4 we introduce the symbolic analysis domain and the notion of symbolic execution along program paths. Section 5 describes the main contribution of this paper, namely the mapping to the symbolic domain through path expressions. In Sect. 6 we discuss experimental results of the SPEC95 benchmark suite. Section 7 surveys related work. Finally, in Sect. 8 we draw our conclusions and outline future work. The proofs of the theorems stated in the paper have been made available in [11].

2   Background and Notation

We use $\mathbb{N}$ to denote the natural numbers, $\mathbb{Z}$ to denote the integers, and $\mathbb{B} = \{true, false\}$ to denote the truth values from Boolean algebra. The finite set of program variables is denoted by $\mathbb{V}$. $\mathcal{D}om$ denotes the domain of a function. A *control flow graph (CFG)* is a directed labelled graph $G = \langle N, E, n_e, n_x \rangle$ with node set N and edge set $E \subseteq N \times N$. Each edge $e \in E$ has a *head* $h(e) \in N$ and a *tail* $t(e) \in N$. The set of incoming edges for a given node $n \in N$ is defined as $in(n) = \{e \in E : t(e) = n\}$. Likewise we define the set of outgoing edges for a node $n \in N$ as $out(n) = \{e \in E : h(e) = n\}$. *Entry* (n_e) and *Exit* (n_x) are distinguished CFG nodes used to denote the start and terminal node. The start node n_e has no incoming edges $(in(n_e) = \emptyset)$, whereas the terminal node n_x has no outgoing edges $(out(n_x) = \emptyset)$. We require that every node n is contained in a program path from n_e to n_x, where a *program path* $\pi = \langle e_1, e_2, \ldots, e_k \rangle$ is a sequence of edges such that $t(e_r) = h(e_{r+1})$ for $1 \leq r \leq k - 1$.

It is shown in [34] how program paths can be represented as regular expressions: Let Σ be a finite alphabet disjoint from $\{\Lambda, \emptyset, (,)\}$. A *regular expression* is any expression built by applying the following rules:

(1a) "Λ" and "$\emptyset$" are *atomic* regular expressions; for any $a \in \Sigma$, "a" is an atomic regular expression.
(1b) If R_1 and R_2 are regular expressions, then $(R_1 + R_2)$, $(R_1 \cdot R_2)$, and $(R_1)^*$ are *compound* regular expressions.

In a regular expression, Λ denotes the empty string, $\emptyset$ denotes the empty set, $+$ denotes union, $\cdot$ denotes concatenation, and * denotes reflexive, transitive closure under concatenation. We use $L(R)$ to denote the set of strings defined by the regular expression R over Σ. A regular expression R is *simple* if $R = \emptyset$ or R does not contain $\emptyset$ as a subexpression. Given a CFG $G = \langle N, E, n_e, n_x \rangle$, we can regard any path π in G as a string over E, but not all strings over E are paths in G. A *path expression* P of type (v, w) is a simple regular expression over E such that every string in $L(P)$ is a program path from node v to node w. Standard algorithms such as Gaussian elimination can be applied to compute path expressions from a CFG (cf. e.g., [25,34]).

The following notational convention is used throughout the paper: to distinguish between corresponding entities from the standard semantic and symbolic domain, we subscript the first with the letter c and the latter with the letter s.

3   Standard Semantic Program Execution

An environment *env* of our Flow language maps a program variable $v \in \mathbb{V}$ to its value $z \in \mathbb{Z}$. The set of possible environments can be represented by a

pred   :   Predicate   assign   :   Assignment
pred ::= true | false | not pred | pred or pred   assign ::= id := exp
    | pred and pred | exp rel-op exp

Fig. 2. Syntactic Domain of the Flow Language

function class $Env \subseteq \{env : \mathbb{V} \to \mathbb{Z}\}$. Functions $pred_c : E \to (Env \to \mathbb{B})$ and $\sigma_c : E \to (Env \to Env)$ associate with each edge $e \in E$ a branch-predicate and a side-effect. The syntax of Flow branch predicates and side-effects is depicted in Fig. 2.

The valuation functions $pred_c$: Predicate $\to (Env \to \mathbb{B})$ and $assign_c$: Assignment $\to (Env \to Env)$ map predicates and side-effects to the semantic domain; due to space considerations we refer to [11, Sect. 3] for their definitions.

Control progresses from node h(e) to t(e) iff $pred_c(e)(env) = true$, which means that the predicate associated with edge e evaluates to $true$ within environment env. We require that for every node $n \neq n_x$ and environment env the branch-predicate of exactly one outgoing edge evaluates to true.

The transition function δ is of arity $(N \times Env) \to (N \times Env)$. Execution of a transition $(n, env) \to (n', env')$ via an edge e is defined as

$$(n, env) \to (n', env') :$$
$$\left(\exists e \in out(n) :\ t(e) = n' \wedge pred_c(e)(env)\right) \qquad (1)$$
$$\Rightarrow env' = \sigma_c(e)(env),$$

where $\Rightarrow$ denotes *implication*. The iterated transition function $\delta^* : (N \times Env) \to (N \times Env)$ is defined by $\delta^*(n_x, env) = (n_x, env)$ and $\delta^*(n, env) = \delta^*(\delta(n, env))$. For any graph $G = \langle N, E, n_e, n_x \rangle$ the environment env_x of the terminal node n_x represents the result of standard semantic program execution along the sequence of transitions $(n_e, env_e) \overset{*}{\to} (n_x, env_x)$. Depending on the structure of G and the initial environment env_e such a transition sequence may not exist. Deciding on its existence is in general equivalent to the halting problem.

4   Semantics of Symbolic Program Execution

The representation of variable values constitutes the main difference between standard semantics and symbolic semantics. Whereas with standard semantics the value of a variable is described by a concrete value $z \in \mathbb{Z}$, symbolic semantics employs symbolic expressions. The relation between standard semantics and semantics of symbolic program execution is depicted in (2).

The standard semantics of a program P is derived by the valuation function S_{con} that takes a program P as argument and returns a standard-semantic functional description of the side-effect of P. The side-effect $S_{con}[\![P]\!]$ is a function that maps a concrete input to a concrete output, written as $S_{con}[\![P]\!](In) = Out$, where $In, Out \in Env$. Given the standard semantics of Flow programs from Sect. 3, the computation of $S_{con}[\![P]\!](In)$ is equivalent to an application of the iterated transition function δ^* to start node n_e and environment In.

$$In \xrightarrow{\text{sym}} In_s$$

$$S_{\text{con}}[\![P]\!] \Bigg\downarrow \qquad\qquad \Bigg\downarrow S_{\text{sym}}[\![P]\!] \qquad\qquad (2)$$

$$Out \xleftarrow{\text{con}} Out_s$$

Similarly we derive the semantics of symbolic program execution for program P, denoted by $S_{\text{sym}}[\![P]\!]$. It is the purpose of function S_{sym} to transform P into a representation that is based on symbolic values instead of concrete ones. The side-effect $S_{\text{sym}}[\![P]\!]$ of this representation is therefore a function that maps a symbolic input In_s to the corresponding symbolic output Out_s. Symbolic input and output belong to the class Env_s of *symbolic environments* that replaces the concrete environments $env : \mathbb{V} \to \mathbb{Z}$ which are not able to bind identifiers to symbolic expressions.

The diagram in (2) contains two additional functions, sym and con, that we need in order to relate input and output of the functional descriptions $S_{\text{con}}[\![P]\!]$ and $S_{\text{sym}}[\![P]\!]$. Function sym transfers a concrete environment to the symbolic domain, whereas function con *instantiates* a symbolic environment with a concrete one. The commutation of concrete and symbolic execution depicted in (2) can then be formalised as

$$S_{\text{con}}[\![P]\!](In) = \text{con}\big(In, S_{\text{sym}}[\![P]\!](\text{sym}(In))\big), \qquad (3)$$

which means that the result of the symbolically executed program $S_{\text{sym}}[\![P]\!]$ over input $In_s = \text{sym}(In)$ and instantiated by In must be the same as the result from standard semantic program execution $S_{\text{con}}[\![P]\!](In)$.

4.1   The Domain for Symbolic Program Execution

To be able to distinguish between a variable and its *initial value*, we introduce the set $\underline{\mathbb{V}}$ of initial value variables. This set is isomorphic to $\mathbb{V}$. Its purpose is to represent the initial values for the variables in $\mathbb{V}$. The initial value operator $\_ : \mathbb{V} \to \underline{\mathbb{V}}$ maps a variable $v \in \mathbb{V}$ to the corresponding variable in $\underline{\mathbb{V}}$. As a shorthand notation we write $\underline{v}$ for the application of the initial value operator to variable v.

The *standard semantic* model of the Flow language is based on *integer arithmetics*. Transferring this property to the symbolic domain requires symbolic expressions to be *integer-valued* as well.

Given the operations of addition and multiplication it follows that the multivariate polynomials from the ring $\mathbb{Z}[\mathbf{x}]$, with indeterminates $\mathbf{x} = (x_1, \ldots, x_\nu) \in \underline{\mathbb{V}}^\nu$, are integer-valued expressions.

To support division, the ring $\mathbb{Z}[\mathbf{x}]$ is extended to the quotient field $Q(\mathbb{Z}[\mathbf{x}])$ (cf. [18]). By means of the rounding operation Rnd we can "wrap" a rational function x/y to obtain an integer-valued expression $\text{Rnd}(x/y)$[1]. Hence we can model the integer division of two symbolic expressions x and y, $y \neq 0$, as

---

[1]   Simplifications of expressions involving operation Rnd have been investigated in [11, Sect. 4.1], they are however outside the scope of this paper.

$x \operatorname{div}_s y = \operatorname{Rnd}(x / y)$, where the symbolic division operator div_s denotes the counterpart of the integer division operator div of the Flow standard semantics.

Let $f^{(n)} \in \{+^{(2)}, -^{(2)}, -^{(1)}, \cdot^{(2)}\}$ denote functions corresponding to the Flow arithmetic operations, where (n) denotes the respective arity. They constitute the corresponding operations on multivariate polynomials and rational functions, with the only extension that they do accept arguments "wrapped" by the rounding operator Rnd.

Definition 1. *The set of integer-valued symbolic expressions of the domain SymExpr is inductively defined by*

- $\mathbb{Z}[\mathbf{x}] \subset SymExpr$
- *for all $f^{(n)}$ and all $e_1, \ldots, e_n \in SymExpr$, $f^{(n)}(e_1, \ldots, e_n) \in SymExpr$ (i.e., application of functions $f^{(n)}$ to symbolic expressions yields symbolic expressions),*
- *for all $e_1, e_2 \in SymExpr$, we have $e_1/e_2 \in SymExpr$, iff e_1/e_2 is an integer-valued symbolic expression,*
- *for all $e_1, e_2 \in SymExpr$, we have $\operatorname{Rnd}(e_1/e_2) \in SymExpr$.*

Let $f \in \{<, \leq, =, \geq, >\}$ denote functions corresponding to the relational connectives of the Flow language. They are extensions of their standard semantic counterparts which operate on values of the symbolic expression domain SymExpr, and return values of the symbolic predicate domain SymPred, e.g., $\leq$: SymExpr$\times$SymExpr $\to$ SymPred. Moreover, let $l^{(n)} \in \{\wedge^{(2)}, \vee^{(2)}, \neg^{(1)}\}$ denote the logical connectives of conjunction, disjunction and negation. They are extensions of their standard semantic counterparts that operate on values of the symbolic predicate domain SymPred.

Definition 2. *The set of symbolic predicates of SymPred, the symbolic predicate domain, is inductively defined as*

- $\mathbb{B} \subset SymPred$ *(i.e., true and false are symbolic predicates),*
- *for all f and all $e_1, e_2 \in SymExpr$, we have $f(e_1, e_2) \in SymPred$ (i.e., application of relational connectives to symbolic expressions yields symbolic predicates),*
- *for all l and all $e_1, \ldots e_n \in SymPred$, we have $l(e_1, \ldots, e_n) \in SymPred$ (i.e., application of logical connectives to symbolic predicates yields symbolic predicates).*

It is shown in [11, Sect. 4.1] that the domain SymPred constitutes a Boolean algebra.

Definition 3. *A state $s \in S$ is a function that maps a program variable to the corresponding symbolic expression. The set of possible states can be represented by a function class $S \subseteq \{f : \mathbb{V} \to SymExpr\}$. A clean slate state s maps all variables in its domain to the corresponding initial value variables: $\forall v \in \mathcal{D}om(s) : s(v) = \underline{v}$. Note that if we restrict our interest to a subset of $\mathbb{V}$ then states are partial functions.*

Definition 4. *A context $c \in C \subseteq [S \times SymPred]$ is defined by an ordered tuple $[s,p]$ where s denotes a state, and pathcondition $p \in SymPred$ describes the condition for which the variable bindings specified through s hold (cf. [4,17]). We make use of the functions* pc $: C \rightarrow SymPred$ *and* st $: C \rightarrow S$ *to access a context's pathcondition and state. A clean slate context consists of a clean slate state and a* true *pathcondition.*

Standard semantic and symbolic side-effects and branch-predicates share the syntactic domain depicted in Fig. 2. Due to space considerations we refer to [11, Sect. 4.2] for an exhaustive description of the valuation functions into the symbolic domain that are introduced in brief below. Equation (4) defines valuation function assign$_s$ which maps the derivation tree of an assignment statement to the corresponding side-effect in the symbolic domain. This side-effect is a function that transforms its argument context $[s,p]$ by updating the state s with a new symbolic expression at id[[id]].

$$\text{assign}_s : \text{Assignment} \rightarrow (C \rightarrow C)$$
$$\text{assign}_s[[\text{id}:=\text{exp}]](c) = \lambda[s,p].[\lambda s_1.s_1 [\text{id}[[\text{id}]] \mapsto \exp_s[[\exp]](s_1)](s), p](c) \tag{4}$$

Branch-predicates are treated according to (5). The valuation function pred$_s$ maps the derivation tree t of a branch-predicate to a function $f : C \rightarrow C$. Application of f to the argument-context $[s,p]$ results in a context $[s,p \wedge p']$, where $p' \in SymPred$ is a symbolic predicate corresponding to tree t.

$$\text{pred}_s : \text{Predicate} \rightarrow (C \rightarrow C)$$
$$\cdots$$
$$\text{pred}_s[[\text{pred}_1 \text{ and } \text{pred}_2]](c) = $$
$$\lambda[s,p].[s,p \wedge (\text{pc}\,(\text{pred}_s[[\text{pred}_1]]([s,\textit{true}]))$$
$$\wedge \, \text{pc}\,(\text{pred}_s[[\text{pred}_2]]([s,\textit{true}])))]\,(c) \tag{5}$$

4.2 Single-Edge Symbolic Execution

We express the effect of a computational step associated with a single edge e by a member of the function class $F_s \subseteq \{f : C \rightarrow C\}$. F_s contains the identity function ι which can be envisioned as a null-statement without any computational effect. We require F_s to be closed under composition, which allows us to compose the computational steps of edges along program paths.

An edge transition function $M_s : E \rightarrow F_s$ assigns a function $f \in F_s$ to each edge $e \in E$ of the CFG. The valuation function edge$_s$[[...]] maps syntactic constructs associated with CFG edges to the respective valuation functions for branch predicates and side-effects, which allows us to specify functions $f \in F_s$ as follows.

$$f = M_s(e)(c) = \sigma_s(e) \circ pred_s(e)(c) = $$
$$= \text{edge}_s[[e : \text{pred} \Rightarrow \text{assign}]](c) = \tag{6}$$
$$= \text{assign}_s[[\text{assign}]]\,(\text{pred}_s[[\text{pred}]](c))$$

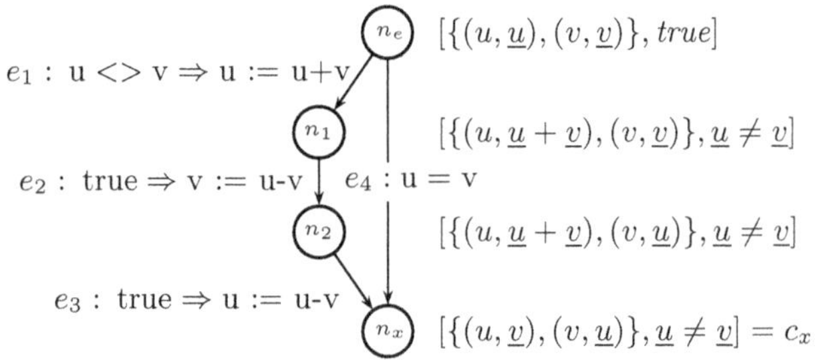

$$e_1 : u <> v \Rightarrow u := u+v$$

$n_e \quad [\{(u,\underline{u}),(v,\underline{v})\}, \textit{true}]$

$n_1 \quad [\{(u,\underline{u}+\underline{v}),(v,\underline{v})\}, \underline{u} \neq \underline{v}]$

$$e_2 : \text{true} \Rightarrow v := u-v \qquad e_4 : u = v$$

$n_2 \quad [\{(u,\underline{u}+\underline{v}),(v,\underline{u})\}, \underline{u} \neq \underline{v}]$

$$e_3 : \text{true} \Rightarrow u := u-v$$

$n_x \quad [\{(u,\underline{v}),(v,\underline{u})\}, \underline{u} \neq \underline{v}] = c_x$

Fig. 3. Symbolic Execution along Path $\pi_1 = \langle e_1, e_2, e_3 \rangle$

It follows immediately from the preceding denotational definitions of side-effects and branch predicates that functions specified in the above way fulfil the properties required for function class F_s.

Figure 3 depicts our running example for which we determine the transition function f for edge e_1. Applying (6) and the valuation functions for branch predicates and side-effects, we get

$$f = M_s(e_1)(c) = \text{edge}_s[\![e_1 : u <> v \Rightarrow u := u+v]\!](c) =$$
$$= \text{assign}_s[\![u := u+v]\!]\big(\text{pred}_s[\![u <> v]\!](c)\big) =$$
$$= \lambda[s,p].\big[s[u \mapsto s(u) + s(v)], p \wedge s(u) \neq s(v)\big](c).$$

4.3   Single-Path Symbolic Execution

For a forward data-flow problem we can extend the transition function M_s from edges e to program paths π as follows.

$$M_s(\pi) = \begin{cases} \iota, & \text{if } \pi \text{ is the empty path} \\ M_s(e_k) \circ \cdots \circ M_s(e_1), & \text{if } \pi = \langle e_1, \ldots, e_k \rangle \end{cases} \tag{7}$$

As a shorthand notation we may also use f_e for $M_s(e)$ and f_π for $M_s(\pi)$. Clearly if the computational effect of a single statement of a Flow program is described by a function $f \in F_s$, the computational effect of program execution along a path π is defined by $M_s(\pi)(c_e)$, where c_e denotes the initial context on entry to π. (*Proof by induction on the length of π omitted.*)

In the previous example we determined the result of the transition function $M_s(e_1)$ which represents the effect of symbolic program execution along edge e_1 of our running example. After evaluation of all edge transition functions along the program path $\pi_1 = \langle e_1, e_2, e_3 \rangle$ we use function $M_s(\pi_1)$ to calculate the effect of symbolic execution along path π_1. We assume that the initial context c_e passed as argument to $M_s(\pi_1)$ contains two program variables u and v holding their initial values $\underline{u}$ and $\underline{v}$. Then the contexts depicted in Fig. 3 illustrate the transformation of the initial context c_e during symbolic execution along program path $\pi_1{}^2$. The context shown with node n_x represents the result for $M_s(\pi_1)(c_e)$.

4.4   Multi-path Symbolic Execution

In the preceding example we have omitted symbolic execution along edge e_4. As long as we cannot decide that this path is infeasible, we have to analyse it for our symbolic solution to be complete. Symbolic execution along edge e_4 yields a further program context $c'_x = [\{(u, \underline{u}), (v, \underline{v})\}, \underline{u} = \underline{v}]$.

As can be seen from this example, the description of the symbolic solution in terms of contexts increases with the number of program paths through a CFG; each program path from the entry node n_e to a given node n contributes one context to the symbolic solution at node n. As long as CFGs are acyclic, the number of contexts of this symbolic solution is finite. With the introduction of cycles the number of program paths from the entry node to a given node n, and hence the number of contexts of the symbolic solution at node n, becomes infinite. In order to describe the joint effects of execution along several program paths, we introduce a structure that allows us to aggregate contexts.

Definition 5. *A supercontext $sc \in SC$ is a collection of contexts $c \in C$ and can be envisioned as a (possibly) infinite set*

$$sc = \{c_1, \ldots, c_k, \ldots\} = \{[s_1, p_1], \ldots, [s_k, p_k], \ldots\}.$$

We write $c \in sc$ to denote that context c is an element of the supercontext sc. For supercontexts $sc_1, sc_2 \in SC$ the supercontext union operation $sc_1 \cup sc_2$ contains those contexts that are either in sc_1, or in sc_2, or in both. If we regard single contexts as one-element supercontexts, we can use the supercontext union operation to denote a supercontext sc through union over its context elements, arriving at the following notation for supercontexts.

$$sc \in SC = \left[\bigcup_{k=0}^{\infty} [s_k, p_k] \right] \tag{8}$$

Note that supercontexts correspond to the notion of *symbolic environments* used in the introduction of this section.

Because a supercontext consists of an arbitrary (even infinite) number of contexts, it can represent the result of symbolic execution along an arbitrary (even infinite) number of program paths. According to [24] the *meet over all paths (MOP) solution* for a given CFG node n is the maximum information, relevant to the problem at hand, which can be derived from every possible execution path from the entry node n_e to n. The MOP-solution of symbolic execution for a given node n can then be written as

$$\mathrm{mop}(n) = \bigcup_{\pi \in \mathrm{Path}(n_e, n)} M_s(\pi)(c_e), \tag{9}$$

---

[2] As a notational convention we depict the *graphs* of the contained states instead of the states themselves.

with $\mathrm{Path}(n_e, n)$ denoting the set of all program paths from node n_e to node n, $\cup$ denoting supercontext union, and c_e denoting the initial argument context. A correctness proof for the symbolic MOP-solution is given in [11].

5   Symbolic Evaluation

The symbolic execution approach of Sect. 4 is capable of computing the MOP-solution for arbitrary CFG nodes. It is however not constructive in the sense that we have not specified a method to obtain the set of program paths needed by this approach. Furthermore, the MOP-solution delivered is infinite. In this section we define a method to compute the MOP-solution that is both constructive and finite. It is based on the regular expression algebra of Sect. 2, which we use to model the program paths of a given CFG. The structure of regular expressions imposes a horizontal functional decomposition of the CFG in contrast to the approach of the previous section in which our functional decomposition was vertically along whole program paths. As a consequence we have to extend domain and codomain of the function class F_s introduced in Sect. 4.2 from contexts to supercontexts, yielding a new function class F_{sc}:

$$F_{\mathrm{sc}} \subseteq \{f_{\mathrm{sc}} : SC \to SC\}. \tag{10}$$

We achieve this extension with the help of the wrapping operator wrap which constructs a function $f_{\mathrm{sc}} \in F_{\mathrm{sc}}$ of arity $SC \to SC$ from a function $f_s \in F_s$ of arity $C \to C$ in passing each context of the supercontext-argument of f_{sc} through f_s:

$$\mathrm{wrap} : (C \to C) \to (SC \to SC)$$

$$\mathrm{wrap}(f_s)(sc) ::= f_{\mathrm{sc}}\left(\left[\bigcup_{i=0}^{\infty}[s_i, p_i]\right]\right) = \left[\bigcup_{i=0}^{\infty} f_s([s_i, p_i])\right].$$

The function class F_{sc} has the following properties, which are easily verified from the definition of the wrapping operator, the properties of supercontexts (cf. Definition 5), and the properties of the function class F_s on which F_{sc} is based.

F1) F_{sc} contains the identity function ι.
F2) F_{sc} is closed under $\cup$: $\forall f, g \in F_{\mathrm{sc}} : (f \cup g)(x) = f(x) \cup g(x)$.
F3) F_{sc} is closed under composition: $\forall f, g \in F_{\mathrm{sc}} : f \circ g \in F_{\mathrm{sc}}$.
F4) F_{sc} is closed under iterated composition (with $f^0 = \iota$ and $f^i = f^{i-1} \circ f$):

$$f^*(x) = \left[\bigcup_{i \geq 0} f^i(x)\right]. \tag{11}$$

F5) Continuity of $f \in F_{\mathrm{sc}}$ across supercontext union $\cup$:

$$\forall f \in F_{\mathrm{sc}} \text{ and } X \subseteq SC : f(\cup X) = \left[\bigcup_{x \in sc} f(x)\right].$$

Based on the edge transition function M_s (cf. Sect. 4.2) we define a new edge transition function M_{sc} that encapsulates the wrapping operator inside:

$$M_{sc} : E \to F_{sc}$$
$$M_{sc}(e) ::= \mathrm{wrap}(M_s(e)). \tag{12}$$

We can compose edge transition functions from function class F_{sc} along program paths in the same way shown for function class F_s in (7). In a similar way we use the shorthand notation f_e for $M_{sc}(e)$, and f_π for $M_{sc}(\pi)$.

Let $P \neq \emptyset$ be a path expression of type (v, w). For all $x \in SC$, we define a mapping ϕ as follows.

$$\phi(\Lambda) = \iota, \tag{13}$$
$$\phi(e) = M_{sc}(e) = f_e, \tag{14}$$
$$\phi(P_1 + P_2) = \phi(P_1) \cup \phi(P_2), \tag{15}$$
$$\phi(P_1 \cdot P_2) = \phi(P_2) \circ \phi(P_1), \tag{16}$$
$$\phi(P_1^*) = \phi(P_1)^*. \tag{17}$$

Lemma 1. *Let $P \neq \emptyset$ be a path expression of type (v, w). Then for all $x \in SC$,*

$$\phi(P)(x) = \left[\bigcup_{\pi \in L(P)} f_\pi(x) \right].$$

Proof in [11]. Based on Lemma 1 we establish that the mapping ϕ is a homomorphism from the regular expression algebra to the function class F_{sc} of (10), and that the computed solution corresponds to the MOP-solution for symbolic execution of (9).

Theorem 1. *For any node n let $P(n_e, n)$ be a path expression representing all paths from n_e to n. Then $\mathrm{mop}(n) = \phi(P(n_e, n))(c_e)$, where c_e denotes the initial context[3] valid at entry node n_e.*

Proof in [11]. It should be noted that Theorem 1 does not impose a restriction on path expression $P(n_e, n)$. As a consequence, Theorem 1 holds for path expressions corresponding to CFGs with *irreducible* graph portions. Furthermore it holds for arbitrary graph nodes, even within loops and nested loops.

5.1   Finite Supercontexts

It has been pointed out in Sect. 4.4 that the MOP solution becomes infinite with the introduction of CFG cycles. CFG cycles induce $*$ operators in path expressions; due to the iterated composition that is implied by the right-hand side of (17), each $*$ operator induces an infinite number of contexts in the resulting supercontext.

---

[3] Since program contexts are one-element supercontexts, c_e is a valid argument for functions from class F_{sc}.

In changing the mapping ϕ by replacing (17) with

$$\phi(P_1^*) = \phi(P_1)^\circledR, \tag{18}$$

we introduce a new operation $\circledR$ which replaces the iterated composition operation from (11) by a composition operation that generates a finite representation
for the result of symbolic evaluation of the CFG cycle corresponding to path expression P_1. This finite representation is an extension of a context by a system
of symbolic recurrences [26] and is called a *closure context*. As will be pointed
out below, a system of symbolic recurrences makes a closure context an *exact*
representation of the infinite set of contexts that is due to a CFG cycle. In this
way (18) changes our representation of a supercontext from an *infinite set* of
contexts to a *finite set* of *closure contexts*. The purpose of this change is to have
a compact representation of supercontexts that facilitates domain-specific static
program analyses and that can be implemented with CASs.

The remainder of this section is devoted to the definition of closure contexts
and the $\circledR$ operation.

In analogy to the set $\mathbb{V}$ of program variables we define the set $\mathbb{L}$, $\mathbb{V} \cap \mathbb{L} = \emptyset$,
of *loop index variables*. We use lowercase letters, e.g., l, m, n, to denote elements
from $\mathbb{L}$. Conceptually a loop index variable can be envisioned as an artificial
program variable that is assigned the value 0 upon entry of the loop body. After
each iteration of the loop body, its value is increased by one.

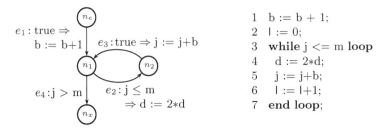

Fig. 4. Example Loop: Implicit vs. Explicit Loop Index Variable

Figure 4 depicts a Flow example loop together with a textual representation
where the loop index variable has been made explicit (cf. line 2 and 6). Associated
with a loop index variable l is a *symbolic* upper bound, denoted by l_ω. This
symbolic upper bound represents the number of loop iterations[4]. Specifically,
an upper bound of $l_\omega = 0$ implies zero loop iterations, as can be inferred from
Fig. 4[5]. Endless loops can be modelled by defining $l_\omega = +\infty$.

---

[4] Computing a *symbolic* upper bound for the number of loop iterations is beyond the
scope of this paper. It is discussed, among others, in [17,5].
[5] This contrasts the notion of range expressions in contemporary programming languages, where **range** L..U denotes the interval [L, U] .

Definition 6. *The set of symbolic expressions (cf. Definition 1) is extended by*

- $\mathbb{L} \subset SymExpr$ (*i.e., loop index variables are symbolic expressions*), *and*
- *for all $v_i \in \mathbb{V}$, and $\mathsf{l} \in \mathbb{L}$, $v_i(0) \in SymExpr$, $v_i(\mathsf{l}) \in SymExpr$, $v_i(\mathsf{l}+1) \in SymExpr$, and $v_i(\mathsf{l}-1) \in SymExpr$ (i.e., dereferencing the value of a program variable to specify a recurrence relation yields a symbolic expression).*

Definition 7. *A* range expression *is a symbolic expression of the form $0 \leq \mathsf{l} \leq \mathsf{l}_\omega$, with loop index variable $\mathsf{l} \in \mathbb{L}$, and l_ω being the symbolic upper bound of l. We extend the set of symbolic predicates of the domain SymPred (cf. Definition 2) by the following rule to include range expressions: for all $\mathsf{l} \in \mathbb{L}$, $0 \leq \mathsf{l} \leq \mathsf{l}_\omega \subset SymPred$ (i.e., range expressions constitute symbolic predicates).*

We denote a *recurrence system* over loop index variable l by $rs(\mathsf{l})$. We can construct a *recurrence system set* r of k recurrence systems by

$$r ::= \bigcup_{1 \leq j \leq k} rs(\mathsf{l}_j).$$

Recurrence system sets can be nested, and the set of all recurrence system sets is denoted by R. For our purpose it is furthermore beneficial to impose a total order $\leq$ on the elements of a recurrence system set in order to obtain the semantics of a list.

Definition 8. *A* closure context *$\bar{c}$ is an element of the set $\overline{C} = S \times SymPred \times R$, denoted by $[s, p, r]$. For a clean slate closure context the state s is a clean slate state, p is a true pathcondition, and r is the empty set. A context can be considered a special case of a closure context with $r = \emptyset$. A* supercontext *consisting of a finite number of closure contexts is denoted by $\overline{sc}$, for the set of all such finite supercontexts we write $\overline{SC}$.*

Definition 9. *We define operation $\circledast$ of (18) in terms of the input/output-behaviour of the function resulting from the application of operation $\circledast$ to $\phi(P_1)$, that is, $\phi(P_1)^\circledast$. Let $f = \phi(P_1)$ be a functional description of the accumulated side-effect of one iteration of the loop body represented by the path expression P_1. For a given closure context $\overline{c_{in}} = [s_{in}, p_{in}, r_{in}]$ we define the properties of the closure context $\overline{c_{out}} = [s_{out}, p_{out}, r_{out}]$ resulting from the application of $f^\circledast$ to $\overline{c_{in}}$, that is,*

$$\overline{c_{out}} = \phi(P_1^*)(\overline{c_{in}}) = \phi(P_1)^\circledast(\overline{c_{in}}) = f^\circledast(\overline{c_{in}}). \tag{19}$$

One iteration of the loop body determines the recurrence system that is due to the induction variables of the loop body. Hence we start with a clean slate closure context $\overline{c_0} = [s_0, p_0, r_0]$ and compute the result of symbolic evaluation of one iteration of the loop body, denoted by $\overline{c_1}$.

$$\overline{c_1} = [s_1, p_1, r_1] = f(\overline{c_0}). \tag{20}$$

A substitution $\sigma_{s,e}$ for a given state s and an expression $e \in SymExpr$ is defined such that $\sigma_{s,e} = \{v_1 \mapsto v_1(e), \ldots, v_j \mapsto v_j(e)\}$, with $\underset{1 \leq i \leq j}{v_i} \in \mathcal{D}om(s)$.

What follows is the description of $\overline{c_{out}}$ in terms of its state s_{out}, its pathcondition p_{out}, and its recurrence system set r_{out}.

State: The state s_{out} is computed from s_{in} by replacing the symbolic expressions that describe the values of the variables v_i by the value of the recurrence relation for v_i over loop index variable I.

$$\forall v_i \in \mathcal{D}om(s_{in}) : \quad s_{out} ::= s_{in}[v_i \mapsto v_i(I)] \tag{21}$$

Hence we get $graph(s_{out}) = \{(v_1, v_1(I)), \ldots, (v_n, v_n(I))\}$.

Pathcondition: The pathcondition p_{out} of closure context $\overline{c_{out}}$ has the form

$$p_{in} \wedge (0 \le I \le I_\omega) \wedge \bigwedge_{1 \le I' \le I} p(I' - 1). \tag{22}$$

Therein the term p_{in} constitutes the pathcondition of closure context $\overline{c_{in}}$. The second term is a range expression according to Definition 7. It defines the value of the loop index variable I to be in the interval $[0, I_\omega]$. The third term denotes the pathcondition accumulated during I iterations of the loop. It is actually a conjunction of I instances of the pathcondition p_1 from (20), where the I'^{th} instance corresponds to $\sigma_{s_{in},(I'-1)}(p_1)$.

An example will illustrate this. Assume the pathcondition $p_1 = j \le m$ from Fig. 4. After $I > 0$ iterations the third term in the above equation will read

$$j(0) \le m(0) \wedge j(1) \le m(1) \wedge \cdots \wedge j(I-1) \le m(I-1)$$
$$= \bigwedge_{1 \le I' \le I} (j(I'-1) \le m(I'-1)).$$

Recurrence System: Let IV denote the set of induction variables of the loop under consideration. We set up a recurrence system over the loop index variable I, from which we construct a recurrence system set r as follows.

$$r = \left\{ \begin{bmatrix} \forall v_i \in IV : \begin{cases} v_i(0) ::= s_{in}(v_i) \\ v_i(I+1) ::= \sigma_{s_{in},I}(s_1(v_i)) \end{cases} (1) \\ rc ::= \sigma_{s_{in},I}(p_1) \qquad\qquad\qquad\quad (2) \end{bmatrix} \right\} \tag{23}$$

Part (1) denotes the recurrence for induction variable v_i. The boundary value of a variable upon entry of the loop body is the variable's value from the "incoming" context ($\overline{c_{in}}$ in our case). We derive the recurrence relation for variable v_i as follows. State s_1 contains the variable bindings after the first iteration of the loop body. In replacing all occurrences of the initial value variables $v_i \in \mathbb{V}$ by their recursive counterpart $v_i(I)$, we obtain the bindings after iteration $I + 1$, denoted by $v_i(I+1)$. If we can derive a closed form for the recurrence relation of variable v_i, Part (1) consists only of a symbolic closed form expression over loop index variable I. Part (2) holds the recurrence condition rc for this recurrence system. The condition is basically a symbolic predicate obtained by replacing the initial value variables in the pathcondition p_1 (cf. (20)) by their recursive counterparts.

Having set up the recurrence system set r according to (23), the recurrence system set r_{out} of closure context $\overline{c_{out}}$ is derived from r_{in} by appending r to it.

A recurrence system set can be simplified if we are able to derive closed forms for the recurrence relations of the involved induction variables. There exists a vast body of literature on this topic, e.g., [21,26,37,36,22,19]. These methods are directly applicable to the recurrence system sets of our symbolic analysis framework. Modern CASs such as Mathematica [38] provide an ideal platform for the implementation of these methods.

Due to space limitations we refer to [11] for the details involved with the construction of recurrence system sets for nested loops.

Returning to the running example of Fig. 4, we seek the MOP-solution for node n_1. The MOP-solution of this node is due to the path expression $e_1 \cdot (e_2 \cdot e_3)^*$ of type (n_e, n_1). Starting with the clean slate closure context $\overline{c_e} = [s, p, r] = [\{(b, \underline{b}), (d, \underline{d}), (j, \underline{j}), (m, \underline{m})\}, true, \emptyset]$, we compute $\phi(e_1 \cdot (e_2 \cdot e_3)^*)(\overline{c_e}) = (f_{e_3} \circ f_{e_2})^\circledast \circ f_{e_1}(\overline{c_e})$. Function application $f_{e_1}(\overline{c_e})$ yields the closure context $\overline{c_{in}} = [\{(b, \underline{b}+1), (d, \underline{d}), (j, \underline{j}), (m, \underline{m})\}, true, \emptyset]$, which reduces our computation to $(f_{e_3} \circ f_{e_2})^\circledast(\overline{c_{in}})$. To apply operation $\circledast$ we proceed according to Definition 9. Due to (20) we have to compute the result of symbolic evaluation of one iteration of the loop body to derive the underlying recurrence relations. For this we can reuse the clean slate closure context $\overline{c_e}$ by defining $\overline{c_0} :: = \overline{c_e}$ and proceed with the calculation of $\overline{c_1} = (f_{e_3} \circ f_{e_2})(\overline{c_0}) = [\{(b, \underline{b}), (d, 2 \cdot \underline{d}), (j, \underline{j} + \underline{b}), (m, \underline{m})\}, j \leq \underline{m}, \emptyset]$. The closure context $\overline{c_{out}}$ resulting from the computation of $\overline{c_{out}} = (f_{e_3} \circ f_{e_2})^\circledast(\overline{c_{in}})$ can then be described in terms of its state s_{out}, its pathcondition p_{out}, and its recurrence system set r_{out}. The loop index variable for this loop is l.

State: The state of $\overline{c_{out}}$ is obtained from the state of $\overline{c_{in}}$ by replacing the symbolic expressions that describe the values of the induction variables $v_i \in IV = \{d, j\}$ by the value of the recurrence relation for v_i over loop index variable l. Hence we get $s_{out} = \{(b, \underline{b} + 1), (d, d(l)), (j, j(l)), (m, \underline{m})\}$.

Pathcondition: According to (22) we get the pathcondition $p_{out} = true \wedge (0 \leq l \leq l_w) \wedge \bigwedge_{1 \leq l' \leq l} (j(l' - 1) \leq \underline{m})$.

Recurrence System: According to (23) we arrive at the one-element recurrence system set r', with $s_{in} = st(\overline{c_{in}})$ and $s_1 = st(\overline{c_1})$ already substituted.

$$r' = \left\{ \begin{bmatrix} \begin{cases} d(0) :: = \underline{d} \\ d(l+1) :: = 2 \cdot d(l) \end{cases} & (1a) \\ \begin{cases} j(0) :: = \underline{j} \\ j(l+1) :: = j(l) + \underline{b} + 1 \end{cases} & (1b) \\ rc :: = j(l) \leq \underline{m} & (2) \end{bmatrix} \right\}$$

Applying standard methods to solve the recurrence relations for the induction variables d and j, we arrive at

$$r = \left\{ \begin{bmatrix} \{ d(l) :: = 2^l \cdot \underline{d} & (1a) \\ \{ j(l) :: = \underline{j} + l \cdot (\underline{b} + 1) & (1b) \\ rc :: = j(l) \leq \underline{m} & (2) \end{bmatrix} \right\}.$$

Combining state s_{out}, pathcondition p_{out} and the recurrence system set r yields

$$[\{(b, \underline{b} + 1), (d, d(l)), (j, j(l)), (m, \underline{m})\}, (0 \leq l \leq l_w) \wedge \bigwedge_{1 \leq l' \leq l} (j(l' - 1) \leq \underline{m}), \{r\}]$$

as the solution for the closure context $\overline{c_{out}}$, which is also the MOP-solution for node n_1. The intuitive meaning of this closure context unveils if we consider the range expression $(0 \leq 1 \leq 1_\omega)$ that is part of its pathcondition: as loop index variable 1 ranges from 0 to 1_ω, the recurrence system r generates the variable bindings of the respective context[6] c_1 valid after 1 loop iterations, i.e. $c_1 = (f_{e_3} \circ f_{e_2})^1 \circ f_{e_1}(\overline{c_e})$. Hence the closure context $\overline{c_{out}}$ represents a total number of $1_\omega + 1$ contexts valid at node n_1. Formally the closure context $\overline{c_{out}}$ can be viewed as a predicate $\forall b \forall d \forall j \forall m \forall 1 : \overline{c_{out}}$, where the set $\{x \mid 0 \leq x \leq 1_\omega)\} \subseteq \mathbb{N}$ is the universe of discourse for loop index variable 1.

The above closure context describes all variable bindings valid at node n_1 of Fig. 4. It yields important information for static program analysis, e.g.,

- at node n_1 the variables b and m assume the values $\underline{b} + 1$ and $\underline{m}$ respectively during all loop iterations,
- the induction variables d and j assume monotonically increasing/decreasing sequences of values (depending on the initial values of variables d and b),
- the symbolic values of the induction variables d and j during each iteration of the loop,
- a symbolic upper bound 1_ω for the number of loop iterations (computed from the recurrence condition as described in [17]), and therefore
- symbolic lower and upper bounds for the induction variables d and j.

It is instructive to consider a closure context once the associated loop L has been exited. Upon exit of a loop via a given edge e, the pathcondition p associated with e implies that $1 = 1_\omega$. In other words, the conjunction of p and the pathcondition of a closure context from node $h(e)$ collapses the set of contexts represented by the resulting closure context to the single context valid after execution of the loop.

Returning to the example of Fig. 4, once we exit the loop via edge e_4, the fact that $1 = 1_\omega$ simplifies the closure context valid at node n_x to

$$[\{(b, \underline{b} + 1), (d, d(1_\omega)), (j, j(1_\omega)), (m, \underline{m})\}, \bigwedge_{1 \leq 1' \leq 1_\omega} (j(1' - 1) \leq \underline{m}) \wedge j(1_\omega) > \underline{m}, \{r\}],$$

which represents the single context valid after execution of the loop. It should be noted that the determination of loop exit edges is done based on path expressions, which makes the above simplification a purely mechanical step in our symbolic analysis method.

6   Experiments

The prototype implementation of our symbolic analysis framework constitutes a term rewrite system based on OBJ3 ([3,20]) and Mathematica [38]. Together with the analysis results of Flow sample programs, we have made it available at [14].

---

[6] Not to be mistaken with a closure context.

Since the practicality of our symbolic analysis method critically depends on the size of the path expressions occurring in practice, we have surveyed the problem sizes arising from the programs of the complete SPEC95 benchmark suite (cf. [33]). The SPEC95 benchmark suite consists of 18 benchmark programs with GCC and the Perl interpreter among them. Overall, we investigated all 5053 procedures, in an attempt to make the survey representative both in quantity and in the problem sizes of the investigated programs.

The technical part of this survey comprised the definition of a metric to compute the symbolic analysis problem sizes (i.e., the number of closure contexts resulting from a given path expression), and to apply this metric to the path expressions of the procedures from the SPEC95 benchmark code.

We compute the number of program paths of a path expression corresponding to an acyclic CFG through the mapping $ncc(e) = 1$, $ncc(P_1 + P_2) = ncc(P_1) + ncc(P_2)$, and $ncc(P_1 \cdot P_2) = ncc(P_1) \cdot ncc(P_2)$. Every such program path induces the generation of one closure context during symbolic analysis[7]. Our *accumulated* ncc metric (ancc) starts with the innermost nested loop of a path expression P and computes the ncc count for its body. Thereafter the subexpression in P that corresponds to this loop is replaced by a single edge and the ancc metric is applied to the resulting expression. This is done for all loops across all nesting levels, and for the topmost remaining loopless path expression itself. The ancc-value for P then equals the sum of the calculated ncc counts.

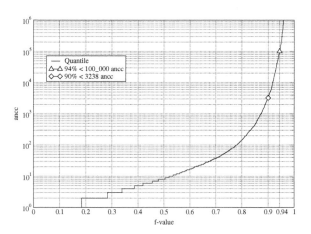

Fig. 5. Quantile Plot for SPEC95 Programs

In our survey each SPEC95 procedure has been accounted for through its path expression of type (n_e, n_x). Figure 5 contains a quantile plot of the ancc values of the SPEC95 procedures. It has been scaled to exclude outliers with an ancc-value above 10^6. It shows that the distribution of ancc values starts at the lowest possible value (1) and increases modestly up to the 0.94 quantile. Thereafter we

---

[7] Hence the name ncc which stands for *number of closure contexts*.

can observe an excessive increase of quantiles which indicates that the final 6 percent of the distribution represent costly outliers. The two distinguished data points in the upper right corner represent the 0.9 quantile and the 0.94 quantile. It follows from those data points that 90 percent of the SPEC95 procedures show an ancc-value below 3238, and for 0.94 percent it is still below 100, 000. This means that the problem sizes of more than 94 percent of the procedures from the SPEC95 benchmark suite constitute no problem at all for symbolic analysis, and that the ancc values for 90 percent of all procedures are indeed very small. Due to space limitations we refer to [12] for a description of the whole range of experiments carried out on the SPEC95 benchmark suite.

7   Related Work

P. and R. Cousot [16] pioneered abstract interpretation as a theory of semantic approximation for semantic data and control flow analysis. The main differences between abstract interpretation and our symbolic analysis are as follows: our symbolic analysis framework precisely represents the values of program variables whereas abstract interpretation commonly approximates a program's computations. Second, path conditions guarding conditional variable values are not included in abstract interpretation. Third, applications of abstract interpretation are faced with a trade-off between the level of abstraction and the precision of the analysis, and its approximated information may not be accurate enough to be useful.

Haghighat and Polychronopoulos [22] base their symbolic analysis techniques on abstract interpretation. The information of all incoming paths to a node is intersected at the cost of analysis accuracy. Their method does not maintain predicates to guard the values of variables and it is restricted to reducible CFGs. No correctness proof of the used algorithms is given.

Van Engelen et al. [37,36] use chains of recurrences [39,2] to model symbolic expressions. Analysis is carried out directly on the CFG, with loops being analysed in two phases. In the first phase recurrence relations are collected, whereas in the second phase the recurrence relations are solved in CR form. The analysis method is restricted to reducible CFGs, which makes it less general than our approach. In comparison, our algebra-centered approach uses only standard mathematical methods instead of specialised analysis algorithms. It provides for a seamless integration of the chains of recurrences algebra to solve recurrence relations, but it is not restricted to it.

The algorithms developed with both Haghighat's and van Engelen's approaches are tailored around the intended application (i.e., analysis problem). In contrast we advocate a generic method that allows the formulation of arbitrary domain-specific static analysis problems based on the MOP-solution.

In [4] symbolic evaluation is used for estimating the worst-case execution time of sequential real-time programs. Symbolic evaluation is set up as a data-flow problem, with equations describing the solutions at the respective CFG nodes.

In [17] a symbolic representation for contexts is introduced. Closure contexts are an extension of this algebraic structure.

Tu and Padua [35] developed a system for computing symbolic values of expressions using a demand-driven backward analysis based on G-SSA form. Their analysis can be more efficient than our approach if local analysis information suffices to obtain a result, otherwise they may have to examine large portions of a program. Tu and Padua require additional analysis to determine path conditions in contrast to our approach that directly represents path conditions in the context. For recurrences, Tu and Padua cannot directly determine the corresponding recurrence system from a given G-SSA form. With our approach the extraction of recurrence systems is an integral operation provided in the symbolic domain.

Menon et al. [27] describe a technique for dependence analysis that verifies the legality of program transformations. They apply symbolic analysis to establish equality of a program and its transformation. Their symbolic analysis engine is limited to affine symbolic expressions and predicates consisting of conjunctions and disjunctions of affine inequalities. Blume and Eigenmann [10] apply symbolic ranges to disprove carried dependences of permuted loop nests. They use abstract interpretation to compute the ranges for variables at each program point. Gerlek et al. [19] describe a general induction variable recognition method based on a demand-driven SSA form. Rugina and Rinard [31] carry out symbolic bounds analysis for accessed memory regions. With their method they set up a system of symbolic constraints that describe the lower and upper bounds of pointers, array indices, and accessed memory regions. This system of constraints is then solved using ILP. The Omega test [28] developed by W. Pugh is an integer programming method that operates on a system of linear inequalities to determine whether a dependence between variables exists. It has been extended to nonlinear tests in [30,29].

8   Conclusions and Future Work

In this paper we have presented a generic symbolic analysis framework for imperative programming languages. At the center of our framework is a comprehensive and compact algebraic structure called supercontext. Supercontexts describe the complete control and data flow analysis information valid at a given program point. This information is invaluable for all kinds of static program analyses, such as memory leak detection [32], program parallelisation [17,22,37,10], detection of superfluous bound checks, variable aliases and task deadlocks [31,13,6,7], and for worst-case execution time analysis [4,8].

At present our framework accurately models assignment statements, branches, and loop constructs of imperative programming languages. It can easily be extended to the inter-procedural case (as discussed in [17,6]).

Our approach is more general than existing methods because it can derive solutions for arbitrary nodes (even within loops) of reducible and irreducible CFGs.

We proved (cf. also [11]) the correctness of our symbolic analysis method using a two-step verification based on the MOP-solution for symbolic execution and path-expression-based symbolic evaluation.

Our approach is based purely on algebra and is fully automated. The detection of recurrences is decoupled from the process of finding closed forms. This separation facilitates the extension of our recurrence solver with new classes of recurrence relations. Our novel representation of program semantics closes the gap between program analysis and computer algebra systems, which makes supercontexts an ideal intermediate representation for all domain-specific static program analyses.

The experiments conducted with our prototype implementation showed that the problem sizes of real-world programs such as those from the SPEC95 benchmark suite are tractable for our symbolic analysis framework. It has been shown in [9] that symbolic analysis has a vast improvement potential in the area of contemporary data-flow based analyses of sequential and concurrent programs. We are therefore facing two research tiers that we plan to pursue in the future, namely (1) the extension of our method to incorporate concurrent programming language constructs, and (2) the application of our method to domain-specific static program analysis problems.

References

1. A. V. Aho, R. Sethi, and J. D. Ullman. *Compilers—Principles, Techniques, and Tools*. Addison-Wesley, 1986.
2. O. Bachmann, P. S. Wang, and E. V. Zima. Chains of Recurrences — A Method to Expedite the Evaluation of Closed-Form Functions. In *Proc. of the Internat. Symposium on Symbolic and Algebraic Computation*, pages 242–249. ACM Press, 1994.
3. F. Baader and T. Nipkow. *Term Rewriting and All That*. Cambridge University Press, New York, 1998.
4. J. Blieberger. Data-Flow Frameworks for Worst-Case Execution Time Analysis. *Real-Time Systems*, 22:183–227, 2002.
5. J. Blieberger. Discrete Loops and Worst Case Performance. *Computer Languages*, 20(3):193–212, 1994.
6. J. Blieberger, B. Burgstaller, and B. Scholz. Interprocedural Symbolic Evaluation of Ada Programs with Aliases. In *Proc. of the Ada-Europe International Conference on Reliable Software Technologies*, pages 136–145, Santander, Spain, June 1999.
7. J. Blieberger, B. Burgstaller, and B. Scholz. Symbolic Data Flow Analysis for Detecting Deadlocks in Ada Tasking Programs. In *Proc. of the Ada-Europe International Conference on Reliable Software Technologies*, pages 225–237. Springer-Verlag, 2000.
8. J. Blieberger, T. Fahringer, and B. Scholz. Symbolic Cache Analysis for Real-Time Systems. *Real-Time Systems*, 18(2/3):181–215, 2000.
9. B. Burgstaller, J. Blieberger, and R. Mittermayr. Static Detection of Access Anomalies in Ada95. In *Proc. of the Ada-Europe International Conference on Reliable Software Technologies*, pages 40–55. Springer-Verlag, 2006.
10. W. Blume and R. Eigenmann. Nonlinear and Symbolic Data Dependence Testing. *IEEE Transactions on Parallel and Distributed Systems*, 9(12):1180–1194, 1998.

11. B. Burgstaller. Symbolic Evaluation of Imperative Programming Languages. Technical Report 183/1-138, Department of Automation, Vienna University of Technology, June 2005. http://www.auto.tuwien.ac.at/~bburg/reports.html.

12. B. Burgstaller, B. Scholz, and J. Blieberger. Tour de Spec — A Collection of Spec95 Program Paths and Associated Costs for Symbolic Evaluation. Technical Report 183/1-137, Department of Automation, Vienna University of Technology, June 2004. http://www.auto.tuwien.ac.at/~bburg/reports.html.

13. J. Blieberger and B. Burgstaller. Eliminating Redundant Range Checks in GNAT Using Symbolic Evaluation. In *Proc. of the Ada-Europe International Conference on Reliable Software Technologies*, pages 153–167, Toulouse, France, June 2003.

14. http://www.it.usyd.edu.au/~bburg/symanalysis.html.

15. L. A. Clarke and D. J. Richardson. Symbolic Evaluation Methods for Program Analysis. In Steven S. Muchnick and Neil D. Jones, editors, *Program Flow Analysis: Theory and Applications*, pages 264–300. Prentice-Hall, 1981.

16. P. Cousot and R. Cousot. Abstract Intrepretation: a Unified Lattice Model for Static Analysis of Programs by Construction or Approximation of Fixpoints. In *Proc. of POPL*, pages 238–252, January 1977.

17. T. Fahringer and B. Scholz. *Advanced Symbolic Analysis for Compilers*, volume 2628. LNCS, Springer-Verlag, 2003.

18. K. O. Geddes, S. R. Czapor, and G. Labahn. *Algorithms for Computer Algebra*. Kluwer Academic Publishers, 1992.

19. M. P. Gerlek, E. Stoltz, and M. Wolfe. Beyond Induction Variables: Detecting and Classifying Sequences Using a Demand-Driven SSA Form. *TOPLAS*, 17(1):85–122, January 1995.

20. J. Goguen, T. Winkler, J. Meseguer, K. Futatsugi, and J. Jouannaud. Introducing OBJ. Draft, Oxford University Computing Laboratory, 1993.

21. D. Greene and D. E. Knuth. *Mathematics For the Analysis of Algorithms*. Birkhäuser, second edition, 1982.

22. M. R. Haghighat and C. D. Polychronopoulos. Symbolic Analysis for Parallelizing Compilers. *TOPLAS*, 18(4):477–518, July 1996.

23. P. Havlak. *Interprocedural Symbolic Analysis*. PhD thesis, Dept. of Computer Science, Rice University, May 1994.

24. M. S. Hecht. *Flow Analysis of Computer Programs*. Elsevier, 1977.

25. J. E. Hopcroft and J. D. Ullman. *Introduction to Automata Theory, Languages, and Computation*. Addison-Wesley, N. Reading, MA, 1979.

26. George S. Lueker. Some Techniques for Solving Recurrences. *ACM Computing Surveys (CSUR)*, 12(4):419–436, 1980.

27. V. Menon, K. Pingali, and N. Mateev. Fractal Symbolic Analysis. *TOPLAS*, 25(6):776–813, 2003.

28. W. Pugh. The Omega Test: A Fast and Practical Integer Programming Algorithm for Dependence Analysis. *Communications of the ACM*, 35(8):102–114, 1992.

29. W. Pugh. Counting Solutions To Presburger Formulas: How and Why. In *Proc. of PLDI*, pages 121–134, 1994.

30. W. Pugh and D. Wonnacott. Nonlinear Array Dependence Analysis. Technical report, College Park, MD, USA, 1994.

31. R. Rugina and M. Rinard. Symbolic Bounds Analysis of Pointers, Array Indices, and Accessed Memory Regions. In *Proc. of PLDI*, pages 182–195, 2000.

32. B. Scholz, J. Blieberger, and T. Fahringer. Symbolic Pointer Analysis for Detecting Memory Leaks. In *ACM SIGPLAN Workshop on "Partial Evaluation and Semantics-Based Program Manipulation" (PEPM'00)*, Boston, January 2000.

33. SPEC CPU95 Benchmark Suite, Version 1.10, August 1995.

34. R. E. Tarjan. A Unified Approach to Path Problems. *Journal of the ACM*, 28(3):577–593, 1981.
35. P. Tu and D. A. Padua. Gated SAA-Based Demand-Driven Symbolic Analysis for Parallelizing Compilers. In *International Conference on Supercomputing*, pages 414–423, 1995.
36. R. A. van Engelen. The CR# Algebra and its Application in Loop Analysis and Optimization. Technical Report TR-041223, Department of Computer Science, Florida State University, December 2004.
37. R. A. van Engelen, J. Birch, Y. Shou, B. Walsh, and K. A. Gallivan. A Unified Framework for Nonlinear Dependence Testing and Symbolic Analysis. In *ICS '04: Proc. of the 18th Annual International Conference on Supercomputing*, pages 106–115. ACM Press, 2004.
38. Stephen Wolfram. *The Mathematica Book*. Wolfram Media, Incorporated, 2003.
39. E. V. Zima. Simplification and Optimization Transformations of Chains of Recurrences. In *ISSAC '95: Proc. of the 1995 International Symposium on Symbolic and Algebraic Computation*, pages 42–50. ACM Press, 1995.
40. H. Zima and B. Chapman. *Supercompilers for Parallel and Vector Computers*. ACM Press, New York, 1991.

Array-Structured Object Types for Mathematical Programming

Felix Friedrich and Jürg Gutknecht

Computer Systems Institute, ETH Zürich, Switzerland
{felix.friedrich, gutknecht}@inf.ethz.ch

Abstract. In this paper a concept for structured mathematical programming within an object-oriented language is presented. It leads to better readable, more natural and more compact code in typical linear algebra applications and provides options for optimized implementation. We also discuss the realization of this concept as an extension of the programming language Active Oberon.

We define new built-in array types that provide a slight modification of classical arrays in Oberon. By introducing range-valued indices as array designators, we permit the use of regular sub-domains of arrays as parameters of operators and procedures. The built-in types are complemented by *custom* array structured object types. The latter can be specified by the programmer and are designed to be syntactically compatible with the former. They provide the needed flexibility for the language.

1 Introduction

There are already concepts for mathematical programming proposed both in multi-purpose languages, such as Fortran, Zpl and Chapel, and in special purpose packages like Matlab, Mathematica and R, just to mention a few. Concepts in common mathematical languages are too specific and functionality is too complex for a general purpose language. However, these approaches must not be ignored but rather be used for inspiration.

Besides other advantages of the programming language Oberon, its clarity and readability is undoubtedly a good reason to go for it. Because it is more abstract and closer to mathematics than system near languages such as C/C++, Java etc., it permits to implement mathematical algorithms in very clear and structured form. However, by experience and inspection of code, in particular for linear algebra and imaging applications, we discovered that a small extension of the language can significantly increase efficiency and readability.

We cannot present a solution that satisfies all possible needs. Although it is tempting to implement as much functionality as possible, we aim at a coherent, self-contained concept that avoids redundant language constructs and programming pitfalls. To achieve such a lean model, we attach equally much importance to constructs that we provide and to functionality that we deliberately *omit*.

D. Lightfoot and C. Szyperski (Eds.): JMLC 2006, LNCS 4228, pp. 195–210, 2006.

We believe that a programmer can enhance an implementation considerably without having to deal with system near constructs: The ideal case is of course the development of theoretically better algorithms providing lower complexity and lower run-times. But also using the structure inherent to a problem in the implementation can be of high value. For instance, in the context of array operations, existing code can be made considerably clearer and more efficient by exploiting that certain operations can be performed block-wise. We are not aiming at an automatic enhancement on the code generation level (as, for instance, in ATLAS, cf. [2]) but want to give the programmer tools at hand with which he can incorporate his expert knowledge about the structure of the matter.

The objective of this paper is to establish an object oriented concept of (multidimensional) array-structured types. Purpose is intuitive and efficient mathematical programming. The paper is organized as follows: Section 2 has a motivating nature. It provides some preliminary examples of our language extensions and contains conceptional considerations. The new language constructs are then presented in Section 3 in detail. This last part comprises the formal specification of built-in and custom array types, of operators on and between them, of range-valued indices used as array designators and some implementation specific notes. The paper ends with a conclusion.

2   Preliminary Conceptual Considerations

The first part of this section contains examples providing a quick insight to our new language constructs. In the second part we will give reasons for the design that is then particularized in Section 3. The current state of the art in Oberon is recapitulated in the third part.

2.1   Illustration

In this paragraph, we examine code from a typical Oberon linear algebra implementation and illustrate our approach by ways of these examples. The examples are not exhaustive and anticipate notions that will be explained in Section 3.

Operators: Matrix Multiplication. The most prominent example of a linear algebra operation is certainly the multiplication of two matrices. A naïve Oberon version is displayed in Fig. 1 and a version with elimination of the inner loop is depicted in Fig. 2. It is obvious that, having readability in mind, this construct in general has to be replaced by a call to a procedure or better by a language-integrated multiplication operator as displayed in Fig. 3. But not only this can be learned from the displayed algorithm: If L and R are large matrices then cache misses are highly probable in the inner loop, since R is processed column-wise. Operators between arrays and dimensions-permuted storage formats are of benefit here and possible in the new approach.

```
VAR A,B,Res: POINTER TO ARRAY OF ARRAY OF REAL;
    i,j,k: LONGINT;
    temp: REAL;
(* ... *)
(* check shapes *)
FOR i := 0 TO LEN(L,0)-1 DO
 FOR j := 0 TO LEN(R,1)-1 DO
  temp := 0;
  FOR k := 0 TO LEN(R,0)-1 DO
   temp := temp + L[i,k]*R[k,j];
  END;
  Res[i,j] := temp;
 END;
END;
```

Fig. 1. Naïve matrix multiplication

```
VAR A,B,Res: POINTER TO ARRAY OF ARRAY OF REAL;
    i,j: LONGINT;
(* ... *)
(* check shapes *)
FOR i := 0 TO LEN(L,0)-1 DO
 FOR j := 0 TO LEN(R,1)-1 DO
  Res[i,j] := L[i,..]+*R[..,j]; (* pseudo scalar product *)
 END;
END;
```

Fig. 2. Naïve matrix multiplication,inner loop eliminated

```
VAR A,B,Res: ARRAY [..,..] OF REAL;
(* ... *)
Res := A*B;
```

Fig. 3. Matrix multiplication with natural notation

Sub-array Structures. Very often operations are not performed on the complete array but rather on sub-array structures, such as (parts of) columns or rows of a matrix. A first example with operation on rows and columns of a matrix has already been displayed in Fig. 2.

The singular value decomposition algorithm provided by LAPACK is one prominent example consisting of many such operations. In Fig. 4 a small portion of the code is displayed. Our approach includes range-valued indices that, applied to an array, form a designator of certain substructures, see Fig. 5.

```
VAR u: POINTER TO ARRAY OF ARRAY OF REAL;
    s,h,f: REAL; i,j,k,l,m,n: LONGINT;
(* ... *)
FOR j := 1 TO n DO
  s := 0.0;
  FOR k := i TO m DO
   s := s + u[k, i] * u[k, j]
  END;
  f := s / h;
  FOR k := i TO m DO
   u[k, j] := u[k, j] + f * u[k, i]
  END;
END;
```

Fig. 4. Small part of SVD in classical notation

```
VAR u: ARRAY [..,..] OF REAL; s,h: REAL; i,j,l,m,n: LONGINT;
(* ... *)
FOR j := 1 TO n DO
  S := u[i..m,i]+*u[i..m,j];                (* scalar product *)
  u[i..m,j] := u[i..m,j] + s/h* u[i..m,i]; (* element-wise operations *)
END;
```

Fig. 5. Code from Fig. 4 using new approach

Custom Array Types. Since not all possible features can be implemented in a built-in array type, we have made provision for the implementation of custom array types. Figure 7 contains a sample implementation of a sparse matrix, i.e. a two dimensional array that only has a small number of nonzero elements. In Fig. 6 it is shown how such a new type harmonizes with the concept of 'normal' arrays. Note that the two dimensional array structure and the element type is constituted in the (array) type declaration of SparseMatrix.

```
VAR A: ARRAY [10,10] OF REAL; B: SparseMatrix; i: LONGINT;
  (* ... *)
  A := 1;                        (* fill matrix A with ones *)
  NEW(B,1000,1000);              (* sparse matrix of size 1000x1000 *)
  FOR i := 0 TO 999 BY 10 DO
   B[i..i+9,i..i+9] := A;        (* fill blocks along diagonal *)
  END;
```

Fig. 6. Using custom array types. Implementation of SparseMatrix suggested in Fig. 7

```
TYPE
 SparseMatrix*= ARRAY [..,..] OF REAL (* 2d array structure with element type real *)
 VAR d: Data; len0,len1: LONGINT; (* assume type Data is defined elsewhere *)

 PROCEDURE NEW(i,j: LONGINT); (* allocation *)
 BEGIN
  (* create data structure *)
  len0 := i; len1 := j;
 END NEW;

 PROCEDURE LEN(i: LONGINT): LONGINT; (* sizes, shape *)
 (* ... *)
 END LEN;

 PROCEDURE "[]"(i,j: LONGINT): REAL;
 BEGIN
  (* range check *)
  RETURN Get(d,i,j)
 END "[]";

 PROCEDURE "[]"(i,j: LONGINT; r: REAL);
 BEGIN
  (* range check *)
  Put(d,i,j,r);
 END "[]";

 (* matrix extraction *)
 PROCEDURE "[]"(a1..b1 BY c1,a2..b2 BY c2: LONGINT): ARRAY [..,..] OF REAL;
 VAR A: ARRAY [..,..] OF REAL; (* in this implementation: extract block as built-in array *)
 BEGIN
  IF a1 = MIN(LONGINT) THEN a1 := 0 END; (* defaults *)
  IF b1 = MAX(LONGINT) THEN b1 := len0-1 END; (* defaults *)
  (* same for a2,b2 *)
  (* range check *)
  NEW(A,(b1-a1) DIV c1,(b2-va2) DIV c2);
  Extract(d,A,a1..b1 BY c1; a2..b2 BY c2);
  RETURN A;
 END "[]";

 (* submatrix assignment *)
 PROCEDURE "[]"(a1..b1 BY c1,a2..b2 BY c2: LONGINT; VAR A:ARRAY [..,..] OF REAL);
 BEGIN
  (* defaults, range check *)
  Insert(A,d,a1..b1 BY c1, a2..b2 BY c2);
 END "[]";

END SparseMatrix;

(* Get, Set, Extract, Insert routines skipped *)

(* operator overloading *)
PROCEDURE '*' (A,B: SparseMatrix): SparseMatrix;
(* ... *)
END '*';

PROCEDURE '*' (A: SparseMatrix; VAR B: ARRAY [..,..] OF REAL): ARRAY [..,..] OF REAL;
(* ... *)
END '*';

(* ... *)
```

Fig. 7. Draft of a sparse matrix implementation

2.2   Design Objectives

In this paragraph we state basic conditions and establish a concept that is in compliance with them.

Requisites. Our goal is an approach that, in particular for arrays, supports the following general key requirements.

1. *Efficiency.* It should be possible that expert knowledge about the structure of an algorithm is incorporated into an implementation to achieve efficiency.
2. *Notational simplicity.* Mathematical programs must well be readable and notation should conform with usual mathematical conventions.
3. *Structural simplicity.* A programmer must not need to handle system matters like complicated pointer arithmetics and memory management.
4. *Extensibility.* The built-in features of a language cannot satisfy all possible needs. It should thus be possible to add arbitrary functionality on an implementation level if it agrees with stipulated syntax and semantics.
5. *Safety.* Typical safety features, such as range- and type-checking must be preserved by the extension of the language.

To achieve efficient implementations of array-based algorithms, fast single element accesses are obviously necessary in the first place. Also the availability of optimized block-wise operations on sub-array configurations can improve speed considerably in many cases. The most prominent example is the generalized matrix multiplication identified to be the main performance kernel of the Basic Linear Algebra Subprograms (BLAS), cf. [2], p. 10. Figure 8 illustrates the gain of speed reached by using an optimized matrix multiplication using Intel's Streaming SIMD extensions (SSE), which add vector-oriented capabilities to general purpose processors. The displayed measurements refer to inline assembler code within an optimized Oberon module. Optimizations of this and similar kind will be done by the compiler and can in principle be applied to any type of regular array substructure. A discussion of optimization techniques in detail is beyond the scope of this paper.

Another important issue for efficiency is the avoidance of cache missing and cache trashing when dealing with large data, cf. [7]. Notational simplicity implies that block-wise operations have to be denoted in a common form and that specific optimizations, such as the avoidance of cache missing, must happen behind the scene and should not affect the notation. In the context of array handling, extensibility implies the implementation facility of arrays that cannot be represented as a linear piece of memory. Typical examples are sparse matrices or images with special boundary conditions such as 'periodic', 'mirrored' etc. Regarding safety, array range checks are indispensable as they are substantial for debugging and vital for system safety.

2.3   Concepts of the New Array Types

To comply with the aforementioned requisites, we decided to extend the functionality of Oberon *built-in* arrays and complement them by compatible

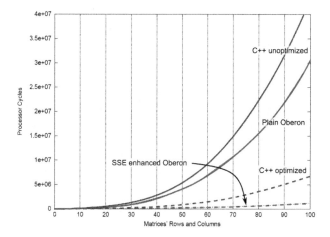

Fig. 8. Processor cycles of matrix multiplication. Oberon vs. C++ vs. optimized C++ vs. Oberon using SSE instructions, source: [14].

(programmer-definable) *custom* array-structured types. To explicitly discriminate the newly proposed built-in arrays from the classical array types in Oberon, we will in this text now and then denote them as *special* arrays. Special arrays permit the use of ranged indices as array designators. This construct allows to pass regular sub-domains of arrays to procedures and to use them as operands in expressions. This, together with the availability of efficient operators, leads to more readable and efficient code in linear algebra applications. Moreover, it allows the identification of independent pieces of code that can be optimized, for example being executed in parallel. As a further positive side effect, the needed array memory representation permits a dimension-permuted storage scheme that can be utilized for the avoidance of cache missing. Range checks are performed for each single element access and can be optimized to one single check for the access to an entire sub-structure. Safety is thus preserved while efficiency can be achieved by using the concept of ranges and operators.

For mathematical programming we generally prefer value semantics to reference semantics as it assures unambiguity of operations, in particular assignment and test for equality. Consequently, special arrays are value types (like records), rather than reference types (like objects). Memory allocation and pointer mechanisms are performed on behalf of the programmer behind the scenes. The programmer is only confronted with the definition and usage of fix- or variable-sized arrays. As a consequence, dynamic arrays are not exposed as pointers to an array structure: an array may well be of length zero but physically it invariably consists at least of the descriptor containing information about its shape. The decision for value semantics does not imply a severe restriction since arrays may still be wrapped into records or objects. For shared access this would be necessary anyway since concurrent access is managed by mutual exclusion on an object level in Oberon. Value semantics can also be regarded as additional protection against unintentional concurrent access to an array.

Custom array types can be specified by the programmer and are designed to be syntactically compatible with the built-in arrays. They provide the needed flexibility for the language. For operations on and between array types we use the already implemented operator concept of Oberon together with the facility of overloading. Internally, a custom array type is designed like a *value object type whose signature explicitly contains the array structure*. In this respect it is not regarded as an extension of a built-in array, but merely as a custom type that *mimics* the behavior of an array. Custom array types are abstract data types that may contain variables and procedures, but cannot be extended. The most important difference to the indexer concept of C# is that the array access structure of a custom array type is provided and fixed by its signature. We regard array structure as not only a property but merely as very immanent feature that must be statically tied to the respective object. In particular it allows to define substructures of object types in a clean way and prevents the misuse of mathematical 'indexers' for general purposes.

The dimension of an array is statically determined, i.e. cannot be changed at runtime, neither for built-in types nor in the programmer-definable form.

We repeat the main achievements of this concept. It permits

1. notational compactness in linear algebra applications,
2. optimizations by utilizing block-wise operations while preserving safety,
3. a clean implementation of (non-contiguous) custom array structures.

Discarded Ideas. Arrays in general stand for data of the form E^S, where E is a set of possible single states and S is a subset of $\mathbb{Z}^d$. Thus the specification of an array type A requires the definition of an element type B (referring to the set of single states E), a specification of the index set S and access patterns for elements of A. Although it somehow reflects the mathematical nature of E^S, for the sake of simplicity we do not introduce a separate type for the domain S as for example done in the programming language Chapel [4] and (partially) in ZPL [5].

The following features are of interest in some applications and can be implemented with custom array types. For built-in types, however, we decided against them: Customizable lower bounds for arrays provide potential pitfalls in programming, therefore built-in arrays have a fixed lower bound of zero. Free boundary conditions, such as "mirrored", "wrapped" etc., cannot be set for the built-in arrays, because it would generally prohibit efficiency for single element access. Built-in arrays do not permit the appending, insertion and deletion of elements since this requires a complex data type. (A reasonable implementation is provided by the software package Voyager, cf. [16]). The same holds for a built-in type of a sparse array representation. Having a common type for both 'normal' and sparse arrays would represent a dilemma for efficiency. Moreover, there are various forms of matrix storage schemes, such as Compressed Row/-Column Storage, Jagged Diagonal Storage etc., cf. [8]. We therefore decided to provide the flexible and efficient sparse matrix specification according to [3] as *sample implementation* using custom array-structured types.

Another approach that we discussed was the support of *properties* (built-in attributes) of arrays / matrices such as 'diagonal', 'symmetric' etc. on a language level. For example, the (dynamic) array structure could be taken into account to optimize the execution speed of operators like multiplication. On a static level this is already possible using custom array types. However we decided that the rare cases where a dynamic optimization would be possible are not worth the enormous computational effort and discarded this idea.

We also discarded the uses of indexers, as for instance provided by C#, because taking substructures would not be possible in a clean way, compare previous paragraph.

3   Specification of the Language Extension

In this section the syntax of the new built-in arrays and custom array types in Oberon is provided. Further some implementation specific notes are stated. We first recapitulate the status quo of Oberon: In classical Oberon it is not possible to address sub-arrays that do not form a contiguous block. New array types with different element access rules, such as sparse matrices, cannot be added to the system. The dimension order in memory coincides with that of the notation. From the view of mathematical programming the pointer notation used in Oberon for dynamic arrays is somewhat unnatural.

3.1   Built-In Arrays

Special arrays do not replace the classical arrays of Oberon but are added to the language. A special array type is determined by a statement that is compliant with the EBNF rule

$$\text{ARRAY "[" Length\{"," Length\} "]" OF Type ";"} . \tag{1}$$

where Length is either given by an expression or two periods:

$$\text{Length = ".." | Expression} . \tag{2}$$

The index set of an array is a rectangular d-dimensional set. The lower bound is zero in each dimension. Special arrays can be defined statically, semi-dynamically, dynamically and open. They are regarded as value types. Unallocated dynamic arrays have zero length dimensions. Constant arrays can also be specified like displayed in Fig. 9.

Operators. There are unary and binary operators predefined. Binary operators apply to two arrays or an array and a base type. Most important is the operator ':=': Special arrays may be assigned to each other. Since they are of value type, assignment infers copy of content. For any operation on two arrays with a compatibility requirement, such as assignment, the shape of the arrays must

```
A: ARRAY [..,..] OF REAL  (* declaration of dynamic size matrix *)
B: ARRAY [3,5] OF REAL    (* declaration of static size matrix *)
LEN(B,i)                  (* length of dimension i, LEN(B)=LEN(B,0) *)
NEW(A,3,5)                (* allocation of dynamic size matrix *)
[[1,2,3],[4,5,6]]         (* constant array *)
r := A[i,j]               (* element read access *)
A[i,j] := r               (* element write access *)
```

Fig. 9. Some examples regarding the notation of special arrays

match, that is `dim(A)=dim(B)` and `LEN(A,i)=LEN(B,i)` for all $0 \leq i < $ `dim(A)`, and the element types must be compatible w.r.t. the operation. The predefined operators on and between arrays are displayed in Fig. 10 and 11. With respect to efficiency, the objective of having operators is to leave open the possibility of fast (potentially parallel) execution of operations that usually require many single element accesses. The displayed operators (together with the special cases for matrices, see below) are chosen from typical applications in linear algebra and are promising with respect to significant speed-up of most frequently used routines. The notation is deliberately designed to be near to that of MatLab.

operator	operand	result	meaning
'-'	array of number	array	element-wise negation
'~'	array of boolean	array	element-wise inversion
'ABS'	array of number	array	element-wise absolute value
'MIN' , 'MAX'	array of number	scalar	minimal and maximal element
'SUM'	array of number	scalar	sum of elements
'PRODUCT'	array of number	scalar	product of elements

Fig. 10. Unary array operators

operator	operands	result	meaning
':='	scalar,array	array	assignment of value to each element
':='	array,array	array	assignment of same sized arrays
'+' , '-' , '*' '/' , 'MOD' , 'DIV'	array,scalar	array	element-wise scalar operation
'+' , '-' , '.*' '/' , 'MOD' , 'DIV'	array,array	array	element-wise operation
'+*'	array,array	scalar	pseudo scalar product
'='	array,array	boolean	test of equality

Fig. 11. Binary array operators

For arrays of non-arithmetic types, the operators are still undefined (but can be overloaded). The definition of the (pseudo-) scalar product `A +* B` is necessary for performance reasons: `SUM(A .* B)` requires array allocation while

```
VAR A,B: ARRAY [..,..] OF REAL; r: REAL; b: BOOLEAN;
(* ... *)
B:= -A;        (* element wise negative of A *)
B:= ABS(A);    (* element wise absolute value of A *)
MIN(A), MAX(A) (* minimal / maximal element of A *)
A + B, A - B   (* sum and difference *)
A .* B, A./ B  (* element-wise product and quotient *)
A +* B         (* (pseudo) scalar product *)
b := A=B;      (* equality *)
```

Fig. 12. Operators on and between special arrays

A +* B does not. Examples regarding notation of operators are displayed in Fig. 12.

Special Case: Matrix Operators. According to [1] and [2], the most important and time-critical operation in the Basic Linear Algebra Subroutines (BLAS) package is the one for generalized matrix multiplication. Moreover, the solution of matrix equations as displayed below is also a prominent example, again the notation follows MatLab. The following operators are defined for two dimensional arrays. The unary operator "'" does not create a copy of the data but only a designator to the same array with toggled dimensions. This is possible due to the internal format of the array references, cf. paragraph 3.3. Examples are given in Fig. 14.

Remark: "/" and "\" will not necessarily be provided as built-in operators.

operator	operands	result	meaning
' (postfix)	2d array	2d array	transposed of matrix
*	2d array,2d array	2d array	matrix product
/	2d array,2d array	2d array	solution of equation system
\	2d array,2d array	2d array	solution of equation system

Fig. 13. Operators on two dimensional arrays

```
VAR A,B,C,X: ARRAY [..,..] OF REAL;
C := A * B; (* matrix product *)
X := B / A; (* solution of equation X*A=B, read: B*A^(-1) *)
X := A \ B; (* solution of equation A*X=B, read: A^(-1)*B *)
A := B';   (* B' is reference to transposed of B, copy by ":=" *)
```

Fig. 14. Operators on and between two dimensional arrays

Ranges. A range is denoted by an expression of the form

$$[Expression]..[Expression][BY Expression]. \qquad (3)$$

Consider the range a..b BY c. Here the symbols a, b and c (c > 0) must be integer valued constants or integer variables. The range a..b BY c stands for the set

$$\{a + i \cdot c : i \in \mathbb{N}, 0 \leq i \cdot c \leq b - a\}.$$

The usage of this notation is limited to the call and declaration of procedures and of the index operators ' [] '. If c is not specified, then a value of 1 is assumed. If a or b is not given, then – depending on the context – the smallest or largest appropriate value is imputed. If not specified but explicitly referred to, a value of MIN(LONGINT) and MAX(LONGINT) is presumed on a or b, respectively. For instance the call TestRange(..) of the procedure

PROCEDURE TestRange(a..b BY c: LONGINT)

results in a=MIN(LONGINT), b=MAX(LONGINT), c=1 in the procedure body.

Ranges on Arrays. Ranges can be applied to special arrays. A variable specified by the expression

Identifier[Range|ConstExpr{,Range|ConstExpr}]   (4)

is formally of array type with dimension equal to the number of ranges given. It is a designator and is therefore not necessarily materialized but only stands for a certain part of the array. As in the case of ordinary indices, a designator is applicable for read and write access.

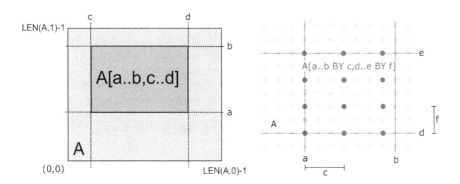

Fig. 15. Illustrations of domain extraction

Note that there is a substantial difference between a number i and a range a..b BY c in the specification of a sub-domain. A[a..b,c..d] stands for a two dimensional array, even if a=b or c=d, while A[a..b,i] stands for a one dimensional array and A[i,j] stands for a number.

Sub-domain specifications, such as A[a..b,c..d] refer to the same data as the referenced object (A). So referring to A[a..b,c..d] in the procedure declaration with a VAR parameter allows to modify the content of A. However, the statement sequence

$$B \ := \ A[..,..]; \ B[2,2]:= \ r$$

does not modify the content of A since the assignment operator ':=' stands for copy operation. More examples are displayed in Fig. 16.

```
VAR V: ARRAY [..] OF REAL; A: ARRAY [..,..] OF REAL;
V[..10] (* stands for V[0..10], is of type ARRAY [..] OF REAL *)
V[3..] (* stands for V[3..LEN(A)-1] *)
V[.. BY 2] (* stands for V[0..LEN(A)-1 BY 2] *)
A[a1..b1 BY c1, a2..b2 BY c2] (* two dimensional subdomain of A *)
A[a1..b1,a2..b2] := [[1,2,3],[4,5,6],[7,8,9]]; (* assignment of const *)
V := A[a1..b1,a2]; (* copy of piece of column *)
V := A[a1,a2..b2]; (* copy of piece of row *)
(* assume PROCEDURE MyProc(v: ARRAY [..] OR REAL); *)
MyProc(A[..,5]); (* call procedure, pass 6th column of A as parameter *)
```

Fig. 16. Examples regarding use of ranges

3.2   Custom Array Types

Besides the built-in functionalities, provision is made for the free specification of structured array types and operators. In this paragraph the syntax and semantics are defined.

Definition of Custom Array-Structured Types. A custom array type may be defined by the programmer like an object type. Inheritance and polymorphism is not supported. Moreover, custom array types cannot have an (active) body in Active Oberon. The reason for this decision is clearness of the language definition: built-in array types and custom array types must be handled equivalently and the atomic evaluation of operators is not guaranteed for the first. Synchronization has to be done on an object level if references are used for the arrays. As mentioned previously, this is additionally ensured by the value semantics used.

A custom array is specified with the pattern

TYPE ident "≙" ARRAY "[" ..{,..} "]" OF Type   DeclSeq   END ident.

(5)

The minimal ingredients that are usually implemented are the procedures NEW, LEN and read- and write-access methods "[]" as displayed in Fig. 17.

Ranges on Custom Array Types. For custom array-structured types, typically the procedures depicted in Fig. 18 would be implemented to obtain range accesses. The compiler discriminates between different forms of '[]' by their different signatures. Generally, only the array specific operators LEN and the index operators are directly declared within array scope whereas other operators have to be declared outside in module scope.

```
TYPE SparseMatrix = ARRAY [..,..] OF REAL
VAR (* ... *) (* allocation variables etc. *)
  PROCEDURE NEW(i,j: LONGINT); (* initialization, allocation *)
  PROCEDURE "[]"(i,j: LONGINT): REAL; (* read access *)
  PROCEDURE "[]"(i,j: LONGINT; r: REAL) (* write access *)
  PROCEDURE LEN(i: LONGINT): LONGINT; (* shape *)
END SparseMatrix;
```

Fig. 17. Custom array type definition I

```
TYPE
Matrix= ARRAY [..,..] OF REAL;
Vector= ARRAY [..] OF REAL;

SparseMatrix = ARRAY [..,..] OF REAL
  ...
  (* read access routines *)
  PROCEDURE "[]"(a1..b1 BY c1, a2..b2 BY c2: LONGINT): Matrix;
  PROCEDURE "[]"(a1..b1 BY c1, i: LONGINT): Vector;
  PROCEDURE "[]"(i, a2..b2 BY c2: LONGINT): Vector;
  (* write access routines *)
  PROCEDURE "[]"(a1..b1 BY c1, a2..b2 BY c2: LONGINT; VAR A: Matrix);
  PROCEDURE "[]"(a1..b1 BY c1, i: LONGINT; VAR A: Vector);
  PROCEDURE "[]"(i, a2..b2 BY c2: LONGINT; VAR A: Vector);
END SparseMatrix;
```

Fig. 18. Custom array type definition II

Operators. Generic operators can also be defined for custom array types. As mentioned, operators must be defined within the array type module scope. At least one of the operands must be part of the current scope. The definition of overloaded operators follows the current Active Oberon convention. For the SparseMatrix example, operators would typically be defined as in Fig. 19.

```
PROCEDURE ":=" (VAR dest: ARRAY [..,..] OF REAL; src: SparseMatrix);
PROCEDURE "*" (src1,src2: SparseMatrix): ARRAY [..,..] OF REAL;
PROCEDURE "*" (l: SparseMatrix; r: REAL): SparseMatrix;
PROCEDURE "+*" (l,r: SparseMatrix): REAL;
```

Fig. 19. Overloading operators for custom array types

3.3   Notes on Implementation

The implementation of the compiler modifications necessary for providing all language constructs presented in this paper is, at the time of submission, still work in progress. Nevertheless, in this paragraph we comment on some implementation specific details. For the built-in array types we decided – notionally - for a consistent memory representation that does not depend on array allocation kind such as dynamic, semi-dynamic, open or static. Since a special array is of value type, it at least consist of an array descriptor that includes the information about the array shape. An empty array A is characterized by LEN(A)=0. A schematic view of the memory structure is displayed in Fig. 20. The increment fields in the array descriptor are necessary for the sub-domain operations.

adr offset	description
...	type descriptor
+0	base address of data, points to *dataaddr* if array is on stack
+4	increment of dimension d-1
+8	length of dimension d-1
...	
$+8 \cdot (d-1) + 4$	increment of dimension 0
$+8 \cdot (d-1) + 8$	length of dimension 0
...	(padding)
$+dataaddr$	data base-address if array is on stack

Fig. 20. Schematic memory layout of built-in arrays

We give a short example of how range-valued indices are implemented: consider the assignment A[a..b] := B[c,a..b]. Both range valued indices A[a..b] and B[c,a..b] are of (one dimensional) array type; After range checks, corresponding increments $I_1 = \text{Inc}(A, 0)$ and $I_2 = \text{Inc}(A, 1)$, lengths $L_1 = L_2 = b - a + 1$, and base addresses $M_1 = \text{Adr}(A) + a \cdot \text{Inc}(A, 0)$ and $M_2 = \text{Adr}(B) + c \cdot \text{Inc}(B, 0) + a \cdot \text{Inc}(B, 1)$ are computed (according to the designators) and the two array descriptors are pushed on the stack. These are then used as arguments for the copy operation.

Note that it is not assumed that $\text{Inc}(i) < \text{Inc}(j)$ for $i < j$. This permits an arbitrary assignment of the contiguous part in the memory to a particular index, which is potentially useful for avoidance of cache missing. By introducing additional fields for an offset in each dimension, it would have easily, and without significant loss of efficiency, been possible to offer customizable lower bounds in arrays. However, for the given reasons (cf. Sect. 2), we decided against them.

Note that the displayed memory structure is only a very slight modification of the memory structure of classical arrays in Oberon. This can be regarded as confirmation of our maxims simplicity and efficiency.

4   Conclusion

The presented extension of the programming language Oberon is a further step in the direction of more intuitive and efficient mathematical programming. The introduction of a more flexible built-in array concept, including range-valued indices, leads to more compact and readable notation for computing with vectors, matrices etc. Being still safe it also has a high potential w.r.t. efficiency for the reasons of block-wise operations and the possible avoidance of cache missing. Flexibility and extensibility is granted by the introduction of custom array types that can be specified by the programmer and are syntactically compatible with the built-in array constructs.

References

1. R. Clint Whaley, Antoine Petitet. *Minimizing development and maintenance costs in supporting persistently optimized BLAS*, Software: Practice and Experience, Vol 35, No 2, (2005), pp. 101-121, John Wiley & Sons (2005)
2. R. Clint Whaley, Antoine Petitet, Jack J. Dongarra, *Automated empirical optimizations of software and the ATLAS project*, Parallel Computing 27 (1-2), 2001, pp. 3-35, Elsevier Science Publishers B.V. (North Holland): Amsterdam-London-New York-Oxford-Paris-Shannon-Tokyo
3. Bradford L. Chamberlain, Lawrence Snyder, *Array language support for parallel sparse computation*, Proceedings of the 15th international conference on Supercomputing, Sorrento, Italy, pp. 133 - 145 (2001), ACM Press New York
4. Specification of the Programming language *Chapel*, from http://chapel.cs.washington.edu/.
5. Bradford L. Chamberlain. *The Design and Implementation of a Region-Based Parallel Language*, PhD thesis, University of Washington (2001).
6. Malik Silva and Richard Wait, *Cache Aware Data Layouts*, IITC2000, Colombo, January 2001
7. Malik Silva and Richard Wait, *Go for Both types of Data Locality!*, HPCAsia, Bangalore, December 2002
8. Alik Silva, *Sparse matrix storage revisited*, Proceedings of the 2nd conference on Computing frontiers, pp.230-235, Ischia, Italy (2005)
9. MATLAB documentation web site. http://www.mathworks.com/access/helpdesk/help/techdoc/
10. R Language Definition and Introduction on http://www.r-project.org.
11. Peter Januschke, *Oberon-XSC – Eine Programmiersprache und Arithmetikbibliothek für das Wissenschaftliche Rechnen*, PhD Thesis, Universität Karlsruhe, 1998.
12. Robert Griesemer, *A Programming Language for Vector Computers*, PhD Thesis, ETH Zürich, 1993.
13. Bernd Mösli,*A Comparison of C++, FORTRAN 90 and Oberon-2 for Scientific Programming*, GISI 95, editors: Friedbert Huber-Wäschle, Helmut Schauer, Peter Widmayer Berlin, Springer, p. 740-748, 1995.
14. Michael Baumgartner, *Erweiterung des Active Oberon Compilers und Software Entwicklungssystems im Hinblick auf die Ausnutzung der Intel SSE2 Vektoroperationen für mathematische Anwendungen*, Diploma Thesis, ETH Zürich, 2003.
15. Roberto Morelli, *Integration of OberonX in Oberon*, Diploma Thesis, ETH Zürich, 1997.
16. Günther Sawitzki, *Extensible Statistical Software: On a Voyage to Oberon*, J.Computational and Graphical Statistics, 5(3):263-283,1996.

MetaModelica: A Unified Equation-Based Semantical and Mathematical Modeling Language*

Adrian Pop and Peter Fritzson

Programming Environment Laboratory
Department of Computer and Information Science
Linköping University, 58183 Linköping, Sweden
`{adrpo, petfr}@ida.liu.se`

Abstract. For a long time, one of the major research goals in the computer science research community has been to raise the level of abstraction power of specification languages/programming languages. Many specification languages and formalisms have been invented, but unfortunately very few of those are practically useful, due to limited computer support of these languages and/or inefficient implementations. Thus, one important goal is executable specification languages of high abstraction power and with high performance, good enough for practical usage and comparable in execution speed to hand implementations of applications in low-level languages such as C or C++. In this paper we briefly describe our work in creating efficient executable specification languages for two application domains. The first area is formal specification of programming language semantics, whereas the second is formal specification of complex systems for which we have developed an object-oriented mathematical modeling language called Modelica, including architectural support for components and connectors. Based on these efforts, we are currently working on a unified equation-based mathematical modeling language that can handle modeling of items as diverse as programming languages, computer algebra, event-driven systems, and continuous-time physical systems. The key unifying feature is the notion of equation. In this paper we describe the design and implementation of the unified language. A compiler implementation is already up and running, and used for substantial applications.

1 Introduction

For a long time, one of the major research goals in the computer science research community has been to raise the level of abstraction power of specification languages/programming languages. Many specification languages and formalisms have been invented, but unfortunately very few of those are practically useful, due to limited computer support of these languages and/or inefficient implementations.

In this paper we briefly describe our existing work in creating efficient executable specification languages for two application domains and propose an integration of this work within a unified language for mathematical and semantical modeling.

---

* This work was supported by the SSF RISE project, the Vinnova SWEBPROD project, and by the CUGS graduate school.

D. Lightfoot and C. Szyperski (Eds.): JMLC 2006, LNCS 4228, pp. 211–229, 2006.
© Springer-Verlag Berlin Heidelberg 2006

Thus, the main goal of this work is the design and development of a *general executable mathematical modeling and semantics meta-modeling language*. This language should have a clean semantics as in the case of Modelica and Natural Semantics (RML), and should be compiled to code of high performance. This language will allow expressing mathematical models but also meta-models and meta-programs that specify composition of models, transformation of models, model constraints, etc. This language is based on Modelica extended with several new language constructs that allows program language specification. The unified language is called MetaModelica.

The paper is structured as follows: In the next section we present the starting background for the development of the MetaModelica unified language. Section 3 presents the proposed mathematical/semantical unified modeling language. In Section 4 we present the implementation of the MetaModelica compiler for the unified language. Section 5 presents performance evaluation of our generated code. Section 6 presents future work. Conclusions and Future work are presented in Section 7.

2   Background

About sixteen years ago, our research group has selected two application domains for research on high-level specification languages:

- Specification languages for programming language semantics. Much work has been done in that area, but there is still no standard class of compiler-compiler tools around, as successful as parser generators based on grammars in BNF form like lex (flex), yacc (bison), ANTLR, etc.
- Equation-based specification languages for mathematical modeling of complex (physical) systems.

In the following sections we briefly describe the main achievements of this work.

2.1   Natural Semantics and the Relational Meta-Language (RML)

Concerning *specification languages for programming language semantics*, compiler generators based on denotational semantics (Pettersson and Fritzson 1992 [24]) (Ringström et al. 1994 [29]), were investigated and developed with some success. However this formalism has certain usage problems, and Operational Semantics/Natural Semantics started to become the dominant formalism in common literature. Therefore a meta-language and compiler generator called RML (Relational Meta Language) (Fritzson 1998 [8], PELAB 1994-2005 [21], Pettersson 1995 [25], 1999 [26]) for Natural Semantics was developed, which we have used extensively for full-scale specifications of languages like Java (object oriented), C subset with pointer arithmetic, functional, and equation-based languages (Modelica). Generated implementations are comparable in performance to hand implementations. However, it turned out that development environment support is needed also for specification languages. Recent developments include a debugger for Natural Semantics specifications (Pop and Fritzson 2005 [28]).

Natural Semantics (Kahn 1988 [16]) is a specification formalism that is used to specify the semantics of programming languages, i.e., type systems, dynamic semantics, translational semantics, static semantics (Despeyroux 1984 [4], Glesner and Zimmermann 2004 [14]), etc. Natural Semantics is an operational semantics derived from the Plotkin (Plotkin 1981 [27]) structural operational semantics combined with the sequent calculus for natural deduction. There are few systems implemented that compile or interpret Natural Semantics.

One of these systems is Centaur (Borras et al. 1988 [1]) with its implementation of Natural Semantics called Typol (Despeyroux 1984 [4], 1988 [5]). This system is translating the Natural Semantics inference rules to Prolog.

The Relational Meta-Language (RML) is a much more efficient implementation of Natural Semantics, with a performance of the generated code that is several orders of magnitude better than Typol. The RML language is compiled to highly efficient C code by the rml2c compiler. In this way large parts of a compiler can be automatically generated from their Natural Semantics specifications. RML is successfully used for specifying and generating practically usable compilers from Natural Semantics for Java, Modelica, MiniML (Clément et al. 1986 [3]), Mini-Freja (Pettersson 1995 [25]) and other languages.

2.1.1   An Example of Natural Semantics and RML

As a simple example of using Natural Semantics and the Relational Meta-Language (RML) we present a trivial expression (Exp1) language and its specification in Natural Semantics and RML. A specification in Natural Semantics has two parts:

- Declarations of syntactic and semantic objects involved.
- Groups of inference rules which can be grouped together into relations.

In our example language we have expressions built from numbers. The abstract syntax of this language is declared in the following way:

integers:

$v \in Int$

expressions (abstract syntax):

$e \in Exp ::= v \mid e1 + e2 \mid e1 - e2 \mid e1 * e2 \mid e1 / e2 \mid -e$

The inference rules for our language are bundled together in a judgment $e => v$ in the following way (we do not present here the similar rules for the other operators.):

(1) $v \Rightarrow v$

(2) $\dfrac{e1 \Rightarrow v1 \ e2 \Rightarrow v2 \ v1+v2 \Rightarrow v3}{e1+e2 \Rightarrow v3}$

RML modules have two parts, an interface comprising datatype declarations (abstract syntax) and signatures of relations (judgments) that operate on such datatypes, followed by the declarations of the actual relations which group together rules and axioms. In RML, the Natural Semantics specification shown above is represented as follows:

```
module Exp1:

   (* Abstract syntax of the language Exp1 *)
   datatype Exp =   RCONST of real
                  |  ADD    of Exp * Exp
                  |  SUB    of Exp * Exp
                  |  MUL    of Exp * Exp
                  |  DIV    of Exp * Exp
                  |  NEG    of Exp
   relation eval: Exp => real
end
(* Evaluation semantics of Exp1 *)
relation eval: Exp => real  =

   (* Evaluation of a real node is the real number itself *)
   axiom eval(RCONST(rval)) => rval

   (* Evaluation of an addition node ADD is v3, if v3 is the result of
      adding the evaluated results of its children e1 and e2. *)
   rule   eval(e1) => v1 & eval(e2) => v2 &   v1 + v2 => v3
          ----------------------------------------------
          eval( ADD(e1, e2) ) => v3

   rule   eval(e1) => v1 & eval(e2) => v2 &   v1 - v2 => v3
          ----------------------------------------------
          eval( SUB(e1, e2) ) => v3

   rule   eval(e1) => v1 & eval(e2) => v2 &   v1 * v2 => v3
          ----------------------------------------------
          eval( MUL(e1, e2) ) => v3

   rule   eval(e1) => v1 & eval(e2) => v2 &   v1 / v2 => v3
          ----------------------------------------------
          eval( DIV(e1, e2) ) => v3

   rule   eval(e) => v & -v => vneg
          -----------------------
          eval( NEG(e) ) => vneg

end (* eval *)
```

A proof-theoretic interpretation can be assigned to this specification. We interpret inference rules as recipes for constructing proofs. We wish to prove that there is a value v such that $1 + 2 \Rightarrow v$ holds for this specification. To prove this proposition we need an inference rule that has a conclusion, which can be instantiated (matched) to the proposition. The only proposition that matches is the second proposition (2), which is instantiated as follows:

$$\frac{1 \Rightarrow v1 \quad 2 \Rightarrow v2 \quad v1 + v2 \Rightarrow v}{1 + 2 \Rightarrow v}$$

To continue the proof, we need to apply the first proposition (axiom) several times, and we soon reach the conclusion. One can observe that debugging of Natural Semantics comprise proof-tree understanding.

2.1.2 Specification of Syntax

Regarding the specification of lexical and syntatic rules for a new language, we use external tools such as Lex, Yacc, Flex, Bison, etc., to generate those modules. The parser builds abstract syntax by calling RML-defined constructors. The abstract syntax is then passed from the parser to the RML-generated modules. We currently use the same approach for languages defined using MetaModelica.

2.2 Modelica – An Object-Oriented Equation-Based Component Language

Starting 1989, we developed an equation-based specification language for mathematical modeling called ObjectMath (Viklund et al. 1992 [36]), using Mathematica as a basis and a frontend, but adding object orientation and efficient code generation was developed. Following this path our group joined effort with several other groups in object oriented mathematical modeling to start a design-group for developing an internationally viable declarative mathematical modeling language. The language resulted from this effort is called *Modelica*. Modelica (Elmqvist et al. 1999 [7], Fritzson 2004 [13], Fritzson and Engelson 1998 [9], Modelica-Association 1996-2005 [18], Tiller 2001 [35]) is an object-oriented modeling language for declarative equation-based mathematical modeling of large and heterogeneous physical systems. For modeling with Modelica, commercial software products such as MathModelica (MathCore [17]) or Dymola (Dynasim 2005 [6]) have been developed. Also open-source implementations like the OpenModelica system (Fritzson et al. 2002 [10], PELAB 2002-2005 [22]) are available.

The Modelica language has been designed to allow tools to generate efficient simulation code automatically with the main objective of facilitating exchange of models, model libraries and simulation specifications. The definition of simulation models is expressed in a declarative manner, modularly and hierarchically. Various formalisms can be combined with the more general Modelica formalism. In this respect Modelica has a multi-domain modeling capability which gives the user the possibility to combine electrical, mechanical, hydraulic, thermodynamic, etc., model components within the same application model. Compared to most other modeling languages available today, Modelica offers several important advantages from the simulation practitioner's point of view:

- Acausal modeling based on ordinary differential equations (ODE) and differential algebraic equations and discrete equations (DAE). There is also ongoing research to include partial differential equations (PDE) in the language syntax and semantics (Saldamli et al. 2002 [31]), (Saldamli 2002 [30], Saldamli et al. 2005 [32]).
- Multi-domain modeling capability, which gives the user the possibility to combine electrical, mechanical, thermodynamic, hydraulic etc., model components within the same application model.
- A general type system that unifies object-orientation, multiple inheritance, and generics templates within a single class construct. This facilitates reuse of components and evolution of models.
- A strong software component model, with constructs for creating and connecting components. Thus the language is ideally suited as an architectural description language for complex physical systems, and to some extent for software systems.

- Visual drag & drop and connect composition of models from components present in different libraries targeted to different domains (electrical, mechanical, etc).

The language is strongly typed and declarative. See (Modelica-Association 1996-2005 [18]), (Modelica-Association 2005 [19]), (Tiller 2001 [35]), and (Fritzson 2004 [13]) for a complete description of the language and its functionality from the perspective of the motivations and design goals of the researchers who developed it. Shorter overviews of the language are available in (Elmqvist et al. 1999 [7]), (Fritzson and Engelson 1998 [9]), and (Fritzson and Bunus 2002 [12]).

2.2.1 An Example Modelica Model

The following is an example Lotka Volterra Modelica model containing two differential equations relating the sizes of rabbit and fox populations which are represented by the variables `rabbits` and `foxes`: The rabbits multiply; the foxes eat rabbits. Eventually there are enough foxes eating rabbits causing a decrease in the rabbit population, etc., causing cyclic population sizes. The model is simulated and the sizes of the rabbit and fox populations as a function of time are plotted in Fig. 1.

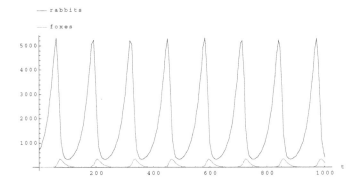

Fig. 1. Number of rabbits – prey animals, and foxes - predators, as a function of time simulated from the PredatorPrey model

The notation `der(rabbits)` means time derivative of the `rabbits` (population) variable.

```
class LotkaVolterra
  parameter Real g_r =0.04     "Natural growth rate for rabbits";
  parameter Real d_rf=0.0005   "Death rate of rabbits due to foxes";
  parameter Real d_f =0.09     "Natural deathrate for foxes";
  parameter Real g_fr=0.1      "Efficency in growing foxes from
  rabbits";
  Real      rabbits(start=700) "Rabbits,(R) with start population
  700";
  Real      foxes(start=10)    "Foxes,(F) with start population 10";
equation
  der(rabbits) = g_r*rabbits - d_rf*rabbits*foxes;
  der(foxes)   = g_fr*d_rf*rabbits*foxes - d_f*foxes;
end LotkaVolterra;
```

2.2.2 Modelica as a Component Language

Modelica offers quite a powerful software component model that is on par with hardware component systems in flexibility and potential for reuse. The key to this increased flexibility is the fact that Modelica classes are based on equations, i.e., acausal connections for which the direction of data flow across the connection is not fixed. Components are connected via the connection mechanism, which can be visualized in connection diagrams. The component framework realizes components and connections, and ensures that communication works and constraints are maintained over the connections. For systems composed of acausal components the direction of data flow, i.e., the causality is automatically deduced by the compiler at composition time.

Two types of coupling can be established by connections depending on whether the variables in the connected connectors are nonflow (default), or declared using the flow prefix:

1. Equality coupling, for nonflow variables, according to Kirchhoff's first law.

2. Sum-to-zero coupling, for flow variables, according to Kirchhoff's current law.

For example, the keyword flow for the variable i of type Current in the Pin connector class indicates that all currents in connected pins are summed to zero, according to Kirchhoff's current law.

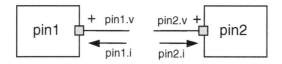

Fig. 2. Connecting two components that have electrical pins

Connection equations are used to connect instances of connection classes. A connection equation connect (pin1,pin2), with pin1 and pin2 of connector class Pin, connects the two pins (Fig. 2) so that they form one node. This produces two equations, namely:

```
pin1.v = pin2.v
pin1.i + pin2.i = 0
```

The first equation says that the voltages of the connected wire ends are the same. The second equation corresponds to Kirchhoff's second law, saying that the currents sum to zero at a node (assuming positive value while flowing into the component). The sum-to-zero equations are generated when the prefix flow is used. Similar laws apply to flows in piping networks and to forces and torques in mechanical systems.

3 MetaModelica – A Unified Equation-Based Modeling Language

The idea to define a unified equation-based mathematical and semantical modeling language started from the development of the OpenModelica compiler (Fritzson et al.

2002 [11]). The entire compiler is generated from a Natural Semantics specification written in RML. The open source OpenModelica compiler has its users in the Modelica community which have detailed knowledge of Modelica but very little knowledge of RML and Natural Semantics. In order to allow people from the Modelica community to contribute to the OpenModelica compiler we retargeted the development language from RML to MetaModelica, which is based on the Modelica language with several extensions. We already translated the OpenModelica compiler from RML to the MetaModelica using an automated translator (Carlsson 2005 [2]) implemented in RML. We also developed a compiler which can handle the entire OpenModelica compiler specification (~105000 lines of code) defined in MetaModelica. An evaluation of the performance of the generated code is presented in section 6.

The basic idea behind the unified language is to use equations as the unifying feature. Most declarative formalisms, including functional languages, support some kind of limited equations even though people often do not regard these as equations, e.g. single-assignment equations.

Using the meta-programming facilities, usual tasks like generation, composition and querying of Modelica models can be automated.

The MetaModelica language inherits all the strong component capabilities Modelica. Components can be reused in different contexts because the causality is not fixed in equations and is up to the compiler to decide it.

3.1 The Types of Equations in the Unified Language

In the following we present the current types of equations already present in Modelica and detail the addition of the equations that support the definition of semantic specifications.

3.1.1 Mathematical Equations

Mathematical models almost always contain equations. There are basically four main kinds of mathematical equations in Modelica which we detail below.

Differential equations contain time derivatives such as $\frac{dx}{dt}$, usually denoted $\dot{x}$:

$$\dot{x} = a \cdot x + 3 \tag{1}$$

Algebraic equations do not include any differentiated variables:

$$x^2 + y^2 = L^2 \tag{2}$$

Partial differential equations also contain derivatives with respect to other variables than time:

$$\frac{\partial a}{\partial t} = \frac{\partial^2 a}{\partial z^2} \tag{3}$$

Difference equations express relations between variables, e.g. at different points in time:

$$x(t+1) = 3x(t) + 2 \tag{4}$$

3.1.2 Conditional Equations and Events

Behavior can develop continuously over time or as discrete changes at certain points in time, usually called events. It is possible to express events and discrete behavior solely based on conditional equations. An event in Modelica is something that happens that has the following four properties:

- A point in time that is instantaneous, i.e., has zero duration.
- An event condition that switches from false to true for the event to happen.
- A set of variables that are associated with the event, i.e., are referenced or explicitly changed by equations associated with the event.
- Some behavior associated with the event, expressed as conditional equations that become active or are deactivated at the event. Instantaneous equations are a special case of conditional equations that are active only at events.

Modelica has several constructs to express conditional equations, e.g. if-then-else equations for conditional equations that are active during certain time durations, or when-equations for instantaneous equations.

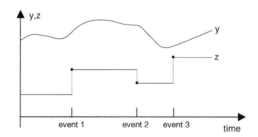

Fig. 3. A discrete-time variable z changes value only at event instants, whereas continuous-time variables like y may change both between and at events

3.1.3 Single-Assignment Equations

A single-assignment equation is quite close to an assignment, e.g.:

```
x = eval_expr(env, e);
```

but with the difference that the unbound variable (here x) which obtains a value by solving the equation, only gets its value once, whereas a variable in an assignment may obtain its value several times, e.g.:

```
x := eval_expr(env, e); x := eval_expr2(env, x);
```

3.1.4 Pattern Equations in Match Expressions

In this section we present our addition to the Modelica language which allows definitions of semantic specifications. The new language features are pattern equations, match expressions and union datatypes.

Pattern equations are a more general case than single-assignment equations, e.g.:

```
Env.BOOLVAL(x,y) = eval_something(env, e);
```

Unbound variables get their values by using pattern-matching (i.e., unification) to solve for the unbound variables in the pattern equation. For example, x and e might be unbound and solved for in the equations, whereas y and env could be bound and just supply values.

The following extension to Modelica is essential for specifying semantics of language constructs represented as abstract syntax trees:

- Match expressions with pattern-matching case rules, local declarations, and local equations.

It has the following general structure:

```
match expression  optional-local-declarations
  case pattern-expression opt-local-declarations
    optional-local-equations then value-expression;
    ...
  else optional-local-declarations
    optional-local-equations then value-expression;
end match;
```

The then keyword precedes the value to be returned in each branch. The local declarations started by the local keyword, as well as the equations started by the equation keyword are optional. There should be at least one case...then branch, but the else-branch is optional.

A match expression is closely related to pattern matching in functional languages, but is also related to switch statements in C or Java. It has two important advantages over traditional switch statements:

- A match expression can appear in any of the three Modelica contexts: expressions, statements, or in equations.
- The selection in the case branches is based on pattern matching, which reduces to equality testing in simple cases, but is unification in the general case.

Local equations in match expressions have the following properties:

- Only algebraic equations are allowed as local equations, no differential equations.
- Only locally declared variables (local unknowns) declared by local declarations within the case expression are solved for, or may appear as pattern variables.
- Equations are solved in the order they are declared (this restriction may be removed in the future, allowing more general local algebraic systems of equations).
- If an equation or an expression in a case-branch of a match-expression fails, all local variables become unbound, and matching continues with the next branch.

We also need to introduce the possibility to declare recursive tree data structures in Modelica, e.g.:

```
uniontype Exp
  record RCONST Real x1; end RCONST;
  record PLUS  Exp x1; Exp x2; end PLUS;
```

```
    record SUB    Exp x1; Exp x2; end SUB;
    record MUL    Exp x1; Exp x2; end MUL;
    record DIV    Exp x1; Exp x2; end DIV;
    record NEG    Exp x1;          end NEG;
  end Exp;
```

A small expression tree, of the expression `12+5*13`, is depicted in Fig. 4. Using the record constructors PLUS, MUL, RCONST, this tree can be constructed by the expression `PLUS(RCONST(12), MUL( RCONST(5), RCONST(13)))`

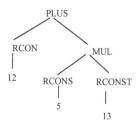

Fig. 4. Abstract syntax tree of the expression `12+5*13`

The `uniontype` construct has the following properties:

- Union types can be recursive, i.e., reference themselves. This is the case in the above Exp example, where Exp is referenced inside its member record types.
- Record declarations declared within a union type are automatically inherited into the enclosing scope of the union type declaration.
- Union types can be polymorphic
- A record type may currently only belong to one union type. This restriction may be removed in the future, by introducing polymorphic variants.

This is a preliminary union type design, which however is very close (just different syntax) to similar datatype constructs in declarative languages such as Haskell, Standard ML, OCaml, and RML. The uniontypes can model any abstract syntax tree while the match expressions are used to model the semantics, composition or transformation of the specified language.

3.2 Solution of Equations

The process of solving systems of equations is central for the execution of equation-based languages. For example:

- Differential equations are solved by numeric differential equation solvers.
- Differential-algebraic equations are solved by numeric DAE solvers.
- Algebraic equations are solved by symbolic manipulation and/or numeric solution
- Single-assignment equations are solved by performing an assignment.
- Pattern equations are solved by the process of unification which assigns values to unbound variables in the patterns.

The first three solution procedures are used in current Modelica. By the addition of local equations (Section 3.1.4) in match expressions to be solved at run-time, we generalize the allowable kinds of equations in Modelica.

3.3 Evaluator for the Exp1 Language in the Unified Language

As an example of the meta-modeling and meta-programming capabilities of the MetaModelica we give a very simple example. The semantics of the operations in the small expression language Exp1 follows below, expressed as an interpretative language specification in Modelica in a style close to Natural and/or Operational Semantics, see Exp1 specified in RML in Section 2.1.1. Such specifications typically consist of a number of functions, each of which contains a match expression with one or more cases, also called rules. In this simple example there is only one function, here called `eval`, since we specify an expression evaluator.

```
function eval
  input  Exp  in_exp;
  output Real out_real;
algorithm
 out_real :=
  match in_exp
    local Real v1,v2,v3;  Exp e1,e2;
    case RCONST(v1) then v1;
    case ADD(e1,e2) equation
      v1 = eval(e1);  v2 = eval(e2); v3 = v1 + v2;  then v3;
    case SUB(e1,e2) equation
      v1 = eval(e1);  v2 = eval(e2); v3 = v1 - v2;  then v3;
    case MUL(e1,e2) equation
      v1 = eval(e1);  v2 = eval(e2); v3 = v1 * v2;  then v3;
    case DIV(e1,e2) equation
      v1 = eval(e1);  v2 = eval(e2); v3 = v1 / v2;  then v3;
    case NEG(e1) equation
      v1 = eval(e1); v2 =  -v1;  then v2;
    end match;
  end eval;
```

As usual in Modelica the equations are not directional, e.g. the two equations `v1 = eval(e1)` and `eval(e1) = v1` are equivalent. The compiler will select one of the forms based on input/output parameters and data dependencies.

There are some design considerations behind the above match-expression construct that may need some motivation.

- Why do we have local variable declarations within the match-expression? The main reason is clear and understandable semantics. In all three usage contexts (equations, statements, expressions) it should be easy to understand for the user and for the compiler which variables are unknowns (i.e., unbound local variables) in pattern expressions or in local equations. Another reason for declaring the types of local variables is better documentation of the code – the modeler/programmer is relieved of the burden of doing manual type-inference to understand the code.
- Why the `then` keyword before the returned value? The code becomes easier to read if there is a keyword before the returned value-expression. Note that most functional languages use the `in` keyword instead in this context, which is less

intuitive, and would conflict with the set or array element membership meaning the Modelica in keyword.

4 Details of the Compiler Implementation

The current compiler for the MetaModelica language is based on OpenModelica compiler which was extended with code from the RML compiler (for meta-modeling/meta-programming facilities like pattern matching, unification, higher order functions, optimizations, etc). In the current version the meta-programming code can appear only in functions which can be called by Modelica code in the way an external function is called.

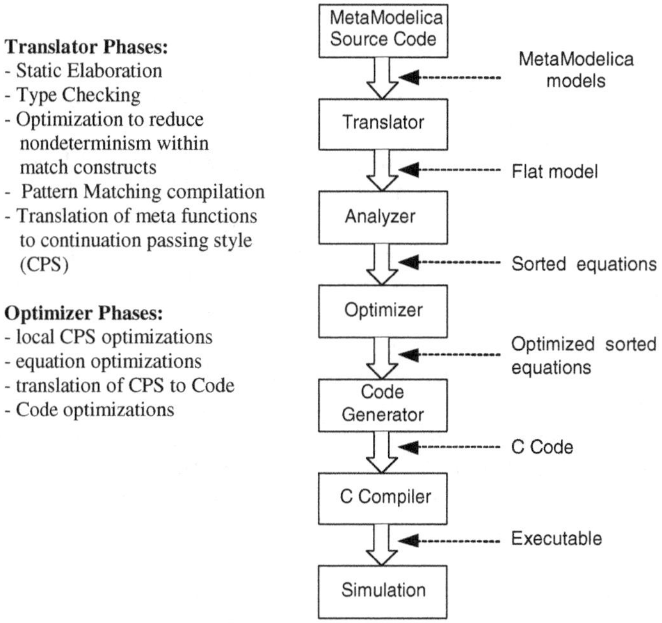

Translator Phases:
- Static Elaboration
- Type Checking
- Optimization to reduce
  nondeterminism within
  match constructs
- Pattern Matching compilation
- Translation of meta functions
  to continuation passing style
  (CPS)

Optimizer Phases:
- local CPS optimizations
- equation optimizations
- translation of CPS to Code
- Code optimizations

MetaModelica
Source Code

Translator

Analyzer

Optimizer

Code
Generator

C Compiler

Simulation

MetaModelica
models

Flat model

Sorted equations

Optimized sorted
equations

C Code

Executable

Fig. 5. The stages of translation and execution of a MetaModelica model

All variable values are boxed to be distinguished by the garbage collector. Every boxed value has a small integer as a header. Composite values are boxed structures. The structure header contains a small integer tag which is used for pattern matching. Logical variables are represented as boxed references. A different header is used to represent unbounded or bounded logical variables.

The MetaModelica source code is first translated into a so-called "*flat model*". This phase includes type checking, performing all object-oriented operations such as in-heritance, modifications, compilation of pattern matching, translation of meta functions to continuation passing style. The flat model includes a set of equations declarations, functions and meta functions, with all object-oriented structure removed, apart from the dot notation within the names. This process is called the "*partial instantiation*" of the model.

The next step is to solve the system of equations. First the equations need to be transformed into a suitable form for the numerical solvers. This is done by the symbolic and the numerical module of the compiler. The simulation code generator takes as input the flattened form of the equations. The equations are mapped into an internal data structure that permits simple symbolic manipulations such as: common subexpresions elimination, algebraic simplifications, constant folding, etc. These symbolic operations decrease substantially the complexity of the system of equations. After this stage the Block Lower Triangular form of the system of equations is computed.

Finally, in the last phase, the procedural code (in our implementation C code), is generated based on the previously computed BLT blocks when each block is linked to a numerical solver and the runtime for the meta functions. Within the C code the meta functions are called like normal functions.

5   Performance Evaluation of the MetaModelica Compiler

We are not aware of any language that is similar with the MetaModelica language. However, the meta-modeling and meta-programming parts of the MetaModelica language are close to a logic/functional language. Backtracking is used within the match construct to select the correct case and the specifications can contain logical variables. The uniontypes are similar with the SML datatype definitions, however MetaModelica functions have multiple inputs and outputs not just one argument like in SML. Also, because a reordering phase is applied to the MetaModelica code there is no need to explicitly declare mutually recursive types and functions.

All the information, the test code and the files needed to reproduce our results are available online at: **http://www.ida.liu.se/~adrpo/jmlc2006**. Please contact the authors for any additional information regarding the performance evaluation tests.

We have compared the execution speed of our generated code with SWI-Prolog 5.6.9 (SWI-Prolog [34]), SICStus Prolog 3.11.2 (Science [33]), Maude MSOS Tool (MMT) on top of Maude 2.1.1 (Illinois [15]). The Maude MSOS Tool (MMT) is an execution environment for Modular Structural Operational Semantics (MSOS) (Mosses 2004 [20]) specifications that brings the power of analysis available in the Maude system to MSOS specifications. The Maude MSOS Mini-Freja translation was implemented by Fabricio Chalub and Christiano Braga and is available as a case study together with sources from http://maude-msos-tool.sourceforge.net/. SWI-Prolog is a widely known open source implementation of Prolog. SICStus Prolog is a commercial Prolog implementation.

The closest match to the meta-modeling and meta-programming facilities of the MetaModelica compiler is the Maude MSOS Tool.

The test case is based on an executable specification of the Mini-Freja language (Pettersson 1999 [26]) running a test program based on the sieve of Eratosthenes. Mini-Freja is a call-by-name pure functional language. The test program calculates prime numbers.

The Prolog translation (mf.pl) was implemented by Mikael Pettersson and this author corrected a minor mistake.

Table 1. Execution time in seconds. The – sign represents out of memory.

	MetaModelica	SICStus	SWI	Maude MSOS Tool
8	0.00	0.05	0.00	2.92
10	0.00	0.10	0.03	5.60
30	0.02	1.42	1.79	226.77
40	0.06	3.48	3.879	-
50	0.13	-	11.339	-
100	1.25	-	-	-
200	16.32	-	-	-

The comparison was performed on a Fedora Core4 Linux machine with two AMD Athlon(TM) XP 1800+ processors at 1500 MHz and 1.5GB of memory.

The memory consumption was at peak 9Mb for MetaModelica and the others consumed the entire 1.5Gb of memory and aborted at arround 40 prime numbers. With this test we stressed only the meta-programming and meta-modeling part of the compiler. The Modelica part of the compiler was already able to handle huge models with thousands of equations.

6   Related Work

As related work we can consider the Unified Modeling Language (UML). Modeling in the UML sense has more emphasis on graphical notation for modeling rather than precise mathematical model definitions as in the modeling languages mentioned in the previous section. Initially, execution support was lacking, but during recent years code generators from UML2 has appeared. Also, during recent years, there has been an increased interest in model-driven developments and the OMG has launched model-driven architectures, primarily based on UML models. The idea of meta-modeling has attracted increased interest: a meta-model describes the structure of models at the next lower abstraction level. Meta-modeling and meta-programming allows transformations and composition of models and programs, which is becoming increasingly relevant in order to specify and manage complex industrial software and system applications. However, UML has developed into a rather heterogeneous collection of modeling notations. Also, precise mathematically defined semantics is not always available for these graphical notations. By contrast, MetaModelica is defined exclusively based on equations, functions and meta functions. Similar meta-programming facilities are present in functional languages like SML, Haskell and OCaml but the execution strategy is different in these languages as they do not support backtracking to select cases.

In the area of mathematical modeling the most important general de-facto standards for different dynamic simulation modes are:

- Continuous: Matlab/Simulink, MatrixX/SystemBuild, Scilab/Scicos for general systems, SPICE and its derivates for electrical circuits, ADAMS, DADS/Motion, SimPack for multi-body mechanical systems.
- Discrete: general-purpose simulators based on the discrete-event GPSS line, VHDL- and Verilog simulators in digital electronics, etc.
- Hybrid (discrete + continuous): Modelica/Dymola, AnyLogic, VHDL-AMS and Verilog-AMS simulators (not only for electronics but also for multi-physics problems).

The insufficient power and generality of the former modeling languages stimulated the development of Modelica (as a true object-oriented, multi-physics language) and VHDL-AMS/Verilog-AMS (multi-physics but strongly influenced by electronics).

The rapid increase in new requirements to handle the dynamics of highly complex, heterogeneous systems requires enhanced efforts in developing new language features (based on existing languages!). Especially the efficient simulation of hardware-software systems and model structural dynamics are yet unsolved problems. In electronics and telecommunications, therefore, the development of SystemC-AMS has been launched but these attempts are far from the multi-physics and multi-domain applications which are addressed by Modelica.

7   Conclusions and Future Work

We have presented two executable specification languages: RML for Natural Semantics specifications of programming languages, and Modelica for equation-based semantics and mathematical modeling of complex systems. We have also described MetaModelica as a unified mathematical and semantical modeling language by generalizing the concept of equation and introducing local equations and match expressions in the Modelica language. This gives interesting perspectives for the future regarding meta-modeling, model transformations and compositions during simulation, etc.

The current status of this work is that the OpenModelica compiler has been ported to the new unified Modelica modeling language, resulting in ~105000 lines of code expressed in the unified language. A compiler for MetaModelica has been completed at the time of this writing. We have also developed an integrated development environment based on Eclipse which facilitates writing and debugging of MetaModelica code (PELAB 2006 [23]). The MetaModelica language can be used to write semantic specifications for a broad spectrum of languages ranging from functional to imperative languages. We have also translated all our RML specification examples to MetaModelica in order to provide teaching material for the new language. The current specifications include imperative, functional, equation-based, and object-oriented languages.

The unified MetaModelica language gives new perspectives for a broad range of items, from programming and modeling languages to physical systems, but also including model transformations and composition. Apart from language specification to generate interpreters and compilers, symbolic differentiation rules for differentiating expressions and equations have been specified in MetaModelica and is in use.

Our near future plans are to extend MetaModelica with exceptions and reflection. The long term goal for MetaModelica is to achieve the generation of compilers for any language by drag and drop semantic components from libraries and connect them together in a similar way the physical systems are modeled today in Modelica.

References

[1] Patrik Borras, Dominique Clement, Thierry Despeyroux, Janet Incerpi, Gilles Kahn, Bernard Lang, and Valérie Pascual. *CENTAUR: The System.* ed. P. Henderson, Proceedings of ACM SIGSOFT/SIGPLAN Software Engineering Symposium on Practical Software Development Environments, February, 1988, vol. 24 of SIGPLAN, p.: 14-24

[2] Emil Carlsson, *Translating Natural Semantics to MetaModelica*, Department of Computer and Information Science. 2005, Linköping University, Linköping, Master's Thesis.

[3] Dominique Clément, Joëlle Despeyroux, Thierry Despeyroux, and Gilles Kahn. *A Simple Applicative Language: Mini-ML*, Proceedings of the ACM Conference on Lisp and Functional Programming, August, 1986. also available as research report RR-529, INRIA, Sophia-Antipolis, May 1986.

[4] Thierry Despeyroux. *Executable Specification of Static Semantics.* ed. Gilles Kahn, Proceedings of Semantics of Data Types, 1984. Berlin, Germany, Springer-Verlag, Lecture Notes in Computer Science, vol. 173, p.: 215-233

[5] Thierry Despeyroux, *TYPOL: A Formalism to Implement Natural Semantics*, INRIA, Sofia-Antipolis, Report: RR 94, 1988, www: http://www.inria.fr/rrrt/rt-0094.html.

[6] Dynasim, *Dymola*, Last Accessed: 2005, www: http://www.dynasim.se/.

[7] Hilding Elmqvist, Sven Erik Mattsson, and Martin Otter. *Modelica - A Language for Physical System Modeling, Visualization and Interaction*, Proceedings of IEEE Symposium on Computer-Aided Control System Design, August 22-27, 1999. Hawaii, USA

[8] Peter Fritzson, *Efficient Language Implementation by Natural Semantics*. 1998, http://www.ida.liu.se/~pelab/rml.

[9] Peter Fritzson and Vadim Engelson. *Modelica, a general Object-Oriented Language for Continuous and Discrete-Event System Modeling and Simulation*, Proceedings of 12th European Conference on Object-Oriented Programming (ECOOP'98), July 20-24, 1998. Brussels, Belgium

[10] Peter Fritzson, Peter Aronsson, Peter Bunus, Vadim Engelson, Levon Saldamli, Henrik Johansson, and Andreas Karstöm. *The Open Source Modelica Project*, Proceedings of Proceedings of The 2th International Modelica Conference, March 18-19, 2002. Munich, Germany

[11] Peter Fritzson, Peter Aronsson, Peter Bunus, Vadim Engelson, Levon Saldamli, Henrik Johansson, and Andreas Karstöm. *The Open Source Modelica Project*, Proceedings of the 2nd International Modelica Conference, March 18-19, 2002. Munich, Germany, Modelica Association, www: http://www.modelica.org/events/Conference2002/, Open Modelica System: http://www.ida.liu.se/~pelab/modelica/

[12] Peter Fritzson and Peter Bunus. *Modelica, a General Object-Oriented Language for Continuous and Discrete-Event System Modeling and Simulation*, Proceedings of 35th Annual Simulation Symposium, April 14-18, 2002. San Diego, California

[13] Peter Fritzson, *Principles of Object-Oriented Modeling and Simulation with Modelica 2.1*. 2004, Wiley-IEEE Press. 940 pages, ISBN:0-471-471631, Book home page: http://www.mathcore.com/drmodelica.

[14] Sabine Glesner and Wolf Zimmermann, *Natural semantics as a static program analysis framework*. ACM Transactions on Programming Languages and Systems (TOPLAS), 2004. vol: 26(3), p.: 510-577.

[15] University of Illinois, *The Maude System Website*, Last Accessed, www: http://maude.cs.uiuc.edu/.

[16] Gilles Kahn, *Natural Semantics*, in Programming of Future Generation Computers, ed. Niva M. 1988, Elsevier Science Publishers, North Holland. p. 237-258.

[17] MathCore, *MathModelica*, Last Accessed: 2005, MathCore, www: http://www.mathcore.se/.

[18] Modelica-Association, *Modelica: A Unified Object-Oriented Language for Physical Systems Modeling, Language Specification 2.2*, Last Accessed: 2005, www: http://www.modelica.org/.

[19] Modelica-Association, *Modelica - A Unified Object-Oriented Language for Physical Systems Modeling - Tutorial and Design Rationale Version 2.0*, Last Accessed: 2005, www: http://www.modelica.org/.

[20] Peter D. Mosses, *Modular structural operational semantics*. Journal of Functional Programming and Algebraic Programming. Special issue on SOS., 2004. vol: 60-61, p.: 195-228.

[21] PELAB, *Relational Meta-Language (RML) Environment*, Last Accessed: 2005, Programming Environments Laboratory (PELAB), www: http://www.ida.liu.se/~pelab/rml.

[22] PELAB, *Open Modelica System*, Last Accessed: 2005, Programming Environments Laboratory, www: http://www.ida.liu.se/~pelab/modelica.

[23] PELAB, *Modelica Development Tooling (MDT)*, Last Accessed: April, 2006, PELAB, www: http://www.ida.liu.se/~pelab/modelica/OpenModelica/MDT/.

[24] Mikael Pettersson and Peter Fritzson. *DML - A Meta-language and System for the Generation of Practical and Efficient Compilers from Denotational Specifications*, Proceedings of the 1992 International Conference on Computer Languages, April 20-23, 1992. Oakland, California

[25] Mikael Pettersson, *Compiling Natural Semantics*, Department of Computer and Information Science. 1995, Linköping University, Linköping, PhD. Thesis.

[26] Mikael Pettersson, *Compiling Natural Semantics*. Lecture Notes in Computer Science (LNCS). Vol. 1549. 1999, Springer-Verlag.

[27] Gordon Plotkin, *A structural approach to operational semantics*, Århus University, Report: DAIMI FN-19, 1981

[28] Adrian Pop and Peter Fritzson. *Debugging Natural Semantics Specifications*, Proceedings of Sixth International Symposium on Automated and Analysis-Driven Debugging, September 19-21, 2005. Monterey, California

[29] Johan Ringström, Peter Fritzson, and Mikael Pettersson. *Generating an Efficient Compiler for a Data Parallel Language from Denotational Specifications*, Proceedings of Int. Conf. of Compiler Construction, April, 1994. Edinburgh, Springer Verlag, vol. LNCS 786

[30] Levon Saldamli, *PDEModelica - Towards a High-Level Language for Modeling with Partial Differential Equations*, Department of Computer and Information Science. 2002, Linköping University, Linköping, Licenciate Thesis.

[31] Levon Saldamli, Peter Fritzson, and Bernhard Bachmann. *Extending Modelica for Partial Differential Equations*, Proceedings of 2nd International Modelica Conference, March. 18-29, 2002. Munich, Gernany

[32] Levon Saldamli, Bernhard Bachmann, Peter Fritzson, and Hansjürg Wiesmann. *A Framework for Describing and Solving PDE Models in Modelica*. ed. Gerhard Schmitz, Proceedings of 4th International Modelica Conference, 2005. Hamburg-Harburg, Modelica Association, www: http://www.modelica.org/events/Conference2005/

[33] SICS - Swedish Institute of Computer Science, *SICStus Prolog Website*, Last Accessed: April, 2006, www: http://www.sics.se/sicstus/.

[34] SWI-Prolog, *SWI-Prolog Website*, Last Accessed: April, 2006, University of Amsterdam, www: http://www.swi-prolog.org/.

[35] Michael M. Tiller, *Introduction to Physical Modeling with Modelica.* 2001, Kluwer Academic Publishers.

[36] Lars Viklund, Johan Herber, and Peter Fritzson. *The implementation of ObjectMath - a hight-level programming enviornment for scientific computing.* ed. Uwe Kastens and Peter Pfahler, Proceedings of Compiler Construction - 4th International Conference (CC'92), 1992, Springer-Verlag, Lecture Notes in Computer Science (LNCS), vol. 641, p.: 312-318

A Component Language for
Structured Parallel Programming

Luc Bläser

Computer Systems Institute, ETH Zurich, Switzerland
`blaeser@inf.ethz.ch`

Abstract. Current programming languages are still underdeveloped for the construction of well-structured concurrent software systems. They typically impose many unnecessary and unacceptable compromises and/or workarounds due to a multiplicity of different suboptimal concepts. With regard to object-orientation, one can identify references, methods and inheritance as such inappropriate constructs.

To overcome this unfavourable situation, we have designed and implemented a substantially new programming language which integrates a general component notion. Three fundamental relations govern components in this language: (1) hierarchical composition, (2) symmetric connections with a dual concept of *offered* and *required* interfaces and, (3) communication-based interactions. With the use of various examples, the advantage of the new component language is demonstrated in this paper.

1 Motivation

The current trend within the field of software engineering is steadily evolving towards programming languages which possess an increasing number of different and unfortunately, counterproductive concepts. This growing conceptual incoherence often implicates such high complexity, that it decisively limits the flexible construction of structured parallel programs. With regard to the current most prevalent object-oriented programming paradigm, we are confronted with three fundamental problems:

- *References*
  References (or pointers) form semantically very weak constructs for describing relations between dynamically created object instances. Arbitrary interlinking of object instances is therewith promoted, leading to an object graph of non-hierarchical shape[1]. Clear program structures and general encapsulations remain unsupported: any abstraction that consists of a dynamic structure of sub-elements is not adequately representable as a hierarchically composed object. Instead, this has to be forcibly modelled as a reference-linked conglomerate of elementary object instances, constituting an

---

[1] C.A.R. Hoare unequivocally criticizes the unstructured nature of references and calls their introduction in high-level programming languages a step backwards [17, page 20].

D. Lightfoot and C. Szyperski (Eds.): JMLC 2006, LNCS 4228, pp. 230–250, 2006.

undifferentiated part in the common overall and flat object graph. As a consequence, incautious reference copying may quickly lead to incorrect program dependencies (aliasing problems [16, 4, 11, 8, 22, 2]). Moreover, object exchangeability is strongly impacted by dependencies of outgoing object references which are unspecified in object interfaces[2].

- *Methods*
  Methods fail the realization of a true message passing paradigm, as they in fact only constitute procedures (with an implicit reference to the containing object). An object is not capable of maintaining an arbitrarily long state-full interaction with multiple clients individually, but can only hold a client-specific context during a method invocation[3]. The pattern of a method for a client-specific interaction is however oversimplified, having only one parameterised input followed by one possible output, with generally only one value. Methods additionally obstruct concurrency by blocking the invocator during their entire execution, instead of running at the expense of the actual containing object.

- *Inheritance*
  The main object-oriented mechanism for type polymorphism, known as inheritance, enforces a groundless hierarchisation and classification of object types at compile-time. Unlike a symmetric polymorphism, objects can not be represented by multiple, equally important facets, without artificially preferring some facets as sub-types of others. Inheritance also unsuitably combines the two antagonistic concerns of polymorphism and code reuse, often resulting in mutual imports of different classes. A special object class, which needs to be inherited from a general class for the purpose of type polymorphism, should not be obligated to also inherit the general implementation of the super-class, as the special class' code is naturally more specific than that of the general class[4].

This unfavourable situation demands a total revision of the conceptual basis of current programming languages. We are challenged to design new languages, which base on a new more powerful paradigm that uniformly enables structured, dynamic, and safe software development. Clearly, this requires the liberation of the language concepts from the often unreasonable close binding to a concrete machine model. Instead, there is a need for real high-level programming languages, which are still effectively implementable on different computer platforms.

In order to achieve this ideal, we have designed and implemented a substantially new programming language, which integrates a general high-level component notion. Three simple but fundamental relations govern components in this language: (1)

---

[2] Every element of public visibility in the object may be considered as part of the object's interface.

[3] The iteration over a collection stands for a client-individual state-full interaction that can not be accurately expressed with methods (cf. 3.2).

[4] Clearly, the example of a rectangle and square shows this contradiction: a square is a geometrical special-case (modelled as a *sub-class* of a rectangle but on the other hand, should not inherit the general rectangle implementation (with the two variables *length* and *width*).

hierarchical composition without use of explicit pointers, (2) symmetric connections with a dual concept of *offered* and *required* interfaces and, (3) communication-based interactions. The new *component language* takes a completely different path in comparison to existing component models, architecture description languages, and object structure specification models (see Section 5). As innovation, it provides a fully-fledged programming language, which only features high-level concepts for the implementation of components. The component language inherently abolishes the fundamental deficiencies of current programming models and offers the following attractive features:

- *Hierarchical encapsulation*
  A component is able to contain any (static or dynamic) structures of components and program logic of any complexity. The hierarchically contained components and the relations among them are thereby fully encapsulated and exclusively managed by the surrounding component.
- *Expressive structural relations*
  All structures of components are described by semantically rich relations, such that classical references (and pointers) can be entirely abandoned without loss of expressiveness: each component contains its own arbitrary network of sub-components. This prohibits uncontrolled program dependencies (such as aliasing problems).
- *Intrinsic concurrency*
  Concurrency inherently results from the language model, in which all components run fully autonomously and have their own intrinsic activities. Components only interact via bidirectional message communications (with non-blocking message sending).
- *Unrestricted polymorphism*
  Components can be represented by an arbitrary set of independent interfaces, activating unrestricted symmetric polymorphism in total separation from implementation reuse. A new type description ensures the correct handling of polymorphic components.
- *Interoperability*
  Although the component language is designed for general purposes (except machine-close programming) and common programs are entirely developable in components, the language also permits safe interoperability due to the guaranteed encapsulation. Terminal components, which do not contain sub-components, may be just as well implemented in any programming language, such as for the purpose of machine-specific implementations.

1.1 Contributions

The contributions of this paper can be summarised as follows:

- The presentation of a new programming language with an integrated general component notion for structured parallel programming.
- A comparison of the new language with classical object-orientation, showing the advantage by means of practical examples.

- The description of a complete implementation of the programming language, comprising compiler and runtime system.

The remainder of the paper is organised as follows; Section 2 presents the concepts of the new programming language and explains them by means of illustrative examples. Section 3 shows practical examples of the new language and compares them with object-orientation. Section 4 describes the implementation of the programming language and also gives an experimental evaluation of the system. Section 5 discusses related work, which is finally followed by a conclusion.

2 Component Language

The new programming language follows the principle that any program forms a component which may be constructed again from an assembly of components and so on. With this paradigm of stepwise refinement, complex systems can be built with abstract program elements that hide detailed logic from a higher abstraction level.

A *component*[5] constitutes a closed program unit (*black box*) that encapsulates an arbitrary assembly of sub-components, together with runtime state and behaviour. Components are only allowed to have external program dependencies over explicitly defined interfaces. An *interface* represents an external facet of a component and thus establishes an explicit interaction point between the component and its exterior environment. Each component *offers* an arbitrary number of own interfaces and also *requires* an arbitrary number of foreign interfaces that belong to other external components[6].

By way of a first example, let us consider a standard house, which has the external facets of a residence and a parking space, requiring both electricity and water supplies from outside. The house may be described as a component called *StandardHouse*, which offers both a *Residence* and *ParkingSpace* interface (see Fig. 1). In addition, the house requires the foreign *Electricity* and *Water* interfaces from other external components. Clearly, all interfaces of the component have equal rights, i.e. there is no artificially preferred interface. With regard to the example, this means that the characterizations of a residence and parking space are equally important facets of the house.

```
INTERFACE Residence; (* ... *)
INTERFACE ParkingSpace; (* ... *)
INTERFACE Electricity; (* ... *)
INTERFACE Water; (* ... *)

COMPONENT StandardHouse
 OFFERS Residence, ParkingSpace
 REQUIRES Electricity, Water;
 (* implementation *)
END StandardHouse;
```

---

[5] A component here always means a runtime instance of a component template.
[6] A variety of other component definitions can be found in [26, Chapter 11].

Fig. 1. A component

Arbitrarily many *component instances* (also simply called *components*) can be created from the same *component template* (also called *component type*[7]). In the example above, the program describes the component template, which can in turn be used to create as many house component instances as needed. One such possible instance of a house is depicted by the diagram in Fig. 1.

The component language is based upon three fundamental relations between components:

- *Hierarchical composition*
  Each component can be hierarchically composed, by containing an arbitrary assembly of component instances. The contained sub-components are fully encapsulated by the surrounding super-component.
- *Interface connections*
  An arbitrary network of components can be built by connecting the required interfaces of components to corresponding offered interfaces of other components. A component only constructs the network of its sub-components.
- *Communication-based interactions*
  Components can interact via interfaces by message communications. An individual communication channel is maintained between a component, which offers an interface, and each component, which uses the interface[8].

The component notion is designed to cover any conceivable encapsulated program unit and to enable higher generality than the classical component abstractions of objects and modules. For that reason, the general components establish the sole building units of the language.

2.1 Component Instances

Component instances must always be declared in the program scope of their containing super-component. The declaration of an instance requires a description of the corresponding component type (component template), in order to ensure the correct handling of instances. The concrete component type is one possibility for such a description. For example, *house1* and *house2* can be declared as two instances of the *StandardHouse* component type:

house1, house2: StandardHouse

In many cases, it is however necessary to declare component instances without statically fixing a specific type. Therefore, as another possibility, a component

---

[7] A component instance has only one type, i.e. the concrete template from which it is created.

[8] Notably, the communication between components is fully symmetric and does not entail "inverse programming" by means of event-orientation.

instance is also declarable in abstract terms, by simply postulating a set of offered and required interfaces. The example below shows such an abstract declaration of a *building* component instance, with the postulated offered interfaces *Residence* and *ParkingSpace*, and the required interfaces *Electricity* and *Water*.

building: ANY(Residence, ParkingSpace | Electricity, Water)

Using this declaration, the component instance can be of *any* component type that fulfils the following requirements:

1. The component type *offers at least* the interfaces which are postulated as offered by the declaration (i.e. *Residence* and *ParkingSpace*). These interfaces are always guaranteed to be provided by the declared component instance.
2. The component type *requires at most* the interfaces which are postulated as required by the declaration (i.e. *Electricity* and *Water*). These interfaces have to be provided by the environment of the declared component instance, before the component's offered interfaces can be used.

Applying the rules above, the following *townHouse* component may well be of the *StandardHouse* type. Conversely, the *oldHouse* component can not represent a *StandardHouse* as no required *Electricity* interface is postulated.

townHouse: ANY(Residence | Electricity, Water, CentralHeating);
oldHouse: ANY(Residence | Water)

A static declaration of component instances is not always applicable as in some cases, the number of component instances may be determined only at runtime. Hence, it is also possible to declare a dynamic *collection* of component instances with the same type description. An *index*, qualified by a list of comparable data values, thereby allows the dynamic identification of a component within the collection. For example, the following declaration defines a collection of components of the *StandardHouse* type, requiring a street number and name to identify an instance.

house[number: INTEGER, street: TEXT]: StandardHouse

With this declaration, the following component instances (amongst others) may be accessed.

house[12, "Market Street"]   house[3, "First Avenue"]   house[100, "Grand Boulevard"]

2.2 Hierarchical Composition

A component can be hierarchically composed, by containing an arbitrary static or dynamic number of sub-components. The sub-components are fully encapsulated and exclusively managed by the surrounding super-component, such that the inner components are completely invisible and inaccessible outside the super-component.

The program below delineates a hierarchical composition with the example of a *StandardHouse* component, which contains a garage and two floors as sub-components (see Fig. 1). In this language, variables enable hierarchical compositions by representing *separate containers*, in which a component instance with a compatible type can be stored.

```
COMPONENT StandardHouse OFFERS Residence, ParkingSpace REQUIRES Electricity, Water;
 VARIABLE garage: StandardGarage; groundFloor, firstFloor: ANY(Rooms | Electricity, Water);
 BEGIN
  NEW(garage); NEW(groundFloor, Floor); NEW(firstFloor, Floor)
 END StandardHouse;
```

As a variable is empty by default, a component instance has to be created within it by the NEW-statement. If an abstract type description is declared for the variable (ANY-construct), the component type has to be explicitly specified as second parameter (see the two last NEW-statements in the example above).

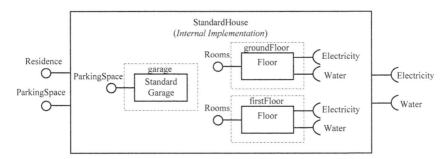

Fig. 2. A hierarchical composition of components

Naturally, a variable is also capable of storing a dynamic collection of component instances:

```
VARIABLE room[number: INTEGER]: HotelRoom;
FOR i := 1 TO N DO NEW(room[i]) END
```

Variables are only defined locally in a program scope, such that they directly imply a hierarchical lifetime dependency between the surrounding instance and the internal components.

2.3 Component Networks

Components systematically decompose programs into separated logical parts, with precisely defined dependencies in the form of offered and required interfaces. Networks of component instances can be built by explicitly connecting each required interface to one with an equal name which is offered by another component. The following example of a small city demonstrates the construction of such a network of component instances. By means of the CONNECT-statement, the required *Water* interface of *house1* is for instance connected to the offered *Water* interface of *river1*. (The offered interface is thereby implicitly defined by the first argument.) The resulting component network is visualised in Fig. 3.

```
COMPONENT HydroelectricPowerPlant OFFERS Electricity REQUIRES Water; (* ... *)
COMPONENT River OFFERS Water; (* ... *)

VARIABLE
 house1, house2: StandardHouse;
 powerPlant: HydroelectricPowerPlant;
```

river1, river2: River;

BEGIN
  NEW(house1); NEW(house2); NEW(powerPlant); NEW(river1); NEW(river2);
  CONNECT(Water(house1), river1); CONNECT(Electricity(house1), powerPlant);
  CONNECT(Water(house2), river2); CONNECT(Electricity(house2), powerPlant);
  CONNECT(Water(powerPlant), river2)

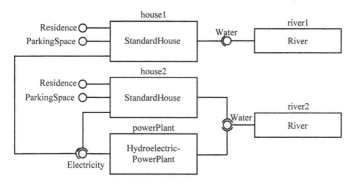

Fig. 3. A component network

Component networks can of course also be constructed with a dynamic number of component instances, as illustrated by the following program[9].

VARIABLE
  house[postalAddress: TEXT]: StandardHouse;
  powerPlant: HydroelectricPowerPlant;
  river[number: INTEGER]: River;

BEGIN
  FOR n := 1 TO N DO NEW(river[n]) END; (* N >= 1 *)
  NEW(powerPlant); CONNECT(Water(powerPlant), river[1]);
  REPEAT
    location := *postal address of the new house*;
    NEW(house[location]); CONNECT(Electricity(house[location]), powerPlant);
    n := *number of nearest river*;
    CONNECT(Water(house[location]), river[n])
  UNTIL *no free building site available*

Furthermore, a component may also *redirect* the implementation of its own offered external interfaces to its sub-components. For this purpose, an offered external interface (e.g. *ParkingSpace* of the *StandardHouse* below) can be connected to an offered interface with the same name that belongs to a sub-component (e.g. *garage*). Analogously, a required interface of a sub-component (e.g. the *Water* interface of the *groundFloor*) is also connectable to a corresponding interface, which is required by the super-component from outside.

COMPONENT **StandardHouse** OFFERS **Residence**, **ParkingSpace** REQUIRES **Electricity**, **Water**;
  VARIABLE garage: StandardGarage; groundFloor, firstFloor: ANY(Rooms | Electricity, Water);
  BEGIN
    NEW(garage); NEW(groundFloor, Floor); NEW(firstFloor, Floor);

---

[9] The elementary statements of the language are similar to the Oberon language [30, 31].

CONNECT(ParkingSpace, ParkingSpace(garage));
CONNECT(Electricity(groundFloor), Electricity); CONNECT(Water(groundFloor), Water);
CONNECT(Electricity(firstFloor), Electricity); CONNECT(Water(firstFloor), Water)
END StandardHouse;

Fig. 4 depicts the corresponding connections for the example above. As can be seen, hierarchical composition inherently enables implementation reuse. The *StandardHouse* component can be flexibly built by integrating the existing *StandardGarage* implementation as a sub-component and by redirecting the *ParkingSpace* interface correspondingly. In contrast to object-oriented inheritance, the concerns of reuse and polymorphism are fully separated here.

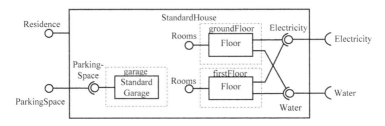

Fig. 4. Redirected interfaces

In the preceding examples, the pointer issue of ordinary programming languages is overcome: interface connections can arrange arbitrary component networks, which are always fully encapsulated by the surrounding component. This is due to the following two important distinctions:

1. A connection only constitutes a link which is exclusively set and controlled by the surrounding component, whereas a pointer (and a classical reference) forms a data value that can be freely copied from one to another object.
2. A connection establishes a symmetric link between a required and an offered interface, whereas a reference/pointer asymmetrically links a target from the reference holder and may not be visible outside the holder.

2.4 Communication-Based Interactions

Interfaces enable arbitrarily general communication-based interactions between components. Two components, which are connected by a required and offered interface, can communicate over the interface by bidirectional message exchange. The feasible sequences of message transmissions during the communication have to be explicitly defined by a protocol in the interface. As an example, the *HotelService* interface below describes the protocol for the communication between a component, which offers this interface, and an external component, which uses it (see the scenario in Fig. 5).

```
INTERFACE HotelService;
  {
    IN CheckIn
    (
      OUT AssignedRoom(number: INTEGER)
      { IN EnterRoom IN ExitRoom }
      IN CheckOut OUT Bill(price: INTEGER) [ IN DirectPayment(m: Money) ]
    | OUT FullyBooked
    )
  }
END HotelService;
```

A protocol is specified as a regular expression in the Extended Backus Naur Formalism (EBNF) [29][10]. The symbols in the protocol denote messages that are exchanged during the communication. Each message has a declared transmission direction (either IN or OUT), an identifier (e.g. *CheckIn*), and an optional list of parameters (e.g. *number*). The IN-direction defines that a message is sent to the component offering the interface, while the OUT-direction characterises the opposite direction of transmission. According to this, the communication protocol of the *HotelService* interface can be understood as the temporal series of messages outlined in Fig. 5.

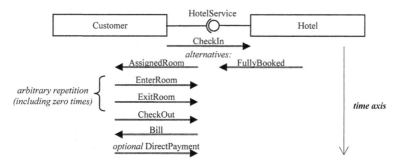

Fig. 5. Message communication via an interface

The parameters of a message represent component instances that are carried within a message. Transmitted instances are always sent as *copies* which have the same internal state and network of sub-components like the original (*deep copy*), and can in turn be safely plugged into the receiver. Naturally, really huge instances (e.g. files) should not to be transmitted as copies but should be rather represented by *unique identifiers* (e.g. file descriptors or invariant file path expressions). Such identifiers however do not form inbuilt language constructs (such as classical pointers) but have to be explicitly defined by the programmer itself, using normal data values or components. Consequently, a unique identifier can be utilised to interact (via

---

[10] In EBNF, a concatenation of expressions represents a sequence, square brackets [ ] indicate an optional expression, curly brackets { } describe a repetition of zero or arbitrary times, and a vertical bar | denotes an alternative between two expressions. By default, concatenation has a stronger binding than an alternative. The default binding order can be explicitly changed with round brackets ( ).

connected interfaces) with the component that contains the actual huge instance (e.g. with the file system).

An offered interface of a component can be used in parallel by all the components which are connected to the corresponding interface, as well as by the containing super-component itself. The component which offers the interface plays the role of the *server* of the interface, whereas the other components which use the interface act as *clients* of this interface. For each client of an interface, the server automatically maintains a separate state-full[11] communication channel. Hence, some *Customer* components may simultaneously perform their individual hotel check-in, while other clients are in another state of communication with the same *Hotel* instance (see Fig. 6).

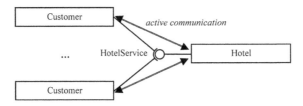

Fig. 6. Multiple parallel client communications

The following program code sketches the implementation of a communication between a *Customer* and a *Hotel* component. The *Hotel* component contains an implementation block for the offered *HotelService* interface. This implementation block is automatically incarnated *as a separate process for each client* and runs as an individual *service agent* for the client. Alternatively, the *Customer* component may directly communicate via its required interface.

```
COMPONENT Customer REQUIRES HotelService;        COMPONENT Hotel OFFERS HotelService;
BEGIN                                            IMPLEMENTATION HotelService;
  HotelService!CheckIn; (* send message *)       BEGIN
  IF HotelService?AssignedRoom THEN(*receive test*)  WHILE ?CheckIn DO {EXCLUSIVE}
  HotelService?AssignedRoom(n) (*accept message*)      ?CheckIn; (* accept message *)
  (* ... *)                                           IF (*free room*) THEN !AssignedRoom(n)
  ELSE (* fully booked *)                              ELSE !FullyBooked END
  HotelService?FullyBooked (* accept message *)     END
  END                                            END HotelService;
END Customer;                                    END Hotel;
```

The send statement (denoted with "!"), delivers a message to the other communication side, by filling the message with copies of the specified parameter arguments. A copy forms an identical clone of the original, such that the clone contains the same internal state, which includes the network of sub-components. These internal components are again recursively copied. Conversely, the receive statement (denoted with "?") awaits the arrival of a specific message from the other communication side and accepts the message on arrival. The contained component

---

[11] State-full means that the component saves the context for the interaction with each individual client.

instances of the received message are eventually assigned to the corresponding variables, which are specified as parameter arguments. A receive statement blocks the execution as long as the message is not received. The receive-test function (an expression denoted with "?")[12], tests whether a specific message can be received from a specific interface by first awaiting any message input. The receive-test function hence blocks the execution until the arrival of any message from the interface but does not yet accept the message nor assign the message parameters[13].

Within the implementation block, the send- and receive-statements without specified interface directly refer to the corresponding client, which is served by the block. Conversely, for the communication in the role of a client, the interface has to be explicitly specified.

It is dynamically checked that all required interfaces of a component are connected when a communication is initiated via one of its offered interface. During a communication between a client and server, all messages have to be sent and received according to the defined protocol. The fulfilment of the protocol is dynamically monitored for each communication, and in the case of a violation, a runtime error is generated. When a client is disconnected from a component, the implicit END message (without parameters), is automatically delivered to the server side and may be optionally accepted by the server.

In the course of the subsequent application of the component language, some of the aforementioned elements for component implementations will be explained in more detail when required. Those, who desire a complete specification of the component language, are referred to the language report [9].

3 Examples

This section illustrates practical examples of the component language, by contrasting them to corresponding object-oriented solutions.

3.1 Producer-Consumer

The first example demonstrates a *producer-consumer* scenario, where both producer and consumer autonomously interact in parallel with a common bounded buffer.

```
COMPONENT Producer REQUIRES DataAcceptor;
 VARIABLE i: INTEGER;
 BEGIN FOR i := 1 TO 100000 DO DataAcceptor!Element(i) END
END Producer;

INTERFACE DataAcceptor;
 { IN Element(x: INTEGER) }
END DataAcceptor;

COMPONENT Consumer REQUIRES DataSource;
 VARIABLE i: INTEGER;
 BEGIN WHILE DataSource?Element DO DataSource?Element(i) END
END Consumer;
```

---

[12] Notably, a receive-test function is uniquely distinguishable from a receive-statement, as it forms a syntactical expression and not a statement.

[13] Additionally, there is also a non-blocking INPUT-function to check the arrival of a message.

```
INTERFACE DataSource;
 { OUT Element(x: INTEGER) }
END DataSource;

COMPONENT BoundedBuffer OFFERS DataAcceptor, DataSource;
 CONSTANT Capacity = 10;
 VARIABLE a[position: INTEGER]: INTEGER; first, last: INTEGER; finished: BOOLEAN;

 IMPLEMENTATION DataAcceptor;
 BEGIN
  WHILE ?Element DO {EXCLUSIVE}
   AWAIT(last-first < Capacity); ?Element(a[last MOD Capacity]); INC(last)
  END;
  BEGIN {EXCLUSIVE} finished := TRUE END
 END DataAcceptor;

 IMPLEMENTATION DataSource;
 BEGIN
  REPEAT {EXCLUSIVE}
   AWAIT((first < last) OR finished);
   IF first < last THEN !Element(a[first MOD Capacity]); INC(first) END
  UNTIL finished
 END DataSource;

 BEGIN first := 0; last := 0; finished := FALSE
END BoundedBuffer;
```

In the previous example, the component body of the *BoundedBuffer* initialises the buffer, before interactions over offered interfaces are accepted. The server-side processes (*service agents*) of the offered interfaces are internally synchronised by using an exclusive *monitor lock* on the component instance, in combination with AWAIT-statements. An AWAIT-statement blocks the execution until the fulfilment of a local condition, by temporarily releasing the monitor lock. This monitor-oriented synchronization is only applicable inside the component instance, and forms a supplement to inter-component interactions, which are merely communication-based. The consumer-producer program may consequently be set up as follows (see Fig. 7):

```
COMPONENT Simulation;
 VARIABLE buffer: BoundedBuffer; producer: Producer; consumer: Consumer;
 BEGIN
  NEW(buffer); NEW(producer); NEW(consumer);
  CONNECT(DataAcceptor(producer), buffer); CONNECT(DataSource(consumer), buffer)
 END Simulation;
```

Producer and consumer immediately start to interact with the buffer, when the *Simulation* is created and the components have been appropriately connected. Naturally, one can also connect multiple producers and multiple consumers to the same buffer.

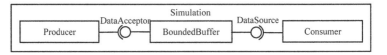

Fig. 7. Producer-consumer scenario

In object-orientated languages, such a scenario entails the explicit incarnation of *threads*, which run as concurrent procedural executions on the passive objects.

Concurrency is therewith not only poorly supported as a secondary programming element (mostly provided by a separate library) but thread interactions are also only insufficiently describable. Threads may only interact implicitly by operations on shared resources, whereas the autonomously running components of our language interact in a clearly defined way by bilateral message exchange according to a formal protocol.

3.2 Digital Library

By way of a second example, we program a digital library which contains a dynamic collection of books. In the library, generic books with the offered *Book* interface can be stored. The library is usable in parallel by an arbitrary number of connected customer components (see Fig. 8), which may request digital copies of books or may also list the book catalogue. Book references are directly modelled as what they really are: unique identities in the form of international standard book numbers (ISBNs). These real references do not involve any specific language concept but only form self-defined identifiers of component instances. Hence, real references imply neither a direct access link nor an existence guarantee. An identified book can be transmitted as a copy within a message from the library to the corresponding customer. The program code for the digital library is:

```
INTERFACE Library;
  { IN RequestBook(isbn: TEXT) (OUT Book(b: ANY(Book)) | OUT Unavailable)
  | IN ListCatalogue { OUT BookReference(isbn: TEXT) } OUT EndOfList }
END Library;

COMPONENT DigitalLibrary OFFERS Library;
  VARIABLE book[isbn: TEXT]: ANY(Book);

  IMPLEMENTATION Library;
  VARIABLE isbn: TEXT; b: ANY(Book);
  BEGIN
    WHILE ?RequestBook OR ?ListCatalogue DO
     IF ?RequestBook THEN {EXCLUSIVE}
      ?RequestBook(isbn);
      IF EXISTS(book[isbn]) THEN !Book(book[isbn]) ELSE !Unavailable END
     ELSE {SHARED}
      ?ListCatalogue; FOREACH isbn OF book DO !BookReference(isbn) END; !EndOfList
     END
    END
  END Library;
END DigitalLibrary;
```

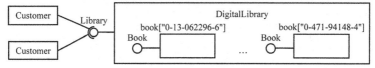

Fig. 8. Encapsulated library

Again, a few explanatory remarks may be helpful. The books in the library are stored within a dynamic component collection (cf. Section 2.1). To identify the contained instances in the collection, ISBNs are used as indexes. The inbuilt EXISTS-function tests whether a defined element is contained in the dynamic collection. If present, a copy of the appropriate book is sent. Note that the case of an inexistent book can be accurately communicated by an alternative message (named *Unavailable*), whereas in object-orientation, an artificial *null* reference often represents this case. The state-full process of listing the book catalogue, involves a shared lock of the library, permitting concurrent iterations by other users. During iterations, any modification is however prevented by exclusive locks. The FOREACH-statement allows the iteration over all instances in a collection, where each iteration step assigns a valid index to the specified iteration variable.

3.2.1 An Object-Oriented Library as Contrast

Unlike our language, an object-oriented program can not accurately describe the encapsulation of dynamic object structures inside other objects, as object-orientation does not feature a hierarchical composition relation. Therefore, an object-oriented language can not guarantee the encapsulation of books in the library but compels the programmer to allocate the internal books of the library as normal objects in the system-wide flat object graph. Very cautious programming is then required to prevent passing out references to internal books of the library in error. The following object-oriented program illustrates this situation:

```
class Book {
  string isbn; string content; Book[] references;
  void Annotate(string note) { content += note; }
}
class Library {
  Book[] books;
  Book RequestBook(string isbn) {
    for (int i = 0; i < books.Length; i++)
    { if ((books[i] != null) && (books[i].isbn == isbn)) { return books[i].Clone(); }  }
    return null; /* null means unavailable */
  }
}
```

Analogous to the component-oriented program, the requested book objects are also transferred as copies between the library and the customer, as the client could otherwise modify the original book in the library. However, despite this precaution, the (directly or indirectly) referenced books in the library may then still be incorrectly accessed by an external customer (see following program fragment and also Fig. 9).

```
class Customer {
  Library library;
  void IncorrectUse {
    Book book = library.RequestBook("3-468-11124-2");
    Book x = book.reference[0];
    read(x.content); /* forbidden reading use of an internal book of the library */
    x.Annotate("personal note"); /* forbidden modifying use of an internal book of the library */
  }
}
```

This demonstrates how vulnerable object-oriented programs are, by the fact that references can conceptually link arbitrary objects in the system and can be freely

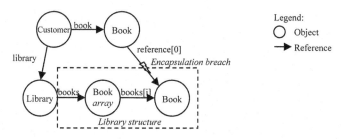

Fig. 9. Incorrect referencing

copied around. Hence, it may be argued that object-oriented references ought not to be used to represent book references in this example. Another approach of only passing *read-only* references [22], does not give any sustainable solution either, since books may still be read without permission.

Catalogue listing is also only inadequately realizable in object-orientation, because the client-individual iteration process has to be forcibly outsourced to an artificial *iterator* object. As a consequence, the external iterator has to store then a reference (or other specific information) that directly breaks into the internal library structure (see Fig. 10). (This encapsulation breach is often considered as a counter-example for the proposed object-oriented encapsulation mechanisms [11, 22].)

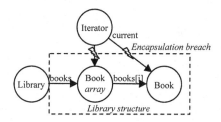

Fig. 10. Iterator object

4   Language Implementation

The presented component language has been completely implemented, comprising a compiler and runtime system, which are based on the Bluebottle operating system [10, 23]. The runtime system is designed as a stack-based virtual machine, supporting an intermediate language that consists of a sensibly selected combination of both primitive functionality (e.g. integer addition) and more complex functionality (e.g. message sending and receiving). These complex instructions directly correspond to fundamental high-level language abstractions. The compiler generates the inter-mediate code, which is in turn automatically transformed to the backend machine code by the virtual machine. Backend code generation is only initiated at the time when the intermediate code is loaded.

For hierarchical composition, component instances are dynamically organised in the linear heap memory with appropriate memory indirections. An internal data structure automatically manages an indexed collection of component instances. Here, an adaptive data structure may be reasonable, e.g. a simple linear list for small collection sizes and a B-tree for larger sizes. Due to the hierarchical lifetime dependencies of compositions, automatic garbage collection for memory-safe runtime management is no longer needed. Components can be directly de-allocated on the disposal of the super-component, without suffering extensive (and generally system-blocking) garbage collection.

High and efficient parallelism is most critical for the adequate runtime support of component instances and their internal processes. For this purpose, the Active Object technology [23] of the Bluebottle operating system is advantageous, as it provides particularly light-weighted parallelism with low-cost context switches. Of course, there is still much potential and need for further improvement of concurrency.

The communication between two components is implemented by an internal bidirectional message channel. These channels have bounded buffer sizes, to avoid dynamic memory allocations on message sending. The communication protocol is dynamically monitored by using a finite state machine, that is automatically generated by the backend compiler from the protocol specification.

Table 1 gives an impression of the system's performance and scalability by means of experimental measurements with three test applications (available at [9]): (1) a producer-consumer scenario with 100,000 exchanged elements, (2) a small city simulation (as in Section 2) with 100 houses, each consuming 1,000 units of water and electricity, and (3) a large city simulation with 1,000 houses. Whereas the small city simulation only involves about 500 components and 300 processes, the large city requires more than 5,000 components and 3,000 processes. The results are first compared to analogous programs written in Active C# [13] and to a Windows implementation of AOS (called WinAOS [12]). On a Intel P4, 2.6GHz with 2 logical processors, our component system shows a substantially higher performance than the Windows-based systems and also scales higher with regard to the number of parallel processes. The performance advantage is mainly due to the fast context switches of processes in the underlying Bluebottle system; direct context switches are for example performed on message sending and receiving, if the other communication partner is already waiting for a message transfer. Compared to the traditional thread-based systems, the higher scalability results from the lower stack overhead of the active object technology. To estimate the costs of the virtual machine of the component system, the performance is also measured with analogous Active Oberon programs, which directly run on the native Bluebottle system (whereon our virtual machine runs as well). As the difference between both systems shows, the overhead of component language is relatively small, i.e. not higher than about 10 percent.

Table 1. Comparison of execution times (in seconds)

Test application	Component System	Active C#	WinAOS	Native Bluebottle
Producer-consumer	1.6	4.4	10	1.6
Small city simulation	2.9	360	24	2.7
Large city simulation	30	- (out of memory)	- (out of memory)	28

5 Related Work

The presented language is to our knowledge, the first general-purpose programming language which directly integrates a general component notion with only high-level programming concepts, and which is free of the classical problematic constructs of references, methods and inheritance (see Section 1). Some fundamental concepts of this language are however similar to previous works.

Interface connections. The Microsoft COM [27, 28] wiring mechanism (see [26], Section 10.3) with incoming and outgoing interfaces has similarities to the offered and required interfaces in our language, but is only designed to support asynchronous events using classical method calls. Hence, conventional pointers (or references) still establish the typical component relations in COM. The model of provided and required interfaces is also often used in architecture description languages [3, 20, 21]. However, these languages do not form real programming languages but just allow the formal description and specification of software architectures. Dynamic structures of components are generally not describable, as the number of components is either static or fixed by a parameter. Moreover, interactions have to be either inadequately represented by method-based interfaces [21], or by low-level message channels (called ports), which are often even unidirectional (like electronic wires) [20]. Other architecture description languages [3] do not have dual provided and required interfaces, but instead necessitate artificial constraints (called glue) to bind a set of ports. With these low-level ports, each client requires a separate interface port for individual communication but a component is typically unable to support an arbitrary (dynamic) number of ports.

Symmetric polymorphism. The symmetric support of offered interfaces is comparable to COM and Zonnon, but in our language, interfaces are merely communication-oriented. Interfaces are also often provided together with a special concept of reusable implementation parts, such as mixins [5] or traits [24]. However, in our language, composition and interface redirection inherently permit flexible implementation reuse without needing such an artificial code mixing mechanism.

Communication-based interactions. The paradigm of message communication has been introduced with CSP [18] and realised in Occam [19]. However, a decisive distinction to our language model is that a component (called process) in CSP/Occam can not interact with multiple interface clients individually, but has to explicitly handle all possible overlapping of client interactions via a time-multiplexed communication channel. The formal Actor model [15, 1], which also proposes communicating parallel components, requires the explicit identification of communication partners by means of references (called mail addresses). This does not only impede clearly described client-individual communications, but also implicates the elementary problems of references like in object-orientation. Our communication model with individual clients is rather influenced from the activity concept of Active C# [13] and Zonnon [14]. Though, in Active C# and Zonnon, clients have to explicitly invoke an activity and interact with the returned dialog, whereas this component language permits direct client-individual communications via interfaces. A further distinction can be made as the component language supports explicit messages with a set of data values and instances that are carried in parameters.

Conversely, data values and explicit tokens/tags have to be transmitted as single items in Zonnon, Active C#, CSP, and Occam.

Component systems. A variety of other component models have been invented to enhance structuring, deployment, extendibility and reusability of software [26]. Java Beans, Enterprise Java Beans, CORBA, Microsoft COM, and the Microsoft .NET framework are only some representatives of popular component systems. All these models however have the same fundamental deficiencies with regard to references and methods (see Section 1). With the exception of COM, object-oriented component models also integrate the inheritance relation and its discussed disadvantages.

Other related work. In addition, many efforts have been made to tackle the problems of references with visibility restrictions [8], ownership models [16, 4, 11, 22, 6, 2], region models [7], encapsulation policies [24] and many more. The common problem of all these approaches is that they are still based on the classical low-level model of references and thus require complicated rule systems (mostly integrated in type systems), to ensure structural conditions. Moreover, these models can generally not describe state-full and client-individual interactions (c.f. iterators in Section 3.2), such that the encapsulation has to be forcibly broken up, by using read-only references [22], dynamic parameter aliasing [16, 4], or simply normal unrestricted references. As conventional references are still supported as standard constructs in these models, the majority of objects may nevertheless be exposed as part of the system-wide flat object graph.

6 Conclusion

The presented component language is a radically new approach for more powerful and structured programming. It integrates a general component notion with appropriate high-level programming concepts, to enable structural clarity, high dynamicity, together with inherent parallelism. As a result, immanent solutions to the various shortcomings of the currently prevalent object-oriented programming paradigm can be gained. The complete implementation and the detailed report of the component language can be found at [9].

Acknowledgments

I am particularly grateful to Prof. Dr. Jürg Gutknecht for his support and helpful advice during this work and for this paper. Many thanks are also due to Dr. Thomas Frey, Dr. Felix Friedrich and other colleagues for their constructive reviews and suggestions for improvement.

References[14]

1. G. Agha. Actors: A Model of Concurrent Computation in Distributed Systems. MIT Press, 1986.
2. J. Aldrich and C. Chambers. Ownership Domains: Separating Aliasing Policy from Mechanism. In European Conference on Object-Oriented Programming (ECOOP), June 2004.

---

[14] With regard to the discussion in Section 3.2, this section lists real references.

3. R. Allen and D. Garlan. A Formal Basis for Architectural Connection. ACM Transactions on Software Engineering and Methodology, 6(3): 213-249, July 1997.
4. P.S. Almeida. Balloon Types: Controlling Sharing of State in Data Types. In European Conference on Object-Oriented Programming (ECOOP), June 1997.
5. G. Bracha and W. Cook. Mixin-based Inheritance. In Object-Oriented Programming Systems, Languages, and Applications (OOPSLA), October 1990.
6. C. Boyapati, R. Lee, and M. Rinard. Ownership Types for Safe Programming: Preventing Data Races and Deadlocks. In Object-Oriented Programming Systems, Languages, and Applications (OOPSLA), November 2002.
7. C. Boyapati, A. Salcianu, W. Beebee, M. Rinard. Ownership Types for Safe Region-Based Memory Management in Real-Time Java. In Programming Language Design and Implementation (PLDI), June 2003.
8. B. Bokowski and J. Vitek. Confined Types. In Object-Oriented Programming Systems, Languages, and Applications (OOPSLA), November 1999.
9. L. Bläser. The Component Language. ETH Zurich, Switzerland, 2006. Available from http://www.jg.inf.ethz.ch/components.
10. J. Gutknecht, P. J. Muller, T. M. Frey, et al. The Bluebottle Operating System. ETH Zurich, Switzerland. Available from http://www.bluebottle.ethz.ch.
11. D.G. Clarke, J.M. Potter, and J.Noble. Ownership Types for Flexible Alias Protection. In Object-Oriented Programming Systems, Languages, and Applications (OOPSLA), October 1998.
12. F. Friedrich. The WinAOS Oberon System. ETH Zurich, Switzerland. Available from http://www.bluebottle.ethz.ch/winaos.
13. R. Güntensperger and J. Gutknecht. Active C#. .NET Technologies, May 2004.
14. J. Gutknecht and E. Zueff, Zonnon Language Report, ETH Zurich, Switzerland, October 2004. Available from http://www.zonnon.ethz.ch.
15. C. Hewitt, P. Bishop and R. Steiger. A Universal Modular Actor Formalism for Artificial Intelligence, International Joint Conference on Artificial Intelligence (IJCAI), 1973.
16. J. Hogg. Islands: Aliasing Protection in Object-Oriented Languages. In Object-Oriented Programming Systems, Languages, and Applications (OOPSLA), October 1991.
17. C.A.R. Hoare. Hints on Programming Language Design. Stanford Artificial Intelligence Laboratory Memo AIM-224 or STAN-CS-73-403, Stanford University, Stanford, California, December 1973.
18. C.A.R. Hoare. Communicating Sequential Processes. Communications of the ACM, 21(8):666-677, 1978.
19. Inmos Ltd. Occam 2 Reference Manual. Prentice-Hall, 1988.
20. J. Magee and J. Kramer. Dynamic Structure in Software Architectures. In Fourth Symposium on the Foundations of Software Engineering (FSE), October 1996.
21. N. Medvidovic, D. S. Rosenblum, and R. N. Taylor. A Language and Environment for Architecture-Based Software Development and Evolution. In International Conference on Software Engineering (ICSE), May 1999.
22. P. Müller and A. Poetzsch-Heffter. A Type System for Alias and Dependency Control. Technical Report 279, Fernuniversität Hagen, 2001.
23. P. J. Muller. The Active Object System. Design and Multiprocessor Implementation. PhD thesis 14755, Department of Computer Science, ETH Zurich, 2002.
24. N. Schärli, S. Ducasse, O. Nierstrasz, and A. P. Black. Traits: Composable Units of Behaviour. In European Conference on Object-Oriented Programming (ECOOP), July 2003.

25. N. Schärli, S. Ducasse, O. Nierstrasz, and R. Wuyts. Composable encapsulation policies. In European Conference on Object-Oriented Programming (ECOOP), June 2004.
26. C. Szyperski. Component Software, Beyond Object-Oriented Programming. Addison-Wesley, 1998.
27. A. Williams. Dealing with the Unknown – or – Type Safety in a Dynamically Extensible Class Library. Draft, Microsoft Application Division, 1988. Available from research.microsoft.com/comapps/docs/ Unknown.doc.
28. A. Williams. On Inheritance: What It Means and How to Use It. Draft, Applications Architecture Group, Microsoft Research, 1990. Available from research.microsoft.com/comapps/docs/Inherit.doc.
29. N. Wirth. What can we do about the unnecessary diversity of notation for syntactic definitions? Communications of the ACM, 20(11): 822, 823, November 1977.
30. N. Wirth and J. Gutknecht. The Oberon System. Software – Practice and Experience, 19(9): 857-893, September 1989.
31. N. Wirth. The Programming Language Oberon. Software - Practice and Experience, 18(7): 671-690, July 1988.

Internal and External Token-Based Synchronization in Object-Oriented Languages

Franz Puntigam

Technische Universität Wien, Institut für Computersprachen
Argentinierstraße 8, 1040 Vienna, Austria
franz@complang.tuwien.ac.at

Abstract. We expect interfaces in programming languages to expose essential parts of the objects' internal synchronization as well as required external synchronization. Clients need this information to provide required and avoid conflicting synchronization. We propose a mixed static and dynamic token-based approach to uniformly specify internal and external synchronization in a simplified Java-like language. This concept gives us much flexibility on token management, ensures race-free programs without any need for complete aliasing information, and supports static type checking of synchronization using a rich notion of subtyping.

1 Introduction

Synchronization is essentially a means to enforce data dependences in control flows: If there is a dependence between data accesses in two threads of control, then one of the threads must wait until the other has caught up to meet at a synchronization point where data are consistent. Providing proper synchronization is difficult. Omitted synchronization statements can from time to time result in reading inconsistent data (these are races). It is very difficult to catch such bugs. Programmers often apply synchronization and restrict concurrency much more than necessary to prevent the danger of races and because of missing knowledge about data dependences. Unnecessary synchronization affects program efficiency and increases the danger of deadlocks and other undesirable program behavior.

Good knowledge of the whole program and its synchronization structure reduces the problem. Many programs consist of independently developed components, each treating synchronization in its own way. Component interfaces are the best place to provide synchronization information. Substituting a component for another one requires synchronization in the two components to be compatible, this is, their interfaces must be in a subtype relationship. In this paper we deal with synchronization information in interfaces and subtype relations as well as static type checking to ensure race-free programs. We explore interfaces of simple objects, but all results hold also for component interfaces.

Most programming languages support internal synchronization within objects, while required external synchronization (to be provided by clients) can be expressed only as comments. Since especially required external synchronization is important to clients and for subtyping, we propose language support for it.

D. Lightfoot and C. Szyperski (Eds.): JMLC 2006, LNCS 4228, pp. 251–270, 2006.

An important topic is the representation of synchronization information. Direct representation of dependences is hardly tractable and exposes too many implementation details to clients. Therefore, we prefer an abstract representation based on tokens as proposed for process types [1,2]. This type system allows us to specify required external synchronization in types and statically ensures that clients observe required dependences.

In Sect. 2 we analyze internal and external synchronization and introduce a corresponding language. Next, in Sect. 3 we propose a concept of internal synchronization resembling more conventional synchronization, and in Sect. 4 we address the problem of encoding changing synchronization information into the types of instance variables. We consider synchronization information together with subtyping in Sect. 5. A discussion of related work follows in Sect. 6.

2   The Basis: Synchronization, Tokens, and Language

We develop a simple Java-like language using tokens for synchronization as basis for further analysis. First. we explore the synchronization information we need in interfaces. Then, we introduce the language mainly by examples.

2.1   Responsibility for Synchronization

We use a broad notion of synchronization and distinguish between the following kinds based on the roles of objects as clients and servers and their responsibilities:

Internal Synchronization: This is any means to enforce data dependences in control flows within an object as server – synchronization in a narrow sense. Thereby, the execution of a thread can be blocked. In Java we use synchronized methods (or statements) together with wait and notify for internal synchronization. For example, java.util.Hashtable uses internal synchronization to ensure consistent updates of its instances. Internal synchronization determines when an invoked method gets executed. Only the object itself is responsible for providing this kind of synchronization.

Required External Synchronization: This is synchronization an object requires to be provided by each client. A method can be invoked only if a synchronization condition is satisfied, and within the method this condition is regarded as satisfied. For example, java.util.HashMap requires external synchronization to ensure consistent updates. Required external synchronization determines when a method can be invoked. All clients are responsible for providing required synchronization.

Provided External Synchronization: A client of the object under consideration provides this synchronization. Regarded as server a client does so by internal or external synchronization, or simply by invoking methods in a specific order. Clients usually provide more synchronization than required. Unrequired external synchronization can be in conflict with internal synchronization. For example, we get a deadlock if a simple buffer with a single slot uses internal synchronization to ensure put and get to be executed only in alternation, and clients provide external synchronization by invoking get only after put has been executed twice. Provided external synchronization determines if and when an invokable method actually is invoked.

Clients must know the server's internal synchronization that can be in conflict with provided synchronization. Fortunately, not every internal synchronization can be in conflict with provided synchronization:

Simple Mutex Synchronization: This kind of internal synchronization ensures just that only a single thread can execute a critical section at any time. The execution of the critical section must terminate, and the synchronization condition must not depend on anything else than the number of threads in the critical section. Examples are synchronized methods in Java that do not invoke wait. It is a good idea to demand such critical sections to terminate in a short period of time; otherwise the execution of the whole system can be blocked. Simple mutex synchronization can delay execution, but cannot prevent it. Hence, simple mutex synchronization is not in conflict with provided external synchronization and need not be visible to clients.

Dependent Internal Synchronization: Synchronization conditions depend on the program state in a more complex way. For example, synchronized methods in Java invoking wait depend on an invocation of notify in another thread. Clients must know about such dependences to avoid conflicting synchronization (through simultaneous executions of methods invoking notify).

In simple cases like buffers we usually prefer internal synchronization where only the server decides when to perform an operation. External synchronization gives clients better control. Clients having sufficient information about dependences can get better performance from external than from internal synchronization.

There are useful relationships between the different kinds of synchronization. For example, a proxy as client of an object can convert the object's required external synchronization into internal synchronization in the proxy. Programmers can decide case by case whether they prefer direct access to an object with required external synchronization or indirect access through a proxy providing the required synchronization. Because of such techniques servers requiring external synchronization give clients all possibilities.

2.2   A Simple Language with Tokens

In our language we use tokens as proposed for process types [1,2]. This type system statically ensures that users observe all required external synchronization conditions without any need for complete aliasing information.

Fig. 1 shows the grammar of our language. Throughout this paper, $u, \ldots, z$ (possibly quoted and indexed) denote names, t token specifications, c pre- and post-condition pairs on tokens, d dependent tokens, τ types, p formal parameters, s statements, e expressions, and $i, \ldots, n$ natural numbers (including zero and the special symbol ∞). We differentiate between classes and interfaces as named

$$P ::= gdef^+$$
$$gdef ::= [t^*] \text{ interface } u \; \{decl^*\} \mid [t^*] \text{ class } u \; \{ldef^+\}$$
$$decl ::= \tau \, x(p^*) \text{ with } c_1 \text{ when } c_2 \mid \text{void } x(p^*) \text{ with } c_1 \text{ when } c_2$$
$$ldef ::= \tau \, d^* \, v \mid decl \; \{s^*\} \mid \text{new}(p^*) \text{ with } \rightarrow t^* \; \{s^*\}$$
$$d ::= [t_1^+ \text{ for } t_2^+]$$
$$p ::= u[c] \; v$$
$$c ::= t_1^* \rightarrow t_2^*$$
$$t ::= (n)x$$
$$\tau ::= u[t^*]$$
$$s ::= v = e \mid v.x(w^*) \mid \text{fork } v.x(w^*) \mid \text{with } c \; \{s^*\} \mid \text{return } e$$
$$e ::= v \mid v.x(w^*) \mid u.\text{new}(w^*) \mid \text{null}$$

Fig. 1. Syntax of our Language

basic units in a program. Subtyping is inferred from the structure of classes and interfaces; there are no explicit supertype specifications. For syntactic simplicity we avoid commas and semicolons as separators. To create a new object we invoke a constructor (beginning with new) in a class. As shown by the examples below, initial internal tokens (those specified in front of the class or interface key word) and when-clauses determine internal synchronization. Tokens associated with types and with-clauses determine required external synchronization.

In our examples we take the liberty to omit with-clauses, when-clauses, and square brackets not containing any tokens. We often write just x instead of $(1)x$ (one token of name x) and usually avoid to write down $(0)x$ (no token of name x). The first example shows how to specify required external synchronization:

```
interface Window {
        void iconify() with displayed → iconified
        void display() with iconified → displayed
}
```

We assume windows to be displayed on a screen or just represented by icons. Two methods switch between these states. According to the with-clause we can invoke iconify only if we have a token displayed; this token is removed on invocation, and iconified is added on return. For a variable v of type Window[displayed] we can invoke v.iconify(). This invocation changes the type of v to Window[iconified]. Afterwords we can invoke v.display(), then again v.iconify(), and so on. Simple static type checking enforces the methods to be invoked only in alternation. Typically a button causing an icon to be replaced with a displayed window does not exist at the same time as one causing the window to become an icon. In this case it is very natural to statically express the expected state of the window in its type, and there is no need for synchronization at run time.

Types can be associated with several tokens. For example, let an instance of Window[(8)displayed (7)iconified] be a window manager iconifying and displaying any of its at least 15 windows. This object accepts iconify and display in all sequences such that never more that 15 or less than zero windows are displayed.

2.3   Moving Static Tokens Around

We handle tokens in parameter types in a similar way as in with-clauses:

```
class Parameters {
    void foo(Window[displayed iconified → (2)displayed] w) {
        w.iconify()   w.display()   w.display()
    }
}
```

Arrows in parameter types relate tokens required on invocation with those available on return. Let v be a variable of type Window[(2)iconified (2)displayed] and x one of Parameters. An invocation of x.foo(v) first iconifies a window and then displays two of them. The variable w in foo is known to have at least a displayed and a iconified token on invocation and two displayed tokens on return. Removing the tokens to the left of the arrow on invocation causes the type of v to become Window[displayed iconified], and adding those to the right on return causes it to become Window[(3)displayed iconified]. Tokens move from argument types to formal parameter types on invocation and vice versa on return. Only with-clauses (and for this section when-clauses, see below) add and remove tokens. Each object produces and consumes only its own tokens.

A statement 'fork x.foo(v)' spawns a new thread executing x.foo(v). Since execution continues without waiting for termination of the new thread, fork statements cannot return result values and tokens. The type of v changes on invocation from just to Window[displayed iconified]. Everything to the right of the arrow in the formal parameter type is ignored. Thereby, the old type of v is split into two types – the new type of v and the type of the formal parameter w. Both threads can invoke methods in the same object without affecting each other concerning type information.

Assignment resembles parameter passing when spawning threads: We split an assigned value's type into two types. One type becomes the variable's type, and the other becomes the assigned value's new type. Tokens move from the value's to the variable's type. For example, if a variable w is expected to be of type Window[(2)iconified] and v is of Window[(2)displayed (2)iconified], then the execution of 'w = v' causes the type of v to become Window[(2)displayed].

With-clauses in constructors play an important role in introducing tokens:

```
class MyWindow {
    int test
    void iconify() with displayed → iconified { test = 0 }
    void display() with iconified → displayed) { test = 1 }
    new() with → displayed { test = 1 }
}
```

An invocation of MyWindow.new returns a new object with a single token. No other token is available for this object. Since invocations of iconify and display consume a token before they issue another one, there exists always at most one token. This property ensures that each method invocation switches the value of test between 0 and 1, and there cannot be simultaneous accesses of test.

2.4   Simplified Internal Synchronization

For the rest of this section we use a simplified view of internal synchronization, and we will reconsider it in the next section. We associate each object with a dynamically manipulated pool of internal tokens. Classes and interfaces specify initial internal tokens of new instances (in front of the key words class and interface). Tokens to the left of the arrow in when-clauses must be available and are removed from this pool before executing the method body, and tokens to the right are added on return. If required tokens are not available, then the execution is blocked until other threads cause the tokens to become available. Checks for the availability of· these tokens occur only at run time.

The following buffer example uses internal synchronization to ensure mutual exclusion and to avoid buffer overflow and underflow:

```
[sync (10)empty] class BufferDyn {
     ListElem head
     new() { head = null }
     void increment() when → (10)empty {}
     void decrement() when (10)empty → {}
     void put(Elem e) when sync empty → sync filled {/* add to list */}
     Elem get() when sync filled → sync empty {/* get from list */}
}
```

Instances get some empty tokens and a single token sync on creation. Both put and get remove sync at the begin and issue a new one on return and thereby ensure exclusive access to head. Tokens filled and empty dynamically ensure that a buffer never contains more than the maximum or less than zero elements. Execution blocks until these conditions are satisfied. The maximum capacity of the buffer can be changed by (repeatedly) invoking increment and decrement.

2.5   Usual Uses of Tokens and Infinity

The above examples use tokens as counters in a similar way as semaphores are essentially counters, no matter whether we use internal or external synchronization. More often we use tokens as binary semaphores where at most one token of some name can exist for each object. Names of such tokens usually abstract over (specific aspects of) the objects' current states as in the next example:

```
class ShowStates {
     new() with → justCreated {...}
     void init1() with justCreated → partlyInitialized {...}
     void init2() with partlyInitialized → (∞)ready {...}
     void doSomething() with ready → {...}
}
```

Immediately after creation an instance is in state justCreated. On execution of init1 (which can occur at most once) the state changes to partlyInitialized, and on executing init2 (at most once) to (∞)ready – an unlimited number of tokens ready. We can invoke doSomething as often as we want, even simultaneously. As with-clause of doSomething we can have (n)ready $\rightarrow$ (m)ready with any $n \geq 1$ and $m \geq 0$ without changing the semantics.

To meet our expectations we define (for all natural numbers n including 0 and ∞) $\infty \geq n$ to be true, $\infty + n = \infty$, and $\infty - n = \infty$ (implying $\infty - \infty = \infty$).

As in the example we usually use unlimited numbers of tokens to indicate that corresponding (aspects of) object states do not change anymore. Major reasons for using ∞ instead of 1 as token numbers include

- no limitation of simultaneous execution,
- and type splitting (for external synchronization) where each of the split types has full information about available tokens.

In type splitting for assignment and forking we usually must decide which client gets which tokens. With unlimited token numbers all clients can have complete information. For example, ShowStates[(∞)ready] can be split into twice the same type because of $\infty - \infty = \infty$.

3   Internal Synchronization Reconsidered

3.1   Atomic Actions and Their Problems

Token-based internal synchronization as introduced in the previous section and in [3] has desired properties especially for dependent internal synchronization (see Sect. 2.1) and some weaknesses for simple mutex synchronization and in relating internal with required external synchronization:

Atomic Actions: When-clauses (and with-clauses) specify atomic actions. Synchronization is guaranteed by removing tokens at the begin and adding new tokens only at the end. Atomic actions are quite valuable in programming because they clearly specify points in the program where we expect object states to be consistent. Between these points we have to regard states as inconsistent. This principle is enforced also for nested (possibly recursive) method invocations. Unfortunately, if the when-clause of the outer method invocation removed tokens needed by the inner invocation, then the execution can easily be in a deadlock: The outer invocation waits for termination of the inner invocation, and the inner invocation waits for tokens to be added at the end of the outer invocation. In general, such situations are erroneous: We expect the object to be in a consistent state on invocation of the inner method, but actually it is possibly in an inconsistent state. Therefore, program termination or raising an exception is useful program behavior in this case. However, if we use tokens just to ensure mutual exclusion (this is simple mutex synchronization), then missing tokens do not imply inconsistent states. Provided that the missing tokens were removed within the same thread, we expect the execution to continue in this case. To improve the model we must distinguish between dependent internal synchronization and simple mutex synchronization.

This: Tokens for internal and external synchronization are strictly separated: Only with-clauses manipulate external tokens, and only when-clauses internal tokens. The self-reference this naturally breaks the separation: This implicitly refers to an instance of the most specific type of the object it occurs within. We can regard internal tokens to be at the same time tokens in the implicit type of this. When invoking a method through this, the with-clause of the invoked method takes required tokens from the pool of internal tokens and puts added tokens back to this pool. The use of this as formal parameter can also manipulate internal tokens. Unfortunately, requiring internal tokens from the pool can block the execution (if required tokens are not available). Thereby, synchronization points occur within atomic actions – not necessarily at the begin of atomic actions. We regard such blocking as undesirable. To improve the model we must statically ensure availability of all tokens needed in the implicit type of this.

3.2   Thread-Specific Token Pools

With a more advanced concept of internal synchronization we treat both problems: In addition to the general pool of internal tokens in each object we use a token pool per thread and object. We redefine the semantics of when-clauses such that they just move tokens from the general token pool to the thread-specific token pool on invocation and vice versa on return instead of removing and adding them. There is no need to wait for the availability of tokens in the general pool if they are already in the thread-specific pool. Only tokens in the thread-specific pool are regarded as available in the implicit type of this. The following abstract example demonstrates the new semantics of when-clauses:

```
[sync] class InternExtern {
       void makeIntern() when sync → sync dep { ... this.makeExtern() ... }
       void makeExtern() with → dep when sync → sync {...}
       void useIntern() when sync dep → sync { ... this.useExtern() ... }
       void useExtern() with dep → when sync → sync {...}
       ...
}
```

We assume that each of the four methods accesses a shared critical resource protected by an internal token sync that ensures mutual exclusion. With a token dep we let useExtern only be invokable as often as makeExtern was invoked before. An invocation of makeIntern causes the token produced in an invocation of this.makeExtern to become available as internal token, and an invocation of useIntern consumes an internal token dep in an invocation of this.useExtern.

On invocation of makeIntern the when-clause first looks if sync is available in the thread-specific token pool. In this case execution immediately continues with the method body. Otherwise execution is blocked until sync becomes available in the general pool; then sync will be removed from the general pool and added to the thread-specific pool before execution continues. When invoking makeExtern through this in the body of makeIntern, sync will be available in the thread-specific pool and the body of makeExtern can be executed without delay. On return from makeExtern a new token dep specified in the with-clause is added to the thread-specific pool because the tokens in the implicit type of this correspond to the thread-specific pool. On return from makeIntern the tokens sync and dep must be available in the thread-specific pool as specified to the right of the arrow in the when-clause. Then, dep is removed from the thread-specific pool and added to the general pool in any case, and sync is removed from the thread-specific and added to the general pool only if it was not available in the thread-specific pool when invoking makeIntern; otherwise sync remains in the thread-specific pool.

On invocation of useIntern the token dep must be moved from the general to the thread-specific pool even if there is already such a token: We expect the thread-specific pool to contain the same tokens on invocation and return. Since the execution of useIntern just removes dep, this token would not be in the thread-specific pool on return if it was token from this pool.

Note that we use sync in makeExtern and useExtern only to demonstrate nesting of when-clauses. We omit them where we need no mutual exclusion.

Quite often methods like makeExtern and useExtern need not be used from outside. In this case we can simplify the syntax by using with-statements instead of with-clauses in methods:

```
void makeIntern() when sync → sync dep { ... with → dep {...} ... }
void useIntern() when sync dep → sync { ... with dep → {...} ... }
```

With-statements are essentially syntactic sugar inlining methods that would otherwise be invoked through this. Tokens in with-statements are taken from and added to the thread-specific pool.

3.3 New Semantics of when-Clauses

We differentiate between three kinds of tokens in when-clauses:

Remove-Tokens occur only to the left of the arrow.
Add-Tokens occur only to the right of the arrow.
Through-Tokens occur on both sides of the arrow.

This is the new semantics of the when-clause in each method:

- On method invocation the when-clause moves these tokens from the general to the thread-specific pool of the current thread:
  - all remove-tokens and
  - through-tokens not yet being in the thread-specific pool.
  Execution blocks until all tokens to be moved are simultaneously available in the general pool. Then, these tokens are moved atomically. To be concrete, they must be removed from the global pool in an indivisible step while adding them to the thread-specific pool need not be atomic.
- On return from the method the when-clause moves these tokens from the thread-specific to the general pool (not necessarily atomically):

- all add-tokens and
- through-tokens moved to the thread-specific pool on method invocation.
- Static type checking ensures that all tokens occurring to the right of the arrow will be available in the thread-specific pool on return from the method if tokens to the left were available on method invocation. To perform static type checking we treat this as any other instance variable and assume the tokens to the left of the arrow in the when-clause as being available in the type of this at the begin of checking the method. After checking the method, the type of this must contain at least all tokens to the right. Each instance variable is assumed to have some tokens at the begin and some (other) tokens at the end of method checking (see Sect. 4).

We regard tokens of some name as relevant for internal synchronization in a class or interface if at least one token of this name occurs to the left of the arrow in any when-clause in the class or interface. Accordingly we regard tokens as relevant for required external synchronization if at least one token of this name occurs to the left of the arrow in any with-clause. All tokens occurring in when-clauses must be relevant for internal synchronization. Other tokens cannot influence internal synchronization. In contrast, tokens (to the right of the arrow) in with-clauses must be relevant for internal or required external synchronization: Methods invoked through this can add such tokens to the internal token pool.

The semantics of when-clauses imposes a natural differentiation between tokens possibly relevant for dependent internal synchronization and those relevant only for simple mutex synchronization: Tokens relevant for internal synchronization are possibly relevant for dependent internal synchronization if they

- occur as remove-tokens,
- or are also relevant for required external synchronization.

Add-tokens are necessarily relevant for both internal and required external synchronization; otherwise they cannot become available in the type of this. All other tokens relevant for internal synchronization (they can only be through-tokens) are relevant only for simple mutex synchronization. Such tokens need not be considered in subtyping (see Sect. 5). In all examples used so far, sync is relevant only for internal synchronization while internal tokens of other names are possibly relevant for dependent internal synchronization.

The semantics of when-clauses is compatible with semantics of more conventional synchronization concepts: Synchronized methods in Java correspond essentially to methods with when-clauses containing only a single token relevant for simple mutex synchronization (monitor concept). The wait-operation can easily be simulated using remove-tokens, and the notify-operation with add-tokens.

4   Accessing Instance Variables

Instance variables are declared only once, but they can be accessed (possibly simultaneously) in several methods, each expecting different tokens to be available in the variables' types at different points in time. Uses of variables can cause changes of the tokens encoded into types. In this section we address corresponding problems and show how to avoid races.

4.1   Read-Access to Instance Variables with Dependent Tokens

In Sect.2.1 we mentioned that a proxy can convert required external synchronization into internal synchronization. When implementing such synchronization proxy we face a problem: We need an instance variable referring to the object requiring external synchronization. Tokens in the type of this variable change over time as does the state of the object. Because of internal synchronization in the proxy the tokens in the variable's type depend on internal tokens available in the proxy. The next example shows the implementation of a buffer and a proxy using dependent tokens to connect the external tokens of the buffer with the internal tokens of the proxy:

```
interface BufferStat {
    void put(Elem e) with empty → filled
    Elem get() with filled → empty
}
[sync] class BufferStatImpl {
    ListElem head
    new() { head = null }
    void increment() with → (10)empty {}
    void put(Elem e) with empty → filled when sync → sync {/* add to list */}
    Elem get() with filled → empty when sync → sync {/* get from list */}
}
[(50)pe] class Proxy {
    BufferStat[empty for pe][filled for pf] buffer
    new(BufferStat[(50)empty →]) { buffer = b }
    void put(Elem e) when pe → pf { with pe → pf { buffer.put(e) }}
    Elem get() when pf → pe { with pf → pe { return buffer.get() }}
}
```

In class BufferStatImpl, internal synchronization ensures mutual exclusion, and required external synchronization avoids over- and underflows. As we will see in Sect. 5 BufferStatImpl is a subtype of BufferStat, an interface not showing simple mutex synchronization.

Dependent tokens in the type of buffer specify that within each method in Proxy we assume an empty to be available for each pe in the corresponding with-clause, and a filled for each pf. In the with-statement in put the variable is of type BufferStat[empty] at the begin and of BufferStat[filled] at the end. An execution of buffer.put(e) causes the type change. In the with-statement in get the type of buffer changes from BufferStat[filled] to BufferStat[empty]. On return from the constructor, buffer must be of type BufferStat[(50)empty] because of the initial internal tokens (and, in general, tokens in the constructor's with-clause). By strictly coupling tokens in the variable's type to the containing object's initial tokens and all changes through with-clauses we ensure the object's tokens to actually reflect the variable's tokens. Static type checking guarantees this property.

We need with-statements in put and get because dependent tokens depend only on tokens in with-clauses. It is impossible to assume dependences on tokens in when-clauses since several atomic actions can see the same tokens (occurring in a thread-specific pool) causing tokens in the variables' types to be implicitly duplicated. Token duplication would destroy soundness.

Dependent tokens support concurrent read accesses. For example, instances of Proxy support up to 50 simultaneous executions of put and get, each reading and changing the state encoded in the type of buffer.

We compute the tokens in the type of instance variables by repeatedly applying dependences (for-clauses) specified in variable declarations in arbitrary ordering. We start with the multi-set of tokens in the with-clause. If we have the tokens to the right of a for-clause in this multi-set, then we delete these tokens from the multi-set and add the tokens to the left of the for-clause to the tokens assumed to be available for the variable. We repeat this step as long as there are appropriate for-clauses. To ensure the results to be unique we require that if at least one token of some name occurs to the right of for in a dependence, then no token of this name occurs in another dependence in the same variable declaration. Furthermore, there must be at least one token to the right of for.

4.2   Write-Access to Instance Variables with Dependent Tokens

Dependent tokens require the absence of concurrent or overlapping accesses to instance variables when writing them. Neither put nor get can write buffer. When added to Proxy the following method writes buffer:

```
void update(BufferStat[(50)empty →] b) when (50)pe → (50)pe
      { with (50)pe → (50)pe { buffer = b }}
```

Because each instance of Proxy always has at most 50 tokens there are no tokens left that would allow put, get, or another invocation of update to run simultaneously. Since each instance has at most 50 tokens it is sufficient for the assigned value to provide 50 tokens empty. In general, we must find out

- that no concurrent access can occur when writing a variable (see Sect. 4.3),
- which tokens can be available for an object,
- and which tokens must be provided when writing to an instance variable.

There is a simple fixed-point algorithm to compute upper bounds of token sets that can become available for an object [3]. It extends initial token sets to upper bounds according to each pre-/post-condition pair in with-clauses where the precondition is satisfied. For example, when applied to Proxy the algorithm computes the set of token sets

$$\{[(i)\mathsf{pe}\ (50-i)\mathsf{pf}] \mid 0 \leq i \leq 50\}$$

and applied to BufferStatImpl we get

$$\{[\mathsf{sync}\ (\infty)\mathsf{empty}\ (\infty)\mathsf{filled}]\}.$$

The algorithm uses as input only information available in a single class (and hence supports separate compilation) and is accurate in the sense that

- if it generates a token set containing only a finite number of tokens, then we can construct clients invoking methods such that this set of tokens actually becomes available,
- and if it generates a token set containing an unlimited (∞) number of tokens, then we can select arbitrary numbers i and construct clients invoking methods such that more than i of these tokens become available.

We apply this algorithm to find out which token sets can become available for an instance of a class. From each of these sets we compute the tokens expected to be available in the type of an instance variable at the end of an atomic action (this is the end of a method or with-statement). Unfortunately, in general we do not know exactly which one of the token sets applies in the current situation. This is, we cannot know at compilation time (and probably we do not know at run time, too) which tokens are available for the object within the whole system. Thus, we use a conservative approximation to compute the tokens expected to be available: We compute the maximum of tokens within all sets returned by our algorithm that satisfy the precondition (this is, that contain all tokens to the left of the arrow in the with-clause). Static type checking ensures corresponding tokens to be available in the variable's type at the end of the method.

In instances of Proxy we can write to buffer whenever we have 50 tokens – any mixture of tokens pe and pf. For update we require (50)pe; hence, writing is actually possible. However, adding a method increment to Proxy (as in BufferStatImpl) would cause update to be no longer type-safe since in this case unlimited numbers of tokens can become available.

4.3   Variable Accesses and Race Avoidance

We must ensure not to write an instance variable simultaneously with other accesses of the same variable. A single criterion is sufficient to ensure this property: No preconditions in with-clauses and when-clauses of two methods accessing the same variable can be satisfied at the same time if at least one of the methods writes to the variable. This criterion implies race-free programs.

As basis of a corresponding analysis we use again upper bounds of token sets that can become available for an object. In contrast to the fixed-point algorithm applied in Sect. 4.2 we compute these sets by extending initial token sets according to each pre-/post-condition pair in with- and when-clauses (not just with-clauses). Otherwise the algorithm remains unchanged.

For (1) each instance variable in the analyzed class, (2) each method writing to this variable, and (3) each method accessing the variable (reading or writing, including the method considered in (2)) we build the union of all tokens occurring to the left of the arrow in the with- and when-clauses of the methods considered in (2) and (3). If the resulting token set is covered by a token set returned by the fixed-point algorithm, then it is possible that the methods considered in (2) and (3) run concurrently. We regard this case as a program error. Otherwise writing of instance variables cannot occur simultaneously with other accesses to the variable because there cannot exist enough tokens allowing us to do so. We analyze each class separately. All needed information is available in the code of the class, and we need no aliasing information.

By including information in when-clauses we get more flexibility. To ensure the absence of races it is not necessary for atomic actions to run completely in isolation: If an action A is executed in the same thread as another thread B and B starts after A and terminates before B, then B is nested into A. In contrast to with-clauses, when-clauses support nested actions. Values written to instance variables in A before starting B are visible in B, and values written in B are visible in A after termination of B. Nonetheless, type consistency is ensured because dependent tokens depend only on preconditions of with-clauses which do not support nesting. It is impossible to write to the same variable in A and B because at most one of the actions can have got all tokens necessary to do so.

5   Subtyping

5.1   Definition of Subtyping with Tokens

Subtyping has to consider internal as well as required external synchronization information. If we use an instance of a subtype where an instance of a supertype was expected, then the instance of the subtype

- accepts at least all method invocations in all orders that clients of an instance of the supertype can invoke, and
- the when-clause of an invoked method in the subtype can block execution for a possibly unlimited amount of time only if also the corresponding when-clause in the supertype can do so.

These conditions are necessary to ensure that clients knowing only supertypes have enough information to provide all required external synchronization and to avoid conflicting synchronization. Synchronization conditions in subtypes can only be less restrictive than corresponding conditions in supertypes.

In Fig. 2 we give a formal definition of subtyping. A type τ_1 is subtype of τ_2 in a program P if $P; \emptyset \vdash \tau_1 \leq \tau_2$ holds. Beyond the usual conditions for subtype relationships (contravariant formal parameter types, covariant result types, etc.) we require

- subtypes to have at least the same (or more) internal and external tokens as supertypes, respectively,
- when- and with-clauses in subtypes to contain at most the same (or less) tokens to the left of the arrow as corresponding clauses in supertypes,
- and when- and with-clauses in subtypes to contain at least the same (or more) tokens to the right of the arrow as corresponding clauses in supertypes.

Two exceptions from these rules improve the flexibility of subtyping:

$$\frac{}{P;\Gamma \vdash \tau \leq \tau} \qquad \frac{P;\Gamma \vdash \tau_1 \leq \tau_2 \quad P;\Gamma \vdash \tau_2 \leq \tau_3}{P;\Gamma \vdash \tau_1 \leq \tau_3} \qquad \frac{}{P;\Gamma,\tau_1 \leq \tau_2 \vdash \tau_1 \leq \tau_2}$$

$$\frac{RI_P^{u|v} \vdash Tok_P^u \geq Tok_P^v \quad \forall dec_2 \in Sig_P^v \cdot \exists dec_1 \in Sig_P^u \cdot P;\Gamma, u[] \leq v[] \vdash u.dec_1 \leq v.dec_2}{P;\Gamma \vdash u[] \leq v[]}$$

$$\frac{P;\Gamma \vdash u[] \leq v[] \quad RE_P^{u|v} \vdash t_1^* \geq t_2^*}{P;\Gamma \vdash u[t_1^*] \leq v[t_2^*]}$$

$$\frac{P;\Gamma \vdash \tau_1 \leq \tau_2 \quad P;\Gamma \vdash p_2^* \leq p_1^* \quad RE_P^{u|v} \vdash c_2 \geq c_1 \quad RI_P^{u|v} \vdash c_4 \geq c_3}{P;\Gamma \vdash u.\tau_1\ x(p_1^*)\ \text{with}\ c_1\ \text{when}\ c_3 \leq v.\tau_2\ x(p_2^*)\ \text{with}\ c_2\ \text{when}\ c_4}$$

$$\frac{}{P;\Gamma \vdash \epsilon \leq \epsilon} \qquad \frac{P;\Gamma \vdash u_1[] \leq u_2[] \quad RE_P^{u_1|u_2} \vdash c_1 \geq c_2 \quad P;\Gamma \vdash p_1^* \leq p_2^*}{P;\Gamma \vdash u_1[c_1]\,v\,p_1^* \leq u_2[c_2]\,v\,p_2^*}$$

$$\frac{\forall 1 \leq i \leq j \cdot x_i \in R \ \Rightarrow\ (n_i^1 \geq n_i^2 \ \wedge\ n_i^4 + n_i^1 - n_i^2 \geq n_i^3)}{R \vdash (n_1^1)x_1 \dots (n_j^1)x_j\,t_1^* \rightarrow (n_1^3)x_1 \dots (n_j^3)x_j \geq (n_1^2)x_1 \dots (n_j^2)x_j \rightarrow (n_1^4)x_1 \dots (n_j^4)x_j\,t_2^*}$$

$$\frac{\forall 1 \leq i \leq j \cdot x_i \in R \ \Rightarrow\ n_i^1 \geq n_i^2}{R \vdash (n_1^1)x_1 \dots (n_j^1)x_j\,t^* \geq (n_1^2)x_1 \dots (n_j^2)x_j}$$

Tok_P^u = initial tokens declared in class u in program P

Sig_P^u = set of method signatures in class u in program P

$RI_P^{u|v}$ = {tokens relevant for dependent internal synchronization in u and v in P}

$RE_P^{u|v}$ = $RI_P^{u|v} \cap$ {tokens relevant for external synchronization in u and v in P}

Fig. 2. Subtyping

- We consider only tokens relevant for external synchronization as well as tokens possibly relevant for dependent internal synchronization (see Sect. 3.3), and we consider only tokens relevant for both the subtype and the supertype. Tokens relevant only for simple mutex synchronization as well as tokens relevant only in one of the two types need not be considered.
- If a when- or with-clause in a subtype does not contain some token to the left of the arrow that occurs there in the corresponding clause in the supertype, then the clause in the subtype need not contain this token also to the right of the arrow. Invoking the method in the subtype where we expect to invoke the method in the supertype simply does not touch this token while we expect it to be removed on invocation and added on return.

According to this definition, BufferStat[empty] is subtype of BufferStat[(2)empty], and BufferStatImpl[(i)empty)] is subtype of BufferStat[(j)empty) (k)filled] for all $i \leq j$. However, the types BufferStat[empty], BufferStat[filled], and BufferDyn are not related by subtyping.

5.2   Semantics of Subtyping

Concerning required external synchronization, subtypes specify essentially the same or more sets of acceptable message sequences (supported orders of method invocations) than supertypes [2]. Subtypes cannot strengthen synchronization constraints. This restriction is a direct consequence of the substitution principle:

An instance of a subtype can be used where an instance of a supertype was expected [4,5]. If a client provides the required external synchronization when invoking a method in a supertype, then the required external synchronization of all corresponding methods in subtypes are also satisfied.

We need not consider tokens irrelevant in the supertype because they can be relevant in the subtype only for methods not invokable according to the supertype. In this case the substitution principle does not apply. We need not consider tokens irrelevant in the subtype because no method depends on them; the subtype supports more orders of method invocations than the supertype.

Internal synchronization does not restrict message orders. Nonetheless subtypes must not strengthen internal synchronization to get this property: If sequences of method invocations in an instance of a supertype do not enforce synchronization conflicting with internal synchronization, then these sequences of invocations do not enforce conflicting synchronization in an instance of a subtype. For example, an internally synchronized buffer can safely substitute another one with less slots, but substituting one with more slots can lead to unexpected deadlocks because of stronger synchronization constraints. If two objects of two types execute the same method invocations in the same order, then the instance of the subtype always contains at least the same (or more) internal tokens than the instance of the supertype after executing the same methods. This is because the instance of the subtype has at least the same initial internal tokens, and each method removes the same or less tokens on invocation and adds the same or more tokens on return than the instance of the supertype.

Of course, this property holds only for synchronization possibly conflicting with the when-clauses in corresponding methods in sub- and supertypes. Subtyping cannot avoid that a different implementation of the method in the subtype introduces errors like conflicting synchronization when invoking further methods. Currently static type checking does not avoid conflicting synchronization.

For internal synchronization we consider only tokens relevant in both the subtype and the supertype for essentially the same reason as for required external synchronization. However, we consider only tokens possibly relevant for dependent internal synchronization. Simple mutex synchronization need not be considered because from the client's point of view its only effect is to delay execution for a finite amount of time under the simplifying assumption that all methods depending on these tokens terminate in finite (and for practical reasons short) time. It is the programmer's obligation to ensure termination.

Subtyping does not consider instance variables because they are only accessible within objects containing them (at the presence of dependent tokens). Otherwise we would not be able to resolve dependences between tokens. It is always possible to circumvent this restriction by using setter and getter methods.

6   Related Work and Contribution

A huge number of language features for synchronization has been proposed, most of them concentrating on server synchronization [6,7]. Conventional synchronization concepts like semaphores express synchronization directly while other concepts express what groups of operations must be executed in isolation [8,9]. Petri Nets have been explored for nearly half of a century as a basis of token-based synchronization [10]. External synchronization and especially static type checking of external synchronization was addressed only recently [11,12,13,14,1].

With- and when-clauses in our approach resemble assertions in Eiffel [15]. Especially preconditions can be regarded as synchronization conditions (for internal synchronization) that must be satisfied before entering a routine [16,17]. They use Boolean expressions as synchronization conditions rather directly. Similar as in our approach, synchronization conditions in subtypes can be less restrictive, and unnecessary exposure of implementation details to clients can be avoided by assigning names to synchronization conditions. There is no separation between internal and required external synchronization. While preconditions require all conditions to be explicit in program code (local to an object) they can remain on a more abstract level in our approach. When-clauses (synchronization conditions) of protected types in Ada [18] are similar to preconditions in Eiffel except that Ada does not support subtyping on protected types.

The Fugue protocol checker [11] uses a different approach to specify client-server protocols: Rules for using interfaces are recorded as declarative specifications. These rules can limit the order in which methods are called (implying required external synchronization) as well as specify pre- and post-conditions. Since there is no complete aliasing information and no concept resembling type splitting (as in our approach), the checker cannot statically ensure all methods to be invoked in specified orders. In these cases the checker introduces pre- and post-conditions to be executed at run time.

Many proposals ensure race-free programs [19,6,20]. Some approaches depend on explicit type annotations [20] while others perform type inference [19]. Usually only simple mutex synchronization is considered. Such techniques can lead to more locks because no approach accurately decides between necessary and unnecessary locks. Program optimization can remove some unnecessary locks [21,22]. Unfortunately, we usually must analyze complete programs for good results.

Process types [14,1,2] were developed as abstractions over expressions in object-oriented process calculi like Actors [23]. Static type checking ensures that only acceptable messages can be sent and thereby enforces required external synchronization. Process types allow us to specify arbitrary constraints on the acceptability of messages. We consider types to be partial behavior specifications [4,24] especially valuable to specify the behavior of software components [25,26,27].

There are several approaches similar to process types. Some approaches ensure subtypes to show the same deadlock behavior as supertypes, but do not enforce message acceptability [28,27]. Other approaches consider dynamic changes of message acceptability, but do not guarantee message acceptability in all cases [16,29,30]. Few approaches ensure all sent messages to be acceptable [12,13]. All of these approaches specify constraints on the acceptability of messages in a rather direct way and do not make use of a token concept.

Recently several programming languages [31,32,33] were developed based on the Join calculus [34]. For example, in Polymorphic C# [31] we combine methods like put and get in a buffer to a chord to be executed as a single unit. Clients can see how methods in a chord are synchronized. Since only one method in a chord is executed synchronously and all other methods are asynchronous, only a specific form of internal synchronization is supported. There is no way to express required external synchronization. For example, it is easy to program a buffer with unlimited capacity using chords, but a buffer with limited capacity (even when using only internal synchronization) and a window changing state between iconified and displayed (see Sect. 2) cannot easily be written. Communication in Polymorphic C# and similar languages resembles that of the rendezvous concept while our approach extends monitors.

The present work extends previous work on separating client synchronization from server synchronization [3]. Major improvements over this work are the proposal of a more advanced concept of internal synchronization, the support of dependent types, and a richer notion of subtyping. These contributions are important for the following reasons:

– We regard the new concept of internal synchronization as an extension of more conventional synchronization concepts like that in Java. Synchronized Java methods correspond to methods with a clause "when sync → sync", and wait and notify can be modelled by when-clauses and with-statements with conditions of the form "token →" and "→ token", respectively. This property can be the basis for slow migration to the new concept which provides more expressiveness and safety than conventional synchronization.
– Dependent types solve an old problem of process types together with instance variables: They allow us to express states in types of variables depending on the states of objects where the variables belong to. Thereby, the coupling between the objects becomes evident, and corresponding type information becomes usable in static type checking.
– It is well-known that subtyping has to consider object behavior to provide substitutability [4]. However, it is still not clear which aspects of the behavior must be considered. Our notion of subtyping distinguishes between simple mutex synchronization (that can be ignored) and dependent internal as well as required external synchronization (which must be considered). Unfortunately, Java-like languages make essentially simple mutex synchronization (through synchronized methods) clearly visible while dependent internal synchronization (through wait and notify) are less visible and required external synchronization is not even expressible in program code.

Much work remains to be done. The most important work planed for the future is an implementation of the proposed concept. Other future work includes a rigorous formalization of the approach and the development of further consistency checks (for example, to guarantee continuity and liveness properties) on this basis.

7   Conclusions

Differentiation between internal and required external synchronization allows us to clearly specify who is responsible for which synchronization. Clients need all synchronization information except of simple mutex synchronization to use objects as expected. Subtyping considers dependent internal and required external synchronization, but ignores simple mutex synchronization. Dependent tokens in types of instance variables give us the flexibility to use more available synchronization information in providing external synchronization. Static type checking uses all kinds of synchronization information (without any need for aliasing information) to ensure race-free programs while supporting separate compilation.

References

1. Puntigam, F.: Coordination requirements expressed in types for active objects. In Aksit, M., Matsuoka, S., eds.: Proceedings ECOOP'97. Number 1241 in Lecture Notes in Computer Science, Jyväskylä, Finland, Springer-Verlag (1997) 367–388
2. Puntigam, F.: Concurrent Object-Oriented Programming with Process Types. Der Andere Verlag, Osnabrück, Germany (2000)
3. Puntigam, F.: Client and server synchronization expressed in types. In: Proceedings of the OOPSLA 2005 Workshop on Synchronization and Concurrency in Object-Oriented Languages (SCOOL), San Diego, USA (2005)
4. Liskov, B., Wing, J.M.: Specifications and their use in defining subtypes. ACM SIGPLAN Notices **28** (1993) 16–28 Proceedings OOPSLA'93.
5. Wegner, P., Zdonik, S.B.: Inheritance as an incremental modification mechanism or what like is and isn't like. In Gjessing, S., Nygaard, K., eds.: Proceedings ECOOP'88. Number 322 in Lecture Notes in Computer Science, Springer-Verlag (1988) 55–77
6. Brinch-Hansen, P.: The programming language Concurrent Pascal. IEEE Transactions on Software Engineering **1** (1975) 199–207
7. Hoare, C.A.R.: Communicating sequential processes. Communications of the ACM **21** (1978) 666–677
8. Harris, T., Fraser, K.: Language support for leightweight transactions. In: OOP-SLA'93, Anaheim, California, USA, ACM (2003) 388–402
9. Liskov, B., Scheifler, R.: Guardians and actions: Linguistic support for robust, distributed programs. ACM Transactions on Programming Languages and Systems **5** (1983) 381–404
10. Murata, T.: Petri nets: Properties, analysis and applications. Proceedings of the IEEE **77** (1989) 541–580
11. DeLine, R., Fähndrich, M.: The fugue protocol checker: Is your software baroque? Technical report, Microsoft Research (2004) http://www.research.microsoft.com.
12. Kobayashi, N., Pierce, B., Turner, D.: Linearity and the pi-calculus. ACM Transactions on Programming Languages and Systems **21** (1999) 914–947
13. Najm, E., Nimour, A.: A calculus of object bindings. In: Proceedings FMOODS'97, Canterbury, United Kingdom, Chapman & Hall (1997)
14. Puntigam, F.: Type specifications with processes. In: Proceedings FORTE'95, Montreal, Canada, IFIP WG 6.1, Chapman & Hall (1995)

15. Meyer, B.: Eiffel: The Language. Prentice Hall (1992)
16. Caromel, D.: Toward a method of object-oriented concurrent programming. Communications of the ACM **36** (1993) 90–101
17. Meyer, B.: Systematic concurrent object-oriented programming. Communications of the ACM **36** (1993) 56–80
18. ISO/IEC 8652:1995: Annotated ada reference manual. Intermetrics, Inc. (1995)
19. Bacon, D.F., Strom, R.E., Tarafdar, A.: Guava: A dialect of Java without data races. In: OOPSLA 2000. (2000)
20. Flanagan, F., Abadi, M.: Types for safe locking. In: Proceedings ESOP'99, Amsterdam, The Netherlands (1999)
21. Choi, J.D., Gupta, M., Serrano, M., Sreedhar, V.C., Midkiff, S.: Escape analysis for Java. In: OOPSLA'99, Denver, Colorado (1999)
22. von Praun, C., Gross, T.R.: Static conflict analysis for multi-threaded object-oriented programs. In: PLDI '03, ACM Press (2003) 115–128
23. Agha, G., Mason, I.A., Smith, S., Talcott, C.: Towards a theory of actor computation. In: Proceedings CONCUR'92. Number 630 in Lecture Notes in Computer Science, Springer-Verlag (1992) 565–579
24. Meyer, B.: Object-Oriented Software Construction. Second edition edn. Prentice Hall (1997)
25. Arbab, F.: Abstract behavior types: A foundation model for components and their composition. Science of Computer Programming **55** (2005) 3–52
26. Lee, E.A., Xiong, Y.: A behavioral type system and its application in Ptolemy II. Formal Aspects of Computing **16** (2004) 210–237
27. Nierstrasz, O.: Regular types for active objects. ACM SIGPLAN Notices **28** (1993) 1–15 Proceedings OOPSLA'93.
28. Nielson, F., Nielson, H.R.: From CML to process algebras. In: Proceedings CONCUR'93. Number 715 in Lecture Notes in Computer Science, Springer-Verlag (1993) 493–508
29. Colaco, J.L., Pantel, M., Salle, P.: A set-constraint-based analysis of actors. In: Proceedings FMOODS'97, Canterbury, United Kingdom, Chapman & Hall (1997)
30. Ravara, A., Vasconcelos, V.T.: Behavioural types for a calculus of concurrent objects. In: Proceedings Euro-Par'97. Number 1300 in Lecture Notes in Computer Science, Springer-Verlag (1997) 554–561
31. Benton, N., Cardelli, L., Fournet, C.: Modern concurrency abstractions for C#. ACM Transactions on Programming Languages and Systems **26** (2004) 269–804
32. Drossopoulou, S., Petrounias, A., Buckley, A., Eisenbach, S.: School: A small chorded object-oriented language. In: Proceedings of ICALP Workshop on Developments in Computational Models. (2005)
33. Odersky, M.: Functional nets. In: Proceedings of the European Symposium on Programming, Springer-Verlag (2000)
34. Fournet, C., Gonthier, G.: The reflexive cham and the join-calculus. In: Proceedings of the 23rd ACM Symposium on Principles of Programming Languages. (1996) 372–385

A New Component-Oriented Programming Language with the First-Class Connector

Bo Chen[1], ZhouJun Li[2], and HuoWang Chen[1]

[1] Computer College of National University of Defense Technology,
Changsha, Hunan, P.R. China
{chenbo, hwchen}@nudt.edu.cn
[2] School of Computer Science and Engineering, Beihang University,
Beijing, P.R. China
lizj@buaa.edu.cn

Abstract. The idea of a connector, which explicitly describes the interactions among components, is one of the important contributions of the research on software architecture. The importance of the connector as a first-class entity in software architecture has been increasingly recognized. In this paper we argue that such an important abstraction also deserves first-class support from programming languages. We present a new component-oriented programming language, SAJ (Software Architecture based Java), which integrates some architectural concepts such as the component, the port and particularly the connector into Java. The connector is treated as a first-class entity in SAJ as is the component so that software architecture can be made more explicit at implementation level and the simultaneous reuse of the component and the connector can be realized. The component model and the connector model underlying SAJ are also discussed in detail. We formalize our language giving both the type system and operational semantics and prove the type soundness property.

1 Introduction

The idea of a connector, which explicitly describes the interactions among components, is one of the important contributions of the research on software architecture. The importance of the connector as a first-class entity in software architecture has been increasingly recognized. In this paper from another perspective, that of a component-oriented programming language, we argue that such an important abstraction also deserves first-class support from programming languages. Our notion is based on the recognition that the interactions among components are as important as (even more important than) the components themselves and that the first-class treatment of the connector in a programming language can make these two concepts clear and improve their reusability. Providing the connector for explicitly specifying the interactions among components in a programming language addresses the following problems:

Making interactions (connectors) and computations (components) separate to increase the reusability of both components and connectors. When components with certain services are connected in order to interact, certain functionality is

D. Lightfoot and C. Szyperski (Eds.): JMLC 2006, LNCS 4228, pp. 271 – 286, 2006.

inherently the responsibility of the connector and should not be in the component. The different responsibilities make it necessary to keep the connector separate from the component. Furthermore, keeping them separate favors the reuse of the component and the connector. Ideally, the components are independent of the different interactions in which they could engage, and the same component can be used in a variety of environments with different connectors. Similarly, as we shall see, the same connector can provide communication and coordination services for different components. It is possible to increase the reusability of the component and the connector simultaneously by separating them. The straightforward way to keep them separate is to provide explicit support for the connector in a programming language which has direct influence on the implementation of the software system. However, up to now, the connector has not been considered as a first-class entity in any programming language, to the best of our knowledge. Hence, the connector behavior is scattered in components, which greatly reduces reusability.

Enforcing conformance between architectural specification and implementation to support more effective reengineering and evolution. During the phase of software architecture description, almost all the existing Architectural Description Languages (ADL) offer support for the connector and they can be used to describe, analyze and verify the connector formally[1][2][3]. However, description and design information about the connector are lost as it gets spread out into the participating components in the implementation. The loss of this information makes the implementation opaque with respect to the architecture specification, and traceability, intelligibility and maintainability of the software system are lost to a great extent, while the constraints and non-functional properties that the ADL described, analyzed and verified are not likely to be held in the implementation, doing nothing for reengineering and evolution. Having a general-purpose programming language that more directly supports the connector will bring more explicit intuition about the architecture into the implementation, which will help make the realization phase a smooth continuation of the software architecture description and design process.

Support for developing communication-centric (or interaction-centric) software. In the age of web service and peer-to-peer computing, communication (interaction, collaboration) among distributed software entities (distributed components) is crucial. New complexities, such as ensuring correct construction of complex communication from communication primitives and guaranteeing that a communication protocol is deadlock-free, have become significant. The first-class treatment of the connector can be a first step towards communication-centric programming.

To meet the above challenges, a new component-oriented programming language, SAJ—an extension of Java—has been designed and developed in which some architectural structures, such as the component, the port and particularly the connector are integrated into the Java language.

It may be noted that even though special components called by communication components or connector components are sometimes used to represent particular connections among components instead of using a connector abstraction, which seems to blur the distinction between the component and the connector, there are other good reasons for the first-class treatment of the connector: (1) Interaction and computation are two different concepts, they should have different semantics and roles in a programming language. A programming language needs not only structures to specify computation but also structures to specify interaction, which supports separation of concerns and software reuse. The emerging interaction-based formal models and programming languages have fully shown this [4] [5]. Using the special component to simulate the connector may lead to further obscuring their distinct nature and confusion of the component definition which has not yet been reached a consensus; (2) Connectors enrich design vocabulary and directly support concepts embodied in several design patterns; (3) The lack of the connector abstraction can lead to various problems, such as increase in the complexity of the components, etc [6].

The rest of this paper is organized as follows. In Sect.2, the component model and the connector model underlying SAJ are discussed. The SAJ language is introduced in Sect.3, where the syntax, semantics and type system of SAJ are presented in detail. In Sec.4, a case study is presented. Finally, in Sect.5 and Sect.6, we compare our approach with related work and discuss ongoing work.

2   The Component and the Connector Model Underlying SAJ

In the same way that a component model defines what a component is and how to construct a composite component, so a connector model defines what a connector is and how to construct a composite connector.

There is a kind of consensus about what a component is: a component is a unit of composition with contractually specified interfaces and explicit context dependencies. A software component can be deployed independently and is subject to composition by third parties [7].Each component may have multiple interfaces called ports. Each port represents a logical point of interaction between the component and the external world. A port declares two kinds of interfaces: provided interfaces and required interfaces. Required interfaces clearly declared can make dependencies explicit, reduce coupling among components and promote understanding of the component in isolation. The concept of the port is favorable for information hiding and the interface segregation principle, and we provide support for it in SAJ, which is different from other component-oriented programming languages.

With regard to the connector, there is little consensus yet in its definition, or even on the necessity of making it a first-class model entity. Our connector model is based on the following definition of connectors: connectors mediate interactions among components; that is, they establish the rules that govern component interaction and specify any auxiliary mechanisms required [8]. Each connector has a group of roles and interaction protocols. A role, which represents the external behavior that the component participating in the interaction should have, is the abstraction of the component that is capable of playing the role: any component that can play the role (strictly speaking, any component that can play the role through a certain port) is able to connect to the connector and participate in the interaction. An interaction protocol, which describes how roles collaborate, localizes information about the interaction: the interaction among components happens in the connector. In SAJ, the role is the interface in its general meaning, and the interaction is implemented by the isolated codes in the connector.

In our connector model we distinguish two kinds of connectors according to the relationship between the component and the connector: the active connector (or the exogenous connector [9]) and the passive connector. The main difference between the active connector and the passive connector is that the former initiates and coordinates control whereas the latter does not. The active connector describes collaborations among roles, and the component connects to the connector to play the corresponding role through the port, which has substantively formed the active/passive relationship between the connector and the component. More importantly, it is active connectors rather than components themselves that initiate service invocations in the components, and handle accompanying data flow, so that any control flow among components is encapsulated by active connectors. More visibly, through separating control and computation with active connectors, the problem of mixing control and computation in components which occurs in existing component models is solved. Thereby, the coupling between components is reduced greatly, and simultaneously reusing components and connectors can be realized. Active connectors represent the long-lived connection relationships among components though all the components have little knowledge about each other. This kind of connector suits to be used in the systems with centralized architecture, such as intra-enterprise applications.

On the other hand, the passive connector represents short-lived binary interaction, and it can be created only when one component wants to invoke required services which are provided by another component and to be destroyed when all the interactions between the two parties are completed. The passive connector is responsible for transparently delivering the services the component required to the corresponding port of another component and returning the result. In other words, the passive connector is a private channel that offers services of data and control transfer (i.e. encapsulates communication), while the component encapsulates control and computation. The passive connector is applicable to the dynamic systems with decentralized architecture, such as p2p computing and web service.

Table 1. The differences between active connectors and passive connectors

	Active Connectors	**Passive Connectors**
Relationship with Component	active	passive
Lifetime	long-lived	mostly short-lived
Control Flow	encapsulate control	control transfer
Data Flow	knowing the meaning of data	not knowing the meaning of data
Applicable Context	centralized architecture	decentralized architecture

The differences of active connectors and passive connectors are listed in Table 1. We believe that the interactions among components are various and apt to change and that two kinds of connectors which are complementary to each other suit to different environments respectively. In SAJ, both of them are supported.

SAJ also provides support for the concepts of the composite component and the composite connector. The composite component is different from the basic component in that it has an internal architecture which consists of sub-components and connectors, and that the services it provides for the external world are accomplished through the collaborations among the sub-components connected by the connectors. In the composite component, the connector, particularly the active connector, is used as a composition operator which has much richer semantics than simple composition operators such as Mixin [10]. Although the composite connector also has internal architecture, the internals of it are composed of methods, component instances and connector instances, which are used to implement cross-cutting feature services, while most of these services, such as security, log and so on, are common services which are orthogonal to the business logic.

A method of inheritance and incremental composition in constructing user-defined (composite) connectors is adopted in SAJ. According to the classification of connectors [11], the primitive connectors (procedure call, pipeline, data stream and the like) are predefined in SAJ. We believe that however complex the interaction among components is, it always belongs to a certain type as a whole. After the user-defined connector inherits the pre-defined connector in such a type, various common services are added to it in order to implement complex interactions and communication protocols. These common services possess the property of universal applicability, so generic programming and aspect-oriented programming are adopted in the implementation of the common services.

3   Formalization

In this section, we formalize our language by giving both the type system and operational semantics and prove the type soundness property. The core of SAJ is based on RelJ[12], a "middleweight" subset of Java. The reason for our choosing RelJ as our basis from a number of calculi proposed for Java [13] [14] [15] is that it is "big enough to include the essential imperative features of Java and yet small enough that formal proofs are still feasible" [12] (We should point it out that many definitions in the following sections are directly derived from RelJ). On the basis of RelJ, component, connector, port, role (interface) and some other architecture concepts are added.

3.1 Syntax

The partial syntax of SAJ is given in Fig.1. We distinguish user syntax, *i.e.,* source-level code and runtime syntax, which includes runtime instance and heaps. The meta-variable c ranges over component class names; d ranges over connector class names; r, r', R, P and I range over interface names, where r and r' are typically used to represent role types; n ranges over component class names, connector class names and interface names; z ranges over port names; t ranges over types; f ranges over fields; m ranges over the set of method names; x ranges over the set of variable names which contains the element *this* that cannot be on the left-hand side of an assignment; u and v range over values; e ranges over expressions; s ranges over statements; as a shorthand, an overbar is used to represent a sequence.

$p \in$ Program	$::=$com* con*
com	$::=$Component Class c extends c' $\{\overline{t\ f}, \overline{M}, \overline{z}\}$
con	$::=$Connector Class d extends d' $(r, r')\{\overline{t\ f}, \overline{M}\}$
Primtype	$::=$int I booleanIvoidI....
$n \in$ RefType	$::=c$IdII (interface-name)
$t \in$ Type	$::=$ PrimtypeI RefType
M	$::=t\ m(\overline{t\ x})\ mb$
$mb \in$ MethBody	$::=\{s\ return\ e;\}$
$mt \in$ Methtype	$::=\overline{t} \rightarrow t$
r, r', R, P, I	$::=\{\overline{m{:}mt}\}$
z	$::=\{$Required R, Provided $P\}$
$u, v \in$ Value	$::=pv$Inull$l$I$l\ (address)$
$pv \in$ PrimValue	$::=intvalue \mid boolvalue \mid ....$
var	$::=x$I$e.f$
$e \in$ Expression	$::=v$IvarIse
$se \in$ StatementExp	$::=var{=}e$I$e.m(\overline{e})$I$e.z.m(\overline{e})$I$e.r.m(\overline{e})$Inew $c()$ Inew $d(r, r')$
$s \in$ Statement	$::=\varepsilon \mid se;s_1$ I if (e) then $\{s_1\}$ else$\{s_2\};s_3$
	// runtime syntax
$o \in$ Instance	$::={<}{<}c\|f_1{:}v_1, f_2{:}v_2, ...f_n{:}v_n {>}{>}I{<}{<}d, l_1, z_1, l_2, z_2 \|f_1{:}v_1, f_2{:}v_2, ...f_n{:}v_n{>}{>}$
σ	$::=\{l \rightarrow o \mid l \in dom(\sigma)\}$
ρ	$::=\{l_1 \times z_1 \times l_2 \times z_2 \rightarrow l\}$
λ	$::=\{x \rightarrow v\}$

Fig. 1. The partial syntax of SAJ

As usual for such language formalizations, we assume that given a SAJ program P, the component class and connector class declarations give rise to component and connector tables that are denoted by C_p and D_p, respectively. A component (connector) table is a map from a component (connector) class name to a component (connector) definition.

A component class definition is a tuple, (c', F, M, Z), where c' is the superclass; F is a map from field names to field types; and M is a map from method names to method definitions. Z is a map from port names to port definitions. Method definitions are tuples $(\overline{t\ y}, L, t', mb)$, where y is the parameter; t is the parameter type; L is a map from local variable names to their types; t' is the return type; and mb is the method body. For brevity, we write F_c, M_c and Z_c for the field, method and port definition maps of class c.

A connector class definition is a tuple, (d', r, r', F, M), where d' is the superclass, r, r' represent the role's type in the connector (to be for simplicity, we assume that there are two roles in each connector and that each connector connects two components). $r(r')$ is represented by the pair (c, z) in which c represents the type of the

$C \in$ ComponentTable : CompontClassName $\rightarrow$ CompontClassName $\times$ FieldMap $\times$ MethMap
$\times$ PortMap

$D \in$ ConnectorTable : ConnectorClassName $\rightarrow$ ConnectorClassName $\times$ RoleType $\times$ RoleType
$\times$ FieldMap $\times$ MethMap

$F \in$ FieldMap : FldName $\rightarrow$ Type

$M \in$ MethMap : MethName $\rightarrow$ ParameterList $\times$ LocalMap $\times$ TypeList $\times$ Type $\times$ MethBody

$Z \in$ PortMap : PortName $\rightarrow$ ReqInterface $\times$ ProInterface

$L \in$ LocalMap : VarName $\rightarrow$ Type

Fig. 2. Signatures of component and connector class tables

component participating in the interaction and z represents the port that is connected to the connector; F, M are the same to the above. Signatures for these maps are presented in Fig. 2.

Values represent irreducible computational results, including primitive values (*e.g.* literals such as true, false, 1, *etc*). Expressions include component-instance creation expressions, connector-instance creation expressions, field accesses, method invocations etc. For compactness, only conditional statements and statement sequences are considered.

The runtime syntax extends the user syntax: it extends values to allow for address l and introduces runtime instances and heaps. Runtime instances, ranged over by o, are either component instances or connector instances. Component instances are written as an annotated pair $<< c \| f_1 : v_1, f_2 : v_2, ... f_n : v_n >>$, where c represents the dynamic type of component instance, f_i and v_i represent the name and the value of field respectively.

Connector instances are written as an annotated 6-tuple $<< d, l_1, z_1, l_2, z_2 \| f_1 : v_1, f_2 : v_2 .... f_n : v_n >>$, d represents the dynamic type of connector instance; l_1, l_2 represent the addresses of the component instances participating in the connection, while z_1, z_2 represent the ports through which the component instances work.

A heap σ, is a map from addresses to instances (component instances and connector instances), while local variables are given values by a locals store λ. A connection relationship heap ρ maps connection-relationship tuples (l_1, z_1, l_2, z_2) to addresses.

3.2 Semantics

This section presents the operational semantics of SAJ, which is inspired by the standard small step reduction of [13] [16] [17].We start by listing the evaluation contexts to specify evaluation order.

$$E_e ::= [] \mid x = E_e \mid E_e . f \mid E_e . f = e \mid u.f = E_e \mid E_e . m(\bar{e}) \mid u.m(\bar{u}, E_e, \bar{e}) \mid E_e . z.m(\bar{e}) \mid u.z.m(\bar{u}, E_e, \bar{e})$$
$$\mid E_e . r.m(\bar{e}) \mid E_e . r.m(\bar{u}, E_e, \bar{e}) \mid \{E \text{ return } e;\} \mid \{\text{return } E_e;\}$$
$$E_s ::= E_e; s \mid \text{if } (E_e) \text{ then } \{s_1\} \text{ else } \{s_2\}; s_3$$

A program configuration *config* $< \Gamma, \sigma, \rho, \lambda, s >$ in the semantics is a 5-tuple of typing environment Γ (which is a finite map from variables to types), heap σ, connection relationship heap ρ, locals map λ, and a statement s. An error configuration is a configuration $< \Gamma, \sigma, \rho, \lambda, Error >$, with an error in a statement sequence. Program execution is described with $< \Gamma, \sigma, \rho, \lambda, s > \leadsto < \Gamma', \sigma', \rho', \lambda', s' >$.

Expression execution proceeds when a sub-expression may be reduced, as specified by OSContextE, and similarly for statements in OSContextS:

$$\text{(OSContextE)} \quad \frac{< \Gamma, \sigma, \rho, \lambda, e > \leadsto < \Gamma, \sigma, \rho, \lambda, e' >}{< \Gamma, \sigma, \rho, \lambda, E_e[e] > \leadsto < \Gamma, \sigma, \rho, \lambda, E_e[e'] >}$$

$$\text{(OSContextS)} \quad \frac{< \Gamma, \sigma, \rho, \lambda, e > \leadsto < \Gamma, \sigma, \rho, \lambda, e' >}{< \Gamma, \sigma, \rho, \lambda, E_s[e] > \leadsto < \Gamma, \sigma, \rho, \lambda, E_s[e'] >}$$

In the following, the base cases for the operational semantics will be defined. Only the more interesting reduction rules in Fig.3 are discussed here.

OSNewActCon gives the semantics to the creation of an active connector instance. The OSNewActCon rule reduces a new expression to a fresh address. The heap is updated at that address to refer to a new connector instance with its fields set to the initial values and its roles set to the pairs formed by the connected component and port. The connection-relationship heap is added an entry which represents the map from the newly created connection-relationship tuple to the address of the new connector instance. A passive connector instance is created when one component wants to invoke a required service which is provided by another component and the semantics of its creation are similar to that of the active connector except that l_1 represents the value of *this*. However, as we shall see, the typing rule of the creation of the passive connector instance is different.

The interactions among components begin after the connector instance has been created. We first consider the interactions between components connected by the passive-connector instance. The rule OSCallReqMeth gives the semantics for calling required methods in the port. Only the component instance itself is able to call the required methods in the connected port which is then delivered by the passive connector instance (rule OSTranReqMeth) to the corresponding port of another component instance.

The OSCallProMeth rule is straightforward. The semantics for the method invocation of the component instance are given by OSCallComMeth. The rule OSCallComMeth determines the correct method body to invoke. Then the method invocation is replaced with the appropriate method body. In the method body, all occurrences of the formal method parameters and *this* are replaced with the actual arguments and the receiver respectively.

Finally, we consider method invocations in the active connector whose methods describe the interactions among components. The rule OSCallActConMeth of the active connector is the same as the rule OSCallComMeth except that the roles of the active-connector instance are replaced with actual component instances (when the component instance plays a role through a certain port, only its provided methods at this port can be invoked in the connector methods). Here, only the OSCallActConMeth rule is given.

(OSNewActCon) $< \Gamma, \sigma_1, \rho_1, \lambda, New\, d(l_1, z_1, l_2, z_2) > \leadsto < \Gamma, \sigma_2, \rho_2, \lambda, l_3 >$

where $\sigma_2 = \sigma_1[l \mapsto << d, l_1, z_1, l_2, z_2 \mid f_i : Initial(FD_c(f_i)) >>]$

$\rho_2 = \rho_1[(l_1, z_1, l_2, z_2) \mapsto l]\quad l \notin dom(\sigma_1)$

(OSCallReqMeth) $< \Gamma, \sigma, \rho, \lambda, l_1.z_1.m(\overline{u}) > \leadsto < \Gamma, \sigma, \rho, \lambda, l.m(\overline{u}) >$

where $\sigma(l_1) = << c \parallel ... >>\quad m \in \{c.z_1.R_1 \mid z_1 \in dom(Z_c)\}$

$\rho(l_1, z_1, \_, \_) = l \Rightarrow l \neq Null$

(OSTranReqMeth) $< \Gamma, \sigma, \rho, \lambda, l.m(\overline{u}) > \leadsto < \Gamma, \sigma, \rho, \lambda, l_2.z_2.m(\overline{u}) >$

where $\sigma(l) = << d, l_1, z_1, l_2, z_2 \parallel ... >>$

$\rho(l_1, z_1, l_2, z_2) = l\quad l_1 \neq Null \wedge l_2 \neq Null$

$\sigma(l_j) = << c' \parallel ... >>\quad m \in \{c'.z_2.P_2 \mid z_2 \in dom(Z_{c'})\}$

(OSCallProMeth) $< \Gamma, \sigma, \rho, \lambda, l.z_i.m(\overline{u}) > \leadsto < \Gamma, \sigma, \rho, \lambda, l.m(\overline{u}) >$

where $\sigma(l) = << c \parallel ... >>\quad m \in \{c.z_i.P_i \mid z_i \in dom(Z_c)\}$

(OSCallActConMeth) $< \Gamma_1, \sigma, \rho, \lambda_1, l.m(\overline{u}) > \leadsto < \Gamma_2, \sigma, \rho, \lambda_2, \{s_3\ return\ e_3;\} >$

where

$\sigma(l) = << d, l_1, z_1, l_2, z_2 \parallel ... >>\quad MD_d(m) = (\overline{t\ y}, L, t', s_1\ return\ e_l)$

$dom(L) = \overline{x'}\quad\quad \overline{u'}, x'_{this}, x' \notin dom(\lambda_1)$

$\Gamma_2 = \Gamma_1[\overline{u' \mapsto t}][x'_{this} \mapsto d][x' \mapsto L(x)]$

$\lambda_2 = \lambda_1[\overline{u' \mapsto u}][x'_{this} \mapsto l][\overline{x' \mapsto Inital(L(x))}]$

$s_2 = s_1[\overline{u'/y}][x'_{this}/this][\overline{x'/x}]\quad\quad e_2 = e_l[\overline{u'/y}][x'_{this}/this][\overline{x'/x}]$

$s_3 = s_2[l_1.z_1/x'_{this}.r][l_2.z_2/x'_{this}.r']\quad\quad e_3 = e_2[l_1.z_1/x'_{this}.r][l_2.z_2/x'_{this}.r']$

Fig. 3. Some more interesting reduction rules

3.3 Type System

Component is provided for the root of the component class hierarchy, and **Connector** as its counterpart in the connector class hierarchy. **PassiveConnector** and **ActiveConnector** are subtypes of **Connector**. The subtyping rules are omitted here because they are similar to those of [12] [14]. We type expressions and statements in the presence of a typing environment Γ and only some typing rules deserving particular attention are presented in Fig.4.

When an active connector instance is created, each component instance connected by this connector instance is passed to the connector constructor. The typing rule TSNewActCon verifies that the type of the provided interface in the connected port of each component instance should be the subtype of role $r's$ type and $r''s$ type respectively, while the type of the required interface should be the supertype of role $r''s$ type and $r's$ type respectively.

The typing rule TSNewPasCon for creation of a passive-connector instance is different, only checking that the type of the provided interface of one connected port needs to be subtype of the required interface of the other connected port and vice versa. The reason why we do not consider the role's type in this rule is that the passive-connector instance has no special requirement about the role's type, only requiring two connected ports to be compatible.

TSCallMeth looks up the invoked method's type using the *mtype* function, and verifies that the actual argument types are subtypes of the method's parameter types. If the invocation is through a port and the invoked method belongs to the required interfaces, the rule TSCallPortMeth verifies that the instance expression must be *this* .

$$\text{(TSNewActCon)}$$

$$d \in dom(D_p) \qquad D_p(d) = (d',r,r',F,M)$$

$$\Gamma \vdash e_1 : c_1 \qquad \Gamma \vdash e_2 : c_2 \quad \Gamma \vdash c_1.z_1.P_1 \le r \qquad \Gamma \vdash c_2.z_2.P_2 \le r'$$

$$\frac{\Gamma \vdash r' \le c_1.z_1.R_1 \qquad \Gamma \vdash r \le c_2.z_2.R_2}{\Gamma \vdash New\ d(e_1.z_1,e_2,z_2):d}$$

$$\text{(TSNewPasCon)}$$

$$d \in dom(D_p) \qquad D_p(d) = (d',r,r',F,M)$$

$$\Gamma \vdash e_1 : c_1 \qquad \Gamma \vdash e_2 : c_2$$

$$\frac{\Gamma \vdash c_1.z_1.P_1 \le c_2.z_2.R_2 \qquad \Gamma \vdash c_2.z_2.P_2 \le c_1.z_1.R_1}{\Gamma \vdash New\ d(e_1.z_1,e_2,z_2):d}$$

(TSCallPortMeth)   (TSCallMeth)

$$\Gamma \vdash e:c \quad \Gamma \vdash \bar{e}:\bar{t'} \qquad\qquad \Gamma \vdash e:n$$

$$c \in dom(C_p) \quad z \in dom(Z_c) \qquad \frac{\Gamma \vdash \bar{e}:\bar{t'}}{}$$

$$m \in c.z.R \Rightarrow e = this \qquad mtype(m,n) = \bar{t} \rightarrow t$$

$$\frac{mtype(m,c,z) = \bar{t} \rightarrow t \quad \bar{t'} \le \bar{t}}{\Gamma \vdash e.z.m(\bar{e}):t} \qquad \frac{\bar{t'} \le \bar{t}}{\Gamma \vdash e.m(\bar{e}):t}$$

Fig. 4. Typing rules for connector instance creation and method invocation

Next, the rules for well-formed component class definition and connector class definition are given in Fig.5. Firstly, ports are checked in the presence of their enclosing component class and then fields and methods are checked in the presence of their enclosing component class or connector class (Only the TSPort rule is presented here).

TSPort checks that a port is well-formed by verifying that only a subclass of **Component** can define new ports and that the intersection of the required interface and the provided interface at the same port is empty.

TSCom specifies that a component class type is well-formed if its superclass is well-formed, its ports are well-formed, and if all of its methods and fields are well-typed. TSActCon imposes many of the same restrictions as TSCom except without checking ports. TSActCon also requires that only a subclass of a pre-defined connector in SAJ can define new roles. The rule for the passive connector is the same as TSActCon except without checking condition 1.

It seems that too many restrictions are imposed on well-formed component class definition and connector class definition. For example, only a subclass of **Component** can define new ports and only a subclass of a pre-defined connector in SAJ can define new roles. There are two considerations for these restrictions: (1) we want SAJ to

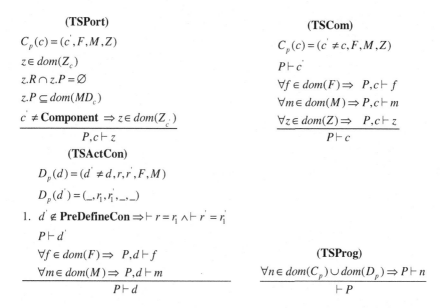

Fig. 5. Port, component class, connector class and program typing

have the type soundness property; (2) we favor composition over inheritance. In other words, we use component composition and connector composition to construct software systems, and restrictions on inheritance have little influence on us.

TSProg specifies that a program is well-formed if all of its component classes and connector classes are well-formed.

Finally, the rules for the well-formed heap σ, the connection relationship heap ρ and the locals map λ are given. For the heap σ, we ensure all the runtime instances (component instance and connector instance) stored in it are well formed. The rule for the well-formed component instance is the same as WFOBJECT2 in RelJ. The rule for the well-formed active connector instance WFActConInst is presented below:

(WFActConInst)

1. $D_p(d) = (d', r, r', F, M)$ $\forall f \in dom(FD_d) \Rightarrow P, \sigma, o \vdash f_{\Diamond fld}$

2. $\sigma(l_1) = \ll c \parallel ... \gg \Rightarrow P, \sigma \vdash \ll c \parallel ... \gg_{\Diamond inst}$

   $\sigma(l_2) = \ll c' \parallel ... \gg \Rightarrow P, \sigma \vdash \ll c' \parallel ... \gg_{\Diamond inst}$

3. $\vdash dynType(\sigma(l_1)).z_1.P \leq r$

   $\vdash dynType(\sigma(l_2)).z_2.P \leq r'$

$$\overline{P, \sigma \vdash \ll d, l_1, z_1, l_2, z_2 \parallel f_1 : v_1 .... f_n : v_n \gg_{\Diamond inst}}$$

WFActConInst ensures that (1) all fields that the connector instance has, including those inherited from its superclasses, are well-formed (the rule for well-formed field is the same as that of RelJ);(2) component instances connected by the connector instance are well-formed;(3) the type of the provided interface at the connected port of each component instance is a subtype of the type of the role that the component instance plays. The WFPasConInst rule for the well-formed passive connector instance is the same as WFActConInst except without checking condition 3.

We then map the conditions for well-formed instances and local variables over the heap σ, the connection relationship heap ρ, and the locals map λ:

(WFHeap)

$$\frac{\forall l \in dom(\sigma) \Rightarrow P, \sigma \vdash \sigma(l)_{\Diamond inst}}{P \vdash \sigma_{\Diamond heap}}$$

(WFLocals)

$$\frac{\forall x \in dom(\Gamma) \Rightarrow P, \sigma, \Gamma \vdash \lambda(x): \Gamma(x)}{P, \sigma, \Gamma \vdash \lambda_{\Diamond locals}}$$

(WFConHeap)

$$\frac{\forall(l_1, z_1, l_2, z_2) \in dom(\rho) \Rightarrow P, \sigma \vdash \sigma(l_1)_{\Diamond inst} \wedge P, \sigma \vdash \sigma(l_2)_{\Diamond inst} \wedge P, \sigma \vdash \sigma(\rho(l_1, z_1, l_2, z_2))_{\Diamond inst}}{P, \sigma \vdash \rho_{\Diamond conheap}}$$

We consider a program configuration $< \Gamma, \sigma, \rho, \lambda, s >$ to be well-formed when σ, ρ and λ are well-formed, and when s is type-correct.

3.4 Soundness

We prove type soundness using standard theorems of type preservation and progress, and the proofs for the two theorems are left for another paper due to limitations of space.

Theorem 1 (Type Preservation). *In a well-typed program, P, where configuration $<\Gamma, \sigma, \rho, \lambda, s>$ executes to a new configuration $< \Gamma', \sigma', \rho', \lambda', s' >$, that configuration will be well-formed. Furthermore, all instances in σ retain their dynamic type in σ'.*

Theorem 2 (Progress). *For all well-typed programs, P, all well-formed configurations $<\Gamma, \sigma, \rho, \lambda, s>$ execute to either an error configuration $< \Gamma', \sigma', \rho', \lambda', Error >$ or a new statement configuration $< \Gamma', \sigma', \rho', \lambda', s' >$.*

Together, progress and type preservation imply that well-typed programs do not go wrong.

4 Case Study

In this section, a simple ATM demo system is used to introduce how to construct a system with SAJ. The ATM is used to deal with the transactions between the ATM client and the bank, such as audit, deposit, withdraw and so on. After a customer inserts his card into the ATM client, the information in the card is read, and the ATM client will ask the customer to input the password. Then the bank server will check the correctness of the password. The customer who passes the check is able to go on with his audit and other transactions on the ATM client.

The software architecture style of the ATM demo system is client-server (for simplicity, we assume that both the ATM client and the bank are in the same machine.) As Fig.6 shows, the client and the server interact through procedure calls, so we choose the pre-defined procedure-call connector (ConProcCall) as the superclass of the ATM connector. The main components of the system include the ATM component, the Bank component and so on. The ATM component had two ports, PA and PC, which respectively interact with the Bank component and the card. Port PA has two sets of interfaces: IBank (the interface that requires services) and IAtm (the interface that offers services). PB, one of the ports of the Bank component, also has two

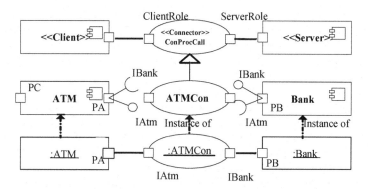

Fig. 6.   The ATM demo system

sets of interfaces: IBank (the interface that offers services) and IAtm (the interface that requires services). Connector ATMCon, which extends ConProcCall, describes the interactions between the ATM component and the Bank component. This is the static model of the ATM demo system, the pseudo-code of which is in Fig.7.

```
Interface IAtm {
  CardInfo  GetCardInfo();
  String    GetPassWord();
  ......
}
Interface IBank{......}
Component Class ATM extends Component{
  Public Port PA{
    Provided IAtm;
    Required IBank;
  }
  Public CardInfo GetCardInfo {......}
  ......
}
Component Class Bank extends Component{
  Public Port PB{
    Provided IBank;
    Required IAtm ;
  }
  ......
}
Connector Class ATMCon extends ConProcCall {
  ......
  void ATMCon(IAtm atm,IBank bank){
    this.IAtm=atm;
    this.IBank=bank;
  }
  Public void Transaction {......}
  ......
}
```

Fig. 7.   The static model of the ATM demo system

The dynamic model of a software system is described by connector methods which describe how the roles cooperate to implement system services. In the ATM demo system, the instance of the ATM plays the IAtm role through port PA and the instance of the Bank plays the IBank role through port PB. The interactions between the component instance of the ATM and that of the Bank are described in the Transaction method of ATMCon, whose pseudo-code is in Fig.8.

From the pseudo-code in Fig.8, we are able to determine that with the separating of control and computation by the connector, control is encapsulated in the connector ATMCon, while computation is encapsulated in the component ATM and Bank. Thus, the coupling between the component ATM and Bank is able to be reduced, and the simultaneously reuse of component and connector can be realized.

In a real ATM system, the ATM and the Bank are distributed at different locations and it is better to use a passive connector than an active connector. Only when the customer inserts his card to require ATM service, is a passive connector instance created between the ATM and the Bank and it is destroyed when the customer completes his transactions. The passive connector instance offers services of data transfer and control transfer as a private channel between the ATM and the Bank.

```
Public void Transaction {
    CardInfo Info=IAtm.GetCardInfo();
    String   PassWord=IAtm.GetPassWord();
    If (IBank.verfyPassWord(Info,PassWord)==Success)
        {
         If (IAtm.GetEvent()==Deposit) then
             {
              IBank.deposit(Info,IAtm.GetDepositMoney());
              ......
             }
         ......
        }
}
```

Fig. 8. The pseudo-code of the Transaction method

5   Related Work

In both the software architecture field and the component technology field, people have been focusing for a long time on component structure, component interface and some other aspects of the component, and research on the connector was completely ignored. Nowadays, people are becoming more and more concerned that for a large-scale complex system, functional properties and non-functional properties of a system usually depend on the interactions among components. Research on the connector has been advanced rapidly in recent years, especially research on how to realize the connector and how to use the connector has already been a hot topic.

Aldrich proposed ArchJava as a programming language integrating architectural concepts into Java [18], which give us some inspirations. Aldrich also proposed an approach to support connector abstraction in ArchJava using a reflection mechanism [19]. User-defined connectors were derived from the pre-defined connectors offered by the ArchJava reflection library, while the "Invoke" function of the connector that described the dynamic semantics of interaction was overridden. Furthermore, it has been argued that offering support for the connector abstraction in a programming language has a flexibility which could greatly improve the reuse of the connector, because almost all kinds of connectors listed in [11] could be realized with the connector abstraction of ArchJava. The main problem of this approach lay in that it was difficult to guarantee the type soundness in the implementation of the connector abstraction by the reflection mechanism.

Exogenous connectors were proposed to solve the problem of mixing computation and control in components [9]. The key distinguishing characteristic of exogenous connectors is that they encapsulate control totally, i.e. control originates from connectors. Exogenous connectors are favorable for reusing components and connectors simultaneously. However, as we have said, exogenous connectors and passive connectors are complementary to each other. Exogenous connectors alone can not solve all the problems.

6 Conclusion

In this paper, we present a new component-oriented programming, SAJ, in which the connector is a first-class entity as well as the component. We formalize our language giving both the type system and operational semantics and prove the type soundness property. Our first-class treatment of the connector is based on the recognition that interactions among components are as important as (even more important than) the components themselves and that the first-class treatment of the connector in a programming language can favor making these two different concepts clear and increasing the reusability of them. The problems mentioned in the introduction section also can be better solved by explicitly supporting the connector in the programming language.

The component model and the connector model underlying SAJ are also given in the paper. We distinguish two kinds of connectors, i.e., active connectors and passive connectors. The difference between them is discussed in detail, which would be helpful to using them correctly.

Our work on SAJ is at a preliminary stage, however. Future tasks include further perfecting our component model and connector model and researching the technique of automatic connector creation. For perfecting the component model and the connector model, we are particularly interested in enriching component and connector specification and offering composition methods or appropriate composition operators to allow construction of the complex connector. Concerning automatic connector creation, we want to propose an approach of creating connectors automatically based on the enriched component and connector specification.

Acknowledgements

We gratefully acknowledge the financial support of the China National Natural Science under Grant Nos. 90104026, 60473057, 90604007. We would like to thank David Lightfoot for amending this paper. We would like also to thank the anonymous reviewers for their helpful comments.

References

1. R. Allen and D. Garlan. A formal basis for architectural connection. ACM Trans. on Software Engineering and Methodology, 6(3): 213~249, 1997.
2. David C. Luckham, John J. Kenney, Larry M. Augustin, James Vera, Doug Bryan, Walter Mann. Specification and Analysis of System Architecture Using Rapide. IEEE Trans. on Software Engineering, 21(4), 336~355, 1995.
3. P. Oreizy, David S. Rosenblum, Richard N. Taylor. On the Role of Connectors in Modeling and Implementing software Architectures. Technical Report UCI-ICS-98-04, University of California, Irvine, 1998.
4. F. Arbab. Abstract Behavior Type: A Foundation Model for Component and Their Composition. Science of Computer Programming, 3~52, 2005.
5. Yu David Liu, Scott F. Smith. Interaction-Based Programming with Classages. In Proceedings of the 20th Conference on Object-Oriented Programming, Systems, Languages and Applications (OOPSLA'05), San Diego, California, October 2005.
6. M. Oussalah, A. Smeda, and T. Khammaci. An Explicit Definition of Connectors for Component-Based Software Architecture. In 11th IEEE International Conference on the Engineering of Computer-Based Systems (ECBS 2004), Brno, Czech Republic, May 2004.
7. C. Szyperski. Component Software - Beyond Object-Oriented Programming. Addison-Wesley, 2003.
8. M. Shaw and D. Garlan. Software Architecture: Perspectives on an Emerging Discipline. Prentice-Hall, 1996.
9. Kung-Kiu Lau, Perla Velasco Elizondo, and ZhengWang. Exogenous Connectors for Software Components. In Eighth International SIGSOFT Symposium on Component-based Software Engineering (CBSE 2005). St. Louis, MO, USA, May, 2005.
10. Vugranam C. Sreedhar. Mixin' Up Components. In Proceedings of the 24th International Conference on Software Engineering. Orlando, Florida, May 2002.
11. N.R. Mehta, N. Medvidovic, and S. Phadke. Towards a taxonomy of software connectors. In Proc. 22nd International Conference on Software Engineering. Limerick, Ireland, June 2000.
12. G. Bierman and A. Wren. First-class relationships in an object-oriented language. In In Proceedings of the 19th European Conference on Object-Oriented Programming. Glasgow, Scotland, 2005.
13. S. Drossopoulou, T. Valkevych, S. Eisenbach. Java type soundness revisited. Technical report, Imperial College London, September 2000.
14. A. Igarashi, B. C. Pierce, and P. Wadler. Featherweight Java: A minimal core calculus for Java and GJ. In Conference on Object-Oriented Programming, Systems, Languages and Applications (OOPSLA), 1999.
15. M. Flatt, S. Krishnamurthi, M. Felleisen. Classes and mixins. In Proceedings of the 25th ACM SIGPLAN-SIGACT Symposium on Principles of Programming Languages, San Diego, California, 1998.
16. A. K. Wright and M. Felleisen. A syntactic approach to type soundness. Information and Computation, 115(1):38–94, 1994.
17. B. C. Pierce. Types and Programming Languages. MIT Press, 2002.
18. J.Aldrich,C.Chambers and D.Notkin. ArchJava: connecting software architecture to implementation. In Proceedings of the 24th International Conference on Software Engineering,Orlando,FL,2002.
19. J.Aldrich,C.Chambers and D.Notkin. Language Support for Connector Abstractions. In Proceedings of the 17th European Conference Object-Oriented Programming, Darmstadt, Germany, 2003.

A Component Plug-In Architecture for the .NET Platform*

Reinhard Wolfinger, Deepak Dhungana, Herbert Prähofer,
and Hanspeter Mössenböck

Christian Doppler Laboratory for Automated Software Engineering
Johannes Kepler University, 4040 Linz, Austria
{wolfinger, dhungana, praehofer, moessenboeck}@ase.jku.at

Abstract. Plug-in architectures and platforms represent a promising approach for building software systems which are extensible and customizable to the particular needs of the individual user. For example, the Eclipse platform, as the most prominent representative of plug-in systems, is based on a unique plug-in and extensibility concept and has succeeded in establishing itself as the leading platform for the development of tool environments. This paper introduces a new plug-in architecture for the .NET platform which shows much resemblance to Eclipse. However, whereas Eclipse is a Java-based system and uses XML to describe extensions, our architecture relies on .NET concepts such as custom attributes and metadata to specify relevant information directly in the source code of an application. We argue that this approach is more readable and easier to maintain. As a case study for our plug-in architecture we present a new plug-in platform for implementation of rich client applications in .NET.

1 Introduction

Originally made popular by Web browsers, plug-in platforms enable the extension of a core application with new features implemented as components that are plugged into the core at load time or even at run time and integrate seamlessly with it. Feature-bloated applications like Microsoft Word evidence what happens if a monolithic application follows the *one-size-fits-all* approach. Microsoft continues to receive user feedback with requests for features that already exist in the product. Typical users struggle to find their 10%-share of the feature set that they really want to use. The plug-in approach on the other hand strives for compact application cores that can be extended with plug-in components tailored to the users' needs. It improves focus and reduces clutter by providing a customized user environment.

Eclipse [7] is certainly the most prominent representative of those plug-in platforms and has driven the idea to its extreme: "Everything is a plug-in!" [1]. Moreover, other interesting approaches exist (see related work below). For example, OSGi [16] is a Java-based technology for deploying and managing coarse-grained components. It also serves as the deployment technique for Eclipse plug-ins. Mozilla [13] represents

---

* This work has been conducted in cooperation with BMD Systemhaus GmbH, Austria, and has been supported by the Christian Doppler Forschungsgesellschaft, Austria.

D. Lightfoot and C. Szyperski (Eds.): JMLC 2006, LNCS 4228, pp. 287 – 305, 2006.

a further interesting plug-in platform where user interface contributions are defined in the declarative language XUL. Despite their diverse technological foundations, all those systems have in common the focus on extensibility of applications.

In addition to facilitating extensibility of applications, plug-in architectures and platforms represent an interesting and promising approach for providing reusable building blocks. Assembling systems from pre-fabricated building blocks has been regarded as an appealing approach to software construction since the very early days of software engineering [11]. Originally, object-oriented technology was supposed to make systematic development of reusable building blocks and wide-scale reuse feasible [2]. Today, it is generally agreed that object-oriented technology as such has not fulfilled those expectations [20]. Although we have seen much progress into this direction in the last decades [19], [3], component-based software engineering still has not reached a level of maturity that is taken for granted in other engineering disciplines.

We argue that plug-in approaches represent a significant progress for making a component-based software development reality. So it seems that Eclipse has succeeded where previous approaches have failed, namely in establishing a real component market. Today a huge community of developers and software vendors has committed itself to Eclipse as the technological basis for developing reusable components and thousands of Eclipse plug-ins can be found on the Web.

The success of Eclipse and similar systems has many reasons, some of which go far beyond pure technical considerations. However, there are several technical features which have contributed to the success of plug-in systems:

- Plug-in components are coarse-grained, i.e., they are like small applications with features which are of direct value for the user. In that, they are mainly self-contained and have limited dependencies on other components.
- There are clear rules on how to specify dependencies and interactions between components. This results in precise documentation on how systems can be extended and how plug-ins shall interact.
- Eclipse and similar systems have demonstrated ways how plug-in components can be integrated seamlessly into working environments. Working environments can grow in a disciplined and determined manner allowing the users to create their individual working environments by selecting from a set of plug-ins.

This paper introduces a new plug-in architecture for the .NET platform which shows much resemblance to Eclipse. However, whereas Eclipse describes extension points and extensions with dedicated XML configuration files, our architecture relies on .NET concepts such as custom attributes and metadata to specify relevant information directly in the source code of an application. We argue that this approach is more readable and easier to maintain. Moreover, it exploits .NET specific features for plug-in deployment and discovery. As a case study for our plug-in architecture we present a new plug-in platform for rich client applications called CAP.NET. We describe its design as well as a prototypical implementation and show how it supports users assembling their individual working environments.

1.1 Related Work

One of the first runtime extensible systems was Emacs ("Editor MACroS") [18]. Emacs extensions are written in *elisp* – a Lisp dialect – and installed by setting paths in an initialization file. In that, Emacs can be described as a readily extensible scripting framework, to which new scripts can be added at runtime.

Many Web browsers make use of the "plugging" concept. Mozilla [13], for example, lets developers define new extensions and makes use of various technologies for this purpose. In Mozilla the user interface is represented by an XML data model. Plug-ins specify their user interface contributions in the declarative language XUL (another XML language) and with the help of JavaScript and XPCOM one can add dynamic behaviour to the UI elements. XPConnect bridges XPCOM [17] and JavaScript by allowing JavaScript to access and manipulate XPCOM objects. Applications built with this technology are not limited to the Mozilla Web browser but range from different Web browsers (FireFox, Mozilla Suite, Netscape), email clients (Thunderbird), calendar applications (Sunbird) to integrated development environments (Kommodo) and Web-design applications (NVU).

OSGi [16] is a Java-based technology for deploying and managing coarse-grained components. The Open Service Gateway Initiative (OSGi) defines several mechanisms that are relevant for a plug-in framework. Lifecycle management of components (referred to as bundles in OSGi) and hot update are possible using OSGi. Additionally, OSGi offers a service concept and a set of service standards for component integration and interaction. Technically, the OSGi service framework can be boiled down to a custom, dynamic Java class loader and a service registry that is globally accessible within a single Java virtual machine [9].

The Eclipse Platform [7] is certainly the most prominent plug-in platform today. Eclipse is built upon a small core and all further functionality is provided by a (usually huge) set of plug-ins. Plug-ins for Eclipse are written in Java and are delivered as JAR libraries. Plug-ins declare their interconnections to other plug-ins using a manifest in XML format. The idea is quite simple: a plug-in declares named extension points and extensions to extension points in other plug-ins. The platform matches extensions with their corresponding extension point declarations by name, discovers plug-in dependencies in this way, and integrates the plug-ins to a comprehensive working environment at start-up without actually loading the code. The resulting plug-in registry is available via the platform API. Any problems, such as extensions to missing extension points, are detected and logged. Eclipse evolved as it moved from version 2.x to 3.0. In version 3.0.7 it adopted the OSGi Service Platform (SP) as a foundation for plug-in management. Backed with OSGi it allows hot updates of plug-ins, i.e., updating the code and reloading a plug-in while the Eclipse system keeps running.

NetBeans [15], as the main competitor of the Eclipse Java development environment, has introduced a plug-in concept which differs significantly from that in Eclipse. In NetBeans, plug-ins are referred to as modules and, as in Eclipse, are JAR libraries contained in a plug-in directory within the NetBeans environment. However, extension mechanisms and plug-in integration are based on a so-called *virtual file system* that, in essence, represents the hierarchical structure of the application. Plug-ins define their extensions in XML documents (called *layer.xml*) by specifying their contributions to the virtual file system. For example, a plug-in which would like to add a menu item "Format" in sub menu "Source" would simply specify that it has a contribution to the virtual directory path "Menu/Source" with name "Format".

1.2 Outline

This paper is structured as follows: Section 2 defines basic terms and concepts and derives requirements for a plug-in architecture and a plug-in platform. In Section 3 we will discuss some .NET features which have been important in our approach. Section 4 introduces the basic concepts of our plug-in architecture, namely extension, deployment, and discovery mechanisms. In Section 5 we validate our approach by a prototypical implementation of a rich client platform. Finally Section 6 discusses our approach and achievements and gives an outlook to future work.

2 Terms and Concepts

2.1 Basic Mechanisms of a Plug-In Platform

A plug-in platform enables components to plug into an application core at load time or at run time. For that purpose the platform requires the following basic mechanisms:

(a) Plugging. An essential principle of a plug-in architecture is that system extensions are carried out in controlled, restricted and determined manner. Therefore, in a plug-in architecture there have to be means which allow specifying explicitly how a component should be extended and how other plug-in components make their contributions. In Eclipse, for example, this is done by extension point and extension specifications in XML. We adopt a notion of extension slot, i.e., the specification how an extension should occur, and the extension, i.e., the specification how a plug-in makes a contribution to a particular slot. System integration, i.e., combining the set of plug-ins at hand into a integrated running system, is solely accomplished by reading and exploiting this information about extension slots and fitting extensions.

(b) Deployment. Plug-in components are like small applications that extend the application core by new services. Nontrivial services may consist of multiple extensions plugging into different slots defined by one or several extension hosts. Extensions that belong together are merged into a single plug-in component that serves as a single unit of deployment and versioning.

(c) Discovery. Safe and easy plug-in activation should not require complicated and error-prone configuration tasks. Therefore, plug-ins are simply moved to a central place called a plug-in repository where they are discovered and activated automatically at application load or run time. Accordingly, removing a plug-in from the repository deactivates it.

2.2 Slots and Extensions

As discussed above, a plug-in is a deployable software unit which has explicit specifications of its slots and extensions. Slot specifications define how other plug-ins are intended to extend the functionality of this plug-in, whereas extension specifications define how this plug-in makes contributions to slots of others. Therefore, slots and extension specifications have to match. In essence, slots declare the types of information a plug-in expects and the extensions fill this information slots accordingly. In its simplest form, a plug-in specification is a structured list of name/value-pairs where the slot specifies the required names and value ranges and the extension specification defines appropriate values for the extension at hand.

The component defining the slot is called the *extension host* and the component implementing the extension is called the *extension contributor*. Extension contributors again can define their own slots where other plug-ins can contribute allowing the whole system to grow. A non-trivial plug-in can contain multiple extensions plugging into different slots.

Usually, plug-in extensions will occur on the level of run-time behavior, i.e., plug-in host and contributor will communicate based on a defined protocol in order to accomplish a particular task. The collaboration between the host and its contributor is defined in the form of required and provided interfaces. The host will define the required interface and the extension contributor has to provide an implementation for it.

Fig. 1 depicts the structure of slot and extension specifications in host and contributor plug-ins. The interface in the host and the implementation class in the contributor specify the agreed collaboration protocol. Additional name/value pairs define other properties that the host requires to make use of the extension.

2.3   Further Services of a Plug-In Platform

A plug-in platform built on the basic mechanisms presented above can also provide the following services:

(a) Hot Plugging. Having to restart an application in order to install new components leads to annoying interrupts of the user's work flow and should be avoided. Hot plugging means the ability to add, update and remove plug-ins while the application is running.

(b) Auto-Update. Patches are a common way of supplying small updates to pieces of software in order to update it or to fix problems. If the update process is automated users are relieved from this tedious and error-prone task. A plug-in platform can therefore periodically scan the plug-in repository and compare version information with an installation repository. If newer versions of plug-ins are available, they are copied from the installation to the plug-in repository and are reactivated when the application is restarted. If hot plugging is supported, no restart is required.

(c) Sandboxing. Malicious or unreliable plug-ins represent a security hazard for the application. A sandbox is a secure environment for safely running plug-ins within well-defined limitations to their possible set of actions.

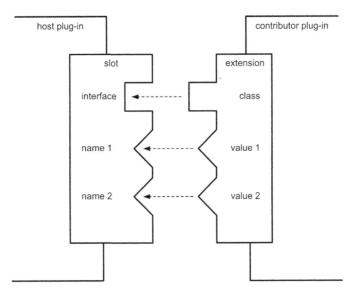

Fig. 1. Slot and extension in host and contributor plug-in

3 .NET Framework Concepts

The .NET Framework offers advanced concepts which form a technological basis for
the plug-in approach presented. Those are .NET custom attributes, assemblies, metadata and reflection. We shortly discuss those topics now.

(a) Custom attributes

Custom attributes are pieces of meta-information that can be attached to language
constructs such as classes, interfaces, methods or fields in the source code of an application. At run time the attributes attached to a language construct can be retrieved
using reflection [12]. In addition to pre-defined attributes programmers can declare
custom attributes by implementing attribute classes with arbitrary properties whose
values can be set when the attribute is attached to a language construct.

Adding custom metadata that can be evaluated by development tools is a common
usage scenario in .NET. A well-known example is the WebMethod attribute which
indicates that a method is exposed as part of an XML Web service.

```
public class StockTicker : WebService {
  [WebMethod]
  public double GetQuote(string symbol) { ... }
}
```

The Web Services Description Language tool (wsdl.exe) is an example of a development tool that uses reflection to read out the WebMethod attribute for identifying a
method as a Web method and, from this information, creating contract files or proxy
code.

Our plug-in architecture makes similar use of attributes for representing information about slots or extensions in plug-in code (see Section 4.1).

(b) Assemblies

An assembly is the basic packaging unit in .NET. It is the smallest unit for loading, deployment, versioning and security. Assemblies can come as executables (*.exe) or as library components (*.dll). They contain metadata describing types, resources and referenced assemblies. Because assemblies are self-describing, assembly component deployment is as simple as an copy operation. There are no issues with class or type library registration as in traditional COM deployment. Lack of registry dependency and support for side-by-side component deployment avoids the problem known as "DLL hell" [10].

Strong name identification and assembly version information are used to identify components. An assembly version number is represented as a four-part number. For example, version 1.5.1254.0 indicates 1 as the major version, 5 as the minor version, 1254 as the build number, and 0 as the revision number. To give an example a version number is attached to the `StockTicker` program (see above) through the AssemblyVersion-Attribute.

```
[assembly: AssemblyVersion("1.5.1254.0")]
public class StockTicker { ... }
```

A component update service can acquire the component version using reflection like this:

```
Version v =
  AssemblName.GetAssemblName("ticker.dll").Version;
```

In our plug-in architecture a dll assembly is used as a container for a plug-in component. Strong name identification and assembly version information are used to identify plug-ins and to facilitate auto-update.

(c) Metadata.

An assembly does not only store code but also metadata describing the symbolic information of all types, methods, fields and other entities in the assembly. An assembly's metadata is generated automatically by the compiler from the source code. .NET makes it possible to retrieve the metadata of an assembly at run time using reflection [10]. The sample code below demonstrates how a tool can search the `StockTicker` class (see above) for methods with the `WebMethod` attribute attached. For all the methods in the `StockTicker` class it will retrieve all the attributes of type `WebMethodAttribute` using the reflection method `GetCustomAttributes`. If the length of the array returned is greater than 0, the first array element is accessed and casted to the `WebMethodAttribute` type.

```
foreach(MethodInfo mi in
typeof(StockTicker).GetMethods()) {
  object[] webMethodAttrs = mi.GetCustomAttributes(
                           typeof(WebMethodAttribute),
  true);
```

```
  if(webMethodAttrs.Length > 0) {
    WebMethodAttribute webMethodAttr =
            (WebMethodAttribute) webMethodAttrs[0];
    // use WebMethodAttribute
  }
}
```

Our plug-in platform uses reflection for discovery. The discovery service scans the plug-in repository and activates extensions by reading their extension definition from metadata.

4   A Plug–In Architecture for .NET

In this section we will show how the .NET-specific concepts described in Section 3 can be used to implement the basic mechanisms of a plug-in platform as described in Section 2. In particular, we show

- how to define slots and extensions with .NET attributes,
- how to use .NET assemblies for plug-in packaging and deployment, and
- how to use reflection for plug-in discovery and activation.

We will showcase this approach with two sample extensions. The first example defines an extension slot for pluggable logging functionality. An extension contributor will receive logging information from the host and logs this information in its specific way. The second extended example introduces an additional custom property to differentiate various message types (e.g. error, warning, info).

4.1   Defining Slots and Extensions with .NET Attributes

Our specification of slots and extensions is based on .NET attributes. In Section 2 we have seen that a slot can specify one or more interfaces, which have to be implemented by the extension. In our first example the extension host defines an interface ILog and applies the attribute Slot with a name "Log" to the interface.

```
[Slot("Log")]
public interface ILog {
  void Write(string msg);
}
```

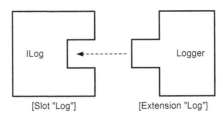

Fig. 2. Simple logger slot and extension

The `Slot` attribute is predefined by our plug-in platform. It is used to tag any program elements which belong to a particular slot. The slot is identified by a unique name. In the example above, the `Slot` attribute simply says that the `ILog` interface is an interface of the slot with the name `"Log"`. The following code shows the definition of the `Slot` attribute.

```
class SlotAttribute : Attribute {
  public SlotAttribute(string name) { ... }
  private string name;
}
```

The interface `ILog` declares a method `Write` which the host calls to log messages and which has to be implemented by contributor plug-ins. The sample extension `Logger` writes messages to the console. The class `Logger` provides an implementation for the required interface `ILog`.

```
[Extension("Log")]
public class Logger : ILog {
  public void Write(string msg) {
    Console.WriteLine(msg);
  }
}
```

Extensions in contributor plug-ins have to be tagged by the custom attribute `Extension` which is also predefined in the platform. The same name as in the slot is used to uniquely identify the slot to be extended. The following code shows the definition of the `Extension` attribute.

```
class ExtensionAttribute : Attribute {
  public ExtensionAttribute(string name) { ... }
  private string name;
}
```

In the example above, the class `Logger` is now referred to as an extension of the slot `"Log"` because it is associated to this slot by the attribute `Extension`. Furthermore, it is a valid extension that conforms to the requirements of the `Slot` declaration as it implements the interface `ILog`.

Logger with a Custom Property

The previous example is now extended to demonstrate the use of custom properties. In this example, we assume that the host allows the extension to choose between different message types which should be logged. For example, if the extension specifies `Info`, `Warning` or `Error` as its message types, the host will forward only the respective logging information.

The host defines a custom attribute class `MessageType`. The standard `AttributeUsage` attribute specifies that `MessageType` can only be attached to class definitions. The `Slot` attribute defines that `MessageType` is associated to a `"Log"` slot.

```
public enum MessageTypeEnum {Info, Warning, Error}
```

```
[Slot("Log")]
[AttributeUsage(AttributeTargets.Class)]
public class MessageType : Attribute {
  public MessageType(MessageTypeEnum type) { ... }
  private MessageTypeEnum type;
}
```

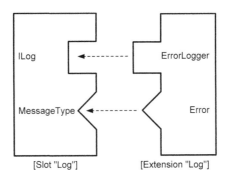

Fig. 3. Logger with custom property

A contributor plug-in can use this custom attribute in the extension implementation. In the following ErrorLogger implementation the Slot attribute is used to specify that this class is an extension to the "Log" slot and the MessageType attribute is used to specify that this logger implementation is intended to accept error logs only.

```
[Extension("Log")]
[MessageType(MessageTypeEnum.Error)]
public class ErrorLogger: ILog {
  public void Write(string msg){
    // do something
  }
}
```

In summary, specifying slots and extensions works as follows. In an extension host a slot is specified in the following way:

- There is a Slot attribute which is used to tag program elements of the host, i.e. interfaces and custom attribute classes, which belong to a particular slot that is identified by a unique name.
- The host will define one or several interfaces which are intended to be implemented by the extension contributors. They are marked with the Slot attribute.
- In most cases the host will also define one or several custom attribute classes which are intended to be used by the extension contributors to provide static information. That means, custom attributes are used to embody the name/value pairs. Again the Slot attribute is used to assign the attribute class to a particular slot.

In an extension contributor the extension is specified as follows:

- There is an `Extension` attribute that is used to tag the class of the contributor in order to make a contribution to a particular slot. Thereby, the unique slot identifier given in the `Slot` attribute is used.
- For a slot interface there is a class implementing that interface in the contributor. This class is tagged with the `Extension` attribute denoting that it is an extension of a particular slot.
- The custom attributes defined in the slot specification will be used in the contributor to provide the respective static extension information. They are also attached to the extending class.

4.2 Deployment and Update

The class that provides an extension is packed into a plug-in assembly for deployment. To prepare for automatic plug-in update, we need to add version information to the plug-in assembly. We continue with the error logger example from the previous section and add version information.

```
using System;
using System.Reflection;

[assembly: AssemblyVersion("0.1.*")]

[Extension("Log")]
[MessageType(MessageTypeEnum.Error)]
public class ErrorLogger : ILog {
  public void Write(string msg) {
    // do something
  }
}
```

Major version is 0, minor version is 1, and by specifying a wildcard for build and revision number, the compiler will insert adequate values. The following command builds the error logger plug-in.

```
csc /reference:platform.dll /target:library
/out:errorlogger.dll errorlogger.cs
```

The plug-in `errorlogger.dll` contains the extension and version information and is ready for deployment. Deployment means to move the plug-in into the repository. A repository is a folder in the file system that contains all active plug-ins for an extension host. When a plug-in is moved to the repository, the plug-in platform will automatically discover the newly installed plug-in and activate it (see Section 4.3).

Plug-in providers may provide updates with new features or fixes for problems. The Auto-Update service uses reflection to acquire the version info of plug-ins in the repository. It compares the version number of the currently installed plug-in and compares it to a installation repository that provides updated plug-ins. If updates are available, the update service replaces the plug-in in the repository with the newer version from the server.

```
Version v1 = AssemblyName.
  GetAssemblyName("errorlogger.dll").Version;
Version v2 = AssemblyName.
  GetAssemblyName("\\install\errorlogger.dll").Version;
if(v2 > v1) {
  // do update
}
```

The update process requires the plug-in platform to be restarted. An active plug-in means that its assembly is load in an application domain. As of .NET 2.0, assemblies cannot be individually unloaded. Consequently the update service shuts down the extension host, installs updated plug-in in the repository and restarts the extension host.

4.3 Discovery and Activation

At start-up the extension host searches the plug-in repository to discover plug-ins. It uses reflection to browse all classes in plug-in assemblies to look for Extension attributes. Classes with that attribute attached contain extensions. A conformance test checks if the extension provides the required interfaces and properties. Valid plug-ins are represented in the *plug-in registry*, which is a data structure that represents relations between slots and extensions, as well as inter-extension dependencies. The source code below shows a simplified discovery routine.

```
foreach(string filename in Directory.GetFiles(
        "plugins", "*.dll")) {
  Assembly a = Assembly.ReflectionOnlyLoadFrom(filename);
  foreach(Type t in a.GetTypes()) {
    object[] attrs = t.GetCustomAttributes(
                        typeof(ExtensionAttribute),true);
    if(attrs.Length > 0) {
      // check conformance
      // add it to the registry
    }
  }
}
```

Discovery uses the reflection-only context, which means that none of the plug-ins are actually loaded yet. Our plug-in platform supports lazy-loading, which means that extensions are loaded at the latest possible point in time. For example, when lazy-loading is applied to user interface elements, the plug-in is not loaded until the user performs an action on the user interface element and activates the respective function.

The code sample below shows how a plug-in is loaded and an extension is instantiated and used.

```
Assembly a = Assembly.LoadFrom("plugin\\errorlogger.dll");
ILog log = a.CreateInstance("ErrorLogger");
log.Write("Hello world!");
```

5   CAP.NET: A Rich Client Application Platform in .NET

CAP.NET (Client Application Platform .NET) is a platform for the realization of rich client applications in .NET and has been developed primarily for the validation of the plug-in architectural concepts as presented in Section 4. The idea of CAP.NET is to lay a basis for the realization of plug-in components for rich client workbenches, to allow the selection of an individual set of plug-in components by a user, and the integration of this set into a comprehensive and seamless user interface.

CAP.NET focuses on user interface integration, plug-in component deployment and life-cycle management. It is designed and built to meet the following requirements:

- integrate a variety of plug-ins for different tasks into a single rich client application
- facilitate seamless integration of user interface elements contributed by different plug-ins
- provide an update mechanism for plug-ins
- provide a framework for rapid application development of rich client components.

In addition to the plug-in mechanism presented in Section 4 CAP.NET provides the following features:

- a concrete plug-in discovery, deployment and update mechanism which uses a Web-Service interface on the download server
- a workbench component based on a well-defined user interface paradigm which provides several extension slots for plugging in user interface elements as plug-in components.

Fig. 4 shows the architecture of the CAP.NET platform. The platform core implements the plug-in discovery and start-up mechanisms and contains the plug-in registry. Additionally, the security component is responsible for managing rights and roles of plug-ins.

Everything else in CAP.NET is a plug-in. The core provides one extension slot `"cap.ui.workbench"`, which is intended to be filled by a workbench component.

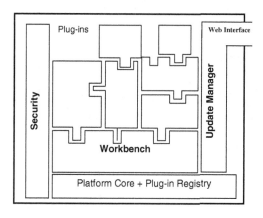

Fig. 4. Architecture of CAP.NET

So far we have implemented just one kind of workbench component, but other workbench components following different UI paradigms could be implemented and plugged in as well. The realized `Workbench` component has several extension slots allowing further components to plug-in and in this way make contributions to the overall working environment, as we will see in Section 5.4. The update manager is also a plug-in and handles assembly deployment and update.

In the following we will present CAP.NET in some detail. First, we will outline the platform core which implements the basic mechanisms. Then we will present the UI paradigm and the workbench components as well as the workbench extension slots and how the UI extensions are integrated. Finally, we will show some example plug-ins and an example user workbench.

5.1 Platform Core

At start-up, the platform core discovers the available plug-ins. It looks in the installation directory for files named `*.dll`. These plug-in assemblies are loaded using `ReflectionOnlyLoad` and scanned for slot and extension attributes.

The plug-ins discovered during this process are stored in the plug-in registry, which is basically a set of `Plugin` objects. The platform core is responsible for registering and managing plug-in assemblies and allows easy access to data and resources from the framework, including resources shared among plug-ins.

The plug-in registry simplifies the integration of extensions. A host component that defines a certain slot can find out if extensions to this slot are available using the plug-in registry which holds the static descriptions of the available extensions.

5.2 Update Manager

The update manager is also a plug-in. It periodically connects to an update Web Service running on an installation server. This Web Service checks whether newer versions of the installed plug-ins are available on the server and returns them to the update manager which installs them into the client's plug-in directory. This makes the update process extremely simple. The system administrator at the server side simply copies new versions of plug-ins into the server's plug-in directory. Any clients relying on these plug-ins detect the new versions automatically and copy them over.

5.3 User Interface Paradigm and Workbench Plug-In

User interface integration is about integrating different contributions into an overall user interface. To make this work, user interface integration has to be based on a general user interface paradigm, i.e. a general set-up and a general working principle that all applications obey. We have defined such a user interface paradigm for rich client applications. It focuses on the notion of *user tasks*, i.e., tasks that a user wants to work on. Depending on the chosen tasks the working environment will present itself in different ways. In general, a CAP.NET user interface consists of the following four panes: task navigation, task content, task commands, and views (see Fig. 5).

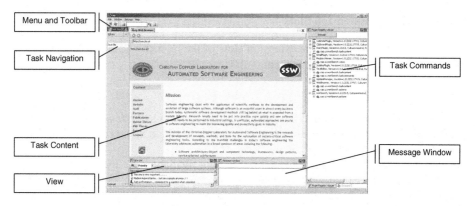

Fig. 5. CAP.NET Workbench

Task navigation
This is a UI element which allows navigation between different tasks in a hierarchical manner and is usually placed on the left side of the working environment. It shows all available tasks in a hierarchical arrangement and is always visible.

Task content
The task content window is the working window for a particular task. It will be either some sort of editor or an input form allowing the manipulation of data and objects. It can display the data graphically, textually, in forms etc. and can react on commands to change the data. Task content elements are based on the model-view-controller (MVC) pattern and allow the user to open, edit and save data objects. They follow an open-save-close life cycle much like file-system-based tools.

Task commands
It is common to have a set of commands for every task (e.g. a search command and a replace command for a text editor). These commands are displayed in task command windows, which are little control panes usually placed to the right of the task content window. There can be several task command windows for one task content.

Views
Views are UI elements which provide different views on a task's data. They can be used for navigation but not for changing data. For example, in a development environment there could be different views of the code that is being written. One view could display the variables and methods while another view could display properties and their values. A view may also augment other views by providing information about the currently selected object.

In addition to these special UI elements there are standard menus and toolbars as well as standard windows such as a message window or a to-do list. The `Workbench` plug-in realizes this UI paradigm and provides extension slots for tasks, commands, views and other elements, allowing custom plug-ins to make their UI contributions.

5.4 Workbench Extension Slots

In the following we outline the extension slots of the Workbench plug-in and show
how contributor plug-ins can use them.

cap.ui.workbench.actions

Additions to the menu bar and the toolbar are referred to as *actions*. This is because
they represent some kind of user interaction, e.g. selecting a menu command or clicking a button in the toolbar.

In order to make a new menu or toolbar item available, the user has to provide
code that has to be called, whenever the user clicks on that item. For that purpose an
interface IAction has to be defined. This interface contains a method OnClick,
which is called when the menu or toolbar item is clicked.

Since this slot can serve two purposes, i.e. the installation of a menu item or a toolbar item, there are two different attributes (MenuAction and ToolBarAction)
that are used to provide the required information for UI integration. With the help of
these attributes, the framework can extract the static information required for user
interface integration without having to load the code.

The following code shows how a menu item is installed into the workbench. The
class UpdateMenuPlugin extends the slot cap.ui.workbench.actions.
The MenuAction attribute specifies the location where the new menu item should
be inserted into the menus of the workbench.

```
[Extension("cap.ui.workbench.actions")]
[MenuAction(MenuPath = "Settings/Web")]
class UpdateMenuPlugin : IAction {
  public void OnClick(object sender, EventArgs args) {
  ... }
}
```

This will insert a menu item "Web" into the "Settings" menu. If the user selects this
menu item the class UpdateMenuPlugin will be loaded and the OnClick method
will be called.

cap.ui.workbench.taskcontent

For contributing a new task content element there is the slot "cap.ui.work-
bench.taskcontent" as well as the interface ITaskContent which defines
methods for handling task content elements. Methods like OnNew, OnSave etc. are
intended to be called when the respective actions on the content element are carried
out. These operations apply to the currently active content. An extension to this slot
has to implement the following interface ITaskContent.

```
[Slot("cap.ui.workbench.taskcontent")]
public interface ITaskContent{
  void OnNew();
  void OnSave();
  void OnSaveAs();
  void OnOpen(String filename);
```

```
    void OnClose(object sender, FormClosingEventArgs e);
    void OnTitleChanged(object sender, EventArgs e);
}
```

A `TaskContent` attribute can be used to provide information such as the file extension the task content is related to. For example, for a text editor plug-in the `Task-Content` attribute can be used as follows:

```
[Extension("cap.ui.workbench.taskcontent")]
[TaskContent(FileExtension="txt", Name="Text file")]
public class TextEditorContent : ITaskContent { ... }
```

The `TaskContent` attribute tells the workbench to create a menu item "Text file". It also notifies the framework about the capability of the plug-in to deal with `.txt` files.

cap.ui.workbench.taskcommands

The `"cap.ui.workbench.taskcommands"` slot is intended to be used for contributing a task command dialog for a particular task content. Task command dialogs are implemented as extensions of .NET's `Form` class. As a task dialog refers to a particular task content window, it is required to identify the task content. This is done with the `TaskCommandFor` attribute. For example, the following code shows a task command extension for the text editor plug-in.

```
[Extension ("cap.ui.workbench.taskcommands")]
[TaskCommandFor("at.dhungana.plugins.texteditor")]
public partial class TextEditorCommands : Form { ... }
```

cap.ui.workbench.views

In order to add new views to the workbench, clients have to use the extension slot `cap.ui.workbench.views`. The attribute `WorkbenchView` is used to inform the workbench about the availability of a new view. This attribute can be used to specify the name of the view, which is then listed as a menu item in the menu where all other views are listed.

```
[Extension("cap.ui.workbench.views")]
[WorkbenchView("CAP Clipboard")]
public class ClipboardView : Form { ... }
```

5.5   Example Plug-Ins and Working Environment

To test and demonstrate the platform, a set of plug-ins for a typical rich client workbench have been realized (see Fig. 5 for a sample screenshot) . These are:

- a simple text editor plug-in,
- a web browser plug-in (a public domain implementation has been wrapped and packaged as a CAP.NET plug-in),
- a calendar plug-in,
- a diary plug-in,

- an email plug-in,
- a Sudoku game plug-in,
- and a registry view plug-in for browsing the plug-in registry.

By these plug-in developments it was possible to show that CAP.NET fulfills the requirements of an integration platform for rich client applications and that the user interface paradigm is a simple but appropriate interaction model for typical user tasks.

6 Summary and Discussion

In this paper we presented a plug-in architecture and a rich client platform for the .NET platform. Adopting ideas similar to Eclipse, our approach relies on .NET-specific features such as custom attributes, assemblies, metadata and reflection. We argue that the use of these .NET features results in a better plug-in architecture. In particular, we argue that our approach of specifying slots and extensions using custom attributes is more readable and easier to maintain that the Eclipse approach using XML specifications.

In our approach the extension host uses a `Slot` attribute to tag any interfaces that are to be implemented by the contributor. It also uses custom attributes for specifying properties for which the contributor has to provide values. This makes it easy for a contributor to describe an extension. The contributor has to implement the slot's interface by a class and tag this class with the `Extension` attribute. Moreover, the contributor can use the custom attributes defined for the slot to provide values for the required properties. Slots and extensions are specified directly in the source code of an application which makes it easier to keep them in sync with the implementation.

.NET assemblies, as the unit of deployment and versioning, are a most adequate and natural means for the implementation of plug-in components. Furthermore, assemblies can contain arbitrary metadata allowing us to include plug-in specific information. Plug-in discovery is based on .NET metadata and reflection. In .NET 2.0 programmers can load metadata of an assembly without actually loading the code (method `ReflectionOnlyLoad`). This allowed us to realize a lazy loading strategy as in Eclipse, i.e., plug-in integration occurs at start-up time based on metadata without actually loading the code. The code is only loaded when it is activated for the first time.

Hot update means that an old version of a plug-in is unloaded and a new version of it is loaded while the system keeps running. In Eclipse this is accomplished by the OSGi implementation and by the fact that each plug-in is loaded by its own class loader. When the plug-in should be unloaded, the class loader is just disposed and with it the loaded plug-in. .NET works differently in this respect. In .NET, assemblies are loaded into so-called application domains (objects of type `AppDomain`). To unload code one would have to delete the `AppDomain` object. However, application domains also represent memory boundaries and method calls between objects in different application domains have be done using remote method invocation. For that reason, it would represent an unacceptable overhead to load each assembly into its own application domain. Assemblies therefore cannot be unloaded individually. How to realize hot updates in .NET remains an problem that is still to be solved.

References

1. Beck, K., and Gamma, E.: Contributing to Eclipse. Addison-Wesley, 2003.
2. Cox, B.J.: Planning the software industrial revolution. IEEE Software 7(6), 1990.
3. Crnkovic, I. et al. (eds.): Special Issue: Automated Component-based Software Engineering. Journal of Systems and Software, 74 (1), Elsevier, 2005.
4. Dean, D.: The Security of Static Typing with Dynamic Linking. In Proceedings of the Fourth ACM Conference on Computer and Communications Security, Zurich, Switzerland, April 1997.
5. Dewan, P. and Choudhary, R.: Coupling the user interfaces of a multiuser program. ACM Transactions on Computer Human Interaction, 1995
6. Dhungana, D.: CAP.NET – Client Application Platform in .NET. Master thesis, Johannes Kepler University, Linz, Austria (2006).
7. Eclipse Platform Technical Overview. Object Technology International, Inc., http://www.eclipse.org, February 2003.
8. Ghezzi, C., Monga, M.: Fostering component evolution with C# attributes. International Workshop on Principles of Software Evolution (IWPSE) 2002.
9. Hall, R. S, Cervantes H: An OSGi Implementation and Experience Report; Consumer Communications and Networking Conference, 2004
10. Löwy, J.: Programming .NET Components. O'Reilly Media, Sebastopol (2003)
11. McIllroy, M. D.: Mass produced software components. In: Proceedings of the Nato Software Engineering Conference. 1968, pp. 138-155.
12. Microsoft: Microsoft C# Language Specifications. Microsoft Press, Redmond (2001).
13. mozilla.org: An Introduction To Hacking Mozilla. http://www.mozilla.org/hacking/coding-introduction.html.
14. Mössenböck, H., Beer W., Birngruber, D., Wöß, A.: .NET Application Development. Pearson Addison Wesley, 2004.
15. NetBeans Project: http://www.netbeans.org/index.html
16. OSGi Service Platform, Release 3. The Open Services Gateway Initiative, March 2003, http://www.osgi.org.
17. Shaver, M., and Ang, M.: Inside the Lizard: A Look at the Mozilla Technology and Architecture. http://www.mozilla.org, 2000.
18. Stallman, R.: EMACS: The Extensible, Customizable Display Editor. ACM Conference on Text Processing, 1981.
19. Syperski, C.: Component Software, Beyond Object-Oriented Programming, 2nd edn. Addison-Wesley, 2002.
20. Udell, J.: Component Software. BYTE, 19 (5), 1994, pp. 46-55.

Improve Component-Based Programs with Connectors

Joachim H. Fröhlich[1] and Manuel Schwarzinger[2]

[1] Department of Business Informatics - Software Engineering,
Johannes Kepler University of Linz,
Altenbergerstr. 69, A-4040 Linz, Austria
joachim.froehlich@acm.org
[2] Racon Software GmbH,
Goethestr. 80, A-4021 Linz, Austria
schwarzinger@racon-linz.at

Abstract. Interfaces rather than components carry component-based software architectures. This follows directly from the design of component interfaces and contractual obligations before the implementation of components. We suggest separating component interfaces and component services such as protocol checking, synchronization, parallelization and caching into dedicated components which we call connectors. Connectors channel the communication so that components do not communicate directly with each other. Thus connectors foster the standardization of identifiable component contracts, accelerate the development of complementing or competing components, and improve the testability, portability and maintainability of component-based programs.

1 Introduction

Interfaces are core architectural constructs. Interfaces and contractual obligations are needed to build, analyze, test and configure programs. This holds especially for component-based software architectures. Blurring classes and components—as today's major component platforms like Java Beans and .NET do—impacts negatively on component architectures. This is best indicated by heavyweight, intrusive component containers; they attach component services directly to components (classes) via special base classes, marker interfaces, and/or attributes (.NET) or annotations (Java). Thus components are coupled to the component container and so restrain testability, reusability and portability.

Component-based programming remains exotic for many programmers because they have grown accustomed to object-oriented programming with its dominantly white-box style of reuse especially due to frameworks. In contrast, component-based programming extensively employs black-box reuse, interfaces (types) and contracts. The interplay between component-based programming and object-oriented programming has not been clearly elaborated, as demonstrated by the prevalent confusion around key terms like component, class object and component objects. The confusion derives partly from object-orientated techniques being well-suited for component implementations. However, object-oriented languages lack constructs necessary for defining functional and nonfunctional properties in sharp, coherent component

D. Lightfoot and C. Szyperski (Eds.): JMLC 2006, LNCS 4228, pp. 306–325, 2006.

interfaces. Whether language constructs are applied so as to reap the full benefits of component-based programs depends to a considerable degree on the skills of the programmer.

It is fundamentally clear that components should be designed with high cohesion and low coupling. This leads to advantages well-known from proper class and method design. Functional diversity unfolded at component interfaces as lengthy or deeply structured public classes packed into large deployment units (.NET assemblies or Java jar-files) complicates the application and implementation of components. The resulting problems are documented in complicated test procedures—most evidently for components wired into intrusive application servers (component containers). These components are loaded with operations that are foreign to their core business. To overcome these difficulties, lightweight component containers have been emerging. In the Java world, the Spring framework [8] serves as a prototypical example of promoting testable program architectures that revolve around interfaces.

Interfaces should be independent pivotal elements because they connect two or more communicating components. In practice, however, interfaces are attached either to service-providing components or to service-requiring components. This asymmetry impairs the specification, testing and development of independently installable and replaceable components. In the long run this hampers the widespread adoption of component technology. To overcome this obstacle, we propose an architectural style where every pair of interacting components is fully separated by independent, special-purpose components called *connectors* that isolate component interfaces. Connectors optionally implement nonfunctional component services such as checking communication protocols, sequencing or branching operation requests, and distributing load. Components communicating across connectors can focus on domain-specific tasks. Components that do not need such services use type-compatible connectors that omit some or all component services.

The paper is organized as follows: A presentation of related work in Section 2 elaborates open issues. Section 3 details the goals that drive the proposed architecture style. Section 4 presents basic concepts of the connector/component style. Section 5 sketches a typical connector application. Section 6 presents the basic design of connectors. Section 7 sketches two variants of a configurable program for analyzing data streams and how they profit from the connector/component style. Discussion and consequences conclude the paper. We back the presentation with prototypical code snippets in .NET/C# and semantically rich diagrams documenting parts of real system implementations.

2 Related Work

Our work revolves around grouping related component interfaces in separate deployment units which we call connectors. Connectors as separate development and deployment units of coherent programs are scarcely discussed in the literature. However, the basic idea of including interfaces in separate components is not new. Szyperski et al. [15] emphasize the importance of viewing interfaces in isolation from any specific component that might implement or use such interfaces, but does not discuss further-reaching concepts or implementation techniques. In the context of .NET,

Löwy [9] suggests assemblies with interfaces to parallelize the development of adjacent components. Wienholt [16] proposes a similar technique for .NET to shorten load time of assemblies and to reduce the memory usage. He puts frequently and occasionally used types of an assembly into different netmodules[1] and separates them by netmodules that consist only of interfaces, which leads to multi-module components.

Connectors are broadly known as a means of communication. In the context of coherent programs, connectors occur at the abstraction level of a programming language as shared variables, buffers and procedure calls [10, 13]. In the context of distributed programs, connectors are manifested as parts of the underlying infrastructure, e.g., in the form of sockets, pipes, networking protocols, SQL links between a database server and a database application program, event buses, message brokers, and even as complete middleware like COM+ or CORBA [2, 4, 10, 13]. Service–oriented architectures (SOA) provide the plumbing for the integration of components running on different technological platforms; component interfaces are published, queried and translated into executable code for calling services across the Internet [14].

UML 2.0 introduces connectors at the conceptual level as a means for wiring components together based on interface compatibility [11]. Components can offer ports that enable the definition of named sets of interfaces either provided or required by a component. Delegation connectors link external contracts of a component (specified by its ports) to the internal realization parts. Assembly connectors are established between two components and define the services that one component provides and another component requires. UML blurs components and classes by defining a component as a subtype of a class in order for a component to have operations and attributes and to be able to participate in associations and generalization/specialization hierarchies. Catalysis is a development method that applies components, ports and connectors in the UML sense for constructing component-based systems [4].

Component specification architectures as suggested by Cheesman and Daniels [1] adhere to a UML dialect that packs component specifications and interfaces in separate conceptual units. These units are defined and combined to software architectures before implementing them. Interface information models specify state changes of component objects (instances created from an installed component) caused by interface operations. Contractual obligations are specified with OCL (object constraint language).

Interfaces play an important role in the realm of lightweight, non-intrusive component containers. Spring [8] is a good example. It decouples components in the form of classes (beans) by externalizing object creation and injecting objects at dedicated points of collaborating classes (dependency injection). Collaborating classes announce these points with interfaces. Spring abandons subclassing for Spring-compliant components because the Spring Core (the basic bean container) heavily applies reflective programming techniques for identifying, instantiating and binding classes. Spring hides the complexity of underlying J2EE environments, so that components are almost like plain Java classes. Simple component services can be interwoven by means of an additional package supporting AOP (aspect-oriented programming). Spring does not treat interfaces as contracts that are independent of component implementations.

---

[1] A netmodule is a *raw* module that must be associated with a full-fledged component (assembly) prior to deployment.

3 Goals

We seek an architectural style that enables components to focus on their business without being distracted by intrusive component containers. Such a style must enable economically feasible structuring of general-purpose programs as well as domain- or application-specific programs. Thereby a program is either self-contained or embedded in a component container (application server). The architectural style must facilitate separate specification, implementation, testing, guarding, installation, substitution and monitoring of components and their interactions. Component services must be transparent: the mechanisms enabling this architectural style must be configurable in a way that leaves components using these mechanisms completely untouched, i.e., even decorating components with attributes is not necessary. Thereby, these mechanisms shall cost only as much in resources as needed in various program variants or stages (e.g., development, testing, launch, production). The architectural style must enable independent component evolution in in-house and open-market situations. For practicability, existing container technologies, if needed at all, should be supplemented rather than be replaced.

4 Connector Basics

We view software architectures as systems of component interfaces that optionally or temporarily service components. Like components, we treat component interfaces as binary, identifiable and separately deployable units that we call *connectors*. Technically, a connector contains at least one interface in the sense of the construct of the same name in modern object-oriented programming languages. Operations declared in interfaces of a connector form a functional closure; i.e., operations of connector interfaces use only parameters of basic data types, interfaces contained in the same connector, or interfaces in other connectors. In special cases types used in the signature of component interface operations are interfaces of application-neutral parts of the underlying class library, with collection interfaces and classes as the most evident examples. Additionally, connectors can monitor, guard or change operation invocations and data transmissions across component boundaries as long as they conform to the contracted communication protocol without distracting adjacent components. Figure 1 illustrates the idea by means of a component (C_1) surrounded by several connector components (A_1, A_2 and A_3) conforming to the architectural style and a style-violating component (C_2).

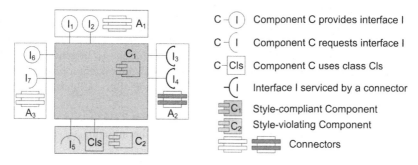

Fig. 1. A component surrounded by connectors

In the constellation shown in Figure 1, connector A_1 contains interfaces that component C_1 must implement (provided interfaces). Connector A_2 contains interfaces that component C_1 uses (requested interfaces). Connector A_2 services these interfaces, e.g., in order to monitor the communication protocol and map unexpected exceptions raised by the component that provides interfaces I_3 and I_4 to exceptions contracted in the connector. We call connectors *heavy connectors* if they wrap interfaces (like connector A_2 in Figure 1) in order to hook component services like logging, profiling, security checks and protocol checks. We call connectors *light connectors* if they contain only interface declarations (like connectors A_1 and A_3 in Figure 1). Light connectors can be exchanged for type (interface) compatible heavy connectors by means of program reconfiguration before run time.

An executable program applying one connector obviously consists of at least two communicating components. We call these components *functional components* (components for short where it is unambiguous) because they directly or indirectly implement functions that comprise the core business of a program. We speak of a *symmetric connector* when a functional component on the client side of connector uses the same interface(s) as the functional component on the provider side for communication. We speak of an *asymmetric connector* when a client component and a provider component use different interfaces and the connector maps interface concepts during communication. This article focuses on symmetric connectors. Figure 2 illustrates a program that is minimal in terms of components and connectors and exposes the internal plumbing of a light connector.

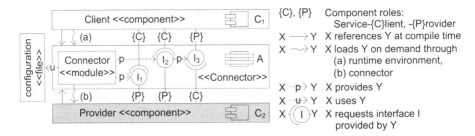

Fig. 2. Connector and functional components

The connector in Figure 2 completely channels the communication between the component playing the role of a service client (component that requests interfaces I_1 and I_2) and the component playing the role of a service provider (component that provides interfaces I_1 and I_2). Note that during an application session functional components may change roles as in Figure 2 for callback interface I_3. In general we call a component initiating a session a *client* and the triggered component a *provider*. Usually providers implement the interfaces that a connector offers. Clients only implement callback interfaces, if any.

The primary task of the connector module[2] (see Figure 2) is to load a service provider silently in the background during first access by the initiating service client. To

---

[2] Modules are classes with (static) class members only.

this end the connector module processes data from a configuration file in order to relieve service clients as well as the connector itself from referencing concrete classes in the program code, which otherwise would directly couple client components and connectors to provider components. The resulting constellation is characterized as follows:

- Components do not depend on each other.
- Components depend on connectors.
- Connectors do not depend on components.

The compilation procedure in .NET/C# illuminates the constellation (see Table 1):

Table 1. Compilation procedure with a self-containing connector

Compilation procedure	Reference structure
csc /out:Connector.dll /t:library ... csc /out:Provider.dll /t:library /r:Connector.dll ... csc /out:Client.exe /t:exe /r:Connector.dll ...	 C_1 = Client.exe, C_2 = Provider.dll A = Connector.dll

Obviously, if a connector A1 refers to interfaces of another connector A2, an adjacent component C refers to both connectors (see Table 2):

Table 2. Compilation procedure with a partial connector

Compilation procedure	Reference structure
csc /out:A1.dll /t:library ... csc /out:A2.dll /t:library /r:A1.dll... csc /out:C.dll /t:library /r:A2.dll;A1.dll...	

Connectors remove direct coupling between functional components and break circular dependencies. Connectors that are capable of loading several service providers (*multiple-part connectors*) instead of loading at most one service provider as discussed so far (*single-part connectors*) reduce the complexity of each of the service-providing components. Figure 3 illustrates a multiple-part connector.

Upon exceeding a certain breadth, the component interface defined by a connector ($I_1 \ldots I_n$ in Figure 3) can be implemented by several components (C_2 and C_3 in Figure 3) instead of just one component. These components build a group. A component group is defined by a common connector and one or more partitioning attributes. Each component of a group must publish a value for each partitioning attribute. The combination of attribute values characterizes a component within a component group. Thus partitioning attributes are used to diversify components. Diversification narrows the application scope of a single functional component, which eases its implementation while raising the domain-specific service level. A provider selection strategy [6] implemented either by the connector as part of the contract or by a client component selects the best-fitting service provider. Table 3 provides examples of multi-part connectors and partitioning attributes whose values can be determined either statically or dynamically.

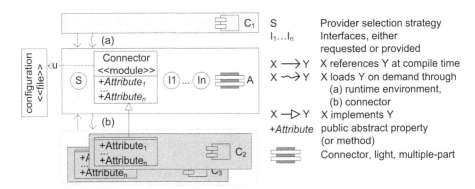

Fig. 3. Multiple-part connector

Table 3. Attributes of multi-part connectors

Multi-part connector	Attributes
String matchers	automaton, e.g., NFA, DFA
Report generators	file format, e.g. PDF, HTML, CSV
Memory systems	access time, durability
Numeric systems	accuracy, precision, run time
Information brokers	current server load, round-trip time, availability, cost

Provider components to hook into a multiple-part connector are specified in the configuration file with multiple-value entries such as

```
<connector name="A">
  <provider name="C1"/>
  <provider name="C2"/>
</connector>
```

From the presentation so far it should be obvious that neither functional components nor connectors reference functional components. Because they realize independent component specifications with optionally built-in component services, connectors become the points of variation of a program at which components can on demand be loaded, registered, monitored, controlled and unloaded. Figure 4 sketches a program whose architecture follows the connector/component-style.

Figure 4 introduces a new kind of connector and the connector manager. Connector A_3 is a heavy, multi-part connector; i.e., it can manage several functional components ($C_4 \ldots C_6$ in Figure 2) and service them. This kind of connector is typically applied to secure premature or third-party components in a sandbox. Consequently, we distinguish four kinds of connectors (see Table 4).

The connector manager is a new component with essentially two tasks.

- It factors out code common to all connectors, e.g., code for loading functional components specified in the configuration file.

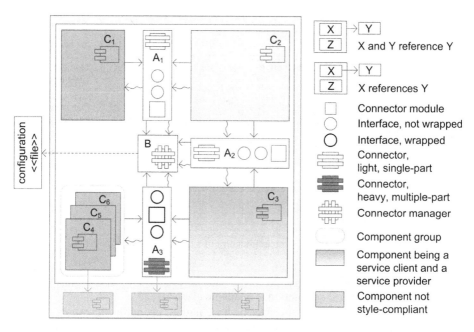

Fig. 4. A connector/component-architecture

- It provides a communication interface by which external clients can monitor and control connectors, e.g., temporarily switching component services on and off.

Note that the connector manager is optional. Functional components are indifferent to the existence of a connector manager. If installed, the connector manager improves nonfunctional properties of a program such as maintainability and dynamic adaptability.

Table 4. Kinds of connectors

Connector kinds	*light Connector:* no component services	*heavy Connector:* with component services
single-part Connector: at most one provider		
multiple-part Connector: any number of providers		

5   A Connector in Test Use

Before delving into some details of various kinds of connectors, we examine a usage scenario by means of a simplistic but demonstrative bank application. Section 7 will introduce two variants of a more demanding application relying heavily on the connector/component architecture style. Figure 5 sketches the architecture of the bank application. It applies a light, single-part connector and omits a connector manager;

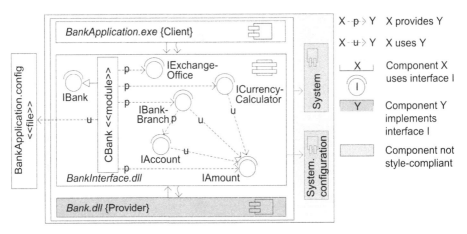

Fig. 5. Connector/component architecture of a bank application in test use

the simple configuration is typical for component testing. The complete implementation of an almost identical application is available elsewhere [5].

The connector offers several interfaces whose names, operation signatures and relations directly reflect the application's view of the bank domain, consisting of branches, currency exchange offices and accounts. In this example the operations of all interfaces build a functional closure, i.e., involve only basic data types and interfaces declared in this (self-contained) connector:

```
namespace BankInterface { // Connector (BankInterface.dll in Figure 5)
  public interface IBank {
    void Provide(out IBankBranch branch);
    void Provide(out IAmount money, double value, string currency);
    ...
  }
  public interface IBankBranch {
    IAccount SetupAccount(IAmount initialValue);
    IAccount SetupAccount(); // initialValue= 0.00 EUR
    bool Transfer(IAmount money, IAccount source, IAccount target);
    ...
  }
  public interface IAccount {
    string Owner { get; set; }
    bool Deposit(IAmount money);
    ...
  }
  ...
} // BankInterface
```

The concrete bank implementation providing the services as specified by these interfaces is configured before run time in the configuration file:

```
<connector name="BankInterface"> <provider name="Bank"/> </connector>
```

A test scenario illustrates the coding style, which resembles that prevailing for clients of COM components. In this scenario several customers transfer various amounts of money from their accounts to a common target account. The code is kept close to the connector and with it close to the object under test:

```
namespace BankApplication { // Client (BankApplication.exe in Figure 5)
// 1. Set up bank branch and target account
IBank bank= CBank.Get();
  // during first access the connector loads Bank.dll and creates reflectively a bank object
IBankBranch branch; bank.Provide(out branch);
IAccount target= branch.SetupAccount(); // initial amount 0.00 Euro

// 2. Transfer 1000.00
IAmount amount1; bank.Provide(out amount1, 1000.00, "EUR");
IAmount amount2; bank.Provide(out amount2, 1500.00, "EUR");
IAccount source= branch.SetupAccount(amount2); // initial amount 1500.00 Euro
branch.Transfer(amount1, source, target);

  ...
}
```

The service provider (Bank.dll) can be reconfigured by substituting an interface- and contract-matching component without changing the client's implementation. In this way a test stub that is applied during development of a bank client can be replaced with a production version for integration tests. The light connector can be replaced with a type-compatible heavy connector which can, e.g., check accounts for being issued by the same bank.

6 Connectors in Detail

6.1 Light Connectors

The defining task of a connector is to isolate logically coherent interfaces and (optionally) contractual obligations into a separate component. Furthermore, each connector must implement just one nonfunctional task: the establishment of the first connection between a service-using and a service-providing component while preserving their independence as well as its own independence. For this purpose a connector contains what, at the conceptual level, we have called a connector module. At the implementation level it is represented as a *provider-independent connector class* (CPiC). Figure 6 sketches the basic design of a light, single-part connector offering one interface (I_1).

A provider-independent connector class essentially has two tasks. On the one hand CPiC acts as a module with

- class methods that load a provider and create a provider-identifying object, and
- class variables for anchoring a provider-identifying object.

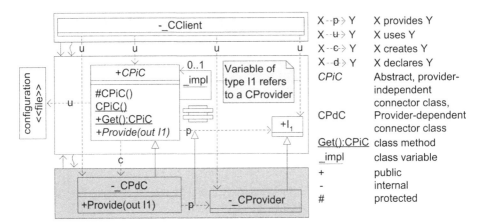

Fig. 6. Light, single-part connector

On the other hand CPiC is a type that declares factory methods [6] for letting providers deliver first objects (root objects) of business process chains (application sessions). Whether a provider starts a new business process per client request or reuses an existing one is determined in the contract between clients and providers.

In any case, each provider must subclass exactly one *provider-dependent connector class* (CPdC in Figure 6) per supported connector. The provider-independent connector class uses reflection techniques to create the sole object of this class (a singleton [6]), the connector object. This object is created automatically in the background during the first access to a provider (triggered, e.g., by bank= CBank.Get() in the bank application and executed by the class constructor of the CPiC) immediately after the provider component specified in the configuration file is loaded. Once the connector has supplied the connector object, a client queries it for the first business object by means of a factory method (e.g., via bank.Provide(out IBankBranch) in the bank application) declared in the provider-independent connector class and implemented in the provider-dependent connector subclass.

The implementation of the managing aspects of a light connector as discussed so far is delightfully cheap. Implemented in C# it costs about 10 lines of code executed once on first access (see the implementation of the CPiC CBank in Bank.src\Bank-Interface\CBank.cs [5]) with a negligible increase for light, multi-part connectors due to loading, instantiating and anchoring several providers in a loop. All other operation calls connect functional components (client components and provider components) directly, but only for provider-independent operations declared in interfaces offered by the light connector. Thus light connectors completely separate communicating functional components with no run-time overhead.

6.2 Heavy Connectors

A connector is the place to factor out nonfunctional services from functional components. Typical services are logging, profiling, security checks, and checks of operation parameters and operation sequences (protocol checks). Adjacent functional components must have contracted these services. If not contracted, these services dare not disturb the normal flow of operations and data between components communicating across heavy connectors. Logging and profiling are services that fulfill these requirements from a functional point of view. However, the implementation of these services must be optimized for run-time performance in order to avoid timeouts that would change the behavior of a program in irregular ways. In any case, all calls between communicating components must be trapped in the connector. For this purpose Figure 7 extends the design shown in Figure 6 with proxy classes [6] around interfaces and template methods [6] in the provider-independent connector class (CPiC). Alone these wrapping techniques comprise the basic plumbing of every heavy connector. Syntactically, hooks and connected services are completely hidden in the connector and therefore invisible to functional components.

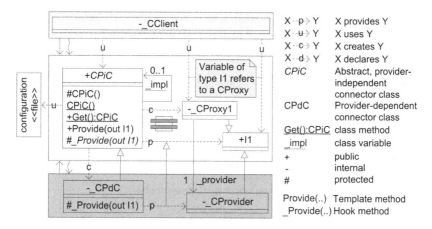

Fig. 7. Heavy, single-part connector

Remember that a connector approves two-way communication expressed by call interfaces and callback interfaces. Connectors wrap both kinds of interfaces in the same way but at different moments: call interfaces on the way out of an operation and callback interfaces on the way into an operation. The following excerpt from the implementation of a CPiC demonstrates this by wrapping the root object of a business process chain.

```
namespace Connector { // e.g. BankInterface in the bank example
  public abstract class CPiC { // e.g., CBank in the bank example
    public void Provide(out I1 p) { // the template method
      I1 q; // the service provider
      this._Provide(out q);
      p= new _CProxy1(q, this);
      // 1.) I1 is a call interface, so wrap the return value q of type I1 on the way out
      // 2.) tell the proxy to which connector it belongs (this is a parameter of the constructor)
    }
    protected abstract void _Provide(out I1 q);
    // the primitive operation of the template method to be implemented by CPdC
    ...
```

```
    } // CPiC
    public interface I1 { ... }
    internal class _CProxy1 : I1 { ... }
    ...
  } // Connector
```

This is the starting point for hooking any kind and number of nonfunctional services. We demonstrate this with a component service that checks objects passed as parameters of manipulating operations for being issued by the same functional component. On violation of this constraint, the connector throws an exception signaling an error in the communication protocol. The exception is part of the contract between the communicating components. Components that cast types of parameter objects to component-specific type implementations need this service to ensure their integrity. The bank example provides another illustrating rationale for the usefulness of this service: A bank manages only accounts issued by one of its bank branches.

```
namespace Connector {
  internal class _CProxy1 : I1 {
    internal _CProxy1(I1 provider, CPiC connector) {
      this._provider= provider;
      this._connector= connector;
      this._connector.Register(this);
    }
    public void Process(I2 p) { // operation defined in public interface I1
      if (!this._connector.IsRegistered(p))
        throw new CProtocolException("unknown parameter object");
      this._provider.Process(p);
    }
    public I2 Deliver() { // operation defined in public interface I1
      I2 p= this._provider.Deliver();
      return new _CProxy2(p, this._connector);
    }
    private I1 _provider;
    private CPiC _connector;
  } // _CProxy1
  internal class _CProxy2 : I2 {
    internal _CProxy2(I2 provider, CPiC connector) {
      this._provider= provider;
      this._connector= connector;
      this._connector.Register(this);
    }
    ...
  } // _CProxy2
  public abstract class CPiC {
    ... // as implemented in the code snippet above
    internal void Register(Object p) { ... }
    internal bool IsRegistered(Object p) { ... }
```

```
} // CPiC
} // Connector
```

A service for checking complete application sessions is a more advanced example. We sketch the design and implementation of this service by means of a generic data stream analyzer.

7 Connectors in Action

Connector/component architectures lend themselves for building families of programs out of common components and varying components. Indeed the first incarnation of this architecture-style arose from our work on post-mortem analysis of limited data streams (logs). The first version of a generic log analyzer consisted of only light, single-part connectors. We outline the application domain before we sketch the architectures of two different log analyzers.

In multithreaded and distributed environments, programs abound in components that interact in complex ways. These programs often exhibit fancy features and subtle errors during development and operation. Logs containing sequences of name/type/value log entries are commonly used for testing and debugging such programs. However, these logs vary in format and contents. Different stakeholders of a program, e.g., software developers, testers and operators, have different interests that are expressed by different analysis processes.

The separation of the analyzers into analysis-neutral and analysis-specific components is an essential prerequisite for a broad application scope. Analysis-neutral components

- merge, sort, filter and split logs,
- check logs against restrictions of hypothetical log patterns,
- trigger actions on matching log entries, and
- evaluate analysis steps statistically.

Analysis-specific components

- transform logs between external (proprietary) and internal (general) formats, and
- provide specific actions that can be triggered on matching log entries.

7.1 Generic Log Analyzer with a Connector-Based Tier Architecture

From a functional point of view, the outstanding characteristic of the first analyzer variant is its support of interactive analyses applied to rather unfamiliar logs and automatic analyses applied to rather familiar logs (see Figure 8).

From a nonfunctional point view, the outstanding characteristic is the arrangement of -the components in four tiers as Table 5 illustrates.

This variant is actually a productive analyzer used, e.g., to examine logs of a distributed program controlling a steel mill. To provide the big picture of the control program's dynamics, the analyzer must be capable of loading and transforming several logs of different types. Thus the analyzer uses a multi-part connector (A_3) for connecting several log adapters (SAD). It uses heavy connectors (A_3, A_5) for protocol checks to shield application-neutral components from external, application-specific components, i.e., log adapters (SAD) and action providers (ACT). Note that all components communicate exclusively through connectors, such as MEN surrounded by connectors A_2, A_4, A_5, A_6, A_7 and A_8. Furthermore, the analyzer uses a connector manager, but only for factoring out code common to all connectors. A post-mortem analyzer does not need dynamic configurability (dynamic loading and unloading of components) or online monitoring of its operations.

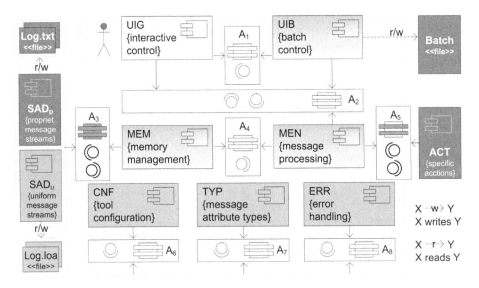

Fig. 8. Generic log analyzer with a connector-based tier architecture

Table 5. Generic tier log analyzer of common components and *variable* components

Tier		Components
1	User interface	UIG, UIB
2	Business logic	MEN, *ACT*
3	Data management	MEM
4	Data import / export	*SAD$_p$*, SAD$_u$

A crucial part of the analyzer's architecture is the interface between the business logic encapsulated in MEN and the components that accept user commands and depict results, namely UIG and UIB. Because of the complexity of this interface, we have experimented with a heavy connector for testing the communication protocol during the development and testing phases of the analyzer. The testing service applies the state pattern [6]. Figure 9 illustrates the design of those parts of the testing service that check the protocol of undoable user commands.

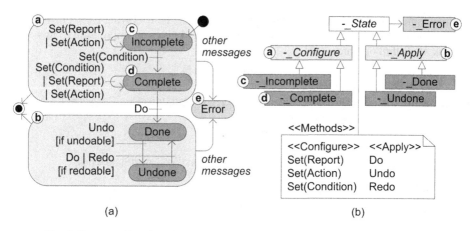

(a)   (b)

Fig. 9. State machine that checks the communication between UIG/UIB and MEN

The testing service is directly hooked into proxies of user commands in the form of objects belonging to concrete subclasses of class _State (see Figure 9b).

```
namespace MEN.Interface { // connector (A₂ in Figure 8)
  internal class _CCommandProxy : ICommand {
    internal _ CCommandProxy (ICommand cmd) { this._provider= cmd; }
    internal void Set(ICondition condition) {
      this._currentState.Set(this, true, condition);
      this._provider.Set(condition);
      this._currentState.Set(this, false, condition);
    }
    internal void Do() {
      this._currentState.Do(this, true);
      this._provider.Do();
      this._currentState.Do(this, false);
    }
    ...
    internal _State _currentState= _CIncomplete.Instance;
    internal _State _nextState= null;
    internal ICommand _provider;
  } // _ CCommandProxy
    ...
} // MEN.Interface
```

State objects check call sequences against the specified communication protocol. Whenever a client calls a method of a command object, the command's state is changed. If a message is valid in the current state (at the beginning of a state transition), an eavesdropping state object replaces itself in the command proxy with the object that represents the target of a state transition. If the current state is not valid, the target state is the error state. The state objects that a command proxy references one after another (in instance variable _currentState) reflect a communication course. When used this way for checking a communication protocol, state objects can be implemented as singletons [6] (_CIncomplete.Instance). The following excerpt from the class that models the starting state of a user command gives an impression of how the check algorithm operates.

```
namespace MEN.Interface { // connector (A₂ in Figure 8)
  internal class _CIncomplete : _CConfigure {
    internal void Set(_CCommandProxy cmdPrxy, bool startTransition, ICondition) {
      if (startTransition) // start state change
        cmdPrxy._nextState = _CComplete.Instance;
      else { // end state change
        cmdPrxy._currentState = cmdPrxy._nextState; cmdPrxy._nextState = null;
      }
    }
    internal void Do(_CCmdProxy cmdPrxy, bool)
    {
      cmdPrxy._currentState = _CError.Instance;
      throw new CProtocolException("execute incomplete cmd");
    }
    ...
  } // _CIncomplete
} // MEN.Interface
```

7.2 Generic Log Analyzer with a Connector-Based Pipeline Architecture

The second variant of a log analyzer is directed towards automatic analysis of data streams. From a nonfunctional point view, the outstanding characteristic is the arrangement of component objects in pipelines consisting of analysis commands alternating with data (message) transporting channels. Figure 10 shows the connector/component architecture of this analyzer variant.

In general, analyzers applying the pipeline architecture can be configured in two ways. (1) A developer can extend the set of command types (modeled by Action connector), such as sort and filter. To broaden the analysis scope, a developer could introduce a translator that unifies different date formats. (2) An end user configures application-specific analysis processes in the form of analyzer pipelines with the commands and channels available such as:

```
<pipeline>
 <dataprocess>
  <command id="1">
   <type>TransformX</type><parameters>....</parameters><outchannel>A</outchannel>
  </command>
  <command id="2">
   <type>Filter</type> ...  <inchannel>A</inchannel><outchannel>...</outchannel>
  </command>
  ...
 </dataprocess>
 <datatransport>
  <channel id="A"><type>RingBuffer</type> ... </channel>
  ...
```

```
</datatransport>
</pipeline>
```

The pipeline variant of the generic data stream analyzer is geared towards analysis of continuous data streams. Online monitoring is essential for analyses of continuous data streams. Therefore we extended the core parts of a pipeline, namely components Command, Channel and Data, with a Sensor component. The heavy, multi-part connector at the back end of the Sensor component (Monitor in Figure 10) provides a special service: it pushes sensed data about a pipeline's healthiness to all connected monitors concurrently. A connector manager can support continuous analyses of data streams well. An operator instructs the Action connector via the connector manager to dynamically load new application-specific command types. This provides a pipeline with much flexibility, provided that the component responsible for the configuration of a pipeline (the Pipeline Configurator in Figure 10) supports on-the-fly alterations of the pipeline layout.

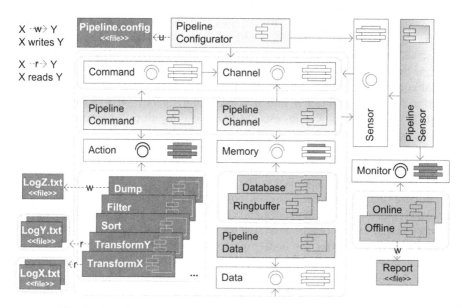

Fig. 10. Generic log analyzer with a connector-based pipeline architecture

8 Discussion and Consequences

Connectors as discussed in this article are special-purpose components that embody interfaces of functional components in the form of binary contracts. This allows functional components to focus on their core business without being distracted by details of component containers. Connectors improve programs in several respects. With connectors functional components can be

- specified and tested separately
- developed in several alternate or supplementary variants
- relieved of nonfunctional services like monitoring and protocol checking

Connectors can interpose nonfunctional services between functional components in a completely non-intrusive manner. This is achieved by means of a pattern language [3] that combines several design patterns [6], such as factory method, template method, proxy, strategy and state, and by encapsulating pattern implementations in separate deployment units. Two more design patterns lend themselves for queuing up several nonfunctional services in a connector: chain of responsibility and observer.

Connectors promote architecture-centric project development [12]. Due to their focus on rather stable component interfaces, connectors enable easier adaptation of programs to changing requirements. Program functionally can be delivered and updated incrementally. Multi-part connectors allow diversification (specialization) of functional components with regard to certain business characteristics (attributes). Diversification narrows the application scope of a single component, thus reducing its complexity. This simplifies its implementation, raises the domain-specific service level of a program, and improves the manageability of projects.

Connectors with integrated life-cycle management enable embedded components to be unloaded during run time. This requires heavy connectors with essentially two services: protocol checks and object reference checks. Proxy objects around each component object embed component and perform these checks silently. A connector manager links connectors so that component services can, e.g., be coordinated among several connectors. On basis of .NET, unloading a component requires it to be installed in a separate application domain [7], i.e., in a separate .NET process, which of course increases communication costs due to marshalling all calls between application domains.

Even demanding services such as parallelizing operation requests among several service-providing components can be included in heavy, multi-part connectors without distracting adjacent components. The implementation is straightforward for one-way control- and data-flows. However, non-blocking, concurrent operations that return data require advanced implementation techniques such as asymmetric connectors (connectors that offer different interfaces for client components and provider components) or futures (proxies for undetermined results of a concurrent computations which automatically block accesses until the values become determined). Related problems are outside our current work because so far they have not been relevant to our pilot project, the generic data stream analyzer.

Programs that do not need connectors offering advanced component services simply use light connectors. The implementation of the skeletal structure of a light connector is almost for free with regard to both development time and run-time efficiency while still providing the fundamental advantages of connectors, i.e., separate specification, testing and development of functional components. Variants of a generic data stream analyzer prove the practical feasibility of the connector/component architecture style. Life-cycle management of components coordinated by connectors that are linked to a central connector manager is a key issue of our current work. Linking connectors this way to a connector framework and enabling this framework to dynamically control connectors and the set of components further improves program adaptability and operability.

References

1. Cheesmann J., and Daniels J.: UML Components. Addison-Wesley, 2001
2. Clements P., Bachmann F., Bass L., Garlan D., Ivers J., Little R., Nord R., and Stafford J.: Documenting Software Architectures – Views and Beyond. Addison-Wesley, 2002
3. Cunnigham W.: Design Methodology for Object-Oriented Programming. Addendum to the Proceedings of OOPSLA'87, ACM SIGPLAN Notices, 23(5), 1987, 94-95
4. D'Souza D.F., and Wills A.C.: Objects, Components and Frameworks with UML: The Catalysis Approach. Addison-Wesley, 1999
5. Fröhlich, J.H., and Wolfinger, R.: .NET Profiling: Write Profilers with Ease Using High-Level Wrapper Classes. MSDN Magazine 21(5), 2006, 85-93
6. Gamma E., Helm R., Johnson R., and Vlissides J.: Design Patterns: Elements of Reusable Object-Oriented Software. Addison-Wesley, 1995
7. Gunnerson, E.: AppDomains and Dynamic Loading. http://msdn.microsoft.com/library/en-us/dncscol/html/csharp05162002.asp, 2002
8. Harrop, R., and Machacek, J.: Pro Spring. Apress, 2005
9. Löwy J.: Programming .NET Components. O'Reilly, 2003
10. Mehta M.R., Medvidovic N., and Phadke S.: Towards a Taxonomy of Connectors. ICSE 2000, Proceedings of the 22nd International Conference on Software Engineering, Limerick Ireland, June 4-11, 2000, 178-187
11. Object Management Group: Unified Modeling Language: Superstructure. Version 2.0, http://www.omg.org/cgi-bin/apps/doc?formal/05-07-04.pdf, 2005
12. Paulish D.J.: Architecture-Centric Software Project Management. Addison-Wesley, 2002
13. Shaw M., and Garlan D.: Software Architecture-Perspectives on an Emerging Discipline. Prentice-Hall, 1996
14. Skonnard, A.: SOA: More Integration, Less Renovation. MSDN Magazine 20 (2), 2005, 107-111
15. Szyperski C., Gruntz D., and Murer S.: Component Software: Beyond Object-Oriented Programming. Addison-Wesley, 2002
16. Wienholt N.: Maximizing .NET Performance. Apress, 2003

Automatic Object Colocation Based on Read Barriers[*]

Christian Wimmer and Hanspeter Mössenböck

Institute for System Software
Christian Doppler Laboratory for Automated Software Engineering
Johannes Kepler University Linz
Linz, Austria
{wimmer, moessenboeck}@ssw.jku.at

Abstract. *Object colocation* is an optimization that reduces memory access costs by grouping together heap objects so that their order in memory matches their access order in the program. We implemented this optimization for Sun Microsystems' Java HotSpot[TM] VM. The garbage collector, which moves objects during collection, assigns consecutive addresses to connected objects and handles them as atomic units.

We use read barriers inserted by the just-in-time compiler to detect the most frequently accessed fields per class. These "hot fields" are added to so-called *hot-field tables*, which are then used by the garbage collector for colocation decisions. Read barriers that are no longer needed are removed in order to reduce the overhead. Our analysis is performed automatically at run time and requires no actions on the side of the programmer.

We measured the impact of object colocation on the young and the old generation of the garbage collector, as well as the difference between dynamic colocation using read barriers and a static colocation strategy where colocation decisions are done at compile time. Our measurements show that object colocation works best for the young generation using a read-barrier-based approach.

1 Introduction

Object-oriented applications tend to allocate large numbers of objects that reference each other. If these objects are spread out randomly across the heap, their access is likely to produce a large number of cache misses. This can be avoided if objects that reference each other are located consecutively. Changing the object order so that related objects are next to each other is called *object colocation*. It is conveniently implemented as part of garbage collection where live objects are moved to new locations. In general, the access pattern of objects cannot be determined statically because it depends on how the program is used and which classes are dynamically loaded. Therefore the analysis of access patterns must be done at run time.

---

[*] This work was supported by Sun Microsystems, Inc.

D. Lightfoot and C. Szyperski (Eds.): JMLC 2006, LNCS 4228, pp. 326–345, 2006.
© Springer-Verlag Berlin Heidelberg 2006

Figure 1 shows an example of an object graph taken from the benchmark _227_mtrt of the SPECjvm98 benchmark suite [12]. Objects of the instance classes OctNode, Face and Point as well as of the array classes Face[] and Point[] form an access path that accounts for 70% of all reference field loads. The objects have a size of 16 to 40 bytes, so up to four objects fit in a typical cache line of 64 bytes. Colocating the objects reachable from an OctNode object therefore reduces the memory access costs when a Point of an OctNode is accessed.

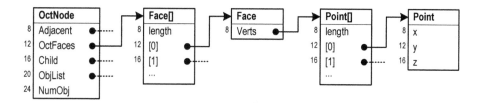

Fig. 1. Motivating example for object colocation

A static colocation strategy, e.g. one that always colocates the object referenced by the first field of another object, is only suitable for simple data structures. For objects with more than one reference field, the first field is typically not the most frequently accessed one. For example, the field OctFaces of OctNode objects has a 10 times higher access frequency than the first field Adjacent.

We implemented a dynamic analysis for Sun Microsystems' Java HotSpot™ VM that identifies frequently accessed "hot fields" on a per-class basis using read barriers. If a field counter reaches a certain threshold, the field is added to the *hot-field table* of the according class. The read barriers are inserted into the machine code by the just-in-time compiler. To minimize the run-time overhead, read barriers that are no longer needed are removed.

The garbage collector uses the hot-field tables to decide which objects should be colocated and assigns consecutive addresses to these objects when they are moved during collection. This goes beyond previous approaches that modify only the order in which a copying collector processes reference fields: We treat a set of colocated objects as an atomic unit and guarantee that it is not separated in a later garbage collection run. This paper contributes the following novel aspects:

- We implemented object colocation in a system with dynamic class loading and different garbage collection algorithms.
- We use read barriers inserted by the just-in-time compiler to get a dynamic field access profile with a negligible run-time impact.
- We evaluate our implementation and compare different configurations of the garbage collector. We also compare the dynamic read-barrier-based approach with a static colocation strategy.

2   System Overview

Figure 2 shows the structure of the Java HotSpot^{TM} VM with the relevant subsystems. We modified the default configuration for interactive desktop applications, called the *Client VM*, which uses a fast just-in-time compiler and a generational garbage collector with two generations. The Client VM is available for Intel's IA-32 and Sun's SPARC architecture, but object colocation is currently only implemented for the IA-32 architecture because the code patterns for the read barriers are platform dependent.

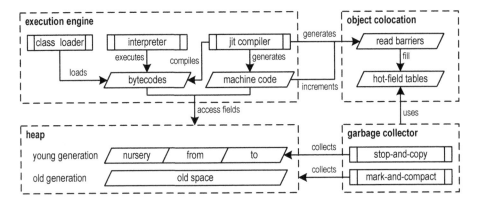

Fig. 2. System structure of the Java HotSpot^{TM} VM

Methods are loaded by the class loader and start being executed by the interpreter. Only frequently executed methods are compiled to minimize the compilation overhead. Both interpreted and compiled methods access objects in the heap, which is divided in a young and an old generation. The young generation is collected using a stop-and-copy algorithm that copies live objects between alternating spaces. A full collection of both generations is done using a mark-and-compact algorithm [7]. Section 4 presents details of these algorithms.

The garbage collector accesses the hot-field tables that store parent-child relationships of classes whose objects should be colocated. The access profile of fields is collected by read barriers, which are emitted by the just-in-time compiler into the generated machine code and increment a counter for each field load. Fields with high counter values are added to the hot-field tables. Section 3 presents the code patterns used for the read barriers.

A parent object and the child object referenced by the parent's most frequently accessed field are placed next to each other in the heap. If a second field also has high access counts, the corresponding child is placed consecutively to the first one, and so on. Objects referenced by fields with low access counts are not colocated because the optimization of rarely accessed data structures does not pay off.

Accesses to array elements are counted in the same way as field accesses. However, the colocation of objects referenced by array elements is more complicated because all elements are usually accessed with similar frequencies. As a pragmatic solution, we colocate only the object referenced by the first element.

2.1   Hot-Field Tables

A hot-field table is a VM-global data structure that is built for every class with hot fields. It is rooted in the data structure maintained by the VM for each loaded class, which already stores information such as super- and subclasses, fields and methods of the class.

Figure 3 shows a fragment of the hot-field tables for our example benchmark _227_mtrt. The table for a *parent class* stores a list of child entries for its hot fields. Each entry holds the offset (*off*) of the field as well as the field's declared *child class*. The order of the children is important: The first entry of the list is processed first by the garbage collector, so the first child is placed consecutively to the parent.

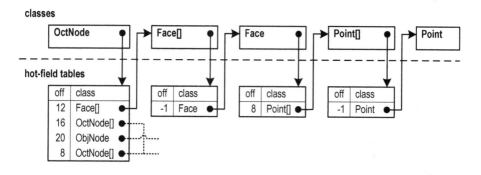

Fig. 3. Example of hot-field tables

The list contains only frequently accessed children because optimizing rarely accessed data structures only introduces overhead to the garbage collector. There is no table for the class Point because this class only stores scalar fields. Since array classes do not have a list of fields with according field offsets, the special marker value -1 is used as the offset in the table. It is replaced by the index of the first non-null array element when an actual object graph is constructed.

A hot-field table does not contain child entries for fields declared in a superclass. Instead, the superclass has its own hot-field table. Similarly, a table contains only direct children. Indirect children are only implicitly visible: the class of a child entry also has its own hot-field table. In our example, a Face[] object is a direct child of an OctNode object, while Face, Point[] and Point objects are indirect children of this OctNode. During garbage collection, all direct and indirect children of an object are captured by a separate table, which is discussed in Sect. 4.1.

2.2 Identifying Hot Field Loads

The hot-field tables are filled dynamically at run time. To achieve the best results, they should contain only the most frequently accessed fields in the correct order. We use read barriers emitted by the just-in-time compiler to detect hot field accesses. Section 3.1 presents the code that is inserted by the compiler. We count only field loads and not field stores because a high number of stores can indicate a frequently changing data structure where object colocation is difficult or even impossible. Furthermore, we ignore loads of scalar fields and emit read barriers only for loads of reference fields.

We also experimented with a static approach to object colocation where the just-in-time compiler fills the hot-field tables with all fields that are accessed in compiled methods instead of emitting read barriers. The resulting hot-field tables are bigger, but still useful because only a small fraction of methods is compiled and the tables do not contain fields that are accessed only by interpreted methods. In Sect. 5.2 we compare the two approaches.

3 Read Barriers

Read barriers allow dynamic measurements of an application's memory access behavior. A read barrier is a piece of machine code that is inserted after the code that performs the actual load of a reference field. We use two different kinds of read barriers:

- A *simple read barrier* identifies frequently accessed fields that are worth being optimized by object colocation.
- A *detailed read barrier* collects data for the analysis and verification of the optimizations. It counts the number of field accesses where a parent object and its child objects are colocated as well as in the same cache line.

Simple read barriers are a prerequisite of our object colocation and therefore always enabled. In contrast, detailed read barriers are currently not intended for production use. When analyzing the impact of object colocation, as presented in Sect. 5.2, detailed read barriers are enabled via a VM flag.

The read barriers are inserted by the just-in-time compiler because it has full information about fields: The instruction for a field access in the compiler's intermediate representation contains the class that declares the field (the parent class), the field offset and the type of the field (the child class). With this information, a unique counter is created for each field. When the same field is accessed in different methods, the same counter is used. The few field accesses that are performed by the interpreter are thus not counted, but this does not affect the precision of the measurements.

The address of a counter is statically known and can be directly emitted into the machine code. This allows a read barrier to be efficiently implemented as a single increment instruction, which nevertheless counts only accesses to a particular field of a class. Section 3.1 shows the details of the emitted instructions.

Our read barriers take compiler optimizations into account: The compiler eliminates a field load if the value of the field is known at compile time or if the load is redundant, and also does not emit a read barrier for these loads. So the resulting counter values can be lower than a naive counting using an instrumented interpreter, but they better reflect the actual behavior of an application.

3.1 Code Patterns for Read Barriers

Figure 4 shows the code pattern for a simple read barrier that increments a counter for a field load. Assume that the field at offset 8 is to be loaded, that the object's address is already in register **eax**, and that the counter is located at the fixed address 5000h. The IA-32 instruction set allows instructions to operate on memory operands [6], so it is not necessary to load the counter value into a register. Only a single instruction is emitted for the increment.

```
    ...                         // eax: base address of object
    mov  ebx, ptr [eax+8]       // access field at offset 8
    inc  ptr [5000h]            // increment counter
    ...                         // ebx: result of field load
```

Fig. 4. Code pattern for a simple read barrier

A simple read barrier is sufficient for identifying hot fields, but for the evaluation of object colocation we are also interested in statistical data about colocated objects and the cache behavior. Figure 5 shows the code pattern for a detailed read barrier that checks if a parent object and a child object are located in the same cache line.

```
          ...                          // eax: base address of object
          mov  ebx, ptr [eax+8]        // access field at offset 8
          dec  ptr [4000h]             // decrement slowcase counter
          jle  slowcase                // slowcase if counter reaches 0
continue: ...                          // ebx: result of field load

slowcase: mov  ptr [4000h], 1000       // reset slowcase counter
          inc  ptr [5000h]             // increment total counter
          lea  esi, ptr [eax+8]        // compute address of field
          xor  esi, ebx                // check if address and value of
          and  esi, 0FFFFFFC0h         //   field are in same cache line
          jne  skip_inc
          inc  ptr [5004h]             // increment cache line counter
skip_inc: ...                          // check for object colocation
          jmp  continue
```

Fig. 5. Code pattern for a detailed read barrier

Executing the complete sequence of more than 15 instructions for each field load would be too expensive. Therefore, the code is placed in a *slow case* [4] that collects data only for every 1000th field load. A global counter is decremented at each field load. Assume that the address of this counter is 4000h. When the counter reaches 0, the slow case is executed.

The slow case resets the counter to 1000 and increments a *total counter* at the address 5000h. The address of the referencing field is loaded to esi, and the address of the referenced object is already in ebx. These addresses are in the same cache line with a size of 64 bytes if all but their lower 6 bits are identical, which is checked using the xor and and instructions. In this case the *cache line counter* at the address 5004h is incremented. Dividing the cache line counter by the total counter yields the percentage of objects that are in the same cache line.

The slow case also computes a *colocation counter* that counts the number of cases in which the parent object and its child are colocated. This part of the code has been omitted from Fig. 5 because it is similar to the code for computing the cache line counter. If the base address of the parent object (which is in eax) plus the size of the object (which is retrieved via the class pointer stored in the object's header) equals the address of the child object (which is in ebx), the objects are colocated and the counter is incremented.

3.2   Processing of Counters

When the counter of a field has exceeded a certain threshold at the time of the next garbage collection, the field is recorded in the hot-field table of the parent class. The time between two garbage collections is used as the measurement interval. We want to record fields that are accessed frequently in this period, and to filter out the large number of fields that are accessed infrequently. As a heuristic, a field is added to the hot-field table if it accounts for more than 6% of all field loads in the last period.

The heuristic fills the tables iteratively: At the first garbage collection, fields with an exceptionally high access frequency (and therefore a high percentage) are added to the hot-field tables. Their read barrier counters are then invalidated and ignored when computing the percentages at the second garbage collection, so the next fields with still a high access frequency are added. This is repeated until a stable state is reached where most fields have similar access frequencies, so no single one is above 6%.

Incrementing a counter for each field load involves some run-time overhead. Therefore, read barriers are removed as soon as they are no longer needed, i.e. after the corresponding field was added to the hot-field table or if the access count was low for a long time. This is done by recompiling all methods that increment the read barrier's counter. The machine code of those methods is marked so that the compiler is invoked when the method is called the next time. Because read barriers whose counters were invalidated are ignored during compilation, the new code does not contain these read barriers anymore.

4   Modifications of Garbage Collection Algorithms

The Java HotSpot^{TM} VM uses a generational garbage collection system with different collection algorithms. The default configuration uses two generations with a *stop-and-copy* algorithm for the young generation and a *mark-and-compact* algorithm for a full collection of both generations.

When the young generation is collected, live objects are copied between two alternating spaces, called the *from-space* and the *to-space*. After several copying cycles, an object is promoted to the old generation. New objects are allocated in a separate *nursery space* of the young generation that is treated as a part of the from-space during collection.

When the old generation is full, the entire heap is collected by a mark-and-compact algorithm. All live objects are marked and then moved towards the beginning of the heap in order to eliminate gaps between live objects. This takes more time than a collection of the young generation, but it is only necessary if no more space is available for the promotion of young objects.

We integrated our object colocation algorithm into both algorithms and allow switching it on and off independently. This allows us to evaluate the benefits of the optimization in both generations. However, enabling object colocation for the young generation also affects the old generation: Groups of colocated objects are promoted together, so the order of objects in the old generation is also partly optimized. Because the unmodified mark-and-compact algorithm does not change the object order, the optimized order is preserved.

4.1   Colocation Tables

The hot-field tables introduced in Sect. 2.1 are easy to maintain because they store only direct children. However, it is expensive to detect all direct and indirect children that should be colocated to a particular parent object. To limit the overhead during garbage collection, an additional *colocation table* is created from the hot-field table for each class. Figure 6 shows the colocation tables for the running example of _227_mtrt.

Each table contains a flat list of all fields that should be colocated for a given class. It is created once before garbage collection, and filled with objects multiple times during garbage collection. The first entry stores the parent object for which the table is filled; all other entries are direct or indirect children of this object. The columns contain the following information:

- Field offset (*off*): The offset of the field whose value is stored in this entry, or -1 as a marker for arrays.
- Parent entry (*par*): The index of this object's immediate parent in the same table. It is 0 for direct children and greater than 0 for indirect children of the parent object for which the table is filled.
- Object (*obj*): The actual object that is referenced by this field. It is filled in during garbage collection.

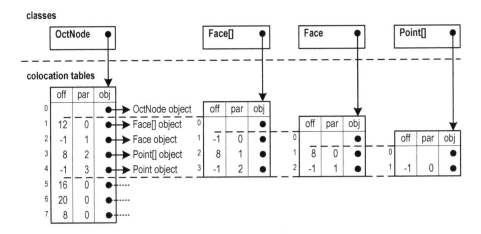

Fig. 6. Example of colocation tables used during garbage collection

In our example, all information required for the colocation of direct and in-direct children of an OctNode object is contained in the colocation table for OctNode: The entries with the indices 1, 5, 6 and 7 denote fields that reference direct children of the OctNode object with the index 0. The entries 2, 3 and 4 denote indirect children of the OctNode object as shown in Fig. 1. They are direct children of the entries 1, 2 and 3, respectively.

If a Face[] object is not colocated to an OctNode object, we need the coloca-tion table of Face[]. This table is smaller because it contains only the objects that are colocatable to a Face[] object. Similarly, there are colocation tables for the classes Face and Point[]. These tables contain a part of the information of the bigger tables, indicated by the dashed lines in Fig. 6.

The algorithm GETCHILDREN of Fig. 7 is used during garbage collection to fill a colocation table with the children of a specific parent: After the parent object has been stored in the first entry, all its children are iterated. Because the immediate parent of a child is always located before this child, $c.par$ has already been added to the table before c and the field with the offset $c.off$ of the object $c.par.obj$ can be accessed.

```
GETCHILDREN(obj)
    tab = colocation table for class of obj
    if tab not found then
        return empty table

    tab[0].obj = obj                        // initialize first entry, which holds the parent
    for i = 1 to tab.length - 1 do          // iterate all entries except the first
        c = tab[i]                          // get the entry of the current child
        c.obj = c.par.obj.fieldAt(c.off)    // access the field at the specified offset

    return tab
```

Fig. 7. Algorithm for filling a colocation table during garbage collection

4.2   Stop-and-Copy Collection of the Young Generation

Figure 8 shows the basic STOPANDCOPY algorithm. First, all objects referenced by root pointers are copied from the from-space to the to-space using COPYOB-JECT. Allocating memory in the to-space requires only an increment of the *end* pointer. Each object of the from-space that has been copied stores a forwarding pointer to its new location. All objects referenced by copied objects are also alive and must therefore be copied as well. The algorithm uses the to-space as a queue and scans all copied objects in sequential order. The forwarding pointer is used to prevent copying an object twice.

```
STOPANDCOPY                              COPYOBJECT(obj)
    toSpace.end = toSpace.begin              if obj is forwarded then
    for each root pointer r do                   return obj.forwardee
        r = COPYOBJECT(r)
                                             newObj = toSpace.end
    obj = toSpace.begin                      toSpace.end += obj.size
    while obj < toSpace.end do               memmove(obj, newObj, obj.size)
        for each reference r in obj do       obj.forwardee = newObj
            r = COPYOBJECT(r)                 return newObj
        obj += obj.size
```

Fig. 8. Stop-and-copy algorithm used for collection of the young generation

This breath-first copying scheme is simple and efficient, but it leads to a random order of copied objects in the to-space. An object is copied when the first reference to it is scanned. A depth-first copying scheme, where all referenced objects are copied immediately after the object itself, would result in a better object order, but it would require an explicit stack of objects to be scanned.

We extended the breath-first copying so that it processes groups of objects instead of individual objects. When a parent object has to be copied, the colocation table is filled using the algorithm GETCHILDREN. All child objects in the table are copied together with their parent object. The necessary memory for the object group is allocated at once. Figure 9 shows the modified algorithm for COPYOBJECT. The handling of child objects that are already in the old generation has been omitted from the algorithm; such children are simply ignored.

The root pointers are processed in an arbitrary order. If both the parent object and a child object are referenced by a root pointer, it can happen that the child object is copied before the parent. Because an object must not be copied twice, the two objects cannot be colocated in this garbage collection run. This is checked in the algorithm before colocating a child.

To avoid children that are copied before their parent, objects that were once detected to be colocation children are tagged with a dedicated bit in the object header, referred to as *isColocationChild* in the algorithm. The copying of tagged objects is delayed until the parent object is processed, so the colocation succeeds. Because all children keep the tag for their entire lifetime, objects are guaranteed to stay colocated even if new root pointers to children are introduced.

```
COPYOBJECT(obj)
    if obj is forwarded then
        return obj.forwardee              // prevent copying an object twice
    if obj.isColocationChild then
        return fixupMarker        // delay copying; a fixup is done when obj is copied later

    tab = GETCHILDREN(obj)                // get children of obj (may return empty table)
    allocSize = obj.size                  // computation of total allocation size
    for i = 1 to tab.length - 1 do
        tab[i].obj.isColocationChild = true   // tagging of object as colocation child
        if tab[i].obj is not forwarded then
            allocSize += tab[i].obj.size  // only non-forwarded objects can be colocated

    newObj = toSpace.end                  // allocate memory for parent and all children
    toSpace.end += allocSize

    memmove(obj, newObj, obj.size)        // copy and forward parent object
    obj.forwardee = newObj
    offset = obj.size
    for i = 1 to tab.length - 1 do        // copy and forward all children
        if tab[i].obj is not forwarded then
            memmove(tab[i].obj, newObj + offset, tab[i].obj.size)
            tab[i].obj.forwardee = newObj + offset
            offset += tab[i].obj.size

    return newObj
```

Fig. 9. Object colocation for the stop-and-copy algorithm

When the copying of a child object is delayed, the references to the child require a later fixup. `CopyObject` returns a fixup marker and the reference is added to a list. When the scan of the to-space is completed, these references are updated to the forwarding pointer of the child object that was set during the colocated copying. In rare cases it can happen that the parent object died, but the child object is still alive because another object holds a reference to the child. Similarly, a field update of the parent object can install a new child object and leave the old one without a parent. Such objects are still uncopied in the fixup phase, so they are copied before the fixup and the colocation bit is cleared.

4.3 Mark-and-Compact Collection of the Old Generation

The stop-and-copy collection of the young generation also affects the old generation because colocated objects are promoted together and are therefore already partly colocated in the old generation. However, a collection of the young generation can only colocate a group of objects if all members of this group are still in the young generation. If a child has already been promoted, it cannot be colocated. In contrast, a collection of the entire heap can colocate all objects.

The mark-and-compact algorithm processes all live objects of the old and the young generation. Because it places all objects contiguously into the old generation, this is called a collection of the old generation. It requires four phases:

1. *Mark live objects*: The heap is traversed recursively starting with the root pointers to mark all live objects.
2. *Compute new addresses*: In a linear walk through the heap each object is assigned a new address, which is stored in the object's forwarding pointer. Because gaps between live objects are removed, objects move towards the beginning of the heap.
3. *Adjust pointers*: All root pointers and inner pointers of objects are updated to point to the new addresses stored in the forwarding pointers of the referenced objects.
4. *Move objects*: In another linear walk through the heap the objects are copied to their new locations. Because objects move only towards the beginning of the heap, the memory of the new location can be overwritten without precautions.

The basic mark-and-compact algorithm preserves the order of objects. This simplifies object colocation because the correct order needs to be established only once. We extended the basic algorithm by modifying the phases 1, 2 and 4 in the following way:

In phase 1, all parents and children are detected. For each object whose class has a colocation table, we use GETCHILDREN (see Fig. 7) to fill the table with the actual children of this object. The children are then tagged as in the stop-and-copy algorithm.

When a parent object is processed in phase 2, GETCHILDREN must be called again because there is only one colocation table per class. All children of this object get consecutive addresses assigned. This may change the order of objects in the heap. With the help of the tags that are set in phase 1, the processing of a child is delayed when it would be processed before its parent. So a child object never gets a new address assigned before its parent. As a result, child objects can now move also towards the end of the heap.

Since objects can now also move towards the end of the heap, phase 4 must take precautions to rescue such objects. They are first copied into a scratch area and then copied back to their final location after all other objects were processed. However, this is only necessary for a small number of objects because at the next collection the object order is already correct, so no reordering and no rescuing is necessary.

5   Evaluation

We integrated our object colocation algorithm in the Java HotSpot^{TM} VM of Sun Microsystems, using a development snapshot of the upcoming Java SE 6 called Mustang [14]. Currently, we work with the Mustang build 66 from January 2006. Compared with the current JDK 5.0, the VM of this build includes optimizations such as a new object locking scheme called biased locking, and an improved just-in-time compiler using an intermediate representation in static single assignment form and a linear scan register allocator [16].

All measurements were performed on an Intel Pentium D processor 830 with two cores running at 3.0 GHz. Each core has a separate L1 data cache of 16 KByte and an L2-cache of 1 MByte. The cache line size is 64 bytes for both caches. The main memory of 2 GByte DDR2 RAM is shared by the two cores. Microsoft Windows XP Professional was used as the operating system. Both garbage collection algorithms are neither parallel nor concurrent. Therefore, the second core of the processor is idle during garbage collection. We evaluated our work with the SPECjbb2005 benchmark [13] and the SPECjvm98 benchmark suite [12].

The SPECjbb2005 benchmark[1] emulates a client/server application. The resulting metric is the average number of transactions per second executed on a memory-resident database. Since the default maximum heap size of the HotSpot^{TM} VM is too small for this benchmark, the heap was enlarged to 512 MByte via a VM flag.

The SPECjvm98 benchmark suite[2] consists of seven benchmarks derived from real-world applications, which cover a broad range of scenarios where Java applications are deployed. They are executed repeatedly until there is no significant change in the execution time any more. The speedup of the fastest run compared to a reference platform is reported as the metric for each benchmark, and the geometric mean of all metrics is computed.

Scientific applications usually operate on large arrays, so no performance gain can be expected from object colocation. However, there should also be no slowdown due to read barriers or additional garbage collection overhead. In order to verify this, we performed all measurements of the next sections also for SciMark 2.0 [11], a benchmark for scientific applications that executes several numerical kernels. All configurations of read barriers and object colocation showed the same results.

5.1   Read Barriers

Read barriers impose a run-time overhead because additional code must be executed for each field load. Table 1 compares the baseline version where all our changes are disabled, simple read barriers as described in Sect. 3.1 that are always enabled, and simple read barriers that are removed when the counters reach the threshold as described in Sect. 3.2. Object colocation was disabled for all measurements, so no optimizations were performed.

Counting all field loads leads to an average overhead of 30%, with a maximum slowdown of nearly 80% for the field-access-intensive benchmark _227_mtrt. This shows that such a naive read barrier is unfeasible, so we have to remove unnecessary read barriers. When read barriers are removed, the slowdown is reasonably small, with an average of 1%.

---

[1] All SPECjbb2005 results were valid runs according to the run rules. The measurements were performed with one JVM instance.

[2] All SPECjvm98 results are not approved metrics, but adhere to the run rules for research use. The input size 100 was used for all measurements.

Table 1. Benchmark results for read barriers (higher is better)

	baseline	read barriers always enabled		read barriers with removal	
SPECjvm98 mean	216.6	150.2	-30.6%	214.4	-1.0%
_227_mtrt	591.9	119.6	-79.8%	583.1	-1.5%
_202_jess	267.2	222.1	-16.9%	260.9	-2.4%
_201_compress	217.7	165.1	-24.1%	219.3	0,7%
_209_db	56.7	53.1	-6.4%	56.7	0.1%
_222_mpegaudio	389.5	323.3	-17.0%	386.8	-0.7%
_228_jack	234.9	208.7	-11.1%	232.1	-1.2%
_213_javac	125.2	110.0	-12.1%	122.8	-1.9%
SPECjbb2005	14,292	9,179	-35.8%	14,152	-1.0%

The maximum slowdown is 2.4% for _202_jess. This benchmark loads a large number of fields with a low frequency, so the corresponding read barriers are not removed because the recompilation overhead would be too high. The slight speedup of some benchmarks is the result of improved optimizations during the recompilation, e.g. a better inlining of methods.

The recompilation of methods increases the total number of method compilations by 23.4% (from 1005 to 1240) for SPECjvm98 and by 48.5% (from 540 to 802) for SPECjbb2005. The additional compilation time has no significant impact on the overall performance, especially for long-running applications.

5.2 Access Counts of Colocated Fields

Object colocation can be performed independently for the young and for the old generation. This allows us to experiment with different scenarios: We measured the impact of object colocation when it is performed only for the young generation, only for the old generation, or for both generations. We also experimented with different strategies for filling the hot-field tables and compared our read-barrier-based approach with a static colocation strategy: Instead of emitting read barriers, the just-in-time compiler adds all fields accessed in compiled code directly to the hot-field tables.

To assess the quality of our object colocation, we counted the number of field accesses where the parent and the child object were colocated and where they were in the same cache line. We use this as an approximation of the memory access costs: When a reference field is loaded, the result of the load is typically used for another field load in the near future. So it is beneficial if the address of a loaded field and the value of the field are in the same cache line. In that case, the subsequent load accesses a memory location that has already been put into the cache during the first load.

Table 2 shows the number of fields and array elements that were loaded for the benchmarks as well as the percentages of the loads that were colocated and that were in the same cache line. The numbers were collected using the detailed read barriers presented in Sect. 3.1. With object colocation the percentages are

Table 2. Field loads of colocated objects and objects in same cache line

	num. loads (x 1,000)	baseline		read barriers young gen.		read barriers old gen.		read barriers both gen.		static young gen.	
		coloc.	cache	coloc.	cache	coloc.	cache	coloc.	cache	coloc.	cache
SPECjvm98 mean	2,078,900	7%	6%	21%	17%	18%	13%	21%	16%	20%	17%
_227_mtrt	167,000	7%	5%	59%	42%	58%	41%	59%	42%	52%	37%
_202_jess	171,100	19%	13%	39%	29%	19%	13%	39%	29%	41%	31%
_201_compress	774,900	4%	6%	4%	6%	4%	6%	4%	6%	4%	6%
_209_db	356,800	0%	0%	40%	32%	37%	29%	43%	34%	41%	32%
_222_mpegaudio	436,500	9%	5%	9%	5%	9%	5%	9%	5%	9%	5%
_228_jack	61,400	22%	19%	29%	25%	26%	22%	32%	27%	36%	28%
_213_javac	111,200	9%	7%	24%	20%	15%	13%	26%	19%	24%	17%
SPECjbb2005	—	2%	3%	33%	21%	23%	16%	33%	21%	32%	21%

significantly higher for most benchmarks. This shows that object colocation improves both the locality of objects and the cache behavior. The detailed read barriers collect data only for every 1000th field load, so all results are approximate numbers. Because of the large number of loads they are nevertheless significant.

SPECjbb2005 uses a large memory-resident database implemented as trees of objects. Object colocation succeeds to optimize these trees and increases the percentage of colocated objects from 2% to 33%. Performing object colocation in the young generation outperforms object colocation in the old generation because the benchmark accesses a high number of objects located in the young generation. Enabling object colocation in both generations does not improve the numbers further. The number of field loads is not reported because the benchmark does not execute a fixed workload, but runs for a fixed time.

For the benchmark _227_mtrt the percentage of colocated objects increases from 7% to nearly 60%. Table 3 lists the most frequently accessed fields of the benchmark. Four fields form the hot access path and account for 70% of all field loads. These are the fields that were used in the running example of this paper. Object colocation succeeds to colocate a high percentage of them. For the array class `Face[]`, only 18% (about 1/6) of the array accesses load a colocated element because all six elements are accessed with the same frequency and only the first element is colocated.

All three garbage collection configurations basically show the same results. The static colocation strategy leads to the same results as the dynamic strategy for classes with only one reference field. However, it fails to colocate the field `OctNode.OctFaces` because it is not the first one.

The seven fields listed in Table 3 for the benchmark _209_db account for 99.9% of all field loads. In the hot path a `Vector` of `String`s that is stored in an `Entry` of a `Database` is accessed. Colocation is possible for three of the seven fields. The other four fields are typical examples where object colocation is not possible: large arrays (`Entry[]`), frequently changing fields (`Database.index`), fields or arrays of the type `Object` or `Object[]`, and fields of short-living temporary objects such as iterators (`Vector$1.this$0`).

Table 3. Frequently accessed fields of _227_mtrt and _209_db

	num. loads (x 1,000)	baseline		read barriers young gen.		read barriers old gen.		read barriers both gen.		static young gen.	
		coloc.	cache	coloc.	cache	coloc.	cache	coloc.	cache	coloc.	cache
_227_mtrt	167,000	7%	5%	59%	42%	58%	41%	59%	42%	52%	37%
Face[]	33,200	0%	0%	18%	9%	17%	9%	18%	6%	18%	9%
Face.Verts	32,900	2%	2%	100%	88%	100%	87%	100%	88%	100%	89%
Point[]	32,600	0%	0%	99%	61%	98%	61%	99%	61%	99%	62%
OctNode.OctFaces	15,700	0%	0%	93%	58%	91%	56%	92%	60%	0%	0%
_209_db	356,800	0%	0%	40%	32%	37%	29%	43%	34%	41%	32%
Entry[]	66,400	0%	0%	0%	0%	0%	0%	0%	0%	0%	0%
Database.index	61,100	0%	0%	0%	0%	0%	0%	0%	0%	0%	0%
Vector.elementData	54,900	0%	0%	87%	74%	89%	68%	100%	80%	88%	74%
Object[]	54,500	0%	0%	0%	0%	0%	0%	0%	0%	0%	0%
Entry.items	51,100	0%	0%	100%	79%	88%	74%	100%	84%	100%	79%
String.value	45,500	0%	0%	100%	75%	87%	65%	100%	75%	100%	75%
Vector$1.this$0	23,200	0%	0%	0%	0%	0%	0%	0%	0%	0%	0%

For _202_jess and _213_javac, performing object colocation in the young generation outperforms object colocation of the old generation. The collection of the old generation comes too late because the benchmarks primarily access objects in the young generation. Enabling object colocation in both generations leads to the same results as performing colocation only in the young generation.

Object colocation cannot optimize applications that require no garbage collection. Both _201_compress and _222_mpegaudio operate on a small, fixed set of objects that are allocated at the beginning of the execution, so the percentages are low for all configurations.

Each benchmark is executed once to collect the counters, so this run also includes the construction of the hot-field tables. For the benchmark _228_jack the static colocation strategy has an advantage because the tables are filled when methods are compiled and not when counters overflow. This is early enough to optimize a larger data structure that is created at startup. However, both strategies show the same results starting with the second execution of the benchmark.

5.3   Run-Time Impact of Object Colocation

Table 4 shows the run-time results of the various object colocation scenarios. Some benchmarks are very sensitive to garbage collection time. Because object colocation requires additional operations for each object copied during garbage collection, the improved cache behavior is countervailed by the garbage collection overhead. The old generation contains much more objects than the young generation, so the overhead is higher when performing object colocation for the old generation. However, there is still potential for optimizing the garbage collection algorithms so that the slowdown for these benchmarks can probably be eliminated in the future.

Table 4. Benchmark results for object colocation (higher is better)

	baseline	read barriers young gen.		read barriers old gen.		read barriers both gen.		static young gen.	
SPECjvm98 mean	216.6	230.0	+6.2%	224.3	+3.6%	227.8	+5.2%	229.5	+6.0%
_227_mtrt	591.9	620.0	+4.8%	582.9	-1.5%	613.3	+3.6%	613.3	+3.6%
_202_jess	267.2	264.4	-1.1%	259.5	-2.9%	263.7	-1.3%	267.3	+0.0%
_201_compress	217.7	217.4	-0.1%	214.6	-1.4%	214.5	-1.5%	217.4	-0.1%
_209_db	56.7	86.6	+52.8%	83.5	+47.2%	86.8	+53.1%	86.7	+53.0%
_222_mpegaudio	389.5	386.8	-0.7%	387.9	-0.4%	388.5	-0.3%	388.9	-0.1%
_228_jack	234.9	230.7	-1.8%	230.7	-1.8%	227.6	-3.1%	229.3	-2.4%
_213_javac	125.2	123.5	-1.3%	117.8	-6.0%	119.6	-4.5%	121.9	-2.7%
SPECjbb2005	14,292	14,599	+2.1%	14,260	-0.2%	14,512	+1.5%	14,394	+0.7%

The benchmark _209_db benefits most from object colocation. The speedup of more than 50% shows that the cache behavior has a major influence on the total performance of the application. _227_mtrt also shows a significant speedup in most scenarios. As shown in Table 3, both benchmarks have a hot path of frequently accessed fields that can be optimized.

SPECjbb2005 shows a speedup of 2.1%, which proves that object colocation also succeeds to optimize a large heap of a long-running application. The overhead of object colocation is influenced by the number of children that are colocated to a parent. Because the static colocation strategy identifies much more children than the dynamic read-barrier-based approach, the dynamic approach has a lower overhead and outperforms the static one.

For SPECjbb2005, the percentages of colocated objects (see Table 2) are similar for the dynamic and the static approach, but the speedup (see Table 4) is 2.1% for the dynamic approach and 0.7% for the static approach. Using the static approach, there are 113 hot-field tables, with a maximum of 23 hot children for the table of a class with 25 reference fields. In the dynamic approach, there are only 38 tables with a maximum of 4 hot children per table. This shows that the static colocation strategy does not scale well for larger applications, so the read-barrier-based approach is inevitable.

5.4   Summary

All in all, the results show that the read-barrier-based object colocation of the young generation leads to the best results. Optimizing only the old generation finds less colocatable objects because the old generation is collected infrequently. Optimizing both generations increases the overhead, but does not improve the heap layout significantly because colocated objects are promoted and the old generation preserves this optimized object order.

The static colocation strategy does not yield information about the most frequently accessed fields. Therefore, too many parent-child relationships are added to the tables, which increases the garbage collection overhead. The impact is evident especially for larger applications such as SPECjbb2005.

6   Future Work

The evaluation showed that our algorithm improves the object order of the heap, but the speedup of some benchmarks is lower than one would expect. Therefore, we plan to extend our object colocation algorithm to do *object inlining*, which will eliminate the field loads for colocated objects and lead to an additional speedup. The counters collected by the detailed read barriers show that for many fields the referenced objects can always be colocated. In such cases, the address of a child object needs not be read from a field, but can be computed by adding a fixed offset to the address of the parent object.

Eliminating field loads can be implemented easily in the just-in-time compiler. However, a safe execution of the optimized code requires additional effort: While failing to colocate a small number of objects of a class is acceptable for object colocation because it does not have a negative impact on the cache behavior, object inlining requires that *all* objects of a class are colocated.

To guarantee this, object allocation must be modified so that colocated objects are already allocated together. Currently, objects are only colocated after the first garbage collection run. Object inlining also requires that field stores which change a parent-child relationship do not happen. Because fields can also be changed via reflection or by native code using the Java Native Interface, these subsystems must be instrumented to detect such cases. Recent research on optimizations in the Java HotSpot^{TM} VM showed that the safe execution of aggressively optimized code requires extensive support of the run-time system [9].

7   Related Work

Huang et al. describe a system similar to ours called *online object reordering*, implemented for the Jikes RVM [5]. They use the adaptive compilation system of Jikes that periodically records the currently executed methods. Hot fields accessed in these methods are traversed first in their copying garbage collector and thus reordered. The decision which field of a method is hot is based on a static analysis of the method, so it is not as precise as our dynamic numbers obtained from the read barriers. By using the existing interrupts of Jikes, their analysis has a low run-time overhead of 2% to 3%.

Chilimbi et al. use generational garbage collection for *cache-conscious data placement* [3] and present results for the object-oriented programming language Cecil. They use a profiling technique similar to read barriers to construct an object affinity graph that guides a copying garbage collector and report an overhead of about 6% for the profiling. They do not distinguish different fields within the same object, which suffices only for small objects and does not allow colocating the most frequently accessed field of bigger objects.

Lhoták et al. compare different algorithms for *object inlining* and report how many field accesses they optimize [10]. All described algorithms are implemented in static compilers and do not handle dynamic class loading. However, the dynamic class loading of the Java HotSpot^{TM} VM asks for algorithms that do not require a global data flow analysis.

The algorithm for *object combining* by Veldema et al. puts objects together that have the same lifetime [15]. It is more aggressive than object inlining because it also optimizes unrelated objects if they have the same lifetime. This allows the garbage collector to free multiple objects together. Elimination of pointer accesses is performed separately by the compiler. However, the focus is on reducing the overhead of memory allocation and deallocation. This is beneficial for their system because it uses a mark-and-sweep garbage collector where the costs of allocation and deallocation are higher.

Escape analysis is another optimization that reduces the overhead of memory accesses. It detects objects that can be eliminated or allocated on the method stack. It is an orthogonal optimization to object colocation because it optimizes short-living temporary objects, whereas object colocation optimizes long-living data structures. Kotzmann implemented a new escape analysis algorithm for the Java HotSpot^{TM} VM [8]. It is fast enough for a just-in-time compiler and handles all aspects of dynamic class loading. When a class is loaded that lets a previously optimized object escape its scope, all affected methods are deoptimized and recompiled using the same mechanism we use for removing read barriers.

Blackburn et al. measured the dynamic impact of various read and write barriers on different platforms [2]. They focused on barriers that are necessary for current garbage collection algorithms, so a barrier similar to ours that counts field accesses is not measured. A complex conditional read barrier shows an average slowdown of 16% on a Pentium 4 processor, with a maximum slowdown of over 30%.

Arnold et al. presented a general framework for instrumentation sampling to reduce the cost of instrumented code [1]. The framework dynamically switches between the original uninstrumented code and the instrumented code in a fine-grained manner. Instrumentation can be performed continuously with a reported overhead of about 6%. This approach is more sophisticated than our detailed read barriers that always collects data for every 1000th field load, but doubles the code size.

8   Conclusions

We presented an object colocation algorithm implemented for the garbage collector of the Java HotSpot^{TM} VM. The most frequently loaded fields and thus the most promising objects to be colocated are identified using read barriers that are inserted into the machine code by the just-in-time compiler. The read barriers yield precise information about the field access profile with a low run-time overhead of just 1%.

In a generational garbage collection system, object colocation can be performed independently for each generation. Our measurements show that it is sufficient to optimize the young generation. When colocated objects are promoted, they remain colocated in the old generation. A comparison with a static colocation strategy shows that the overhead of optimizing infrequently accessed objects is higher than the benefit.

Acknowledgments

We would like to thank the Java HotSpot^{TM} compiler team at Sun Microsystems, especially Kenneth Russell, Thomas Rodriguez and David Cox, for their persistent support, for contributing many ideas and for helpful comments on all parts of the Java HotSpot^{TM} Virtual Machine.

References

1. Arnold, M., Ryder, B.G.: A framework for reducing the cost of instrumented code. In: Proceedings of the ACM SIGPLAN 2001 conference on Programming language design and implementation, ACM Press (2001) 168–179
2. Blackburn, S.M., Hosking, A.L.: Barriers: friend or foe? In: Proceedings of the 4th international symposium on Memory management, ACM Press (2004) 143–151
3. Chilimbi, T.M., Larus, J.R.: Using generational garbage collection to implement cache-conscious data placement. In: Proceedings of the 1st international symposium on Memory management, ACM Press (1998) 37–48
4. Griesemer, R., Mitrovic, S.: A compiler for the Java HotSpot^{TM} virtual machine. In Böszörményi, L., Gutknecht, J., Pomberger, G., eds.: The School of Niklaus Wirth: The Art of Simplicity. dpunkt.verlag (2000) 133–152
5. Huang, X., Blackburn, S.M., McKinley, K.S., Moss, J.E.B., Wang, Z., Cheng, P.: The garbage collection advantage: improving program locality. In: Proceedings of the 19th annual ACM SIGPLAN conference on Object-oriented programming, systems, languages, and applications, ACM Press (2004) 69–80
6. Intel Corporation: IA-32 Intel Architecture Software Developer's Manual, Volume 1: Basic Architecture. (2006) Order Number 253665-018.
7. Jones, R., Lins, R.: Garbage Collection: Algorithms for Automatic Dynamic Memory Management. John Wiley & Sons (1996)
8. Kotzmann, T., Mössenböck, H.: Escape analysis in the context of dynamic compilation and deoptimization. In: Proceedings of the 1st ACM/USENIX international conference on Virtual execution environments, ACM Press (2005) 111–120
9. Kotzmann, T., Mössenböck, H.: Reallocation and garbage collection support for scalar-replaced and stack-allocated objects. Technical report, Institute for System Software, Johannes Kepler University Linz (2006)
10. Lhoták, O., Hendren, L.: Run-time evaluation of opportunities for object inlining in Java. In: Proceedings of the 2002 joint ACM-ISCOPE conference on Java Grande, ACM Press (2002) 175–184
11. Pozo, R., Miller, B.: SciMark 2.0. (1999) http://math.nist.gov/scimark2/.
12. Standard Performance Evaluation Corporation: The SPEC JVM98 Benchmarks. (1998) http://www.spec.org/jvm98/.
13. Standard Performance Evaluation Corporation: The SPEC JBB2005 Benchmark. (2005) http://www.spec.org/jbb2005/.
14. Sun Microsystems, Inc.: Java SE 6: Mustang Snapshot Releases. (2006) https://mustang.dev.java.net/.
15. Veldema, R., Ceriel, J.H., Rutger, F.H., Henri, E.: Object combining: A new aggressive optimization for object intensive programs. In: Proceedings of the 2002 joint ACM-ISCOPE conference on Java Grande, ACM Press (2002) 165–174
16. Wimmer, C., Mössenböck, H.: Optimized interval splitting in a linear scan register allocator. In: Proceedings of the 1st ACM/USENIX international conference on Virtual execution environments, ACM Press (2005) 132–141

Nearly Optimal Register Allocation with PBQP [*]

Lang Hames and Bernhard Scholz

School of Information Technologies
The University of Sydney, NSW 2006, Australia
{lhames, scholz}@it.usyd.edu.au

Abstract. In this work we present a new heuristic for PBQP which significantly improves the quality of its register allocations and extends the range of viable target architectures. We also introduce a new branch-and-bound technique for PBQP that is able to find optimal register allocations.

We evaluate each of these methods, as well as a state of the art graph colouring method, using SPEC2000 and IA-32 as a testbed. Spill costs are used as a metric for comparison. We provide experimental evidence that our new heuristic allows PBQP to remain effective even for relatively regular architectures such as IA-32, generating results equal to those of a start-of-the-art graph colouring technique. Our method is shown to run 3–4 times slower than graph colouring, however it supports a wide range of irregularities.

Using our branch-and-bound solver for PBQP we were able to solve 97.4% of the functions in SPEC2000 optimally. These results are used as a yardstick to show that both PBQP and graph colouring produce results which are very close to optimal.

1 Introduction

Efficient utilisation of machine resources demands highly optimising compilers as we reach the limits of Moore's law [1]. *Register allocation* is a key optimisation which decides how programs will use the *CPU registers* which form the top level of the memory hierarchy. As increases in CPU speed continue to outstrip reductions in memory latency, the efficient use of registers becomes ever more important for ensuring program performance.

In the intermediate representation of a compiler it is assumed that there are an arbitrary number of symbolic registers available. During the register allocation stage the compiler attempts to map these symbolic registers to real registers. Symbolic registers for which no CPU register can be found (because all are already in use) are forced to reside in memory. Such symbolic registers are said to have been *spilled* to memory. Load and store code must be inserted into the program to retrieve spilled values before they are used, and store them after they are defined. This inserted code, called *spill code*, reduces program performance and is referred to as the *spill cost* of the symbolic register. The challenge of register allocation is to find an assignment which minimises the total spill cost, while terminating within a reasonable time frame. The scope of the register

---

[*] This work has been supported by the ARC Discovery Project Grant "Compilation Techniques for Embedded Systems" under Contract DP 0560190.

D. Lightfoot and C. Szyperski (Eds.): JMLC 2006, LNCS 4228, pp. 346–361, 2006.

allocation is either on the basic block level (also known as *local register allocation*) or over a whole procedure (also known as *global register allocation*).

The classical formulation of the global register allocation problem is NP complete. It has traditionally been solved heuristically using the *graph colouring* method introduced in [2], and extended in [3]. In this method a global register allocation problem is described by an *interference graph* in which nodes represent symbolic registers, and edges represent interference constraints. Using heuristics, the register allocator attempts to compute a k-colouring of the interference graph, where each colour represents a CPU register. If a k-colouring of the graph can be found it is mapped to a register allocation. If no k-colouring can be found then some non-colourable nodes are spilled. Spill code for these symbolic registers is inserted, the interference graph reconstructed and the colouring process is restarted.

Graph colouring methods have been shown to be highly effective at producing allocations for regular register architectures [3,2]. They have also been extended to support architectures with irregularities such as register pairing [4], and register classes and aliasing [5]. However, graph colouring methods generally lack the descriptive power required to accurately model the costs and constraints of more irregular architectures. Several alternative methods of register allocation have been devised to support irregular architectures, including *Integer Linear Programming* (ILP) [6], *Multi-Commodity Flow Network* (MCFN) methods [7], and *Partitioned Boolean Quadratic Programming* (PBQP) [8].

In this work we focus on the underlying mathematical discrete optimisation problem for register allocation. We are interested in how effective current state-of-the-art graph-colouring approaches [5] are in comparison with approaches designed for highly irregular architectures and small embedded system programs [8]. In order to ensure a fair comparison between the methods we have used spill costs as a metric. Using spill costs provides a clear and solid mathematical comparison, and avoids the noise which is introduced by other optimisations run after the register allocation phase. Since spill costs are estimated by the compiler (either a-priori, or based on dynamic profiles) their accuracy is dependant on the accuracy of the estimator. However, since each of the methods we compare relies on the same spill costs this does not affect the fairness of our comparison.

As a testbed we have chosen the register allocation problems in the SPEC2000 benchmark suite, and IA-32 (which is fairly regular) as a target architecture. This combination of architecture and benchmark suite represents a worst case for our method. This extreme case was chosen in order to investigate how the old PBQP heuristic scaled under such conditions, and how the new heuristic would fare. To find a yardstick for the performance of both approaches we employed our optimal solver which can cope with the large register allocation problems in the SPEC2000 benchmark suite, and the constraints of IA-32.

The contributions of this work are outlined in the following:

1. We show that the heuristic introduced in [8] performs poorly for larger register allocation problems.
2. We describe a new heuristic for PBQP that is able to produce allocations of very high quality in reasonable time.

3. We introduce a new branch-and-bound solver for PBQP. Using this solver we are able to generate optimal register allocations for 97.4% of the functions in the SPEC2000 benchmarks.
4. Using the optimal solutions mentioned above we are able to show, for our testbed, i.e., IA-32 and SPEC2000, that the heuristics for graph-colouring and PBQP leave little room for further improvements.

The paper is organised as follows. Section 2 provides background information on the PBQP method of register allocation. Section 3 describes our new heuristic for PBQP. In Section 4 we explain the branch-and-bound algorithm for PBQP. Section 5 provides experimental evidence both for the performance of PBQP with the new heuristic, and the optimality of the achieved solutions. Section 6 surveys related work. In Section 7 we draw our conclusions.

2   Background

2.1   PBQP

The Partitioned Boolean Quadratic Programming (PBQP) problem [8,9] is a specialised Quadratic Assignment Problem (QAP). Consider a set of discrete variables $X = \{x_1, \ldots, x_n\}$ and their finite domains $\{\mathbb{D}_1, \ldots, \mathbb{D}_n\}$ where $m_i = |\mathbb{D}_i|$. A solution of PBQP is a simple function $h : X \to \mathcal{D}$ where $\mathcal{D}$ is $\mathbb{D}_1 \cup \ldots \cup \mathbb{D}_n$; for each variable x_i we choose an element d_i in $\mathbb{D}_i$. By imposing a total order for each discrete variable domain, sometimes we refer d_i by its ordinal number ranging from 1 to m_i.

The quality of a solution is based on the contribution of two sets of terms:

1. for assigning variable x_i to the element d_i in $\mathbb{D}_i$. The quality of the assignment is measured by a *local cost function* $c(x_i, d_i)$.
2. for assigning two related variables x_i and x_j to the elements d_i in $\mathbb{D}_i$ and d_j in $\mathbb{D}_j$. The quality of the assignment is measured by a *related cost function* $C(x_i, x_j, d_i, d_j)$.

Thus, the total cost of a solution h is given below:

$$f = \sum_{1 \leq i \leq n} c(x_i, h(x_i)) + \sum_{1 \leq i < j \leq n} C(x_i, x_j, h(x_i), h(x_j)) \tag{1}$$

The PBQP problem asks for an assignment of a minimum total cost.

We solve PBQP using matrix notation. A discrete variable x_i becomes a boolean vector $\boldsymbol{x_i}$ whose elements are zeros and ones and whose length is determined by the number of elements in its domain $\mathbb{D}_i$. Each 0-1 element of $\boldsymbol{x_i}$ corresponds to an element of $\mathbb{D}_i$. An assignment of x_i to d_i is represented by setting all elements of $\boldsymbol{x_i}$ to zero except the element of d_i, which is set to one. Hence, a possible assignment for a variable x_i is modelled by the constraint $\boldsymbol{x_i}^T \cdot \boldsymbol{1} = 1$ that restricts vectors $\boldsymbol{x_i}$ such that exactly one element of the vectors is assigned one; all other elements are set to zero.

The related cost function $C(x_i, x_j, d_i, d_j)$ is decomposed for each pair (x_i, x_j). The costs for the pair are represented as a matrix $\overline{C}_{ij}$. An element in the matrix corresponds to an assignment (d_i, d_j). Similarly, the local cost function $c(x_i, d_i)$ is mapped to cost vectors c_i. Quadratic forms and scalar products are employed to rewrite the objective function of Eq. (1) to

$$s.t. \ \forall 1 \leq i \leq n : x_i \in \{0, 1\}^{|\mathbb{D}_i|}$$
$$\forall 1 \leq i \leq n : x_i^T \cdot \mathbf{1} = 1$$
$$\min f = \sum_{1 \leq i \leq n} x_i^T \cdot c_i + \sum_{1 \leq i < j \leq n} x_i^T \overline{C}_{ij} x_j \qquad (2)$$

In [8,9] a solver was introduced, which solves a sub-class of these problems optimally in $\mathcal{O}(nm^3)$, where n is the number of discrete variables and m is the maximal number of elements in their domains, i.e. $m = \max(m_1, \dots, m_n)$. For a given problem, the solver eliminates stepwise discrete variables until the problem is trivially solvable, i.e. all quadratic forms $x_i^T \overline{C}_{ij} x_j$ are eliminated. Each elimination step requires a reduction. The solver has reductions R0, RI, RII, which are not always applicable. If no reduction can be applied, the problem becomes irreducible and a heuristic is applied, which is called RN. The heuristic chooses a beneficial discrete variable x_i and a good assignment for it by searching for local minima. The solution found is guaranteed to be optimal when the reduction RN is not used. Once the PBQP graph has been fully reduced the *backpropagation* phase is invoked to compute a final solution by reconstructing the original PBQP problem.

A PBQP problem can be represented as an undirected *PBQP graph* $G\langle N, E \rangle$. The nodes of the PBQP graph are discrete variables x_i, for all i ($1 \leq i \leq n$). In the graph there exists an edge (i, j) for $i < j$ if matrix $\overline{C}_{ij}$ is not the zero matrix.

2.2   PBQP for Register Allocation

Previous work in [9,8] described how the register allocation problem for irregular architectures can be mapped to PBQP. To understand this mapping it is easiest to view the PBQP graph as an extension of the interference graph.

Nodes in the PBQP graph represent symbolic registers as in an interference graph. In addition each node u has an associated cost vector c_u which describes the costs of each allocation option for u. In this work we assume that the first element of this vector will contain the cost of the spill option sp, and subsequent elements will contain the costs of each CPU register that is valid for u.

Edges in the PBQP graph represent constraints on the register allocation problem as before. There are usually two types of edges in an interference graph, interference or coalesce edges (which indicate that there is a benefit to assigning two non-interfering symbolic registers to the same CPU register). Edges in PBQP graphs have no explicit type, but are associated with cost matrices $\overline{C}_{uv}$. Each cost matrix $\overline{C}_{uv}$ represents the cost of pairs of allocations for nodes u and v. The contents of each cost matrix determines the effect of its edge on the final solution. Several common matrix forms for register allocation were given in [8].

For our work we employ only *interference matrices*. Interference matrices describe the costs of combinations of assignments for pairs of nodes which interfere. For two interfering nodes u and v the cost of an allocation (a_i, a_j) is infinite if a_i and a_j *alias*.

Pairs of registers r_i and r_j are said to alias if writing to one may affect the value of the other. By definition a register aliases with itself, and the spill option aliases with nothing (not even itself). For allocations where a_i and a_j do not alias the cost is zero. The interference matrix for nodes u and v is thus given by

$$\bar{I}_{uv}(i,j) = \begin{cases} 0, & \text{if } a_i \text{ aliases } a_j \\ \infty, & \text{otherwise.} \end{cases} \tag{3}$$

As an example, consider the following subset of the IA-32 register architecture. It contains three 16bit registers named AX, BX and CX, each of which is aliased by two 8bit registers as depicted below.

AX		BX		CX	
AH	AL	BH	BL	CH	CL

If two nodes u and v have register option sets $\{sp, AH, AL, BL, CL\}$ and $\{sp, AX, BX\}$ respectively, the interference matrix I_{uv} is given by

$$I_{uv} = \begin{matrix} & sp\ AX\ BX \\ & \downarrow\ \ \downarrow\ \ \ \downarrow \\ \begin{vmatrix} 0 & 0 & 0 \\ 0 & \infty & 0 \\ 0 & \infty & 0 \\ 0 & 0 & \infty \\ 0 & 0 & 0 \end{vmatrix} & \begin{matrix} \leftarrow sp \\ \leftarrow AH \\ \leftarrow AL \\ \leftarrow BL \\ \leftarrow CL \end{matrix} \end{matrix} \tag{4}$$

The rows of the matrix represent each allocation option for u (sp, AH, AL, BL and CL respectively). The columns represent each allocation option for v (sp, AX and BX respectively). Each element (i, j) gives the cost of an allocation (a_i, a_j).

The costs in the first row and column are all zero, since the spill option does not alias with anything. The second column contains two infinities since the AX register option for v aliases with both the AH and AL options for u. The third column contains only a single infinity since the BX register option for v only aliases with the BL option for u (we assume that the BH option has been denied to u by a register exclusion). The final row, representing the CL option for u, contains all zeros, because no register option for v aliases with CL.

Neither hardware registers nor register exclusions are explicitly represented in a PBQP graph. Instead, register exclusions remove options from nodes, reducing the length of the cost vectors and matrices. This in turn improves the speed of the PBQP solver.

3 PBQP Heuristic

Our initial experiments using PBQP to allocate registers for SPEC2000 revealed that the heuristic described in [8], Maximal Degree Minimum Solution (MDMS), performed poorly for these benchmarks.

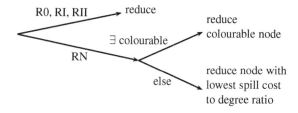

Fig. 1. Reduction Decision Tree

Previous work, presented in [9], showed that better results can be obtained by pre-computing an RN reduction order using a traditional graph colouring approach. (Graph colouring approaches select and remove *colourable* nodes before *non-colourable* ones; a node u is considered colourable if no allocation of registers to u's neighbours precludes an allocation of a register to u itself.)

In the following we present a heuristic which is able to dynamically determine a reduction order for RN nodes based on colourability. At the core of our heuristic is an efficient and accurate method of determining colourability for irregular architectures.

The reduction order produced by our method is similar, though not identical, to that produced by graph colouring. Our reduction order is determined during the reduction phase based on the decision diagram depicted in Figure 1. During the reduction phase nodes of degree two or less are removed by the R0, RI and RII reductions. These reductions are performed irrespective of the colourability of nodes (on irregular architectures even low degree nodes may be non-colourable due to large register exclusion sets). Once all remaining nodes are of degree three or higher our RN heuristic is invoked to decide which node to reduce.

Our RN heuristic sorts the remaining nodes in descending order of degree. Based on this order it searches for a colourable node. If a colourable node is found it is removed from the PBQP graph and placed on the reduction stack. Sorting the nodes by degree ensures that the colourable node of highest degree is reduced. This improves the performance of the reduction process by maximising the number of nodes whose degrees are reduced.

If no colourable node is found we apply Brigg's spill heuristic [3] to reduce the node with the lowest ratio of spill cost to degree. No register assignment is made at this stage; instead our heuristic is optimistic in the sense that it defers the actual assignment until the backpropagation phase.

At the end of the reduction phase all nodes reside on the reduction stack. During the backpropagation phase the PBQP solver pops nodes from the reduction stack and reinserts them into the PBQP graph. As nodes are reinserted, the solver selects a decision vector that minimises the cost of the final solution. All nodes that we have classified as colourable (cf. the path via predicate "∃ colourable" in Figure 1) are guaranteed to be allocated a register. Nodes reduced by the R0, RI or RII reductions are solved optimally, and will be allocated a register if one is available. Nodes reduced due to the spill heuristic may or may not be allocated a register. Nodes which cannot be assigned a register will be assigned the *sp* option.

The performance of our heuristic depends on the efficient determination of colourability. For regular architectures colourability can be determined by comparing the degree of a node u to the number of available registers k. If $degree(u) < k$ then the node is colourable. For irregular architectures this condition is insufficient because each neighbour of u may exclude more than one register option from u (due to register aliasing). We describe below a fast and accurate method to determine the colourability of nodes for irregular architectures. Our method is based on the PBQP graph and its associated cost matrices.

We observe that a node u is colourable if either of the following two conditions hold.

(1) *The maximum number of colours which could be denied to u by a colouring of u's neighbours is less than the total number of colours available for u.*
(2) *There is at least one colour which is a valid choice for u, but not for any neighbour of u.*

To determine whether Condition (1) holds we calculate the maximum number of register choices that can be denied to node u by a colouring of u's neighbours. It is not practical to calculate this value exactly, because this would require enumerating all colourings of the neighbours of u. Instead we calculate a safe upper bound on Condition (1) by examining the worst case colourings of each of u's neighbours considered individually. This upper bound we call the impact upon u, denoted by $impact_u$.

If the adjacency set of a node u is given by $adj(u)$, and the impact of a single neighbour v by $impact_u(v)$, then the impact upon u by its neighbours is given by

$$impact_u = \sum_{v \in adj(u)} impact_u(v). \tag{5}$$

In order to calculate $impact_u(v)$, we need to look at the columns of the cost matrix $\overline{C}_{uv}$. The number of infinite elements in each column j represents the number of registers which could be denied to node u by selecting register r_j for node v (cf. Eq. (3)). For instance it can be seen in Eq. (4) that selecting the AX register for v (column 2) removes two options from u, whereas selecting the BX option (column 3) removes only one option, and the sp option (column 1) removes none.

We write $inf\_count(\overline{C}_{uv}, j)$ for the number of infinite cost elements in column j of matrix $\overline{C}_{uv}$, and m_u for the number allocation options for u. Then $impact_u(v)$ is given by

$$impact_u(v) = \max_{1 \le j \le m_u} \{inf\_count(\overline{C}_{uv}, j)\}. \tag{6}$$

To determine whether Condition (2) holds for node u we determine the set of registers which cannot be denied to u by any colouring of its neighbours. This set we call $safe\_regs_u$. For Condition (2) to hold the cardinality of $safe\_regs_u$ must be greater than zero. To determine whether register r_i resides in $safe\_regs_u$, we examine row i of each of the neighbouring cost matrices of u. If row i of a matrix $\overline{C}_{uv}$ contains an infinite element, then r_i may be denied to u by some selection for v, thus r_i must be removed from $safe\_regs_u$.

In order to calculate $safe\_regs_u$, we place all register options except the spill element in $safe\_regs_u$. For each neighbour v of u we examine the cost matrix $\overline{C}_{uv}$. Each of the rows of this matrix represents a valid register choice for u. For each row i that contains an infinite element we remove the corresponding register r_i from $safe\_regs_u$, since a certain colouring of v could exclude r_i from u. At the end of this process the registers remaining in $safe\_regs_u$ are those whose rows contained no infinite elements in any of the neighbouring matrices of u.

In Eq. (4) it can be seen that register AH (row 1) must not be in $safe\_regs_u$, since row 1 contains an infinity. Likewise registers AL and BL must not be in $safe\_regs_u$ because rows 2 and 3 contain infinities. Row 4 however, representing the CL option, does not contain an infinity, so CL is in $safe\_regs_u$.

Because the cost matrix construction process takes into account register classes and aliasing, these phenomena are implicitly considered in the determination of colourability. In addition, a positive effect of register exclusions, not considered in [3] and [5], is accounted for: if all neighbours of a node u are excluded from occupying a register that is a valid option for u, then u is colourable. On regular architectures register exclusions are rare and this effect would not significantly improve accuracy. However, for irregular architectures register exclusions are common and register sets are typically small. Considering this register exclusion effect can therefore yield a small increase in the accuracy of the colourability criterion.

An algorithm to calculate the colourability criterion according to Conditions (1) and (2) is given below. Therein $options(u)$ denotes the valid allocation options for node u, and sp denotes the spill element.

4   Branch-and-Bound for PBQP

Branch-and-bound is a general technique for solving discrete and combinatorial optimisation problems [10]. The general idea of branch-and-bound relies on two concepts. First, *branching* is a decomposition of the problem into sub-problems. Since branching is applied recursively to each of the sub-problems, the generated sub-problems form a tree called a *search tree*. Second, *bounding* is a fast way of finding lower bounds and upper bounds, respectively, for the optimal solution within sub-problems.

The branch-and-bound algorithm prunes sub-problems whose lower bounds are greater than the upper bound for any other sub-problem. If an upper bound for a sub-problem matches its lower bound, then the sub-problem has been solved. For finding the minimum all sub-problems of the search tree are either pruned or solved. Due to limited computational resources, sometimes not all sub-problems of the search-tree are either pruned or solved, and the branch-and-bound algorithm is terminated before finding the minimum of the objective function. In this case, the minimum lower bound and the minimum upper bound, among all non-pruned sub-problems, bound the minimum of the objective function. For branch-and-bound methods there are different ways to bound sub-problems and how to create and inspect the nodes in the search tree.

We extend the PBQP solver with branch-and-bound techniques. The approach introduced in [8] solves a PBQP problem optimally if R0, RI and RII reductions entirely decompose the problem. If no R0, RI or RII reduction can be applied in the reduction phase, the PBQP becomes irreducible and a heuristic selects a discrete variable x_l and chooses a concrete solution for x_l in $\mathbb{D}_l$. We refer to this step as RN reduction. If the

---

Algorithm 1. Colourability Criterion

Input: PBQP Graph G, node $u \in G$.
Output: Boolean value describing the colourability of u.

1: $impact_u \leftarrow 0$
2: $safe\_regs_u \leftarrow options(u) \backslash sp$
3: **for all** $v \in adj(u)$ **do**
4:     $impact_u(v) \leftarrow 0$
5:     **for all** $j \in \{1, \ldots, |\mathbb{D}_v|\}$ **do**
6:         $inf\_count(\overline{C}_{uv}, j) \leftarrow 0$
7:         **for all** $i \in \{1, \ldots, |\mathbb{D}_u|\}$ **do**
8:             **if** $\overline{C}_{uv}(i, j) = \infty$ **then**
9:                 $inf\_count(\overline{C}_{uv}, j) \leftarrow inf\_count(\overline{C}_{uv}, j) + 1$
10:                $safe\text{-}regs_u \leftarrow safe\text{-}regs_u \backslash r_i$
11:            **end if**
12:        **end for**
13:        **if** $inf\_count(\overline{C}_{uv}, j) > impact_u(v)$ **then**
14:            $impact_u(v) \leftarrow inf\_count(\overline{C}_{uv}, j)$
15:        **end if**
16:    **end for**
17:    $impact_u \leftarrow impact_u + impact_u(v)$
18: **end for**
19: **if** $(|safe\text{-}regs_u| > 0) \lor (|impact_u| < |options(u)|)$ **then**
20:    $colourable \leftarrow true$
21: **else**
22:    $colourable \leftarrow false$
23: **end if**

---

problem domain is known, RN reductions based on heuristics are highly efficient and effective.

To find an optimal solution exhaustive enumeration was employed in [11]. The underlying idea of exhaustive enumeration is to use the ideas of the heuristic approach, i.e., R0, RI and RII reductions are applied until the problem is trivially solvable or an RN reduction needs to be applied. Instead of choosing a single solution for a discrete variable reduced by RN, all possible assignments of the discrete variable are enumerated. The complexity of exhaustive enumeration grows exponentially with the number of discrete variables reduced by RN. Despite the fact that for smaller problems with a small number of RN reductions this approach works sufficiently well, it becomes intractable for huge register allocation problems.

For PBQP a branch-and-bound approach is superior to an exhaustive enumeration approach because many assignments of discrete variables reduced by RN will be pruned. Furthermore, the solving techniques for PBQP allow a natural formulation of a branch-and-bound algorithm: A sub-problem is a PBQP problem which (1) cannot be further reduced by R0, RI and RII, and (2) is not trivially solvable. To each sub-problem we associate the discrete variable x_l which is selected by the RN reduction in the next reduction step and its concrete assignment.

A fragment of a search tree is depicted in Figure 2. The root of the tree represents the overall problem to be solved. If a problem has no RN reduction, the problem has no sub-problems and the tree consists of the root node only. Otherwise the reduced discrete variable x_{i_1} and its possible assignments ranging from 1 to m_{i_1} of the first RN reduction constitute the children of the root node. The discrete variable of the second RN reduction and its assignments constitute the grandchildren of the root node and so forth.

Note that a child of a sub-problem is a new sub-problem for which the discrete variable of its parent sub-problem was reduced, and R0, RI and RII reductions had been applied until the problem became irreducible. For the branch-and-bound algorithm we need to find lower and upper bounds of sub-problems, denoted by $\langle f_{i_k}^l, f_{i_k}^u \rangle$.

Before discussing the specific problem of finding lower and upper bounds of sub-problems, we derive the computation of lower and upper bounds of a general PBQP problem in matrix notation (see Eq. (2)). More formally, we want to find a lower bound f^l and upper bound f^u of f such that

$$f^l < f(x_1, \ldots, x_n) < f^u \tag{7}$$

holds for all possible assignments for discrete variables $x_i \in \mathbb{D}_i$, $(1 \leq i \leq n)$. Bounds can be simply derived by the observation that only one element of a cost vector c_i and matrix $\overline{C}_{ij}$ respectively, contributes to the objective function. Thus, lower and upper bounds of f are given by

$$f^l = \sum_{1 \leq i \leq n} \min c_i + \sum_{1 \leq i < j \leq n} \min \overline{C}_{ij} \tag{8}$$

$$f^u = \sum_{1 \leq i \leq n} \max c_i + \sum_{1 \leq i < j \leq n} \max \overline{C}_{ij}, \tag{9}$$

where $\min c_i$ is the smallest element in c_i and in $\overline{C}_{ij}$, respectively, and $\max c_i$ is the greatest element in c_i and in $\overline{C}_{ij}$, respectively.

The bounds for a sub-problem are computed by reducing the node x_l. We choose a concrete element for vector x_l as assignment in $\mathbb{D}_l$. For a given assignment of x_l a sub-problem represented in matrix notation as given in Eq. (2) reduces to

$$s.t. \ \forall 1 \leq i \leq n, i \neq l : x_i \in \{0,1\}^{|\mathbb{D}_i|}$$
$$\forall 1 \leq i \leq n, i \neq l : x_i^T \mathbf{1} = 1$$
$$\min f = \alpha + \sum_{1 \leq i \leq n, i \neq l} x_i^T (c_i + \Delta_i) + \sum_{1 \leq i < j \leq n, i \neq l, j \neq l} x_i^T \overline{C}_{ij} x_j, \tag{10}$$

where α is a constant, i.e., $\alpha = x_l^T c_l$, and Δ_i is a cost vector, i.e.,

$$\Delta_i = \begin{cases} \overline{C}_{il} x_l, & \text{if } i < l \\ x_l^T \overline{C}_{li}, & \text{otherwise.} \end{cases} \tag{11}$$

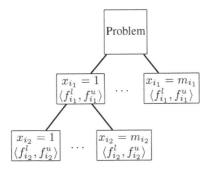

Fig. 2. Search Tree for PBQP

Because the discrete variable x_l is set to a concrete value, quadratic forms involving x_l become scalar products. Applying the lower and upper bounds of Eq. (8) and Eq. (9), we can deduce the following lower and upper bounds for a sub-problem.

$$f^l = \alpha + \sum_{1 \le i \le n, i \ne l} \min(c_i + \Delta_i) + \sum_{1 \le i < j \le n, i \ne l, j \ne l} \min \overline{C}_{ij} \tag{12}$$

$$f^u = \alpha + \sum_{1 \le i \le n, i \ne l} \max(c_i + \Delta_i) + \sum_{1 \le i < j \le n, i \ne l, j \ne l} \max \overline{C}_{ij} \tag{13}$$

The PBQP branch-and-bound algorithm is a standard branch-and-bound algorithm: sub-problems are classified in live and dead nodes in the search tree. Live nodes are leafs of sub-problems, which are not solved yet (i.e., lower and upper bound do not coincide). Dead nodes are nodes whose children have been already expanded. For running the algorithm we need an upper bound for the global minimum of the PBQP problem. The upper bound of the global minimum is initialised with infinity.

The live nodes are stored in a priority queue where the priority is determined by the lower bound of the sub-problem. The live node with the smallest lower bound is expanded first. The expansion of a node includes two steps. First, the children of the sub-problem are added to the tree and inserted to the priority queue if their lower bound is smaller than the upper bound of the global minimum. Second, the node is removed from the priority queue and it becomes dead. The branch-and-bound algorithm terminates if there are no nodes left in the priority queue, or if the upper bound of the global minimum is smaller then the smallest element in the priority queue.

We improved the standard algorithm by using the solution of a heuristic algorithm. In a pre-processing phase the search tree is expanded according to the solution of a given heuristic. Before running the canonical expansion the branch-and-bound algorithm has a tight upper bound for the global minimum and the search space becomes significantly smaller if the heuristic used is close to the optimum.

5   Experiments

In our experiments we compared the performance of three different PBQP solvers, i.e. a PBQP solver using the MDMS heuristic introduced in [8], a PBQP solver using our new

Table 1. Number of Functions in SPEC2000

Benchmark	Total	Pairs	Empty	Remaining
164.gzip	89	1	14	74
175.vpr	266	4	47	215
176.gcc	1965	46	367	1552
181.mcf	26	0	2	24
186.crafty	109	39	9	61
197.parser	323	0	27	296
252.eon	1257	0	570	687
253.perlbmk	1015	1	208	806
254.gap	852	6	122	724
255.vortex	923	10	93	820
256.bzip2	74	0	14	60
300.twolf	191	0	17	174
total	7090	107	1490	5493

heuristic (see Sec. 3), a PBQP solver using branch-and-bound (see Sec. 4), and a state-of-the-art graph colouring method described in [5]. The four approaches are compared in terms of number of spills, spill costs, and solve time. We do not consider the effects of register allocation on code size nor on runtime of benchmark programs since register allocation works in concert with other standard compiler optimisations. Measuring the genuine effects of register allocation on code size and runtime would be overlayed with noise. Taking the spill cost as a measurement gives a solid mathematical comparison.

To obtain a comparison of our methods each solver was used to produce allocations for the SPEC2000 benchmarks. The interference graphs, annotated with spill costs and register constraints, were obtained from the GCC 3.3.6 compiler, and passed to the solvers. Empty interference graphs and graphs requiring register pairs were not taken into account, leaving 5493 graphs for our experiments. A quantitative summary of the interference graphs is given in Table 1. Each solver calculates an allocation and produces a raw assignment of registers and spills to symbolic registers, as well as timing information. Our raw allocations were processed to check for correctness and to extract spill costs and other information.

The cost model used for our experiments is highly regular. Our solvers assign only registers of the same size as the allocation candidate (in contrast to GCC's allocator which stores all non-spilled symbolic registers in 32-bit registers). All valid register options are assumed to have zero cost (except the spill option, whose cost is given by GCC's spill cost estimator), and only interference constraints are modelled. Such a regular cost model represents a worst-case scenario for PBQP, which performs better on more constrained architectures.

Summaries of the allocations produced by each of our solvers are given in Table 2. The first three columns describe the total spill cost for each benchmark individually and overall, using each heuristic solver. The next three columns give the number of spills produced by the solvers. The final three columns show the time taken to produce the allocations.

Table 2. Raw Allocation Results for the SPEC2000 Benchmarks

Benchmark	Spill Cost			Spills			Allocation Time (ms)		
	MDMS	New	GrCo	MDMS	New	GrCo	MDMS	New	GrCo
164.gzip	120438	60175	60838	121	114	118	6.9	9.2	3.1
175.vpr	521770	330724	328358	690	710	704	27.5	39.8	12.4
176.gcc	1431081	720548	728731	3078	3341	3335	322.6	532.4	133.2
181.mcf	98796	69440	69445	81	82	83	2.4	3.2	1.1
186.crafty	73491	27978	28267	149	153	153	10.5	15.1	4.9
197.parser	221732	162962	168847	508	525	525	35.9	52.9	15.1
252.eon	446646	366810	367965	815	826	816	34.7	53.0	16.6
253.perlbmk	758888	323161	334957	910	925	921	93.4	126.4	38.8
254.gap	1873241	1090693	1099054	1822	1929	1947	118.8	163.9	49.5
255.vortex	424300	238188	239328	972	983	977	49.9	64.8	23.6
256.bzip2	67531	26944	27349	134	146	146	7.1	10.1	3.2
300.twolf	1085151	560064	564956	1110	1194	1203	91.7	155.7	33.1
total	7123065	3977687	4018095	10390	10928	10928	801.5	1226.5	334.5

It can be seen from the final row of Table 2 that our new heuristic produces a spill cost 44% lower than that of the MDMS heuristic, and 1% lower than graph colouring. This result represents a large improvement over the previous heuristic, and places PBQP on a par with graph colouring in terms of the allocations generated.

The poor performance, in terms of spill cost, of the MDMS heuristic compared to graph colouring has not been observed before. Previous work on PBQP for register allocation using this heuristic, given in [8], was carried out using embedded systems benchmarks. These benchmarks have smaller interference graphs than those of SPEC2000. For such graphs the RN reduction rule is seldom invoked, and the choice of RN heuristic has less impact upon the final result.

The MDMS heuristic generates fewer spills overall than either of the other methods, despite producing a worse allocation overall. This occurs because the MDMS heuristic always reduces the node of highest degree, regardless of whether the node is colourable. Choosing such a node lowers the degree of the maximum number of neighbours, reducing the chance of further spills. No effort is made to decide whether this is a good spill decision however, which leads to a poor final allocation.

Both PBQP heuristics are considerably slower than graph colouring. The MDMS heuristic takes a factor of 2.4 times longer than graph colouring over all benchmarks. An original naive implementation of our heuristic required a factor of 25 times longer than graph colouring. We determined however that most of this time was spent in unnecessary re-evaluations of matrices. By implementing a caching strategy for per-matrix information and using lazy evaluation to update these caches we were able to reduce the time taken to the present factor of 3.7 times longer than graph colouring. Previous work on register allocation [12] showed that the time taken to solve the graph colouring problem is only a small fraction of the overall allocation time. As such we would not expect our method to significantly increase the total compile time.

Table 3 gives the results produced by each solver for those functions which we were able to solve optimally. The first column gives the number of functions solved optimally

Table 3. Optimal Costs, Spills and Comparisons

Benchmark	Functions	Spill Cost			Spills		
		Optimal	New	GrCo	Optimal	New	GrCo
164.gzip	73	47603	47605	48268	105	104	108
175.vpr	207	286466	291553	289036	600	605	599
176.gcc	1491	595785	602444	611952	2212	2281	2272
181.mcf	24	69404	69440	69445	81	82	83
186.crafty	59	23702	23789	24078	120	121	123
197.parser	280	144464	148540	154400	320	329	329
252.eon	686	366613	366723	367874	775	782	775
253.perlbmk	800	429530	441131	451981	795	825	833
254.gap	710	1033923	1042452	1049729	1634	1672	1688
255.vortex	815	225461	228250	229673	862	875	869
256.bzip2	58	23179	24344	27349	92	99	97
300.twolf	149	368726	375961	378710	528	544	547
total	5352	3614856	3662232	3699885	8124	8319	8323

for each benchmark and overall. The next three columns give the spill costs for the optimal solution, PBQP using our new heuristic, and graph colouring. The final three columns give the number of spills generated by each of the methods.

Overall we were able to solve 97.4% of the functions in the SPEC2000 benchmarks optimally over a period of about a day. From the final row it can be seen that the optimal spill cost is 1.3% lower than that produced by our heuristic, and 2.3% lower than that of graph colouring. Our heuristic never generated spill costs more than 3% above the optimal for any benchmark (the highest was perlbmk at 2.7%). Graph colouring never generated an allocation more than 7% above the optimal for any benchmark (the highest was parser at 6.9%). The small margins between the optimal spill costs and the heuristics show that there is little room for improvements for a fairly regular architecture such as IA-32.

6   Related Work

Graph colouring approaches [2,3] are a success story for RISC architectures with large register banks and an orthogonal instruction set. However, attempts to adapt graph colouring to irregular architectures have produced ad-hoc modifications which fail to provide a unified method for dealing with irregularities. Each of these methods is able to deal with a certain subset of irregularities at the expense of breaking from the simple graph colouring analogy.

Smith et al. [5] introduced a new colourability criterion for irregular architectures which is able to determine colourability for architectures featuring register classes and aliasing. However, their approach cannot deal with complex constraints between two symbolic registers such as pairing or dedicated registers. Runeson and Nyström [13] present a retargetable graph-colouring register allocator based on the $\langle p, q \rangle$ test, which is similar to the work in [5]. Other techniques for graph colouring such as the technique introduced by Koseki et al. [14] modifies the selection phase to increase the likelihood that symbolic registers are given their preferred registers. However, their algorithm can only deal with certain aspects of irregular architectures.

Register allocation based on Integer Linear Programming (ILP) was introduced by Goodwin and Wilken [15]. The approach maps the register allocation problem to an integer linear program, which is solved by CPLEX, a commercial solver for generic ILP problems. The work was extended by Kong and Wilken [6] for irregular architectures. Recently, in [16], an approach was introduced which uses a progressive solver for solving register allocation problems based on multi commodity network flows. With their approach not all possible constraints occurring in irregular architectures can be modelled.

Recently, register allocation approaches exploiting the tree structure of SSA graphs have been investigated [17] stating that the graph colouring problem is solvable in polynomial time without considering coalescing costs at phi-nodes. However these approaches do not consider any irregularities.

Most of the work in this paper builds on work described in [8,11]. The PBQP optimisation problem accommodates for the needs of solving the register allocation problem for a wide range of irregularities. It is a fairly comprehensive approach. However, the exhaustive enumeration approach introduced in [11] is intractable for larger benchmarks and the approach introduced in [8] has a poorly performing heuristic for larger benchmarks and more regular architectures. Both problems have been resolved by this work.

7   Future Work and Conclusion

In this paper we have presented a new PBQP heuristic for register allocation. For larger benchmarks and moderately irregular architectures the new heuristic performs significantly better than the MDMS heuristic introduced in [8]. We also describe a new algorithm for PBQP based on branch-and-bound. The branch-and-bound algorithm was extended to use a heuristic to find a tight upper bound for its global minimum. With this technique we show that 97.4% of the register allocation problems in the SPEC2000 integer benchmark suite can be solved optimally in less than a day.

With the given framework there is still the algorithmic challenge to solve every register allocation problem in SPEC2000 optimally. This challenge might be achieved by exploring some decomposition properties of PBQP, i.e. a PBQP problem disintegrates into independent sub-problems during the reduction phase. By solving the sub-problems independently the search space of the branch-and-bound solver will be significantly reduced.

We plan to integrate this method into a modern optimising compiler in order to evaluate our method's effects on code size and execution speed. Given the closeness of the spill costs we have seen we do not expect significant deviation between our method and graph colouring for IA-32 using these metrics. However we plan to apply both methods to more irregular architectures where we would expect a greater variation.

With the optimal solution as a yardstick we have shown that current graph colouring heuristics [5] for irregular architectures and the new PBQP heuristic introduced in this work are on average 2% from the optimal solution. In future there will be very little room for further progress in finding better optimisation heuristics for moderately irregular architectures.

References

1. Moore, G.: 40th Anniversary of Moore's Law. Press Conference (2005)
2. Chaitin, G.J., Auslander, M.A., Chandra, A.K., Cocke, J., Hopkins, M.E., Markstein, P.W.: Register allocation via coloring. Computer Languages **6** (1981) 47–57
3. Briggs, P., Cooper, K.D., Torczon, L.: Improvements to graph coloring register allocation. ACM Trans. Program. Lang. Syst. **16**(3) (1994) 428–455
4. Briggs, P., Cooper, K.D., Torczon, L.: Coloring register pairs. ACM Lett. Program. Lang. Syst. **1**(1) (1992) 3–13
5. Smith, M.D., Ramsey, N., Holloway, G.: A generalized algorithm for graph-coloring register allocation. In: PLDI '04: Proceedings of the ACM SIGPLAN 2004 Conference on Programming Language Design and Implementation, New York, NY, USA, ACM Press (2004) 277–288
6. Kong, T., Wilken, K.D.: Precise register allocation for irregular architectures. In: MICRO 31: Proceedings of the 31st annual ACM/IEEE international symposium on Microarchitectures, Los Alamitos, CA, USA, IEEE Computer Society Press (1998) 297–307
7. Koes, D., Goldstein, S.C.: A progressive register allocator for irregular architectures. In: CGO '05: Proceedings of the international symposium on Code generation and optimization, Washington, DC, USA, IEEE Computer Society (2005) 269–280
8. Scholz, B., Eckstein, E.: Register allocation for irregular architectures. In: LCTES/SCOPES '02: Proceedings of the joint conference on Languages, compilers and tools for embedded systems, New York, NY, USA, ACM Press (2002) 139–148
9. Eckstein, E.: Code Optimizations for Digital Signal Processors. PhD thesis, Institute of Computer Languages, Compilers and Languages Group, Vienna University of Technology (2003)
10. Murty, K.G.: Operations Research: Deterministic Optimization Models. Prentice Hall (1995)
11. Hirnschrott, U., Krall, A., Scholz, B.: Graph -coloring vs.optimal register allocation for optimizing compilers. Proceedings of the Joint Modular Language Conference (2003) 202–213
12. Briggs, P.: Register allocation via graph coloring. Technical Report TR92-183, Department of Computer Science, Rice University (1998)
13. Runeson, J., Nyström, S.: In Software and Compilers for Embedded Systems (SCOPES). In: Retargetable Graph-Coloring Register Allocation for Irregular Architectures. Volume 2826 of Lecture Notes in Computer Science. Springer Press, Klagenfurt, Austria. (2003) 240–254
14. Koseki, A., Komatsu, H., Nakatani, T.: Preference-directed graph coloring. In: PLDI '02: Proceedings of the ACM SIGPLAN 2002 Conference on Programming language design and implementation, New York, NY, USA, ACM Press (2002) 33–44
15. Goodwin, D.W., Wilken, K.D.: Optimal and near-optimal global register allocations using 0–1 integer programming. Softw. Pract. Exper. **26**(8) (1996) 929–965
16. Koes, D., Goldstein, S.C.: A global progressive register allocator. In: PLDI '06: Proceedings of the ACM SIGPLAN 1990 conference on Programming language design and implementation, Ottawa, ON, Canada, ACM Press (2006) (to appear)
17. Pereira, F.M.Q., Palsberg, J.: Register allocation via coloring of chordal graphs. In: APLAS'05: Proceedings of APLAS'05, Asian Symposium on Programming Languages and Systems, Springer Spress (2005) 315–329

Fast Profile-Based Partial Redundancy Elimination

R. Nigel Horspool[1], David J. Pereira[1], and Bernhard Scholz[2]

[1] Department of Computer Science, University of Victoria
P.O. Box 3055, Victoria, BC, Canada V8W 3P6
{nigelh, djp}@cs.uvic.ca
[2] School of Information Technologies, Madsen Building F09
University of Sydney, Sydney, NSW 2006, Australia
scholz@it.usyd.edu.au

Abstract. Partial Redundancy Elimination (PRE) is a standard program optimization which removes redundant computations via Code Motion. It subsumes and generalizes the optimizations of Global Common Subexpression Elimination (GCSE) and Loop Invariant Code Motion (LICM). Recent work has generalized PRE to become Speculative PRE (SPRE), which uses estimates of execution frequencies to find the optimal places in a program to perform computations. However, the analysis performed by the compiler is computationally intensive and hence impractical for just-in-time (JIT) compilers.

This paper introduces a novel approach which abandons a guarantee of optimality in favour of simplicity and speed of analysis. This new approach, called Isothermal SPRE, achieves results which are close to optimal in practice, yet its analysis time is at least as good as current compiler techniques for code motion. It is a technique suitable for use in JIT compilers.

1 Introduction

The simplest computation performed by a program is the evaluation of an expression, say a+b. If the program contains a sequence of statements similar to

```
x = a+b;
x = x + c*d;
y = a+b;
```

then (assuming complications involving aliasing of variable names do not occur) the second computation of a+b is *fully redundant*, since neither a nor b is modified between the two computations of a+b. A good compiler would translate the code as though it had been written as

```
t1 = a+b;
x = t1;
x = x + c*d;
y = t1;
```

where t1 is a new temporary variable (and which would be a good candidate for implementing as a register).

D. Lightfoot and C. Szyperski (Eds.): JMLC 2006, LNCS 4228, pp. 362–376, 2006.

The generalization to *partial redundancy* occurs if we have a program that contains multiple control flow paths and where a computation is redundant on some path(s) but not on all paths. An example fragment of program with a partially redundant occurrence of a+b is shown in Figure 1(a). In this (meaningless) calculation, the value of a+b computed in the loop condition will usually be the same value as was computed on the previous iteration. A compiler which performs *partial redundancy elimination* optimization will go through a two step process of inserting some additional computations of a+b to produce the intermediate version of Figure 1(b) and then eliminating those occurrences which have become fully redundant to achieve the result shown in Figure 1(c).

```
t1 = a+b;              // inserted
while((a+b) > sum) {
    if (sum % 10 == 0) {
        a = a + 1;
        t1 = a+b;       // inserted
    }
    sum += b;
}
```

(b) After insertions of a+b

```
while((a+b) > sum) {
    if (sum % 10 == 0)
        a = a + 1;
    sum += b;
}
```

(a) Original while loop

```
t1 = a+b;
while(t1 > sum) {  // replaced
    if (sum % 10 == 0) {
        a = a + 1;
        t1 = a+b;
    }
    sum += b;
}
```

(c) After deletion of redundancies

Fig. 1. Application of (classical) PRE to a loop

However, the classical PRE analysis is performed without any knowledge of the relative frequencies of execution of the different paths through the program. Thus PRE is required to be conservative, and will never choose to insert a computation e at a point P in the program unless it is guaranteed that the value of e will be used on every path that continues from point P. After those computations that become fully redundant due to the insertions have been removed, the number of computations of e cannot be greater than in the original program. Usually it will be smaller. Another benefit of the conservative approach is that even *unsafe* expressions can be moved. An unsafe expression is a computation which may cause a run-time exception. For example, an array reference A[i] in Java may cause an exception either because the array A has not been allocated or because the index i is out of range. If the expression does cause an exception at run-time, then the optimized program will at worst raise that exception at an earlier point in the program.[1] In no case would the transformed program raise an exception that would not be raised in the original program.

The conservatism of PRE causes it to miss optimization opportunities that involve *safe expressions*, i.e. expressions that cannot raise an exception when computed. An enumeration of expressions which should be considered safe depends on the semantics of the programming language and on the platform for which the code is compiled. For example, a+b is normally safe in the C language. However a/b would be safe at a point P in a C program only if the compiler can prove that b is non-zero at P or if the integer division instruction on the target platform does not generate a divide-by-zero interrupt. (The PowerPC architecture provides an example of such a platform.)

The example of Figure 2 shows a loop that PRE cannot optimize, but which SPRE will. The transformation from Figure 2(a) to Figure 2(b) cannot be performed by PRE. Without knowledge of execution path frequencies, an insertion of t1=a*a in the *then* clause of the *if* statement might make the program slower. PRE has to consider the possibility, for example, that the *else* clause is never executed. That would introduce 10000 computations in the transformed program that would not have been performed by the original program. However, if SPRE is given profile information which shows that the *else* clause is executed more frequently than the *then* clause, then it will produce the result shown in Figure 2(b) because the total number of computations of a*a would be smaller.

```
for(i=0; i<10000; i++) {
    if (A[i]<0) {  // 1% frequency
        a = a+1;
    } else {       // 99% frequency
        sum += a*a;
    }
}
```
(a) Original code

```
t1 = a*a;
for(i=0; i<10000; i++) {
    if (A[i]<0) {
        a = a+1;
        t1 = a*a;
    } else {
        sum += t1;
    }
}
```
(b) Result from SPRE

Fig. 2. A loop that PRE does not optimize

The SPRE approach is restricted to safe expressions because a compiler should never introduce the possibility of an exception that was not present in the original program. However, there is no reason why a dual approach of using SPRE for safe expressions and PRE for unsafe expressions could not be adopted.

A major obstacle to adopting SPRE in a compiler is that the existing analysis algorithms are computationally intensive. For each candidate expression, the current formulations of SPRE construct a network flow problem and then finds a minimum-cut partition of the network. Given that the number of nodes V in

---

[1] However this may cause other difficulties for Java because it has precise exception semantics and code motion must take this into account.

the network is proportional to the size of the control flow graph of the program being analyzed, and given that standard algorithms for finding the minimum cut have $O(V^3)$ time complexity, finding the solution is costly (even if it finds an optimal solution).

In contrast, PRE uses data flow analyses which can be formulated as *bit-vector* problems. This means that PRE determines solutions for all candidate expressions simultaneously. Furthermore, the worst-case time complexity for solving the data flow equations is quadratic in the size of the control flow graph, with linear time complexity being the norm for almost all control flow graphs that occur in practice.

Although there is undoubtedly scope for implementing faster versions of SPRE, its analysis time is about two orders of magnitude slower than PRE. This may be acceptable for use in a standard optimizing compiler where much effort can be expended to achieve the fastest possible target program. However, it has restricted applicability in a just-in-time compiler where all the analysis must be performed on the fly.

In this paper, we introduce a new formulation of SPRE where the optimality of its final result is sacrificed in order to achieve a very efficient analysis. We call the new formulation *Isothermal Speculative Partial Redundancy Elimination* (ISPRE) for reasons which will be covered later.

ISPRE performs standard data flow analyses which can, again, be implemented as bit vector problems. Furthermore, these analyses are simpler than those performed by PRE. Since ISPRE uses program profile information, it will usually produce results which are better than PRE, though they would usually be a bit worse than those of SPRE. Experimental results included in this paper confirm this expectation. These same results also demonstrate the speed of the implementation of ISPRE, comparing it to the speed of PRE and SPRE.

2   Background and Related Work

Common Subexpression Elimination (CSE) has existed as a standard compiler optimization since the early Fortran compilers [1,2]. The first formulation of Global Common Sub-expression Elimination (GCSE), via an available expressions analysis, is described in [4].

The generalization from GCSE to partial redundancy elimination (i.e. PRE) was first described by Morel and Renvoise [10]. They later extended their analyses to the interprocedural case [11].

There have been several developments to PRE that have both improved its implementation in compilers and the quality of the transformed program. These include the reformulation of PRE as a set of *uni*directional analyses [16], and the establishment of critical-edge splitting [5] as a crucial component in increasing the power of PRE. Finally, Lazy Code Motion (LCM) [8,9] is a PRE formulation which is optimal with respect to lifetimes of the temporary variables introduced to hold expression values. Since these temporaries would often be implemented as registers, LCM has the smallest impact on register pressure. LCM is presently the algorithm of choice in modern optimizing compilers.

The idea of using profiling information to improve the expected performance of PRE is due to Horspool and Ho [6]. Subsequent work has shown that the problem can be mapped to a form of network flow problem known as Stone's Problem [15]. The name *Speculative Partial Redundancy Elimination* (SPRE) has been applied to the problem, and algorithms for finding optimal solutions have been presented [3,13]. These optimal solutions minimize the expected number of computations of the candidate expressions, based on the execution frequencies of the different paths through the program obtained from the program profile. A secondary, but still very important, concern is in minimizing register pressure. Xue and Cai [17] have developed a variation on SPRE which minimizes the lifetimes of the temporary variables while still maintaining optimality.

3   Notation and Terminology

In this paper, we present an *intraprocedural* analysis algorithm. That is, each procedure of a program will be transformed by ISPRE independently of the other procedures. Extension of ISPRE to the interprocedural case should be straightforward and is left for future work [12, sec. 19.2].

We assume that each procedure is translated into an intermediate representation (IR) by the compiler and that machine independent optimizations such as ISPRE are applied to the IR form. For the purposes of this paper, we assume that IR statements have these forms only:

```
L:                       // a label
    x = c                // assign a constant
    x = y                // assign a variable
    x = y op z           // assign a simple expression
    goto L               // unconditional branch)
    if (a op b) goto L   // conditional branch
```

where *op* represents a simple operation like addition or multiplication, or like less-than when used in a conditional branch. The precise details are unimportant when describing ISPRE.

The sequence of IR instructions for a procedure is partitioned into basic blocks. A basic block is a maximal sequence of instructions through which the only flow of control is sequential. This implies that the first instruction in a basic block must be either a labelled instruction or an instruction which follows a conditional branch. It also implies that the last instruction in a basic block is a branch, either conditional or unconditional.

The basic blocks of a procedure form a control flow graph (CFG). A CFG is a directed graph with the node set N, where each node $b \in N$ represents a basic block. The CFG has an edge set $E \subseteq N \times N$, and two distinguished nodes: $s \in N$, a unique start (or entry) node, and $f \in N$, which is a unique final (or exit) node. Edges $(u, v) \in E$ represent the branching structure of the CFG. The functions $succs(u) = \{v | (u, v) \in E\}$ and $preds(u) = \{v | (v, u) \in E\}$ represent the *immediate successors* and *immediate predecessors* of node u.

4   Isothermal Speculative Partial Redundancy Elimination

Isothermal SPRE (ISPRE) is a complete reformulation of SPRE. It is, by design, an approximate technique for performing code motion using information obtained from program profiles. The major part of the performance gains achieved by ISPRE are made in one transformation pass over the flowgraph. Further improvements can be made with additional passes, but a law of diminishing returns apply. We distinguish two versions of ISPRE with the names *Single Pass ISPRE* and *Multipass ISPRE*, according to whether just one pass or several transformation passes over the program are performed. In the following, and in our experiments, we describe single pass ISPRE.

ISPRE initially uses profile information to divide a CFG G into two subgraphs — a **hot** region G_{hot} consisting of the nodes and the edges executed more frequently than a given threshold frequency Θ, and a **cold** region G_{cold} consisting of the remaining nodes and edges. A pictorial representation of a division of a CFG into its hot and cold regions is shown in Figure 3. In this picture, the black region represents G_{hot} and the grey region represents G_{cold}.

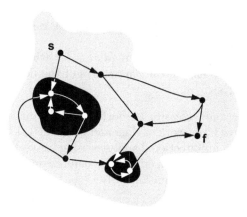

Fig. 3. Dividing a CFG into Hot and Cold Subgraphs

The example illustrates that either subgraph may consist of disconnected components. As shown here, the components of G_{hot} would usually correspond to loops. However, that is not necessarily the case because an isolated node with several predecessors and several successors could be hot while its immediate neighbours are all cold. It is also possible for a cold component to consist of just a single edge, to provide a second example of a degenerate case.

More formally,

$$G_{hot} = \langle N_H, E_H \rangle$$
$$G_{cold} = \langle N_C, E_C \rangle$$

where

$$N_H = \{u \mid u \in N \wedge \mathrm{freq}(u) > \Theta\}$$
$$E_H = \{e \mid e \in E \wedge \mathrm{freq}(e) > \Theta\}$$
$$N_C = N - N_H$$
$$E_C = E - E_H$$

Given that division into hot and cold subgraphs, we define the *Ingress* edges as

$$\mathrm{Ingress} = \{(u,v) \mid u \in N_C \wedge v \in N_H\}$$

That is, the *Ingress* set consists of those edges which transfer control from a cold node to a hot node. Note that $\mathrm{Ingress} \subseteq E_C$ must hold (because every edge adjacent to a cold node must be cold).

ISPRE operates by inserting expressions on edges in the *Ingress* set, and thus making some expressions in hot nodes become fully redundant. If those fully redundant expressions are then replaced by references to temporaries which hold saved values of the expressions, we have achieved code motion from G_{hot} to G_{cold}.

The code motion is driven by the results of two analyses:

removability, which deduces instances of computations in the hot region that can be deleted; and

necessity, which deduces edges in the *Ingress* set where computations must be inserted, so as to ensure the correctness of the deletions determined by removability analysis.

Both *removability* and *necessity* are formulated as analyses that fall within the monotone dataflow framework of Kam and Ullman [7]. This implies that they can be implemented as unidirectional analyses using bit-vector representations of sets of expressions. That is, we can efficiently compute removability and necessity for all candidate expressions simultaneously.

4.1   Removability Analysis

An expression e is a possible candidate for removal if (1) e is a *safe* expression and (2) there is an *upwards exposed* use of e in at least one node $u \in N_H$. As mentioned previously, an expression is safe at a particular program point if computing it at that point cannot generate an exception. Exactly which expressions can be considered safe is both language and platform dependent, and is beyond the scope of this paper. An expression a op b, for some operator *op* is upwards exposed in a basic block if it is not preceded in that basic block by any assignments to a or b (or, in the terminology of dataflow analysis, is not preceded by any statements which kill e).

Our removability analysis is based on the assumption that *every* candidate expression is available on *every* edge in the *Ingress* set. An expression e is available at a point P if it has been computed on every edge leading to P without being subsequently killed (i.e. no operand of e has been modified). The necessity analysis will ensure that our assumption is satisfied.

Given the assumption, removability analysis just becomes available expressions analysis [1]. A candidate expression e is removable from node u if and only if u contains an upwards exposed use of e and if e is available on entry to u. The dataflow equations, with modifications to incorporate our assumption, can now be stated.

First, the following sets are computed for each basic block by processing the intermediate code in the block.

$$\text{XUSES}(b) \quad \overset{\text{def}}{=} \quad \{\, e \mid \text{expression } e \text{ occurs in } b \text{ and is not preceded} \\ \qquad\qquad \text{by any redefinitions of operands of } e \qquad \}$$

$$\text{GEN}(b) \quad \overset{\text{def}}{=} \quad \{\, e \mid \text{expression } e \text{ occurs in } b \text{ and is not followed} \\ \qquad\qquad \text{by any redefinitions of operands of } e \qquad \}$$

$$\text{KILL}(b) \quad \overset{\text{def}}{=} \quad \{\, e \mid \text{block } b \text{ contains a statement which} \\ \qquad\qquad \text{may redefine an operand of } e \qquad \}$$

Then the following dataflow equations are solved by finding a least fixed point solution.

$$\forall b \in N :$$
$$\text{AVOUT}(b) \quad = \quad (\text{AVIN}(b) - \text{KILL}(b)) \cup \text{GEN}(b)$$

$$\text{AVIN}(b) \quad = \quad \bigcap_{p \in preds(b)} \begin{cases} \text{Candidates} & \text{if } (p, b) \in \text{Ingress} \\ \text{AVOUT}(p) & \text{otherwise} \end{cases}$$

$$\forall b \in N_H :$$
$$\text{Removable}(b) \quad = \quad \text{AVIN}(b) \cap \text{XUSES}(b)$$

In the above equations, *Candidates* represents the set of all candidate expressions. The solutions to the equations for *Removable* indicate which upwards exposed uses of expressions can be removed from each node in G_{hot}.

Note that the equations for *AVIN* and *AVOUT* are solved for all blocks in the CFG, not just in the hot region. This is because the expression availability within the cold region is useful in completing the necessity analysis.

4.2 Necessity Analysis

The solutions for the *Removable* sets assume that computations of all candidate expressions are available on the *Ingress* edges. That assumption could be satisfied by inserting the computations on all those edges. However, that would be a suboptimal solution because not all the insertions would be needed. There are two reasons why inserting an expression e on an edge (u, v) in the *Ingress* set may be unnecessary.

1. *It is useless:* the expression may not reach any exposed use of e in the hot region which has been deemed to be removable, or
2. *It is redundant:* the expression e may already be available at the end of block u.

The dataflow equations for *NEEDIN* and *NEEDOUT* determine whether insertions of the candidate expressions would be useless or not. When they have been solved, their results are used to construct the *Insert* sets. The calculation of these sets takes into account whether the insertion would be redundant or not.

$$
\begin{aligned}
\forall b \in N_H : \\
\text{NEEDIN}(b) \quad &= \quad (\text{NEEDOUT}(b) - \text{GEN}(b)) \cup \text{Removable}(b) \\[2mm]
\text{NEEDOUT}(b) \quad &= \quad \bigcup_{s \in succs(b)} \text{NEEDIN}(s) \\[2mm]
\forall (u, v) \in \text{Ingress} : \\
\text{Insert}(u, v) \quad &= \quad \text{NEEDIN}(v) - \text{AVOUT}(u)
\end{aligned}
$$

4.3 An ISPRE Example

An example CFG to be optimized by Isothermal SPRE is shown in Figure 4(a). For the example, we use a threshold value Θ of 900. Thus the hot region G_{hot} consists of blocks b2, b3, and b4, and edges b2→b3, b3→b5, and b5→b2, while the *Ingress* set consists of edges b1→b2 and b4→b5. ISPRE assumes that the result of the computation of a+b is available in temporary variable t0 on edges b1→b2 and b4→b5. Although ISPRE does not actually transform the CFG at this stage, the removability analysis assumes the existence of the extra computations on the *Ingress* edges, as shown in Figure 4(b).

Removability analysis then finds that the computation of a+b in block b3 would be redundant and can be replaced with t0. The result is shown in Figure 4(c).

Finally, we can clean up the CFG. We should, whenever possible, avoid inserting new code on edges because that implies the creation of new basic blocks and that, in turn, may cause the compiler to generate more branch instructions. In our example, the code to be inserted in edge b1→b2 can be moved to the bottom of block b1; similarly the code to be inserted on b4→b5 can be moved to the bottom of node b4. The result is shown in Figure 4(d).

4.4 Multipass ISPRE

The analysis described above partitions the CFG into two regions: a hot region and a cold regions. Once the code motions implied by that partitioning have been completed, there is no reason why the same process should not be repeated with a smaller threshold value. The smaller value for Θ will select a larger subgraph for G_{hot}, one that contains the previous G_{hot} region. The ISPRE transformations

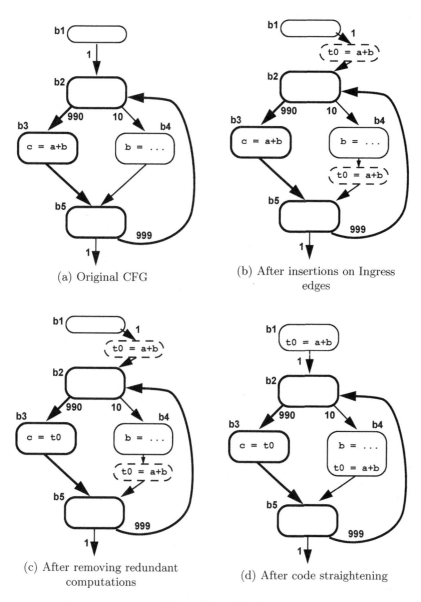

(a) Original CFG

(b) After insertions on Ingress edges

(c) After removing redundant computations

(d) After code straightening

Fig. 4. Example of ISPRE

for the second pass will again move computations from the hot region to the cold region, improving the overall performance of the program.

We propose, but we do not yet have experimental justification for, the halving of the threshold value on each pass until the expected performance gains become unimportant.

The structure of multipass ISPRE would be as follows:

$\Theta = 0.90 * maximum\ frequency$
repeat
  perform ISPRE on the CFG
  $\Theta = \Theta / 2$
until Θ *is small*

Much of the analysis for the second and subsequent iterations of ISPRE can reuse the results of the dataflow analyses from the previous iteration, just updating the solutions.

5 Experimental Results

For our experiments, we used the `gcc` compiler (version 4.1.0) when applied to various programs from the SPEC CPU2000 benchmark suite.[14] For these preliminary experiments, the `test` subsection of the suite has been used. (We plan to use the full `ref` suite in future experiments.)

Table 1 compares the effects of different PRE optimization algorithms. The column labelled *LCM* shows the execution times when compiled by `gcc` using its PRE algorithm, which is an implementation of LCM [8]. The two columns labelled *SPRE* show the (a) times when an optimal speculative PRE algorithm is used by the compiler, and (b) those times as compared to LCM. (The implementation of SPRE follows that given in [13].) Finally, the two columns labelled *ISPRE* show the results achieved by the method described in this paper. In the comparisons with LCM, a negative percentage value shows a smaller time than LCM while a positive value shows the converse.

For all the ISPRE experiments reported here, a single partitioning of the CFG was performed. That is, the multipass ISPRE was not tested in these experiments. The threshold parameter Θ was always set to be 90% of the highest node frequency in the CFG. We observe that even a single pass of ISPRE produces execution times which are very similar to those for SPRE. Taken over the set of twelve benchmarks, ISPRE produces slightly better results than SPRE.

One might ask how it is possible that an approximate technique like ISPRE could produce better timings than SPRE which is provably optimal. A partial answer is that SPRE is optimal only with respect to the expected number of evaluations of the candidate expressions when the program is run. The dynamic number of evaluations is not perfectly correlated with execution time because of interactions between PRE and other compiler optimizations, and there are interactions with the code generation phase of the compiler. We suspect that the dominant interaction effect is register pressure. The version of SPRE implemented for these experiments does not take register pressure into account. On the other hand, LCM keeps the lifetimes of the introduced temporary variables to a minimum and is therefore minimizing its effect on register pressure. We also believe that ISPRE naturally chooses insertion points for new computations at places which do not have a severe impact on register pressure.

Table 1. Execution Times of Optimized Programs

Benchmark	LCM time (seconds)	SPRE time (seconds)	relative to LCM	ISPRE time (seconds)	relative to LCM
164.gzip	1.183	1.266	7.02%	1.190	0.59%
181.mcf	0.118	0.119	0.85%	0.115	-2.54%
197.parser	1.418	1.416	-0.14%	1.305	-7.97%
253.perlbmk	4.364	4.363	-0.02%	4.373	0.21%
255.vortex	3.376	3.203	-5.12%	3.194	-5.39%
300.twolf	0.145	0.144	-0.69%	0.146	0.69%
173.applu	0.149	0.150	0.67%	0.150	0.67%
178.galgel	4.930	4.750	-3.65%	4.770	-3.25%
183.equake	0.553	0.532	-3.80%	0.532	-3.80%
188.ammp	5.688	5.281	-7.16%	5.213	-8.35%
189.lucas	7.102	7.094	-0.11%	7.202	1.41%
301.apsi	4.128	4.150	0.53%	4.164	0.87%
Summary	33.154	32.468	-2.07%	32.354	-2.41%

Table 2. Compilation Times

Benchmark	LCM time (seconds)	SPRE time (seconds)	relative to LCM	ISPRE time (seconds)	relative to LCM
164.gzip	2.300	2.460	6.96%	2.330	1.30%
181.mcf	1.200	1.240	3.33%	1.190	-0.83%
197.parser	8.370	9.150	9.32%	8.370	0.00%
253.perlbmk	28.630	33.430	16.77%	28.600	-0.10%
255.vortex	23.150	24.200	4.54%	23.270	0.52%
300.twolf	12.890	14.660	13.73%	12.840	-0.39%
173.applu	2.930	2.920	-0.34%	2.930	0.00%
178.galgel	10.580	10.760	1.70%	10.550	-0.28%
183.equake	1.110	1.330	19.82%	1.050	-5.41%
188.ammp	6.600	7.280	10.30%	6.730	1.97%
189.lucas	1.900	1.940	2.11%	1.940	2.11%
301.apsi	6.230	6.190	-0.64%	6.200	-0.48%
Summary	105.890	115.560	9.13%	106.000	0.10%

One of the claims made in this paper is that the analysis performed by ISPRE is much faster than SPRE and similar to that of the standard implementations of PRE. This claim is supported by the timings shown in Table 2. These timings show the total compilation times for the benchmark programs. In the environment of JIT compilation, all the initial phases of a compiler (lexical analysis, syntactic analysis, semantic analysis and IR code generation) would have been performed before the program begins execution. Thus the time spent on performing code optimization becomes much more significant.

Table 3. Compilation Times for PRE Optimization Phase Only

Benchmark	LCM time (seconds)	SPRE time (seconds)	SPRE relative to LCM	ISPRE time (seconds)	ISPRE relative to LCM
164.gzip	0.010	0.140	14.00	0.010	1.00
181.mcf	0.020	0.300	15.00	0.010	0.50
197.parser	0.040	0.680	17.00	0.040	1.00
253.perlbmk	0.230	4.760	20.70	0.340	1.48
255.vortex	0.130	1.040	8.00	0.210	1.62
300.twolf	0.060	1.740	29.00	0.130	2.17
173.applu	0.030	0.050	1.67	ϵ	-
178.galgel	0.270	0.270	1.00	0.310	1.15
183.equake	ϵ	0.160	-	0.200	-
188.ammp	0.060	0.590	9.83	0.020	0.33
189.lucas	0.040	0.020	0.50	0.030	0.75
301.apsi	0.030	0.040	1.33	0.070	2.33
Summary	0.920	9.630	10.47	1.170	1.27

To further reveal the difference in analysis times between the three different PRE implementations, Table 3 shows just the times spent in performing the PRE optimization during compilation. The columns which show relative performance are displayed as ratios (not as percentage differences) because most ratios are large numbers. The large ratios for SPRE, e.g. 29 for the 300.twolf benchmark, occur with the benchmarks which contain large CFGs and are a symptom of the cubic time computational complexity of the SPRE analysis. In a couple of cases, the benchmark programs are small and the measured times are negligible. In these cases, the times are shown as ϵ and the ratios between the times are left blank.

The case of 183.equake shows a negligible compilation time with LCM but a much larger compilation time with ISPRE – even larger than the compilation time with SPRE. It is currently under investigation.

6   Conclusions and Further Work

This paper has introduced a new way to implement partial redundancy elimination in a compiler. Unlike other PRE implementations, there is no claim of optimality for any cost metric (not lifetimes of saved expression values, not expected number of expression computations). However, we do claim that the method is simple to implement, is fast, and produces results that are close to those produced by the optimal SPRE algorithm. We claim the the technique is fast enough to be used by JIT compilers.

We have much further work to do, including: evaluation of multipass ISPRE, selection of threshold values, analysis of register pressure and lifetime issues, incorporating unsafe expressions into the framework, and optimizing in the presence of Java or C# exception handling.

We believe that ISPRE has the potential to become the code motion optimization algorithm of choice in future compilers, especially just-in-time compilers.

Acknowledgements

The authors gratefully acknowledge funding for this research received from the IBM Center for Advanced Studies and the Natural Sciences and Engineering Research Council of Canada.

References

1. A. Aho, R. Sethi, and J. Ullman. *Compilers: Principles, Techniques, and Tools.* Addison-Wesley, 1986.
2. M. Breuer. Generation of optimal code for expressions via factorization. *CACM*, 12(6):333–340, 1969.
3. Q. Cai and J. Xue. Optimal and efficient speculation-based partial redundancy elimination. In *CGO '03: Proceedings of the ACM/IEEE 2003 Symposium on Code Generation and Optimization*, pages 91–104, 2003.
4. J. Cocke. Global common subexpression elimination. In *Proceedings of a symposium on compiler optimization*, pages 20–24, 1970.
5. D. Dhamdhere. Practical adaptation of the global optimization algorithm of Morel and Renvoise. *ACM Transactions on Programming Languages and Systems*, 13(2):291–294, 1991.
6. R. Horspool and H. Ho. Partial redundancy elimination driven by a cost-benefit analysis. In *Proceedings of the 8th Israeli Conference on Computer Systems and Software Engineering*, pages 111–118, 1997.
7. J. B. Kam and J. D. Ullman. Monotone data flow analysis frameworks. *Acta Informatica*, 7:309–317, 1977.
8. J. Knoop, O. Ruthing, and B. Steffen. Lazy code motion. In *PLDI '92: Proceedings of the ACM SIGPLAN 1992 conference on Programming Language Design and Implementation*, pages 224–234, 1992.
9. J. Knoop, O. Ruthing, and B. Steffen. Optimal code motion: theory and practice. *ACM Transactions on Programming Languages and Systems*, 16(4):1117–1155, 1994.
10. E. Morel and C. Renvoise. Global optimization by suppression of partial redundancies. *CACM*, 22(2):96–103, 1979.
11. E. Morel and C. Renvoise. Interprocedural elimination of partial redundancies. In S. Muchnik and N. Jones, editors, *Program Flow Analysis: Theory and Applications*, pages 160–188. Prentice Hall, June 1981.
12. S. Muchnik. *Advanced Compiler Design and Implementation.* Morgan Kaufmann, 1997.
13. B. Scholz, N. Horspool, and J. Knoop. Optimizing for space and time usage with speculative partial redundancy elimination. In *LCTES '04: Proceedings of ACM SIGPLAN/SIGBED 2004 Conference on Languages, Compilers, and Tools for Embedded Systems*, pages 221–230, 2004.
14. Standard Performance Evaluation Corporation. Cpu2000. http://www.spec.org, 2006.

15. Harold Stone. Multiprocessor scheduling with the aid of network flow algorithms. *IEEE Transactions on Software Engineering*, SE-3(1):85–93, January 1977.
16. M. Wolfe. Partial redundancy elimination is not bidirectional. *SIGPLAN Notices*, 34(6):43–46, 1999.
17. Jingling Xue and Qiong Cai. A lifetime optimal algorithm for speculative pre. *ACM Transactions on Architecture and Code Generation*, page (to appear), 2006.

The Dining Philosophers Problem Revisited

Jürg Gutknecht

ETH Zürich
gutknecht@inf.ethz.ch

Abstract. We present an alternative solution to the Dining Philosophers problem that is based on Peterson's mutual exclusion algorithm for N processes, with the benefit of not using any ingredients beyond atomic read and write operations. We proceed in two steps towards a comprehensible, symmetric, and starvation-free algorithm that does neither rely on atomic test-and-set instructions nor on synchronization constructs such as monitors, signals, semaphores, locks, etc.

1 Introduction

Ever since E. W. Dijkstra posed the story of the dining philosophers as an exercise in concurrent programming in the early 1970s [1], this problem has attracted and challenged both theoreticians and programmers, and a variety of different solutions have been developed, most of them using some kind of synchronization mechanism (typically a semaphore) to control accesses to chopsticks by hungry philosophers, see for example [2]. Amazingly, although this problem is unmistakably a restricted mutual exclusion problem, we could not find any solution that makes direct use of a classical mutual exclusion algorithm. Therefore, we took the bait and tried to reuse Peterson's simple but ingenious solution to mutual exclusion published in 1981 [3].

2 Peterson's Filter Algorithm

Peterson's algorithm guarantees mutual exclusion among a fixed number of N processes with respect to their critical section, without making use of any synchronization constructs. The state of each process $0,..., N - 1$ is captured by an array structured variable named *claiming*. For i fixed, *claiming[i]* serves as an "escalator" for process i to travel from "floor" 0 (non-critical section) to "floor" N (entrance to the critical section). On each floor, the shared variable *mark* is used by a newly arriving process to leave a "footprint". Using a notional Pascal-like syntax, our version of the Peterson algorithm for N processes looks like this:

Program 1. Peterson's mutual exclusion algorithm for N processes

```
(* state space *)
var claiming, mark: array N of integer;
(* initialization *)
var i: integer;
```

D. Lightfoot and C. Szyperski (Eds.): JMLC 2006, LNCS 4228, pp. 377–382, 2006.
© Springer-Verlag Berlin Heidelberg 2006

```
begin
  for i := 0 to N-1 do claiming[i] := 0 end
end

(* process nr. i *)
var k: integer;
begin
  loop
    ... (* non-critical section *)
    (* entry protocol to critical section *)
    for k := 1 to N-1 do
      claiming[i] := k; mark[k] := i;
      while (exists j: j # i:
        (claiming[j] >= k) & (mark[k] = i)) do
      end
    end;
    claiming[i] := N;
    ... (* critical section *)
    claiming[i] := 0 (* relinquish exclusivity *)
  end
end
```

This algorithm is also called the *filter* algorithm, see [4]. The reason is that for each floor i from 1 to $N - 1$ the last process arriving at this floor (the one that left the last footprint", that is, the one that set *mark[k]* to i most recently) is a "victim" that cannot proceed. As a consequence, at most $N - i + 1$ processes can simultaneously be on floor i and, as a corollary, at most one process can be on floor N at any time, so that mutual exclusion is guaranteed. As a fine point note that the statement *claiming[i] := N* can be omitted without loss.

It is shown in [3] that the algorithm is free from *starvation* (and *deadlock*), under the obvious assumption that each process is always guaranteed to get a chance to proceed after some finite amount of time. However, note that the algorithm does not guarantee first-in-first-out handling because one process within the entry protocol can easily pass another.

3 Peterson Modified for the Dining Philosophers

Let us first recall E. W. Dijkstra's invention of the Dining Philosophers that is illustrated in Figure 1. The original formulation of the problem was this: "Five philosophers sit around a circular table. Each philosopher is alternately thinking and eating. In the centre of the table is a large plate of noodles. A philosopher needs two chopsticks to eat a helping of noodles. Unfortunately, only five chopsticks are available. One chopstick is placed between each pair of philosophers, and each agrees only to use the two chopsticks on their immediate right and left side".

Because each adjacent pair of philosophers is forced to share one chopstick but requires two of them in order to eat, appropriate synchronization of the philosophers' access to them is necessary. Therefore, at a fundamental level, we have a restricted mutual exclusion problem, and so we now try to adapt Peterson's filter algorithm to solve it.

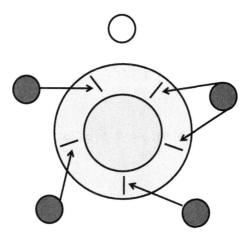

Fig. 1. A possible scenario of the Dining Philosophers: one philosopher is eating, three philosophers are waiting for their second chopstick, and one philosopher is thinking

Obviously, the *thinking* phase and *eating* phase of a philosopher's process correspond to the *non-critical* and the *critical* section of a process in the abstract setting above. The key idea of how to apply Peterson's algorithm to the philosophers problem is now straightforward: reinterpret the permission of entrance into the critical section as a mere chance to enter, and have the applicant restart his entry protocol in the case when at least one of his two neighbors is critically engaged (that is *eating*).

Keeping in mind that $(i - 1)$ *(mod 5)* and $(i + 1)$ *mod* 5 are the numbers of philosopher i's neighbors (due to a linear array being used to represent the circular table) and using abbreviations c for *claiming* and m for *mark*, we deduce the following attempt to solve the Dining Philosophers problem for five diners:

Program 2. Attempt of a Peterson based Dining Philosopher solution

```
(* state space *)
var c, m: array 5 of integer;
(* initialization *)
var i: integer;
begin
  for i := 0 to 4 do c[i] := 0 end
end

(* activity of philosopher nr. i *)
var k: integer;
begin
  loop
    (* think *)
    loop (* claim access to chopsticks *)
      for k := 1 to 4 do
        c[i] := k; m[k] := i;
```

```
    while ((c[(i + 1) mod 5] >= k)
         | (c[(i + 2) mod 5] >= k)
         | (c[(i + 3) mod 5] >= k)
         | (c[(i + 4) mod 5] >= k))
       & (m[k] = i) do
     end
   end;
   c[i] := 5;
   if c[(i - 1) mod 5] >= 0 & c[(i + 1) mod 5] >= 0
     then exit
   end
 end;
 c[i] := -1;
 (* eat *)
 c[i] := 0
end
end
```

According to this algorithm, each philosopher i is continuously cycling through the states $c[i] = 0, 1, 2, 3, 4, 5, 1, 2, 3, 4, 5, 1, 2, 3, 4, 5, ..., 1, 2, 3, 4, 5, -1, 0, 1, 2, ...$ whose semantics are described in Table 1.

Table 1. State diagram for philosopher processes

State c	Semantics
0	thinking
1	hungry, starting entry protocol
2	progressing in entry protocol
3	progressing in entry protocol
4	progressing in entry protocol
5	chance to eat if no neighbor eats
-1	eating

From our above discussion of the filter algorithm we know that the statements in state $c[i] = 5$ (in bold type face) run under mutual exclusion, which means that $c[i] < 0$ invariantly implies $c[(i - 1) \bmod 5] >= 0$ and $c[(i + 1) \bmod 5] >= 0$ or, in other words, that, whenever philosopher i is in his critical section, none of his two neighbors $(i - 1) \bmod 5$ and $(i + 1) \bmod 5$ are in their critical section.

However, the above solution is not free from potential starvation, as the following scenario demonstrates: an applicant P detects that one of his neighbors, say Q, is busy in his critical section and therefore immediately restarts the entry protocol. At roughly the same time, Q exits the critical section and, because he is still hungry, immediately requests entrance to the critical section again. This leads to a race between P and Q that might be won by Q because, as we know, the filter algorithm does not prevent one algorithm from passing another. Because this situation may recur any arbitrary number of times, *P* may finally starve due to the "race hazard".

Therefore, the algorithm needs further refinement. One way to remedy the race hazard is adding a variant of the "bakery algorithm" by introducing a ticket-numbering system that (roughly) indicates the order of the processes starting the entry protocol. However, ticket-numbering may have a transitive (global) effect that prevents an otherwise unblocked philosopher from starting to eat merely because of his high ticket-number. A better refinement of Program 2 is based on a mechanism that allows a hungry but blocked philosopher in the state $c[i] = 5$ to raise a flag. For this purpose, Boolean arrays *l* and *r* are added with the following semantics:

- $l[i] \Leftrightarrow$ philosopher *i* would be allowed to eat but is blocked by his left neighbor
- $r[i] \Leftrightarrow$ philosopher *i* would be allowed to eat but is blocked by his right neighbor

An additional guard at the end of the filter loop is now used to request each philosopher to yield to any of his neighbors who was previously blocked. The following argument shows that the resulting algorithm is free from starvation: assume that some philosopher process *i* cannot proceed from state *5* to the critical section due to one or both neighbors who are in their critical section. Then, after some finite amount of time, these neighbors will leave their critical section and will not be able to enter again before philosopher *i* has removed his flags $l[i]$ and $r[i]$ and has passed the critical section himself.

Program 3. The Final Program Solving the Dining Philosophers Program

```
(* state space *)
var l, r: array 5 of Boolean;
   c, m: array 5 of integer;

(* initialization *)
var i: integer;
begin
  for i := 0 to 4 do
    l[i] := false; r[i] := false; c[i] := 0
  end
end

(* activity of philosopher nr. i *)
var k: integer;
begin
  loop
    (* think *)
    loop (* enter room and claim access *)
      for k := 1 to 4 do
        c[i] := k; m[k] := i;
        while ((c[(i + 1) mod 5] >= k)
             |  (c[(i + 2) mod 5] >= k)
             |  (c[(i + 3) mod 5] >= k)
             |  (c[(i + 4) mod 5] >= k))
             & (m[k] = i) do
      end
```

```
        end;
        c[i] := 5;
        if c[(i - 1) mod 5] < 0 then l[i] := true
        elsif c[(i + 1) mod 5] < 0) then r[i] := true
        elsif ~r[(i - 1) mod 5] & ~l[(i + 1) mod 5])
        then exit
        end
      end;
      c[i] := -1; l[i] := false; r[i] := false;
      (* eat *)
      c[i] := 0
    end
end
```

3 Conclusion

We have demonstrated the approach of adapting a well-proved generic mutual exclusion algorithm to a restricted mutual exclusion problem, with the benefit of automatically inheriting its correctness and other qualities. This approach contrasts with the usual approach of handcrafting an algorithm that solves a singular concurrency problem but inherently carries the dangers of errors due to overlooked scenarios. The net result is an elegant, symmetric, and starvation-free solution to the Dining Philosophers' problem that does neither rely on synchronization constructs nor on hardware support for atomic memory updates.

Acknowledgement

I gratefully acknowledge the hint from Daniel Kröning on Nir Shavit's proof of Peterson's filter algorithm. Also, I thank Ulrike Glavitsch, Gerardo Tauriello and Svend Knudsen for their critical inspection of the algorithm, and Brian Kirk for his constructive review of earlier versions of this paper.

References

1. Dijkstra, E. W.: Hierarchical Ordering of Sequential Processes, Acts Informatica I, 115 – 138 (1971)
2. Silberschatz, A., Peterson, J. L.: Operating Systems Concepts, Addison-Wesley (1988)
3. Peterson, G. L.: Myths About the Mutual Exclusion Problem, IPL 12(3), 115 – 116 (1981)
4. Shavit, N.: Lecture Notes for Lecture 2, Chapter 2.4.1., Tel-Aviv University, http://www.cs.tau.ac.il/~shanir/multiprocessor-synch-2003/

A Mobile Agent Service-Oriented Scripting Language Encoded on a Process Calculus

Hervé Paulino[1] and Luís Lopes[2]

[1] Departamento de Informática, Faculdade de Ciências e Tecnologia,
Universidade Nova de Lisboa, Portugal
herve@di.fct.unl.pt
[2] Departamento de Ciência de Computadores, Faculdade de Ciências,
Universidade do Porto, Portugal
lblopes@dcc.fc.up.pt

Abstract. We present a service-oriented scripting language for programming mobile agents in distributed systems. The main novelty of the language we call MOB, is the integration of the service-oriented and mobile agent paradigms. MOB is also encoded onto a process calculus with a well studied semantics. The encoding provides a specification for the front-end of the language compiler and allows us to use, for the back-end and for the run-time system, a compiler and a virtual machine previously developed for the process calculus.

1 Introduction and Motivation

Service-Oriented Computing (SOC) builds on the pre-existing concepts of object-oriented and component-based programming, and the client-server paradigm. The programming model is borrowed from the object-oriented paradigm, as services are accessed much in the same way that objects are. Services are described in a platform independent way by contracts (service interfaces), which are negotiated by the components of an application. Inter-component communication is based on the client-server paradigm. However, unlike typical client-server architectures where a client is linked to a given server during the entire operation, in service-oriented architectures the client-server model is used to request services in a peer-to-peer organization. A component is not tied to a single server and there are no client-server hierarchies between the components that provide and require services. Most of the first service-oriented architectures were built resorting to DCOM [1] or to CORBA [2]. Component-based systems have recently received a lot of attention for distributed systems, namely with the .NET [3], Jini [4] and Openwings [5] platforms.

Another major technology for Web applications is that of *mobile agents* (MA). Mobile agents are computations that have the ability to travel through a network, by halting their execution, saving their state and then restoring it in a new host. As they travel along the network, mobile agents use resources (e.g., data, servers) thus focusing on local, rather than remote, communication. This contrasts with the usual communication paradigms (e.g., client-server), that require costly remote sessions to be maintained.

D. Lightfoot and C. Szyperski (Eds.): JMLC 2006, LNCS 4228, pp. 383–402, 2006.

Programming languages for mobile agents come in two flavors: those *designed by hand* and those based on formal systems. In the first set we have systems such as Aglets [6], Mole [7] and Voyager [8] that mostly extend Java classes to define an agent's behavior. Since it is not possible to access the state of the Java Virtual Machine (JVM), and modifying it would mean losing portability, all these systems resort to a weaker kind of migration. Instead of moving the whole computation to the new location and resuming the execution in the exact same point where it was interrupted, only code and data are moved, forcing the programmer to implement *receiver code* that re-activates the agent after a migration. Another approach, still in the same set, is that of scripting languages such as D'Agents [9] or Ara [10], that fully support agent migration but require specific virtual machine support.

Providing a demonstrably sound semantics for all these systems is rather difficult given the gap between the implementation and an adequate formal model.

Languages in the second set are based on formal systems, mostly some form or extension of the π-calculus [11,12]. This process calculus provides the theoretical framework upon which researchers can build solid specifications for programming languages. Languages can thus be proved correct *by design* relative to some base calculus with a well established theory, by providing an adequate encoding. Examples of such languages have been implemented in recent years, namely, JoCaml [13], TyCO [14], X-Klaim [15], Nomadic Pict [16], Acute [17] and Alice [18]. Although process calculi are ideal formal tools for the development of mobile agent frameworks, their constructs are very low-level and high-level idioms that provide more intuitive abstractions for programming are desirable.

In [19] we first introduced Mob, a programming language for developing applications based on mobile agents. Here we extend Mob with another main abstraction, *services*, thus uniting two major paradigms for Web applications. Services, whose contracts are interfaces implemented by agents, and (mobile) agents are the main abstractions of the language. Agents provide and require services dynamically as they move through the network. It is our belief that combining the SOC and MA paradigms in a programming language provides a useful tool for high-level programming of mobile agents. For instance, using a service-oriented language, programmers are not required to keep track of agent names. This makes applications more resilient since the same service may be provided transparently by several agents in the network.

Moreover, the new formulation of the Mob language has been encoded onto a calculus that extends the LSD (Lexically Scoped Distributed) π-calculus [20] with basic objects, expressions, and a strong migration primitive. The LSDπ-calculus is, in turn, a form of the π-calculus extended with support for distributed execution and mobility of resources and, with a well-studied semantics. Although this is not the focus of this paper, we hope to use the encoding to prove the soundness of the operational semantics of the language. This is particularly important as it provides a form of language security, in the sense of being *correct by design*, not readily available in related languages.

Last, but not least, the encoding onto the process calculus provides a full specification of the front-end of the compiler for MOB. The output of this front-end is the MOB source programs written into equivalent programs in the DiTyCO language [14], a concrete implementation of the LSDπ model. This allowed us to use both the compiler and the run-time system previously developed for DiTyCO [21], respectively, as the back-end of the MOB compiler and as the basis for the run-time system for MOB.

The remainder of the paper is structured as follows: the next section describes the syntax and semantics of the MOB programming language; section 3 describes the MOB language compiler and run-time system; section 4 presents two programming examples in MOB to demonstrate its expressiveness; section 5 compares our approach to existing work in the area, and; finally, we present some conclusions and future work in section 6.

2   Introducing Mob

MOB is a service-oriented mobile agent programming language, whose main abstractions are agents and services. Agents are objects with an associated run-time. Following an object-oriented approach, they are abstracted in classes defined by the **agent** construct, while instances are created with the **new** construct. Definitions for common objects are given by the **class** construct, and instances are created also with the **new** construct.

Agents may move through the network and this is controlled explicitly, at high-level, by the programmer using a primitive **go** (similar to the one found in Telescript [22]). A strong migration mechanism is used, thus the movement of an agent involves moving its whole state (code, data and execution state) to the target host in the network. On arrival the execution resumes transparently at the exact point where it was interrupted. An agent always carries the closure for its code, thus enabling disconnected autonomous execution.

Agents may provide (**provides**) services to other agents and, simultaneously, require (**requires**) services provided by other agents. There is absolutely no distinction between clients and servers. As service providers, agents must be able to handle multiple incoming requests. To cope with this demand MOB agents are multi-threaded. Threads can be explicitly created by an agent, through the **fork** instruction, or implicitly created, e.g., in a remote method invocation. The threads running in an agent have unique identifiers and share the agent's address space. Synchronization with the parent thread can be achieved with the **join** instruction. Another form of synchronization is provided by the instructions **lock** and **unlock** that support a simple form of mutual exclusion in data access.

The interface for services is defined by the **service** construct. The interface is the contract for the service, the base for all service-oriented programming in MOB. By providing and requiring services, agents become the components of a service-oriented architecture. Checking that the interface of a service is correctly implemented is done at compile time by connecting to a network name service. The types inferred by the MOB compiler are matched with those assumed for the service in the network. Well-typed MOB programs do not have run-time protocol errors, i.e., method invocations are guaranteed to invoke existing methods in objects and agents, with the right number of arguments and with the correct types for the arguments.

To access a service, an agent must get a binding for an agent that provides that service. The binding is obtained dynamically through the primitive **bind** that asks the network name service for an agent that provides the required service. When the binding is received, interaction through method invocation can happen (much like Java RMI [23]).

MOB can also be used as a coordination language. For that we support the interaction with external services through the **exec** primitive. We supply an interface of seven actions that allow initializing a session with a service, interacting with it, and ultimately terminating it. This interface can be used, for instance, to execute services implemented in other languages, or interact with network services, such as WWW queries, FTP transactions, or e-mail communication.

The remainder of the language constructs provide fairly standard support for control flow, expression evaluation and built-in types.

Syntax and Semantics

Here, we describe the abstract syntax for MOB, an extension of the MOB core language [24], obtained by providing derived constructs for higher-level programming. The derived constructs keep the underlying semantics of the core language and are used, for example, to introduce new data-types such as arrays and hashes (associative arrays). Due to space constraints we will briefly describe the syntax and semantics of the language. The full definition of the language and its operational semantics may be found in [24].

The syntax for a MOB program is presented in figure 1. The language defines a set of reserved words identified in bold-face. The main syntactic categories are: constants (booleans, integers and strings) ranged over by c; variables, ranged over by x; agent and class identifiers, ranged over by X; service identifiers, ranged over by S; method names, ranged over by m; expressions, ranged over by e, and; instructions, ranged over by P. A sequence of elements of a syntactic category α is denoted $\tilde{\alpha}$. With this syntax, constant arrays are denoted by $[\tilde{e}]$ and constant hashes by $\{\tilde{e} \Rightarrow \tilde{e}\}$. Naturally, the concrete syntax of MOB imposes some restrictions to this syntax, e.g., class, agent and service declarations are allowed only at the beginning of programs.

We exemplify the syntax with a small example of a server and a client for a Time service. The server (listing 1) provides the service Time with a single method getTime(). Note that the **main** method may be empty since MOB agents run as daemons and some external action is required to terminate their execution. Here **mob** is a built-in object, available to every MOB program. It provides an implementation for basic operations (e.g., input/output) and a simple interface based on sessions to run external programs. For example, in listing 1, the execp method encapsulates the execution of a command in the local file-system and returns a handle for a session in the variable proc. Methods can then be executed

$$P \quad ::= \quad \textbf{agent } X(\tilde{x}) \text{ [\textbf{provides} } \tilde{S}] \text{ [\textbf{requires} } \tilde{S}] \; \{ \, [G] \, [M] \, \} \quad | \quad \textbf{class } X(\tilde{x}) \; \{ \, [G] \, [M] \, \}$$
$$| \quad \textbf{service } S \, \{\tilde{m}\} \quad | \quad \textbf{requires } \tilde{S} \quad | \quad \textbf{join } (x) \quad | \quad \textbf{lock } (x) \quad | \quad \textbf{unlock } (x)$$
$$| \quad \textbf{go } (e) \quad | \quad \textbf{if } (e) \; \{ \, P \, \} \; [\textbf{else} \; \{ \, P \, \}] \quad | \quad \textbf{while } (e) \; \{ \, P \, \} \quad | \quad \textbf{for } (x \textbf{ in } e) \; \{ \, P \, \}$$
$$| \quad \textbf{for } (G \; ; \; e \; ; \; G) \; \{ \, P \, \} \quad | \quad \textbf{break} \quad | \quad \textbf{return } e \quad | \quad \textbf{exit}() \quad | \quad d = e \quad | \quad C$$
$$| \quad P \; ; \; P \quad | \quad \epsilon$$
$$G \quad ::= \quad x_1 = e_1 \; ... \; x_n = e_n$$
$$M \quad ::= \quad m_1(\tilde{x}_1) \; \{ \, P_1 \, \} \; ... \; m_n(\tilde{x}_n) \; \{ \, P_n \, \}$$
$$C \quad ::= \quad \textbf{new } X(\tilde{e}) \quad | \quad \textbf{fork } \{ \, P \, \} \quad | \quad \textbf{bind } (S, \, e) \quad | \quad \textbf{bind } (S) \quad | \quad \textbf{host}()$$
$$| \quad \textbf{exec } (\tilde{e}) \quad | \quad e.m \; (\tilde{e})$$
$$e \quad ::= \quad C \quad | \quad \{\tilde{e} \Rightarrow \tilde{e}\} \quad | \quad [\tilde{e}] \quad | \quad e \; bop \; e \quad | \quad uop \; e \quad | \quad d \quad | \quad c \quad | \quad \textbf{self} \quad | \quad \textbf{mob}$$
$$| \quad \textbf{null}$$
$$d \quad ::= \quad x \quad | \quad e[e] \quad | \quad e\{e\} \quad | \quad d.d$$

Fig. 1. The syntax of the MOB programming language

on this handle according to the kind of session provided: the readln method reads the result of the command getTimeApp, and; kill terminates the session.

Listing 1. A time server agent

```
service Time { getTime }
agent TimeServer() provides Time {
 main { }
 getTime() {
   proc = mob.execp("getTimeApp");
   line = proc.readln();
   proc.kill();
   return line;
 }
}
new TimeServer()
```

The client (listing 2) requires the Time service and takes an array of hosts as an argument. The agent performs a cycle in which it moves to each of the hosts provided, setting the current time to the value retrieved from the TimeServer.

Listing 2. A time client agent

```
agent TimeClient(hosts) requires Time {
 main() {
   timeServer = bind(Time);
   for (hostname in hosts) {
     go(hostname);
     proc = mob.execp("setTimeApp " ^ timeServer.getTime());
     proc.kill();
   }
 }
}
new TimeClient(["host1", "host2", "host3", "host4"]);
```

The semantics for the MOB core language is provided in the form of a static type system and an abstract machine. The later describes state transitions between network configurations. It is not possible to provide a detailed description of the abstract machine here, due to space constraints. We refer the reader to [24] for an in depth presentation and, instead briefly sketch the abstract machine here.

A MOB network N is composed of a set of agents A running concurrently, together with a name service R. This service keeps two maps. The first, R_h, keeps track of the current host for each agent. The second, R_s, keeps, for each service, its type and the set of agents currently running in the network that provide it. Thus a network may be written as $A_1 \mid \ldots \mid A_n, R$ (where $\mid$ is the concurrent composition operation).

Each agent is internally composed of an agent key k (used to identify the agent in the network), a host identifier h (the name of the host the agent is currently running on), the code C required for the execution of the agent, a heap H (to keep run-time data-structures), a pool of running threads $T_1 \mid \ldots \mid T_n$ and, a set of suspended threads W (waiting on resources). Thus, we write an agent as a tuple of the form $A \overset{\text{def}}{=} (k, h, C, H, T_1 \mid \ldots \mid T_n, W)$.

Threads T are composed of a thread identifier t (a synchronization point for the thread), a stack Q (composed of closures of code blocks waiting to be executed) and, a heap reference r where the result of the execution of the thread is to be placed. Thus, a thread may be written as a tuple of the form: $T \overset{\text{def}}{=} (t, Q, r)$.

The abstract machine describes MOB computations with rules of the form $A, R \rightarrow A', R'$. This top-level reduction operation is most often obtained in terms of reduction within agents $A \rightarrow A'$ when the instructions executed by the agent do not involve the name service, or other agents. With this description, the initial state of the execution of a program P is:

$$(k, h, \emptyset, \emptyset, (t, (\emptyset, P), null), \emptyset) \mid A, R$$

where k is a fresh agent key, t is a fresh thread identifier, h is the local host and, P is the sequence of instructions of the program. At the end of the sequence of instructions of a program the configuration of the network will be of the form:

$$(k, h, \_, \_, (t, \epsilon, null), \emptyset) \mid A', R'$$

This state may not be further simplified to A', R', since the agent may provide services to the network. It simply means that the services have been setup. The agent now runs as a daemon at host h. To end the execution of an agent the programmer must explicitly do so with an **exit** command.

As an example, we present the rules for the **go** and **bind** primitives. The **go** primitive takes an argument that must be evaluated as a string and that names a host (h') in the network. The rule takes the host name and changes the name service map R_h by mapping the agent binding r' to the host h'. This change is reflected in the current hostname for the agent.

$$\frac{\mathsf{eval}(H,t,B,v) = h' \quad B(\mathbf{self}) = r' \quad r' \in dom(R_h) \quad h' \in \mathrm{Host}}{(k,h,C,H,(t,(B,\mathbf{go}(v)\ ;P) :: Q,r) \mid T,W) \mid A,(R_h,R_s) \rightarrow \atop (k,h',C,H,(t,(B,P) :: Q,r) \mid T,W) \mid A,(R_h + \{r' : h'\},R_s)}$$

The **bind** primitive takes a service name as its argument and provides a binding for an agent that implements the service. So, the rule for **bind**, consults the R_s component of the name server with S as key, and retrieves a binding for one of the available agents. Here we assume that any agent will do. However, in an implementation, the choice criteria can be customized.

$$\frac{R_s(S) = (\alpha, \{r_1, \ldots, r_n\}) \quad r' \in \{r_1, \ldots, r_n\}}{(k,h,C,H,(t,(B,x = \mathbf{bind}(S)\ ;P) :: Q,r) \mid T,W) \mid A,(R_h,R_s) \rightarrow \atop (k,h,C,H,(t,(B + \{x : r'\},P) :: Q,r) \mid T,W) \mid A,(R_h,R_s)}$$

Finally, the abstract machine was encoded onto the DiTyCO process calculus [14] by defining a map from networks in MOB onto networks in DiTyCO. This encoding forms the specification for the front-end of the MOB compiler which we will describe in the next section.

3   Compiler and Run-Time System

The Compiler
The compilation of a MOB program is a two stage process (figure 2). First, the front-end of the compiler takes the MOB source code and outputs the corresponding code in the DiTyCO language, as specified by the encoding of MOB in LSDπ. The back-end of the MOB compiler is just the compiler for the DiTyCO language [21]. The DiTyCO compiler outputs code written in an intermediate language called MIL (Multi-threaded Intermediate Language [25]), which is compiled *just-in-time* by the run-time system before being executed.

The *front-end* of the compiler performs type inference on the MOB source code and in particular finds the types for both the services provided and required by each agent defined in a program. At this point in the compilation, the network name service is contacted and a type-check is performed. The types inferred by the compiler are matched against those assumed for the services in the network. If the agent provides a non-existing service, the interface provided becomes *the* interface for that service. This level of type verification provides some form of program security in remote method invocation. If the type-check succeeds, the source MOB program is transformed into a program written in the DiTyCO programming language.

Along with the DiTyCO code for a MOB program, one extra DiTyCO program may be produced for certain agents. These are *proxies* that, when compiled and executed, allow users to locate a particular agent in the network and to interact with it. Proxies are generated only for agents that define a special proxyKey attribute, that is used to locate the agent in the network. Proxies can be executed in any MOB-enabled host.

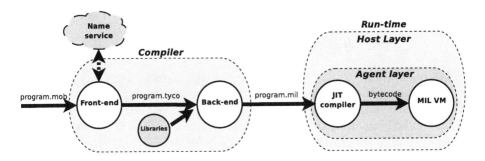

Fig. 2. The compilation and execution of a MOB program

The back-end of the compiler, takes the DiTyCO code generated by the front-end and processes it with the DiTyCO language compiler to produce .mil files for each agent and its proxy. Only well-typed DiTyCO programs are successfully compiled into the final MIL code. The MIL code thus generated is executed by the run-time system for the DiTyCO programming language [26] with extensions to support strong mobility (figure 2).

The Run-Time System

Agents run within the boundaries of hosts. In MOB, this host layer is implemented on every MOB-enabled host in a network and on top of the DiTyCO run-time system (figure 3). This layer is responsible for managing agents within hosts and supporting their mobility. It is implemented as a service, identified by a unique, network-wide port, and provides the means to create, execute, marshall, send, unmarshall and receive agents. Its implementation takes advantage of the fact that the MIL virtual machine is implemented on top of the JVM. This, for instance, enables the access to the full state of an agent and makes the (un)marshalling operations quite straightforward to implement besides preserving portability. For example, the MOB run-time system can provide a strong migration mechanism in a simple and transparent way by stopping and serializing a running agent that executes the **go** primitive.

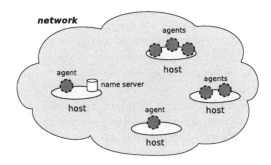

Fig. 3. A MOB network

DiTyCO run-time system

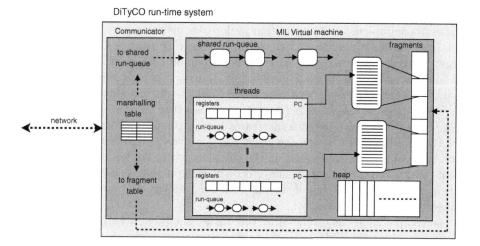

Fig. 4. The DiTyCO run-time system (site)

The next layer corresponds to the agents themselves and the name service. Both the agents and the name service are implemented with DiTyCO run-time systems. Each DiTyCO run-time system (site) has two components; the first is an instance of the MIL virtual machine that runs the MIL code for the agent or for the name service; the second, is called the *communicator* and is a JVM thread responsible for handling network communication for the MIL virtual machine (figure 4).

Internally, the MIL virtual machine is composed of a heap, a hash of MIL program fragments, and a pool of JVM threads that consume/produce tasks from/for a set of local run-queues. The tasks are activation records for fragments of MIL code compiled from the original MOB program. They are scheduled for execution in the run-queues and executed by idle threads [26].

A shared run-queue also exists to allow for load-balancing between the threads running the virtual machine (figure 4).

The migration of sites introduces a problem in the management of the coherence of the state of the network, since other sites may hold bindings to resources from the site about to move. We handle this problem with a lazy reconfiguration of the network's topology. When a client tries to establish a connection to an agent (a site) that is no longer where expected, an exception is thrown. In response to this exception, a query is sent to the DiTyCO run-time infrastructure to find the new location of the agent. The run-time system provides the new location of the agent and updates all the bindings for the resources imported from that agent in the client. If the agent is not found, the run-time system reports an error to the client.

4   Programming with MOB

In this section we present two programming examples that illustrate the expressiveness of the language.

A Mobile Number Cruncher

The example implements an agent that performs some computationally intensive task (e.g., *number crunching*) that requires a large amount of CPU time. The target hardware system in this example is a common LAN, in which computers are idle for substantial periods of time (e.g., during the night, weekends, lunch hour). To obtain the resources it requires to complete the computation, the agent moves through the LAN looking for idle machines that voluntarily donate their CPU cycles. This example also illustrates how MOB may be used to program just the coordination between the agent and the underlying network infrastructure, thus completely encapsulating the computation to be performed. Allowing agents to dynamically move to computers where the required resources are available increases the usefulness of the platform considerably and potentially allows almost uninterrupted execution.

The computation encapsulated by the worker agents may be implemented in a language other than MOB. The only assumption we make on the application is that it periodically checkpoints its state into a file and that this file may be used (as input) to resume the computation once the agent has moved to another host. The application is divided into three MOB modules.

The PortalAgent (listing 3) supplies an entry point to the network. Its purpose is to welcome the registry of new hosts to the network and to allow the execution of new applications. The Portal service defines methods to allow new hosts to join the network (enter), to retrieve the currently registered hosts (getHosts), to obtain the number of hosts participating in the cluster (getNoOfHosts), and which of these are currently available to receive work (getNoOfHostsAvailable). This data is collected by interacting with MonitorAgent installed on each host of the LAN.

Listing 3. The PortalAgent agent

```
service Portal {enter, getHosts, getNoOfHosts, getNoOfHostsAvailable}

agent PortalAgent() provides Portal {
  hosts = [];  // The hosts registered in the portal

  enter(h) { hosts.put(h); }
  getHosts() { return hosts; }
  getNoOfHosts() { return hosts.size(); }

  getNoOfHostsAvailable() {
    result = 0;
    for (h in hosts)
      if (h.getLoad() != -1)
        result++;
    return result;
  }
}
new PortalAgent();
```

A MonitorAgent (listing 4) begins by locating the portal and joining the network. At startup, it specifies the maximum computational load allowed for applications in the local node. Then, it periodically checks the load of the host and uses it to decide whether it is possible to host an application. If the load is higher than the limit and a worker is running, the later is notified that it must leave the host. The Monitor service provides methods to retrieve the name of the host it is monitoring (getHost), to reserve the host for an incoming agent (reserve), to allow a worker to register itself in the host and store a file with given contents in the local file-system (registerAndStoreFile), to load a data file to memory (loadFile), and to retrieve the computational load of the host (getLoad). The reserve method ensures that the migration from one host to another is atomic, setting the target host as unavailable to any other request during the operation.

Listing 4. The MonitorAgent agent

```
service Monitor {getHost, reserve, getLoad, registerAndStoreFile, loadFile}

agent MonitorAgent(portalHost, maxLoad) provides Monitor requires Portal {
  worker = null;                              // The worker currently executing in the host
  load = 0;                                    // The current work load
  available = true;                            // Availability of the host

  main() {
    portal = bind(portalHost, Portal);        // Locate portal
    portal.enter(self);                        // Enter the network
    while (true) {
      load = readLoad();                       // Read the host's load
      if (worker != null) {                    // If a worker is running
        if (load > maxLoad) {
          worker.leave();                      // Command agent to leave
          worker = null;
        }
      }
      else                                     // If no a worker is running
        if (load > maxLoad)  available = false; // Not available
        else   available = true;               // Available
      mob.sleep(1000);                         // Sleep 1 second
    }
  }

  registerAndStoreFile(w, fileName, data) {
    worker = w;                                // Register worker
    // Open file and store contents
  }

  loadFile(fileName) { /* Read and return file contents */ }

  getHost() { return host();  }

  reserve() { available = false; }

  getLoad() { if (available) return load; else return -1; }

  readLoad() {
    proc = mob.execp("getLoad");               // Obtain the load of the host
    result = new String(proc.readln()).toInt(); // Convert it to an integer
    proc.kill();                               // Terminate execution of getLoad
    return result;                             // Return result
  }
}
new MonitorAgent($1, new String($2).toInt());
```

Finally, a WorkerAgent (listing 5) encapsulates the application to be executed in a given host. Its parameters are: the name of the portal, the name of the application to execute and, the name of the checkpoint file for the application.

Listing 5. The WorkerAgent agent

```
service Worker { leave }

agent WorkerAgent ( portalHost , app , dataFile ) provides Worker requires Portal {
   portal ;                                  // The agent supplying the Portal service
   monitor ;                                 // The monitor of the current host
   data ;                                    // The data collected by the agent
   runningApp ;                              // The process running the application
   MAX_LOAD = 1000                           // A top for the load

   main ( ) {
      portal = bind ( portalHost , Portal );      // Locate portal
      data = monitor . loadFile ( dataFile );     // Load file to memory
      findHostAndGo ( );                          // Find a host to execute the application
   }

   leave ( ) {
      runningApp . kill ( );                      // Terminate the execution of the application
      data = monitor . loadFile ( dataFile );     // Load file to memory
      findHostAndGo ( );                          // Find new host
   }

   findHostAndGo ( ) {
      found = false ;
      hosts = portal . getHosts ( )               // Get hosts in the network
      monitor = null ;
      while ( ! found ) {
         load = MAX_LOAD;
         for ( h in hosts ) {                     // For each host in the network
            aux = h . getLoad ( );                // Obtain load of the host
            if ( aux != −1 && aux < load ) {      // Check if it is the one with a lower load
               monitor = h ;
               load = aux ;
            }
         }
         if ( monitor != null )
            found = monitor . reserve ( );        // Mark host as reserved
      }
      go ( monitor . getHost ( ));                            // Migrate to host
      monitor . registerAndStoreFile ( self , dataFile , data );  // Store data to file
      runningApp = mob . execp ( app );                       // Run application
   }
}
new WorkerAgent ( $1 , $2 , $3 );                 // Create worker agent
```

The **main** method locates the portal and calls findHostAndGo to find a suitable host to install the computation. Once the host is selected in the later method, the agent moves to it, saves the checkpoint data to a file and executes the application. The host where the application is deployed is selected based on the loads reported by the monitors of each host registered in the portal. In this example, the host with the lowest load is reserved. The reservation will only fail if another worker as already reserved the host. The leave method is used to suspend the execution of the application in the current host when it ceases to provide the computational resources necessary to run it (for example, the owner of the host restarts using it). The method suspends the execution of the application and looks for a new host by querying the portal. Note that the method only returns once the migration is complete, and thus the later is a synchronous operation.

A Mobile RPM Installer

In this section we present an example that provides a simple way to dynamically update the software (in the form of RPM files) in a network. For simplicity we assume that all target hosts have the same operating system and distribution, and thus no version control is required. We also do not implement user authentication, since it is not the focus of the example. The application is divided into four components.

The Repository agent manages a repository of software files (listing 6). It implements the SoftRepository service that provides methods to store (put) and retrieve files (get), and to obtain the agent's location (getHost). Method get takes a list of file names and creates and returns an hash in which the keys are the file names and the values are the contents of the files. The method put method adds files to the repository.

Listing 6. The Repository agent

```
service SoftRepository { put get getHost }

agent Repository() provides SoftRepository {

  main() {  }

  put(fileName, fileContents) { ... }

  get(files) {
    result = {};
    for (fileName in files)                    // Place the contents of the files in the map
      result.put(fileName, readFile(fileName));
    return result;                             // Return map
  }

  getHost() { return host(); }

  readFile(fileName) { /* Read the file to memory */ }
}
new Repository();
```

Every host willing to be updated must execute an agent that implements the SoftInstaller service. This agent, Installer, is the base station for other agents to come and install the software. The SoftInstaller service is composed by two methods: install and getDeps. In their implementation in the Installer agent, the install method performs the actual installation of the software given as argument. It creates a new file to hold the RPM to install, installs it by executing the `rpm -i` command, and finally removes the RPM file from the file-system. It returns the message given by the RPM installation, or an error message, if the file could not be created. The getDeps method, returns an array holding the dependencies of the given file. The implementation is similar to install.

Listing 7. The Installer agent

```
service SoftInstaller { install, getDeps }

agent Installer(targetHost) provides SoftInstaller {
  main() { go(targetHost); }

  install(fileContents) {
    fileName = createFile(fileContents);        // Create file
    proc = mob.execp("rpm -i " ^ fileName);     // Install file
    proc.wait();                                // Wait for completion
    result = proc.readln();
    removeFile(fileName);                       // Remove file
    return result;                              // Return result
  }

  getDeps(fileContents) {
    fileName = createFile(fileContents);        // Create file
    proc = mob.execp("rpmDeps " ^ fileName);    // Get dependencies
    proc.wait();                                // Wait for completion
    result = new String(proc.readln()).toArray(); // Create array from string
    removeFile(fileName);                       // Remove file
    return result;                              // Return result
  }

  createFile(fileContents) { /* Create new temporary file */ }
  removeFile(fileName) { /* Delete file from folder */ }
}
for (i = 1; i < $$; i++)                        // For each host given as argument
  new Installer($i);                            // Launch installer
```

Client is a component that locates a network agent that provides the Soft-Deployer service and instructs him to install a set of files in a set of hosts. Its implementation (listing 8) receives a string with the hosts ($1) and, a string with the names of the files to install ($2) from the command line.

Listing 8. The Client script

```
requires SoftDeployer
bind(SoftDeployer).deploy( new String($1).toArray(), new String($2).toArray());
```

Finally, a Deployer agent is launched into the network and waits for installation requests. As the name suggests, the agent deploys the files required by the local instances of Installer agents. Requests get exclusive access to the agent and thus are serviced one at a time. A call to the deploy method first resolves the location of the software repository and the Deployer agent moves to that host, in order to obtain the desired RPM files. Then, it moves through the list of hosts given in the call. At each host it obtains a bind for a local agent implementing the SoftInstaller service. Then, for each file to install, it checks for unresolved dependencies. The result (deps) will be matched against the list of files installed in the previous host (the keys of the cachedFiles hash). Once this operation is completed, the deps list will contain the name of the files required from the repository and, the cachedFiles hash the dependencies for the files that are already owned by the agent. If deps is not empty, another trip to the repository is required to obtain the missing files.

These will also be placed in cachedFiles, which keeps track of the dependencies to be resolved before installing the software. The actual installation is done by iterating through the cachedFiles and toDeploy hashes and calling install in the local Installer agent to install the packages involved. The use of both hashes separates the static set of requested files from the host-dependent, dynamically gathered dependencies.

Listing 9. The Deployer agent

```
service  SoftDeployer { deploy }

agent  Deployer() provides SoftDeployer requires SoftRepository, SoftInstaller {

  main() { }
  deploy(fileNames, hosts) {
    lock(self);
    rep = bind(SoftRepository);              // Discover the repository
    repHost = rep.getHost();                 // Obtain the host where it is located
    go(repHost);                             // Migrate to its location
    toDeploy = rep.get(fileNames);           // Get files to install
    cachedFiles = {};
    deps = {};
    for (h in hosts) {
      go(h);                                 // Migrate to a target host
      installer = bind(SoftInstaller, h);    // Obtain a binding for the local base station
      for (file in toDeploy) {               // Get dependencies
        deps = installer.getDeps(file);
        for (fileName in cachedFiles.keys())  // Check if all dependencies are fulfilled
          if (deps.contains(fileName))
            deps.remove(fileName);
          else
            cachedFiles.remove(fileName);
        if (! deps.isEmpty()) {              // Dependencies are not fulfilled
          go(repHost);                       // Migrate to the repository
          cachedFiles.put(rep.get(deps));    // Get dependency files
          go(h);                             // Migrate back to the host
        }
      }
      for (file in cachedFiles)              // Install dependencies
        installer.install(file);
      for (file in toDeploy)                 // Install requested files
        installer.install(file);
    }
    unlock(self);
  }
}
new Deployer();
```

Running MOB applications is easy. The mob command may be used to run scripts. A MOB program is run by specifying its .mil file, the host where it should run (which must be MOB-enabled) and the command line arguments the program takes. The command that follows creates a new DiTyCO run-time system to run agentCode.mil at ahost.anet with arguments arg1 arg2 ... argn.

> mob agentCode.mil ahost.anet arg1 arg2 ... argn

Similarly, when a proxy is run, a new DiTyCO run-time system is created. The proxy takes the key of the agent as argument, resolves its current location using the underlying DiTyCO infra-structure and gets a binding for it. After the binding is obtained, communication through remote method invocation is possible. The following command starts the proxy program, agentProxy.mil, that connects to the agent with key agentKey.

> mob agentProxy.mil agentKey

5   Related Work

In this section we describe recent research that we feel relates more closely to this work. In the field of languages and systems based on process calculi there are several languages that have been proposed. None of these languages use the concept of service-orientation.

Jocaml [13] is a programming language based on the Join calculus that provides support for distributed and mobile agent based applications. The language uses a custom virtual machine and supports the migration of trees of computations (an agent and its tree of sub-agents) between hosts in a network. Just as in MOB, type-checking is mostly done at compile time except for interaction with other modules which is done dynamically. The required type information is annotated in the source program.

The M-Calculus [27] is an extension of the Distributed Join calculus, that incorporates several new notions, such as programmable localities and dynamic binding. It does not support mobile computations but rather code mobility. Its focus is on resource access control and safe communication, defining localities composed of a membrane and a content. The current implementation uses a distributed abstract machine called CLAM (CeLular Abstract Machine), and provides a centralized implementation, the C-VM (Cellular Virtual Machine) [28], which was developed on top of the JVM. Each location is executed by a single dedicated Java thread. In MOB, we defined the MOB abstract machine, and implemented it resorting to the DiTyCO distributed implementation. Each MOB agent is encoded into a DiTyCO site (run-time system) which is executed, by the MOB host service. Each site is itself multi-threaded [26].

The X-KLAIM [15] programming language is an implementation of the KLAIM model with ad-hoc extensions to incorporate higher-order constructs, asynchronous reading of tuple-spaces and hierarchical structured networks. Programs in X-KLAIM are compiled into Java classes that resort to a package, KLAVA, to run. A mobile agent in X-KLAIM is a process with a single execution flow, rather than the multi-threaded agents found in MOB. This makes the migration of a multi-threaded agent, scattered among several processes at a given site, a complex and user aware operation.

Nomadic Pict [16] is perhaps the closest to our work in that it grows from another process calculus based language, Pict [29], and adds primitives for programming mobile computations such as agent creation, agent migration and asynchronous communication between agents. Nomadic Pict also focuses on verification and a proof of correctness for an instance of the infrastructure has been achieved [30]. Despite the similar approach, our emphasis is on producing a compact, user-friendly, scripting language that abstracts away from network location dependent information. In this respect we feel that MOB, even in its core language is higher level than Nomadic-Pict, providing built-in multi-threaded agents and a service-oriented paradigm.

Acute [17] is a programming language for mobile agents built on top of the Objective Caml programming language. The language provides type-safety through a mixed static/dynamic type checking scheme, e.g., on module linking. Moving computations is achieved through an atomic operation that captures a collection of threads in a structure (a *thunk*) that can afterwards be marshalled and moved across the network. This contrasts with MOB where marshalling of objects or agents is transparent to the programmer. In the case of MOB agents the primitive *go* implements the marshalling required for sending the agent to another node in the network. The MOB service on that node will be responsible for unmarshalling the agent and restart it. In this respect Acute provides a finer, lower level, control over migration and marshalling than MOB.

Alice is a programming language based on Oz and its implementation, Mozart [18] (itself based on Standard ML). The functionality provided by Alice is similar to that of Acute, supporting dynamically linked modules, type-safe marshalling, concurrent execution but with some differences, e.g., it lacks rebinding. The front-end of the Alice compiler produces Oz intermediate code so that the Oz run-time, Mozart, is used to run Alice applications. The approach is similar to the one we use since the front-end of the MOB compiler produces DiTyCO code that is then executed with DiTyCO's run-time system.

Java based systems such as Aglets [6], Mole [7] and Voyager [8] supply a set of Java classes which the programmer must extend to implement applications. As in MOB, the run-time architecture of these systems is based on abstractions for IP nodes running a hosting service.

In Aglets [6], inter-agent communication is done by dispatching instances of a *Message* class, which are relayed by a proxy on the target agent's side, much like in MOB. Communication is point-to-point and group communication is not supported. Each agent is executed in an independent Java thread.

Mole [7] agents are clusters of objects. References to agents in Mole are symbolic, each agent being identified by a unique network-wide name. In MOB, references to agents are true heap references and are kept by the agent as it moves through the network. Communication in Mole uses a set of pre-defined mechanisms supported by Java such as RMI or asynchronous message-passing.

In Voyager [8] an agent is also a collection of objects. However, objects (including agents) may be created remotely without implementing any special interface. Voyager generates all the required files, and handles all messaging. Communication is done by method invocation or through a shared space. As in MOB, Voyager supplies basic communication mechanisms, reserving higher-level communication or protocols to the application programmer.

Two other systems that have some features akin to MOB are D'Agents and Ara. A mobile agent in D'Agents [9] (former Agent Tcl) may be written in any language, although TCL is the one mostly used. All the services and resources required by an agent (e.g., state capture, migration, communication, disk access) are made available at each host by a dedicated server. D'Agents implements a weak form of migration since, although agents resume execution in the next instruction of the program after a migration, no state is carried by the agent.

Mobile agents in Ara [10] are programmed in an interpreted language. The interpreter for this language is a special run-time system for agents called the *core*. A special core call allows agents to migrate at any point of their execution, and the agent carries the full state of the computation with it (as opposed to D'Agents).

6   Conclusions and Future Work

We introduced MOB, a programming language for developing applications based on mobile agents that uses a service-oriented approach to resource discovery. The combination of both paradigms in a programming language and run-time system provides a very high level model for programming distributed applications for today's networks. It allows, for example, to abstract away from the physical locations and even from the identifiers of individual network agents. Interaction is based on service contracts. Services are provided to the network and are required from the network.

We have implemented a compiler and a run-time system for the MOB language. The abstract machine for MOB was encoded onto a process calculus and this allowed us to use this encoding as a specification for the front-end of the MOB compiler. It also allowed us to use the run-time system developed for the calculus as the basis for the development of the MOB run-time system.

Currently, we are preparing a release of the platform with the prototypes of both the compiler and the run-time. We are also extending the language with APIs for interaction with external services. This will allow MOB to act as a coordination language for mobile agents that interact with web services using such protocols as SMTP, FTP, or HTTP and, to interact with network databases.

From a more formal point of view, we aim to prove the soundness of the MOB language. In other words, given our encoding $[\![\cdot]\!]$, from MOB abstract-machine states into the extended LSDπ-calculus, we wish to prove the following conjecture:

Conjecture (Soundness.) Let N and N' be network configurations in the MOB abstract-machine. If $N \rightarrow N'$ (*reduces to* in MOB) then, $[\![N]\!] \equiv [\![N']\!]$ (*is congruent to* in the calculus) or $[\![N]\!] \rightarrow [\![N']\!]$ (*reduces to* in the calculus).

References

1. Horstmann, M., Kirtland, M.: DCOM Architecture. Microsoft. (1997)
2. Object Management Group: The Common Object Request Broker: Architecture and Specification. Object Management Group. (2001)
3. Platt, D.: Introducing Microsoft .NET, Third Edition. Microsoft Press (2003)

4. Waldo, J.: The Jini Architecture for Network-Centric Computing. Commun. ACM **42**(7) (1999) 76–82
5. Openwings: Openwings: A Service-Oriented Component Architecture for Self-Forming, Self-Healing, Network-Centric Systems (Rev 2.0). http://www.openwings.org (2001)
6. Lange, D.B., Oshima, M.: Programming and Deploying Java Mobile Agents with Aglets. Addison-Wesley (1998)
7. Straber, M., Baumann, J., Hohl, F.: Mole - A Java Based Mobile Agent System. In M., M., ed.: Special Issues in Object Oriented Programming. (1997) 301–308
8. Glass, G.: Overview of Voyager: ObjectSpace's Product Family for State-of-the-art Distributed Computing. Technical report, CTO ObjectSpace (1999)
9. Gray, R.S.: Agent Tcl: A Transportable Agent System. In: Proceedings of the CIKM Workshop on Intelligent Information Agents, Fourth International Conference on Information and Knowledge Management (CIKM 95). (1995)
10. Peine, H., Stolpmann, T.: The Architecture of the Ara Platform for Mobile Agents. In: Proc. of the First International Workshop on Mobile Agents MA'97. Volume 1219 of Lecture Notes in Computer Science., Springer-Verlag (1997) 316–323
11. Honda, K., Tokoro, M.: An Object Calculus for Asynchronous Communication. In: European Conference on Object-Oriented Programming (ECOOP'91). Volume 512 of Lecture Notes in Computer Science., Springer-Verlag (1991) 141–162
12. Milner, R., Parrow, J., Walker, D.: A Calculus of Mobile Processes (parts I and II). Information and Computation **100**(1) (1992) 1–77
13. Conchon, S., Fessant, F.L.: Jocaml: Mobile Agents for Objective-Caml. In: ASA/MA'99, IEEE Computer Society (1999) 22–29
14. Vasconcelos, V., Lopes, L., Silva, F.: Distribution and Mobility with Lexical Scoping in Process Calculi. In: Workshop on High Level Programming Languages (HLCL'98). Volume 16(3) of Electronic Notes in Theoretical Computer Science., Elsevier Science (1998) 19–34
15. Bettini, L., de Nicola, R., Pugliese, R.: X-Klaim and Klava: Programming Mobile Code. In: TOSCA 2001. Volume 62., Elsevier Science (2001)
16. Wojciechowski, P.T., Sewell, P.: Nomadic Pict: Language and Infrastructure Design for Mobile Agents. IEEE Concurrency **8**(2) (2000) 42–52
17. Sewell, P., Leifer, J.J., Wansbrough, K., Zappa Nardelli, F., Allen-Williams, M., Habouzit, P., Vafeiadis, V.: Acute: High-level Programming Language Design for Distributed Computation. In: ICFP '05: Proceedings of The 10th ACM SIGPLAN International Conference on Functional Programming, ACM Press (2005) 15–26
18. Smolka, G.: Concurrent Constraint Programming Based on Functional Programming. In Hankin, C., ed.: Programming Languages and Systems. Volume 1381 of Lecture Notes in Computer Science., Springer-Verlag (1998) 1–11
19. Paulino, H., Lopes, L., Silva, F.: Mob: A Scripting Language for Mobile Agents Based on a Process Calculus. In: Web Engineering - International Conference, ICWE 2003. Volume 2272 of Lecture Notes in Computer Science., Springer-Verlag (2003) 40–43
20. Ravara, A., Matos, A., Vasconcelos, V., Lopes, L.: Lexically Scoped Distribution: What You See Is What You Get. In: FGC: Foundations of Global Computing. Volume 85(1) of Electronic Notes in Theoretical Computer Science., Elsevier Science (2003)
21. TyCO (Typed Concurrent Objects) Programming Language. (Available at http://www.dcc.fc.up.pt/tyco/)
22. White, J.E.: Telescript Technology: Scenes from the Electronic Marketplace. General Magic White Paper. General Magic edn. (1995)

23. Java Remote Method Invocation (Java RMI). (http://java.sun.com/products/jdk/rmi/)
24. Paulino, H., Lopes, L.: Mob Core Language and Virtual Machine. Technical Report DCC-2005-05, DCC - FC & LIACC, Universidade do Porto, http://www.dcc.fc.up.pt/Pubs/treports.html (2005)
25. Vasconcelos, V., Lopes, L.: A Multi-threaded Assembly Language: Intermediate Language and Virtual Machine. (Unpublished)
26. Paulino, H., Marques, P., Lopes, L., Vasconcelos, V., Silva, F.: A Multi-Threaded Asynchronous Language. In: 7th International Conference on Parallel Computing Technologies (PaCT'03). Volume 2763 of Lecture Notes in Computer Science., Springer-Verlag (2003) 316–323
27. Schmitt, A., Stefani, J.B.: The M-calculus: A Higher-Order Distributed Process Calculus. In: Proceedings 30th Annual ACM Symposium on Principles of Programming Languages (POPL). (2003)
28. Germain, F., Lacoste, M., Stefani, J.B.: An Abstract Machine for a Higher-Order Distributed Process Calculus. In: EATCS Workshop on Foundations of Wide Area Network Computing (FWAN'02). Volume 66.3., Elsevier (2002)
29. Pierce, B., Turner, D.: Pict: A Programming Language Based on the Pi-Calculus. In: Proof, Language and Interaction: Essays in Honour of Robin Milner, MIT Press (2000) 455–494
30. Asis Unyapoth: Nomadic Pi Calculi: Expressing and Verifying Infrastructure for Mobile Computation. PhD thesis, University of Cambridge (2001)

A Case Study in Concurrent Programming with Active Objects

Ulrike Glavitsch and Thomas M. Frey

Computer Systems Institute, ETH Zurich,
8092 Zurich, Switzerland
ulrike.glavitsch@inf.ethz.ch, thomas.frey@alumni.ethz.ch

Abstract. The recent product development of processors shows that multi-core computer architectures are rapidly becoming reality. Therefore, in order to use the available processing power, operating systems and programming languages supporting the development of multi-threaded software will be needed. In this paper, we present a small case study that shows how elegant and safe concurrent programming can be if a powerful programming language and thread-safe libraries are used. The case study is a simple search tool written in Active Oberon. The application uses a thread-safe GUI framework that relieves the programmer from synchronizing requests.

1 Introduction

Present and future multi-core computer architectures require multi-processor operating systems and support for multi-threading on the level of the programming language and the environment. Current operating systems are capable to schedule processing tasks to multiple processors. The complexity is hidden, thus, giving the IT user benefits in terms of efficiency and response times. The structuring of a programming task into threads and their synchronization is one of the challenges of current programming and can hardly be automated. In standard programming languages and environments (Java, C#/.NET), multi-threading is supported by a number of specialized library or language calls. However, their use is cumbersome and very often, the programmer has to understand the implementation to make correct use of them. In addition, standard libraries and frameworks for graphical user interfaces (GUI) are seldom thread-safe (e.g. Java Swing, .NET WinForms). This means that it is the programmer's responsibility to synchronize threads that operate on the same component. What is desirable is a programming environment in that developing complex multi-threaded applications becomes more focused on the actual problem and releases the programmer from burdens that can be performed effectively by the environment.

Active Oberon is a type-safe, modular object-oriented programming language that contains dedicated language constructs for threads and their synchronization [1]. Threads are declared as activities encapsulated in objects. Such an active object contains variables and methods like a regular object but its body is executed as a separate thread. In addition, there exist language constructs to declare critical sections with respect to an object scope and a powerful wait statement that allows waiting for a

D. Lightfoot and C. Szyperski (Eds.): JMLC 2006, LNCS 4228, pp. 403–414, 2006.
© Springer-Verlag Berlin Heidelberg 2006

conditional expression to become true instead of waiting for a primitive signal like it is commonly used in other languages and threading libraries. With these, it is possible that an object or a module performs like a monitor [1][2]. It has been shown that these multi-threading specific language constructs can be adopted by other programming languages [3].

Bluebottle is an operating system consisting of a lean multiprocessor kernel and a thread-safe multimedia and GUI framework [1][4]. It is fully programmed in Active Oberon. The particular thread-safety mechanism of Bluebottle's GUI framework makes developing applications easier. Programmers do not need to explicitly synchronize requests to the same GUI component. This built-in synchronization strategy uses a message queue for asynchronous events, a thread for processing the messages and a lock for ensuring a consistent view on inter-component relations [5].

This paper presents the design and implementation of a sample application programmed in Active Oberon under Bluebottle. This application, a search tool, is a typical concurrent GUI application. We demonstrate that the combination of the language constructs of Active Oberon and the synchronization strategy of Bluebottle's GUI framework is perfectly well suited for this type of problem. While the implementation of this application in other environments is typically complex and cumbersome, the program code in Active Oberon becomes clear and concise, and thus, less error-prone.

2 Sample Application

Our case study is a GUI application that allows the user to search for files that contain a given character string. The GUI of the search tool is shown in Fig. 1. The input

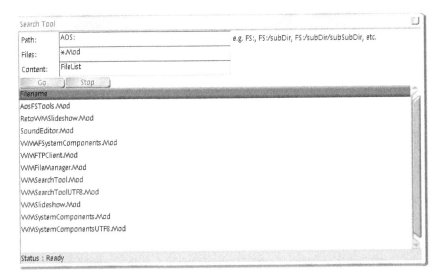

Fig. 1. Graphical user interface of search tool. It shows the results of a search request given the directory path "AOS:", the file mask "*.Mod" and the search string "FileList".

parameters of a search request are a directory path, a file mask (e.g. *.Mod), and a search string. The search is started by pressing the start button labeled with "Go" and interrupted by clicking on the button "Stop". The search results are displayed as soon as they are found. A status line at the bottom of the window indicates the status of an ongoing request. It can either show "Processing" or "Ready". As searching through files is time-consuming it is possible to open some of the found files while the search is still ongoing.

A user may open multiple instances of the search tool on his desktop and start several search requests in parallel.

3 Design

The graphical user interface of the search tool is built using Bluebottle's GUI components. Bluebottle provides a number of standard GUI components to build the most common user interfaces. The search tool uses two threads for searching through the files and for displaying the results. The two threads communicate by a buffer and, thus, represent a classical producer-consumer scheme. The current search results are written to the GUI using a model-view-controller (MVC) pattern. The consumer process updates the model of the GUI component. Changes to the model implicitly lead to an update of the views. Fig. 2 shows the threads (active objects) and the main regular objects involved in this application. The arrows between objects represent method calls.

The singleton object *WindowManager* receives asynchronous mouse and keyboard events and forwards them to the corresponding window [4]. In our case, starting and stopping a search request as well as opening a file for inspection are triggered by mouse clicks.

The main window of the search tool is represented by an object of base type *Form-Window*. It contains the GUI components ordered in a hierarchical structure that control the appearance of the application. For instance, the top element of the component hierarchy is a component of type *Panel* that among others contains a *StringGrid* component to display the search results on the GUI.

The active object *Searcher* processes a search request. It traverses all files that match the given mask and checks if the provided string is contained. The *Searcher* object waits for a new request after finishing a search task. The results are written to a buffer of type *ListBuffer*. The active object *Dispatcher* reads the elements of the buffer chunk by chunk as soon as they are available and updates the object *String-GridModel*. The object *StringGridModel* represents the model in the MVC pattern whereas the view is a GUI component of type *StringGrid* that is part of the component hierarchy contained in object *FormWindow*. The model *StringGridModel* manages a dynamic two-dimensional array of strings that are linked with some more context data. Every change to the object *StringGridModel* automatically leads to an update of its view in the *FormWindow* object.

Status messages are displayed in the GUI component by means of delegate procedures that are registered with the *Dispatcher* object.

Requests to the search tool window are serialized. This means that mouse events from the *WindowManager* object, requests to update the view and status messages are implicitly synchronized. This is done by a sequencing mechanism implemented by a sequencer object that is stored with each *FormWindow* object. The sequencer object contains a thread, a message queue and a lock that protects the hierarchy of GUI components [5]. Each request to the *FormWindow* object that is not called by the sequencer thread is put in the message queue that is processed by the sequencer thread. The object *FormWindow* corresponds to the Active Object pattern that decouples method execution from method invocation in order to allow synchronized access to an object that resides in its own thread of control [6].

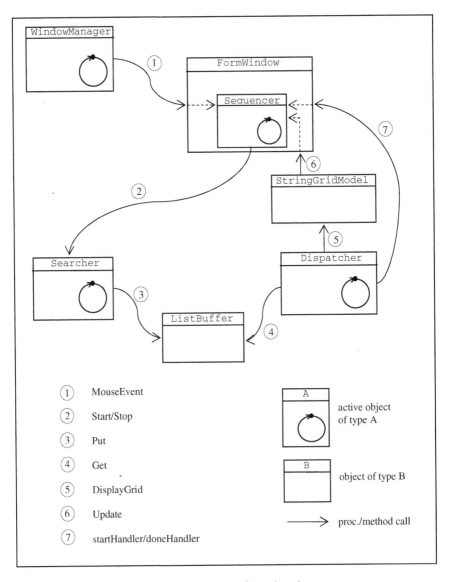

Fig. 2. Call graph of search tool

4 Implementation

The following section presents the implementation of the objects *Searcher, Dispatcher* and *Listbuffer*. It describes the mechanism used to update the *StringGridModel* object and the status display. Finally, we explain the wiring of the objects.

Recall that the object *Searcher* administers the search actions. Results are written to the object *ListBuffer* and are forwarded by the object *Dispatcher* to the model *StringGridModel*.

4.1 Searcher

The active object *Searcher* executes an infinite loop that waits for a new search request, then copies the input parameters from the new search request to those of the current request, resets the buffer and starts the search. It notifies the end of the search request to the buffer and waits for the next search request.

Active objects are declared as regular objects but their body is annotated by the keyword *ACTIVE* to denote that the object body is executed as a separate thread. The active object *Searcher* contains some state variables, the parameters of the ongoing and the new search request and a reference to the *Listbuffer* object. The parameters of a search request are packed in a record type *SearchPar* for ease of use. The *Searcher* object acts as monitor that requests mutual exclusion for its methods [2]. Mutual exclusion for a method is denoted by the keyword *EXCLUSIVE* after the first *BEGIN*. A new search request is started by calling the method *Start* and is interrupted by calling the method *Stop*. The relevant code fragments of the Searcher object are given in the following. The language constructs that support multi-threading are highlighted.

```
TYPE
  SearchPar = RECORD
    path, fmask, content : ARRAY 1024 OF CHAR
  END;

Searcher = OBJECT
VAR
  newlyStarted, stopped : BOOLEAN;
  currentPar, newPar : SearchPar;
  lb : ListBuffer;

PROCEDURE &Init(lb : ListBuffer);   (* constructor *)
BEGIN
  newlyStarted := FALSE;
  stopped := FALSE;
  SELF.lb := lb
END Init;

PROCEDURE Start(VAR searchPar : SearchPar);
BEGIN {EXCLUSIVE}
  newPar := searchPar;
  newlyStarted := TRUE
END Start;
```

```
PROCEDURE AwaitNewStart;
BEGIN {EXCLUSIVE}
  AWAIT(newlyStarted);
  newlyStarted := FALSE;
  stopped := FALSE
END AwaitNewStart;

PROCEDURE CopySearchParams;
BEGIN {EXCLUSIVE}
  currentPar := newPar;
END CopySearchParams;

PROCEDURE Stop;
BEGIN {EXCLUSIVE}
  stopped := TRUE
END Stop;

PROCEDURE HasStopped() : BOOLEAN;
BEGIN {EXCLUSIVE}
  RETURN stopped
END HasStopped;

PROCEDURE SearchPath;
VAR mask, name : ARRAY 1024 OF CHAR;
    e : AosFS.Enumerator;
    d : DirEntry;
BEGIN
  ...
  NEW(e);
  e.Open(mask, {});
  WHILE e.HasMoreEntries() DO
    IF HasStopped() THEN RETURN END;
    IF e.GetEntry(name, ...) THEN
      IF ContainsStr(name, currentPar.content) THEN
        NEW(d);
        ...
        lb.Put(d);
      END
    END
  END
END SearchPath;


BEGIN {ACTIVE} (* body *)
  LOOP
    AwaitNewStart;
    CopySearchParams;
    lb.Reset;
    SearchPath;
    lb.Finished
  END
END Searcher;
```

The *AWAIT* statement as in procedure *AwaitNewStart* is noteworthy. If the condition in the argument of *AWAIT* returns false, the current process is suspended and put in a list of waiting processes. Additionally to the process, a helper function and the base pointer of the current stack frame are stored. The helper function is generated by the compiler and is used to evaluate the condition of the *AWAIT* statement in a given stack frame. When a process leaves the end of a critical section, the runtime system traverses the list of waiting processes and for each process evaluates the condition using the helper function. If a condition of a waiting process evaluates to true, the lock of the process that leaves the critical section is atomically transferred to the waiting process which is then scheduled [1]. In C#/.NET and Java, suspending a process and waking up one or all waiting processes are realized by special library calls and built-in procedures, respectively. In both C# and Java, the programmer has to place the statements for waking up waiting processes at each location in the code where a condition for any of the waiting processes may become true. This is a burden for the programmer and, in fact, these statements are easily forgotten while developing concurrent C# or Java programs. In addition, if there are processes waiting on different conditions and only one of the conditions becomes true there is no other way than to wake up all waiting processes and to suspend those whose condition is not satisfied yet. Besides that the programs thereby become less readable and less compact this may result in a number of unnecessary context switches that reduce the efficiency of the system. Active Oberon wakes up exactly one of those waiting processes whose condition has become true. Thus, unnecessary context switches are avoided. The cost is that the conditions of waiting processes are evaluated every time a process leaves a critical section. Since these evaluations can be performed without a context switch, this overhead is comparatively small [1].

The procedure *SearchPath* performs the actual search over all files that match the given directory path and the file mask. Before inspecting the next file, *SearchPath* checks whether the flag *stopped* is set and returns if this is the case. The algorithm for finding the occurrence of a given string in a file is the Boyer-Moore string search algorithm.

4.2 Dispatcher

The *Dispatcher* thread waits for a new search request and then continuously reads the search results from the buffer and updates the model of the GUI component that displays the results. It displays status messages to the GUI of the search tool denoting that a search is ongoing and when it has finished. The search results are read from the buffer in chunks to avoid too frequent model updates in the case of very frequently occurring search strings. The delegate mechanism of Active Oberon is used for both the model and the status updates. Delegates are declared similar to procedure types [2]. Formally, a delegate variable is a pair of references that point to an object and to a type-bound procedure.

A new data type *RetrievedList* to contain chunks of the buffer is defined. A buffer element is of type *DirEntry* (see Sec. 4.3). It is a record structure that contains the directory information of a file, e.g. the file name, its size, creation date, etc.. Fragments of the program code of *Dispatcher* are shown below. Dedicated language constructs are again highlighted.

```
TYPE
  RetrievedList = RECORD
    data : ARRAY RListSize OF DirEntry;
    noEl : INTEGER
  END;

  TYPE
    GridDisplayHandler = PROCEDURE {DELEGATE} (VAR rl :
  RetrievedList);

    SearchStatusHandler = PROCEDURE {DELEGATE} ();

    Dispatcher = OBJECT
    VAR
      newlyStarted, stopped : BOOLEAN;
      rl : RetrievedList;
      display : GridDisplayHandler;
      startHandler, doneHandler : SearchStatusHandler;
      lb : ListBuffer;

      (* constructor *)
      PROCEDURE &Init(lb : ListBuffer;
                      d : GridDisplayHandler;
                      sh, dh : SearchStatusHandler);
      BEGIN
        SELF.lb := lb;
        display := d;
        startHandler := sh;
        doneHandler := dh;
        stopped := FALSE
      END Init;

      ...
      (* procedures Start, AwaitNewStart, Stop and
         HasStopped as in Searcher *)
      ...

    BEGIN {ACTIVE}
      LOOP
        AwaitNewStart;
        startHandler;
        LOOP
          lb.Get(rl);
          IF rl.noEl = 0 OR HasStopped() THEN EXIT END;
          display(rl);
        END;
        doneHandler;
      END
    END GridDisplayHandler;
```

4.3 ListBuffer

The *ListBuffer* data structure is implemented as a circular buffer. The *Searcher* thread puts the search results into the buffer one by one whereas the *Dispatcher* thread consumes them in chunks.

The variables and signatures of the methods of *ListBuffer* are given below. The *Listbuffer* object contains a variable *chunkSize* that denotes the minimum number of buffer elements returned by procedure *Get* in case of an ongoing search request. This number is computed dynamically. It is initialized to 1 and adapted after each call to *Get*. Procedure *Get* returns only if the number of available elements in the buffer are greater or equal to *chunkSize* or if the search is finished. If the number of available buffer elements is greater than *chunkSize* the variable *chunkSize* is adapted. All methods can only be accessed by one process at a time, i.e. they are declared with the *EXCLUSIVE* keyword. Thus, an instance of *ListBuffer* like the instances of *Searcher* and *Dispatcher* acts as a monitor.

```
TYPE ListBuffer = OBJECT
  VAR data : ARRAY RListSize OF DirEntry;
    in, out, chunkSize : INTEGER;
    finished : BOOLEAN;

  PROCEDURE &Reset; (* constructor *)

  PROCEDURE Put(d : DirEntry); (* produce *)

  PROCEDURE Get(VAR rl : RetrievedList); (* consume *)

  PROCEDURE Finished(); (* signal end of searching *)
END ListBuffer;
```

4.4 StringGridModel Update

The model of the GUI component that displays the search results is updated by the delegate *DisplayGrid* that is a method of the type *FileList*. The *FileList* declaration contains the GUI component, its view, as a variable and provides further methods like opening a file in the GUI component.

Excerpts of the program code of *DisplayGrid* and how it is embedded in the declaration of *FileList* is shown below. The variable *grid* denotes the GUI component that shows the search results. It has a reference to the underlying model and provides a locking mechanism such that changes to the model are synchronized. The methods to lock the model are *Acquire* and *Release*. They are highlighted in the code fragment below. The method *Release* implicitly performs an upcall to the observers of the model to update the view.

```
TYPE FileList = OBJECT
  ...
  grid : WMStringGrids;
  ...

  (* delegate *)
  PROCEDURE DisplayGrid(VAR rl : RetrievedList);
```

```
VAR i : LONGINT;
   d : DirEntry;
BEGIN
  grid.model.Acquire;
  FOR i := 0 TO rl.noEl - 1 DO
     d := rl.data[i];
     ...
     (* add the new search result d to the model *)
     ...
  END;
  grid.model.Release (* performs an implicit update
                         of the view *)
END DisplayGrid;

  ...

END FileList;
```

4.5 Status Messages and Interconnection of Objects

The delegates for displaying the status messages of the search tool are two very short methods of the object of type *FormWindow*. The constructor of *FormWindow* creates the instances of type *Searcher*, *Dispatcher* and *ListBuffer* and connects them as shown in Fig. 2. The buffer of type *ListBuffer* is registered with the active objects *Searcher* and *Dispatcher* and the delegate procedures are installed with the object *Dispatcher*. The following program code shows fragments of the constructor that creates the objects and their connections. We also present the two delegate procedures that display the status messages. The important pieces of code are marked with highlighted comments.

```
TYPE
  Window = OBJECT(WMComponents.FormWindow)
  VAR
     (* GUI component that displays status messages *)
     label : WMStandardComponents.Label;
     ...
     filelist : WMSystemComponents.FileList;
     lb : ListBuffer;
     s : Searcher;
     d : Displayer;
     ...

     PROCEDURE &New();
     BEGIN
        ...
        NEW(filelist);    (* object creation and wiring *)
        NEW(lb);
        NEW(s, lb);
        NEW(d, lb, filelist.DisplayGrid,
            SearchStartHandler, SearchDoneHandler);
        ...
     END New;
```

```
(* delegate *)
PROCEDURE SearchStartHandler;
BEGIN
  label.caption.SetAOC("Status: Processing ...")
END SearchStartHandler;

(* delegate *)
PROCEDURE SearchDoneHandler;
BEGIN
  label.caption.SetAOC("Status: Ready ...")
END SearchDoneHandler;
...
END Window;
```

It must be noted that this easy way of programming the updating of status messages is due to the synchronization mechanism of Bluebottle's GUI framework. The delegate procedures *SearchStartHandler* and *SearchStopHandler* are called from the *Dispatcher* thread and are executed in the context of the GUI thread, i.e. the sequencer thread of *FormWindow*.

Behind the scenes, the GUI framework checks whether the calling process is the same as the sequencer thread. If this is the case, it puts the method call into the message queue of the sequencer thread. Otherwise, the call is executed immediately within the sequencer thread. Checking this condition costs only a few clock cycles in Bluebottle and, thus, can easily be done within the framework [4].

In C#/.NET, the programmer has to check explicitly whether a context switch to the GUI process is required and is forced to handle the two cases appropriately. Correct handling of these cases requires knowledge of the GUI framework that in our opinion should be hidden from the programmer. Bluebottle's GUI framework is a set of libraries where the programmer does not need to know any implementation details to perform his task.

5 Conclusions

We showed that concurrent programs written in a powerful programming language (Active Oberon) using thread-safe libraries (Bluebottle's GUI framework) are compact, readable and less error-prone. The constructs for multi-threading are integrated in the programming language which facilitates their use. In addition, the dedicated language constructs are lean and very effective such that the program code remains clear and concise. The thread-safety of the GUI framework relieves the program developer from synchronizing requests to the same component. This contributes in a similar way to the readability and compactness of the program code.

References

1. Muller, P. J.: The Active Object System – Design and Multiprocessor Implementation. Ph.D. thesis, Institut für Computersysteme, ETH Zürich (2002)
2. Hoare, C. A. R.: Monitors: An operating systems structuring concept. Comm. ACM (1974) 17(10):549-557

3. Güntensperger, R., Gutknecht, J.: Activities and channels: C# language extensions for concurrency control and remote object communication. IEE Proceedings – Software 150(5):315-322 (2003)
4. Frey, T.: Bluebottle: A Thread-safe Multimedia and GUI Framework for Active Oberon. Ph.D. thesis, Institut für Computersysteme, ETH Zürich (2005)
5. Frey, T. M.: Architectural Aspects of a Thread-safe Graphical Component System Based on Aos. Lecture Notes in Computer Science 2789, Springer (2003)
6. Lavender, R. G., Schmidt, D. C.: Active Object: An Object Behavioral Pattern for Concurrent Programming. In Pattern Languages of Program Design 2 (J. O. Coplien, J. Vlissides, and N. Kerth, eds.), Addison Wesley (1996)

Author Index

Lecture Notes in Computer Science

For information about Vols. 1–4077

please contact your bookseller or Springer

Vol. 4131: S. Kollias, A. Stafylopatis, W. Duch, E. Oja (Eds.), Artificial Neural Networks – ICANN 2006, Part I. XXXIV, 1008 pages. 2006.

Vol. 4130: U. Furbach, N. Shankar (Eds.), Automated Reasoning. XV, 680 pages. 2006. (Sublibrary LNAI).

Vol. 4129: D. McGookin, S. Brewster (Eds.), Haptic and Audio Interaction Design. XII, 167 pages. 2006.

Vol. 4128: W.E. Nagel, W.V. Walter, W. Lehner (Eds.), Euro-Par 2006 Parallel Processing. XXXIII, 1221 pages. 2006.

Vol. 4127: E. Damiani, P. Liu (Eds.), Data and Applications Security XX. X, 319 pages. 2006.

Vol. 4126: P. Barahona, F. Bry, E. Franconi, N. Henze, U. Sattler, Reasoning Web. X, 269 pages. 2006.

Vol. 4124: H. de Meer, J.P. G. Sterbenz (Eds.), Self-Organizing Systems. XIV, 261 pages. 2006.

Vol. 4121: A. Biere, C.P. Gomes (Eds.), Theory and Applications of Satisfiability Testing - SAT 2006. XII, 438 pages. 2006.

Vol. 4119: C. Dony, J.L. Knudsen, A. Romanovsky, A. Tripathi (Eds.), Advanced Topics in Exception Handling Components. X, 302 pages. 2006.

Vol. 4117: C. Dwork (Ed.), Advances in Cryptology - CRYPTO 2006. XIII, 621 pages. 2006.

Vol. 4116: R. De Prisco, M. Yung (Eds.), Security and Cryptography for Networks. XI, 366 pages. 2006.

Vol. 4115: D.-S. Huang, K. Li, G.W. Irwin (Eds.), Computational Intelligence and Bioinformatics, Part III. XXI, 803 pages. 2006. (Sublibrary LNBI).

Vol. 4114: D.-S. Huang, K. Li, G.W. Irwin (Eds.), Computational Intelligence, Part II. XXVII, 1337 pages. 2006. (Sublibrary LNAI).

Vol. 4113: D.-S. Huang, K. Li, G.W. Irwin (Eds.), Intelligent Computing, Part I. XXVII, 1331 pages. 2006.

Vol. 4112: D.Z. Chen, D. T. Lee (Eds.), Computing and Combinatorics. XIV, 528 pages. 2006.

Vol. 4111: F.S. de Boer, M.M. Bonsangue, S. Graf, W.-P. de Roever (Eds.), Formal Methods for Components and Objects. VIII, 447 pages. 2006.

Vol. 4110: J. Díaz, K. Jansen, J.D.P. Rolim, U. Zwick (Eds.), Approximation, Randomization, and Combinatorial Optimization. XII, 522 pages. 2006.

Vol. 4109: D.-Y. Yeung, J.T. Kwok, A. Fred, F. Roli, D. de Ridder (Eds.), Structural, Syntactic, and Statistical Pattern Recognition. XXI, 939 pages. 2006.

Vol. 4108: J.M. Borwein, W.M. Farmer (Eds.), Mathematical Knowledge Management. VIII, 295 pages. 2006. (Sublibrary LNAI).

Vol. 4106: T.R. Roth-Berghofer, M.H. Göker, H. A. Güvenir (Eds.), Advances in Case-Based Reasoning. XIV, 566 pages. 2006. (Sublibrary LNAI).

Vol. 4105: B. Gunsel, A.K. Jain, A. M. Tekalp, B. Sankur (Eds.), Multimedia, Content Representation, Classification and Security. XIX, 804 pages. 2006.

Vol. 4104: T. Kunz, S.S. Ravi (Eds.), Ad-Hoc, Mobile, and Wireless Networks. XII, 474 pages. 2006.

Vol. 4103: J. Eder, S. Dustdar (Eds.), Business Process Management Workshops. XI, 508 pages. 2006.

Vol. 4102: S. Dustdar, J.L. Fiadeiro, A. Sheth (Eds.), Business Process Management. XV, 486 pages. 2006.

Vol. 4099: Q. Yang, G. Webb (Eds.), PRICAI 2006: Trends in Artificial Intelligence. XXVIII, 1263 pages. 2006. (Sublibrary LNAI).

Vol. 4098: F. Pfenning (Ed.), Term Rewriting and Applications. XIII, 415 pages. 2006.

Vol. 4097: X. Zhou, O. Sokolsky, L. Yan, E.-S. Jung, Z. Shao, Y. Mu, D.C. Lee, D. Kim, Y.-S. Jeong, C.-Z. Xu (Eds.), Emerging Directions in Embedded and Ubiquitous Computing. XXVII, 1034 pages. 2006.

Vol. 4096: E. Sha, S.-K. Han, C.-Z. Xu, M.H. Kim, L.T. Yang, B. Xiao (Eds.), Embedded and Ubiquitous Computing. XXIV, 1170 pages. 2006.

Vol. 4095: S. Nolfi, G. Baldassare, R. Calabretta, D. Marocco, D. Parisi, J.C. T. Hallam, O. Miglino, J.-A. Meyer (Eds.), From Animals to Animats 9. XV, 869 pages. 2006. (Sublibrary LNAI).

Vol. 4094: O. H. Ibarra, H.-C. Yen (Eds.), Implementation and Application of Automata. XIII, 291 pages. 2006.

Vol. 4093: X. Li, O.R. Zaïane, Z. Li (Eds.), Advanced Data Mining and Applications. XXI, 1110 pages. 2006. (Sublibrary LNAI).

Vol. 4092: J. Lang, F. Lin, J. Wang (Eds.), Knowledge Science, Engineering and Management. XV, 664 pages. 2006. (Sublibrary LNAI).

Vol. 4091: G.-Z. Yang, T. Jiang, D. Shen, L. Gu, J. Yang (Eds.), Medical Imaging and Augmented Reality. XIII, 399 pages. 2006.

Vol. 4090: S. Spaccapietra, K. Aberer, P. Cudré-Mauroux (Eds.), Journal on Data Semantics VI. XI, 211 pages. 2006.

Vol. 4089: W. Löwe, M. Südholt (Eds.), Software Composition. X, 339 pages. 2006.

Vol. 4088: Z.-Z. Shi, R. Sadananda (Eds.), Agent Computing and Multi-Agent Systems. XVII, 827 pages. 2006. (Sublibrary LNAI).

Vol. 4087: F. Schwenker, S. Marinai (Eds.), Artificial Neural Networks in Pattern Recognition. IX, 299 pages. 2006. (Sublibrary LNAI).

Vol. 4085: J. Misra, T. Nipkow, E. Sekerinski (Eds.), FM 2006: Formal Methods. XV, 620 pages. 2006.

Vol. 4084: M.A. Wimmer, H.J. Scholl, Å. Grönlund, K.V. Andersen (Eds.), Electronic Government. XV, 353 pages. 2006.

Vol. 4083: S. Fischer-Hübner, S. Furnell, C. Lambrinoudakis (Eds.), Trust and Privacy in Digital Business. XIII, 243 pages. 2006.

Vol. 4082: K. Bauknecht, B. Pröll, H. Werthner (Eds.), E-Commerce and Web Technologies. XIII, 243 pages. 2006.

Vol. 4081: A. M. Tjoa, J. Trujillo (Eds.), Data Warehousing and Knowledge Discovery. XVII, 578 pages. 2006.

Vol. 4080: S. Bressan, J. Küng, R. Wagner (Eds.), Database and Expert Systems Applications. XXI, 959 pages. 2006.

Vol. 4079: S. Etalle, M. Truszczyński (Eds.), Logic Programming. XIV, 474 pages. 2006.